Mummies around the World

Mummies around the World

AN ENCYCLOPEDIA OF MUMMIES IN HISTORY, RELIGION, AND POPULAR CULTURE

Matt Cardin, Editor

ABC-CLIO

Santa Barbara, California • Denver, Colorado • Oxford, England

Library of Congress Cataloging-in-Publication Data

Mummies around the world : an encyclopedia of mummies in history, religion, and popular culture / Matt Cardin, editor.

pages cm

Includes bibliographical references and index.

ISBN 978–1–61069–419–3 (hardback) — ISBN 978–1–61069–420–9 (ebook)

1. Mummies—Encyclopedias. I. Cardin, Matt, editor of compilation.

GN293.M655   2015

393′.3—dc23   2014020076

ISBN: 978–1–61069–419–3
EISBN: 978–1–61069–420–9

19 18 17 16 15   1 2 3 4 5

This book is also available on the World Wide Web as an eBook.
Visit www.abc-clio.com for details.

ABC-CLIO, LLC
130 Cremona Drive, P.O. Box 1911
Santa Barbara, California 93116-1911

This book is printed on acid-free paper ∞

Manufactured in the United States of America

Contents

List of Entries

Guide to Related Topics

Mummies of Egypt

Egyptian mummies

Egyptian mummification methods

Gebelein Man

Nesyamun or Natsef-amun, the Leeds mummy

Royal mummies of Egypt, Part One: Third to Eighteenth Dynasties

Royal mummies of Egypt, Part Two: Nineteenth to Twenty-fifth Dynasties

Tutankhamun ("King Tut")

Mummies of Europe

Alexander, Tenth Duke of Hamilton

Bentham, Jeremy

Bog bodies

Cladh Hallan mummies

Crypt mummies of Sommersdorf Castle

Grauballe Man

Incorruptibles

Lenin, Vladimir

Lindow Man

The Manchester Mummy (Hannah Beswick)

Mummies of Europe

Mummies of Ferentillo

Mummies of Lithuania

Mummies of Venzone

Ötzi the Iceman

Siberian Ice Maiden/Ukok princess

Tollund Man

von Kahlbutz, Christian Friedrich

Windeby Girl

Mummies of Latin America

Chinchorro mummies

Inca mummies

Juanita, the Inca Ice Maiden

Mummies of Guanajuato

Mummies of Latin America

Nasca mummies

Other Mummies

Animal mummies

Buddhist self-mummification

Fire Mummies: The Ibaloy mummies of the Philippines

Ice mummies

Smoked Bodies of Papua New Guinea

Egyptian Antiquities Museum

Egyptian collection, the British Museum

German Mummy Project

Manchester Egyptian Mummy Project

Mummies of the World: The Exhibition

Summum

Swiss Mummy Project

Vatican Mummy Project

The World Congresses on Mummy Studies

Places

Bahariya Oasis: Valley of the Golden Mummies

Capuchin Catacombs of Palermo

Church of the Dead

Hierakonpolis

Theban Necropolis

Valley of the Kings

Religion and Mythology

Anubis

Book of the Dead

Coffin Texts

Isis

Opening of the Mouth

Osiris

Religion and mummies

Seth

Topical Essays

Collecting mummies

Displaying mummies

Egyptomania

Embalming

Experimental mummification

Genetic study of mummies

Medical imaging of mummies

Medicine and mummies

The mummy in popular culture

Mummy portraits

Mummy unwrappings

Mummy's curse

Napoleon and the birth of Egyptology

Natural mummification

Rosetta Stone

Preface

All around the world, from the most ancient of times, people of various cultures and civilizations have practiced the art, science, and religious ritual of mummification: the preparation and preservation of corpses to resist corruption. As readers of this book will be well aware, this is hardly a subject whose interest is limited to scientists, since in modern times it has increasingly caught the popular imagination as well. The same holds true, significantly, for the phenomenon of natural mummification, where environmental conditions result in the spontaneous preservation of human and animal remains. Today the scientific study of mummies of all types is a booming field, and it is accompanied a surge of popular interest. Mummy-related books, conferences, museum exhibits, university degrees, and television documentaries now form their own established genre.

But beyond all of this, in the collective consciousness of Western societies, mummies have surpassed their purely historical and scientific foundations to become a bona fide cultural icon. Beginning with the new surge of "Egyptomania" that washed across Europe and America in the early nineteenth century, the ancient, sacred practice of preserving the dead underwent a kind of cultural-alchemical transmutation and soon emerged as an entertainment trope centered in supernatural horror. The "mummy novel" stands today as an established and venerable genre reaching well back into the 1800s, and the "mummy movie" has been around formally since 1932, with roots extending into the silent film era. And this is not even to mention the widespread prevalence of "The Mummy"— an iconic figure deserving proper noun caps—throughout the rest of popular culture, in comic books, television series, plastic models, trading cards, Halloween decorations, and more.

Mummies around the World: An Encyclopedia of Mummies in History, Religion, and Popular Culture is a comprehensive encyclopedia relating to all of these aspects of mummies: their ancient and modern history, their scientific study, their occurrence in cultures and civilizations around the globe, the religious and cultural beliefs surrounding them, and their long and varied career in fiction, film, and pop culture at large.

What are the motivations and methods behind the traditions of mummification? Who are the peoples who have practiced it, and what beliefs and worldviews have driven them? How did our modern awareness of mummies take shape? What role has it played in the development of our cultures? What advances in technology have helped it along? Who were the scientists, explorers, adventurers, academics, authors, filmmakers, actors, and artists who shaped it? What are some of the most famous mummies that have driven not only historical and scientific study but popular myths and entertainments? How does the symbolic and literal reality of the mummy speak to our often uneasy awareness of mortality and our strange relationship with our physical bodies?

These questions and more are addressed by *Mummies around the World*, an encyclopedia that unites history and science with religion and popular culture to illuminate this fascinating figure from humanity's dreams and nightmares.

Introduction

The Dream of Eternal Life

The question of human mortality and how to deal with it is as old as recorded history. In fact, recorded history begins with this very theme: the Egyptian *Pyramid Texts*, dating to the third millennium BCE, are among the world's oldest writings, and they consist of spells and other items used in the Egyptian mummification process to help guarantee the continued survival of the deceased in the afterlife. From a cousin culture just east of Egypt, the Babylonian *Epic of Gilgamesh*, also dating to the third millennium BCE, is the oldest surviving work of literature as such, and it tells of the dangerous (and ultimately fruitless) quest of the eponymous king to discover the secret of eternal life.

Given this, it is unsurprising that the subject of mummies has arguably exerted a more enduring influence on the human imagination than any other topic, subject, or figure in history. The practice of artificial mummification is older than written records and prevalent in cultures around the world. Natural mummies—bodies that have been spontaneously preserved by environmental conditions—have likewise occurred everywhere, and have been objects of great interest and even veneration. As indicated by the subtitle of the groundbreaking Mummies of the World exhibition that toured the United States from 2010 to 2014 (and that appeared in different forms in other countries), the deep meaning or "message" of mummies and mummification is that they speak directly to humanity's "dream of eternal life." In preparing the bodies of the dead to resist corruption, and in viewing and studying bodies that have been thus preserved, and in producing and consuming works of art and entertainment about such things, we engage directly with the most primal beliefs, questions, fears, and hopes of the human race.

Mummies, in short, have always been with us. They are part of our cultural and psychological DNA.

Mummies: The Double Helix

In much the same way that DNA consists of a spiraling double helix, mummies have led a dual existence in human culture, characterized by two discrete but deeply intertwined strands of identity. On the one hand, there is the historical reality of mummies and the roles they have played in human societies. This encompasses the beliefs and practices associated with mummies and mummification, which stand as concrete illustrations of the overarching systems of religion and culture in which they have existed. It also encompasses the currently thriving and growing field of scientific mummy studies. On the other hand, there is the imaginative reality of mummies in popular art and entertainment, converging on the singularly iconic figure of "The Mummy," envisioned as a monstrous, shambling, bandage-swathed creature that has been revived from the dead by a supernatural curse to exact revenge on those who disturbed its tomb. Both of these realities, the historical-factual and the mythic-imaginative, are central to any general discussion of mummies and their meaning.

The present book provides just such a discussion. Its contents cover a vast span of territory encompassing multiple aspects of mummies in history, religion, and popular culture. The attentive reader will find that each individual article and essay fits together neatly with the others, so that they form a kind of puzzle whose pieces, when assembled, reveal a striking figure that is a hybrid of the shambling Mummy of classic horror entertainment and the collective totality of the real-life mummies of history, religion, and scientific study. One can dip into this encyclopedia at any point and find much fascinating and useful information in its own right, but each article gains its full measure of meaning in the context of the bigger picture that is formed by all of them together.

What follows is intended to give the reader a preliminary glimpse of that bigger picture, beginning with a summary of the practice of artificial mummification.

Mummies in Fact

Artificial Mummies

Various mummification traditions of great importance have existed in the past and continue to exist today, including—to name just three examples that have their own separate entries in this encyclopedia—the "Fire Mummies" of the Ibaloy people in the Philippines, the smoked body tradition of Papua New Guinea, and the Buddhist practice of self-mummification. But the largest and most extensively studied have been those of Latin America and ancient Egypt.

The earliest practice of artificial mummification, so far as we currently know, existed among the Chinchorro people of southern Peru and northern Chile. As far back as 5000 BCE, the Chinchorro were intentionally mummifying their dead in various ways. The formal scientific study of these mummies was first conducted by Max Uhle in the early twentieth century CE, and his decision to classify the Chinchorro mummies into different types was adopted by later scientists; today we speak of the "black mummies" and "red mummies," and also the "bandaged mummies" and "mud mummies," of the Chinchorro. The study of these mummies and what they reveal about the Chinchorro people is a subfield of great significance.

The Chinchorro were not the only people of Latin America to practice intentional mummification. Various peoples from the west Amazon region (Ecuador, Venezuela, Bolivia, and Colombia) and the Andean region (largely made up of Chile and Peru) mummified their dead in various ways, many of them producing what are now called "mummy bundles" by encasing their dead in some form of cloth. Some Latin American peoples produced mummified heads. Some only mummified their royalty or practiced special forms of mummification on them. Today the field of Latin American mummy studies is one of the most rich and thriving areas in the discipline as a whole, with many scientists hard at work, many books and journals being published, many documentary films and television programs being produced, and many museums set up to preserve the mummies of this part of the world and educate the general public about their nature and significance.

Almost as old as the Latin American mummification traditions is the more widely known tradition of mummification that was practiced in ancient Egypt over a span of 3,000 years. Egyptian mummification began, like many other such traditions around the world, when people started deliberately treating the bodies of their dead to aid the natural mummification process that sometimes occurred. For the Egyptians, this meant finding ways to enhance what they had observed when bodies were sometimes found to have been preserved by burial in the arid Egyptian desert. Today the evolution of Egyptian mummification methods, and also the way this evolution reveals many important facts about ancient Egyptian culture and society as a whole, is understood in extensive detail thanks to the efforts of many dedicated scientists and scholars from many different countries over the past 300 years. From early practices such as eviscerating bodies and wrapping them in plaster-soaked linen, to later practices such as drying bodies with natron, applying oils, and using wigs, fake eyes, paint, and stuffing, the Egyptians created one of the most elaborate mummification traditions the world has ever seen. Nor did they use it only on human beings; they also mummified literally millions of animals to serve as religious offerings, companions, and/or food for humans in the afterlife.

Natural Mummies

Although it is artificial mummies that have been most prominent in popular awareness, a number of natural mummies have also caught the popular imagination in recent decades. The scientific study of such mummies has been invaluable to archaeology, anthropology, and newly emerging fields such as paleopathology (the study of ancient diseases and sicknesses).

While the Latin American and Egyptian artificial mummification traditions are identified with specific geographical areas, the history of natural mummification spans the entire planet. Natural mummies of great importance have been discovered in Egypt, such as the famed Gebelein Man, discovered in 1896, and in Latin America, such as the 111 natural mummies currently housed in the *Museo de las Momias* (English: Museum of the Mummies) in Guanajuato, Mexico. But they have also been discovered in Europe, North America, and elsewhere.

In Europe, some of the most important discoveries have been bog bodies, that is, bodies that were preserved by being immersed in peat bogs. These have been found in Germany, the Netherlands, Denmark, the United Kingdom, and Ireland, and some of them, such as Tollund Man and Lindow Man (and also Grauballe Man, the Weerdinge Men, the Yde Girl, and the Windeby Girl), have become objects of real public fascination. They have also been of great value to science. Although theories about the origins of these mummies are tentative, the most common assumption for their presence in these bogs is that they were placed there as ritual offerings to the gods. Other bog bodies have been found in Norway, Poland, and Florida.

Ice mummies—those found frozen in glaciers or other frigid environments—are another important category of natural mummies. Among these, the most famous is almost certainly Ötzi the Iceman, a.k.a. The Tyrolean Iceman, who was discovered in the Tyrolean Alps in 1991, and who is, at 5,100 years old, Europe's oldest natural mummy. Ötzi has proved invaluable in advancing our understanding of the time period and human culture in which he lived because of the extensive number of artifacts that were discovered with him, Other notable ice mummies include the Canadian Ice Man discovered in 1999, the eight bodies discovered in Greenland in 1992, and Juanita, the so-called "Inca Ice Maiden" who was discovered in the Peruvian Andes in 1995, who apparently died around 1400 CE, and who, like Ötzi, proved particularly potent in capturing the public imagination.

Also of great interest and importance are the numerous crypt mummies that have been found all over Europe. These include many of the mummies in the Capuchin Catacombs of Palermo, Sicily, which were deposited there over a span of three centuries; the 15 mummies at the Church of the Dead in Urbania, Italy; the crypt mummies of Sommersdorf Castle in southern Germany; the mummies in the Dominican church of Vác, Hungary; most of the mummies at the Dominican Church of the Holy Spirit in Vilnius, Lithuania; and many more. Conditions in churches and crypts often prove conducive to natural mummification, and so many of these mummies have been produced over the centuries. In recent years they have been recovered, treated, examined, and respectfully used as objects of scientific study and public display.

Mummymania

The Egyptian mummification tradition was formally ended in the year 392 CE when the Roman Emperor Theodosius I decreed a ban on mummification, but the story of Egyptian mummies was hardly over. With their 3,000 years of preserved bodies locked away in tombs everywhere, the ancient Egyptians had effectively seeded history with a mummy tradition that would one day sprout again to intrigue and inspire people in new and diverse ways.

The seventeenth and eighteenth centuries saw the birth of science itself coincide with the birth of scientific mummy studies, as various scientists began to unwrap and study Egyptian mummies. The practice intensified in the nineteenth century and was accompanied by the birth of Egyptology as a proper science when the translation of the famed Rosetta Stone, discovered during Napoleon's Egyptian campaign in 1799, unlocked ancient Egyptian writing and made available a wealth of knowledge that was formerly unavailable. Scientists and showmen—roles that were united, in some cases, in a single individual—began to conduct public mummy unwrappings and mummy exhibitions in England, Europe, and America. Archaeologists and explorers traipsed across Egypt seeking lost tombs and treasures.

By the dawn of the twentieth century, many important discoveries had been made and many important mummies and associated items had been excavated and collected. Such events as the founding of the Egyptian Antiquities Museum in Cairo and the founding of the Egypt Exploration Society in England were emblematic of the rising importance of ancient Egyptian studies, while popular culture in America and Europe was saturated with awareness of mummies, particularly of the Egyptian variety, which generally stood as a symbol of all things ancient, exotic, dark, and mysterious. The public fascination with mummy unwrappings and related events reached such heights of intensity that it has sometimes been termed "mummymania."

Mummies in Fiction

It was inevitable that a cultural force of this magnitude would have an impact on the artistic imagination, and so the mingled advent of mummy science and mummymania was accompanied by the advent of an associated new genre of literature and drama that was devoted to the same subject, but in a greatly romanticized and exoticized form.

The first English novel featuring a mummy, Jane Webb Loudon's *The Mummy! A Tale of the Twenty-Second Century*, was published in 1827, and was soon followed by stories from the likes of French author Theophile Gautier, American author Edgar Allan Poe, and even Louisa May Alcott, who, although she is far more famous today for having written *Little Women*, produced one of the first fictional explorations of the idea of a "mummy curse" in her 1869 short story "Lost in a Pyramid; or, The Mummy's Curse." Similarly, Arthur Conan Doyle, famed as the author of the Sherlock Holmes stories, wrote two significant mummy stories, "The Ring of Thoth" (1890) and "Lot No. 249 (1892)." Bram Stoker, most famous as the author of *Dracula*, wrote what has come to be widely recognized in just the past few decades as perhaps the greatest mummy horror novel, *The Jewel of Seven Stars* (1903). Fast forward to the year 2013, and, with many years of intervening mummy fiction standing between them, Stoker's novel was joined by *The Book of the Dead*, the first anthology of all-original mummy fiction, published by Jurassic London in cooperation with the Egypt Exploration Society.

The artistic influence of the mummy was not, of course, limited to literature alone. Several stage plays were written and produced in the 1800s that involved mummies, but it was in the new art-and-entertainment medium of the movies that the mummy would achieve perhaps its greatest stature as a mythic, iconic figure of the human imagination. After appearing in numerous films (mostly in incidental roles) during the silent era, mummies rose to major prominence in 1932 in Universal Studios' *The Mummy*, starring Boris Karloff and written by John Balderston—one of the journalists who had covered the opening of Tutankhamun's tomb a decade earlier, which had occasioned a worldwide media sensation. The film instantly immortalized the mummy, specifically the Egyptian variety, as a movie icon, and it spawned an enduring subgenre of cinematic mummy horror as Universal followed *The Mummy* with several more mummy films in the 1940s (and one in the 1950s, the parody film *Abbott and Costello Meet the Mummy*). Then England's Hammer Films produced their own mummy series beginning in 1959, during the decade when Universal's earlier films were being introduced to a new generation of viewers by the "creature feature" phenomenon on late-night American television. The by-then classic character of "The Mummy," mostly in its 1940s guise, also began appearing in comic books, on trading cards, and elsewhere, and suddenly it was the case that a monster born on movie screens (and influenced by literature and stage plays) just a couple of decades earlier had become a pervasive and instantly recognizable icon of horror entertainment. By the time Universal rebooted its classic and long-dormant mummy series in 1999 with a new version of *The Mummy*, the creature pioneered by Karloff had become the stuff of cultural legend.

Mummies at Critical Mass

Today the story of mummies is hardly over. In fact, one could plausibly argue that it is only just beginning. The field of mummy science, for example, has fairly exploded in the past 30 years. When the late Dr. Arthur Aufderheide published his seminal book *The Scientific Study of Mummies* in 2003, he was, in effect, simultaneously summing up what had gone before and heralding the advent of a new era.

Studies of mummies using medical imaging technology, for example, were limited for a century to X-rays, but since the 1980s new technologies such as CTscanning, MRI, and terahertz imaging have been added to the mix, and their use has accelerated dramatically in the twenty-first century. The new field of genetic studies is likewise being employed to harvest enormous amounts of previously unavailable information from both recently discovered mummies and ones that were studied in former eras using older techniques. At the same time, advances in anthropology, archaeology, and other fields continue to be made, and they act in harmony with medical imaging and genetic studies to deliver a veritable treasure trove of new information from around the world that is providing new perspectives and insights on an almost daily basis.

The trajectory of the iconic Mummy of fiction and pop culture likewise appears to be reaching a point of critical mass in the early twenty-first century. As mentioned above, the world's first anthology of all-new fiction about mummies was published in 2013, and its connection with the Egypt Exploration Society is much in keeping with a general cultural theme that has emerged in the era of the Internet as trends in science and other "real-world" areas have become visibly, directly, and mutually reinforced by trends in entertainment. As this encyclopedia goes to press, yet another reboot of the original Universal mummy movie series is in the works, and the infotainment-style spate of television mummy documentaries is showing no signs of abating, and may in fact be accelerating.

Mummies, in short, are not only one of the most ancient cultural fascinations but one of the most current as well. This encyclopedia explains and explores the significance of this fact by painting a vivid and detailed picture of mummies from prehistory to the present. It is thus not only about mummies but about ourselves— what we have collectively believed, hoped, and feared. Mummies have always been with us, and today we turn to them with ever more advanced and refined methods of asking them question and learning their deep secrets. For those who are willing to listen, mummies have a great deal to tell us about the oldest and deepest mysteries of life, death, and our primordial fear and desire for what lies beyond both.

Timeline

ca. 5000 BCE	The Chinchorro peoples of northern Chile and southern Peru begin to engage in the earliest known practice of artificial mummification, beginning with "black mummies."
ca. 3600 BCE	Predynastic tombs are built at Hierakonpolis. They will later provide evidence of the earliest Egyptian attempts at artificial mummification.
ca. 2700 BCE	The Old Kingdom period of ancient Egypt begins. Innovations in mummification include evisceration and wrapping bodies in plaster-soaked linen.
ca. 2050 BCE	The Middle Kingdom period of ancient Egypt begins. Innovations in mummification include the widespread use of natron, oils, perfumes, and resins, as well as the regular use of the cartonnage face mask (isolated examples of which appeared somewhat earlier).
ca. 2500–2000 BCE	The Chinchorro in South America begin to produce "red mummies," bandaged mummies, and mud-coated mummies.
ca. 1800 BCE	The Chavin peoples of Peru begin producing mummy bundles.
ca. 1550 BCE	The New Kingdom period of ancient Egypt begins. Innovations in mummification include stuffing the body with various materials to give it a more life-like appearance.
ca. 1070 BCE	The Third Intermediate Period of ancient Egypt begins. Innovations in mummification include attempts to create a lifelike appearance using wigs, fake eyes, stuffing, and paint, as well as separate mummification of internal organs.
ca. 440 BCE	The ancient Greek historian Herodotus describes Egyptian mummification practices in his *Histories*.
332 BCE	The Greco-Roman period of ancient Egypt begins.

200 BCE	The Nasca people of Peru begin producing mummy bundles and mummified heads. Peru's Moche, Tiwanaku, and Huari groups also engage in artificial mummification.
ca. 100–350 CE	The "Fayum mummy portraits" are created in Egypt during the Roman Period.
392 CE	Egyptian mummification is ended by a ban from the Roman emperor Theodosius I.
ca. 1000 CE	In Peru, the Chiribaya and Chancay peoples and the Moche descendants begin producing mummy bundles.
ca. 1400–1500	The use of crumbled, ground, and/or powdered parts of Egyptian mummies for medicinal purposes comes into common use across Europe and will continue into the late eighteenth century.
ca. 1470–1534	The Inca people of Peru's Late Horizon period mummify their royalty.
1658	One of the earliest recorded unwrappings of an Egyptian mummy takes place in a pharmacy in Breslau (modern-day Wrocław, Poland).
1705	The English surgeon Thomas Greenhill publishes Νεκροκηδεια, or, The art of embalming; wherein is shewn the right of burial, and funeral ceremonies, especially that of preserving bodies after the Egyptian method. The book is intended to professionalize the practice of embalming and encourage more of the nobility to have their bodies embalmed.
1763	The scientist John Hadley unwraps a mummy at his home in London in the presence of the famous doctors William and John Hunter.
1794	The German doctor John Frederick Blumenbach unwraps all the mummies in the British Museum along with several from private collections, and discovers that many of the smaller Egyptian mummies in British collections are actually modern fakes.
1798	Napoleon Bonaparte invades Egypt, setting the stage for the birth of modern scientific Egyptology, including the serious study of Egyptian mummies.
1799	A French soldier in Napoleon's army discovers the Rosetta Stone.
1802	The British Museum acquires the Rosetta Stone from the French.

1804	The Napoleonic Edict of Saint-Cloud forbids burials in churches, resulting in the discovery of many mummies throughout Europe when bodies are excavated for reburial.
1807	The Department of Antiquities is founded at the British Museum.
1809	The first volume of the monumental *Description de l'Egypte* (English: *Description of Egypt*) is published.
1817	In October, Giovanni Belzoni discovers the tomb of Pharaoh Seti I in the Valley of the Kings; by 1821 he is exhibiting and unwrapping mummies in London.
1821	A. B. Granville performs an early, detailed mummy examination in England.
1822	The French scholar Jean François Champollion announces that he has translated portions of the hieroglyphs on the Rosetta Stone.
1823	The first commercial exhibition of an Egyptian mummy in America begins in Boston in May. Frédéric Caillaud unwraps two Egyptian mummies in France before a large audience of scientists and observers.
1824	The first full examination of an Egyptian mummy in the United States takes place in New York.
1825	The Leeds Philosophical and Literary Society performs an autopsy on the 3,000-year-old mummy of Nesyamun.
1827	The novel *The Mummy! A Tale of the Twenty-Second Century* by Jane Webb Loudon is published. It is the first novel in English featuring a revived mummy.
1828	William Osburn's *Account of an Egyptian Mummy*, about the 1825 autopsy on Nesyamun, is published.
1832	The body of English philosopher and political theorist Jeremy Bentham is preserved as an "Auto-Icon."
1833	Thomas Pettigrew hosts his first public unrolling of two Egyptian mummies in the lecture room at Charing Cross Hospital in London. Elsewhere in the city, the earliest known mummy play, a farce titled *The Mummy or The Elixir of Life*, is performed.
1834	Thomas Pettigrew's *A History of Egyptian Mummies* is published.

1837	John Gardner Wilkinson's seminal *Manners and Customs of the Ancient Egyptians* is published, featuring extensive information about ancient Egyptian burial and mummification practices.
1845	The short story "Some Words with a Mummy" by Edgar Allan Poe is published in the April issue of *American Review.*
1851	Auguste Mariette discovers and excavates the Serapeum in Saqqara, Egypt.
1852	Alexander, Tenth Duke of Hamilton, dies on August 18 and is mummified according to his own instructions by Thomas Pettigrew.
1858	Auguste Mariette founds the Egyptian Antiquities Service and becomes its first director.
1863	The first incarnation of the Egyptian Antiquities Museum opens in the Boulaq area of Cairo on October 16 with Auguste Mariette as its director.
1869	The German chemist August Wilhelm von Hofmann conclusively identifies formaldehyde. The short story "Lost in a Pyramid; or, The Mummy's Curse" by Louisa May Alcott is published, becoming perhaps the earliest fictional treatment of the idea of a "mummy curse."
1880	Burials in the Capuchin Catacombs of Palermo, Sicily—home to a large number of mummified human remains—are officially halted but continue into the twentieth century. In January, "My New Year's Eve Among the Mummies" by "J. Arbuthnot Wilson" (pseudonym of Grant Allen) becomes the first known mummy-related short story in a British periodical.
1881	Between July 6 and 8, Emile Brugsch documents the cache of royal mummies uncovered at Deir el-Bahri, Western Thebes. During the same year, Gaston Maspero unwraps many of these mummies.
1882	The Egypt Exploration Fund, based out of England and later to become the Egypt Exploration Society, is founded.
1886	Beginning in October and finishing the following January, H. Rider Haggard's novel *She: A History of Adventure* is published in serial form.
1890	The Boulaq museum in Cairo closes, and antiquities, including the royal mummies, are transferred to the Ghizeh Palace museum.

1894	The Museo de las Momias de Guanajuato (English: The Museum of the Mummies of Guanajuato) is established in Guanajuato, Mexico.
1896	German physicist Walter Koenig conducts the first recorded X-ray of a mummy. Gebelein Man is discovered in Upper Egypt.
1898	A second cache of royal Egyptian mummies is discovered by Victor Loret in the tomb of Amenhotep II.
1899	Director Georges Méliès' silent film *Cleopatra's Tomb* presents the earliest cinematic depiction of a mummy.
1902	Royal mummies and other antiquities are moved to the Egyptian Museum on Tahrir Square.
1903	Bram Stoker's *The Jewel of Seven Stars*, later to be recognized as perhaps the greatest mummy novel, is published. In Cairo, Thutmose IV is the first royal Egyptian mummy to be X-rayed.
1908	Margaret Murray unwraps two Egyptian mummies in front of a standing-room-only crowd at Manchester University, which will go on to become a central institution in the field of mummy studies.
1909	Pathologist M. A. Ruffer begins publishing a series of papers that make significant advancements in the study of mummified tissue.
1912	Max Uhle becomes the first to describe and classify the mummies of northern Chile's Chinchorro culture. Grafton Elliott Smith publishes the Catalogue of Royal Mummies in the Cairo Museum.
1922	Howard Carter discovers the tomb of the pharaoh Tutankhamun in the Valley of the Kings on November 6. News of the find causes a sensation among the general public and the press.
1923	Lord Carnarvon and Howard Carter open Tutankhamun's burial chamber in the Valley of the Kings. Marie Corelli warns in the British press of a punishment to befall violators of tombs. Shortly afterward, Carnarvon dies unexpectedly, becoming the most famous victim of a supposed "mummy curse."
1924	The mummified body of Vladimir Lenin is placed on public display in the Kremlin in Moscow. The book *Egyptian Mummies* by Warren Dawson and Grafton Elliot Smith is published.
1925	Tutankhamun's mummy is autopsied over a span of eight days in November.

1928	Warren Dawson's annotated *Bibliography of Works Relating to Mummification in Egypt* is published.
1932	Universal Studios releases its landmark mummy horror film *The Mummy*.
1940–1944	Universal Studios releases *The Mummy's Hand*, *The Mummy's Tomb*, *The Mummy's Ghost* and *The Mummy's Curse*.
1947	The CBS radio program *Escape* broadcasts an adaptation of Arthur Conan Doyle's 1892 mummy story "The Ring of Thoth."
1949	An adaptation of Theophile Gautier's story "The Mummy's Foot" appears on the television anthology program *Your Show Time* in February, thus becoming the first mummy fiction made for television.
1950	Tollund Man is discovered in a bog near Silkeborg, Denmark.
1951	The first edition of the monumental *Who Was Who in Egyptology* by Warren Dawson is published.
1952	Grauballe Man is discovered in a bog near Grauballe, Denmark. Windeby Girl is discovered in the Domlandsmoor near the town of Windeby in northern Germany.
1957	On American television, *Shock Theater* introduces a new audience to the old Universal monster movies, including the entire mummy series.
1959	Hammer Films releases *The Mummy*—the first in a series of unrelated mummy films that they will release over the next decade.
1964	The first two issues of the comic book *Monster World* feature adaptations of Universal Studios's now-classic *The Mummy* from 1932 and *The Mummy's Hand* from 1940.
1968	Liverpool University anatomist Ronald Harrison X-rays the mummy of Tutankhamun to determine the cause of death.
1970	On February 23, "The Curse of the Mummy" airs as the final episode of the British television anthology series *Mystery and Imagination*; it is the earliest film adaptation of Bram Stoker's *The Jewel of Seven Stars*.
1972	The 2,100-year-old mummified body of the Marquise of Tai is found in a tomb in China's Hunan Province. The movie *El Santo Contra Las Momias de Guanajuato* (released in English as *The Mummies of Guanajuato*) is released. Eight ice mummies dating to ca. 1475 are found in northwestern Greenland.

1973	The Manchester Museum Mummy Project (later to be called the Manchester Egyptian Mummy Project) is founded under the directorship of Rosalie David.
1975	*Doctor Who: Pyramids of Mars* is broadcast between October 25 and November 15. The American religious organization Summum, offering Egyptian-style mummification services for humans and animals, is founded.
1976	An earthquake destroys both the Church of Saint Andrew and the nearby Chapel of Saint Michael in Venzone, Italy; 15 of the more than 20 natural mummies there are rescued and treated for further preservation.
1977	Canadian doctors Derek Harwood-Nash and Peter Lewin become the first to use CT scanning on mummified human remains.
1978	Tutankhamun's head is X-rayed by University of Michigan orthodontist James Harrison.
1980	The royal mummy room at the Cairo Museum is closed on the orders of Egyptian president Anwar Sadat.
1982	*Oh Mummy* from Sinclair/Gem Software and Bandai's handheld *Invaders of the Mummy's Tomb* become two of the earliest video and electronic mummy-based games. Five Inuit ice mummies are found at Utqiagvik (Barrow) in northern Alaska.
1984	Lindow Man is discovered at Lindow Moss bog in northwest England. The graves of three naturally preserved ice mummies from the ill-fated Franklin Expedition of 1845–1848 are excavated on the Beechey Islands in the Canadian Arctic.
1985	The first DNA analysis of mummy tissue is published in the journal *Nature*.
1988	DNA is successfully extracted from the brain of a 7,000-year-old human mummy found in Florida.
1989	The novel *The Mummy or Ramses the Damned* by Anne Rice is published. It becomes the best-selling mummy novel in history.
1990	Rosalie David and the Manchester Egyptian Mummy Project perform medical examinations of Nesyamun—the first in more than a century—using radiology, CT scans, endoscopy, serology, histology dental examination, fingerprinting, and facial reconstruction.

1991	Ötzi the Iceman, the world's oldest known European natural mummy (about 5,100 years old), is discovered on September 19 by two hikers in the Tyrolean Alps.
1992	The first World Congress on Mummy Studies convenes on February 3–6 in Puerto de la Cruz in Tenerife, Spain.
1993	The Siberian Ice Maiden is discovered on the Ukok Plateau in the Altai Mountains, Russia.
1994	Egyptologist Bob Brier and medical doctor Ronald Wade mummify a terminally ill British man using ancient Egyptian techniques and surrounded by extensive media coverage. After new climate-controlled cases are perfected, a new royal mummy room opens at the Cairo Museum with 11 mummies, to be followed by a second room several years later.
1995	The "Valley of the Golden Mummies," containing an estimated 10,000 Egyptian mummies, is discovered in the Bahariya Oasis. Juanita, the Inca Ice Maiden, is discovered in the Peruvian Andes. The Swiss Mummy Project is founded.
1997	The International Ancient Egyptian Mummy Tissue Bank is set up at Britain's Manchester Museum. For Halloween, the U.S. Post Office issues a series of 32-cent stamps highlighting famous Universal monsters, including Boris Karloff as The Mummy.
1998	The Bioanthropology Research Institute is founded.
1999	The Canadian Ice Man is discovered in British Columbia, Canada. Universal Studios reboots its long-dormant movie franchise with a new version of *The Mummy*.
2001	The oldest mummified bodies ever discovered in Britain are found buried in Scotland at Cladh Hallan.
2003	*The Scientific Study of Mummies* by Arthur Aufderheide is published; it immediately becomes a landmark work in the field. The Akhmim Mummy Studies Consortium is founded.
2004	More than 20 human mummies are found in a basement storage area of the Reiss-Engelhorn Museums of Mannheim, Germany, leading to the birth of The German Mummy Project. At its theme parks in Orlando, Florida and Los Angeles, California, Universal Studios debuts *Revenge of the Mummy*, a thrill ride based on their new/rebooted mummy film franchise. In 2010 they will open another one at Universal Studios Singapore.

2005	CT scans are performed on Tutankhamun's mummy in Egypt's Valley of the Kings, in a project funded by National Geographic. An exhibition of Tutankhamun's treasures begins touring the United States.
2007	The Vatican Mummy Project is launched by the Vatican Museums' Department for the Antiquities of Egypt and the Near East. In Mexico, the mayor of Guanajuato launches the Guanajuato Mummy Research Project. In Switzerland, the first examination of multiple mummified tissues using clinical magnetic resonance imaging (MRI) is conducted.
2010	A controversial report on DNA from Tutankhamun and other royal mummies from Egypt's 18th Dynasty is published. "Mummies of the World: The Exhibition" opens at the California Science Center in Los Angeles. The first images of ancient mummies produced by terahertz imaging are published.
2011	The oldest bog body ever found (4,000 years old) is uncovered in County Laois in Cashel, Ireland. The Egyptian Museum in Tahrir Square is looted and some mummies are damaged. Doctors Stephen Buckley and Joanne Fletcher mummify a terminally ill taxi driver by means of a liquid natron bath, at odds with Brier and Wade's previous use of dry natron crystals in 1994.
2012	The genome sequence of Ötzi the Iceman is published. CT scans of all of the mummies at the Manchester Museum are performed using state-of-the-art CT facilities at the Manchester Children's Hospital (a project extending into 2013).
2013	Arthur Aufderheide, a seminal figure in the field of modern scientific mummy studies, dies on August 9. The DNA sequences of five mummies at the University of Tübingen museum are published. The first all-original anthology of mummy fiction, titled *The Book of the Dead*, is published by Jurassic London in conjunction with the Egypt Exploration Society.
2014	In January, "Mummies of the World: The Exhibition" closes at the Maryland Science Center in Baltimore, having toured for nearly four years. In Fusta, Egypt, the National Museum of Egyptian Civilization opens.

2015 (planned)   The Grand Egyptian Museum opens near the pyramids at Giza.

2016 (planned)   Universal Studios launches another reboot of its mummy movie series.

Abbott and Costello Meet the Mummy

Abbott and Costello Meet the Mummy (1955) was directed by Charles Lamont and produced by Howard Christie. It was the last of Universal Studio's original six mummy films and was the only comic mummy film they produced.

The plot begins with Abbott and Costello stranded in Cairo. They agree to bring a mummy back to the United States for an archaeologist, but when they arrive at the archaeologist's home, they learn that he has been murdered and that Klaris, the mummy, has disappeared. Soon they inadvertently become the possessors of a sacred medallion similar to the one seen in Universal Studios' earlier film *The Mummy's Hand*. The medallion turns out to be the key to a buried treasure

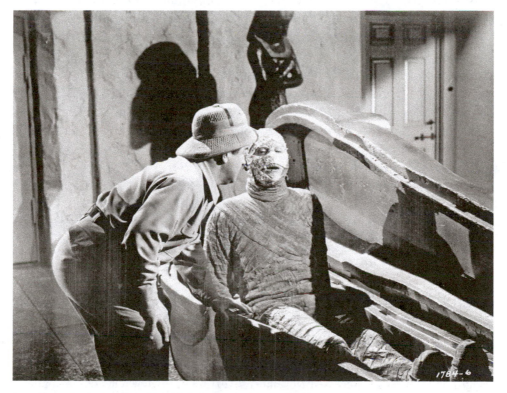

Lou Costello (as Freddie Franklin) confronts Eddie Parker (as Klaris, the mummy) in *Abbott and Costello Meet the Mummy*. (Universal/Photofest)

Kharis, Klaris, Chaney, and Parker

According to rumor, stuntman Eddie Parker, who was billed as playing the stunt double for Lon Chaney, Jr. in the role of the mummy Kharis in Universal's 1940s mummy series, actually played all of the mummy scenes in those films. In *Abbott and Costello Meet the Mummy* he finally got open billing as the mummy, but with the character's named spoofed and changed to "Klaris."

---

in the tomb of the Princess Ara. Eventually it winds up in a hamburger that is eaten by Lou Costello, who, in a hilarious scene, is X-rayed so that the hieroglyphs can be read. But it does not work out as intended, and much trouble ensues. In the end, the tomb is found, but not before a scene in which three mummies (the real Klaris and two imposters) all bump into each other. The treasure is discovered, and the characters decide to turn the tomb into a nightclub.

The sacred medallion is one of several references to elements that appear in Universal's earlier mummy films. In previous films, the mummy was named Kharis, so "Klaris" is a kind of inside joke that mummy fans would easily have recognized. Unlike the mummies in the previous horror films, this one is quite comical. It is never really threatening, and at times it is almost someone the audience can root for.

This was Abbott and Costello's final film for Universal Studios. The same was true for stuntman Eddie Parker, who played Klaris. Parker had served as the stunt double for Lon Chaney, Jr., in several previous entries in Universal's mummy cycle, and there is a long-standing rumor that it was actually him, and not Chaney, who inhabited the bandages in all of the mummy scenes from those films. Whatever the truth of this story may be, in *Abbott and Costello Meet the Mummy* Parker openly played, and received the official credit for, the character of Klaris.

Bob Brier

See also: Chaney, Lon, Jr.; Kharis; *The Mummy's Hand*; Universal Studios mummy series

Further Reading

Cowie, Susan D., and Tom Johnson. 2002. *The Mummy in Fact, Fiction and Film.* Jefferson, NC: McFarland & Co.

Miller, Jeffrey S. 2000. *The Horror Spoofs of Abbott and Costello: A Critical Assessment of the Comedy Team's Monster Films.* Jefferson, NC: McFarland & Co.

Nixon, Rob. "Abbott and Costello Meet the Mummy." Race and Hollywood: Arab Images on Film. *TCM.* Accessed November 7, 2013. http://www.tcm.com/this-month/article/411149|78358/Abbott-and-Costello-Meet-the-Mummy.html.

Akhmim Mummy Studies Consortium

Akhmim Mummy Studies Consortium (AMSC) is an independent research organization located in Carlisle, Pennsylvania, specializing in computerized tomography (CT) research on Egyptian mummies in museum collections worldwide. AMSC developed out of the mummy CT scanning efforts of Carter Lupton of the Milwaukee Public Museum (MPM) from 1986 to 1999. Mummies scanned by AMSC are analyzed full-time and with archival intent and a program of publication. AMSC is a leading proponent of 3D printing technology applied to ancient mummies.

As a result of the source of MPM's two mummies, AMSC, founded in 2003 with start-up funds provided by Westminster College in western Pennsylvania and the Milwaukee Public Museum, originally focused on performing CT scan-based studies on Egyptian mummies associated with the ancient city of Akhmim (Panopolis). Akhmim is an important site sacred to the fertility god Min, located 290 miles (470 km) south of Cairo. Excavations performed in Akhmim's extensive and crowded cemeteries by the French-administered Service des Antiquités, beginning

Jonathan Elias, director of the Harrisburg-based Akhmim Mummy Studies Consortium, explains the background of a three-dimensional model of Pesed, the 2,300-year-old Egyptian mummy at Westminster College in New Wilmington, PA, April 4, 2006. (AP Images/Pittsburgh Tribune-Review/Keith Hodan)

Mummies are a source of enduring fascination not only as sources of bioanthropological information but in connection with the study of ancient Egyptian beliefs about resurrection and the technical means of achieving eternal life. Research on Egyptian mummification is still in its infancy, but is rapidly improving through use of computed tomography (CT) on Ptolemaic mummies, and those of earlier periods. The mummy CT scan (cat-scan) is a powerful tool for new mummy discoveries and for achieving a new understanding about ancient Egyptian views of life and death.

Reference

Elias, Jonathan (Director, Akhmim Mummy Studies Consortium). "Mummy Studies: Continuing Research on the Mummies at Akhmim." Retrieved January 17, 2014. http://amscresearch.com/id3.html.

in March 1884, occurred at a time when mummies were often sold off by officials within weeks of their discovery. Out of 800 mummies reportedly discovered during two weeks of work at Akhmim in 1885, it is estimated that over 100 mummies from Akhmim still exist in collections outside of Egypt. Other mummies were found at Akhmim during the 1890s and quickly approved for sale and export by Emile Brugsch during the era when he administered the Ghizeh Palace Museum (1889–1902).

AMSC organizes CT scanning projects as a means of benefitting smaller museums throughout the world, which may have become repositories for mummies that require professional analysis beyond the normal scope of museum resources. Early AMSC CT projects included the female Ptolemaic mummies of Pesed (Westminster College No. 48), Nefer-ii-ne (Reading Public Museum 30-318-1), and Ta-irty (College of Wooster 01.1a). Since that time, the scans of many other Ptolemaic mummies have been added to the AMSC archives.

In 2005, AMSC initiated the Community of Portraits project, intended to produce a large number of forensic facial reconstructions of the ancient Egyptian population based on rapid prototyped (3D printed) skull models generated from CT data sets. The purpose of this project was to determine the ethnic composition of the ancient Egyptian community in Akhmim. The consortium was assisted in this effort by the Bioanthropology and Digital Analysis Laboratory of the University of Manitoba (BDIAL), which provided 3D printing services from 2005 to 2009. Collaboration with BDIAL resulted in AMSC becoming an early source of rapid prototyping expertise in Egyptian mummy studies.

In 2006, AMSC expanded its research activities significantly, scanning mummies at the Egyptian Antiquities Museum in Cairo and doing background surveys in the cemeteries of Akhmim (2006–2007), while continuing to develop projects on mummies in collections in North America. From 2007 onward, the consortium has begun to assist in the CT scanning of mummies from Egyptian regions beyond Akhmim, including Thebes, and the Fayum. The majority of the now 30 mummies which AMSC has examined date to the 25th Dynasty and later periods, the Ptolemaic age in particular. The consortium has succeeded in identifying two parent-child pairs from Akhmim and has studied the CT scans of these related individuals. The organization has participated in the World Congress on Mummy Studies from 2004 onward, and it specializes in research on subjects related to the evolution of mummification ritual and ancient medical practices. AMSC maintains its own collection of historical documents relating to the history of mummy research spanning the past 500 years and has constructed its own exhibition to display these materials, entitled: *Wrapped! The Search for the Essential Mummy.*

Jonathan Elias

See also: Brugsch, Emile; Collecting mummies; Egyptian mummies; Medical imaging of mummies; The World Congresses on Mummy Studies

Further Reading

Akhmim Mummy Studies Consortium. Accessed November 7, 2013. http://amsc research.com/.

Elias, Jonathan. 2012 online, 2013 print. "Akhmim." In *The Encyclopedia of Ancient History,* edited by R. Bagnall, K. Broderson, C. Champion, A. Erskine, and S. Huebner. Oxford, UK: Wiley Press, Blackwell Publishing Ltd.

Elias Jonathan, and Carter Lupton. 2008. "The Social Parameters of Mummification in Akhmim, Egypt (700–200 BC)." In *Mummies and Science. World Mummies Research: Proceedings of the VIth World Congress on Mummy Studies,* edited by P. Atoche Peña, M. Martin Rodriguez, M. and A. Ramirez Rodriguez, 507–514. Teguise, Lanzarote, Canary Islands. Santa Cruz de Tenerife: Academia Canaria de la Historia.

Alexander, Tenth Duke of Hamilton

The British aristocrat, diplomat, and collector Alexander, Duke of Hamilton (1767–1852) was, following his death, mummified according to his own instructions by the noted anatomist and unroller of Egyptian mummies Thomas Joseph Pettigrew and interred in an Egyptian sarcophagus within the newly appointed family mausoleum.

Alexander Douglas Hamilton, tenth Duke of Hamilton and seventh Duke of Brandon, was born in St. James's Square, London, and went on to be educated at Harrow School and Christ Church, Oxford, although much of his early life was spent in Italy, away from the family seat in central Scotland. Returning to Britain in 1801, Hamilton became a Member of Parliament for Lancaster (1802–1806) before being appointed as British Ambassador to the Russian Court at St. Petersburg (1806–1807).

Alexander Hamilton's fascination with ancient Egyptian mummies was largely inspired by the work of Thomas "Mummy" Pettigrew, famed for his public unrollings and autopsies of mummies before large crowds, so Hamilton arranged to have himself mummified in the Egyptian manner after his death by Pettigrew himself. Years earlier he had acquired the sarcophagus of an ancient Egyptian princess in France, supposedly for the purpose of donating it to the British Museum, but instead he had his own mummy sealed inside it.

Upon the death of his father, Hamilton succeeded to his hereditary titles in 1819 and fulfilled a number of important roles, including that of Keeper of Holyroodhouse in Edinburgh and Lord High Steward at the coronations of both King William IV and Queen Victoria. In 1836 his service was recognized when he was created a Knight of the Garter. Hamilton's fascination with artwork of all periods, doubtless established by his lengthy sojourn in Italy and by sitting for the portraitist Sir Joshua Reynolds in 1782, culminated in his appointment to a variety of roles including Fellowship of the Royal Society, Fellow of the Society of Antiquaries, Vice President of the Royal Institution for the Encouragement of the Fine Arts in Scotland, and, from 1834 until his death, a Trustee of the British Museum.

Hamilton's British Museum connection led to his purchase of the basalt sarcophagus of a Ptolemaic lady named Iretiru on the museum's behalf in 1837. The sarcophagus did not, however, live up to the museum's expectations—they had been hoping for the sarcophagus of Queen Ankhnesneferibre—and he retained it within his collection of artworks at Hamilton Palace, together with that of the High Steward Pabasa of the 26th Dynasty, purchased in 1834.

Hamilton believed himself to be the descendant of the regent of Arran and, as such, the rightful heir to the Scottish throne. Consequently, he engaged the architect David Hamilton to create the suitably imposing Roman-style Hamilton Mausoleum on his estate. The works were eventually completed by David Bryce in 1858, six years following the Duke's demise.

On August 18, 1852, Hamilton died at his London home, 12 Portman Square, where Pettigrew spent the next two weeks mummifying his remains. The Duke's mummy then arrived at Hamilton palace on September 2 and was interred in the sarcophagus of Iretiru on a plinth within the mausoleum, two days later. Unfortunately, Hamilton had been a tall man, and the sarcophagus, although modified, could not accommodate his mummy, and it seems likely that either his feet were removed or his legs broken to ensure a proper fit. By 1921, the settling and sinking of the mausoleum required the removal of the Duke's mummy and sarcophagus for burial in the nearby cemetery of Bent, where they remain today.

Although the Duke had been given his intended Egyptianizing entombment, the sarcophagus of Pabasa, intended to have been the resting place of his wife, remained unused and was subsequently gifted on November 20, 1922, to the Kelvingrove Art Gallery and Museum, Glasgow, where it has since remained on display.

John J. Johnston

See also: Egyptian mummification methods; Pettigrew, Thomas Joseph

Further Reading

Canmore, Royal Commission on the Ancient Historical Monuments of Scotland. "Hamilton Mausoleum." Accessed November 5, 2013. http://canmore.rcahms.gov.uk/en/site/45684/details/hamilton+hamilton+low+parks+mausoleum/.

Dodson, Aidan. 2002. "Duke Alexander's Sarcophagi." *Archiv Orientální*, 70: 340–342.

Dodson, Aidan. 2007. "Legends of a Sarcophagus." In *Egyptian Stories: A British Egyptological Tribute to Alan B Lloyd on the Occasion of his Retirement*, edited by T. Schneider and K. Szpakowska, 21–28. Munster: Ugarit-Verlag.

Sanders, L. C. 2004. "Hamilton, Alexander Douglas, Tenth Duke of Hamilton and Seventh Duke of Brandon (1767–1852)." Revised by K. D. Reynolds. In *Oxford Dictionary of National Biography*, edited by H. C. G. Matthew and Brian Harrison. Oxford University Press. Accessed November 5, 2013. http://www.oxforddnb.com/view/article/7857.

Animal mummies

Animal mummies, including preserved bodies of animals through natural as well as artificially preserved means (true mummies), have been a basic element of Egyptian religion from the Predynastic Period onward. Mummification was a means of preserving the body for eternity so that the soul (*ka* and *ba*) could inhabit it and use it in the afterlife; thus, it is clear that the Egyptians believed animals had souls along with humans. A vast range of animal species were mummified, including cattle, baboons, rams, lions, cats, dogs, hyenas, ichneumon, goats, gazelles, fish, bats, owls, crocodiles, shrews, scarab beetles, ibises, falcons, snakes, lizards, and many different types of birds. Even crocodile eggs and dung balls were wrapped up and presented as offerings.

Although animals were mummified throughout Egyptian history, the majority of such mummies date to the Late and Graeco-Roman Periods (ca. 630 BCE to CE 395). These eras saw an upsurge in animal cults. This may have been the case perhaps because this was a time when Egypt was being invaded by other world powers such as the Assyrians and the Nubians, as well as the Greeks and Romans, thus causing the Egyptians to seek a variety of ways in which to express their own sense of identity, individualism, nationalism, and pride. Additionally, these mummies might also have been a call to local divinities to provide succor during times that were difficult (politically, socially and economically) for the Egyptians.

A cat coffin with mummy, left, and an ibis coffin are displayed as part of the exhibit "Soulful Creatures: Animal Mummies in Ancient Egypt," at the Orange County's Bowers Museum in Santa Ana, Calif. (AP Images/Damian Dovarganes)

Categories of Ancient Egyptian Animal Mummies

Pets. Often buried in the same chamber with their owner (or in the courtyard outside, if their owner died first), complete with elaborate coffins and food offerings, just like humans.

Food. Mummified foods for the deceased, much of it prepared as if ready to be cooked, then put in small "coffinets."

Sacred animals. Animals that were worshiped in life, then mummified and buried after death. Best known examples: Apis Bulls and the Rams of Elephantine.

Votive offerings. Mummies of animals that were totems or symbols of specific gods. They were bought and offered by pilgrims at various temples and then buried in vast catacombs, where they were thought to offer prayers for the pilgrim throughout eternity. Millions have been discovered.

Other. Some animal mummies do not fit into the above categories. Much research is still being conducted to understand their purpose and their methods of mummification.

Animal mummies can be divided into five basic categories: pet, food, sacred, votive, and "other."

Pets were generally buried within the burial chamber of their owner if they died before or immediately after the owner, or in the courtyard outside if they died after the owner's demise, as was the case with a pet monkey excavated outside Theban Tomb 11. Often, like humans, pets enjoyed well-equipped burials, complete with elaborate coffins and food offerings, such as a mare and a baboon, both associated with the family of Senenmut, the architect of the Queen Hatshepsut's Funerary Temple at Deir el-Bahari.

Food or victual mummies are very peculiarly Egyptian and are most common in the New Kingdom. These consist of mummified foods for the deceased, including beef ribs, steaks, ducks, and geese. The meat and poultry are prepared as if they are ready to be cooked: the meat is skinned, the poultry is plucked and eviscerated with the feet and wing-tips removed. After desiccation the liver and giblets are returned to the body cavity. Some of the mummies are colored brown; this roasted/seared appearance might be due to the application of very hot resin to the flesh, which slightly cooks/sears the exterior surface. Tests show that victual mummies were preserved using salt and natron, similar to the way in which beef jerky is prepared. Most of these bandaged meats were placed in individual sycamore-wood "coffinets" carved in the shape of the contents.

Sacred animals were creatures that were worshiped during their lifetime and mummified and entombed in catacombs after their death. The god's "essence" would enter into the body of a chosen animal, identified as the divine recipient by specific markings. Upon the animal's death, the divine spirit would migrate into the body of another similarly marked creature; this is similar to the idea of the eternal soul of the Dalai Lama that remains on earth in a series of different bodies. The best-known sacred animals are Apis Bulls and the Rams of Elephantine.

The majority of animal mummies are votive offerings. Each god had a specific animal that was his or her totem or symbol and was deemed an effective intercessor. These mummified animals were purchased and offered by pilgrims at specific temples (such as those at Saqqara), a custom particularly in vogue during the first millennium BCE. Once consecrated, during a special festival the mummified animals would be taken in procession and buried en masse in vast catacombs that housed millions of such creatures. They (or their souls) would present the prayers of the pilgrim to the god throughout eternity, much in the way that votive candles are used in churches. Many of these animals were deliberately killed prior to being mummified. Practically, this was generated by the high demand. Spiritually, it was viewed as a pious sacrifice of animals that were going to a better and eternal life, united with their deity. Among this group one might also place "false" mummies: bundles that appeared to contain an animal but that on examination actually contained mud, bones from another creature, or feathers or bits of fur. Maybe the priestly embalmers intended to deceive pilgrims intentionally, or perhaps these mummies were made when there was a scarcity of the appropriate animal. In this case, the priests may have used the very Egyptian idea that a part symbolized the whole, and that correct spells and incantations would transform it into a complete offerings for the gods. Alternatively, these bundles might actually contain the detritus of mummification, and as that, too, was sacred, it was interred in a holy place.

The fifth and final category of animal mummy, "other," includes those animal mummies that do not fit comfortably into any of the other categories. Examples include a group of five ducks and geese that were mummified and placed as a foundation offering at the funerary temple of King Thutmoses III (1479–1424 BCE) in Thebes, or the ibis, dog, and monkey found in a tomb surrounding the body of the deceased. More research should allow for a better understanding of this mummy type.

These various types of mummies were prepared in different ways, perhaps due to the different requirements for various creatures engendered by fur, feathers, or fins; economic constraints; the preferences of specific embalming houses; preferences of different towns/cities/villages; or changes in technology over time. As yet, insufficient research has been carried out on well-excavated and well-dated groups of animal mummies to explain satisfactorily the reasons for the variations in mummification.

The main purpose of mummification was to preserve the body so that it could act as a vehicle for the soul. Thus, the central focus of the preparation was to dehydrate and de-fat the body. Natron, a naturally occurring mixture of sodium carbonate and sodium bicarbonate, was the key ingredient in both animal and human mummification. After evisceration through a cut (generally) in the ventral surface, the body cavity was packed with bundles of natron wrapped up in linen, and the body was immersed in powdered natron. For humans this lasted for 40 days; for animals the duration of the immersion probably depended on the size and type of animal. It is also possible that group immersions of creatures took place to fulfill the demand for votive mummies. After desiccation, the animals were removed from the natron, dusted off, and rubbed with sacred oils. Sometimes hot resin mixed with oil was applied to the animals, and then it was wrapped in linen. During the Graeco-Roman era the outermost wrappings could be very elaborate, taking the form of lozenges, coffers, or stripes of different colors, and some animals had cartonnage masks. Sacred animals in particular were masked and adorned with amulets.

Many of the bird mummies might have been produced in a simpler way: the bird was eviscerated, dipped into a mixture of oil and resin, or resin and bitumen, and then wrapped. A few bird mummies that have obviously been treated with resin and oil mixtures are gilded (that is, covered with gold), either entirely or on the heads. No doubt this stressed the association of these birds with the sun god, Ra, or indicate a sacred animal. Other birds were desiccated and then wrapped. Certain large mammals, such as cows, might not have been eviscerated through a cut but rather by dissolving their internal organs by a cedar oil enema that was introduced into the body via the anus and the hole then plugged up. They were then buried in natron for at least 40 days and, once dry, flushed of the cedar oil by pressing the dissolved internal organs out of the anus, and then wrapped in the usual manner.

The production of animal mummies was a major part of the Egyptian economy, particularly during the first millennium BCE. The animals had to be sourced, maintained, and embalmed, often using imported materials. Certainly animal mummification contributed to the wealth of the temples, the embalmers, and all those involved in animal cults.

Despite the vast number of animal mummies found in Egypt, they have only been studied holistically from the end of the twentieth century, when scholars realized just how much information they could glean from these artifacts if properly studied. By identifying species, mode of death, method of mummification, and signs of disease, one can obtain a wealth of information on ancient Egyptian environment, religion, veterinary practices, mummification technology, trade, and culture. Using sophisticated imaging technologies such as X-rays and CT-scans, as well as high temperature gas chromatography and gas chromatography-mass spectrometry (GC-MS) GCS, and DNA analysis, questions concerning mummification technology, trade networks, domestication, the ancient environment, religion, and evolution can all be studied.

Salima Ikram

See also: Egyptian mummification methods; Experimental mummification; Genetic study of mummies; Medical imaging of mummies; Religion and mummies; Theban Necropolis

Further Reading

Armitage, P. L. and J. Clutton-Brock. 1981. "A Radiological and Histological Investigation into the Mummification of Cats from Ancient Egypt." *Journal of Archaeological Science* 8: 185–96.

Flores, D. V. 2003. *Funerary Sacrifice of Animals in the Egyptian Predynastic Period.* Oxford: Archaeopress.

Ikram, Salima. 1995. *Choice Cuts: Meat Production in Ancient Egypt.* Leuven: Peeters.

Ikram, Salima, ed. 2005. *Divine Creatures: Animal Mummies in Ancient Egypt.* Cairo: American University in Cairo Press.

Lortet, L. C. and C. Gaillard. 1903–09. *La faune momifiée de l'ancienne Egypte.* Lyon: Archives du Muséum Histoire Naturelle de Lyon VIII: 2, IX: 2, X: 2.

Rhind, A. H. 1862. *Thebes: Its Tombs and Their Tenants.* London: Longman, Green, Longman, and Roberts.

Anubis

Anubis is the ancient Egyptian god of mummification and guide for the deceased to the underworld. The meaning of the name *Anubis* (Egyptian: *Jnpw*) is debated and remains unclear. Some translate it as "little dog" and others as "Child of the Ruler," the latter based on the identity of the god's parents in Egyptian mythology. Additional names for Anubis are *Imiut* ("The one who is in his mummy wrappings"), "Lord of the sacred land," and "He who is upon his sacred mountain."

Anubis is pictured either as a black jackal or a human with a jackal's head. Two other Egyptian deities also appear as jackals: Upuaut ("Opener of the Ways") and Khenti-Amentiu ("First of the Westerners"), the latter being the local necropolis god of Abydos (see the entry on Osiris). It is often difficult to distinguish among these jackal gods, and over time Anubis overlaid and incorporated the other ones. The fact that jackals and dogs are attracted to burial places was transferred to a divine concept, declaring these animals as protection deities of the necropolis and guardians of the dead.

Anubis was the original funerary god until he was replaced by Osiris. In the Pyramid Texts he plays an important role for the sustenance of the dead king, and his voice makes the king come forth. In the myth of Osiris he is the son of the goddess Nephthys, whose brother Osiris became the protection god of mummification and funerary rituals. In an earlier myth, Anubis was the son of the sun god Ra; later he became a son of Osiris himself. In the Coffin Texts he was declared to be son of the goddess Hesat, while in other stories he was described as son of Seth.

Anubis plays an important role in the myth of Osiris and Isis. After Osiris was killed by Seth, it was Anubis's task to take the dismembered body parts, reassemble them, and thus invent the first mummy. Anubis also performed the funerary rites for his father Osiris, and Egyptian priests used this myth as the pattern for the ritual they performed during the process of mummifying the dead. The leading priest, a funerary priest, wore a jackal mask to impersonate Anubis. Only the priest wearing this mask was entitled to cut, touch, or make changes to the corpse. Anubis is also involved in performing the ritual of the Opening of the Mouth and the cleaning of the dead.

In later periods (Greco-Roman times) Anubis also acted as guide for the deceased and accompanied the souls of the dead to the underworld. (In earlier times this guidance was the task of Upuaut.) Anubis guided the souls to the east and crossed with them the star constellation of Eridanos (a mythical river), which was considered to be the borderline between the living and the cosmic underworld. In the court hall he assisted Osiris, together with Thoth, in the judgment of the heart.

Anubis also uses the title *neb-ta-djeser* ("Lord of the Sacred Land"), making him the ruler of the necropolis. Another title declared him to be the ruler of the "nine bows." This term was used to describe enemy tribes that had to be captured.

These two characteristics are represented in the famous seal of the necropolis administration (a group of officials in charge of the Theban Necropolis), in which Anubis is depicted sitting over nine captives. The seal was used to mark the closed royal tombs, including, most famously, that of Tutankhamun.

Anubis played an important part in the mysteries of Isis and Osiris in the city of Abydos, organizing and controlling the hour watch during the mystery play and, together with Upuaut, defeating the enemies of Osiris. Like Seth, god of the desert, Anubis was also a protection god of the Egyptian military. Especially in later times under the Greeks and Romans, he was also connected with a star constellation that is similar to the contemporary constellation Lepus, south of Orion.

His recognition and worship were localized at various other places in Egypt. For instance, Anubis was the local deity of the 17th Upper Egyptian nome (district) called Anput or Input, the city that later became known as Cynopolis ("City of the Dog") by the Greeks. The Anubeion was a Greco-Roman temple to Anubis in Saqqara, the necropolis of Memphis. The great mortuary temple of Queen Hatshepsut, the "Djeser-djeseru" in Deir el-Bahari, also had a special chapel for the cult of Anubis. All across Egypt, Anubis was worshiped in funerary temples.

In an interesting development, Anubis's name and function have become associated with a couple of modern-day technological innovations. "Anubis" is the name of a 128-bit encryption algorithm. Its creators chose this name because of the god Anubis's title as "Guardian of the Mysteries" or "Master of Secrets," and because of a metaphorical association between embalming and encryption. Separately, engineer Rudolf Gantenbrink led an investigation of the shaft in the great pyramid of Khufu (Cheops) in March 1993 using an exploration robot that he named "Upuaut," after the Egyptian jackal god, which, as described above, was incorporated into Anubis.

Michael E. Habicht

See also: Bahariya Oasis: Valley of the Golden Mummies; Coffin Texts; Isis; Opening of the Mouth; Osiris; Religion and mummies; Rohmer, Sax; Seth; Theban Necropolis

Further Reading

Pinch, Geraldine. 2004. *Egyptian Mythology: A Guide to the Gods, Goddesses, and Traditions of Ancient Egypt*. New York: Oxford University Press.

Wilkinson, Richard H. 2003. *The Complete Gods and Goddesses of Ancient Egypt*. London: Thames & Hudson.

Aufderheide, Arthur Carl

Arthur Carl Aufderheide (1922–2013) was a medical pathologist who, after focusing on diseases of the living for the majority of his career, began to explore how the mummified remains of the dead could contribute to our understanding of modern disease. Driving key research projects and authoring seminal works, he had a passion and a keen intellect that led him to become a motivating force in the growth and professionalization of mummy studies. His scientific contributions were matched by what many experienced as a warm, welcoming personality, and by his mentoring of junior colleagues.

Arthur Carl Aufderheide was born on September 9, 1922, in New Ulm, a small town in rural Minnesota. He decided early on that he wanted to be a medical doctor, and in 1943 he entered medical school at the University of Minnesota, though initially he was not interested in pathology. It was during a tour of duty in the army (1947–1949) that he had the opportunity to study pathology at the Allgemeine Krankenhaus in Vienna. This was a formative experience, for upon his return to the United States he entered a pathology residence.

He went on to hold a number of different positions, and in 1972 he joined the staff at the new Medical School at the University of Minnesota-Duluth. The position required research, but since there was no patient care, Aufderheide had to find another area of investigation. His research in the field of physical anthropology took two directions: elemental analysis of skeletal remains and the paleopathology of mummified remains. While he would continue research in both areas, the latter would remain his primary focus. Fundamentally, his approach was an extension of his medical training and relied on autopsy and the recognition of disease based on morphological changes (i.e., changes to shape and structure). While he acknowledged that nonanatomical methods have the ability to address very specific questions, the specificity of the methods makes them largely secondary tools relative to morphological techniques. In the early 1980s, Aufderheide and his wife and research companion Mary L. Aufderheide (née Buryk), started a life-long journey to seek out and study mummies. The experiences they had, and the friendships they forged, would come to form the foundation for his key contributions to mummy studies.

Aufderheide was instrumental in establishing the World Congress on Mummy Studies. The first meeting was organized after the Aufderheides visited Tenerife in the Canary Islands. The Congress has now met eight times and not only provides an intimate venue where all aspects of research can be shared, but also fosters collaboration and unification across the disciplines involved in mummy studies.

Aufderheide's medical background also likely inspired him to establish the International Mummy Registry. He collected over 6,000 tissue specimens, from eyes to coprolites to hair, from around the world. Through these efforts he helped pioneer the first large-scale, population-based studies of mummies, allowing researchers to discuss prehistoric epidemiology on a scale not previously possible.

Arguably his signature publications are *The Cambridge Encyclopedia of Human Paleopathology* (coauthored with Conrado Rodríguez-Martín) and *The Scientific Study of Mummies*. The former publication was the first to truly define an approach to identifying and understanding the paleopathology of soft tissue; the reader is provided with not only a description of skeletal changes but also a discussion of the gross morphological soft tissue changes. The latter book represents the culmination of a career of research. It is divided into three main sections. In the first he offers the reader a worldwide synopsis of previous mummy research. Following this, he discusses soft tissue taphonomy (i.e., decay) and provides a protocol for conducting an anatomical examination of mummified remains. The last section focuses on the description of soft tissue pathology, liberally illustrated with images from both modern and archaeological contexts. The volume is a manifestation of Aufderheide's legacy and impact on mummy studies, and will not easily be duplicated.

Dr. Aufderheide continued to be active, teaching pathology at the University of Minnesota-Duluth Medical School and attending academic meetings, until his official retirement on December 31, 2008. Even in retirement, however, he continued to publish and contribute to the field he helped to develop and guide. He died on August 9, 2013 in Duluth, Minnesota.

Kenneth C. Nystrom

See also: Medical imaging of mummies; The World Congresses on Mummy Studies

Further Reading

Aufderheide, Arthur C. 2003. *The Scientific Study of Mummies*. Cambridge: Cambridge University Press.

Aufderheide, A.C., and C. Rodríguez-Martín. 1998. *The Cambridge Encyclopedia of Human Paleopathology*. Cambridge: Cambridge University Press.

Endres, Nicole. 2008. "Arthur Aufderheide: Wrapping Up a Career in Paleopathology." *Giving to Medicine and Health*. October 1. Accessed October 28, 2013. http://blog.lib .umn.edu/mmf/news/alumni/2008/arthur-aufderheide-wrapping-up-a-career-in-paleopathology .html.

Krajick, Kevin. 2005. "The Mummy Doctor." *The New Yorker* 81, no. 13: 66–75.

Nystrom, Ken. 2013. "Arthur Aufderheide: 1922–2013." *Paleopathology Newsletter* 164 (December): 16–18.

The Awakening

The Awakening is a 1980 film directed by Nick Murphy and produced by David M. Thompson. It stars Charlton Heston as Matthew Corbeck, an archaeologist searching for the lost tomb of the ancient Egyptian Queen Kara. The film is based on Bram Stoker's 1903 novel *The Jewel of Seven Stars*, but the plot has even more twists than the book. Despite the presence of Hollywood legend Heston, and despite featuring good cinematography, a strong original musical score by Claude Bolling, and some impressive replicas of Tutankhamen's treasures used as props, the movie is generally regarded as a weak entry in the mummy genre.

The film opens with Corbeck and his mistress/assistant Jane (Susannah York) undertaking an archaeological dig in Egypt in 1961. They uncover Kara's tomb,

Charlton Heston in *The Awakening*. (Orion Pictures Corporation/Photofest)

which comes complete with a hieroglyphic curse that reads, "Do Not Approach the Nameless One Lest Your Soul Be Withered." Despite this warning, Corbeck unhesitatingly smashes his way in. With each blow of the sledgehammer, his wife Anne (Jill Townsend), who is back at the camp, experiences a premature contraction in her pregnancy. Corbeck returns to find her unconscious or in a trance.

After dropping Anne off at the hospital, Corbeck returns to the tomb to continue his work. Anne gives birth to a stillborn daughter while Corbeck works to uncover Kara's coffin. At the very moment he opens the coffin, the stillborn girl comes to life, suggesting that Queen Kara has reincarnated in her.

The film then moves 18 years forward, and we learn that Dr. Corbeck, obsessed by Kara's tomb and mummy, has neglected and abandoned both wife and daughter. He learns that the mummy of Queen Kara has a bacterial infestation that must be treated, but when he travels to Egypt and tries to bring the mummy back to England—because he disagrees with the way the Egyptian mummy specialists are trying to treat it—he is blocked when the officials refuses permission. However, this obstacle is removed and Corbeck is able to bring Kara's mummy to England when one of the officials dies in a mysterious accident.

Meanwhile, Corbeck's daughter Margaret, now 18 years old, begins to feel an irrational pull to become acquainted with her father. She goes to meet him in England, where she begins behaving strangely. Eventually she comes to the conclusion—abetted by the fact that her father and Jane tell her all about Kara, including Kara's violent history as a queen and a mythic tale that she was able to reincarnate herself—that she/Kara is responsible for the deaths and accidents that seem to follow her. Corbeck comes to believe that Kara is possessing his daughter, and he realizes that the only way to save Margaret is to resurrect the mummy of the queen by performing an ancient Egyptian ritual involving the canopic jars containing the Queen's internal organs. Margaret is willing to try, but when the ritual is performed, Corbeck realizes the evil queen has tricked him. She completely takes over Margaret's body and kills Corbeck.

The Awakening has an unusual ending for a mummy movie, with the evil queen winning and striding out into the world. The producers were probably leaving the door open for a sequel, but weak acting and the complicated plot led to modest returns at the box office, and no sequel was produced.

Bob Brier

See also: *The Jewel of Seven Stars*

Further Reading and Viewing

The Awakening. 1980. Directed by Mike Newell. Burbank, CA: Warner Home Video, 2012. DVD.

Muir, John Kenneth. 2007. *Horror Films of the 1980s*. Jefferson, NC: McFarland & Co.

B

Bahariya Oasis: Valley of the Golden Mummies

Although all of Egypt's oases saw considerable activity during the Greco-Roman period, Bahariya Oasis is the one best known for its spectacular cemetery of that era, the so-called Valley of the Golden Mummies. The site, initially discovered in 1995, was subsequently dug from 1996 to 1998, and intermittently thereafter.

The cemetery is located in the plains of the oasis, six kilometers southeast of the oasis's main city, Bawiti. It covers some 10 square kilometers and contains an estimated 10,000 burials. The tombs are cut into the desert *tafla* and underlying rock and take the form of multi-niched family (?) tombs as well as simpler shaft and pit tombs. They are undecorated, save for occasional small images of Anubis couchant (i.e., crouching with head upraised) in his animal form painted on the walls. The tombs that have been presumed to be family tombs are entered through

Nine newly discovered 2000-year-old mummies rest in a tomb under the ground at the Valley of the Golden Mummies near Bahariya Oasis in western Egypt, December 12, 2004. (AP Images/Amr Nabil)

The discovery of the burial site popularly known as the "Valley of the Golden Mummies" occurred in the Bahariya Oasis when a camel ridden by an Egyptian Antiquities Guard stumbled in a hole that revealed an opening in the ground. The site was found to contain several buried tombs containing up to 10,000 mummies.

a short sloping passage or a shaft that leads to a large burial chamber. Deep recesses, some with curving (false vaults) roofs that accommodate multiple bodies, are carved into three, and in some cases almost four, sides of the chamber. Bodies were found on the floors of the chambers as well as in the niches. In some instances stone slabs were found at the base of the compartments; presumably these served as basic offering tables. Some of the mummies had a stone beneath the head, as if it were a pillow. Certainly this would be a Greco-Roman variant on the headrest that was more typical of Egyptian burials of the pure Pharaonic era.

A variety of mummy wrappings have been noted, ranging from simple spiral linen bandages to more complex arrangements involving different colored (mainly beige and brown) bandages laid in lozenge or coffered patterns, the centers of which are marked by a small piece of gold or gold leaf. A small number of the mummies have plaster or cartonnage masks that are gilded, with the details of the face, hair, and body ornaments picked out in paint. In some instances floral crowns are modeled in plaster and painted. A few of the mummies—generally not those in the group tombs—are interred in clay coffins. These have the facial features and some decoration along the front of the body modeled; traces of paint were also noted on at least the faces and front.

The overall quality of mummification, regardless of the elaborateness of the external body treatment, seems to be poor, as is often the case with mummies of this period. The bodies were poorly desiccated, anointed with oils and resins, and then wrapped.

As a result, the bodies themselves are in bad condition, and often there has been some pooling of hot resin along the dorsal sides, which, perhaps in combination with occasional dampness of the surface on which the bodies were laid, has resulted in the rotting of the back bandages. Some of these have the crossed-arm position with clenched fists, while others had their arms laid along the sides or their hands placed over the genitals. A range of ages and both sexes are represented.

Salima Ikram

See also: Anubis; Egyptian mummies; Hierakonpolis; Theban Necropolis; Valley of the Kings

Further Reading

Hawass, Zahi. 2000. *Valley of the Golden Mummies*. New York: Harry N. Abrams.

Belzoni, Giovanni

Giovanni Belzoni (1778–1823) was an Italian strongman turned archaeologist who explored and excavated sites throughout Egypt in the nineteenth century. Belzoni acquired many fine objects and artifacts in Egypt, including very large pieces such as a colossal statue of Ramses II ("the Great") for various patrons and employers. Although Belzoni is often criticized for his methods, which by modern standards seem somewhat destructive, much of his work was extremely valuable, and it remains so to this day.

Giovanni Battista Belzoni was born on November 5, 1778, in the city of Padua, Italy. He and his three brothers were all sons of a poor barber, and all were unusually tall and muscular. Belzoni himself eventually grew to nearly 6 ½ feet in height, almost a foot taller than the average of his contemporaries. He worked with his father in the barbershop until he was 16, at which point he left home to further his education and seek his fortune in Rome. Little is known of the subsequent years, though during this time he turned his not inconsiderable intelligence toward hydraulics.

For about 15 years Belzoni traveled throughout Europe, finally ending up in England, where he began to use his extraordinary physique as a way to make money, working as a circus strongman at the Sadler's Wells theater. He got married, and he met Henry Salt, who would later figure prominently in Belzoni's career as an archaeologist.

1778	Giovanni Belzoni is born on November 5 in Padua, Italy.
1803	Belzoni becomes employed in England and Europe as a traveling circus strongman known as "The Great Belzoni."
1815	Belzoni is commissioned to acquire Egyptian antiquities for the British museum.
1817	In October, Belzoni discovers the tomb of Pharaoh Seti I in the Valley of the Kings.
1820	Giovanni Belzoni publishes his journal under the title *Narrative of the Operations and Recent Discoveries within the Pyramids, Temples, tombs, and Excavations in Egypt and Nubia: and of a Journey to the Coast of the Red Sea, in search of the ancient Berenice; and another to the Oasis of Jupiter Ammon.*
1821	Beginning on May 1, Giovanni Belzoni holds an exhibition in Piccadilly, London, in which he displays a full-size copy of two rooms from the tomb of Pharaoh Seti I, along with a scale model of the entire tomb.

Though Belzoni continued to work as a strongman, he still dreamed of being a hydraulic engineer, and so when the opportunity arose to travel to Egypt and present his idea for a hydraulic irrigation wheel to the country's ruler, Mohammed Ali Pasha, he leaped at the chance. In 1815 Belzoni arrived in Egypt, but unfortunately his idea was not picked up by the Egyptian government. However, he was fascinated by Egypt, and particularly by the ancient ruins and antiquities that were visible seemingly everywhere, so he decided to stay there and explore the Nile valley.

While in Egypt, Belzoni was commissioned by Henry Salt and others to acquire Egyptian antiquities for the British Museum. He traveled up and down the Nile valley while keeping a detailed journal of his explorations. He also made sketches and largely accurate, detailed maps, which became especially valuable as the tombs and monuments of Egypt were exposed to more and more visitors and looters. In the famed Valley of the Kings, Belzoni discovered and explored at least five tombs within a span of a several days, including some that contained mummies. He also discovered and excavated other sites in Egypt, such as the entrance to a temple of Ramses the Great, and he participated in the removal of an obelisk from the island temple at Philae. Belzoni collected the finest specimens but left the incomplete and battered objects in the tombs, a common practice during a time when archaeologists were concerned mainly with obtaining intact, museum-quality pieces. He was also responsible for removing and transporting a colossal statue of Ramses II from Thebes (modern Luxor) for the British Museum, as well as numerous other statues.

One of Belzoni's most famous finds was the magnificently decorated tomb of the pharaoh Seti I, widely regarded as the most beautiful tomb in the Valley of the Kings, and the calcite (also called Egyptian alabaster) sarcophagus of that pharaoh. When Belzoni returned to England in 1819, he held an exhibition in which he displayed a full-size copy of two rooms from this tomb and a scale model of the entire tomb. Belzoni also held public mummy unwrappings, a common practice at the time. These events were well-attended and very popular among the British elite, who were enthralled by the exoticism of Egyptian mummies.

Although Belzoni is often criticized for his destructive collecting techniques (for example, he once used a battering ram to open an inaccessible tomb), he was in fact far more conscientious than many of his contemporaries. He also improved and adapted his methods throughout his career, creating excellent maps, plans, and watercolors of tombs and ancient sites. His journal, published in 1820 under the lengthy title *Narrative of the Operations and Recent Discoveries within the Pyramids, Temples, tombs, and Excavations in Egypt and Nubia: and of a Journey to the Coast of the Red Sea, in search of the ancient Berenice; and another to the Oasis of Jupiter Ammon*, provided an entertaining and informative look at ancient Egyptian sites and the state of Egypt and the Middle East during the early nineteenth century. A magnificent volume of color plates accompanied his *Narrative* and remains a fascinating look at Belzoni's travels.

Ever the explorer, Belzoni died in 1823 as he was traveling in western Africa to Timbuktu. His wife, Sarah, exhibited many of his models and drawings after his death, and attempted to keep her husband's memory and achievements alive. Despite the criticisms that were leveled at him, Belzoni's accomplishments were in many ways ahead of his time, and his discoveries remain monumental achievements in Egyptology.

Roselyn Campbell

See also: Egyptian collection, The British Museum; Egyptomania; Mummy unwrappings; Valley of the Kings

Further Reading

Belzoni, G. 1820. *Narrative of the Operations and Recent Discoveries within the Pyramids, Temples, tombs, and Excavations in Egypt and Nubia: and of a Journey to the Coast of the Red Sea, in search of the ancient Berenice; and another to the Oasis of Jupiter Ammon.* London: John Murray, Albemarle-Street.

Bierbrier, M. L. 2012. *Who Was Who in Egyptology.* 4th ed. London: Egypt Exploration Society.

The British Museum. "Giovanni-Battista Belzoni (1778–1823)." Accessed October 18, 2013. http://www.britishmuseum.org/explore/highlights/article_index/g/giovanni -battista_belzoni_177.aspx.

Encyclopaedia Britannica. "Giovanni Battista Belzoni." Accessed October 18, 2013. http://www.britannica.com/EBchecked/topic/60237/Giovanni-Battista-Belzoni.

Hume, Ivor Noël. 2011. *Belzoni: The Giant Archaeologists Love to Hate.* Charlottesville and London: University of Virginia Press.

Mayes, Stanley. 2006 [1959]. *The Great Belzoni: The Circus Strongman Who Discovered Egypt's Treasures.* London: Tauris Park Paperbacks.

Ryan, Donald P. 1986. "BA Portrait: Giovanni Battista Belzoni." *The Biblical Archaeologist* 49, no. 3 (September): 133–138.

Tyldesley, Joyce. 2005. *Egypt: How a Lost Civilization Was Rediscovered.* Berkeley and Los Angeles, California: University of California Press.

Bentham, Jeremy

English philosopher, political theorist, and social reformer Jeremy Bentham (1748–1832) is remembered not only as the chief proponent and expounder of the doctrine of Utility but also for specifying in his will that his body "be put together in such a manner as that the whole figure may be seated in a Chair usually occupied by me when living in the attitude in which I am sitting when engaged in thought in the course of time employed in writing" (Bentham 2002, 8). Bentham's figure is presently on public display in the Cloisters at University College, London,

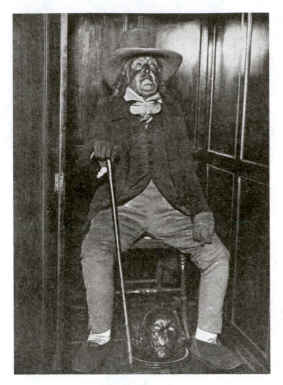

The Auto-Icon of Jeremy Bentham with his embalmed head at his feet, University College, London, 1956. (Print Collector/Getty Images)

and is occasionally to be found in meetings, where he is listed as "present but not voting."

The eldest of seven children, Jeremy Bentham was born on February 4, 1748 (February 15, 1748 OS), in Houndsditch, London. His father, Jeremiah Bentham, was an attorney, and his mother, Alicia Woodward Whitehorne, died when Jeremy was but 11; only one of his siblings, his youngest brother Samuel, survived childhood. A prodigy, Jeremy began learning Latin at the age of 3, was fluent in Latin and Greek at 10, and entered Queen's College, Oxford, at 12; he received his B.A. in 1764 and his M.A. in 1767. He then began the study of law and in 1769 was admitted to the bar and moved to Lincoln's Inn. He began to write in the 1770s, initially offering criticisms on Sir William Blackstone's *Commentaries on the Laws of England* (1765–1769) but ultimately striving to create what he was to call a *pannomion* (a Greek term meaning "all the laws"), a systematic legal approach for England. He was to write voluminously on a variety of subjects including prison reform, for which he proposed a *panopticon*, a prison

When the renowned English philosopher and political theorist Jeremy Bentham arranged to have his body preserved in a quasi-mummified form that he referred to as an "Auto-Icon," he could not have known that the fate of his head would follow a strange and convoluted trajectory. When the preservation process resulted in a grotesque appearance for the head, a French artist was contracted to craft an artificial one from wax, and it is this head that remains on display today with the rest of Bentham's Auto-Icon at University College, London. The real head was also displayed intermittently for many years, sometimes placed on the floor between the body's feet, but pranksters among the students took to stealing it and placing it in unlikely locations around the campus (and elsewhere). Finally, in 2002, concerns about preservation, security, and the ethics of displaying human remains resulted in Bentham's head being locked away in a climate-controlled storeroom.

in which a single watchman could observe all of the prison's inmates without them knowing whether or not they were under observation. Although Bentham spent years trying to realize the panopticon, it was never built. Bentham's writings on political theory, legal reform, capital punishment, economic freedom, animal rights, constitutional law, and the abolition of slavery ultimately lead him to become the leading proponent of the philosophical school called *Utilitarianism*. Although not averse to the opposite sex, Bentham never married and died on June 6, 1832.

As formulated by Bentham, the doctrine of Utility has as its fundamental axiom a moral ethic that "it is the greatest happiness of the greatest number that is the measure of right and wrong" (Bentham 1786, i). Thus, as early as 1769, Bentham had argued that his deceased remains should be dissected "that mankind may reap some small benefit in and by my decease," and at the time of his death, he is said to have carried in his pocket for 20 years the glass eyes that would be used in his head. Nevertheless, the key date in determining Bentham's ultimate decision is usually given as July 1824, when the *Westminster Review* published "Use of the Dead to the Living: An Appeal to the Public and the Legislature, on the Necessity of Affording Dead Bodies to the Schools of Anatomy by Legislative Enactment." Written by Bentham's friend, the physician and reformer Thomas Southwood Smith (1788–1861), the appeal postulates that "the basis of all medical and surgical knowledge is anatomy," and that because "the organs on which all the important functions of the human body depend are concealed from the view," only a thorough knowledge of anatomy can prevent and cure diseases and injuries. Furthermore, because anatomy has been prohibited through superstition and fear, patients have suffered, and "until anatomy be publicly sanctioned in Edinburgh, the school of medicine there can never flourish." Thus, the bodies of the poor must be claimed from hospitals and poorhouses, for "if the dead bodies of the poor are not appropriated for this use, their living bodies will and must be."

In partial response to Smith's essay, and recognizing that death not only curtailed life and happiness but wasted resources, Bentham wrote *Auto-Icon; or, Farther Uses of the Dead to the Living* shortly before his death, arguing that the best benefit to humanity was for the living to make use of the dead resource. Although the words *mummy* and *mummification* had appeared previously in English, Bentham preferred the term *Auto-Icon* in reference to a corpse, arguing in his opening paragraphs that "as in the progress of time, instruction has been given to make 'every man his own broker,' or 'every man his own lawyer': so now may *every man* be *his own statue. Every man is his best biographer.* This is a truth, whose recognition has been followed by volumes of most delightful instruction. *Auto-Icon* – is a word I have created. It is self-explanatory" (Bentham 2002, 2). (This document was not collected in the first edition of Bentham's works and did not see print until a small edition of 1842.)

It is worth mentioning that the preparation of Bentham's Auto-Icon did not go as intended, and there was no actual mummification. Bentham's corpse was left to Smith, who had realized the repugnance of his arguments and accepted that the best solution to the shortage of corpses was voluntary bequests, such as Bentham's. Smith, in his words, "endeavoured to preserve the head untouched, merely drawing away the fluids by placing it under an air pump over sulphuric acid. By this means the head was rendered as hard as the skulls of the New Zealanders, but all expression was of course gone" (Richardson 1987, 196). To permit viewers to see Bentham's benign expression, the services of Dr. Jacques Talrich (d. 1851), a French anatomical modeler, were enlisted, and Talrich prepared a wax head for the figure. Bentham's actual head was initially put into the Auto-Icon's ribcage, then later placed in a box, then finally set at his feet. Bentham's skeleton was cleaned and articulated, then clothed, the figure being padded with such substances as were available: "hay, straw, cotton wool, [wood] wool, and paper ribbon. A bunch of lavender and a bag of naphthalene were added for protection against pests" (Richardson 1987, 196).

Though he is not exactly a mummy, Jeremy Bentham's figure remains the visible embodiment of many of the English ideas and ideals of the late eighteenth and early nineteenth centuries. It is one thing for a man to preach reform, but Bentham chose to practice what he preached, and what he advocated was an ultimately benign doctrine that recognized the values of both life and death and was to influence such notable thinkers and reformers as John Stuart Mill, John Austin, and Robert Owen. Bentham's visible figure is a very profound and tangible legacy.

Richard Bleiler

See also: Embalming

Further Reading

Bentham, Jeremy. 1786. *A Fragment on Government; Being an Examination of What Is Delivered, on the Subject of Government in General.* Dublin: J. Sheppard, W. Whitestone, J. Hort, J. Potts, J. Williams, W. Culles, T. Walker, T. Armitage, W. Spotswood, C. Jenkin, J. Hilary, J. Beatty, and C. Talbot.

Bentham, Jeremy. 2002. *Bentham's Auto-Icon and Related Writings.* Edited and introduced by James E. Crimmins. Bristol, England: Thoemmes Press.

Marmoy, C. F. A. 1958. "The 'Auto-Icon' of Jeremy Bentham at University College, London." *Medical History* II: 77–86. Reprinted as part of the *UCL Bentham Project.* Accessed August 1, 2013. http://www.ucl.ac.uk/Bentham-Project/who/autoicon.

Richardson, Ruth, and Brian Hurwitz. 1987. "Jeremy Bentham's Self Image: An Exemplary Bequest for Dissection." *British Medical Journal* 295: 195–198.

Smith, T. Southwood. 1824. "Uses of the Dead to the Living: An Appeal to the Public and the Legislature, on the Necessity of Affording Dead Bodies to the Schools of Anatomy by Legislative Enactment." *Westminster Review* 2: 59–97.

Bioanthropology Research Institute

The Bioanthropology Research Institute (BRIQ) was formed in 1998 and is administered through the School of Health Sciences at Quinnipiac University in Hamden, Connecticut. Ronald G. Beckett, Professor Emeritus of Biomedical Sciences, Gerald Conlogue, Professor of Diagnostic Imaging, and Jaime Ullinger, Assistant Professor of Anthropology, are the current coexecutive directors of the institute.

The Institute conducts research in biology, archaeology, anthropology, forensics, and paleopathology through paleoimaging applications including diagnostic imaging, video endoscopy, photography, and laboratory analysis. The research is conducted on mummified humans and animals and ancient artifacts without destruction. The codirectors collaborate with bioanthropological and bioarchaeological researchers from around the globe. The institute conducts workshops, gives presentations and conducts field paleoimaging research worldwide.

In the early 1990s Professors Beckett and Conlogue began to collaborate on research projects regarding the medical imaging of mummified remains and artifacts. After conducting laboratory experiments, the two began conducting paleoimaging research at museums and in the field. The researchers adopted the anthropological approach to paleoimaging rather than the medical approach. That is, with the medical approach, the mummified remains or artifacts are brought to the medical facility for imaging analysis. The researchers approach was to take the imaging to the field site in an attempt to retain as much of the original context as possible and thus avoid the potential of disturbing or damaging the mummies or artifacts that were associated with those remains by moving them. By working at the field sites, the internal context, structures and artifacts inside the mummy are less likely to be displaced or damaged. The field paleoimaging approach is also nondestructive, extracting meaningful data while preserving the remains intact. Paleoimaging research has reduced the need to unwrap mummies or to conduct field autopsies in most cases. In this way, cultural respect is maintained while gathering data that can answer a variety of bioarchaeological research questions.

The Institute began presenting its work at Paleopathology Association meetings and found that no one was "making the house calls." Presentations included technical aspects of field work, instrumentation modification, and cultural variance, as well as providing a wide array of bioanthropological information including age at death, sex, dental condition, markers of bio-stress, and paleopathological findings. At these meetings, the team received many invitations to conduct field paleoimaging work around the globe. In an attempt to provide a focal point for requests and for the research, the Bioanthropology Research Institute was established.

Following the establishment of BRIQ, the research caught the attention of the National Geographic Channel. In 2000, a documentary series featuring the work of the Institute and its cofounders and codirectors was funded. The series, the *Mummy Road Show*, was produced by Engle Entertainment, formerly the Engle Brothers (New York), and sponsored by both the domestic and international channels of National Geographic. The series aired for three years (2001–2003) producing 39 episodes as well as a one-hour special (National Geographic Channel 2002). Because of this support, along with continuing invitations to conduct research, individual efforts, and grant awards, BRIQ has researched mummies in nearly all parts of the world and has become a well-known and respected research institute in both bioarchaeology and forensic imaging.

Today, BRIQ-supported research is presented at professional and scientific meetings, including a major presence at annual meetings of the Paleopathology Association, the American Academy of Forensic Sciences, and the World Congress for Mummy Studies. The codirectors of BRIQ have received several grants from the Expeditions Council of the National Geographic Society and their work has been presented in the National Geographic Magazine. The codirectors of BRIQ continue to offer scientific support to various related documentaries.

The cofounders of BRIQ, Beckett and Conlogue, have published two books on their work: *Mummy Dearest: How Two Guys in a Potato Chip Truck Changed the Way the Living See the Dead* and *Paleoimaging: Field Applications for Cultural Remains and Artifacts*, CRC Press (Taylor & Francis), September 2010. The first chronicles the research and experience of their documentary series. In the second book, the authors provide readers with many techniques and adaptive methods as applied to field paleoimaging research developed through their many years of experience.

Ronald G. Beckett and Gerald Conlogue

See also: Medical imaging of mummies; Mummy documentaries; The World Congresses on Mummy Studies

Further Reading

Beckett, Ron, and Jerry Conlogue. 2005. *Mummy Dearest: How Two Guys in a Potato Chip Truck Changed the Way the Living See the Dead*. Guilford, CT: The Lyons Press.

Beckett, Ronald G., and Gerald Conlogue. 2010. *Paleoimaging: Field Applications for Cultural Remains and Artifacts*. Boca Raton, FL: CRC Press, Taylor and Francis.

Bioanthropology Research Institute. Quinnipiac University. 2013. Accessed October 28, 2013. http://www.quinnipiac.edu/institutes-and-centers/bioanthropology-research-institute/.

Shokrian, Rebecca. 2002. "Secrets of *The Mummy Road Show* Unraveled." *National Geographic*, March 27. Accessed October 28, 2013. http://news.nationalgeographic.com/news/2002/03/0326_0327_mummyroadshow.html.

Blackwood, Algernon

English writer Algernon Blackwood (1869–1951) is considered, along with M. R. James and Arthur Machen, to be one of the masters of *fin-de-siècle* supernatural fiction. Like many writers and artists of the time, Blackwood took a personal interest in the occult. Many of his stories bear witness to his concern with what he believed was a thin veil separating the phenomenal world from a supernatural reality. In these tales, under certain circumstances powers from this hidden realm exert their influence on this world. Moreover, human beings are also possessed of latent paranormal faculties.

Born into an evangelical Christian family in London on March 14, 1869, the young Blackwood was never satisfied with his father's narrow views about religion. As an adult he would find himself in the company of theosophists, and for a time he was a member of The Hermetic Order of the Golden Dawn and The Ghost Club in search of truths that could not be answered by Christianity or science. Blackwood's primary education was at the Moravian Brethen school, a strict Christian institute located in the Black Forest of Germany. It was in these ancient woods that Blackwood discovered a love of nature and came to his belief in secret laws that governed the universe. Once he discovered the writings of Eastern mysticism and the Bhagavad Gita, there was no turning back to the Christianity of his family. At the urging of his father, Blackwood studied agriculture and subsequently moved to Canada. He eventually found his way to New York, where he spent time in various career, including farmer and newspaper reporter (among others), and finally found success as a writer.

One of Blackwood's most famous fictional creations was Dr. John Silence, who was a recurring character in several of his stories. Silence was his version of a consulting detective, but Blackwood took this insightful character one step further by imbuing him with psychic powers. The Silence stories were extremely popular and made Blackwood a bit of a celebrity, allowing him the freedom to explore occult

---

It is difficult to say exactly why the sight should have stirred in me so prodigious an emotion of wonder and veneration, for I have had not a little to do with mummies, have unwound scores of them, and even experimented magically with not a few. But there was something in the sight of that grey and silent figure, lying in its modern box of lead and wood at the bottom of this sandy grave, swathed in the bandages of centuries and wrapped in the perfumed linen that the priests of Egypt had prayed over with their mighty enchantments thousands of years before—something in the sight of it lying there and breathing its own spice-laden atmosphere even in the darkness of its exile in this remote land, something that pierced to the very core of my being and touched that root of awe which slumbers in every man near the birth of tears and the passion of true worship.

—From "The Nemesis of Fire" by Algernon Blackwood

and supernatural themes with abandon. The Silence story "The Nemesis of Fire" (1908) was his first tale involving a mummy. Here, Dr. Silence investigates a fire spirit that haunts a colonel and his sister. It is discovered that the origin of the magic is due to a mummy secretly buried by the main characters' brother, who died from mysterious burn-like injuries.

Blackwood was one of the first writers to produce what the scholar Robert Luckhurst calls the Egyptian Gothic tale. During his travels to Egypt beginning in 1912, Blackwood's spiritual imagination was kindled. Mummies and various other artifacts were being excavated from the Egyptian tombs at a tremendous rate, and Blackwood came to see Egypt as a prime example of the lost knowledge and power that had never truly died out of the world since ancient times. He went on to write many stories with Egypt as a theme or plot device, including "Egyptian Antiquities" (1912), "The Wings of Horus" (1914), and "The Egyptian Hornet" (1915).

It is the stories "Sand" (1912) and "Descent into Egypt" (1914), however, that represent Blackwood's most sincere attempt to conjure a spirit of Egypt that is distinct and, in some ways, more "real" than the modern Egypt he visited. In this mythically "true" Egypt, the gods are still present in the modern technological era, and their power merely lies dormant. Both stories involve men seeking access to this power through magic. In both cases the ancient forces of Egypt do not suffer fools gladly, and there are consequences in attempting to extract such secrets. As in many other fictions related to Egypt and mummies, Blackwood's ancient Egypt is a force that cannot be contained and that does not passively allow its treasures to be excavated. But in both stories, the protagonists are looking not for material gain but for spiritual riches, which are shown to be the most dangerous of all when they are sought without the proper intention. "Sand" and "Descent into Egypt" are strangely autobiographical, in the sense that they show Blackwood exposing his own deepest desires and fears related to esoteric matters.

In his Egyptian stories Blackwood continued to explore the themes that haunted him for his whole life. The mystic romance of ancient Egypt offered him a clear and concrete series of images with which to situate the occult reality of the world he so earnestly believed was real. Luckhurst writes that while occult in their framing, Blackwood's Egyptian stories are not meant to be horror stories, but are rather meant to reveal "the yearning for a metaphysical transcendence into a form of eternal life, for which ancient Egyptian permanence is a symbol" (Luckhurst 2012, 81).

Blackwood died on December 10, 1951, and is today remembered as one of the giants of supernatural horror fiction.

Peter Bebergal

See also: The mummy in Western fiction: Beginnings to 1922; Mummy's curse

Further Reading

Ashley, Mike. 2001. *Algernon Blackwood: An Extraordinary Life*. New York: Carroll & Graf.

Luckhurst, Roger. 2012. *The Mummy's Curse: The True History of a Dark Fantasy*. Oxford: Oxford University Press.

Bog bodies

A bog body is a human or animal body that was preserved in a peat environment. All bog bodies are natural mummies: the bodies were preserved solely through the environmental effect of the peat without any human intervention. Despite the presence of bog bodies in a few European museums and in pop culture such as poetry, music, and fiction, these mummies are not well known outside of Europe and are often misunderstood.

In general, bog bodies are rare in comparison to other types of mummies. Although several hundred human bodies excavated from peat bogs have been

A body discovered in a peat bog near Silkeborg, Denmark, May 4, 1952. The man was hanged 2,000 years ago as a sacrifice to the goddess of fertility, according to Professor P. V. Glob and other Danish archaeologists. (AP Images)

documented and confirmed in the past, the exact number is unknown, and estimates vary widely. Many bog bodies were found during the early part of the twentieth century, during the cutting of peat for fuel. Only a small number of the bog bodies ever discovered still survive in museums today: there are around forty-five human bog bodies on display or in museum collections in Europe. Mummified animals from bogs are exceedingly rare. The only known preserved entire animal corpse from a peat bog is a 500-year-old dog from northern Germany. Both skeletal and mummified bodies have been excavated from peat throughout most of northwestern Europe, including northern Germany, the Netherlands, Denmark, the United Kingdom, and Ireland. Many of these bodies date to the Iron Age in northern Europe, around 2,000 years ago. Despite the extent of acidic peat through the United States and Canada, there are no known mummified bog bodies from North America, although several 8,000-year-old skeletons discovered at the Windover Site in Florida had preserved brains.

The extent and quality of preservation of bog bodies is highly variable, and seems to be connected to the specific environmental composition of the site. In an acidic peat environment, soft tissue such as skin, muscle, and connective tissue may be well preserved, but bone will be severely demineralized and easily distorted, or may, in some cases, disappear entirely. In an alkaline peat environment,

---

Four Famous Bog Bodies

Grauballe Man. Discovered in late April 1952 in a bog near Silkeborg, Denmark. Found to be about 2,000 years old. Examined again in 2001 via CT scanning, 3D modeling, endoscopy, and spectroscopy. Subject of the poem "The Grauballe Man" by Irish poet Seamus Heaney. Currently displayed at the Moesgaard Museum in Aarhus, Denmark.

Lindow Man, a.k.a. Lindow II and "Pete Marsh." Discovered in late August 1984 by workers harvesting peat at Lindow Moss bog in northwest England. Facial features reconstructed in 1985 by an expert from the University of Manchester. Freeze-dried after being studied by CT scans, radiocarbon dating, and endoscopic examination. Currently displayed in the British museum.

Tollund Man. Discovered in May 1950 during routine harvesting of peat from a bog near Silkeborg, Denmark. Found to be about 2,000 years old. Promptly subjected to extensive scientific examinations sponsored the National Museum of Denmark. Examined again in 2002 via extensive CT scanning at a local hospital in Silkeborg. Used as the subject of the short science fiction horror story "Tollund" by Adam Roberts, published in the 2013 anthology of all-original mummy fiction, *The Book of the Dead*.

Windeby Girl. Discovered in May 1952 in the Domlandsmoor near the town of Windeby in northern Germany during peat cutting. Results of first scientific examinations published in 1958. Reexamined in 2003 as part of a larger project to reanalyze all of the bog bodies of the Schloss Gottorf collection in Schleswig, northern Germany.

the body will be entirely skeletonized, with no remaining soft tissue. In some cases, the body may be both partially mummified and partially skeletonized. For example, the Tollund Man from Denmark has a well preserved head and feet, but his hands are skeletonized, and the Yde Girl of the Netherlands has extensive soft tissue on her head and upper torso, but most of her lower body is skeletonized.

The environmental processes that lead some bodies in bogs to mummify are not well understood. Most theories center on the presence of tannins in the peat and the lack of oxygen in the bog environment, or a combination of these conditions. In the early 1990s, Terence Painter suggested the "sphagnan hypothesis." According to this theory, a substance known as "sphagnan" is produced during the process of breakdown from living moss to dead moss, and it is sphagnan that is responsible for the demineralization of bones in bog bodies and the dark staining (almost tanning) of the connective tissues of the body. Painter also noted that more than one process was likely necessary to cause soft tissue preservation, and that the age and depth of the peat surrounding the body were also critical elements.

Although Painter's theories have not specifically been tested using humans or animals in a functioning peat bog environment, a few experimental archaeology projects have been undertaken in an attempt to better understand the factors contributing to the preservation of soft tissue in peat bogs (see the article on "experimental mummification" in this volume).

Historical documentation of both existing and lost bog bodies are found in museum and parish records, local newspapers, antiquarian journals, or personal correspondence. Unfortunately, there are numerous "paper bog bodies": bodies that exist in the written record, but of which no physical trace remains today. These bodies may have deteriorated after excavation or been oversampled for research, damaged, or misplaced over time, or lost through catastrophe or conflict. To further complicate the issue of paper bog bodies, one researcher historically known as a leader in the field of bog bodies, Alfred Dieck, fabricated the existence of many of the bodies that he listed in his publications, which severely distorted the number of bodies believed to have been discovered. Furthermore, it is very likely that many bog bodies that were found were never recorded, even informally. If bodies were found during peat cutting, it is possible that superstition may have led to the bodies being reburied or destroyed. Once peat cutting was mechanized, other bodies were lost forever when they were accidentally put through the machinery. In more recent times, peat extraction companies may be reluctant to report finding a body in the bog, fearing police or archaeological intervention that might delay or halt peat harvesting.

With only a very few exceptions, most bog bodies were found decades or centuries ago. Recent finds include five human bodies from Ireland: a pair of legs found in 1998 at Tumbeagh; Clonycavan Man; Old Croghan Man and Derry Cashel Man, found in 2003; and, most recently, the Bronze Age body from Laois, found in

2011. Recently excavated bog bodies have been intensively recorded, analyzed in great detail, and conserved for long-term preservation and museum display.

There are numerous theories to explain the occurrence of bog bodies. Since the bodies from northwestern Europe date primarily to the Iron Age, there are no written records from the cultures associated with the bodies. It is almost impossible to determine exactly why some people became immersed in a peaty environment after death. There are two main interpretations offered as potential explanations for bog bodies: punishment burials and ritual offerings, although there are numerous other possible interpretations.

One idea proposes that bog bodies were those convicted and executed for criminal offences. The writings of the Roman historian Tacitus are often cited as evidence for bog bodies being the result of punishment burials. In *Germania*, Tacitus recorded that some criminals were punished by immersion in marshy areas for crimes defined by some as "abominations" and that sometimes the bodies were to be submerged under a barrier. Since some bog bodies appear to have been "pinned" into the bog with large stones, branches, or sticks, this was viewed as support for the theory of punishment burials. Many bodies were not, however, buried directly in marshy wetlands, but in lakes or other bodies of water that later filled in with vegetation and became a bog. Furthermore, the practicality of weighting down a body in a wet environment at the time of burial to prevent the body floating to the surface cannot be ignored, and may well explain the presence of rocks or sticks with some bog bodies.

The most common interpretation of bog bodies is that they were ritual offerings to the gods. There are numerous publications that present this theory, and this is often the sole theory presented in television documentaries, due, in part, to its dramatic nature. According to this theory, each bog body was an individual human sacrifice to the gods, possibly to secure or give thanks for a successful harvest. There are many examples of votive offerings made in wetlands: pottery, animals, wagon parts, and, occasionally, partial human remains have been excavated from alkaline bog environments. The human and animal remains are skeletonized, since the bodies were placed in open water environments, often with flowing water, such as a river or spring, and these did not become acidic peat bogs, where mummified bog bodies have been found. It is likely that many bog bodies were not votive offerings, since they were not placed in the same type of water environment.

In order for bog bodies to be considered ritual votive offerings, it is important to understand that a ritual requires a pattern of repeated ceremonial behavior. There is, however, great variation in how bog bodies were deposited at different sites in different countries, within the same country, and even at the same site. There is no identifiable pattern in terms of body orientation, position, or placement. This means that it is dangerous and potentially misleading to interpret all bog bodies as ritual offerings. Those who make this interpretation repeatedly cite the same few well-preserved and well-known bodies, and ignore that these bodies are just a few out of more than 300 documented bog bodies.

There are, of course, several other logical interpretations of bodies in peat bogs. It is possible that some bodies represent normal burials, especially in areas with limited land: it makes sense to bury the dead in otherwise unusable land, rather than wasting valuable farmland. Other individuals may have become accidentally mired in peat pools and were unable to free themselves, while others may have been victims of crime.

By far, the most logical approach to interpreting bog bodies should be to consider all of the various possibilities. It is unlikely that any of the theories discussed above could explain every bog body, and each bog body must be interpreted on a case-by-case basis, working from the archaeological and environmental context, whenever possible.

Bog bodies present particular challenges for researchers in mummy studies. First, there is a great deal of variation between bodies, even from the same archaeological site. It is difficult to draw generalizations about preservation or interpretation from a group of bog bodies. Furthermore, there are so few bodies still in existence, and these originate from such a widespread geographic region, that it is not possible to do any type of accurate population study.

Second, the usual methods used to study other types of mummies must be adapted to study bog bodies. For example, the severe demineralization of bog body bones affects the analysis of medical images. Bones may be distorted or missing, and the entire body is usually compressed from the weight of the overlying peat, further distorting the placement of both bones and internal organs.

Many people are fascinated by bog bodies. The environmental processes that lead to bog bodies are not well understood and are further complicated by myths and misconceptions about how the body came to be in the bog. Despite detailed study of bog bodies and new developments in research in the past two decades, the study of the bog bodies has led to more questions than answers.

Heather Gill-Frerking

See also: Cladh Hallan mummies; Experimental mummification; Grauballe Man; Lindow Man; Medical imaging of mummies; Mummies of Europe; Natural mummification; Tollund Man; Windeby Girl

Further Reading

AldhouseGreen, Miranda. 2001. *Dying for the Gods: Human Sacrifice in Iron Age and Roman Europe*. Stroud: Tempus Publishing.

Coles, J. 1988. "An Assembly of Death: Bog Bodies of Northern and Western Europe." In *Wet Site Archaeology*, edited by B. A. Purdy, 219–236. Caldwell: Telford Press.

Gill-Frerking, Heather. 2010. "Bog Bodies: Preserved Bodies from Peat." In *Mummies of the World*. Edited by A. Wieczoreck and W. Rosendahl, 60–70. New York: Prestel.

Glob, P.V. 2004. *The Bog People: Iron-Age Man Preserved*, 1969. Translated by Rupert Bruce-Mitford. New York: The New York Review of Books.

Munksgaard, E. 1984. "Bog Bodies: Brief Survey of Interpretations." *Journal of Danish Archaeology* 3:120–123.

van der Sanden, W. 1996. *Through Nature to Eternity: The Bog Bodies of Northwest Europe*. Amsterdam: Batavia Lion International.

Book of the Dead

The *Book of the Dead* is the most important of all ancient Egyptian religious texts. Its main goal was to protect and reanimate the mummy for continued existence in the next world. It was actually called *The Going Forth by Day* because it was intended to enable the deceased to get up again and resume activities. It was not a single work with a central theme, beginning, and an end. Rather, *Books of the Dead* are rolls of papyrus recording magical spells of which hundreds of versions have been found. The various papyri contain more than 200 spells that have been given standard chapter numbers, so that, for example, any spell dealing with the heart not opposing the deceased when he is being judged will be called Chapter 30.

The *Book of the Dead* is an outgrowth and logical development from two earlier bodies of writing: Pyramid Texts and Coffin Texts. While the Pyramid Texts were magical spells inscribed inside pyramids for royalty only, the Coffin Texts were for anyone who could afford a coffin with magical inscriptions. The problem with placing the spells on the coffins was that space was limited and eventually there

The Egyptian god Osiris, left, is adored by a scribe, Nakht, and his wife Tjuyu, in an illustration from the *Book of the Dead* inked onto a papyrus scroll, dating to the late 18th or 19th dynasty (c. 1350 BCE). (AP Images/Alastair Grant)

The collection of spells known as the *Book of the Dead*, which became the primary funerary texts used in the Egyptian mummification process during ancient Egypt's New Kingdom period (ca. 1500 BCE to ca. 1100 BCE), has proved so enduringly potent down through the millennia that it has crossed over into Western public consciousness and come to symbolize the idea of ancient and exotic Egyptian spiritual mysteries. Included in this phenomenon has been a tendency for the *Book of the Dead* to cross over from the realm of scientific Egyptology and be included in pop cultural presentations of mummies. A significant case in point is Universal Studios's landmark 1932 horror film *The Mummy*, whose plot involves a (fictional) Egyptian text named the "Scroll of Thoth," the reading of which can awaken ancient Egyptian mummies. For the visual image of this text, the filmmakers actually used a copy of the Egyptian *Book of the Dead* that was housed at the British Museum.

were so many different spells intended to protect the deceased that they did not all fit. Thus in the New Kingdom, the *Book of the Dead* came into existence, enabling the deceased to have all of the spells written on a papyrus roll.

Scribes prepared papyrus rolls that told eager customers how to prepare for the next world. In general, the *Book of the Dead* dealt with several different phases of the deceased's existence. The important stages were: (1) Protection of the body in the tomb; (2) Journey to the netherworld; (3) Judgment by the gods; and (4) Existence in the next world.

There is no fixed order in which the spells appear in the various copies of the *Book of the Dead*. It is, however, possible to determine several different geographical areas where differing versions were produced. The most important version is the one known as the Theban Recension of the *Book of the Dead*. During the 18th Dynasty the nobility of Thebes were buried with *Books of the Dead* between the legs of the mummy. These papyrus rolls were almost always written in black ink hieroglyphs running from top to bottom, with lines of the text separated from each other by thin black lines. Across the top of the papyrus sheets, drawings illustrated the spells. Often the scribes did not fully understand what they were writing or were extremely careless. Sometimes the same spell or chapter is repeated twice in the same papyrus. Another common problem was that, at times, the artist was called in first to do the illustrations, and then the scribes would write the appropriate text below. Frequently the artist did not leave enough space for the scribe to enter the entire spell, so the books often contain chapters that are severely abbreviated or condensed, sometimes to the point of being unintelligible. In spite of all these difficulties, these papyri reveal a great deal about the resurrection beliefs of the ancient Egyptians.

Many versions of the *Book of the Dead* contain a praise or hymn to the gods, especially Osiris, god of the dead. Aside from flattering the gods, the hymns served as an introduction to Osiris. An abbreviated example of such a hymn, from the Papyrus of Ani, a scribe of the 18th Dynasty goes as follows:

> Adoration of Re when he appears in the eastern horizon
> of the sky, Behold Osiris, the scribe of the divine offerings
> of all the gods, Ani. He says, praise to thee who has come
> as Khepri, the god of existence who is the creator of the gods
> May he give pleasure and power as one who is dead. The living
> soul of Ani goes forth to see Horus of the two horizons, to the
> soul of Osiris, the scribe Ani, true of voice before Osiris May a
> place be made for me in the boat of the day of going forth of
> the god. May I be received in the presence of Osiris in the land
> of the true of voice of the *ka* of Osiris-Ani.
> (Budge 1967, 1–2)

Aside from general hymns, specific spells described words to be spoken over the mummy at the time of burial, and because the Egyptians were resurrectionists, it was important that the body was intact and functioning. Of all the spells reanimating the body, perhaps the most important was the Opening of the Mouth ceremony. After mummification this was performed by a high priest wearing a leopard skin indicating his office. He touched the mummy's mouth with a tool called an adz and recited:

> My mouth is opened by Ptah. (Said twice.) The local god of my town
> unties the bandages which are over my mouth. Thoth comes, fully
> equipped with magical charms. (Said twice.) with which to unite the
> bandages of Set that fetter my mouth.
> (Budge 1967, 84)

In the spell above, the local god of the deceased is not named. This is because frequently the books would be written before there was an intended customer, so places for the deceased's name were left blank. For the same reason, local gods were not mentioned and were merely referred to as "your local god." After the purchase the deceased's name could be inserted. These were the first written "forms" in history.

The Egyptians were almost encyclopedic in their concern with the various parts of the body. Often the *Book of the Dead* seems to have been written by a priest who sat down and tried to think of every part of the body that would be needed in the next world and who then wrote a spell for each. Thus, there are numerous chapters with titles such as "The Chapter of Not Permitting the Heart of a Man to be Taken

Away" and "The Chapter of Walking with Two Legs and Going Forth from Earth," the latter of which contains the following passage:

> Words spoken by the deceased: Do what thou doest Sokar.
> (Say this twice.) Sokar who is in his dwelling place within
> my legs in the Netherworld. I shine above heaven. I go forth
> from heaven. I sit by the God's spirit. I am weak and feeble.
> (Say this twice.) I walk wearily and am motionless in the
> presence of those whose teeth gnash in the Netherworld.
> (Budge 1967, 118–119)

One of the most famous sections of the Book of the Dead is Chapter 125. Here the deceased will be judged in the Hall of the Double Truth where various gods will be deciding if the deceased is worthy of admittance to the next world. The Book of the Dead instructs the deceased in what to say before the tribunal. Then the person's heart will be weighed against the feather of truth on a balance scale. If it balances, he is declared "True of Voice" and can be admitted to the Netherworld.

Bob Brier

See also: Coffin Texts; Egyptian mummification methods; *The Mummy* (1932); Opening of the Mouth; Osiris; Religion and mummies

Further Reading

Allen, Thomas. 1974. *The Book of the Dead or Going Forth By Day.* Chicago: University Chicago Press.

Budge, E. A. Wallis. 1910. *The Chapters of Going Forth By Day or, The Theban Recension of the Book of the Dead.* London: Kegan, Paul, Trench, Trubner, & Co.

Budge, E. A. Wallis. 1967. *The Egyptian Book of the Dead: The Papyrus of Ani.* New York: Dover.

Champdor, Albert. 1966. *The Book of the Dead: Based on the Ani, Hunefer, and Anhai Papyri in the British Museum.* New York: Garrett Publications.

Davis, Charles. 1901. *The Egyptian Book of the Dead: The Most Ancient and the Most Important of the Two Extant Religious Texts of Ancient Egypt.* New York: G. P. Putnam's Sons.

The Book of the Dead (anthology)

An anthology of short stories taking the theme of the living mummy as their inspiration, *The Book of the Dead* was published as a hardback limited edition, a paperback, and an e-book by Jurassic London in October 2013. It is edited by Jared Shurin and is notable for being the first complete anthology of new and specially commissioned short stories addressing this theme. An earlier anthology, *Mummy!*

A Chrestomathy of Cryptology, published in 1980, contained only six new tales that were presented alongside a selected number of previously published mummy fiction.

The Book of the Dead contains 19 short stories and was published in collaboration with the Egypt Exploration Society, an organization that has made many significant contributions to the archaeological study of ancient Egypt since its founding in 1882 by an employee of the British Museum. Jurassic London, founded by Shurin in 2011, is a small independent publisher with a history of producing works of quality speculative fiction based around a specific theme, frequently in collaboration with a thematically appropriate charity or cultural organization. *The Book of the Dead*, devised by Shurin in early 2012, presents tales by recognized genre authors and less familiar writers who have worked with Jurassic London in the past.

Although the anthology draws heavily on the tropes of literary and cinematic mummy fiction, it nonetheless moves into innovative and challenging territory, allowing the contributors to rework the mummy as a complex and versatile literary creation by presenting a mixture of tales that are genuinely horrific, darkly humorous, and poignant. The full scope of the human condition is explored as the authors utilize the traditional cipher of the living mummy to tackle the emotional and material intricacies of death, loss, remembrance, physical resurrection, and immortality.

The anthology contains the following stories:

"Ramesses on the Frontier" by Paul Cornell is a fictionalized reworking of the 1999 discovery of the mummy of Rameses I in the Michael C. Carlos Museum. It involves the dead king encountering figures from Egyptian mythology as he makes his way across the United States to enter the afterlife.

"Escape from the Mummy's Tomb" by Jesse Bullington presents the lives of a group of London teenagers, obsessed with horror films, and the difficulties of integration encountered by one of their number, an Egyptian boy who is drawn to director Karl Freund's classic 1932 horror film *The Mummy*.

"Old Souls" by David Thomas Moore is set in a British railway café where two ancient Egyptians, reincarnated endlessly throughout the millennia, unwittingly reencounter one another.

"Her Heartbeat, An Echo" by Lou Morgan is concerned with a museum attendant's growing obsession with the mummy of an Egyptian princess that is traveling the world as a temporary loan exhibit.

"Mysterium Tremendum" by Molly Tanzer involves a young librarian in early twentieth century Arkham, whose participation in a theatrical magic show results in the reanimation of the magician's mummified feline familiar.

"Tollund" by Adam Roberts is a story in which nanotechnology from the future reanimates the famous Tollund Man bog body, to the consternation of a team of archaeologists from Egypt, as the fabric of earth's history begins to fragment.

"The Curious Case of the Werewolf that Wasn't, The Mummy that Was and the Cat in the Jar" by Gail Carriger is an episode in the author's "Parasol Protectorate" series involving lycanthropic mummies in nineteenth century Cairo.

"The Cats of Beni Hasan" by Jenni Hill relates a conversation between the pets of two Egyptologists and the vengeance of the titular feline mummies.

"Cerulean Memories" by Maurice Broaddus is the tale of an elderly collector of death-related items in contemporary America who retains the preserved and eviscerated cadaver of his late wife.

"Inner Goddess" by Michael West features the goddess Bast, who assists an academic in exacting revenge on her sadistic lover as the two undertake the analysis of an Egyptian mummy.

"The Roof of the World" by Sarah Newton takes as its inspiration the early twentieth century cosmist, Nikolai Fydorov, who leads a team of Russian explorers into the desolate wastes of the Pamir Mountains, where they encounter a mummy that may be that of Alexander the Great.

"Henry" by Glen Mehn, set in contemporary Cairo and America, details online mummification and uploading to the afterlife by a modern-day necromancer, inspired by, and named for, Conan Doyle's protagonist, Bellingham from the short story "Lot No. 249."

"The Dedication of Sweetheart Abbey" by David Bryher is set on a spacecraft in the distant future and is a more terrible take on the historical tale of Lady Dervorgilla of eleventh century Scotland, who, following the death of her beloved husband, carried his embalmed heart with her thereafter.

"All is Dust" by Den Patrick takes place in contemporary London, where a group of partygoers unwittingly snort, with their cocaine, the dusty remnants of an Egyptian sorceress who utilizes them in her resurrection.

"Bit-U-Men" by Maria Dahvana Headley relates the tale of a mellified mummy whose mesmerizing power is dispersed throughout the United States as fragments of his body are incorporated into a new and addictive confectionary.

"Egyptian death and the afterlife: mummies (Rooms 62–3)" by Jonathan Green is the tale of a devoted and immortal Egyptian who continues to guard the burial assemblage of the 19th Dynasty priestess, Henutmehyt, in the British Museum.

"Akhenaten Goes to Paris" by Louis Greenberg is the poignantly amusing tale of the pharaoh Akhenaten's journey to contemporary Paris to be reconciled with the mummy of his father, Amenhotep III.

"The Thing of Wrath" by Roger Luckhurst is a Victorian thriller-pastiche involving the vengeance of the god Thoth and the historical Egyptologist, Ernest Wallis Budge.

"Three Memories of Death" by Will Hill is set in ancient Egypt during the 19th Dynasty and is a poignant tale of a royal embalmer and his relationship with his subjects in life and death.

The anthology is illustrated by a series of pen and ink drawings from the award-winning artist Garen Ewing and contains an introduction by John J. Johnston, Vice Chair of the Egypt Exploration Society. At time of this writing, it is receiving positive and enthusiastic critical reactions from reviewers.

Also in 2013, Jurassic London published a companion volume in connection with *The Book of the Dead*. Titled *Unearthed* and likewise featuring a lengthy introduction by Johnston, the book brings together 11 classic mummy tales from the past.

John J. Johnston

See also: Freund, Karl; *The Mummy* (1932); The mummy in Western fiction: From 1922 to the twenty-first century; Tollund Man

Further Reading

Johnston, John J., and Jared Shurin, eds. 2013. *Unearthed*. London: Jurassic London.
Shurin, Jared, ed. 2013. *The Book of the Dead*. London: Jurassic London.

Brugsch, Emile

Emile Brugsch (1842–1930) was an influential conservator of Egyptian antiquities within successive national museums based in the vicinity of Cairo, from 1870 until his departure from Egypt in 1914. He is best remembered as the first presiding antiquities official on the scene to document the cache of royal mummies revealed at Deir el-Bahri, Western Thebes in 1881. His success in the burgeoning field of Egyptian archaeology stemmed from training and introductions arranged from his Egyptologist brother Heinrich, 15 years older, and from his own native skills as a photographer. He was granted the Ottoman honorifics *bey* and later *pasha* in recognition of his services to the khedives of Egypt.

Born in Berlin February 24, 1842, and raised in Germany, Emile Charles Albert Brugsch went to Egypt in 1870 to assist Heinrich, a leading historian and epigrapher (scholar of ancient inscriptions), in the management of a school of Egyptology based in Cairo. This activity continued until 1879. Emile had considerable talent and energy, and he came to the notice of the Khedive Ismail Pasha and was included in the delegation that represented Egypt at the American Centennial Exposition in Philadelphia (1876). Although Egyptian financial problems, caused by a crippling conflict with Ethiopia, precipitated an early departure from this venue, Brugsch had managed to make important contacts there, particularly in the field of photography, which had already captured his interest. He returned to Egypt with American photographic equipment.

Although administration of the Egyptian antiquities was under French authority, Brugsch prospered due in no small part to his brother's friendship with the renowned French Egyptologist Auguste Mariette. Along with Urbain Bouriant, Brugsch rose to become coconservator of the Boulaq Museum late in Mariette's tenure as its director. During this period, Brugsch accompanied Ulysses S. Grant as tour guide on his travels in Upper Egypt in January 1878. Brugsch continued in the high administration of the museum under Mariette's successor Gaston Maspero and was in effect a vice-director when, in late June 1881, the Abd er-Rassul family was at last prepared to divulge the location of the cache of royal mummies in a hidden tomb in the southern section of Deir el-Bahri (DB 320). At this time, Maspero, already committed to a foreign trip, empowered the slightly older Brugsch to investigate the find in his absence. Between July 6 and 8, 1881, Brugsch emptied the tomb completely and forever associated himself with the discovery of the mummies of 20 rulers. However, his recording of the archaeological dispositions of the coffined bodies inside the cache was very slight, and for this he is criticized to this day. He undertook two of the three earliest unwrappings of the royal mummies, investigating the mummy of Thutmose III in July 1881, which he rewrapped without making notes. A few years later, Brugsch, apparently alarmed by putrescent odors, unwrapped the early 18th Dynasty queen Ahmose-Nefertari while Maspero was away in September 1885.

While not greatly respected as a mummy analyst, Brugsch is responsible for the often excellent photographs by which the greatest of the royal mummies are remembered, producing an evocative series of silver gelatin prints of Seti I, Rameses II, and Thutmose II and other kings during the main unwrapping phase presided over by Maspero and Daniel Fouquet in June and July 1886. A painting by Marius Michel shows Brugsch photographing mummies in Boulaq, carefully timing the exposure of his plate.

As the economic woes of Egypt mounted after 1885, Brugsch was entrusted with the responsibility of selling mummies that were deemed duplicative of those already in the collection. This activity was stepped up as environmental conditions at the often damp Boulaq Museum worsened. When the Boulaq facility closed in 1889, Brugsch was put in charge of the Ghizeh Palace Museum, which served as the center of museum operations until the Egyptian Museum on Tahrir Square opened in 1902. The Ghizeh Palace Museum included a sales room, where mummies and other antiquities considered to be expendable were sold to raise revenue for the government. Brugsch was to some extent criticized as a profiteer as a result of his involvement in marketing and exporting mummies from Egypt. Whether he specifically benefited or not, his name is doubtless associated with a large number of transactions wherein mummies that had been hastily excavated were transferred to non-Egyptian owners, many of whom were accustomed to seek Brugsch's assistance in such matters. His overarching management of the day-to-day operations of the antiquities service after 1889, which included supervision of new archaeological work by professional excavators and issuing antiquities passes to tourists, greatly facilitated this mummy-selling activity. His influence waned after 1902.

In 1904, Brugsch became briefly involved with the British occultist Aleister Crowley by discussing the 25th Dynasty funerary stela of the priest of Montu Ank-hefenkhons i from Thebes (Cairo A 9422) and arranging for it to be translated. Crowley had become convinced that its old Boulaq museum registry number "666" written on the back of the stela had significance for his religion of Thelema, and he called it the "Stela of Revealing."

Brugsch retired on January 1, 1914, and died at Nice in 1930. He remains one of the most enigmatic behind-the-scenes figures in late nineteenth century mummy collecting.

Jonathan Elias

See also: Akhmim Mummy Studies Consortium; Egyptian Antiquities Museum; Mariette, Auguste; Napoleon and the birth of Egyptology; Royal mummies of Egypt, Part One: Third to Eighteenth Dynasties; Royal mummies of Egypt, Part Two: Nineteenth to Twenty-fifth Dynasties

Further Reading

Graefe, Erhart. 2003. "The Royal Cache and the Tomb Robberies." In *The Theban Necropolis: Past, Present and Future*, edited by Nigel Strudwick and John H. Taylor, 74–82. London: British Museum Press.

Reeves, Nicholas, and John H. Taylor. 1992. *Howard Carter before Tutankhamun*. London: Trustees of the British Museum.

Skinner, Stephen, ed. 1996. *The Magical Diaries of Aleister Crowley, Tunisia 1923*. York Beach, ME: Samuel Weiser, Inc.

Smith, G. E. 2000 [1912]. *The Royal Mummies*. Catalogue General des Antiquités Égyptiennes du Musée du Caire, Nos. 61051–61100. Cairo: Institut Francaise d'Archéologie Orientale. Reprint, London: Duckworth.

Wilson, Edward L. 1882. "Photography and the Orient." *The Photographic Times and American Photographer*, 12: 71–73.

Wilson, Edward L. 1882. "A Drop from the Desert, Photography and the Orient." *The Photographic Times and American Photographer* 12: 196–198.

Wilson, John A. 1964. *Signs and Wonders upon Pharaoh: A History of American Egyptology*. Chicago: University of Chicago Press.

Bubba Ho-Tep

"Bubba Ho-Tep" is a short story written by American author Joe R. Lansdale (born Joe Richard Lansdale in 1951). It tells of an elderly Elvis Presley, now living in an East Texas nursing home named the Mud Creek Shady Rest Convalescent Home,

An ancient Egyptian mummy with a cowboy hat stalks the hallways of an East Texas retirement home in director Don Coscarelli's *Bubba Ho-Tep*, adapted from Joe R. Lansdale's short story. (Photofest Digital Library/Photofest)

as he hunts down and kills the mummy Bubba Ho-Tep, who extends his life by stealing the souls of the nursing home's helpless residents. The story first appeared in the anthology *The King Is Dead: Tales of Elvis Post Mortem* (1994). In 2002 it was made into a film of the same title by director Don Coscarelli that has achieved cult status and is extremely faithful to Lansdale's original.

According to the story, Presley did not actually die in 1977. Instead, before his alleged death, Presley, bored with fame and depressed after his wife had left him, changed lives with Elvis-impersonator Sebastian Haff in a desperate measure to be rid of the crushing weight of celebrity and his sycophantic entourage. As Haff, Presley regained some meaning in his existence, living simply and traveling the country to perform at county fairs as an imitation of himself. However, Haff liked prescription drugs more than Presley did, and when he accidentally overdosed on them in 1977, the world believed that the King was dead, leaving Presley with no way to prove his former identity and reclaim his fortune. After Presley falls and breaks his hip during a show, he ends up in a nursing home, where the staff treat him as a physically and mentally debilitated old man whose claims that he is the King of Rock and Roll are evidence of dementia. In the present-day of the story, every monotonous day is just like the previous one for the residents of the oxymor-onically named convalescent home, where all have been warehoused until they die rather than being sent there to recover from their infirmities. Presley's life only begins to have meaning after he and his friend Jack collaborate to stop Bubba Ho-Tep, the Egyptian mummy who was part of a road show before he disappeared into the Texas landscape when the bus he was traveling on crashed and he escaped.

The mummy Bubba Ho-Tep emerges as a metaphor for the lives of the residents of the Mud Creek Shady Rest Convalescent Home. Their existences are so devoid of meaning, and they are so tyrannized by routine, that they have in essence been mummified alive, just as Bubba Ho-Tep was in life. Bubba Ho-Tep is also similar to Elvis himself, in that both of them, at the height of their fame, lost much of their dignity due to their handlers: Elvis's legendary manager, Colonel Parker, turned him into a caricature of himself by convincing the singer to star in a series of ghastly B-movies, while the mummy of Bubba Ho-Tep, former high priest of Osiris, was dressed in a Stetson, cowboy boots, and a gun belt and dubbed "Bubba" in homage to his displayers' Texas roots.

The parallels also extend to Elvis's friend in the nursing home, Jack, who simi-larly lacks agency and recognition relative to his younger days. Jack, an African-American man, claims to be the former president John Fitzgerald Kennedy, whose enemies convinced the world that he was assassinated in Dallas but secretly put a bag of sand into his head to take the place of the part of his brain containing his memories that was destroyed by the sniper's bullet. According to Jack, then they dyed his skin so that everyone would think he was an inconsequential black man.

Jack and Elvis both recapture some meaning in their lives when they defeat Bubba Ho-Tep so that he can no longer steal the souls of the nursing home's resi-dents defecate the remains of their life forces down the visitor's toilet. Yet Elvis's and Jack's sense of agency is short-lived. Jack dies in the attempt to subdue Bubba Ho-Tep, and Elvis is still old and debilitated and living in obscurity in an East Texas nursing home after the mummy is dead, with the residents none the wiser about his heroism.

Coscarelli's cinematic adaptation of the short story is quite faithful to the original, perhaps because Lansdale was one of the screenwriters. It also features a talented cast, including horror movie legend Bruce Campbell as the aging, fat Elvis and award-winning film and stage actor Ossie Davis as Jack McLaughlin. Peter Travers of *Rolling Stone* and Roger Ebert of *The Chicago Sun-Times* were among the many critics who enthused about the film, singling out as noteworthy Campbell's performance as an aging Elvis who fully appreciates the absurdity of his position.

June Pulliam

See also: The mummy in Western fiction: From 1922 to the twenty-first century; Mummy movies

Further Reading

Crouse, Richard. 2003. *The 100 Best Movies You've Never Seen.* Toronto: ECW.

Lansdale, Joe. 2012. *Bubba Ho-Tep.* Portland: Gere Donovan Press. Kindle book.

Miller, Cynthia J., and A. Bowdoin Van Riper, eds. 2012. *Undead in the West: Vampires, Zombies, Mummies, and Ghosts on the Cinematic Frontier.* Lanham, MD: Scarecrow Press.

Paszylk, Bartlomiej. 2009. *The Pleasure and Pain of Cult Horror Films: An Historical Survey.* Jefferson, NC: McFarland and Co.

Buddhist self-mummification

While many cultures have practiced intentional mummification in one form or another, one group of mummies stands out as being among the most unusual: the self-mummified Buddhist monks. These monks practiced an elaborate ritual of self-deprivation to attain deeper enlightenment. While many who tried did not succeed in self-mummification, there are many who did. The practice is woven into the Buddhist construct of realizing that the body is nothing more than a vessel and that any bodily adversity can be overcome. Among these Buddhists, the process of self-mummification was not seen as taking one's own life, and those who were successful were venerated and referred to as living Buddhas. Those who failed to become mummified were and are deeply respected for their attempt.

The practice of self-mummification dates back into the eleventh century and is thought to have been derived from practices within the Tang dynasty of China. Self-mummified Buddhist monks can be found in a variety of countries. Most notably, numerous self-made mummies are seen in Japan, Thailand, Vietnam, and

---

The core of Buddhism lies in the Four Noble Truths articulated by Siddhartha Gautama in the sixth century BCE:

1. Life is suffering.
2. Suffering is caused by craving and aversion.
3. Suffering can be overcome and happiness attained.
4. The Noble Eightfold Path leads to the end of suffering.

Buddhist mummification practices represent the attempt to realize the goal of Nirvana, the ultimate state of peace and bliss in which the sufferings of bodily existence are transcended.

Cambodia. A law against self-mummification was enacted in the early 1900s in Japan. However, in Thailand a Buddhist monk named Luang Pho Dang mummified himself in the 1970s.

If we are to understand the concept of self-mummification, we need to have at least a cursory understanding of the Buddhist philosophy and way of life. Buddhism is conceptually known as "the middle way"; one strives to be neither at the top nor at the bottom of a social hierarchy.

Buddhism began in the sixth century BCE when Siddhartha Gautama, the son of an Indian warrior-king in Lumbini, Nepal, realized that all the possessions he was privileged to have did not guarantee happiness. At the age of 29, Gautama renounced his title and worldly belongings and set out to seek a true understanding of the world. After his travels he realized that suffering was the final destination of all existence, regardless of one's life path. Furthermore, during a meditation he came to the realization of how to be free from suffering. He soon began to teach what he had come to understand, and thus he became known as the Buddha, "the Enlightened One."

At the core of Buddhist beliefs are the Four Noble Truths and the Noble Eightfold Path. The Four Noble Truths, simply stated, are as follows: (1) life is suffering, (2) suffering is caused by craving and aversion, (3) suffering can be overcome and happiness attained, and (4) the Noble Eightfold Path leads to the end of suffering. In the context of self-mummification, the third Noble Truth is apparent in the monk's attempt at overcoming the suffering brought on by deprivation through prolonged meditation. The monk gives up all bodily cravings in search of true happiness devoid of such needs. In this way the monk, if self-mummification is achieved, has more time in the mummified state to inspire and assist others in their understanding of the Buddhist path. For a monk, this is the achievement of Nirvana, the ultimate state of bliss and peace.

There are several "versions" of Buddhism practiced in the world, with each focusing greater attention on one or more of the Four Noble truths. Thus, there are varied ways in which self-mummification is achieved among the varied Buddhist traditions.

One of the better known processes of self-mummification is that found among the Shingon Buddhists of Japan. The process actually involved a series of processes that began several years prior to the death of the monk. For three years, the monk who desired to attempt self-mummification ate nothing but nuts, seeds, and berries, thus decreasing the fat content of the body. Fat cells are notorious for holding body water, and thus, with less fat there would be less body water to encourage decomposition. Next, the monk would eat tree bark and roots intended to keep the monk in a dehydrated state. These initial stages also involved increased physical activity designed to further reduce body fat. This lasted for several years as well. The monk would then begin to drink a tea made from the *urushi* tree.

This tea was said to have made the body toxic to bacteria. The *urushi* tea also induced vomiting, further reducing body fluids. An interesting note is that the *urushi* tree sap is used as a lacquer and may have had some preservative effect on the body. Finally, the monk, when he perceived that he might die, would place himself in a tomb with a bamboo conduit for air and a bell to ring that would let the other monks know he was still alive. When the bell no longer rang, the monks sealed the tomb and waited several years to see if the self-mummification attempt was successful. Apparently some monks in Japan were buried in a pine coffin filled with salt, which would have drawn any moisture from the body and enhanced the potential for mummification.

Another method is found among the Mahayanna Buddhists. Here the monk, knowing that the time of death was eminent, instructed his disciples to place him in the lotus posture (the cross-legged position of meditation) within a vessel. The vessel was then filled with wood, paper, or lime, all of which would serve to wick the moisture from the body. The body was exhumed after three years, and if mummified, was painted and decorated with gold.

A striking example of the Buddhist practice of self-mummification in modern times can be found in the story of Laung Po Dang, a twentieth-century businessman and family man in Thailand. After his successful career, he sought enlightenment and became a Buddhist monk. Luang Pho Dang was a master at the meditative practices used by the Buddhist monks and was documented to have meditated for 15 days at a time. During these 15-day periods of inactivity with no nourishment and no water, Luang Pho Dang lost weight, both in body fats and muscle, and became severely dehydrated. His physician warned him that this practice was not healthy, and essentially had to fluid resuscitate Luang Pho Dang after each of these prolonged meditation sessions.

Laung Po Dang had a premonition about his death and instructed the other monks and his family that, if he achieved the state of self-mummification, they were to place his body on display at a temple for others to see. In this way, Luang Pho Dang felt that he would become a testament to the power of Buddhist meditation and the belief that the body is merely a vessel.

In the 1970s, at the age of 79, Luang Pho Dang was successful in his quest: he achieved self-mummification. Today his self-mummified body is housed at the Wat Khunaram Temple on the island of Ko Samui in Thailand, where people can come to visit and make offerings to this well-known monk. The mummy resides in a glass case that sits in a special open-air section of the temple dedicated to Luang Pho Dang. The temple also contains a photograph and a statue of him.

Luang Pho Dang's eyes decomposed during the self-mummification process, and children visiting the temple became frightened of the mummy. In response, the monks at the temple decided to place a pair of sunglasses on Laung Po Dang, which appeared to ease the concerns of the temple's younger visitors.

In 2002, a scientific study of Luang Pho Dang was conducted by the Bioanthropology Research Institute (see separate article in this volume), which yielded some very interesting results. Radiographic analysis demonstrated that the internal organs, including brain matter, were present and well preserved, but became smaller from dehydration. These findings attest to the effectiveness of the self-mummification method. Additionally, Luang Pho Dang was still wearing the dentures that he used when alive. Endoscopic visualization revealed that even in death, Luang Pho Dang was practicing the Buddhist belief that all life is to be revered. Behind the sunglasses, within the eye sockets and within the skull, native gecko eggs were seen. Gecko eggs were also present in the oral cavity and in the hypopharynx. Luang Pho Dang's mummified body was providing a safe hatchery for these geckos within his body cavities, housed safely within the glass display case.

The practice of self-mummification defies what we think of as living a long, healthy, and pain-free life. One must remember that attempts at self-mummification required a deep understanding and trust in Buddhist philosophies. The self-control required to attempt the process suggests that an advanced degree of willfulness exists and that overcoming bodily adversities is capable of being achieved. The role of meditation in this achievement cannot be overstated, in that meditation has been scientifically shown to impact major bodily functions, including respiration, heart rate, and blood pressure, as well as having a lasting impact on stress levels.

The process of self-mummification is logical in its procedures, yet it would be difficult to test the process without a willing subject. For all of these reasons, the self-mummified Buddhist monks constitute one of the most fascinating groups of mummies that exist today.

Ronald G. Beckett and Gerald Conlogue

See also: Bioanthropology Research Institute; Medical imaging of mummies

Further Reading

Beckett, Ronald G., and Gerald Conlogue. 2009. *Paleoimaging: Field Applications for Cultural Remains and Artifacts*. USA: CRC Press, Taylor and Francis.

Goldstein, Carly M., Richard Josephson, Susan Xie, and Joel W. Hughes. 2012. "Current Perspectives on the use of Meditation to Reduce Blood Pressure." *International Journal of Hypertension* 1–11. Accessed October 22, 2013. doi: 10.1155/2012/578397.

Jeremiah, Kenneth. 2010. *Living Buddhas: The Self-mummified Monks of Ymagata, Japan*. USA: McFarland & Co., Inc.

Violatti, Cristian. 2013. *Ancient History Encyclopedia*, s.v. "Siddhartha Gautama." February 9. Accessed September 28, 2013. http://www.ancient.eu.com/Siddhartha_Gautama/.

C

Capuchin Catacombs of Palermo

Immortalized in the works of writers such as Ippolito Pindemonte, Alexandre Dumas, Fanny Lewald, and Guy De Maupassant, the Capuchin Catacombs of Palermo, Sicily, are a unique historical site, not only for the huge number of preserved human remains placed there over a span of more than three centuries, but also because this crypt contains pages of utmost importance on the development of mummification and the life and death of illustrious persons who rest in the complex. These include the sculptor Filippo Pennino (d. 1794), the surgeon Salvatore Manzella (d. 1835) and the bishop Agostino Franco (d. 1877).

Founded in the Marche region in the early sixteenth century, the Order of the Capuchin Friars settled in Palermo in 1534 and was granted permission to build its convent next to the preexisting church of Santa Maria della Pace in the same year. In 1599 the opening of a burial next to the church revealed forty-five bodies

A view of mummified corpses in the Capuchin Catacombs in Palermo, Sicily, southern Italy. (AP Images/Alessandro Fucarini)

of religious figures, pristinely preserved. Their incorruptibility was considered to be a sign of God. Forty such bodies were then transferred to a new space excavated under the main altar. Soon, due to the number of friars living and dying in Palermo, it was necessary to obtain another room, and a chapel was excavated in the tuff deposit underneath the area. Hence, a real subterranean dimension was slowly taking shape. By 1732 the Catacombs had almost reached their current configuration, although building works were not completed until 1823.

Initially, this cemetery was only reserved for the friars, but later, in the course of the seventeenth century, other benefactors also began to be admitted, so that the site was eventually subdivided into sectors including friars, men, women, priests, and professionals. There was even an area exclusively devoted to children. As burial there was at a premium, one can guess that the bodies and burials mostly belong to the aristocrats and the emerging middle class, able to afford entombment or exposure within that holy place. Over 1800 subjects are still found along the sides of the corridors forming the site. Many of them are stored in wall niches or shelves, while others lie in wooden coffins, some of which are finely carved.

Burial in the Catacombs was not always immediate, but in most cases consisted of a process similar to that described by sociologist Robert Hertz (1881–1915) in his landmark study on the collective representation of death. The phenomenon of the secondary disposal, typical of some ethnic groups, shows in fact some similarities with certain mortuary practices typical of modern age Sicily, indicating a concept of death as a long, culturally sanctioned process. Shortly after death, the unclothed bodies were placed in special preparation rooms provided with grids made of terracotta tubes, in which they were sealed for a period of about a year to allow dripping of the bodily fluids. After this lapse of time, when desiccation was at an advanced state, the bodies were exposed to the air, washed with vinegar, and dressed. Finally, they were located either in the wall niches or coffins. In case of soft tissue loss, straw, tow, or wool were used to give the bodies a more natural consistency.

Spontaneous mummification, however, was not the only method employed for cadaver preservation. Over time other techniques, including evisceration, immersion, and even injection, were established. For instance, during periods of epidemics, corpses were disinfected with lime. Additionally, in the nineteenth century, preparations involved the use of chemicals introduced into the vascular system and the use of make-up, false eyes, or eye-caps, which would have given the deceased a more realistic and lifelike appearance. Among such methods, the most popular was devised by Sicilian physician Giuseppe Tranchina (1797–1837) who published it in Naples in 1835. His preservative solution included toxic chemicals such as arsenic and mercury.

Requests for burials in the Catacombs peaked in the nineteenth century, so that most of the bodies there today are from that period. But the same century also saw the ending of such burials, which was ordained in 1880. Their full termination, however, was a gradual process; even in the first half of the twentieth century some embalmed and coffined cadavers were "temporarily" admitted in the crypt. It can therefore be speculated that burial within the site was still seen as a sign of privilege. Among the most recent mummies are United States vice-consul Giovanni Paterniti (d. 1911) and Rosalia Lombardo (d. 1920), known as "the Sicilian Sleeping Beauty," both of whom were treated by embalmer Alfredo Salafia (1869–1933) with a formaldehyde-based fluid.

Last, but not least, various funerary items including early photographs, manifold coffins, precious textiles, and marble gravestones can be seen throughout the corridors. Beyond the typically Christian motives such as the holy cross and angels, these items often show zoomorphic (animal-shaped) and phytomorphic (plant-shaped) patterns, as well as symbols related to mortality and resurrection, such as skulls, hourglasses, butterflies, and the Ouroboros.

Today the enormous heritage of the Catacombs is in danger because of humidity, water infiltrations, and acidic formations related to the increased urbanization of the area. Only recently, within the framework of the "Sicily Mummy Project," has the awareness of their value been revived as the mummies have been scientifically investigated with the aim of reconstructing their lives and lifestyles to rescue this precious biocultural source.

Dario Piombino-Mascali

See also: Mummies of Europe; Natural mummification

Further Reading

Panzer, Stephanie, Albert R. Zink, and Dario Piombino-Mascali. 2010. "Radiologic Evidence of Anthropogenic Mummification in the Capuchin Catacombs of Palermo, Sicily." *RadioGraphics* 30, no. 4: 1123–1132.

Piombino-Mascali, Dario, Arthur C. Aufderheide, Melissa Johnson-Williams, and Albert R. Zink. 2009. "The Salafia Method Rediscovered." *Virchows Archiv* 454, no. 3: 355–357.

Piombino-Mascali, Dario, Arthur C. Aufderheide, Stephanie Panzer, and Albert R. Zink. 2010. "Mummies from Palermo." In *Mummies of the World*, edited by Alfried Wieczorek and Wilfried Rosendahl, 357–361. Prestel: New York.

Piombino-Mascali, Dario, Stephanie Panzer, Silvia Marvelli, Sandra Lösch, Arthur C. Aufderheide, and Albert R. Zink. 2011. "The 'Sicily Mummy Project': First Results of the Scientific Campaigns (2007–2010)." In *Geschichte und Tradition der Mumifizierung in Europa*, edited by Reiner Sörries, 25–31. Kassel: Kasseler Studien zur Sepulkralkultur.

Carnarvon, Fifth Earl of (George Herbert)

Carnarvon was one of the last great wealthy amateur excavators in the Valley of the Kings. He was the patron of Howard Carter, with whom he codiscovered the tomb of Tutankhamun in 1922. The global media event of this discovery shifted

February 16, 1923	Lord Carnarvon and Howard Carter break open the doorway of Tutankhamun's burial chamber in the Egyptian Valley of the Kings. The event causes a worldwide sensation in the press (helped along by a savvy publicity campaign mounted by Carnarvon himself).
March 1923	Popular British novelist Marie Corelli, famed for her mystical and occult leanings, warns in the British press that, according to a book of ancient Egyptian lore in her possession, a dire punishment will fall on violators of sealed tombs.
April 5, 1923	Carnarvon becomes the most famous victim of an alleged "mummy curse" when he dies unexpectedly of blood poisoning from an infected mosquito bite, thus appearing to fulfill Corelli's warning.

from wonder to unease when Carnarvon died six weeks after the formal opening of the tomb in April 1923. He remains the most famous victim of an alleged "mummy curse" in popular memory.

George Edward Stanhope Molyneux Herbert (1866–1923) was born to an aristocratic family with a long tradition of public service. Unlike his father, a classical scholar and diplomat, George Herbert was a traveler, sportsman and gambler, rapidly running through the family fortune after his father's death in 1890 and marrying Almina Wombwell for money. Carnarvon wintered in Egypt every year following a serious motor accident in Germany in 1903. In 1906, he was given a permit to excavate ancient sites by Gaston Maspero, and he became a committed amateur archaeologist despite only discovering one mummified cat in his first season. He hired Howard Carter as his expert man in the field in 1907 and for five years excavated in the necropolis at Deir el Bahari, through which Carnarvon built up his private collection, most of which was sold to the New York Metropolitan Museum after his death.

In 1913, wealthy rival explorer Theodore Davis abandoned his concession in the Valley of the Kings, declaring the place exhausted of finds. The Great War intervened, but from 1917 to 1922, Carter and Carnarvon systematically searched a large area in the Valley, using industrial methods to shift over 200,000 tons of rubble. Very early in their last season, Carter found the steps leading to a door of an unknown tomb, sealed with the cartouche of the pharaoh Tutankhamun. Within days, Carnarvon had traveled from England, and the nature of the find had been determined by breaking open a small vantage point through the inner doors. Carnarvon returned to England to prepare for the formal opening and to capitalize on his discovery: he signed an exclusive deal with *The Times* for £5,000 and began negotiations with Samuel Goldwyn for the film rights.

On February 16, 1923, Carnarvon and Carter broke open the doorway of the burial chamber as the world's press waited outside. Carnarvon's exclusive deal ensured rival press agencies had only rumor and speculation to print. Six weeks after the opening, Carnarvon nicked a mosquito bite whilst shaving; he became gravely ill with blood poisoning and then pneumonia and died on April 5, 1923. Superstitions said the electricity in Cairo failed at the moment of his death and his three-legged dog Susie (already unlucky) howled at Highclere (Carnarvon's ancestral home in England) and dropped dead. The press of the time and later the sixth Earl happily fanned the flames of occult and weird happenings around the mummy of Tutankhamun, although Carnarvon never knew that Tutankhamun's body had remained untouched in the tomb, since the sarcophagus was not finally opened until 1925.

Roger Luckhurst

See also: Carter, Howard; Mummy's curse; Tutankhamun ("King Tut"); Valley of the Kings

Further Reading

Carnarvon, Earl of, and Howard Carter. 2004. *Five Years' Explorations at Thebes: A Record of Work Done, 1907–11.* London: Kegan Paul. Includes "Biographical Sketch of the Late Lord Carnarvon," 1–40.

Carter, Howard, and A. C. Mace. 1963. *The Tomb of Tut-Ank-Amen, Discovered by the Late Earl of Carnarvon and Howard Carter.* 3 vols. New York: Cooper Square.

Fagan, B. 2011. "Herbert, George, Fifth Earl of Carnrvon." *Oxford Dictionary of National Biography.* Oxford: Oxford University Press, online edn.

Carter, Howard

Carter was the Egyptologist "cursed" with the fame of being the discoverer of the tomb of Tutankhamun in 1922. A difficult and diffident man, he spent 10 years documenting this extraordinary find, irritably trying to fend off the interference of politicians and journalists. He died disregarded and alone in London in 1939, largely forgotten by the world.

Howard Carter (1874–1939) was the son of a poor English illustrator and artist. His love of Egypt was fired by visiting the greatest private collection of Egyptian antiquities at Didlington Hall, a collection (now dispersed) that included several mummies. He was sent to Egypt to trace out tomb scenes by the Egypt Exploration Society in 1891, and at 17 he helped William Flinders Petrie on an excavation at Tel al-Amarna. He published six volumes on the reliefs of the temple of Queen Hatshepsut, and in 1899 his reputation was such that he was appointed chief inspector of antiquities in Upper Egypt. In 1904, he was held responsible for a scuffle between Egyptian guards and some French visitors to Saqqara. He refused to apologize and was demoted; he resigned a year later and began to work as a

An archaeologist examines the sarcophagus of Tutankhamun in the Valley of the Kings at Luxor. (AP Images)

freelance guide, trader, and excavator. This was typical of his resistance to authority, something that marred his later work on the tomb of Tutankhamun.

In 1909, Carter was recommended to the Fifth Earl of Carnarvon as an expert excavator, and they worked together for the following 14 years, publishing a scholarly study of their digs at Deir al Bahari in 1911. In 1914, Carter and Carnarvon finally acquired a permit for excavations in the Valley of the Kings. Carter was convinced that there were more tombs to uncover. Carter used Carnarvon's wealth to develop a systematic industrialized method of search, employing hundreds of workers to shift thousands of tons of topsoil. In 1922, Carnarvon wanted to abandon the search; Carter offered to pay for one last season himself, and Carnarvon, impressed with this commitment, agreed to fund one more season. Within days, Carter hit the 16 steps that led down to the doors of a tomb marked with the unbroken seals of the pharaoh Tutankhamun.

The media circus that descended on Luxor profoundly irritated Carter. This was also the moment when the first native Egyptian government was coming into power in Cairo after 40 years of British occupation. Carter proved unable to adapt to either intrusion. He made no allies in the press, and when his patron died six weeks after the opening, the story of the "curse" enraged him. Carter was also

Howard Carter's career and persona captured the public imagination in association with his opening of Tutankhamun's tomb and examination of the boy pharaoh's mummy. He has been fictionalized in, portrayed in, and/or incorporated into many different books and films, including the following.

The Curse of King Tut's Tomb: A 1980 movie for American television, partly inspired by the popular touring exhibit of Tutankhamun's treasures in the late 1970s. It presents a fictionalized and exaggerated version of the discovery and opening of Tutankhamun's tomb, and features Howard Carter driving around the Valley of the Kings on a motorcycle.

Cities of the Dead: A 1988 novel by Michael Paine that deals with the mysteries of life and life after death, and that involves the discovery of a child's mummy. It is presented in the form of supposed excerpts from dairies written by Howard Carter in 1903–1904.

The Sleeper in the Sands: A 1998 literary horror novel by Tom Holland that weaves together ancient history with the early twentieth-century discovery and opening of Tutankhamun's tomb. It features Howard Carter as a main character.

The Curse of King Tut's Tomb: A 2006 television miniseries that features Howard Carter as a character and that, like the 1980s television movie of the same title, fictionalizes the discovery and opening of Tutankhamun's tomb. But this version transforms real-life events into a supernatural tale headed by non-historical characters and featuring a horde of flying demons that is unleashed on the modern world after being sealed into an other-dimensional underworld thousands of years ago by King Tut.

Tomb of the Golden Bird: A 2006 novel by Elizabeth Peters that is the 18th title in her popular Amelia Peabody series of historical mysteries. The series follows the adventures of Egyptologist Amelia Peabody Emerson in the late nineteenth and early twentieth centuries, most of them occurring in and around Egypt. *Tomb of the Golden Bird* features Howard Carter and Lord Carnarvon as characters and has Amelia present for their opening of Tutankhamun's tomb. Notably, author "Elizabeth Peters" is the pen name of Egyptologist Barbara Mertz (1920–2013).

periodically locked out of the tomb by the Egyptian authorities. In 1925, he was there to open the sarcophagus of the boy king and conduct the examination of the body, but under transformed political circumstances. With Arthur Mace, he put his name to a three-volume study of the tomb, but he was never to complete publishing his findings after spending 10 years working with the artifacts from it.

Roger Luckhurst

See also: Carnarvon, Fifth Earl of (George Herbert); Mummy's curse; Tutankhamun ("King Tut"); Valley of the Kings

Further Reading

Carter, Howard, and A. C. Mace. 1963. *The Tomb of Tut-Ankh-Amen, Discovered by the Late Earl of Carnarvon and Howard Carter.* 3 vols. New York: Cooper Square.

Colla, Elliott. 2007. *Conflicted Antiquities: Egyptology, Egyptomania, Egyptian Modernity.* Durham: Duke University Press.

James, T. G. H. 2013. "Carter, Howard (1874–1939)." *Oxford Dictionary of National Biography.* Oxford: Oxford University Press, online edn.

Chaney, Lon, Jr.

Lon Chaney, Jr. (1906–1973) was an American character actor renowned for playing the werewolf in Universal Pictures' movie *The Wolf Man* (1941). He was the only actor ever to play all four of Universal's iconic film monsters: Frankenstein's monster, Dracula, the Wolf Man, and the Mummy.

Chaney was born Creighton Tull Chaney on February 10, 1906 in Oklahoma City, Oklahoma, the son of Lon Chaney and Frances Cleveland Creighton Chaney, both traveling stage performers. In 1912, Chaney's father began working in Hollywood and became one of the silent film era's most distinguished actors, originating the title role of *The Phantom of the Opera* (1925), among others.

Chaney's father discouraged him from entering show business and, after attending business college, he worked for his father-in-law at General Water Heater Company, where he rose to the position of secretary treasurer. He married Dorothy Hinckley in 1926 and they had two sons: Lon Ralph Chaney, born in 1928, and Ronald Creighton Chaney, born in 1930.

Following his father's death in 1930, Chaney sought work in Hollywood, signing a contract with RKO in 1932. He appeared uncredited in the serial *The Galloping Ghost* in 1931, and gave his first credited performance, under the name Creighton Chaney, in the 1932 film *Bird of Paradise*. In 1935, hoping to improve his casting chances, Chaney reluctantly began performing as Lon Chaney, Jr., first receiving credit under that name for *Accent on Youth.*

Over the next five years, Chaney acted in more than 40 movies, usually in bit roles. The turning point of his career came in 1939, when he gave a much praised performance as Lennie Small, the mentally challenged migrant ranch hand in the stage adaptation of John Steinbeck's novella *Of Mice and Men.* Chaney reprised the role in the 1939 film adaptation. Although Chaney won the New York Critics Choice Award for his performance, he was typecast to play hulking, brutish characters in many subsequent films.

In 1941, Chaney signed a contract with Universal, the studio that a decade earlier had made *Frankenstein* and *Dracula,* the movies that launched the film careers of Boris Karloff and Bela Lugosi. Hoping to launch a second wave of horror films, Universal cast Chaney as the lead for *Man Made Monster,* in a role that originally had been created with Karloff in mind. In its promotion of the movie, Universal exploited the fact that Chaney was making the film on the same set where his father had made *The Phantom of the Opera*. Later that year, Chaney turned in a signature performance in *The Wolf Man* as the anguished Lawrence Talbot, who, after being bitten by a wolf, turns into a werewolf when the moon is full. Chaney became identified with the character, much as Karloff and Lugosi had with their monster roles, and reprised the Talbot/werewolf character in *Frankenstein Meets the Wolf Man* (1943), *House of Frankenstein* (1944), *House of Dracula* (1945), and finally in the comedy *Abbott and Costello Meet Frankenstein* (1948).

Universal relaunched their mummy film franchise in 1940 with *The Mummy's Hand*. In 1942, Chaney was cast as the mummy Kharis in *The Mummy's Tomb*. He would finish out the film series reprising the role in *The Mummy's Ghost* and *The Mummy's Curse* in 1944. In all of the mummy films, Chaney was so heavily made up that there was little for him to do but play his character as a voiceless, expressionless monster bent on revenge. The same was true of his performance as the monster in *The Ghost of Frankenstein* (1942). By contrast, Chaney's performance as the debonair and seductive Count Dracula (under the name Count Alucard) in *Son of Dracula* made it one of the better Dracula sequels. Beginning with *Calling Dr. Death* (1943), Universal also cast Chaney as the lead in six films spun off from the popular Inner Sanctum radio program between 1943 and 1945, among them *Weird Woman* (1944), the earliest film adaptation of Fritz Leiber's classic witchcraft novel *Conjure Wife*. Once the series ran its course, Universal did not renew Chaney's contract.

Over the next 28 years, Chaney performed in more than 100 movies and television programs, alternating between distinguished films such as *High Noon* (1952) and *The Defiant Ones* (1958) and cheap horror movies such as *The Bride of the Gorilla* (1951), *Indestructible Man* (1956), and *House of the Black Death* (1965). Chaney's last film was *Dracula vs. Frankenstein* (1971). Ill health exacerbated by alcohol dependency dogged him in his final years, and he died of heart failure on July 12, 1973. Although his filmography lists more than 200 appearances, Chaney is remembered primarily for his work in horror films, which comprise only a small percentage of his work on screen.

Stefan R. Dziemianowicz

See also: Kharis; *The Mummy's Ghost* and *The Mummy's Curse*; *The Mummy's Tomb*; Universal Studios mummy series

Further Reading

Landis, John. 2011. *Monsters in the Movies: 100 Years of Cinematic Nightmares*. New York: DK Publishing.

Smith, Don G. 1996. *Lon Chaney, Jr.: Horror Film Star*. Jefferson, NC: McFarland & Co.

Weaver, Tom, Michael Brunas, and John Brunas. 2007. *Universal Horrors: The Studio's Classic Films, 1931–46*. Jefferson, NC: McFarland & Co.

Chinchorro mummies

The Chinchorro culture represents the earliest peoples who inhabited present-day northern Chile and southern Peru, and who engaged in the earliest known practice of artificial mummification, with results that have been of great fascination to twentieth- and twenty-first-century scientists, as well as to a widespread popular audience.

The Chinchorro were an adventurous and resilient people who, without domesticated animals, and with minimal tool technology, were able to explore and conquer the barrenness of the Atacama Desert coast. This pre-pottery culture spread along the coast from Ilo in Peru to Antofagasta in northern Chile. This is a vast territory where freshwater resources are scarce. However, the rich and patchy environment in the small and narrow valleys such as the Caplina, Lluta, San José, and Camarones that drain to the Pacific Ocean provided a diversity of food resources, such as plants, birds, and seafood to allow early human settlement of this region. The localized resources and pristine oases prompted these early populations to settle permanently at river mouths and explore new areas along the coast and narrow valleys. They were skilled hunters and shellfish gatherers who hunted sea lions and wild camelids using dart throwers and harpoons. To harvest from the ocean, they collected and polished fragments of *Choromytilus* shells, transforming them into hooks that were tied to long fishing lines and sunk using polished stone weights. They were master reed weavers as well, and they collected locally available *totora* reeds to manufacture cords, fishing lines, baskets, reed mats, and grass skirts.

The extreme dryness of the desert environment is a product of the crosswinds from the Pacific Ocean pushing the coastal humidity up into the Andes Mountains. The barrenness of the desert landscape contrasts sharply with the small rivers that provide oases of life.

Photo of a Chinchorro mummy (a girl) in the Chilean town of San Pedro de Atacama. (Religious Images/UIG/Getty Images)

Types of Chinchorro Mummies

Black mummies. The oldest and most complex type, produced circa 5000–2500 BCE. Reassembled bodies modeled almost like a statue. Head decorated with a small wig. Skin painted with a black paste of manganese oxide.

Red mummies. Produced circa 2000–1500 BCE. Prepared with less bodily destruction than black mummies. Internal organs removed and replaced by various stuffings. Wooden poles slipped under the skin of arms and legs for rigidity. Wig of human hair added to the head. Body painted with red ochre. Face painted black.

Mud-coated mummies. Produced circa 2000–1700 BCE. Bodies encased in a 1–2 centimeter layer of cement-like mud.

Bandaged mummies. Produced circa 2000 BCE. Similar to red mummies but with skin cut into 1–2 centimeter strips and repositioned in the form of a bandage. In some cases external wrapping of camelid or vegetable fiber cords were used instead of skin.

Yet, thanks to this harsh environment and its absence of rain, today we can observed intact, like a wonderful encyclopedia, many ancient testimonies of yesterday's life: mummies, shell middens, and fishing tools, among other artifacts. All of these archaeological evidences provide a unique picture that aids in reconstructing ancient cultural practices from early South American populations.

For example, the bones of these mummies reveal clues to discover how they lived on a daily basis. They suffered from ear swimmers and bony outgrowth in the ear canal (exostosis), the consequences of diving for shellfish and other marine products. Their bones show microfractures of lower spine vertebrae (spondylolysis), probably the consequences of hyperextending their backs while harpooning sea mammals. Their faces and forearms show healed fractures, likely reflecting interpersonal conflict for territory and mates. Their hair shows a high presence of *Pediculus humanus capitis,* probably the consequence of living in small huts with overcrowding and an absence of combs.

Yet despite this negative health view, one of the most interesting cultural aspects of the Chinchorro is their artificial mummification practices, which is, as stated, the oldest in the world. For reasons still debated, around 5000 BCE the Chinchorro fishers began to artificially mummify their dead in a sophisticated and colorful manner. Scientists who have studied these mummies have postulated that the Arica-Camarones area in northern Chile was the cultural epicenter for this unique funerary practice. The preparation of the body for the next life was a complex process that required gathering of raw materials, much care and dedication, and the expertise of thanatology specialists. The bodies were often dissected to be put together again masterfully with clay, wooden poles, reed cords, and colored earths. These composite materials, particularly the inert clay and pigments, halted decomposition and contributed to the preservation of the body. It was a meaningful mortuary practice undertaken for three to four millennia, with regional and temporal variations. Considering the vast amount of time and territory, Chinchorro mortuary techniques are by no means uniform, and Arriaza (1995) has suggested that the morticians developed at least four types of polychromous mummy preparations: (a) black mummies, (b) red mummies, (c) mummies with bandages, and (d) mud-coated mummies. The first two were the most complex and elaborate types.

The black mummies are the oldest and most complex. Their dating starts at around 5000 BCE, and they disappear around 2500 BCE. They are reassembled bodies, modeled almost like a statue, with an internal structure made of sticks, cord reeds, and whitish clay. Their heads are decorated with a small and short wig. The skin is often replaced and patched with sea lion skin when the person's own skin was not enough. Using a thin (1–2 mm) black paste of manganese oxide, the morticians painted the whole corpse, except the wig, hence the name "black mummy."

By contrast, the red mummies were prepared with less bodily destruction. In general, the organs for these mummies were removed through incisions, and subsequently the cavities were filled with diverse sediments, thereby recovering most of the original volume of the body. Additionally, to provide rigidness to the body the morticians slipped sharp and long wooden poles under the skin of the arms and legs. As a part of the external ornamental features, they added to the head a long wig made of human hair that was secured with a black clay cap. After suturing the incisions, the body was painted with red ochre (iron oxide) and the face was painted black. In some cases the skin was replenished in the form of bandages. These red mummies appeared around 2000 BCE and lasted for almost 500 years. After this period, the mummification techniques were simplified and the bodies were encased with a 1–2 cm layer of cement-like mud, perhaps to minimize decomposition and bad odors. This mud-coated type only lasted a couple of centuries. Another variation was the bandaged mummies (ca. 2000 BCE). They were similar to the red type, but they differed primarily in that the skin was cut into 1–2 cm strips and repositioned in the form of a bandage. Llagostera (2003) also mentions the corded or wrapped mummies. Here the morticians used an external wrapping of camelid or vegetable fiber cords instead of skin, and the bodies had a simple treatment. These type of mummies appeared after 2000 BCE.

The current archaeological evidence and radiocarbon dating suggest that Chinchorro artificial mummification was a local cultural development (rather than an external cultural influence, as several authors have maintained). The oldest Chinchorro mummies have been found in the Camarones Valley, about 100 km south of the modern city of Arica, and all are newborns.

But why did the Chinchorro people develop an artificial mummification practice to begin with? In an article for *Chungara, Revista de Antropología Chilena* (*Journal of Chilean Anthropology*), Arriaza has suggested an environmental-driven hypothesis to explain this cultural phenomenon and the special care given to children.

He argued that the genesis of Chinchorro mummification practices was triggered by high and endemic arsenic levels present in the water of the Camarones Valley, and that the practices were then shaped by the Chinchorro worldview. Camarones water contains 1,000µg /L of arsenic, an extremely high value compared to the10 µg/L recommended by the World Health Organization. Arsenic is a poisonous, odorless, and tasteless chemical element that significantly affects human health, particularly in pregnant women and their fetuses. In pregnant women, the arsenic metal crosses the placenta, causing fetal poisoning, spontaneous abortions, still deaths, and premature births, among other maternal-fetal health complications. Thus, Chinchorro parents faced high and recurrent newborn deaths, which were certainly a mystery to them. Arriaza argues that the high losses of babies caused much parental grief, and as an emotional response, the Chinchorro began caring for the deceased babies, painting and ornamenting them with colored earths. The decorated babies were kept around their camps. The mummies connected the real world with the supernatural and helped the parents and relatives to assuage their otherwise unbearable loss. The decorated bodies provided emotional support to regain the balance of life by producing what was certainly a more pleasant outcome than witnessing the decomposing flesh or the dried-out bodies (natural mummification) produced by the salts and absence of rain of the Atacama Desert. Then, over time, mummification practices spread to nearby areas, especially to Arica, where they became more complex and refined and were applied to all ages and both sexes.

The Chinchorro did not mysteriously disappear, but after thousands of years they gradually abandoned their complex mortuary practices. Their descendants, however, continued to live and flourished along the Pacific Coast, but they took of their dead in a different way. After 1000 BCE the Chinchorro paid less attention to preserving the body and shifted their energy into subsistence strategies such as horticulture. They also paid more attention to the development of new crafts such as headbands, camelids and cotton blankets, early ceramic, and so on. They began burying their dead with minimal treatment, with the bodies lying on their sides and accompanied by more elaborated grave goods such as baskets and textiles. But despite these cultural changes, concerns for death and the afterlife continued, just as they still do among modern-day peoples; death is the cultural umbilical cord that still connects us with ancient cultures.

Today, most Chinchorro mummies are housed in various Chilean museums. The University of Tarapacá in Arica, Chile, has a large ongoing exhibit of these unique mummies. A few mummies are also housed in international museums in the United States and Sweden, as a result of excavations and research undertaken during the 1940s.

Bernardo Arriaza

See also: Mummies of Latin America; Religion and mummies; Uhle, Max

Further Reading

Arriaza, Bernardo. 1995. *Beyond Death: The Chinchorro Mummies of Ancient Chile.* Washington: Smithsonian Institute.

Arriaza, Bernardo. 1995. "Chile's Chinchorro Mummies." *National Geographic*, March. Accessed December 31, 2013. http://ngm.nationalgeographic.com/1995/03/chinchorro-mummies/arriaza-text.

Arriaza, Bernardo. 2005. "Arseniasis as an Environmental Hypothetical Explanation for the Origin of the Oldest Artificial Mummification Practice in the World." *Chungara, Revista de Antropología Chilena* 37, no. 2: 255–260.

Arriaza, Bernardo T., Russell A. Hapke, and Vivien D. Standen. 1998. "Making the Dead Beautiful: Mummies as Art." *Archaeology Magazine*, December 16. Accessed December 31, 2013. http://archive.archaeology.org/online/features/chinchorro.

Llagostera, Agustín. 2003. "Patrones de Momificación Chinchorro en las Colecciones Uhle y Nielsen." *Chungara, Revista de Antropología Chilena* 35, no. 1: 5–22.

Rivera, Mario. 1975. "Una Hipótesis Sobre Movimientos Poblacionales Altiplánicos y Transaltiplánicos a las Costas del Norte de Chile." *Chungara, Revista de Antropología Chilena* 5: 7–31.

Rivera, Mario, and Francisco Rothhammer. 1986. "Evaluación Biológica y Cultural de las Poblaciones Chinchorro. Nuevos Elementos para la Hipótesis de Contactos Transaltiplánicos: Cuenca Amazonas-Costa Pacífico." *Chungara, Revista de Antropología Chilena* 16–17: 295–306.

Schiappacasse, Virgilio, and Hans Niemeyer. 1984. *Descripción y Análisis Interpretativo de un Sitio Arcaico Temprano en la Quebrada de Camarones.* Publicación Ocasional 41. Santiago: Museo Nacional de Historia Natural.

Standen, Vivien. 2003. "Bienes Funerarios del Cementerio Chinchorro Morro 1: Descripción, Análisis e Interpretación." *Chungara, Revista de Antropología Chilena* 35: 175–207.

Standen, Vivien. 1997. "Temprana Complejidad Funeraria en la Cultura Chinchorro: Norte de Chile. Latin American." *Antiquity* 8: 134–156.

Church of the Dead

The Church of the Dead in Urbania, Italy, also known as Chiesa dei Morti, holds a collection of 15 natural mummies and an additional three bodies that are believed to have been artificially mummified. These three mummies are said to have been preserved by a special "potion" intended to stop decomposition. Legend states that Vincenzo Piccini, a chemist and the prior of the Confraternita della Buona Morte (English: Brotherhood of Good Death), developed the potion. He used it first on his son, and then, as per his instructions, it was used on him when he died in 1834 and finally on his wife, Maddalena Gatti, who died in 1836. All three are on display in the church alcoves, with Piccini still wearing the typical robes and cloak of the Brotherhood.

The Church of the Dead was built in 1380 and was originally called the Cappella Cola (English: Cola Chapel). The mummies are displayed behind the altar and

The mummified bodies on display in Italy's Church of the Dead are among many European mummies that were discovered by accident in the early nineteenth century because of a law passed by Napoleon. In 1804 the Edict of Saint-Cloud outlawed burials in churches and populated areas for reasons of health and hygiene. This unintentionally brought many mummies to light in Italy and elsewhere as church tombs were excavated to move the bodies, many of which were found to be naturally mummified.

are in an upright position with each mummy in a glass-enclosed alcove. They were placed on display in the fourth decade of the nineteenth century as a consequence of a Napoleonic edict that cemeteries must be moved out of town. Many individuals had been buried in tombs beneath the church, and when they were exhumed, it was discovered that several had not decomposed. In response, the Brotherhood of Good Death organized the presentation of these naturally preserved remains.

The Brotherhood was founded in 1567. Their tasks included free transport and burial of the dead, tending to those in the dying process, and registering the dead in a special book, as well as collecting and distributing money to the poor and providing seeds to farmers. Most of the dead or dying attended to by the Brotherhood were poor.

The natural mummies on display at the Church of the Dead are thought by some to have been preserved through dehydration by a particular mold, *Hypha bombicina Pers.* This is similar to a hypothesis that has been put forward regarding the natural mummies of Venzone in northeastern Italy (see the separate article in this book). Later theories regarding the formation of natural mummification in this region point to preservation by an extreme pH environment produced by the limestone-rich soil combined with "wicking" provided by the cloth burial wrappings. The dead were provided a funeral, which included a parade through town in a coffin. However, local oral history states that they were not buried in the coffin but only in their grave wrappings. Limestone tombs may have also dehydrated the surrounding air. Coupled with dry season burials, these tomb and environmental forces may have contributed to the natural mummification process.

Sources indicate that the natural mummies at the Church of the Dead come from burials that range from the fourteenth through the nineteenth centuries. Each mummy has a story that has followed him or her through the centuries. One is said to be the baker of the village named Lunano of the eighteenth century. Another is said to be Sebastiano Macci, who was a famous writer and humanist who died in the seventeenth century. A third was thought to have mongoloid features, and a fourth was thought to have to been killed by a knife wound to the thorax and into the heart during a party. The heart supposedly associated with this mummy is stored separately and appears to have a knife cut passing through it. Another story is that of a mummy said to have been buried alive. This idea was based on the observations that he appeared to have "goose flesh" and that his anterior abdominal wall was drawn in and upward, suggesting a struggle for a last breath. Still another was said to have died during a caesarean section. Apparently, at one time a fetus was present in the abdominal cavity, but such remains are no longer at the church.

A study conducted in conjunction with the National Geographic Channel's *The Mummy Road Show* allowed researchers to gather considerable insight into the understanding of this unique group of mummified remains. The gallery of mummies at the Church of the Dead consisted of 18 mummies. For the sake of the study, the mummies were numbered from one to 18, staring from the right and moving left. The collection includes eleven males and seven females. Sex was determined by radiographic assessment of the subpubic angle, sciatic notch, presence or absence of a supraorbital ridge, and external genitalia when present. The age range was approximately 20 to greater than 70 years. The bodies were generally light brown, with the only obvious exception being mummy #8, said to be Vincenzo Piccini, whose surface appearance was white. (A pathologist who inspected this mummy in 1982 suggested that it might have been externally treated with lime—a common practice during periods of epidemic.) The display position was consistent with the burial position with regards to the placement of the arms along the sides, with the females having the arms placed over the pelvic region. The arms were found to be crossed at the breast in three mummies. Internal preservation was generally good with recognizable organ remnants present in many of the mummies.

Radiographic and endoscopic data revealed a variety of paleopathologic conditions (i.e., diseases). Additionally, a coprolite (fossilized feces) sample was taken from mummy #18 and examined for parasites. Chemical analysis of several skin samples was also conducted.

Among the pathologies demonstrated were congenital luxation (dislocation, separation) of the hip, scoliosis, severe thoracic kyphosis (curvature of the upper spine), urolithiasis (stones in the urinary system), arthritic changes, vascular calcifications (calcium deposits that stiffen the muscles lining blood vessels), and pulmonary (lung) pathologies including pulmonary adhesions and apparent consolidations. Whipworm eggs were recovered from a coprolite sample removed from the base of the pelvic cavity of mummy #18.

Chemical analysis of various skin samples from mummies 1, 2, 3, 4, 8, 13, 15, and 16 showed high levels of calcium, a main ingredient in limestone that may have played a key role in the natural mummification of these individuals. The overall state of preservation was good to fair in that the skin and, in most cases, internal organs and structures were still identifiable. The heads of the majority of the mummies were less well preserved than the remainder of the body. The three mummies who were believed to have been artificially mummified, mummies 1, 2, and 8 (the wife and son of the chemist and the chemist himself), were the least well preserved.

In an attempt to relate the prevalence of certain pathologies to the modern residents of Urbania, a comparison was made with cases from the contemporary population that were of similar age and sex. It appears that similar calcifications, arthritic changes, and urolithiasis is still present in modern Urbania.

Ronald G. Beckett and Gerald Conlogue

See also: Mummies of Europe; Mummies of Ferentillo; Mummies of Venzone; Natural mummification

Further Reading

Aufderheide, Arthur C. 2003. *The Scientific Study of Mummies*. Cambridge: Cambridge University Press.

Fornaciari, Gino. 1982. "Natural Mummies in Central Italy: A Preliminary Survey." *Paleopathology Newsletter* 40, no. 1: 11–12.

The Mummy Road Show. 2002. "Mama Mia Mummies." National Geographic Channel. Directed by Larry Engel and written by Alana Campbell. Hosted by Ron Beckett and Jerry Conlogue.

Cladh Hallan mummies

How can archaeologists find out if bodies were once mummified if the soft tissues have now disappeared, leaving only the bones? The answer to this problem came from the discovery of two skeletons from beneath a Late Bronze Age house at Cladh Hallan in the Outer Hebrides off the west coast of Scotland. Even though the soft tissues of these former mummies have long since decayed in the islands' wet, temperate climate, new scientific techniques have revealed that these two Bronze Age burials were previously mummified, most likely by "tanning" of their corpses in a peat bog.

Cladh Hallan is a settlement site on the island of South Uist, in the Outer Hebrides (or Western Isles), that was occupied intermittently between 2000 BCE and 500 BCE. It was also used as a burial place for both cremations and burials. Shortly before 1050 BCE when a row of three or more Late Bronze Age "roundhouses" was built on the site, two bodies were buried below what would later be the northernmost of this north-south line of houses. The underlying geology on

---

"Frankenstein Mummies"

The Cladh Hallan mummies were dubbed "Frankenstein mummies" in the popular press when word got out that they were actually composed of parts from several different individuals that had been assembled together in tightly crouched positions. No one is certain why the bodies were put together in this way, but different theories have been advanced, including the idea that these mummies were meant to symbolize the joining of different families by marriage.

the island's west coast is *machair* sand, formed from sea shells. As a result, it is highly calcareous (chalky), providing excellent conditions for preservation of human bones, but not soft tissues.

Both skeletons were highly unusual because they were composites, each formed from several different individuals. They were so carefully put back together in tightly crouched positions that it was hard to tell that each was made up of body parts from three separate people. The one under the northeast part of the round-house was buried at some time in the period 1440–1260 BCE, and was formed from the torso of one man, the head of another, and the lower jaw (mandible) of a third. This was noticed during excavation because the spine was at a 90 degree angle to the neck vertebrae, and because the lower jaw had a full set of teeth while the upper jaw had none—in fact, many of the teeth in the upper jaw had fallen out long before death, causing the tooth sockets to become reabsorbed. Whereas the upper jaw and skull were those of an old man, the lower jaw was that of an individual in his twenties.

The other skeleton, buried below the south part of the roundhouse, belonged to a woman who died in the period 1310–1130 BCE, but the skull was that of a man who died probably 70 to 200 years earlier. DNA analysis of the bones not only confirmed that they were two separate individuals but also revealed that the woman's right arm actually belonged to a third individual. Two teeth were found to be missing from the man's upper jaw (the left and right lateral incisors). These were found in the skeleton's hands, the left in the left hand and the right in the right hand. Just why this was done remains a mystery, but perhaps it was a further way of linking the male head with the female body.

Evidence that these composite burials were also mummies, or at least collections of mummified body parts, comes from scientific analysis of the bones. Archaeological scientists were able to establish from a variety of techniques that, although bodily decay had begun after death, it was abruptly halted. Although human bones appear solid, they actually contain tiny blood vessels through which bacteria enter the bone when a corpse begins to decay. This results in microbial attack throughout the interior of the bone. Yet the analysis of the Cladh Hallan skeletons revealed an unusual pattern of microbial alteration, with evidence of dense microbial attack just below the bone's surface but not elsewhere. This intense but restricted pattern of attack indicates that there was some initial decay which was then interrupted. The scientific methods used to recognize this were microscopic histological analysis and mercury intrusion porosimetry (HgIP) analysis.

Further confirmation that the corpses' soft tissues had been preserved long after death came from matching of bones from different parts of the Cladh Hallan site. Osteoarchaeologist Christie Willis noticed that the woman's left knee (upper tibia and fibula, patella, and lower femur) had been broken off prior to burial and had been buried in another pit, five meters to the west of the burial pit. Not only was the broken-off knee found in full articulation, indicating that this act was performed while the soft tissues were still in place, but the nature of the fractures indicated that these bones were, in contrast, those of someone already long dead. This is because the bones had already lost much of their collagen, causing them to fracture with a biscuit-like break; the bones of a fresh corpse will, on the other hand, break in a more splintered and angular way. In other words, the bones had lost their elasticity while there was still flesh on them, something that could only happen if the corpse had been mummified.

It now seems likely that the tightly crouched posture of the two bodies was not simply the result of tightly wrapping or tying the body after death but of wrapping their already mummified remains. But how had the corpses been mummified? In many different parts of the world, simple mummification can be achieved by drying corpses over a slow fire, normally after evisceration of the internal organs. In the case of the Cladh Hallan mummies, Fourier transform infrared spectroscopy (FTIR) has demonstrated that the mineral content of the outer three millimeters of the bone's surface had been altered, while small-angle X-ray scattering (SAXS) has shown an unusual thickening of bone mineral crystallites in these areas. These analyses indicate that the bone surface had lost its calcium mineral content, a process that could not have occurred in the alkaline machair sand in which the bodies were buried. However, such a change could have been effected by soaking the corpses in the acidic waters of a Scottish peat bog. Visual evidence of this method of mummification—effectively tanning the corpses—was provided by the orange and dark brown staining of the skeletons' bones, caused by immersion in the peat bog.

It is likely that the Cladh Hallan corpses were immersed in a peat bog for perhaps a few weeks or months, enough to "tan" the soft tissues but not too long for the bones to become completely demineralized. People at this time were already digging peat to use as fuel for their fires; the earliest evidence of peat-digging in Scotland comes coincidentally from the neighboring island of Barra and dates to 1690–1490 BCE. Once the corpses had been retrieved from the peat bog, they must have been allowed to dry. This could have been achieved within a separate "mummy house" or, perhaps more likely on the basis of ethnographic evidence, within a dwelling where they could be suspended among the rafters above the fireplace.

Just why the Cladh Hallan mummies were re-formed into composite bodies is unknown. One possibility is that their integration symbolized the joining of different families through marriage or other alliances. In this way, the ancestors of different kin groups might be merged into a single ancestor. By preserving the dead and keeping them among the living, Bronze Age people were effectively using their remains as historical evidence of who was descended from whom—they could actually look history in the face, at least up until it was decided that the mummies should be buried. Intensification of agriculture and formalized land allotment in Britain's Middle and Late Bronze Age may have provided the motivation for mummification; without written documents, proof of ancestry may have become increasingly important for supporting claims to land and agricultural resources.

Recent scientific analysis of other Bronze Age skeletons by archaeological scientist Tom Booth is showing that mummification may have been more widespread in Britain during the Bronze Age than previously thought. In contrast, there is no such evidence from other periods in British prehistory such as the Neolithic or the Iron Age. It is also very possible that the reason why so few Middle and Late Bronze Age burials are known from Britain is because many of the dead were mummified, so that very few ever ended up in the ground for archaeologists to find.

Without archaeology, there is little indication from historical sources that mummification was carried out in prehistoric Europe. From around 100 BCE, Classical writers such as Poseidonius tell us that the Iron Age Gauls embalmed the heads of their defeated enemies in cedar oil, but there are few other such tales. However, a new range of scientific methods in archaeology is revealing that the bones can tell their own stories, transforming our understanding of the nature and extent of mummification practices in the distant past.

Mike Parker Pearson

See also: Bog bodies; Mummies of Europe; Natural mummification

Further Reading

Hanna, Jayd, Abigail S. Bouwman, Keri A. Brown, Mike P. Pearson, and Terence A. Brown. 2012. "Ancient DNA Typing Shows That a Bronze Age Mummy is a Composite of Different Skeletons." *Journal of Archaeological Science* 39, no. 8: 2774–2779.

Kaufman, Rachel. 2012. "'Frankenstein' Bog Mummies Discovered in Scotland." *National Geographic*, July 6. Accessed November 29, 2013. http://news.nationalgeographic.com/news/2012/07/120706-bog-mummies-body-parts-frankenstein-ancient-science.

Parker Pearson, Mike, Andrew Chamberlain, Matthew Collins, Oliver Craig, Peter Marshall, Jacqui Mulville, Helen Smith, Carolyn Chenery, Gordon Cook, Geoffrey Craig, Jane Evans, Jen Hiller, Janet Montgomery, Jean-Luc Schwenninger, Gillian Taylor, and Timothy Wess. 2005. "Evidence for Mummification in Bronze Age Britain." *Antiquity* 79, no. 305: 529–546.

Parker Pearson, Mike, Andrew Chamberlain, Matthew Collins, Christie Cox, Geoffrey Craig, Oliver Craig, Jen Hiller, Peter Marshall, Jacqui Mulville, and Helen Smith. 2007. "Further Evidence for Mummification in Bronze Age Britain." *Antiquity* 81, no. 312. Accessed November 29, 2013. http://antiquity.ac.uk/ProjGall/parker/index.html.

Parker Pearson, Mike, Niall Sharples, and Jim Symonds. 2004. *South Uist: Archaeology and History of a Hebridean Island*. Stroud: Tempus.

Coffin Texts

"Coffin Texts" (CT) is the modern term for funerary texts of Egypt's First Intermediate Period (ca. 2216–2137 BCE) and the Middle Kingdom (ca. 2137–1781 BCE) that are often found on coffins. Many of them originate from the Pyramid Texts of the Old Kingdom. They have their origin in the theology of Heliopolis.

The Coffin Texts had different functions: They contain rituals for mummification and burial, spells for protection of the mummy, and spiritual maps of the underworld. They later flowed into a new funerary spell collection of the New Kingdom (ca. 1550–1070 BCE), the *Book of the Dead*. Some coffin texts were used until the Late Period (ca. 712–332 BCE). The Coffin Texts were used by commoners and the king alike, as contrasted with the exclusively royal texts (Pyramid Texts, the *Amduat*, the *Book of the Gates*, and others).

Detail from the coffin of Nespawershepi, chief scribe of the Temple of Amun, dating to the 21st dynasty, c. 984 BCE. It shows the sun god Ra in his solar barque and the daily killing of the serpent Apophis, representing the sun's victory over the power of darkness. (Werner Forman/Getty Images)

The Coffin Texts began to replace the Pyramid Texts during ancient Egypt's First Intermediate Period. During the Middle Kingdom they became established as the main texts for use during the ritual of mummification. Containing rites for mummification and burial, spells for protection of the mummy, and spiritual maps of the underworld, the Coffin Texts were not written on paper, but were instead inscribed in coffins, sarcophagi, and tomb chambers. It was not until the famed *Book of the Dead* came to prominence and replaced the Coffin Texts during the New Kingdom period that funerary texts were written down on papyrus.

The Dutch scholar Adriaan de Buck, whose translations and commentary on the Coffin Texts have been highly influential, counted 1185 different spells in them. Some of the spells are only found in one version of the text, while others were apparently very popular (e.g., CT 335 appear in thirty versions). The spells were written on wooden coffins, walls of the tombs, and the funerary equipment. The language used in the Coffin Texts is classic Middle Egyptian, sometimes with older language elements. The spells on coffins were written in special cursive hieroglyphs. Many texts open with the remark, "To be recited over. . . ."

The afterlife is described in these texts as an underworld called Duat, which is ruled by the god Osiris. It was open to everyone, and the deceased who went there became like Osiris. Therefore, deceased individuals are referred in the texts as "Osiris" followed by the person's name. A new theme in the Coffin Texts is the now-famous judgment of Osiris, in which the heart of the deceased is placed on a scale to be weighed against the feather of Maat, the deity or principle of cosmic balance, truth, and the world order. However, the older concept of an afterlife in the cosmic realm was not abandoned; it existed parallel to the Coffin Texts' underworld concept and framed the star constellation of Orion as a cosmic representation of Osiris. The deceased became a member of the crew in the solar boat or even the sun god Ra himself (CT 274) traveling over the sky. On the other hand, and as already described, he or she also became like Osiris (CT 330).

The judgment of Osiris became a vital part of the deceased individual's travel in the afterlife. The difference between the afterlife of Ra and the afterlife of Osiris remains unsolved and parallel in the Coffin Texts, but attempts to unite them were made. Later, the *Book of the Dead* closed the theological gap by connecting them. The afterlife described in the Coffin Texts and the *Book of the Dead* was regarded as a kind of mirror of the life led on earth. Life basically continued there, but in a more perfected way. As part of this, servant figures and shabtis (small statues or figurines), as representatives of the dead, became part of the funerary equipment and were assigned to do all of the manual labor that was required in the land of Rasjetau, the Egyptian version of the Elysian Fields (the afterlife paradise of Greco-Roman religion and mythology). In symbolic expression of this mirror-like effect, funerary books were sometimes written backward so that they would appear in the right direction when reversed in the afterlife.

Michael E. Habicht

See also: Anubis; *Book of the Dead*; Egyptian mummification methods; Osiris; Religion and mummies

Further Reading

Allen, James P., and Adriaan de Buck. 1935–2006. *The Egyptian Coffin Texts*. Vols. 34, 49, 64, 67, 73, 81, 87, 132, Chicago: University of Chicago Press.

Faulkner, R. O. 1972–78. *The Ancient Egyptian Coffin Texts*. Vols. 1–3. Warminster, England: Aris & Phillips Ltd.

Hornung, Erik. 1999. *The Ancient Egyptian Books of the Afterlife*. Translated by David Lorton. Ithaca, NY: Cornell University Press.

Teeter, Emily. 2011. *Religion and Ritual in Ancient Egypt*. New York: Cambridge University Press.

Collecting mummies

In the present day, visitors to the British Museum, the Louvre, the Smithsonian, New York's Metropolitan Museum, or the Oriental Institute at the University of Chicago are confronted with orderly collections of Egyptian antiquities, including mummies of men, women, children, and various animals, from cats to crocodiles. Yet in one way or another, museum collections had to be acquired. How and why were mummies collected, and by whom? And how have attitudes to these prestigious artifacts changed over time?

Many great museums owe their existence to the wealth and obsessive collecting habits of particular individuals. One famous example is the British Museum, founded in 1753 when it received the collection of Sir Hans Sloane (1660–1753), scientist, gentleman collector, and sometime President of both the Royal College of Physicians and the Royal Society. In the previous century, the hard-won collections of the antiquary Elias Ashmole and the Tradescants had come to form Oxford's Ashmolean Museum in 1683, when it was perhaps the first public museum in all of Europe.

In the days when John Tradescant the Elder (d.1638) began collecting artifacts from across the world, John Greaves (1602–1652) was the closest thing Britain had to an Egyptologist. Greaves traveled in the Orient and made detailed measurements of the pyramids, later published in his book *Pyramidographia* (1650). But Greaves does not seem to have attempted mummy collection. To do so at this stage, one had to be both wealthy and intrepid.

Enter the French traveler Monsieur Jean de Thévenot. Early in 1657 Thévenot was grudgingly dispensing bribes to local guides at the mummy pits or "wells" of Saccara (now usually Saqqara), the great necropolis located some 12 miles from modern Cairo.

> When they had removed the sand, they let us down by a rope made fast about our middle, which was held by those that were above, and the pit was two or three pikes length deep; being at the bottom, we crept through a little hole upon our belly, because they had not cleared it sufficiently of the sand, and entered into a little room, walled and arched over with stone. There we found three or four bodies, but only one that was entire, the rest being broken into pieces, which easily convinced us, that that pit had been opened before. We were then for having that opened which was entire, but they would not, unless they were paid for it; and therefore I gave them a piastre, which did not content them. But when they perceived that I was about to break it up in spite of them, without giving them one farthing more, they beat it into pieces. This was a long and large body, in a very thick coffin of wood, shut close on all hands. (Thévenot 1687, 136)

Methods had not changed much when, some time between 1672 and 1676, the German Jesuit, Father Johann Michael Vansleb, could be found dauntlessly probing the caverns of the Egyptian desert. Despite suffering intermittently from a quite severe fever, Vansleb also had himself lowered down into the Saccara mummy pits, where he peered by the wavering light of candles and matches at sarcophagi of sycamore wood or stone; broke open coffins; and unwrapped bodies. Mummies were rifled in search of the funerary idols sometimes lodged within their eviscerated trunks. Vansleb and his comrades were undeterred by either the shadows of death, the occasional foetid air that snuffed their candles, or even the ugly bats—"exceeding a foot in length"—which haunted the burial pits. And they were rewarded by assorted pieces of plunder, including one stone coffin of about eight hundred weight, and another "made of above forty cloths glued or pasted together in thickness, which are not in the least rotten" (Ray 1693, 146).

Such exploits show that both seventeenth-century explorers and their Egyptian guides had little reverence either for mummies as artifacts or for the human individuals who comprised the mummies. Nor was there much precise sense of "Egyptology" among mummy-collectors at this stage. When mummies were cited as part of a collection—then often termed "a cabinet of curiosities"—they were typically just one item in a large, uncategorized, sometimes bizarre assemblage of valuable exotica. A 1664 catalogue of such items gathered by the avid gentleman collector Robert Hubert describes, under the heading "Rarities: Human," both "a mummy, entire, and adorned with hieroglyphics, that shew both the antiquity, and eminent nobility of the person, whose corpse it is, taken out of one of the Egyptian pyramids," and "a giant's thigh-bone, more than four feet in length, found in Syria" (Hubert 1664, 1). Similarly, when English traveller William Mountague visited the famous Leiden anatomical museum in late 1695 and saw "the mummy of an Egyptian Prince, above eighteen hundred years old," he was also confronted by a medley of human and animal relics, including "the head of a sea-horse . . . the bill of a strange bird," and an entire "French nobleman, who ravished his sister, and also murdered her, was beheaded at Paris, and bestowed on the Anatomy by Dr. Bills" (Mountague 1696, 82).

At the same time, the status of the mummy was slowly improving, in relative terms, from the Restoration onward. When Europeans had plundered burial pits around a century before, they had rarely been interested in obtaining "a mummy"; rather, their desire was for "some mummy," to be traded, crumbled, and swallowed in fluid as medicine in Paris or London or Wittenberg (see the article "Mummies and medicine"). By the time of Charles II, people were more likely to talk about "a mummy" as a well-defined, perhaps personalized artifact, rather than about a quantity of mummy that was broken up in an apothecary's mortar. Hence, when the king himself had "an entire Egyptian mummy with all the hieroglyphics and scutcheons upon it" presented to him on Friday, December 20, 1661, "at Whitehall by Captain Hurst, who lately brought it into England from the Libyan sands," the present was described as "the body of a princely young Lady," allegedly preserved at least 2500 years. And, if Hurst had some political motives for the gift, it was also now assumed that this mummy would be an object of general interest; it could, for some time, be seen "by any person of quality, who is delighted in such curiosities, at the sign of the Hand and Comb near Essex house in the Strand" (*Kingdom's Intelligencer*, December 23, 1661).

Whilst Hurst's mummy was clearly a rarity, such sights grew far more common as the eighteenth century progressed. In 1707 the Ashmolean received an Egyptian mummy from the English merchant and traveler, Aaron Goodyear. After his death, the private museum of antiquary John Kemp (1665–1717) was sold at auction in 1721, offering rich collectors the chance to acquire "two of the finest mummies . . . that were ever brought from Egypt" (Anon 1721, 1). And when the property of the late Mrs. Garnier of Pall Mall went under the hammer in October 1742, it was not only the ultra-wealthy who could see "a most perfect mummy of a daughter of Ptolomy," marked with Egyptian hieroglyphics; Londoners were informed that "gentlemen and ladies . . . may have tickets gratis for viewing the mummy" between noon and two each day—this measure being designed "to prevent the curious from being obstructed in their observations" (*London Daily Advertiser*, October 7, 1742).

For all its snobbery, this form of crowd control indicates that the Garnier mummy would have been too popular for its own good in Georgian London.

Yet there are signs that the growing rage for mummy collecting lessened reverence for this Egyptian wonder in some. As early as 1717, a mummy had featured on the London stage in John Gay's farcical and scandalous comedy, *Three Hours After Marriage*. First, an actual mummy is delivered to a medical doctor and collector named "Fossile." This character was in fact a fairly transparent parody of the doctor, natural historian, and antiquary, John Woodward (1665/1668–1728), and when Fossile receives his exotic delivery with the words "Oh! here's my mummy. Set him down. I am in haste," some viewers must have sensed that rich collectors were becoming blasé about the acquisition of Egyptian corpses. Moreover, if collectors themselves could be seen as relatively irreverent about such plunder, both Gay and his chuckling audiences were equally guilty. Rather than being wondrous, or even sinister or dangerous, the figure of the mummy becomes outrightly ridiculous when a character called Plotwell disguises himself as one to evade the doctor's vigilance and enjoy carnal relations with his desirable young wife.

The irreverence of gentlemen collectors (or "connoisseurs") was under attack again in 1754, with the paint barely dry on the newly opened British Museum. An anonymous satirist argued that, "as common malefactors are delivered to the surgeons to be anatomized, I would propose that a Connoisseur should be made into a mummy, and preserved in the Hall of the Royal Society, for the terror and admiration of his brethren" (*The Connoisseur*, May 30, 1754).

Come 1767, when a Captain Clarke was selling the tall slender mummy of an Egyptian woman in Fleet Street, a French soldier found himself involved in a mini-drama turned farce in Paris. Just returned from the East Indies, this unnamed Officer left in a public carriage "a small mummy which he [had] brought from Egypt." Customs officers who examined it took it to be the body of a murdered child, and presently a surgeon was called. Just as the surgeon was about to sign a death certificate in the public morgue, the Officer returned for his property and explained its true origins, prompting the officials to burst into embarrassed laughter (*London Evening Post*, 24 October, 1767).

At the end of the century, the Egyptian campaigns of Napoleon (1790–99), bringing scholars and scientists with them, advanced French Egyptology (see "Napoleon and the Birth of Egyptology"), and come 1823 the first mummy to reach America was greeted by excited crowds as it toured the country. Just a few years earlier, Chicago University had opened its Oriental Institute in 1819, and by the early twentieth century visitors could see an impressive range of human and animal mummies in the Metropolitan Museum in New York. By this stage Egyptology had grown into something resembling Egyptomania in both Europe and America.

Yet it would be a long time before private collectors, museums, or many of the general public grew sensitive to the political and cultural damage that mummy displays could inflict on the host countries or peoples of mummified bodies.

In January 2012, France finally returned 20 mummified Maori heads to New Zealand, decades after they were collected by European travelers in the eighteenth and nineteenth centuries, and some 30 years after the Maoris first requested them during the 1980s. Yet, as Margaret M. Swaney argues, while "current museum policies assert that all institutionalised human remains be treated respectfully . . . museum visitors frequently fail to recognize that Egyptian mummies are both authentic dead bodies, and once living people with unique biographies" (Swaney, *Living Dead*, ii).

Recently, a strange tale from the heyday of British Egyptomania brought a long-buried ethical slip back to light. In the early twentieth century the philanthropic clergyman William MacGregor often stayed in Egypt—partly because of ill-health—and over time amassed a large collection of Egyptian antiquities. Many of these went to the British Museum when the hoard was auctioned in 1922. But not all. MacGregor apparently continued to collect Egyptian artifacts into the 1930s, and in December 2001, a British journalist and historian, John Harper, described the curious fate of two of the vicar's mummies. For some reason (possibly out of respect), MacGregor decided to have them buried in the garden of his home, Bolehall Manor, in Tamworth, Staffordshire. Unused to the less than arid soil of the British midlands, the mummies began to deteriorate and to smell, and MacGregor's gardener (Harper's great-great grandfather) was asked to rebury them. The site chosen was the foundations of the local Palace cinema, then undergoing reconstruction. Harper explains: "the foundations looked like the kind of burial sites [MacGregor] had seen in Egypt, so he asked the foreman if he would mind if he deposited a couple of his mummies in the foundations." The foreman apparently did not mind, but the mummies themselves had no say in the matter. Admittedly, MacGregor's aims seem to have been well-meaning. These mummies were, after all, being buried, unlike all those now exposed to the glare of public attention in the world's museums. A faint flavor of indignity has since been added to the burial site, however. Above the mummies' resting place there is now no longer a cinema, but a McDonald's restaurant. If there is a lesson to be learned from this, it must be that mummies in museums can have their presentation filtered and controlled by sensitive custodians. Some of those outside them clearly cannot.

Richard Sugg

See also: Displaying mummies; Egyptomania; Medicine and mummies; Napoleon and the birth of Egyptology

Further Reading

Anon. 1721. *A Catalogue of the Antiquities of the Late Ingenious Mr. John Kemp.*

"Mummies Buried under Restaurant." 2001. *BBC News*, December 18. Accessed December 3, 2013. http://news.bbc.co.uk/1/hi/england/1718135.stm.

"France Returns 20 Mummified Heads to New Zealand." 2012. *BBC News*, January 24. Accessed December 3, 2013. http://www.bbc.co.uk/news/world-asia-16695330.

The Connoisseur. 1754.

Gay, John. 1717. *Three Hours after Marriage.*

Greaves, John. 1650. *Pyramidographia.*

Hubert, John. 1664. *A Catalogue of Many Natural Rarities.*

Kingdom's Intelligencer. 1661.

London Daily Advertiser. 1742.

London Evening Post. 1767.

Mountague, William. 1696. *The Delights of Holland.*

Ray, John. 1693. *A Collection of Curious Travels.*

Swaney, Margaret M. 2012. *The Living Dead: Egyptian Mummies and the Ethics of Display.* MA dissertation. New York University. Accessed December 3, 2013. http://www.academia.edu/4677578/THE_LIVING_DEAD_EGYPTIAN_MUMMIES_AND_THE_ETHICS_OF_DISPLAY.

Thévenot, Jean de. 1687. *The Travels of Monsieur de Thévenot into the Levant.* Anonymous translator.

Corelli, Marie

Marie Corelli (pen name of Mary Mackay, 1855–1924) was one of the most popular British authors in the late nineteenth and early twentieth centuries. Much of her work focused on melodrama and mysticism, which appealed to the popular occult and supernatural interests of her day, and it occasionally featured mummies. Famously, or perhaps notoriously, she helped to perpetuate the idea of the "mummy's curse" that attended the opening of the tomb of King Tutankhamun.

Born in London on May 1, 1855, Mary Mackay was the illegitimate daughter of the Scottish writer Charles Mackay (remembered today as the author of *Extraordinary Popular Delusions and the Madness of Crowds*) and his servant Mary Elizabeth Mills. Charles Mackay later married Mills after his first wife died. Mary Mackay was educated first at home and then, in her late teens, at a convent school in France, after which she returned to Britain and planned to pursue a career in music. For this purpose, she adopted the stage name Marie Corelli, which she then used as her pen name when she became a journalist and novelist. She died in Stratford-on-Avon on April 22, 1924.

Some of the mummy characters in Corelli's writings were romantic and sensational, such as Ziska, an evil mummy seeking revenge on her reincarnated lover, Gervase. Others stretch the preconceived notions of mummies derived from popular culture, such as her novel *The Soul of Lilith*, in which a character named El-Râmi preserves young Lilith's body with a strange elixir, thereby tethering her soul to the earth so that he can learn the secrets of the afterlife from her. Corelli used these mummy-like characters to explore the nature of the afterlife, the soul, and reincarnation.

Marie Corelli is perhaps more responsible than any other person for helping to popularize the myth of a "mummy's curse." In March of 1923, when Lord Carnarvon had fallen ill from an infected mosquito bite not long after participating in the opening of Tutankhamun's tomb, she wrote a letter that was published in newspapers in London and New York. It hinted at a possible sinister supernatural reason for Carnarvon's illness:

I cannot but think some risks are run by breaking into the last rest of a king in Egypt whose tomb is specially and solemnly guarded, and robbing him of his possessions. According to a rare book I possess, which is not in the British Museum, entitled *The Egyptian History of the Pyramids*, the most dire punishment follows any rash intruder into a sealed tomb. The book . . . names "secret poisons enclosed in boxes in such wise that those who touch them shall not know how they come to suffer." That is why I ask, Was it a mosquito bite that has so seriously infected Lord Carnarvon? . . . "Death comes on wings to he who enters the tomb of a pharaoh."

Carnarvon died of pneumonia two weeks later, making Corelli's words seem prophetic and reinforcing the popular notion that mummies' tombs are guarded by deadly curses.

Ziska, the mysterious femme fatale of *Ziska: The Problem of a Wicked Soul* (1897), is a highly sensual, evil mummy, and instantly attracts many young English men touring Egypt. While the two main characters, Denzil and Gervase, are equally infatuated with Ziska, Corelli uses the skeptical character of Dr. Dean to point out the truth of the situation, which is that Ziska is not in love with anyone. She is setting a trap for Armand Gervase, who is mentioned several times as resembling Araxes, the lover of the ancient Ziska Charmazel, who murdered her. Ziska has apparently waited for centuries for Araxes to be reborn, so she can seek revenge on him, as is evident when she appears as a ghost-like apparition in the very beginning of the novel, and calls for him. Once Gervase sees Ziska, he is doomed to fall in love with her all over again. Ziska appears to be both incorporeal and physical, appearing from nothing in the beginning and mysteriously disappearing after she has killed Gervase, yet when he tries to paint her portrait, he can only paint her true form, which is a hateful corpse. Though the nature of her physical existence is uncertain, she is clearly revived by the desire to avenge her own death. Corelli uses Ziska as an example of immortality through spurned love and hatred. Vengeance, along with the soul, cannot die.

Lilith, in *The Soul of Lilith* (1892), is innocent, yet also mummy-like. Corelli uses her to illustrate to her audience the beauty of a soul freed from its body. El-Râmi takes in an old Egyptian woman named Zaroba, along with her charge, Lilith, who is at the time a young girl. Lilith dies, but instead of burying her, El-Râmi gives her an elixir that not only keeps her body alive but allows her to mature into a beautiful young woman over several years. El-Râmi communicates with her to learn about the afterlife and the nature of death, summoning her spirit through the body as if it were a receiver. He revels in his power over her, and though he does not accept her answers that no matter how far she searches the universe, she cannot find death, he still keeps her tethered to the earth. Corelli chastises him throughout the novel for his feelings of superiority over God, as he considers Lilith his creation, since God left her to die as a child. Finally, he becomes so desperate for proof of the soul that he demands Lilith show him her own. She finally frees herself from her body, and El-Râmi sees a glimpse of the ethereal beauty of her spirit, having focused too long on the loveliness of her preserved body. But when she is free, Lilith's body dies, withering away into ash in only moments. Corelli's saintly mummy shows the superiority of the soul over the body and shows the skeptic, represented by El-Râmi, that truth, peace, beauty, and love all lie in the immortal soul.

Though some considered Corelli's works to be didactic and melodramatic, her novels were very popular in the late Victorian period. Nickianne Moody attributes Corelli's tremendous success to the public's fascination with death and the afterlife and the author's use of contemporary pseudo-sciences in exploring these otherworldly themes. Elaine M. Hartnell notes that the use of sensational themes such as murder and crimes of passion, and even the use of science fiction, appealed to a wide audience.

In 1923, Corelli circulated a warning in the British and American press that, according to a book of ancient Egyptian lore she claimed to possess, intruders into sealed tombs will receive dire punishments. This was in response to the news that Lord Carnarvon, who had financed and spearheaded the recent excavation and opening of Tutankhamun's tomb, had developed blood poisoning from an infected mosquito bite. Less than two weeks after Corelli's warning appeared, Carnarvon died of pneumonia, and Corelli's words, which now appeared prophetic, thus helped to amplify the already spectacular wave of publicity surrounding the Tutankhamun project.

Despite her enormous popularity during life, and despite her crucial role in helping to perpetuate the most famous episode in the long-running myth of the mummy's curse, Corelli's works did not become enduring classics, and today she is largely forgotten. Her books have fallen in recognition and status over the decades, and although a few have received the attention of scholars, most remain out of print and can now be found only in large libraries, online databases such as Project Gutenberg, and occasionally on Amazon.com.

Carolyn Shefcyk

See also: Mummy's curse; Tutankhamun ("King Tut")

Further Reading

Corelli, Marie. 2012. *The Soul of Lilith*, 1892. Library of Alexandria. Kindle Edition.

Corelli, Marie. 2012. *Ziska: The Problem of a Wicked Soul*, 1897. Project Gutenberg. Kindle Edition.

Hartnell, Elaine M. 2006. "Morals and Metaphysics: Marie Corelli, Religion and the Gothic." *Women's Writing* 13, no. 2: 284–303.

Marchant, Jo. 2013. "The Mummy's Curse." *Aeon Magazine*, October 25. Accessed December 4, 2013. http://aeon.co/magazine/altered-states/why-does-the-mummys-curse-refuse-to-die.

Moody, Nickianne. 2006. "Moral Uncertainty and the Afterlife: Explaining the Popularity of Marie Corelli's Early Novels." *Women's Writing* 13, no. 2: 188–205.

Crypt mummies of Sommersdorf Castle

Although crypt mummies in Europe are most often associated with churches, some mummies have been preserved in family crypts of some castles. The crypt of Schloss Sommersdorf (Sommersdorf Castle) in southern Germany holds several coffins, including five containing mummified adults. The current living descendant of several of the mummies, Manfred Baron von Crailsheim, still resides in the castle today and is supportive of the scientific study of his ancestors. The crypt is not open to the public, although two of the mummies from this crypt were included in an exhibition that toured the United States (see the entry on "Mummies of the World: The Exhibition").

Sommersdorf Castle is located near the city of Ansbach, in a southern German region known as Franconia, a part of Bavaria. The first stages of the castle were built prior to 1200; the current moated castle has had only a few major alterations since the late fourteenth century. In an area below the castle church, a crypt was constructed for burials, mainly for members of the von Crailsheim family. Some written records are available, but it is not always possible to identify more than the name and date of death of the individual entombed in the crypt.

The bodies in the crypt were not embalmed, but were naturally mummified. The crypt has open window areas and so the bodies were exposed to a constant flow of air, even inside the coffins. Despite the presence of moisture in the crypt area, the five bodies all have remarkably well preserved skin and muscle tissue. Several other theories were proposed to explain the mummification, ranging from subterranean water courses to radiation, but these explanations seem unlikely.

Some remains of clothing cling to the skin of the mummies, although much of the fabric is fragmentary. The stockings of several of the mummies are better preserved than other clothing. The clothing may have been damaged during the several historical openings of the coffins. It has been reported that Napoleon's army opened the coffins in 1806, and that the coffins were subsequently reopened and screwed or nailed shut again on several occasions. One man, the Baron von Holz, wears exceptional leather boots that reach up to his knees. The boots have diamond-shaped nail heads on the soles, and it appears that they were not worn in life, but were put on the body at the time of his death.

To date, three of the five mummies have undergone some scientific research. The two mummies who have not yet been studied are those of Julius Wilhelm Baron von Crailsheim, who was killed in a hunting accident in 1812, and a woman who may be a von Crailsheim or née von Rauber. Of the three mummies studied, two are women: The Baroness Geyern von Schenck and Sophie Luise von Kniestätt, née von Crailsheim. The final mummy is that of the Baron von Holz, a von Crailsheim relative. The last three mummies date from the early seventeenth century.

The three mummies underwent computed tomography (CT) scans at a German hospital. The data from the CT scans were studied, and researchers generated three-dimensional (3D) virtual models and animations. The Baron von Holz had healed fractures on three ribs on the lower left side of the body. He also had an extra vertebra in his lower back. Although an 1833 lithograph of the mummy in his coffin showed that he was much taller than the other individuals in the crypt, the extra vertebra did not cause this additional height.

The Baroness Schenck von Geyern also had an extra vertebra in her lower back and additional problems with her back: a condition called Diffuse Idiopathic Skeletal Hyperostosis (DISH), which caused five vertebrae in her lower back to fuse together, and a very severe curvature of her spine (kyphoscoliosis). Both of these conditions may have caused back pain and restricted mobility.

Sophie Luise von Kniestätt, who died shortly after giving birth to her eighth child, has claw-like hands and bent toes. One interpretation of the position of Sophie's hands and feet was that she had been buried alive. Examination of the joints of her hands and feet, however, showed that had very severe osteoarthritis that led to the twisting of the joints. There is no evidence that she was buried alive. Sophie also had a very severe curvature of the spine, although her curvature was less severe than that of the Baroness Schenck von Geyern.

More detailed research is still being carried out on all three of the mummies. Samples were taken from the mummies for ancient DNA analysis. The main goal of that research was to attempt to confirm a genetic link between each of the mummies and to living descendants. Preliminary results of this research have, so far, been inconclusive. Since the presence of an extra lumbar vertebra can be a genetic trait, it is possible that the Baron and Baroness are related, although the specific relationship is unclear at this time.

The crypt mummies of Sommersdorf are interesting for various reasons. The mummies are from a small family crypt, not a larger church vault, and a descendant of several of the mummies still resides in the castle. The bodies have naturally mummified in an area in which preservation of soft tissue might not be expected. Over the history of the castle, the coffins of the mummies were repeatedly opened. Radiological studies of the mummies gave researchers the opportunity to identify that the three mummies examined had several anomalies of their spines: extra vertebrae, fused vertebrae, and spinal curvatures.

Heather Gill-Frerking

See also: Genetic study of mummies; Medical imaging of mummies; Mummies of Europe; Mummies of the World: The Exhibition; Natural mummification

Further Reading

Gill-Frerking, Heather, Schanandore, J., and Rosendahl, W. 2011. "Supernumerary Vertebrae and Other Spinal Pathology in Three 17th Century Crypt Mummies from Germany." Unpublished conference paper, American Association for Physical Anthropology. Minneapolis, Minnesota.

von Crailsheim, Baron Manfred. 2010. "The Mummies from Summersdorf Castle." In *Mummies of the World*. Edited by Alfried Wieczorek and Wilfried Rosendahl, 362–364. New York: Prestel.

D

Dawson, Warren Royal

Warren Dawson was a self-educated British Egyptologist and historian, best known for his 1924 volume *Egyptian Mummies*, coauthored with Sir Grafton Elliot Smith, as well as other contributions to the scientific study of mummies and mummification. A painstaking but often rather trusting scholar, Dawson published extensively across a number of fields including the ancient history of medicine and the history of Egyptology.

Born in Ealing, West London in October 1888, Warren Royal Dawson attended the prestigious St. Paul's School, until at the age of 15 his father's death forced him to seek paid employment rather than follow his two older brothers to Oxford University. Dawson worked in insurance for the rest of his career, setting up an underwriting agency in 1922. In 1929 he became in effect a sleeping partner in his own agency, and devoted more of his time to the scholarly pursuits that were always his main interest. He greatly regretted his lack of higher education, and he devoted a great deal of his free time to studying, including in the field of Egyptology.

A turning point in Dawson's studies came when he was befriended by Wallis Budge, then a Keeper at the British Museum responsible for the Egyptian collection. Budge was himself originally self-educated in oriental languages and likely felt a sympathy for Dawson, as Dawson in turn was later to show in his study of the similarly self-taught Thomas Pettigrew. Budge allowed Dawson access to the Egyptian collection at the Museum and guided his scholarship.

Dawson took an early interest in ancient medicine, including the processes of mummification in ancient Egypt and elsewhere. His studies of the techniques and forms of mummification were detailed and penetrating, and he criticized what he perceived to be inaccuracies in early textual accounts of the practice, such as those by Herodotus. Some of his theories have been regarded as fanciful, such as his suggestion that Egyptian embalmers dried bodies inside large jars of natron salts in solution instead of with natron crystals.

Early in his studies of mummification Dawson met Elliot Smith, who had returned from Egypt in 1909 to take up a position in Manchester. Smith's catalogue of the Royal Mummies in Cairo Museum inspired Dawson to focus his Egyptological studies on mummies and mummification. Later, Dawson and Smith decided to collaborate on a popular overview of knowledge and research in mummy studies, which appeared in 1924 as *Egyptian Mummies*. Smith was forced to withdraw from the collaboration and contributed only two chapters, while Dawson wrote the remainder, basing his work to a considerable extent on Smith's earlier writings.

Egyptian Mummies was the first general overview of mummy studies since Pettigrew's *History of Egyptian Mummies* some 90 years earlier. It is richly illustrated with photographs and other illustrations, many of them from mummies unwrapped or examined by Smith during his time in Egypt.

Dawson's studies of mummies and his interest in the history of medicine led him to write and edit biographies and bibliographies of Thomas Pettigrew (1931) and later of Elliot Smith (1938). These biographical studies, together with Budge's reminiscences about the great Egyptologists of times past, led Dawson to produce the first edition of the monumental *Who Was Who in Egyptology*, a fantastic resource for historians and researchers.

Many of Dawson's publications were archive catalogues and bibliographies, and in 1928 he published the still-valuable annotated *Bibliography of Works Relating to Mummification in Egypt*, which brought to light many of the earliest works on mummy studies in several languages. His last work, published just before his death, was the coauthored catalogue of the mummies and human remains in the British Museum.

Dawson's scholarship, though impressive, was marked by a tendency to believe everything that he was told, and to think only the best of those whom he admired. His biography of Pettigrew omits many of the subject's least appealing characteristics, including his dismissal from a hospital post for corruption. Nonetheless Dawson's writings are overwhelmingly a triumph of close observation and painstaking scholarship, and they remain valuable insights into mummy studies and other fields today. Dawson retired to Bletchley in Buckinghamshire in 1936 because of ill health and died in May 1968. His papers are held at the British Library.

Gabriel Moshenska

See also: Egyptian collection, the British Museum; Mummy unwrappings; Pettigrew, Thomas Joseph; Smith, Grafton Elliot

Further Reading

Brier, Bob. 1996. *Egyptian Mummies: Unravelling the Secrets of an Ancient Art.* London: Michael O'Mara.

Dawson, Warren Royal. 1927. "Making a Mummy." *Journal of Egyptian Archaeology* 13: 40–9.

Dawson, Warren Royal. 1929. *A Bibliography of Works Relating to Mummification in Egypt: With Excerpts, Epitomes, Critical and Biographical Notes.* Cairo: Imprimerie de l'Institut français d'archéologie orientale.

Dawson, Warren Royal. 1931. *Memoir of Thomas Joseph Pettigrew F.R.C.S., F.R.S., F.S.A. (1791–1865).* New York: Medical Life Press.

Dawson, Warren Royal (ed.). 1938. *Sir Grafton Elliot Smith: A Biographical Record by his Colleagues*. London: Jonathan Cape.

Dawson, Warren Royal. 1951. *Who Was Who in Egyptology: a biographical index of Egyptologists; of travellers, explorers, and excavators in Egypt; of collectors of and dealers in Egyptian antiquities; of consuls, officials, authors, benefactors, and others whose names occur in the literature of Egyptology, from the year 1500 to the present day, but excluding persons now living*. London: Egypt Exploration Society.

Dawson, Warren Royal, and Peter Hugh Ker Gray. 1968. *Catalogue of Egyptian Antiquities in the British Museum: 1: Mummies and Human Remains*. Oxford: Oxford University Press.

James, T. G. H. 1969. "W. R. Dawson." *Journal of Egyptian Archaeology* 55: 211–4.

Pettigrew, Thomas Joseph. 1834. *A History of Egyptian Mummies*. London: Longman, Rees, Orme, Brown, Green, and Longman.

Smith, Graften Elliot, and Warren R. Dawson. 1924. *Egyptian Mummies*. London: Allen & Unwin.

Displaying mummies

For many people, exposure to mummies may be limited to television documentaries, popular films, and Halloween decorations. Archaeologists and biological anthropologists excavate and study mummies, which are sometimes then put on display for the public to see. Traditionally, mummies are displayed as part of museum collections, but they may also be displayed in other environments, such as libraries, science centers, and commercial exhibitions. The display of mummies is a complex issue. The most important aspects, however, are the protection of the mummies and the respectful treatment of the dead.

Museums are responsible for public presentation of aspects of culture and heritage. At the same time, museums have a particular duty of care for the specimens and objects in their collections, while also providing access to the specimens for researchers and the public. While mummies on display in exhibitions are often popular with visitors, there is a need for the museum to protect mummies through professional conservation and environmental controls.

Many people are so accustomed to seeing real-life mummies displayed in museums, and also presented in books and documentaries, that the sensitive cultural and moral issues associated with displaying the remains of human beings in this way never occurs to them. However, the question of whether it is ethical to display human remains, mummified or otherwise, for public education and/or entertainment is a live one, and has been the subject of an ongoing conversation. Work is ongoing to clarify the issues involved and to establish widely accepted guidelines.

In general, there are few regulations that prohibit the display of human remains as part of museum exhibitions. All museums will adhere to the guidelines and Code of Ethics of the International Council of Museums (ICOM) or other professional standards. The ICOM guidelines, however, provide few details with regards to the ethical display of mummies. In the United States, there are restrictions that usually prevent the display of mummies that originate in North America. These mummies are normally of Native American origin, and under legislation that exists in the United States, Native American human remains cannot usually be displayed.

When human mummies are displayed to the public, they are most often included as examples of a specific cultural custom. Even small local museums often have a mummy or two in their collection; these mummies are nearly always from ancient Egypt and are included in more general exhibitions about the customs of the ancient world. Only rarely are the mummies themselves the central focus of the exhibition (see, for example, the article on "Mummies of the World: The Exhibition" in this volume).

Any display of mummies must be undertaken with an understanding of the public perceptions of the display of the dead. While museums can provide information for visitors, based on archaeological and cultural context, as well as scientific studies, museums cannot tell people what to think about what they are seeing or how to react to the display. Any exhibition that includes a human mummy should be carefully planned to allow the visitor the opportunity to appreciate the mummy as a person, and not just as an object on display. The environmental wall color, lighting, exhibition layout, and ambient noise must be combined to provide a good visitor experience, while maintaining the dignity of, and respect for, the mummy being displayed. Depending on the purpose of the exhibition, the display environment should reflect the importance of respecting the individual mummy while also providing a good visitor experience. It is critical that sensationalism be avoided: visitors must be able to experience mummies that are in their preserved state, as opposed to being altered by stereotypical graphic images or electronic enhancements. Multimedia approaches may include visualization of medical imaging used for research, but these displays should be designed to provide additional information for the visitor and not as gratuitous or cartoonish animations that detract from the mummy being displayed.

Displaying human mummies, however, is not without controversy. Museum exhibition standards have changed over recent decades, and some people now question whether it is ethical and appropriate to display human remains, whether skeletonized or mummified. Others see the display of mummies as a way of exploiting the dead for commercial benefit. Some institutions choose not to display mummies, or to cover part of the mummies so that only the face is visible. Generally, museums in Europe are more willing to display mummies than those in North America, and the visitor attitude toward mummies also seems to vary culturally.

One comparison of visitor perception of the display of bog bodies in Germany versus the United States showed that visitors in Germany were more positive about the display of the bog bodies in a museum than were visitors to an American traveling exhibition that included bog bodies.

Another aspect of the display of mummies that is controversial is merchandise selected for sale in the ubiquitous museum or exhibition gift shop; there is no doubt that the gift shop plays an important role for many exhibitions and museums, as well as for the visitors. While some find souvenirs such as postcards, books, notebooks, or posters acceptable, other items are viewed as tasteless and inappropriate. For example, a bog body exhibition featured such souvenirs as chocolate bars or flavored coffee with the photo of a bog body on the package, and some tee shirts were viewed as disrespectful to the dead because they showed the photograph of one of the bog bodies featured in the exhibition.

It is important that people who do not usually have access to mummies have the opportunity to view them and learn from them. Museum displays and similar exhibitions provide visitors with the chance to face the past through mummies. When human mummies are displayed, however, it is important that the setting is appropriate and respectful, and that there is no risk to any mummy while being exhibited.

Heather Gill-Frerking

See also: Bog bodies; Collecting mummies; Egyptian Antiquities Museum; Egyptian collection, the British Museum; Mummies of the World: The Exhibition

Further Reading

Gill-Frerking, Heather, and Wilfried Rosendahl. Forthcoming. Recommendations for the Public Display and Research of the Mummies. In *Mummy Studies: An Evidence-Based Approach*. Edited by Heather Gill-Frerking. Cambridge: Cambridge University Press.

Gill-Robinson, Heather. 2004. "Bog Bodies on Display." *Journal of Wetland Archaeology* 4: 111–116.

Doctor Who: Pyramids of Mars

Pyramids of Mars is a four-episode serial of the ongoing television drama series *Doctor Who*, which involves murderously ambulant mummies and the attempted restoration of an ancient Egyptian deity. Produced in the United Kingdom by the BBC, *Doctor Who* is the world's longest-running science-fiction television series, relating the adventures of a benevolent alien known as "The Doctor" as he travels through time and space, encountering villainy and alien monstrosities.

This particular serial was originally broadcast on BBC1 between October 25 and November 15, 1975. The story is credited to "Stephen Harris," in fact a pseudonym for the series' script editor Robert Holmes and writer Lewis Greifer, whose original story, based on elements drawn from Egyptian mythology, was deemed to be unworkable within the programme's format.

The Doctor (Tom Baker) and his traveling companion Sarah-Jane Smith (Elisabeth Sladen) arrive in England in 1911 at the country estate of missing Egyptologist Professor Marcus Scarman (Bernard Archard). It rapidly becomes apparent that Sutekh (Gabriel Woolf), the incredibly powerful and destructive sole survivor of an ancient alien race, the Osirans, from the distant planet Phaester Osiris, is attempting to escape his eternal imprisonment using a force of heavily-bandaged robots, resembling Egyptian mummies, and the reanimated corpse of the missing Egyptologist.

Initially dismissive of his companion's indication that she has witnessed "a walking mummy," the Doctor states that mummies are simply "embalmed, eviscerated corpses. They don't walk." It becomes apparent that these mummies are, in fact, service robots, wrapped in "bindings [which] are chemically impregnated to protect the robots against damage and corrosion" and are controlled by a "slave relay" device in the form of a scarab-shaped ring (*Doctor Who* 1975).

Eventually, after traveling to Sutekh's prison beneath a mastaba in Saqqara, Egypt, and then to the titular pyramid of Mars, the Doctor succeeds in capturing Sutekh within his own time tunnel and projecting him into the far future.

While it is evident that *Pyramids of Mars* draws heavily on the tropes and iconography of late nineteenth century mummy fiction, specifically Arthur Conan Doyle's "Lot No. 249," the story's cinematic influences are even more evident, with its general atmosphere of country houses, tweedy but unkempt poachers, and damp bracken echoing that of Hammer Films' *The Mummy* (1959). However, Bernard Archard's physical performance and sepulchral tones stretch further back into the history of cinema, echoing Boris Karloff's desiccated Ardath Bey in director Karl Freund's *The Mummy* (1932). The concept of extraterrestrial intervention on early human development and religion draws on Nigel Kneale's 1956 BBC serial *Quatermass and the Pit*, the 1971 *Doctor Who* serial *The Daemons*, written by Robert Sloman and Producer Barry Letts, and, of course, the famous/notorious theories of Erich von Däniken, espoused in the book *Chariots of the Gods*, published in 1968. During the period 1974–1977, under the guidance of producer Philip Hinchcliffe and the aforementioned Holmes, the series drew substantially on literary and cinematic classics of Gothic horror for inspiration, with director Paddy Russell achieving on a Saturday afternoon a level of horror that had previously only been presented in movie theaters by Hammer Films under the banner of an "X" Certificate.

The mummies' costumes in *Pyramids of Mars*, designed by Barbara Kidd, are heavily stylized with domed heads and enlarged, somewhat pointed chests. As with the costume briefly worn by the reanimated Scarman, the heads of the mummies are clearly modeled on the painting discovered at Tassili Plateau in the Central Sahara in 1958 by French anthropologist Henri Lhote, who jocularly described it as "the Great Martian God" (Lhote 1973, 214), while Sutekh's masked appearance takes as its basis the so-called Barbu de Lyon, dating from 3800–3500 BCE, excavated at Gebelein by Louis Lortet in 1908.

While the contents of Sutekh's tomb/prison are evidently not from the "first dynasties of the pharaohs," as declared by Scarman at the serial's commencement, the use of Egyptian antiquities and iconography is inventive, with the canopic jars containing generator loops, which operate a powerful enclosing force field when placed at the cardinal points of the compass, and the Osiran war-rocket taking the form of a pyramid, which "transposes with its projection" (*Doctor Who*, 1975). These concepts are predicated on the idea that the iconography, if not the purpose, of Osiran technology has been transmitted to Egyptian culture from the time of Sutekh's pre-dynastic imprisonment. The reimagining of mummies as mere unthinking robots, the instruments of another's will, is in keeping with Doyle's conception.

Doctor Who's enduring presence over the past 50 years has ensured its iconic place in British culture, and *Pyramids of Mars*, with its claustrophobic atmosphere, judicious use of location filming, and strong performances from a small (and rapidly dwindling) cast, is regarded as a high point in its history, representing the quintessence of earth-bound stories. The serial received considerable media interest at the time of its broadcast because of its horrific content and broadcast time of 17.45.

Elements of the story have been indirectly referenced in a number of later episodes of *Doctor Who* and directly referenced in the spin-off television series *The Sarah-Jane Adventures* and numerous subsequent novels, published by both the BBC and Virgin. The serial was novelized by Terence Dicks in 1976 and is currently available on DVD.

John J. Johnston

See also: Doyle, Arthur Conan; *The Mummy* (1932); *The Mummy* (1959); The mummy on television

Further Reading

Dicks, T. 1976. *Doctor Who and the Pyramids of Mars*. London: Target.

Doctor Who: Pyramids of Mars. 1975. Directed by Paddy Russell. London: BBC Home Entertainment, 2004. DVD.

Howe, D. J., and S. J. Walker. 2003. *The Television Companion: The Unofficial and Unauthorised Guide to* Doctor Who. Tolworth: Telos.

Kneale, N. 1960. *Quatermass and the Pit*. London: Penguin.

Lhote, H. 1973. *The Search for the Tassili Frescoes: The Story of the Rock Paintings of the Sahara*. 2nd ed. London: Hutchinson.

Miles, L., and T Wood. 2004. *About Time: The Unauthorised Guide to Doctor Who (Seasons 12–17)*. Des Moines: Mad Norwegian Press.

Ziegler, C. (ed.) 2004. *Pharaon*. Paris: Flammarion.

Doyle, Arthur Conan

Edinburgh-born writer Arthur Conan Doyle (1859–1930) is of course famous for the creation of Sherlock Holmes, who remains the most famous literary detective, and the four supernatural novels and fourteen supernatural short stories by him comprise but a small portion of his literary output. Of these fourteen short stories, two feature mummies. A third story, "The Brown Hand" (as "The Story of the Brown Hand," *The Strand Magazine*, May 1899), is sometimes described as involving a mummy, but it is a traditional haunting in which the ghost, an Indian, haunts the surgeon who operated on him, wanting to have his amputated hand returned.

Arthur Ignatius Conan Doyle was born into a wealthy Irish-Catholic family in Edinburgh, Scotland, on May 22, 1859. His father, Charles Doyle, was both a noted figure in the art world and a chronic alcoholic. Arthur's mother, Mary, was well-educated and widely read, and she possessed a gift for dramatic storytelling that she shared regularly with her son, who later credited these performances with igniting his passion for writing. At the age of 9 he was sent to a Jesuit boarding school. He attended Stonyhurst College and then the University of Edinburgh, where he graduated with a medical degree in 1881. While in college he departed from his inherited Roman Catholic faith and gravitated toward a self-professed agnosticism while also developing a keen interest in spiritualism and occultism.

It was clear to John Vansittart Smith that this mummy had never been unswathed before. The operation interested him keenly. He thrilled all over with curiosity, and his bird-like head protruded farther and farther from behind the door. When, however, the last roll had been removed from the 4,000-year-old head, it was all that he could do to stifle an outcry of amazement. First, a cascade of long, black, glossy tresses poured over the workman's hands and arms. A second turn of the bandage revealed a low, white forehead, with a pair of delicately arched eyebrows. A third uncovered a pair of bright, deeply fringed eyes, and a straight, well-cut nose, while a fourth and last showed a sweet, full, sensitive mouth, and a beautifully curved chin. The whole face was one of extraordinary loveliness, save for the one blemish that in the centre of the forehead there was a single irregular, coffee-colored splotch. It was a triumph of the embalmer's art.

—From "The Ring of Thoth" by Arthur Conan Doyle

He also began to write, and although he practiced medicine briefly and successfully after graduation, he eventually abandoned the profession and, following a period of uncertainty and difficulty as he tried to get his work published, achieved enormous fame as the author of the Sherlock Holmes stories. He also remained associated with, and wrote extensively about, the spiritualist movement for the remainder of his life—a fact for which he received much criticism from some quarters, especially when he was duped by several notorious hoaxes. He was knighted by King Edward VII in 1902.

Doyle's two Egyptian stories differ in their presentations and utilizations of the mummy. The first, "The Ring of Thoth" (*The Cornhill Magazine*, January 1890), is seen largely from the perspective of John Vansittart Smith, an Englishman who has studied numerous academic subjects, ultimately settling on Egyptology. Upon visiting the mummies in the Louvre, he notices that the museum attendant is Egyptian, although the attendant denies this. Smith falls asleep and upon awakening in the now-closed museum sees the attendant unwrapping a surprisingly well-preserved mummy and adoring the corpse. Upon his being discovered, Smith is escorted from the room by the attendant and given the history: the attendant is Sosra, born about 1600 BCE, during the reign of Tuthmosis. A brilliant student, Sosra discovered the secret to immortality and gave it to a cat and a young priest, Parmes, then fell in love with Atma, daughter of the Governor, not knowing that Parmes also loved her. Atma would marry Sosra, but the plague kills her. Parmes thereupon reveals that he has discovered a cure for immortality and will die next to Atma, and that the mysterious ingredient necessary to end immortality is hidden in the ring of Thoth, also hidden. Sosra has looked for the ring since the first deaths, and upon learning of the discovery of Atma's mummy and a description of its contents in the newspapers, realizes that the ring has been found. Smith is thereupon ejected from the museum but soon reads in the *Times* an uncomprehending account of the attendant's corpse being found with the mummy, the newspaper concluding that the attendant died in the process of looting the display.

If "The Ring of Thoth" can be said to have a moral, it is an anti-academic one that is expressed explicitly by Sosra, who tells Vansittart that the important aspects of Egyptian life were not the inscriptions or the monuments that Vansittart and his fellow academic contemporaries see and study but the philosophy and mystical knowledge that the Egyptians possessed and which the contemporary Egyptologists ignore. As the events of the story reveal, it is only through intimate acquaintance with the past that the events of the present become comprehensible, and Vansittart (and the reader) realize the flaws in an academic understanding of the past after encountering *The Times*'s mistaken assumptions and conclusions. A message of enduring love is what the past has to offer the present, even if it is not generally recognized.

The majority of "Lot No. 249," Doyle's second Egyptian tale (*Harper's Magazine*, September 1892), takes place in and around Oxford University, in

1884. The story begins with upperclassman Abercrombie Smith learning from his younger friend Jephro Hastie that Smith's downstairs neighbor, Edward Bellingham, though gifted at Eastern languages, is an unpleasant sort. (Bellingham is, however, engaged to Eveline, the lovely sister of his close friend Monkhouse Lee.) A scream emanating from Bellingham's chambers enables Smith to see that the place is "a museum rather than a study" and that Bellingham possesses a mummy, "a horrid, black, withered thing, like a charred head on a gnarled bush" whose very name has been lost and who was the titular lot (No. 249) at the auction at which Bellingham acquired him. Bellingham makes excuses for his fainting, and life resumes, except: Bellingham may have a roommate, though none of the students sees anyone; and somebody attempts to strangle a man who once confronted Bellingham; and Bellingham's engagement is terminated; and somebody attempts to drown Lee; and somebody pursues Smith as he visits a professor at night. Despairing comments from Lee, who has been sworn to silence, lead to Smith realizing that Bellingham has somehow animated the mummy and sent it after those who have offended him, and only chance has kept them alive. Smith calls on Bellingham and forces him to destroy the mummy and the unique roll of papyrus Bellingham used to reanimate it. Bellingham leaves school, and the reader is left frustrated: Abercrombie Smith's anti-intellectualism has emerged triumphant, a narrow priggishness destroying vast and unique knowledge, though Doyle's final sentence does leave open the possibility that Bellingham might yet reappear, for "the wisdom of men is small, and the ways of Nature are strange, and who shall put a bound to the dark things which may be found by those who seek for them?" At the same time, one doubts that Doyle intended this as the message for what is intended to be a story of quiet English heroism.

In addition to the above, one of the curiosities of the stories is that in each the actions are motivated and driven by a frustrated sexuality. In "The Ring of Thoth," this sexuality culminates in a barely concealed act of necrophilia, for though (as we later learn) Sosra has endured for nearly 3,500 years, he has been unable to find another woman or experience a love comparable to that he found with Atma. In his unwrapping of Atma's remarkably well-preserved corpse, a strong death eroticism is established, with the mummy possessing "long, black, glossy tresses . . . a low, white forehead, with a pair of bright, deeply fringed eyes, and a straight, well-cut nose . . . [and] a sweet, full, sensitive mouth, and a beautifully curved chin," and it culminates after Sosra, "hurling himself down upon the ground beside the mummy, he threw his arms around her, and kissed her repeatedly upon the lips and brow." The sexualities depicted in "Lot No. 249" are less explicit and transgressive, but a creepy sexuality is nevertheless present, first in the descriptions of Bellingham, described by Hastie as fat and somehow innately perverse: "My gorge always rises at him. I should have put him down as a man with secret vices—an evil liver." Nevertheless, despite these hints of shady sexuality, Bellingham has managed to become engaged to Eveline Lee, sister of fellow-student Monkhouse Lee, which greatly disgusts Hastie, who refers to them as "a toad and a dove, that's what they always remind me." However, this relationship does not last, for Lee discovers Bellingham's secret and breaks the engagement, thus precipitating Bellingham's using the mummy in his attacks on those who thwarted him.

Although Doyle probably based his stories on his reading of the contemporary archaeological discoveries in Egypt, it seems possible that "The Ring of Thoth" also owes some of its content to H. Rider Haggard's *She* (New York: Harper's Franklin Square Library, 1886; London: Longmans, Green, and Co., 1887). A number of the elements that appear first in *She*—particularly the immortal lover, the death eroticism, and the barely concealed necrophilia—reappear in "The Ring of Thoth," and both stories depict the outcomes of love triangles, although the love triangle in "The Ring of Thoth" (two men and a woman) appears to be a deliberate inversion of that given in *She* (two women and a man). No specific literary model can be established for "Lot No. 249," and Doyle carefully refrains from giving too many details lest he be held accountable for misstatement of error: even the mummy is nameless, reduced to an auctioneer's lot.

Neither "The Ring of Thoth" nor "Lot No. 249" represents Doyle's finest or most imaginative writing, but each is briskly told and possesses a narrative vigor. In addition, because the reanimated mummy of "Lot No. 249" is initially presented realistically, yet also as an icon of horror, with "horribly discoloured" features, "blotched skin," "black, coarse hair," "gaunt ribs," and "a sunken, leaden-hued abdomen, with the long slit where the embalmer had left his mark," the gradual revelation of its supernatural reanimation and its stalking of Smith, in which it is only dimly glimpsed, give it a menace that contrasts quite successfully with the sedate depictions of student life. At the same time, these stories are remembered only because of their author and their subject matter: they are otherwise little more than incidental pieces, minor supernatural fictions of the late Victorian period. Doyle was to write better fiction; others were to write better stories involving reanimated mummies.

Doyle died of a heart attack on July 7, 1930, at his home in Crowborough, East Sussex, England.

Richard Bleiler

See also: Haggard, H. Rider; The mummy in Western fiction: Beginnings to 1922; Mummy movies

Further Reading

Doyle, Arthur Conan. 1979. *The Best Supernatural Tales of Arthur Conan Doyle*. Selected and introduced by E. F. Bleiler. New York: Dover.

Lycett, Andrew. 2007. *The Man Who Created Sherlock Holmes: The Life and Times of Sir Arthur Conan Doyle*. New York: Free Press.

E

Egyptian Antiquities Museum

The Egyptian Antiquities Museum (often known colloquially as the "Cairo Museum") is the largest and oldest museum in Egypt, and has been housed in three different locations in the Cairo conurbation since its foundation. It contains a large collection of mummies, including the majority of the surviving remains of kings.

The concept of a national museum goes back 1835, when an ordinance was made by Muhammed Ali, Ottoman Governor of Egypt, which prohibited the export or destruction of antiquities and founded a national museum. However, for all its fine sentiments, the Ordinance had few lasting effects. An Inspector of Museums, Yousef Zia Effendi, was appointed and a small museum established in the Ezbekiya Gardens, in a small room in the palace of the Deftardar Bay, Minister of Finance, before being moved to the Cairo Citadel. However, items were steadily given away to distinguished visitors, the residue finally being presented to the Austro-Hungarian Archduke Maximillian (later Emperor of Mexico) in 1855, and later became the core of the Egyptian collection of the Kunsthistorisches Museum in Vienna, Austria.

It was not until 1858 that regulation of antiquities was placed on a meaningful basis when Auguste Mariette (1821–1881), was appointed the first Mamûr (Director) of Antiquities Works by Viceroy Said. A new museum was set up in a former warehouse in Cairo's port-suburb, Bulaq, and was formally opened on October 16, 1863. For many years, the Director of the Antiquities Service was also the head of the Museum, which only obtained its own Director on 1941. On the other hand, a Keeper was in charge of its day-to-day running from the outset, the first being Luigi Vassalli (1812–1887).

The Bulaq museum was next to the Nile, and in October 1878 a high Nile inundation flooded it; although most objects were saved, some were ruined by water and some stolen. Nevertheless, the building was expanded and its collections grew rapidly, including the arrival of a large group of royal mummies in 1881. New premises were finally secured in 1890, when a former royal palace on the opposite side of the Nile in Giza (on part of the site now occupied by Cairo Zoo) was taken over. Unfortunately, this building had significant drawbacks, being amongst other things being totally lacking in fire-resistance. It was also still too small, with the discovery of over 150 mummies and their coffins in a tomb known as the

Egyptian Antiquities Museum, Cairo, with a sphinx in the foreground. (Indos82/Dreamstime)

Bab el-Gasus at Deir el-Bahari in 1892 resulting in many of the coffins being given away to foreign museums.

However, a brand-new purpose-built museum was authorized in 1894, the foundation stone being laid at Qasr el-Nil, on the edge of what is now Midan Tahrir, just over two kilometres south of the site of the old museum at Bulaq,

1863	The first incarnation of the Egyptian Antiquities Museum opens on October 16 in a former warehouse in Bulaq, Cairo, headed by Auguste Mariette.
1878	A particularly high seasonal flooding of the Nile River ruins some objects in the museum, although most items are saved.
1890	The museum moves to a new location across the Nile from Cairo, to a former royal palace in Giza.
1902	The museum moves back to its original location in Bulaq, Cairo, to a brand-new purpose-built museum with extensive display and storage capacity.
2014	The Cairo Museum's role becomes more limited and specific as the new National Museum of Egyptian Civilization opens at Fustat and hosts the royal mummies, to be followed by the opening of the Grand Egyptian Museum near the Giza pyramids in 2015.

on April 1, 1897. Built by Italian contractors to the design of the French architect Marcel Dourgnon (1858–1911), it was opened in 1902, and comprised display galleries on two floors, with storage facilities in on a third floor and in an extensive basement area. The lower display floor accommodated principally stone objects, arranged chronologically, while the upper floor was arranged thematically and comprised objects of smaller size and lighter materials: this arrangement still existed in 2013. The building also accommodated an academic library, offices for the curatorial staff and—until 1983—a room in which objects surplus to requirement were sold. The largest stone objects were installed in a full-height atrium, with others in the garden at the front; this also contained a sarcophagus in which Mariette had been buried, surrounded by a pantheon of busts of major Egyptologists. The latter was subsequently added to.

The opening of the new building broadly coincided with the establishment of an international Catalogue Commission to publish the collection. The scheme was far too ambitious to stand a chance of covering all material, but a large series of magnificent volumes have appeared over the decades. The vast majority came out before World War I, and thus only reflect the state of their specific groups of objects at that date, or even earlier. Others continue to be slowly produced, some from manuscripts finished decades ago or continuing a series begun earlier: for example, the second part of the catalogue of the coffins from the Bab el-Gasus appeared (with a different author!) 89 years after the first.

Although far larger than its predecessors, the new museum building was in constant receipt of new material, with a series of upstairs galleries cleared during the 1920s to make way for the objects from the tomb of Tutankhamun. However, few major changes in arrangement have been made subsequently, the main exceptions being two galleries reconstructed to hold some of the royal mummies in the 1990s. These were originally displayed in a large open gallery, but were withdrawn from display in the late 1920s for reasons of respect. Twenty-four of them were then, in 1932, moved to the newly completed mausoleum of the former prime minister Saad Zaghloul (1859–1927), in the Qasr el-Aini district of Cairo, two kilometers to the south, but removed in June 1936 to a temporary location in Heliopolis before later transfer back to the Cairo Museum.

Many of the royal mummies were put back on display in 1947 in a more private side-gallery, until this was closed at the direction of President Anwar Sadat in 1972, once again for reasons of respect. A selection were once again put on view in 1994, having been conserved and partly rewrapped, in a gallery completely refurbished to provide an appropriate ambiance; a similar second gallery was opened in 2006. Apart from these royal mummies, all other mummies on display in the museum are those that remain fully wrapped.

The 1902 museum, although a vast improvement on its predecessors, still had many problems: skylights allowed direct sunlight to strike objects, and had therefore to be covered by wooden shades; the roof leaked, and the basement storage areas were damp and liable to flooding. Thus, a 1925 proposal for a new museum on Zamalek Island, devised by the American Egyptologist James H. Breasted, and proposed and to be funded to the tune of $10 million by John D. Rockefeller, Jr., appeared at first sight welcome. However, the offer was at no point discussed with the Egyptian government, instead being made direct to the King, Fuad I, a constitutional monarch. This political error was further compounded by the fact that the enlarged museum was to be controlled for the first 23 years by an international foundation on which Egyptian officials would be in a minority. An attached research institute would be under the foundation's control for 50 years or even longer. In the context of an Egypt that had finally obtained nominal independence from a British Protectorate in 1922, but was still subordinate to Britain in many key areas, with consequent ongoing resentment against foreign interference in Egyptian affairs, it is hardly surprising that the offer was declined, with the Egyptian Prime Minister from 1924 to 1926, Ahmed Ziwar (1864–1945), concluding that the conditions were "absolutely unacceptable, [as] they infringe upon the sovereignty of Egypt!" Nevertheless, the Chief and Assistant Keeperships of the Museum were held by Englishmen, Rex Engelbach (1888–1946) and Guy Brunton (1878–1948), into the 1940s. However, when the former retired in 1941, he was followed by the Egyptian Mahmud Hamza (1890–1980), as full Director.

Few major changes occurred to the Museum itself between the 1930s and the 1980s, although there were of course minor rearrangements and additions of objects from new excavations. From the late 1980s onward, however, the aforementioned royal mummy rooms and the reconstruction of the rooms holding various collections of precious metals and jewellery were accomplished, while a new exit, bookshop, and catering facilities were added in 2010.

The last quarter of the twentieth century also saw the removal of some objects to provincial Egyptian museums (e.g., that opened in Luxor in 1975), with the aspiration to open additional museums in Cairo, in particular to deal with the increasing numbers of tourists. In the early twenty-first century this crystalized into a new National Museum of Egyptian Civilization (NMEC) at Fustat (which would ultimately also host the royal mummies) and the Grand Egyptian Museum (GEM) near the pyramids at Giza, the latter being a prestige building to hold the great masterpieces and particularly aimed at foreign tourists. The 1902 museum would remain open, but with a more specialist remit, since, even having given up many objects to the new institutions, it will still have massive holdings of important artistic and archaeological material.

The NMEC was begun in 2002 and was structurally complete in 2012; as of 2013, it was due to open in 2014; construction of the GEM began in 2004 with completion scheduled for 2015. However, the ongoing dislocation and economic crisis in the wake of the Egyptian Revolution of 2011 and subsequent events makes these schedules uncertain.

Aidan Dodson

See also: Collecting mummies; Displaying mummies; Mariette, Auguste

Further Reading

Abt, J. 1996. "Towards a Historian's Laboratory: The Breasted-Rockefeller Museum Projects in Egypt, Palestine and America." *Journal of the American Research Center in Egypt* 33: 173–94.

Saleh, M., and H. Sourouzian. 1987. *The Egyptian Museum Cairo: Official Catalogue*. Mainz: Philipp von Zabern.

Egyptian collection, the British Museum

The British Museum, located in London, England, is known as the world's first national public museum. Free to the public, it currently welcomes over six million visitors annually. The museum's total collection, spanning the history of world

The ancient Egyptian priestess Tamut was one of several mummies featured in "Ancient Lives, New Discoveries," an exhibition that opened in 2014 at the British Museum to showcase advances in mummy studies through the use of state-of-the-art scanning and visualization technology. (AP Images/Guy Bell/REX)

culture, is comprised of over eight million objects. It features the world's most extensive collection of Egyptian antiquities, including Egyptian mummies, outside the famed Egyptian Antiquities Museum in Cairo.

The British Museum was founded in 1753 on the death of British physician, Sir Hans Sloane. An avid naturalist and collector, Sloane designated in his will that his collection of 71,000 objects be bequeathed to King George II, with the intention of having the collection preserved and displayed for the public. By an Act of Parliament, the British Museum was founded on June 7, 1753, marking a ground-breaking shift from private collections of the elite to an organization of objects to be enjoyed and studied by the masses.

The initial collection donated by Sloane was divided into three categories: Printed Books, Manuscripts, and Natural and Artificial Productions. To these original objects, King George II donated the "the Old Royal Library" of the monarchs of England, making the first expansion of the collection. These objects were put on display in Montagu House, a seventeenth-century mansion, and the museum opened to the public on January 15, 1759.

Of the original museum collection, 150 objects were from ancient Egypt. As the museum continued to grow through acquisitions, so did the number of Egyptian artifacts. The first Egyptian mummy and coffin was donated by Lieutenant-General William Lethieullier in 1756. One of the first high-profile acquisitions for the museum, and certainly for the Egyptian collection, was the Rosetta Stone. Acquired from the French in 1802, its incorporation into the museum prompted the recognition of the importance of antiquities within the collection. In 1807, the Department of Antiquities was founded.

The Egyptian collection of the British Museum was, at that point, divided between two departments: the Egyptian objects were moved to the newly founded Department of Antiquities, while the Egyptian papyri remained in the Department of Manuscripts. During the early part of the nineteenth-century, the number of Egyptian objects continued to grow by means of purchases and donations.

In 1836, Samuel Birch, an appointee to the Antiquities Department, began the task of cataloguing the growing Egyptian collection. By 1866, Birch had cata-logued over 10,000 objects. In recognition of the need to have a cohesive depart-ment for the Egyptian and other Near Eastern artifacts, the Department of Egyptian and Assyrian Antiquities was established in 1886 with Birch at its head.

Also during the 1880s, the Egypt Exploration Fund (now known as the Egypt Exploration Society) began excavating in Egypt. Many of the archaeological finds from these endeavors were housed in the British Museum. In addition, E. A. Wallis Budge tripled the size of the Egyptian collections through purchase. By the time Budge retired in 1924 as Keeper of the Egyptian collection, there were about 57,000 Egyptian objects in the museum.

During the twentieth century, the British Museum continued to acquire Egyptian objects by means of purchase, donation, and excavation. The last Egyptian acquisition by the museum was a 50th Dynasty granite sarcophagus, obtained in 1990 from a private collection in northern England. The number of Egyptian objects in the museum now stands at over 100,000 artifacts, and while no new objects can be acquired from excavations because of current Egyptian antiquities laws, the British Museum still seeks to expand its Egyptian collection by means of occasional purchases and donations.

Only a fraction of the Egyptian objects under the purview of the British Museum is exhibited. Those objects that are on display are situated within seven of the museum's rooms. The artifacts are largely organized thematically, with two of the seven rooms dedicated to objects pertaining to death and the afterlife. Both human and animal mummies are part of this exhibit, titled "Egyptian Death and Afterlife: Mummies." This exhibit features the Twenty-second Dynasty mummy of a man named Hor, a second century CE mummy of a young woman named Cleopatra of Thebes, and a Ptolemaic mummy of a priest of Amun named Horned-jitef. A mummified cat and bull are also on display. In addition, one predynastic Egyptian mummy, the Gebelein Man, is on display in the Early Egypt gallery. Many additional mummies, of which there are over 140, are in the British Museum's storage facilities, and can be visited by scholars and researchers for academic inquiry.

The British Museum is committed to providing information about the Egyptian Exhibit to both the general public and academic community. The first companion guide to the Egyptian Exhibit was written by then Keeper E.A. Wallis Budge in 1909. Designed to highlight the popular themes of Egyptian life, religion, and history, it cost just one shilling for museum-goers. Since then, Budge's guide has been updated by several Keepers of the Egyptian collection.

In addition, the British Museum Studies in Ancient Egypt and Sudan (BMSAES) journal presents research on all aspects of ancient Egypt and Sudan. This journal presents in-depth studies of the Egyptian collection to a scholarly audience.

Also of an academic undertaking is the *Catalogue of Egyptian Antiquities in the British Museum*. A multivolume publication, the goal of this catalogue is categorize all objects of the Egyptian collection by theme or type in a way that provides scholars with a holistic assemblage of artifacts. This project began in 1968 with the first volume being dedicate to the mummies and human remains of the Egyptian collection. In this volume, a detailed history of many of the museum's mummies, along with photographs and X-rays, were compiled for the publication.

The mummies of the Egyptian collection continue to be the subject of both many academic studies and large public interest. Their display in the Egyptian

Exhibit draws many visitors and provides a historical and social understanding of mummification in ancient Egypt. Having one of the largest Egyptian collections (and largest collection of Egyptian mummies) outside of Cairo places the British Museum at the forefront of Egyptological study, and their collection is of great importance to both scholars and visitors to the museum.

Marissa A. Stevens

See also: Collecting mummies; Displaying mummies; Egyptian Antiquities Museum; Gebelein Man; Lindow Man; Mummy's curse; Rosetta Stone

Further Reading

Andrews, Carol. 2004. *Egyptian Mummies*. London: British Museum Press.

Bierbrier, M. L. 2002. "Travels with His Mummy." *British Museum Magazine-2* 43 (Summer): 31–33.

Budge, E. A. Wallis. 1909. *A Guide to the Egyptian Collections in the British Museum.* London: British Museum Press.

Dawson, W. R., and P. H. K. Gray. 1968. *Catalogue of Egyptian Antiquities in the British Museum 1: Mummies and Human Remains.* London: British Museum Press.

James, T. G. H. 1979. *An Introduction to Ancient Egypt.* London: British Museum Press.

MacGregor, Arthur. 1994. *Sir Hans Sloane: Collector, Scientist, Antiquary.* London: British Museum Press.

Russmann, Edna R. 2001. *External Egypt: Masterworks of Ancient Art from the British Museum.* London: British Museum Press.

Strudwick, Nigel. 2006. *Masterpieces of Ancient Egypt.* London: British Museum Press.

Taylor, John H. 2010. *Egyptian Mummies.* London: British Museum Press.

Taylor, John H., and Nigel Strudwick. 2005. *Mummies: Death and the Afterlife in Ancient Egypt; Treasures from the British Museum.* Santa Ana: Bowers Museum of Cultural Art.

Egyptian mummies

The practice of mummification lasted throughout the history of ancient Egypt. It most likely developed through observing the natural preservation of bodies buried in the desert, and it became a key component of Egyptian conceptions of the afterlife. Believing it was necessary to preserve the body for use after death, the Egyptians used intricate mummification practices to preserve their dead. These efforts resulted in many mummies from all time periods in ancient Egyptian history that show how mummification and burial practices developed.

During the predynastic era, most bodies were placed in a simple pit grave accompanied by grave goods consisting of pottery with food offerings, cosmetic palettes, knives and other small weapons, and beads. The arid sand in which the body was buried was a natural preservation agent. The body, which was normally placed on its side in the fetal position, underwent a process of natural

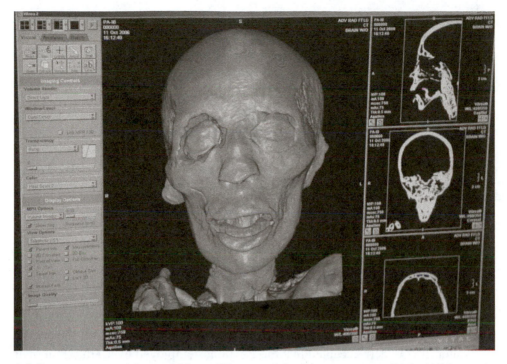

A 3-D computer model created from CT scans of the Egyptian mummy Pa-Ib. (AP Images/ *The Connecticut Post,* Brian A. Pounds)

mummification as it dried within the desert. One of the best known examples of a predynastic mummy is the Gebelein Man in the British Museum. Found at the site of Gebelein in Upper Egypt, his remains have been roughly dated to 3500 BCE.

Shortly after this time, the human remains in the archaeological evidence suggest that the Egyptians were taking active measures to preserve their dead. It has been proposed that these naturally dried bodies were the inspiration for mummification practices in Egypt. The Egyptians could have discovered these naturally preserved bodies through chance occurrences of wild animals or robbers exposing

While many different cultures and civilizations around the world have mummified their dead, it is Egyptian mummies that have long been the most famous type among the general public, and that have exerted the most powerful influence on the popular imagination. Almost (but not quite) the entirety of the mummy horror genre in fiction, film, and popular culture at large has been inspired by and devoted to the mummies of ancient Egypt. Nor is this a recent trend; Western civilization's fascination with Egyptian mummies goes at least as far back as the ancient Greek historian Herodotus, who, in the fifth century BCE, in his now-classic *Histories*—long recognized as one of the founding works in the discipline of history itself— devoted a long section to describing Egyptian mummification techniques and practices.

the remains. After seeing the effects the desert had on the bodies, they might have developed a sense that a preserved body was necessary for the afterlife, and as such, wanted to emulate this natural preservation.

Evidence from the Old Kingdom, mainly from Saqqara and Giza, suggests that bodies were being wrapped in plaster-soaked linen. Oftentimes, this linen was molded to match the bodily features of the dead. Fingers, toes, and the outlines of muscles can be seen in the contours of the wrappings of many mummies from this time period. In some instances, so much linen and plaster were added that the deceased looked very much like a statue. Sometimes, the plaster was painted, with features such as the eyebrows, eyes, and lips being drawn on the face to make the bodies look even more lifelike.

Evisceration was another important development that occurred during the Old Kingdom. The burial of Queen Hetepheres, wife of Sneferu and mother of Khufu, contained the earliest known use of canopic equipment. While her body was never found, the presence of a canopic box is clear indication that her internal organs would have been removed during the mummification process and stored in the canopic box in the tomb. The canopic box's compartments held the remains of Queen Hetepheres's organs, which were preserved in a solution of natron salt and water. It is widely accepted that the Egyptians employed evisceration in their mummification techniques, as they realized that a body preserved in this manner would not putrefy nearly as much as bodies with the internal organs left intact.

As mummification developed during the Middle Kingdom, the heavy use of plaster gave way and was replaced with a more invested effort in the use of natron. A type of salt, natron dried the bodies by pulling out moisture. Coupled with treatments including various oils, perfumes, and resins, natron was a highly effective way of preserving the body—so much so that some female bodies from the Middle Kingdom still clearly show tattoos on their well-preserved skin.

After this preservation treatment, in which the removal of organs was still standard, the body would still have been wrapped in linen. However, instead of using plaster to mold the linen to the features of the deceased, other methods were used. The main innovation to the mummification practices of this period was the cartonnage face mask. Also during this time, it became popular to pour resin over the wrapped mummy. This gives Egyptian mummies their dark, oftentimes black, appearance. It is also the source from which the term "mummy" derives. The Persian word for the thick, resin material used in this process is *mum*. In Arabic, this word is *mumia* or *mumiya*; hence the English word *mummy*.

Some of the best preserved mummies are those of the New Kingdom pharaohs found in the two royal caches in Thebes and that of Tutankhamen in the Valley of the Kings. These mummies, as well as others from the New Kingdom, show expert skill in the level of preservation. Great care was taken during the mummification process; some mummies of the New Kingdom show that the fingernails and toenails were tied onto the digits during mummification so that they would not fall off as the body dried and shrank. Also, during the later part of the New Kingdom and into the Third Intermediate Period, stuffing of the body to give it a more life-like appearance became increasingly popular.

From the Third Intermediate Period, there are hundreds of mummies, mostly from the Theban necropolis. Because of political and economic instability of the time, tomb robbery grew in frequency, and many funerary goods were taken from the dead for either sale or reuse. Coffins were among the long list of objects that were often taken out of tombs. The Egyptians, knowing the likelihood that their coffin would not remain with them forever, began adapting their mummification practices to suit these new conditions. Indeed, more time, effort, and resources were spent on mummification during this period than any other in Egyptian history. The goal was now to make the body look as lifelike as possible, in case it had to spend its afterlife without a coffin and other burial goods. The internal organs were normally mummified separately but returned to the body cavity, instead of being placed in extraneous canopic equipment. Wigs, fake eyes, stuffing, and paint were applied to make the deceased look alert and vibrant.

The Late Period and Greco-Roman Periods saw a continued use of mummification, often with elaborate wrapping patterns that crisscrossed the body. A unique take on the funerary mask, portraits became popular during this time. Most commonly found in the Fayum, these Fayum portraits, as they are often called, show what is arguably an accurate and lifelike portrait of the deceased as they were in life. Highly individualized, these images show a shift away from the idealizing funerary masks that characterized the earlier parts of Egyptian history.

Importantly, the ancient Egyptians did not limit their mummification techniques to humans. Many different animals were mummified. Ibises, cats, falcons, dogs, baboons, and bulls were the most common animals to be mummified by the Egyptians, but even mouse mummies have been found. Oftentimes mummified as part of a particular god's cult, these mummies were placed in tombs or temples as offerings, often housed inside their own coffins or containers. The Apis bulls were mummified and placed into giant stone sarcophagi—a process of interment that required an extreme amount of time, effort, and resources.

Early European explorers in the 1800s often saw Egyptian mummies as great curiosities. An antiquarian's collection was not complete without a mummy or at least part of one. Others, however, were more interested in the many amulets, papyri, jewelry, and other accoutrements that often accompanied the bodies, and many mummies were destroyed in the process of unwrapping and stripping the body of these objects. For a time, mummies were burned as fuel in trains, used as fertilizer for crops, or ground up for use in magical potions and medicinal remedies. Their value as scientific objects were not immediately recognized in these early days of Egyptology, and much information was sadly lost during these renegade times.

The early 1900s saw the recognition of mummies as objects of research. Since then, X-rays, anatomical investigations, CT scans, scopes, 3D imaging and reconstruction, and DNA testing have been performed on many Egyptian (and other) mummies in various museums and institutions around the world, yielding a vast amount of scientific data and firmly securing the mummy's place as a valuable artifact and focus of research.

Marissa A. Stevens

See also: Animal mummies; Collecting mummies; Egyptian mummification methods; Gebelein Man; Genetic study of mummies; Manchester Egyptian Mummy Project; Medical imaging of mummies; Medicine and mummies; Mummy Portraits; Natural mummification; Religion and mummies; Royal mummies of Egypt, Part One: Third to Eighteenth Dynasties; Royal mummies of Egypt, Part Two: Nineteenth to Twenty-fifth Dynasties; Theban Necropolis; Tutankhamun ("King Tut"); Valley of the Kings

Further Reading

Andrews, Carol. 2004. *Egyptian Mummies*. London: British Museum Press.

Chamberlain, Andrew, and Michael Parker Pearson. 2001. *Earthly Remains: The History and Science of Preserved Human Bodies*. New York: Oxford University Press.

Fleming, Stuart James. *The Egyptian Mummy: Secrets and Science*. 1980. University Museum Handbook 1. Philadelphia: University Museum, University of Pennsylvania.

Ikram, Salima, and Aidan Dodson. 1998. *The Mummy in Ancient Egypt: Equipping the Dead for Eternity*. London: Thames & Hudson.

Ikram, Salima, and Mathaf al-Misri. 1997. *Royal Mummies in the Egyptian Museum*. Cairo: American University in Cairo Press.

Leca, Ange Pierre. 1981. *The Egyptian Way of Death: Mummies and the Cult of the Immortal*. New York: Anchor Books.

Strudwick, Nigel and John H. Taylor. 2005. *Mummies: Death and the Afterlife in Ancient Egypt; Treasures from the British Museum*. Santa Ana: Bowers Museum of Cultural Art.

Taylor, John H. 2010. *Egyptian Mummies*. London: British Museum Press.

Egyptian mummification methods

Ancient Egyptian mummies are among the best known and oldest mummified bodies in the world, but the development of the mummification process was a long process of trial and error that continued throughout the Pharaonic period. No intact ancient Egyptian description of mummification has survived to the present day. Instead, a record of embalming techniques used by the ancient Egyptians has been produced mainly from the accounts written by two classical Greek authors (Herodotus and Diodorus Sicculus) and the study of the mummies themselves. For more than three millennia, the ancient Egyptians preserved their dead, refining, developing and changing the techniques they used to produce mummies.

The Evolution of Egyptian Mummification

Predynastic Period	Human remains are buried in shallow graves in the desert. No intentional attempts at preservation are made.
Early Dynastic Period	Early attempts are made to preserve the pharaohs. Bodies are wrapped in resin-soaked or plaster-soaked linen bandages to preserve outward appearance.
Old Kingdom	Bodies are eviscerated and wrapped in plaster-soaked or resin-soaked linen. Bodies and removed organs are dehydrated by applying a dessicant.
Middle Kingdom	Mummification is made available not just to pharaohs but to elite members of Egyptian society. Natron is widely used to dry out the body, and resin is applied directly to the body instead of to bandages. Various oils, perfumes, and resins are also applied. The cartonnage face mask is introduced, as is the practice of removing the brain.
New Kingdom	Body is stuffed with aromatic spices. Fingernails and toenails are tied on.
Third Intermediate Period	The body is carefully stuffed with a variety of materials beneath the skin to give it a more lifelike appearance. Egyptian mummification reaches a peak of finesse and then begins to decline.
Greco-Roman Period	The practice of mummification continues, and Greek settlers embrace it, but quality declines steadily.
392 CE	The Roman emperor Theodosius I formally bans mummification. Egypt's 3,000-year history of embalming is brought to an end.

Egyptian mummification is often discussed in terms of both natural and artificial mummification. The heat of the Egyptian desert frequently led to the natural creation of a mummy by drying the soft tissues, preserving to some extent its outward appearance. This was especially the case during the Predynastic Period, when the ancient Egyptians used shallow graves in the desert. The foundation of the Egyptian state around 3000 BCE, however, led to the development of more complex tomb burials for the reigning pharaoh and his family. This change in burial methods meant the body was less likely to be desiccated naturally, becoming skeletonized instead. As the preservation of the pharaoh's body played an important role in ancient Egyptian religion, an alternative means of preserving the body was sought, and artificial mummification began to develop.

Early attempts at mummification during the Early Dynastic Period (3000–2686 BCE) focused on preserving the outward appearance of the body. Few examples of mummies from this time have survived, but those that have show evidence that the body had been wrapped in resin-soaked linen bandages. This method did not preserve the soft tissues, and mummies from this period usually have a space between the skeleton and the wrappings where the tissues had originally been. Until recently the earliest example of this form of mummification that had been discovered was an arm thought to belong to the pharaoh Djer or his wife, found in his tomb in the royal necropolis of Abydos. However, the discovery of several bodies at Hierakonpolis showing the same method of wrapping now suggests that attempts to preserve the body actually began before the Early Dynastic Period.

The first evidence for the use of a desiccant to dehydrate the body appeared during the Old Kingdom (2686–2160 BCE). Natron was found to have been used to preserve the organs of Queen Hetepheres, wife of the Fourth Dynasty pharaoh, Sneferu. Her mummified organs were found in a canopic chest in her pyramid at Giza, although there was no trace of the rest of her body. It is not known whether natron was used to desiccate the whole body at this time or just the organs, but the viscera of Hetepheres indicate that mummification methods were already quite advanced by this time. Organ removal and preservation had been developed, alongside the use of natron for desiccation and the continued use of resin-soaked linen to mold the features of the body. However, the mummification process was neither complete nor used consistently. Surviving examples from this period include royal mummies with poor soft tissue preservation and other bodies, such as the Sixth Dynasty pharaoh Menenre, that show no attempt at artificial mummification.

During the Old Kingdom, mummification was still a privilege reserved for the royal family. This began to change with the following First Intermediate and Middle Kingdom Periods, when mummification became available to elite members of Egyptian society. Although mummification methods still varied, the molding of bodily features with resin-soaked linen was generally abandoned in favor of the application of resin directly to the body. These resins, most commonly pine resin, are thought to be antibacterial and so would have improved preservation. The Middle Kingdom (2055–1650 BCE) also saw the first appearance of the removal of the brain. This process, known as excerebration, involved the insertion of a metal hook through the nostrils and into the skull to create a hole through which the brain was removed.

The greatest source of information on royal mummification comes from the New Kingdom Period (1550–1069 BCE), due to the discovery of two caches of royal mummies that had been moved from the Valley of Kings to nearby tombs for protection from tomb robbers. These were first studied in the late 1800s by Sir Grafton Elliot Smith and have been the subject of scrutiny ever since. The account written by the historian Herodotus in the fifth century BCE is thought to be most representative of mummification practices during this time. He described three different types of mummification available to the ancient Egyptians. The first method, most likely that used for royalty, involved the removal of the internal organs and the brain, followed by the washing of the body with palm wine and the packing of the body cavities with a range of aromatic spices. Study of the royal mummies shows that embalmers also began to tie on the toe and finger nails, which otherwise frequently dropped off during the desiccation process. Herodotus' other two methods were much simpler and involved removing or cleaning the internal organs via the anus, followed by placing the body in natron. Although mummification became available to a higher proportion of the elite members of Egyptian society during this time, the methods available to them were limited.

Egyptian mummification reached a peak of finesse in the 21st Dynasty (1069–945 BCE) when the Egyptian embalmers began trying to make the body appear more lifelike after mummification. Although the preserving process had been perfected during the New Kingdom, the resulting mummy appeared emaciated due to the desiccation of the soft tissues. To correct this, embalmers began to place packing under the skin to fill out the body. Packing materials have been found to include sawdust, mud, and linen. Only one earlier example of this method has been found so far, in the mummy of the 18th Dynasty pharaoh Amenhotep III. This is thought to have been an experimental technique picked up again and developed in the 21st Dynasty. Mummies during this time were also often painted and given wigs of human hair to help create a lifelike impression. This method lasted only a very short time, however, and by the 22nd Dynasty mummification techniques had begun to decline.

The later centuries of the Pharaonic period were ones of confusion and disruption during which Egypt was periodically controlled by other countries. Finally, in 332 BCE, Egypt came under the control of Alexander the Great, signalling the end of the Pharaonic period. Mummification continued during this time and was embraced by Greek settlers. As more people chose to be mummified, the quality of preservation started to decline. Emphasis was put on the outward appearance of a mummy at the expense of the preservation of soft tissues. Excerebration and evisceration were still carried out, but increasingly rarely. Where organs were removed they were often desiccated, wrapped in linen and returned to the body cavity or placed between the mummy's legs before wrapping. During the Ptolemaic and into the following Roman Period, mummies are characterized by an excessive use of resin to preserve the body. Bodies were often left to decay significantly before mummification began. This resulted in the appearance of restorations: methods used by the embalmers to try and strengthen or repair a mummy. In some cases this resulted in what appears to be a single mummy made up of parts from several different bodies.

The practice of mummification further declined with the rise of Christianity in Roman Egypt because of its association with pagan religious practices. Some mummies from the early Christian period show signs of mummification, but in general the methods used appear to be symbolic rather than practical attempts to preserve the body. Salt is often found sprinkled over these mummies and fruits and spices have been found within the wrappings. The actual method of preservation for Christian period bodies is more likely to have been natural rather than artificial mummification. Then, in 392 CE the Roman emperor Theodosius I placed a ban on mummification, thus bringing to an end more than 3000 years of Egypt's embalming history.

Although much is known about the methods of embalming used by the ancient Egyptians, there is still much to learn. Current understanding naturally focuses on the royal mummies, as these have received the greatest amount of attention. However, new discoveries in Egypt and the growth of scientific investigations of nonroyal mummies will add more detail about how and hopefully why specific mummification techniques were developed. Although broad chronological trends in mummification are quite clear, patterns between mummies from different regions or cities of Egypt have yet to be explored.

Jenefer Cockitt

See also: Egyptian mummies; Embalming; Royal mummies of Egypt, Part One: Third to Eighteenth Dynasties; Royal mummies of Egypt, Part Two: Nineteenth to Twenty-fifth Dynasties; Smith, Grafton Elliot

Further Reading

Aufderheide, Arthur. 2003. *The Scientific Study of Mummies*. Cambridge: Cambridge University Press.

Brier, Bob. 1994. *Egyptian Mummies*. London: Michael O'Mara Books.

David, Rosalie, ed. 2008. *Mummies and Modern Science*. Cambridge: Cambridge University Press.

Smith, Grafton Elliot, and Warren Dawson. 1924. *Egyptian Mummies*. London: George Allen and Unwin.

Egyptomania

Egyptomania is the term, coined in the twentieth century, used to describe a fascination with the iconography of ancient Egypt, usually expressed through the incorporation or wholesale appropriation of recognizably Pharaonic Egyptian motifs into artistic, architectural, or decorative forms throughout the Western world. The word may be utilized in relation to all such instances whether elegantly solemn, such as the Johnston mausoleum in Brooklyn, or trivially kitsch, as in the Harrods department store in London.

There have been three identifiable phases of Egyptomania wherein there was considerable and distinct interest in Egyptianizing forms: Roman, nineteenth century, and early twentieth century.

Roman Egyptomania initially flourished following the defeat of Cleopatra VII and Marc Antony in 31 BCE, after which it became fashionable in Rome to celebrate this victory and the absorption of the great and ancient culture of Egypt into the Roman Empire. This fascination with Egyptian culture is evident today

Egyptomania, Hollywood-style: statues of two pharaohs preside over a crowd of Hebrew peasants and merchants in producer/director Cecil B. DeMille's *The Ten Commandments* (1956). (Mondadori/Getty Images)

through the archaeological remains of public Roman buildings, Egyptian themed statuary, and even the interior decoration of private homes.

The substantial funerary monument of the praetor Gaius Cestius, still strikingly visible in the south of Rome, is in the form of a slim and sharply pointed concrete pyramid, faced with white marble and bearing Latin dedicatory inscriptions on its east and west sides. Built around 12 BCE, it is an approximation of an Egyptian-style pyramid, and its shape provided the template for most Western pyramids built during the eighteenth and nineteenth centuries in funerary and horticultural contexts. Although the tomb of a private individual, it is, by virtue of its size, a very

The phenomenon of Egyptomania—i.e., the cultural fascination with the iconography of ancient Egypt that has caused it to seep into artistic, architectural, and decorative forms—has emerged in three distinct phases or waves at three distinct periods in Western history: ancient Rome in the first several centuries CE; nineteenth-century Europe, Britain, and America; and the early twentieth century. The last of these was largely occasioned by the furor surrounding the discovery and opening of Tutankhamun's tomb in 1922–1923.

public monument, which probably served to commemorate Cestius' involvement in Augusts' Egyptian campaign.

One of the most evident public illustrations of Rome's fascination with Egypt was the major importation and relocation of ancient obelisks into key sites around the city between the reigns of Augustus and Diocletian, in addition to the cutting and inscribing, in Egypt, of at least five purpose-built obelisks, which were erected by the emperors in the centre of Rome.

There are numerous examples of private homes containing exquisite and highly detailed floor mosaics and wall paintings showing fanciful scenes of life on the Nile, usually incorporating hippopotami, crocodiles, and mischievous pygmies amid boats and papyrus thickets. There is frequently a romantic or, indeed, somewhat salacious subtext to these scenes, showing a couple cavorting in a Nile barge.

Egypt was not simply incorporated into the Roman Empire but held special status as the personal property of the emperor. However, its new position ensured the transmission of Egyptian religious cults to many parts of the empire, carried there by devout soldiers, merchants, and settlers, with evidence for the worship of the Egyptian goddess Isis being found in such disparate and far-flung outcrops of the empire as Szombathely in modern Hungary and Tooley Street in London.

Perhaps the most thorough embracing of Roman Egyptomania occurred during the reign of the emperor Hadrian (76–138 CE), who was already much taken by Eastern cultures and religions, and whose fascination increased following the death of his favorite, Antinous, who drowned under suspicious circumstances in the river Nile in 130 CE. Thereafter, Hadrian's palace at Tivoli became not only the probable site of the deified youth's tomb, complete with a specially commissioned dedicatory obelisk, but also a recreation of the Canopus branch of the Nile, to provide a vast lakeside dining area: Egypt in miniature. The Egyptianizing statuary of Antinous excavated from the site in 1793, which depicts him wearing a Pharaonic *shendyt*, kilt, and typical striped *nemes*, or headcloth, (and which is now kept in the *Museo Gregoriano Egiziano* of the Vatican), would go on to provide considerable inspiration for sculptors and artists following their discovery.

Following the Edict of Milan in 313 CE during the reign of Constantine (272–337 CE), the pagan nature of the Roman Empire rapidly dwindled, and the last known hieroglyphic inscription was inscribed in the temple of Philae on August 24, 396. With the eventual fall of the Roman Empire and the subsequent Islamic conquest of Egypt in 649, the country and its ancient history came to acquire a semi-mythical status, with its knowledge largely unknown to all but a handful of Western scholars, whose researches largely tended toward the Biblical or occult in nature, although there was a small trade in antiquities, and specifically in mummified human remains, as evidenced by the medicinal concoctions made from ground mummies that were much favored by the European monarchs Francis

I (1515–1547) of France and Charles II (1630–1685), and also the specimens examined by Hadley and Blumenbach from 1763.

This changed substantially in 1798 when Napoleon Bonaparte (1769–1821) and his force reopened Egypt to the Western gaze, most notably achieved through the subsequent, publication of the 23 volume *Description de l'Egypte*, (1809–1818) prepared by his team of scholars, which ushered in the second great era of Egyptomania. A letter to London's *Morning Chronicle* from 1805 is instructive: "since this accursed Egyptian style came into fashion ... my eldest boy rides on a sphinx instead of a rocking-horse, my youngest has a papboat in the shape of a crocodile, and my husband has built a water closet in the shape of a pyramid, and has his shirts marked with a lotus" (Johnston 2013a, 10).

In 1810, William Bullock opened his Egyptian Hall in London's Piccadilly, while the exertions of Giovanni Battista Belzoni (1778–1823) filled the British Museum with colossal examples of Egyptian sculpture. In addition to Belzoni's re-creation of the tomb of Seti I in Bullock's Egyptian Hall in 1821, this was also the era of public mummy unrollings undertaken by Thomas Joseph Pettigrew (1791–1865) and other noted anatomists of antiquarian inclination. The occasion of the installation of Seti I's alabaster sarcophagus in the museum home of architect and collector Sir John Soane (1753–1837) resulted in a three-day party, attended by some 890 members of London society.

However, the fervor surrounding the rediscovery of ancient Egypt was not restricted to London. Paris erected a number of major monuments, including the *Fontaine du Palmier* in Place du Chatelet and the *Fontaine du Fellah* on the rue des Sevres, the latter taking as its subject the aforementioned Egyptianizing statue of Antinous from Tivoli, enclosed within an Egyptian-style shrine and surmounted by a Napoleonic eagle. Considerable interest in Egyptian forms was also exhibited throughout Eastern Europe and the United States during this period.

Arguably the nineteenth century fascination with Egyptomania continued unabated from the time of Napoleon's incursion: travel to Egypt increased and archaeological investigation developed as an academic discipline, ensuring that Egypt's ancient culture remained a customary topic for newspapers and periodicals. Following a lengthy sojourn in Egypt during the winter of 1873–1874, the novelist Amelia Blandford Edwards founded The Egypt Exploration Fund in 1882, still extant as the Egypt Exploration Society, with the express purpose of recording and preserving the monuments of Egypt through excavation and publication.

Of more, rather more sensational aspect, Egypt's ancient culture provided a fertile basis for numerous novels and short stories, published throughout the century in the genres of romance, thriller, and horror, increasingly dealing with the concept of ambulant mummies.

Egypt's mortuary connotations continued unabated, with mummy unrollings becoming a frequent element of society events and Egyptianizing architecture playing an important role in the development and expansion of purpose-built necropolises throughout the Western world as exemplified by Highgate Cemetery in London and Mount Auburn Cemetery in Massachusetts.

The third major era of Egyptomania came with the entry by Egyptologist Howard Carter (1874–1939) into the tomb of Tutankhamun on November 26, 1922. The beauty of the glittering artifacts found therein and the subsequent press frenzy ensured the ubiquity of ancient Egypt in Western culture until the outbreak of World War II in 1939.

On this occasion, the widespread Egyptomania centred largely on the contents of the tomb and on the mummy itself. The burgeoning American film industry were keen to capitalize on the interest generated by the discovery of the tomb, with director Cecil B DeMille, then working on his first version of *The Ten Commandments* (1923) intending to make Tutankhamun the pharaoh of the Exodus. It was an idea from which he was ultimately dissuaded; however, the film benefitted from the attention being generated by the tomb, and the subsequent events surrounding the alleged curse certainly inspired the screenplay for Universal Studios' *The Mummy* (1932), which was written John Balderston, who, as a journalist in 1922, had attempted to cover the removal of the tomb's contents but was hampered, like most journalists of the period, by the exclusive deal between the London Times newspaper and the expedition's financial backer, the Earl of Carnarvon.

On a wider cultural basis, a substantial number of cinemas built during the 1920s strongly favored Egyptianizing architecture, lending not only a colorful exoticism to the experience of cinema-going but also capitalizing on the dazzling modernity of the Art Deco movement that was sweeping Europe and the United States following the 1925 International Exposition of Modern Industrial and Decorative Arts in Paris, and which incorporated many ancient and exotic motifs, particularly those borrowed from ancient Egypt. Consequently, many elements of ancient Egyptian art and architecture were propelled to the forefront of modern design, as exemplified in everything from Manhattan's Chrysler Building to Cartier brooches, and even dance music in the form of *The Old King Tut* foxtrot, written by Henry Von Tilzer in 1923.

After World War II, the nature of Egyptomania changed and, as with the later nineteenth century, appeared less connected to specific historical events, being more evidently guided by market forces or by the interests of particular artists or designers. In 1950s Hollywood, the announcement that Cecil B. DeMille was engaged in the preparation of a remake of *The Ten Commandments* (eventually released in 1956) resulted in a flurry of similarly themed films, while director Joseph L. Mankiewicz's *Cleopatra* (1963), starring Elizabeth Taylor and featuring designs by the Academy Award winners Irene Sharaf and John De Cuir, inspired almost a decade of clothing and cosmetic fashions for women.

The international touring exhibition of objects from Tutankhamun's tomb, including the famed golden funerary mask, traveled to major venues such as the British Museum and The Metropolitan Museum of Art and was arguably the first such blockbuster art exhibition. It resulted not only in renewed interest in the tomb and its contents but resulted in the marketing of huge numbers of souvenirs and replicas of objects from the tomb.

For reasons that are perhaps self-evident, mummies have tended to feature little in examples of Egyptomania. However, an eroticized example of "mummymania" is to be found in a bronze desk ornament from Vienna, dating from 1900, which features an anthropoid coffin that opens to reveal the tiny bronze statue of a naked woman, smiling coquettishly and adorned with Egyptian jewelry. While the contents of the coffin may seem somewhat unusual now, the concept was quite in keeping with much of the romanticized mummy fiction prevalent from the mid-nineteenth century and in the cinematic works of Georges Méliès. Since the 1990s, variations on this theme, mass-produced in plastic and resin, but containing not Egyptian-esque women but tiny representations of partially wrapped and grotesquely desiccated mummies, have become *de riguer* in museum souvenir shops around the globe.

From 1957, the U.S. television syndication of many of Universal's horror classics that had been produced before 1948, including their mummy feature films, reached a new audience, successfully capitalizing on the substantial publicity generated by Hammer Films' Technicolor reinterpretations of many of Universal's properties. Although broadcast late at night, these horror classics attracted a younger than expected demographic, and in consequence the toy company Aurora began producing a series of plastic model kits based on the Universal's characters, including, in 1963, one modeled on the character of the mummy Kharis from Universal's 1940s films starring Lon Chaney, Jr. While this kit may fall under the heading of "'memorabilia," the Universal branding was relatively discreet, and consequently Kharis appears to have provided the archetype for a slew of mummy toys, Halloween costumes, and comical characters marketed to children, eventually culminating in General Mills' "Fruity Yummy Mummy" breakfast cereal, where the mummy character is essentially divorced from its Egyptological origins and becomes instead a mere, and monstrous, cultural icon, taking its place alongside characters such as the Count from *Sesame Street* and Hermann from *The Munsters*.

Similarly, it is arguable that since the 1970s Egyptomania has, in many respects, joined the mainstream of global cultural influences, with architecture being lumped in with television advertising, toys, and comics, often for little apparent reason, as in Ian Pollard's amusingly kitsch designs for the Homebase DIY store in Earls Court, London, which takes the form of an Egyptian temple, decorated with larger than life reliefs of Egyptian deities with their names spelled out in cartouche enclosed hieroglyphs and partially gilded. The sardonic inclusion of the murderous god Set, holding a power drill in place of an ankh symbol, depicts him as a fearsome figure for the twentieth century and clearly references Abel Ferrara's then-notorious feature film *The Driller Killer* (1979) while discreetly connecting with the purpose and commodities of the story itself.

Interestingly, however, I. M. Pei's gigantic steel and glass pyramid, which has dominated the courtyard of the *Musée du Louvre*, Paris, since 1989, and which appears to directly reference the museum's vast Egyptian collection, has, according to its architect, no such Egyptomaniacal basis.

It remains to be seen whether the three major waves of Egyptomania that have cascaded across the Western world in the past two millennia will be succeeded by a fourth iteration.

John J. Johnston

See also: Belzoni, Giovanni; Carnarvon, Fifth Earl of (George Herbert); Carter, Howard; Collecting mummies; Medicine and mummies; The Mummy in popular culture; Mummy unwrappings; Napoleon and the birth of Egyptology; Pettigrew, Thomas Joseph; Tutankhamun ("King Tut")

Further Reading

Curl, J. S. 2005. *The Egyptian Revival: Ancient Egypt as the Inspiration for Design Motifs in the West*. London: Routledge.

Ebeling, F. 2007. *The Secret History of Hermes Trismegistus: Hermeticism from Ancient to Modern Times*. Ithaca: Cornell University Press.

Elliott, C. et al. 2003. "Egypt in London: Entertainment and Commerce in the 20th Century Metropolis." In *Imhotep Today: Egyptianizing Architecture*, edited by J-M. Humbert and C. Price, 105–121. London: UCL Press.

Frayling, C. 1992. *The Face of Tutankhamun*. London: Faber and Faber.

Humbert, Jean-Marcel, Michael Pantazzi, and Christiane Ziegler, eds. 1994. *Egyptomania: Egypt in Western Art 1730–1930*. Ottowa: National Gallery of Canada.

Humbert, Jean-Marcel. 2003. "The Egyptianizing Pyramid from the 18th to the 20th Century." In *Imhotep Today: Egyptianizing Architecture*, edited by Jean-Marcel Humbert and Clifford Price, 25–39. London: UCL Press.

James, T. G. H., ed. *Excavating in Egypt: The Egypt Exploration Society 1882–1982*. London: British Museum Press.

Johnston, John J. 2013a. "Lost in Time and Space: Unrolling Egypt's Ancient Dead." *The Journal of the Royal Institution of Cornwall*. 7–22.

Johnston, John J. 2013b. "Going Forth by Day." Introduction to *Unearthed*, edited by John J. Johnston and Jared Shurin, 9–42. London: Jurassic London.

Lo Sardo, Eugenio, ed. 2008. *The She-Wolf and the Sphinx: Rome and Egypt from History to Myth*. Translated by Christopher Evans and Richard Sadleir. Rome: Electa.

Luckhurst, Roger. 2012. *The Mummy's Curse: The True Story of a Dark Fantasy*. Oxford: Oxford University Press.

Moser, S. 2006. *Wondrous Curiosities: Ancient Egypt in the British Museum.* Chicago: University of Chicago Press.

Riggs, Christina, ed. 2012. *The Oxford Handbook of Roman Egypt.* Oxford: Oxford University Press.

Wortham, John David. 1971. *British Egyptology 1549–1906.* Newton Abbott: David & Charles.

Embalming

In the ancient world, embalming and mummification were one and the same thing: the preservation of a body using natural materials. Over time, however, the two have become separate ideas. Embalming is now more generally thought of as a method for chemically preserving a body before burial or cremation, preventing decay mainly to allow the body to be viewed by grieving friends and family. Similar methods are also used in preparing cadavers and body parts for anatomical and medical teaching. Today, mummification is carried out mainly for scientific purposes to discover more about how ancient methods worked, as an unusual request by those fascinated by the subject or by natural processes working on the body (see "Experimental mummification").

The popularity of embalming has waxed and waned over the thousands of years of its existence, but it can be broadly divided into two main groups, physical and chemical methods of preservation. The first of these encompasses the more traditional methods of mummification, typified by ancient Egypt but with evidence from numerous other cultures and civilizations. Many of these methods relied on removing water from the body to stop decomposition and preserve the soft tissues of the body. Various other substances would also commonly be used, such as oils, herbs and resins that would both help to preserve the body and reduce any unpleasant odors that would be produced during the process. Some of these have remained aromatic through history, with Egyptian mummies in particular often having a noticeable smell of old resin.

Artificially embalmed mummies from other cultures are not as common as those from ancient Egypt, with many examples being represented by a very small number of bodies. Mummification trends across whole civilizations appear to have been rare in antiquity, though there are several examples where the environment rather than human intervention has allowed quite a large number of mummies to survive to the present day, such as those found high in the Andes. Some of the most famous mummies were produced accidentally, including Gebelein Man, a.k.a. "Ginger" (a preDynastic Egyptian mummy in the British Museum, preserved by the heat of the desert) and Copper Man (the mummy of an ancient Chilean copper miner, preserved by the high copper content in the surrounding rocks). Although ancient Egyptian mummies may be the most famous, they are not the oldest.

The earliest examples of intentional human mummification come again from Chile, where mummies of the Chinchorro people have been found spanning the period from 5000 BCE to 2000 BCE. These are very different from Egyptian mummies, as most of their soft tissues were removed rather than preserved. The bodies were remodeled using mud and adorned with a wig and clay mask to produce an image of the deceased.

Although Egyptian mummification changed greatly over time, some of the stages were fundamental and used throughout most of Pharaonic period. There is evidence that the same basic methods were used to produce many other artificially-created mummies. One example is the Guanche mummies from the Canary Islands, which share many characteristics with Egyptian mummies, such as the removal of the internal organs, stuffing of the body cavity and occasionally, the introduction of packing materials under the skin to make the body appear more life-like. One significant difference is that where the Egyptians used salts for drying the body, Guanche mummies have been preserved by the heat of the volcanic cave they were placed in. Sadly, there are few surviving examples, but as these date from between 400 and 1400 CE, it would appear that the method was in use for a long time. Evisceration is a particularly common feature of artificial mummification, as by removing the digestive tract a large amount of bacteria are also removed from the body, delaying the start of decomposition. Other examples of mummies showing these common stages can be found all over the world, from the Aleutian Islands, Central Asia, the Torres Strait Islands, and a number of regions of South America including Colombia and Peru.

An unusual form of mummification employed by Jivaroan tribes of the Upper Amazon region of South America focused on a particular part of the body to the exclusion of the rest. Shrunken heads, or tsantsas, are trophies made from the heads of an enemy by a laborious preservation process. First, the skin was removed from the skull, then boiled, dried, and turned inside out so that the remaining flesh could be scraped away. Turning it the right way round again, the lips were tied together and hot stones or sand placed inside to actually shrink the head down to about the size of a man's fist. When an active trade in shrunken heads developed during the nineteenth century, supplies of the genuine article became scarce, so traders started to produce forgeries from the heads of animals, such as sloths and monkeys, and even occasionally from humans.

If ancient embalming was a mainly physical process, with water drawn out of the body by salts or heat, the more modern methods have been mainly chemical. The Renaissance brought renewed interest in science and medicine, and with it came demand for anatomical specimens. The origins of modern embalming can be dated back to the seventeenth century, when developments in medicine began to require the preservation of anatomical specimens for teaching and study. William Harvey is credited with being the first to develop methods for the injection of substances into blood vessels to preserve body parts. A number of anatomists developed their own methods, including William and John Hunter, who produced an embalming procedure based on the arterial injection of turpentine, oils of chamomile and lavender, and a vermillion pigment. The body was eviscerated and filled with camphor powder and resin, and aromatic substances were applied to the skin.

As the Hunters' method required evisceration, it had drawbacks for the production of specimens for teaching anatomical dissection. An alternative was developed by Allen Burns, though he kept his exact method to himself. It is known that he used a combination of salt and sugar to dehydrate the body; the surviving examples are referred to as "sugar mummies." Although the next decades saw occasional high-profile examples, such as the preservation of Lord Horatio Nelson's body in a cask of brandy after his death at the Battle of Trafalgar, it was during the American Civil War that embalming once again became popular. As with Lord Nelson, the main driving force was the preservation of the war dead so that they could be buried close to home.

Embalming fluids between the seventeenth and nineteenth centuries were based on toxic heavy metals such as arsenic and mercury, which made them very dangerous to work with. This also created a difficult legal situation, since arsenic poisonings could potentially be covered up by embalming the victim and thus hiding forensic evidence of murder. France banned the use of arsenic in embalming fluids following a trial where a woman accused of poisoning her lover was acquitted after the man who embalmed the corpse confirmed to the court that his methods involved the use of arsenic. America followed suit in the late nineteenth century, after Dr. Thomas Holmes had firmly fixed embalming in the public imagination after reportedly preserving over 4,000 bodies during the Civil War.

It is possible that mercury was used in embalming at a far earlier time, during the Western Han Dynasty in China which spanned the period from 200 BCE to 200 CE. A small number of bodies dating to this time have been discovered that show a remarkable level of preservation. On analysis, the fluid found in their lacquered coffins was determined to contain a small amount of mercury, though the quantity should not have been sufficient to preserve the body by itself. In these cases, it appears that a complex combination of factors must have been responsible for their mummification, but the exact mechanism is still not understood.

With the powerfully toxic heavy metals no longer in use, embalmers turned to another chemical, one identified in 1869 by August von Hofman: formaldehyde. This chemical still forms the basis of modern embalming fluids, used alongside additional chemicals such as phenol and other alcohols. Unfortunately, formaldehyde is also highly toxic, being suspected of causing cancer in addition to other, more immediate effects. It preserves tissues by building chemical bridges between proteins and other molecules, making the tissues resistant to degradation and hardening the body. The toxicity of the fluid also kills bacteria that would otherwise make the body rot. Unfortunately, embalming fluids also change the color of the tissue, so the addition of dyes to the mixture and the application of make-up to the body may be required to produce a more life-like appearance.

The modern embalming process can be split into four main parts. The first of these is the injection of embalming fluid into the blood vessels, typically via the carotid arteries. This stage uses the circulatory system to push preservatives throughout the body. Cavity embalming focuses on the internal organs, with natural fluids sucked out of the body cavity and embalming fluids injected to replace them. Embalming fluids are also injected under the skin (hypodermic embalming) where necessary, and visibly injured parts are treated using surface embalming. Once again, parallels can be drawn to the ancient methods, with attention being paid to the different body parts according to their needs, with particular attention being paid to the viscera. A particularly modern problem is the effect that an autopsy has on the process. As many of the internal organs are removed for examination, including the heart, arterial embalming becomes a more complicated process. Each limb and the head must be preserved separately, with the major blood vessels being used. The organs removed as part of the examination are also treated separately, before being placed back in the body.

The production of specimens for anatomical and surgical teaching uses very similar fluids to funerary embalming, though dyes are not normally included because the appearance of the body is less important than the accuracy of the preservation. Formaldehyde-preserved anatomical specimens remain somewhat fragile; however, and are vulnerable to damage over time. An alternative method for producing stable, hard, and even non-toxic specimens has been developed by Gunther von Hagens and is called plastination. This process takes preserved tissue specimens or whole bodies, removes the embalming fluid, and replaces it with a polymer. The resulting pieces are far more durable than wet-preserved specimens and are safe to handle. The most famous examples of this process are those displayed as part of the "Body Worlds" exhibitions that toured repeatedly through North America, Europe, and Asia in the early 2000s.

As formaldehyde changes the texture and color of the tissues it preserves, it is not ideal for preparing bodies that are to be used for training surgeons. The main alternative preservation method, freezing, does not kill microorganisms, leaving surgeons at risk of infection. Thawed bodies also deteriorate rapidly, so they can only be used for a short period of time. Another method, known as Thiel embalming, which uses a fluid based on boric acid, ethylene glycol, and a small amount of formaldehyde, is now becoming popular as it leaves the body flexible and more realistically colored.

Embalming methods in the past tended to rely on the use of natural resources and the environment to preserve the body, while more recent methods have used a variety of chemicals to achieve more lifelike results. Preservation of the dead has been an important part of human society for millennia, since at least the Chinchorro people of South America. Methods have changed in many ways since then, and it appears highly likely that further changes are yet to be made.

Ryan Metcalfe and Jenefer Cockitt

See also: Chinchorro mummies; Egyptian mummification methods; Experimental mummification; Greenhill, Thomas; Pettigrew, Thomas Joseph

Further Reading

Aufderheide, Arthur. 2003. *The Scientific Study of Mummies*. Cambridge: Cambridge University Press.

Brier, Bob. 1998. *The Encyclopedia of Mummies*. New York: Checkmark Books.

Cockburn, Aidan, Eve Cockburn, and Theodore Reyman. 1998. *Mummies, Disease and Ancient Cultures*. Cambridge: Cambridge University Press.

Experimental mummification

It is often difficult to identify and understand the specific processes leading to mummification, whether natural, artificial, or some combination of the two. Researchers have used experimental mummification projects to try to understand why some bodies preserve as mummies, and exactly how mummification occurs.

Mummies may be naturally or artificially preserved. Natural mummies occur as a result of specific environmental conditions, such as excessively high or low temperatures, a lack of moisture, or a lack of oxygen. Examples of natural mummies include bodies from the arid Atacama Desert of South America, the predynastic bodies of ancient Egypt, and the bog bodies of northwestern Europe.

Artificial mummies are preserved as a result of human intervention in some form. Although the ancient Egyptians produced the best known examples of this type of mummification, many other cultures have used artificial methods to preserve the dead, including the Chinchorro of Chile, some groups in Papua New Guinea, and some bodies in China. In some cases, both the environment and human assistance have led to the preservation of a body. For example, the Sycthian mummies of the Russian Steppes were both eviscerated and stuffed with grasses, and naturally frozen in the excessively cold environment.

One of the most famous moments in the history of experimental mummification came in 1994 when American Egyptologist Bob Brier his colleague Ronald Wade, who was director of the State Anatomy Board in Maryland, collaborated in the mummification of a terminally ill British man using ancient Egyptian methods. They were apparently the first to employ these methods in roughly 2,000 years. They did their work with the full approval of the man and his wife, and their activities drew worldwide media attention.

While it is possible to understand the general principles that enable a body to preserve under certain circumstances, experimental mummification projects allow researchers the opportunity to recreate the conditions as closely as a possible, to determine which factors are most influential. It is possible to recreate experimentally both natural and artificial mummies.

One well-known experiment carried out in the 1990s by American Egyptologist Robert "Bob" Brier followed the mummification techniques traditionally used in ancient Egypt to prepare the entire corpse of a man, with excellent results. More recently, a man in the United Kingdom allowed himself to be mummified using ancient Egyptian techniques, and the entire process was televised in a program titled "Mummifying Alan." The difference between these two projects is interesting: in the first project, the individual was an anonymous donor, while in the second, television viewers came to know the man before his death and then followed the mummification of his body after he died.

Opportunities to use entire human bodies are rare, however, so animal specimens are often used as human substitutes for experimental mummification. One project used rabbits, ducks, and fish when replicating the techniques of ancient Egyptian embalmers. The researchers even followed through with radiological studies of the animal mummies to see how well the process worked.

Animal substitutes have also been used to study various forms of natural mummification. Rats were used to study decomposition and preservation processes in arid desert environments and lowland peat bogs. Pigs are commonly used in studies of experimental mummification, since they most accurately reflect how humans decompose or preserve and can be easily acquired for research.

One of the least understood types of mummification processes is that leading to the preservation of bog bodies of northwestern Europe. To attempt to understand why some bodies in peat bogs were partially or completely preserved, a researcher buried several pigs in bogs in the United Kingdom. The pigs were excavated after periods of time ranging from six months to three years. After only six months, the ribs of piglets had demineralized so completely that it would have been possible to tie them into knots. The skin had already begun to turn a dark brown color similar to that of the human bog bodies that had been excavated over the decades. After three years, the piglets that were still in the bogs had darkened skin and all of the bones were very soft and distorted. The researcher concluded that the level of water affected how much soft tissue survived. Where there was more water, the bodies were generally better preserved. The experimental mummification project not only contributed to understanding why some bodies from peat bogs mummified, but also helped develop scientific protocols for future experimental mummification studies.

Pigs were also used to study why some bodies preserved in oak coffins in the Bronze Age burial mounds of Denmark. In this case, the research allowed archaeologists to determine that the coffins had been buried under a temporary covering of soil while the burial mound was prepared, which ensured that the body was kept in an oxygen-free environment. Since oxygen is necessary for decomposition, the bodies were partially preserved.

Experimental projects to understand natural mummification are complicated. Since the work must be conducted in an environment that replicates the original environment as closely as possible, it is usually impossible to conduct the research in a standard laboratory setting. It is almost impossible to recreate exact environmental conditions, such as those found in a rain-fed peat bog, in a laboratory setting. Experimental projects are also often long term, and it may be several years before researchers are able to record any significant results. Few researchers are able to devote the time and resources necessary to undertake experimental mummification projects. It is also important to be able to record environmental data at every stage and over the duration of the experiments, which may be difficult to do, especially in extreme environments.

Despite all of the apparent drawbacks of experimental mummification projects, the process and results contribute very valuable information for the accurate interpretation of mummies. In many cases, there is no other way to understand the exact conditions and processes that lead to the mummification of humans and animals in certain circumstances, and experimental projects make a very important contribution to the field of mummy studies.

Heather Gill-Frerking

See also: Animal mummies; Bog bodies; Natural mummification

Further Reading

Gill-Frerking, Heather, and Colleen Healey. 2011. "Experimental Archaeology for the Interpretation of Taphonomy Related to Bog Bodies: Lessons Learned from Two Projects Undertaken a Decade Apart." In *Yearbook of Mummy Studies, Volume 1*, edited by Dario Piombino-Mascali, 69–74. Bolzano, Italy: Accademia Europea di Bolzano.

Gill-Robinson, Heather. 2002. "This Little Piggy Went to Cumbria, This Little Piggy Went to Wales: The Tales of 12 piglets in Peat." In *Experimental Archaeology: Replicating Past Objects, Behaviors, and Processes*, edited by J. Mathieu, 111–126. British Archaeological Reports, International Series 1035 (BAR S1035). Oxford: Archaeopress.

Ikram, Salima. 2005. "Manufacturing Divinity: The Technology of Mummification." In *Divine Creatures: Animal Mummies in Ancient Egypt*, ed. by Salima Ikram, 16–43. Cairo: The American University in Cairo Press.

Mummifying Alan: Egypt's Last Secret. First broadcast October 24, 2011 by Channel 4 (UK). Directed by Kenny Scott and written by Gillian Mosely.

Peck, Morgen. 2007. "Mummies: Back from the Dead." *Discover*, October 15. Accessed December 6, 2013. http://discovermagazine.com/2007/oct/mummification-is-back-from-the-dead.

F

Fire mummies: The Ibaloy mummies of the Philippines

The indigenous people known as the Ibaloy inhabit an area of Benguet province of North Luzon, the Philippines, called Kabayan, within the Cordillera region. The ancient Ibaloy practiced an active form of preserving their ancestors, who have come to be known as the Fire Mummies. The Fire Mummy designation arises from the mummification process employed by the Ibaloy. Such bodies are also known as the Igorot mummies. This practice of mummification spans centuries, with the most common time interval reported as the 1700s through the 1900s CE.

Once produced, the mummies were placed in wooden coffins of varied shapes and sizes. Some coffins were large enough to hold the mummified remains of entire family groups. The burials were typically in rock shelters, natural caves, or caves that were hollowed out to accommodate the placement of the coffins. The placement of the deceased in caves within the regional mountains was significant. To the Ibaloy, the mountains were gods, and laying their dead to rest within these mountains symbolized returning the deceased to the mountain god.

Many of the caves have been looted in the past. Perhaps the most famous looting was that of the mummy Apo Anno, said to have been the first to be mummified by the ancients. Apo Anno's story did have a happy ending in that the mummy was recovered and returned to the village. The looting has prompted the living descendants to keep secret the location of many of the existing caves. There is considerable mummy

An Ibaloy mummy at Mt. Timbac, Philippines. (Alexis DUCLOS/Gamma-Rapho/Getty Images)

tourism in the area but only to designated cave sites that can be well protected. Looting is deterred with locked iron gates at the cave entrances. The Ibaloy mummies are an integral part of the Ibaloy national identity, and the interaction with the mummies is conducted with the utmost respect.

Bioanthropological analysis of the mummies of the Kabayan region indicates that individuals of all ages and both sexes were processed. Large family coffins and/or cave complexes were not uncommon among the Ibaloy mummy burials. The state of preservation varies among the mummies, with internal organs being very well preserved at times and poorly preserved in other mummies. The state of preservation among the individuals is likely the result of the quality of the mummification process, the temporal context of the individual, and the taphonomic changes (i.e., changes related to decay and fossilization) occurring over time. Many of the Ibaloy mummies have elaborate tattoos and hyperextended heads, and were not eviscerated as seen in other mummification practices such as the ancient Egyptians.

Mummification Process

The mummification process used by the ancient Ibaloy was indeed complex and required extensive resources and attention. The process has been described primarily through oral histories passed down through the ages. The process begins with the individual being given a saltwater solution to drink near or at the time of death. This initial step has been questioned by scholars, in that salt was scarce and the resulting peristalsis (digestive contractions) needed to distribute the salt solution through the gut of the individual would vary greatly depending on whether the individual was able to swallow or actually dead at the time. Once the saltwater "purge" was achieved, the individual was washed in cold water. The individual was then placed in a seated position in a *sangachil* or death chair and then wrapped in a "death blanket." Additionally, a scarf of the same or similar material was placed over the head. The deceased was secured to the chair with local vines with the head held in position by the scarf. The chair was secured to a ladder and placed near the entrance and facing the front of a traditional stilted house. Under the chair, a low fire was lit (thus the name the Fire Mummies). This position near the house and the associated fire may have created a microenvironment allowing for enhanced dehydration from the heat of the fire and protection from insect infestation because of the smoke. The chemistry of the smoke also played a role in the mummification process. Body fluids were "milked" or expressed from the deceased and were collected in a jar. Once the oozing of body fluids stopped, the body was removed from the *sangachil* and laid out where the relatives performed what is called the *duduan,* the peeling of the epidermis. The body was then returned to the *sangachil* with bodily openings being plugged with the leaves of local plants. The same plants were made into a slurry that was then rubbed over the body. Tobacco smoke was blown into the mouth with the goal of enhancing the mummification of the internal organs. (The effectiveness of blowing smoke on internal mummification is questionable, in that the smoke would not likely travel deeply into the body).

Mummification in the Ibaloy tradition was likely achieved primarily from enhanced dehydration accomplished by the heat from the fire, the position in the death chair, the potential microenvironment, and wicking body fluids into the death blanket. The forces of decomposition may have further been delayed by the smoke chemistry, the increased barrier to insects provided by the smoke, and the plant chemistry. If a salt solution purge was successful, this, too, may have contributed to enhanced dehydration.

Coffin Styles

The Ibaloy used three basic coffin designs. One was ovoid and carved from a local pine tree much like a dugout canoe. Others were rectangular boxes constructed with planks fashioned from the same tree. The larger family-sized coffins were generally of the planked variety. These coffins had patterns carved into them, often in the form animals, such as the snake, and/or human-like depictions.

Funerary Rituals

Today the Ibaloy continue to practice elaborate rituals associated with the dead and many interactions with the dead. Typically, there is a song and dance symbolizing the return of the deceased to the mountain. If one is to visit the caves, several rituals apply. First, songs are chanted and red rice wine is consumed. Forest pigs are sacrificed and their livers and gallbladders are removed and read by the local shaman. The remainder of the pig is shared with the entire village. If the shaman determines that the livers and gallbladders are acceptable, this indicates that the ancestors are agreeable to having a visit. At the cave entrance additional rituals are carried out, including the sacrifice of a chicken, the chanting of another song, and the sharing of more rice wine. The rice wine and bits of food are offered to the ancestors at the mouth of the cave. According to local lore, it is considered taboo to bring the mummies out of the caves, so any visits or scientific work must be conducted within the cave or just inside the cave entrance. The risk, according to the Ibaloy, is that the spirits of the dead may cause trouble for the living.

Current Local Attitudes Regarding the Ibaloy Mummies

The current attitudes toward the Ibaloy mummies vary widely among the inhabitants of Kabayan. Some residents feel that the mummies are sacred and the spirits of the ancestors are very real. The mummified remains must therefore be treated with a great deal of respect, as evidenced by the rituals and traditions surrounding these mummies. If the mummies are not pleased, their spirits can cause periodic calamities. In contrast, some feel that the old ways are dead traditions and that if anything bad happens to the village, the mummies or the spirits of the ancestors have nothing to do with it.

Even with the diverging views, the dead in modern-day Kabayan are not buried in their local cemetery, but rather are buried in their home gardens, thus keeping departed loved ones close to home. This practice suggests that the concept of the spirit still exists among the populace, and that the home burial is a way to continue to show respect and concern for the deceased.

Regardless of belief systems about these Fire Mummies, one attitude is common among nearly all the villagers: these mummies, who are the current villagers' ancestors, have become a symbol of regional identity. Mummy tourism brings much-needed income and jobs to the region. However, problems go hand-in-hand with the mummy industry. Roads need to be maintained with limited funds, the trails are swallowed by the mountains, and the mummies themselves are at risk of deterioration.

This is a very unique group of mummies that represents tremendous effort in their construction, a dedication to the beliefs of the ancients, and a deep-rooted respect for the old ways and the spirit of the Ibaloy.

Ronald G. Beckett, Dario Piombino-Mascali and Gerald Conlogue

See also: Egyptian mummification methods; Embalming

Further Reading

Aufderheide, Arthur C. 2003. *The Scientific Study of Mummies*. Cambridge: Cambridge University Press.

Baucas, Biano L. 2003. *Traditional Beliefs and Cultural Practices in Benguet*. La Trinidad: New Baguio Offset Press.

Beckett, Ronald G., Lohmann, Ulla and Josh Bernstein. 2011. "A Field Report on the Mummification Practices of the Anga of Koke Village, Central Highlands, Papua New Guinea." *Yearbook of Mummy Studies*, 1: 11–17.

Merino, Florentino S. 1989. *The Kabayan Mummies and the Bendiyan Canao*. Kabayan: the Author.

The Mummy Road Show. Episode no. 18, "Cave Mummies of the Philippines," first broadcast October 15, 2002 by National Geographic Channel. Directed by Larry Engel and written by Mary Olive Smith. Hosted by Ron Beckett and Jerry Conlogue.

Picpican, Isikias. 2003. *The Igorot Mummies: A Socio-Cultural and Historical Treatise*. Quezon City: Rex Bookstore Inc.

Freund, Karl

Karl Freund (1890–1969), who was primarily known as a cameraman, also directed eight pictures, including two horror movies, *The Mummy* (1932) and *Mad Love* (1935). Freund worked in both films and later television, and became known as a "pioneer in the development of subjective photography, devising

A publicity poster for Universal Studios' *The Mummy* (1932), directed by Karl Freund. (Archive Photos/Getty Images)

unorthodox techniques (such as strapping the camera to his chest) to capture particular shots" (Brunas). His film *The Mummy*, which starred Boris Karloff (1887–1969), is a classic of the horror genre.

Born in Königinhof in 1890 in what is today the Czech Republic, Freund moved to Berlin as a boy. At 18, he began his career with Pathe, one of the world's largest film equipment and production companies at the time, where he was a newsreel cameraman, a job he would continue to do through World War I. Before immigrating to the United States in 1929, Freund collaborated with expressionist director F. W. Murnau on several films and worked with director Fritz Lang on *Metropolis* (1927). He was the cinematographer for the 1920 version of *The Golem*. A year after arriving in the United States, Freund signed a contract with Universal Pictures, for whom he helped produce *All Quiet on the Western Front* (1930).

Before making his directorial debut in 1932 with *The Mummy*, Freund was the cinematographer for *Dracula* (1931), *The Bad Sister* (1931), *Murders in the Rue Morgue* (1932), and *Air Mail* (1932). His work on *Dracula* and *Murders in the Rue Morgue* impressed the heads of Universal, so they asked him to direct their next monster picture, *The Mummy*. Freund's direction of the film has been described as "succinct and to the point" (Brunas), and it was different from Universal's other horror films in that it was more serious and lacked the element of comic relief. Scholar David J. Skal describes Freund's direction of *The Mummy* less generously, viewing it as a reworking of Browning's *Dracula*. In his words, "virtually every plot element as well as key performers (not to mention some props and set decorations) were recycled" from *Dracula*.

The filming of *The Mummy* was marred by conflicts between Freund and Universal's then head of production, Carl Lammele, Jr., as well as the director's antipathy towards actress Zita Johann (1904–1993), who played the role of Helen Grovesner, the reincarnated Princess Anck-es-en-Amon, Imhotep's lost love. Gavin Schmitt states in his biography of Freund that the director and Lammele, Jr. "almost came to blows over the opening sequence" because "Laemmle wanted the Mummy to come to life and be introduced in a series of stylized close-ups like those that James Whale used in *Frankenstein*," whereas "Freund insisted that the Mummy should not be shown at all after its first stirrings of life in the sarcophagus and that audiences would be far more horrified by the specter of [an archeologist's] descent into madness, and his maniacal laughter, if they didn't see what drove him to it. Fortunately Freund prevailed and the sequence is one of the most revered in Universal's horror classics" (Schmitt).

Freund also had such a stormy relationship with Johann throughout the filming that when Laemmle, Jr. called the actress to enthuse about the final print of *The Mummy* that he had just seen, she told the producer to "do her a favour" and not "pick up [her] option for another picture" (Mank), thus ending her brief relationship with Universal Pictures. Freund, who had a reputation as a "tireless taskmaster" (Brunas), singled out Johann for abuse, treating her as a scapegoat in case the film did not come in on its tight production schedule of a little over three weeks. Freund's harassment of Johann included working her 16 hours a day instead of the usual 12 and even threatening to force her to do a nude scene, which would never have made it past the censors in 1932 and so could never have been part of the finished film. Johann was so exhausted towards the end of production that during the pool scene, where the death and burial of Anck-es-en-Amon is revealed to Helen, the actress collapsed. Freund's dislike of Johann caused him to delete many of her scenes in the film, including a complex montage showing her character remembering several previous lives before her most recent incarnation.

Although Freund was a talented director, he preferred cinematography, which he felt was more artistic. After receiving an Oscar for his direction of *The Good Earth* (1937), he returned to his role as a cameraman and spent the later part of his career working in television. He is known for pioneering the multiple camera set up, which is now a standard filming technique for situation comedies.

June Pulliam

See also: Karloff, Boris; *The Mummy* (1932); Universal Studios mummy series

Further Reading

Fischer, Dennis. 1991. "Karl Freund (1890–1969)." In *Horror Film Directors, 1931–1990*, 428–442. Jefferson, NC: McFarland & Co.

Jacobs, Steven. 2011. *Boris Karloff: More Than a Monster. The Authorized Biography.* Sheffield, England: Tomahawk Press.

Mank, Gregory. 1984. "The Mummy Revisited." *Films in Review*, August/September: 414–421.

Schmitt, Gavin C. 2012. "The Life and Films of Karl Freund, Hollywood Innovator." *The Framing Business*, last modified January 24. Accessed November 4, 2013. http://framingbusiness.net/archives/1056.

Skal, David J. 1993. *The Monster Show: A Cultural History of Horror.* New York: Penguin.

Weaver, Tom, Michael Brunas, and John Brunas. 2007. *Universal Horrors: The Studio's Classic Films, 1931–46.* Jefferson, NC: McFarland & Co.

G

Gautier, Theophile

The noted French poet, critic, and creative writer Pierre-Jules Theophile Gautier (1811–1872), who signed himself Theophile Gautier, wrote a number of fantastic and supernatural works, and made occasional use of Egypt and its mummies in his fiction. The most significant of his tales to feature mummies are "The Mummy's Foot" ("Le Pied de momie," [1840]) and the short novel *The Romance of a Mummy* (*Le Roman de la momie* [1857]).

Pierre-Jules Theophile Gautier was born August 20, 1811, in Tarbes, France. His family moved to Paris, where Gautier attended a school, at College Charlemagne befriending the equally youthful Gerard Labrunie, who was later to achieve fame as Gerard de Nerval. Gautier began to write as a poet and became a noted figure in the nineteenth century French cultural scene, with his friends and acquaintances including such noted figures as Victor Hugo, Honore de Balzac, Alexandre Dumas *père*, Gustav Flaubert, Heinrich Heine, Hector Berlioz, and Giacomo Meyerbeer. He wrote voluminously and diversely, achieving fame for the ballet scenario *Giselle* (1841), for which Adolphe Adam wrote the music.

"The Mummy's Foot" is set in Gautier's France and begins in an astonishingly crowded antique shop in which "all ages and all nations seemed to have made their rendezvous." After the nameless narrator has nearly decided to make his purchase, "hesitating between a porcelain dragon, all constellated with warts . . . and an abominable little Mexican fetich, representing the god Vitziliputzili *au naturel*" (Gautier 1899, 225), he catches sight of a beautiful foot. The shop's strange proprietor identifies it as the foot of the Princess Hermonthis, daughter of the Pharaoh, and sells it to the narrator for a pittance; the narrator uses it as a paperweight. That night, after a friendly engagement with friends, the narrator sees the foot jumping about, and he is soon joined by the lovely Princess Hermonthis, who rebukes her wayward foot. The foot will not return to the Princess, however, for it has been sold, and the poor Princess has no money and cannot redeem her foot. The narrator promptly returns the foot to its rightful owner, and the Princess in gratitude replaces his paperweight with a green paste idol. She takes him to the hollowed mountain occupied by all of the previous Pharaohs, the narrator identifying "Cheops, Chephrenes, Psammetichus, Sesotris, Amenotaph . . . On yet higher thrones sat Chronos and Xixouthros, who was contemporary with the deluge, and Tubal Cain, who reigned before it. . . . further back, through a dusty cloud, I beheld dimly the

At last we found ourselves in a hall so vast, so enormous, so immeasurable, that the eye could not reach its limits. Files of monstrous columns stretched far out of sight on every side, between which twinkled livid stars of yellowish flame; points of light which revealed further depths incalculable in the darkness beyond.

The Princess Hermonthis still held my hand, and graciously saluted the mummies of her acquaintance.

My eyes became accustomed to the dim twilight, and objects became discernible.

I beheld the kings of the subterranean races seated upon thrones—grand old men, though dry, withered, wrinkled like parchment, and blackened with naphtha and bitumen—all wearing pshents of gold, and breastplates and gorgets glittering with precious stones, their eyes immovably fixed like the eyes of sphinxes, and their long beards whitened by the snow of centuries. Behind them stood their peoples, in the stiff and constrained posture enjoined by Egyptian art, all eternally preserving the attitude prescribed by the hieratic code. Behind these nations, the cats, ibixes, and crocodiles contemporary with them—rendered monstrous of aspect by their swathing bands—mewed, flapped their wings, or extended their jaws in a saurian giggle.

—From "The Mummy's Foot" by Theophile Gautier

seventy-two pre-adamite kings, with their seventy-two peoples, forever passed away" (Gautier 1899, 242). As a reward for restoring the Princess's foot, the narrator asks for her hand, a request that strikes all mummies as unreasonable, for as Pharaoh explains, there is not only the age difference but the men of the narrator's generation do not know how to preserve themselves. Pharaoh grips the narrator's hand sufficiently hard that he awakens from his dream to find his friend Alfred shaking him. On his table, however, is the green paste idol.

"The Mummy's Foot" is in many ways a *jeu d'esprit*, a whimsically told and paradoxically structured work that manages to raise a number of issues without resolving them in any way. First, there are the questions of the shop and its proprietor. Early in the description of the shop, the narrator refers to it as "a veritable Capharnaum" and states that "all ages and all nations seemed to have made their rendezvous there" (Gautier 1899, 222), and the descriptions indeed reveal that the shop contains an incredible assortment of artifacts from all times and periods. Gautier is not explicit, but this "veritable Capharnaum" would appear to be an early instance of what has since become recognized as one of the tropes of fantastic fiction, the magic shop. First described and utilized in *La Peu de chagrin* (1830) by Gautier's compatriot and contemporary Honore de Balzac, the magic shop essentially sells items that are genuinely magical or that possess the power to awaken dormant magic. As the events of "The Mummy's Foot" reveal, this is exactly what occurs.

Next, there is the issue of the shop's proprietor and (apparently) sole employee. He is strange in appearance, so strange that the narrator notes that he "had an aspect so thoroughly rabbinical and cabalistic that he would have been burnt on the mere testimony of his face three centuries ago" (Gautier 1899, 224). Not only is the proprietor fantastic and aged in appearance, but his comments about the mummy's foot reveal a great and intriguing knowledge about its origins and hint at a personal acquaintance with the Pharaoh. Indeed, with such statements as "Old Pharaoh will not be well pleased. He loved his daughter, the dear man!" (Gautier 1899, 229) there is the hint that the proprietor is friendly with the Pharaoh himself and knows his likes, dislikes, and will. The narrator's glib response—"You speak as if you were a contemporary of his. You are old enough, goodness knows! but you do not date back to the Pyramids of Egypt" (Gautier 1899, 229)—never resolves the issue, and the reader is left wondering about a shop proprietor who appears to be sufficiently friendly with a Pharaoh to be able to discuss the Pharaoh's feelings.

In addition, there is the question of the story's deliberately ambiguous conclusion. If the events described in the story are all a dream, the mummy's foot should have been present on the table where it was left, but the foot has been replaced by the green paste idol left by the Princess Hermonthis. The presence of the idol means that the narrator's experience was not a dream: and yet, in that the narrator describes his friend shaking him awake from his conversation with the Pharaoh, how can that be?

Contemporary readers of Gautier's tale are likely to accept the fantastic elements without questioning them—today's readership can readily accept magic shops and shop proprietors who might be thousands of years old, and dreams that are not dreams but that may be dreams fail to bewilder—and may seize on as a fantastic element the idea of using a mummy's foot as a paperweight, for mummies are of course to be found in museums, not purchased piecemeal through antique shops. Oddly, this assessment leads to an interpretation that is likely exactly the opposite of Gautier's intention and experience.

At the time Gautier wrote "The Mummy's Foot," mummies were a relative novelty in England and Europe, and while they were recognized as being from Egypt's past, the role of the mummy in Gautier's time was that of a curiosity, a historical souvenir, not a priceless and unique cultural artifact. Mummies were routinely excavated, taken abroad, broken apart, and then offered for sale. More, as historians have noted, "from the 1830's onwards it became popular in England to undertake the unwrapping and dissection of Egyptian mummies publicly in front of paying crowds. Doctor T. J. Pettigrew was particularly famous. He used the large auditorium of Charing Cross Hospital for his 'operations.' This soon became too small and he had to use an even larger exhibition hall" (Seipel 1996, 5). And of course, Pettigrew was far from unique in his operations and depredations: he had rivals. Pettigrew's fascination and obsession led to his writing and publishing a volume, *History of Egyptian Mummies* in 1834, which in turn helped fuel a cultural interest in Egypt and its remnants. As for the remnants of the mummies that were broken up: some of them ended in museums, and some ended in junk stores, and while these junk stores were not literally magic shops, in all probability at least some of them were likely akin to the store visited by the narrator.

The Romance of a Mummy is an historical romance, set in Egypt. It begins in the present, with a lengthy prologue in which European explorers, among them wealthy Englishman Lord Evandale, are led to, excavate, and open a hitherto unopened Egyptian tomb. The discovery is spectacular and mysterious, for the tomb is that of a woman, and the narrative asks explicitly, "how did the woman's coffin come to occupy this royal sarcophagus, in the centre of this cryptic palace worthy of the most illustrious and most powerful of the Pharaohs?" The mummy, unwrapped is a lovely woman in perfect condition, and she is next to a scroll whose translation forms the text of *The Romance of a Mummy.*

The narrative itself is a drama in which the lovely woman—Tahoser of Oph (Thebes)—is beloved by General Ahmosis but loves him not, although her maid Nofre does. Tahoser loves young Poeri, who is a Hebrew, and although the two have met, she has lied to him and led him to think that she is the impoverished orphan Hora, a woman of low rank who needs his assistance. Poeri assists Tahoser, but his heart belongs to Rachel, whom he visits secretly at night. Tahoser collapses in despair at this and is nursed by Rachel, whose old assistant Thamar is suspicious and believes that the young woman may be an Egyptian spy. The Pharaoh has been attempting to learn Tahoser's whereabouts and has questioned the unwitting Poeri, and Thamar realizes Hora is Tahoser. Rachel realizes that Thamar is correct and that Tahoser's actions were motivated by love of Poeri, a situation she encourages, citing the story of Jacob, who had two wives, Rachel and Leah: Tahoser can be Leah. Tahoser accepts this and is willing to give up the worship of the Egyptian gods to follow Poeri's faith, but she is betrayed by Thamar, who leads the Pharaoh to her. He takes Tahoser to his palace and pledges love to her as Thamar staggers away laden with the treasure she received for her betrayal. Moses and Aaron appear before the Pharaoh, and Moses tells Pharaoh to let his people go. The Pharaoh disregards this, but when they return, he demands proof, at which point Aaron throws down his rod, which becomes a serpent. The Pharaoh has his wise men do the same, but Aaron's serpent consumes the Egyptian serpents, and although Tahoser urges the Pharaoh to obey, the proud Pharaoh refuses. A bit later, Aaron shows the power of his god by turning the Nile's waters blood red. After seven days pass, Aaron summons a plague of frogs, and although the Pharaoh initially accedes to their requests for freedom, he breaks his promise and thus more plagues descend on Egypt: lice, boils, hail, darkness, and the death of the first born. The Hebrews are not affected. At the funeral of the Pharaoh's son, the Pharaoh intimates to Tahoser that his days are concluding, for his gods cannot protect him against the God of the Hebrews. When the Hebrews flee, the Pharaoh pursues them; at the Red Sea, the Lord's breath parts the waters for Moses, and the pursuing Egyptians (including the Pharaoh) drown. As Queen, Tahoser reigns, then is buried in the tomb prepared for Pharaoh, the scroll detailing her life left by her side. Lord Evandale has fallen in love with Tahoser and, although the last of his line, never marries.

As the above summary indicates, the narrative of *The Romance of a Mummy* is a combination of staged dramatic events and historical religiosity. It has none of the fantastic verve or brevity found in the earlier "The Mummy's Foot" but is, rather, turgid. Gautier unquestionably did extensive historical researches in the best sources available to him, and Gautier's English translator notes this, stating that his narrative is

> marvellously [sic] accurate. Nothing is easier than to verify his descriptions by reference to the works of Champollion, Mariette, Wilkinson, Rawlinson, Erman, Edwards, and Maspero ... it is evident that he has not trusted alone to what Feydeau told him, or to what he read in his book or in the works of the Egyptologists: he examined the antiquities in the Louvre for himself; he noted carefully the scenes depicted on monuments and sarcophagi; he traced the ornamentation in all its details; he studied the poses, the attitudes, the expressions; he marked the costumes, the accessories. .... [etc.] (DeSumichrast, 4–5)

Unfortunately, to the detriment of the story, and for his readers, then and now, Gautier felt obligated to demonstrate this expertise, and he did it by regurgitating his readings and experiences, at length, at every narrative opportunity: the story described above is buried in a welter of description. Furthermore, and perhaps inevitably, the characterizations do not convince: the characters are not Egyptians but nineteenth-century French with Egyptian names. Finally, there is an unpleasant psychological framework to *The Romance of a Mummy*: because Gautier depicts the discovery of the tomb, the excavation of Tahoser's sarcophagus, and the unwrapping of her body at such length, he creates a scenario in which the death eroticism is highly repellant, the lengthy descriptions of her beautiful and beautifully preserved body bordering on the excessive: and at the conclusion there is no doubt that Lord Evandale is in love with a corpse dead for more than 2,500 years.

Theophile Gautier died on October 23, 1872, without completing his *Histoire du romantisme*. He remains an important and vital figure in any discussion of nineteenth-century French culture and has been and continues to be the subject of much criticism. When Gautier's fantastic works are discussed, critics and readers tend to have dismissed *The Romance of a Mummy* and to have praised "The Mummy's Foot" for its intricacy and cleverness. This situation is unlikely to change.

Richard Bleiler

See also: Collecting mummies; The mummy in Western fiction: Beginnings to 1922; Mummy unwrappings; Pettigrew, Thomas Joseph

Further Reading

Dawson, Warren R. 1934. "Pettigrew's Demonstrations upon Mummies: A Chapter in the History of Egyptology." *The Journal of Egyptian Archaeology* 20: 170–182.

Gautier, Theophile. 1899. *One of Cleopatra's Nights and Other Fantastic Romances*, translated by Lafcadio Hearn. New York: Brentano's.

Gautier, Theophile. 1909. *The Romance of a Mummy*. In *The Complete Works of Theophile Gautier*, volume III. Translated and edited by Professor F. C. DeSumichrast. London and New York: Postlethwaite, Taylor and Knowles.

Grant, Richard E. 1975. *Theophile Gautier*. Boston: Twayne.

Seipel, W. 1996. "Mummies and Ethics in the Museum." In *Human Mummies: A Global Survey of Their Status and the Techniques of Conservation*, edited by K. Spindler et al., 3–7. New York: Springer.

Smith, Albert B. 1977. *Theophile Gautier and the Fantastic*. University, MS: Romance Monographs.

Gebelein Man

Gebelein Man, also known as "Ginger" because of his light-colored hair, is the naturally mummified body of a man from ancient Egypt. The body dates to around 3500 BCE, during the Predynastic Era of Egyptian history, before the establishment of a monarchy and a unified state society. Named for the site of Gebelein, where the body was discovered, Gebelein Man is remarkably well preserved, and is one of the earliest and best known examples of natural mummification from Egypt.

In Predynastic Egypt, before mummification practices were developed, people were normally buried in small pits in the ground. The extremely arid climate of Egypt and the dry sand halted many of the processes of decay, and instead dried out the body to form a natural mummy. Though there are not many examples of these natural mummies, the ones that do exist are generally very well preserved. Gebelein Man's skin, fingernails, and even his eyelashes are still visible, as well as his distinctive "ginger" colored hair (though this color may be due to the process of desiccation rather than the man's natural hair color during life). Like other early Egyptian natural mummies, Gebelein Man was buried in a contracted, or fetal, position, lying on his left side, and may have been wrapped in a mat made of reeds or plant matter. It is likely that he was also accompanied by a few clay pots or other grave goods; even at this early stage of Egyptian history, there seems to have been some sort of belief in an afterlife.

Despite the fact that artificial mummification and ancient Egypt are inextricably linked in the mind of most modern people, the ancient Egyptians themselves recorded almost no information about the history and process of mummification.

The predynastic Egyptian mummy known as Gebelein Man lies in a contracted, fetal position (in accordance with early Egyptian custom) in his reconstructed grave at the British Museum. (Feargus Cooney/Getty Images)

Scholars have long believed that natural mummies such as Gebelein Man probably played a role in the development of artificial mummification. Predynastic graves were often little more than shallow pits, and it is not improbable that the living population occasionally encountered the dead, whether through human or animal activity.

Gebelein Man was discovered at the end of the nineteenth century, probably around 1896, with several other naturally mummified bodies at Gebelein, a site in Upper (southern) Egypt, southwest of modern Luxor. Gebelein Man was placed on display in the British Museum in 1900. In the late 1980s, he was carefully

The naturally mummified body known as Gebelein Man was discovered around 1896 with several other bodies in Upper Egypt. In 1900 he was placed on display in the British Museum. More than eight decades later, in the 1980s, he was treated for further preservation. In 2012 he was taken to a London hospital for CT scanning, which yielded a wealth of previously unknown information. Today Gebelein Man stands as a prominent case study in the evolving field of mummy science, where advances in technology and scientific technique continue to elicit valuable new knowledge from mummies that were first studied decades and even centuries ago.

treated by conservators, who cleaned the body and applied an adhesive to areas where the skin was cracking and pulling apart. An improved, padded mount for the body, which mimicked the inclined plane the body likely occupied during burial, was also created. The display case for Gebelein Man is carefully controlled for temperature and humidity to prevent further damage to the body.

In 2012, Gebelein Man was transported to a London hospital for CT scans. This technology is becoming increasingly popular and useful for studies of mummies, as it provides a noninvasive way to examine mummies literally from the inside out. By examining these scans, Dr. Daniel Antoine was able to determine that Gebelein Man most likely died between the ages of 18 and 21 (based on the state of fusion of the long bones), and suffered from a fractured rib, as well as large indentation in the scapula (shoulder bone). Fragments of the rib had shattered and were lodged in the muscles and tissues of the shoulder and back. The rib fractures and indentation in the scapula led Dr. Antoine to conclude that Gebelein Man most likely died of a stab wound to the back. Several other ribs were broken sometime after Gebelein Man had already died. The CT scans allowed researchers to examine every aspect of Gebelein Man in great detail. Since later mummification techniques dictated that the inner organs be removed, the CT scans of Gebelein Man also allowed scientists an unparalleled opportunity to examine all the organs and tissues.

Gebelein Man is currently housed at the British Museum and is on display with artifacts from the same general time period. The display for Gebelein Man reconstructs what his burial may have looked like and contains several examples of Predynastic Egyptian pottery and artifacts.

Roselyn Campbell

See also: Egyptian collection, the British Museum; Egyptian mummies; Medical imaging of mummies; Natural mummification

Further Reading

British Museum. "Conserving the Body of a Predynastic Egyptian." Accessed October 11 2013. http://www.britishmuseum.org/explore/highlights/article_index/c/conserving_the_body_of_a_predy.aspx.

British Museum. "Gebelein Man." Accessed October 11, 2013. http://www.british museum.org/explore/highlights/highlight_objects/aes/p/gebelein_man.aspx.

British Museum. "Virtual Autopsy: Exploring a Natural Mummy from Early Egypt." Accessed October 11 2013. http://www.britishmuseum.org/channel/exhibitions/2012/virtual_autopsy_gebelein_man.aspx.

David, Rosalie, and Rich Archbold. 2000. *Conversations with Mummies: New Light on the Lives of the Ancient Egyptians*. Toronto, Ontario, Canada: Black Walnut.

Dunand, Françoise, and Roger Lichtenberg. 2006. *Mummies and Death in Egypt*. Translated by David Lorton. Ithaca: Cornell University Press.

Grajetzki, Wolfram. 2007. *Burial Customs in Ancient Egypt: Life in Death for Rich and Poor*. London: Duckworth.

Ikram, Salima. 2003. *Death and Burial in Ancient Egypt*. London: Pearson Education Limited.

McDermott, Bridget. 2006. *Death in Ancient Egypt*. Gloucestershire, United Kingdom: Sutton Publishing.

Taylor, John H. 2001. *Death and the Afterlife in Ancient Egypt*. London: British Museum Press.

Genetic study of mummies

Ever since tools for studying and manipulating genetic material became commonly available in the 1980s, scientists have been entranced by the possibility of using DNA to gain information from ancient mummies. That dream has proved tougher than originally thought. The field has struggled with technical difficulties, not least the need to eliminate contamination with modern DNA. But recent advances in molecular biology have led to some stunning results.

The first published study of DNA from a long-dead organism, published in 1984, was on a quagga (an extinct species of zebra) that had died 140 years before. This was impressive, but a PhD student from the University of Uppsala in Sweden, named Svante Pääbo, believed he could go one better. He persuaded an Egyptology professor at the university to help him take tissue samples from 20 Egyptian mummies at museums in Uppsala and Berlin. Pääbo isolated several chunks of DNA from the mummy of a one-year-old boy, and reported the achievement in *Nature* in 1985.

1984	The first analysis of DNA from a long-dead organism (an extinct species of zebra) is published.
1985	The journal *Nature* publishes results of DNA analysis on tissue samples from 20 Egyptian mummies at museums in Uppsala and Berlin, conducted by Swedish PhD student Svante Pääbo
1988	Pääbo and colleagues use the newly developed technique of polymerase chain reaction to extract DNA from the brain of a 7,000-year-old human mummy found in a Florida bog.
2010	A team put together by Zahi Hawass, led by Albert Zink and Carsten Pusch, and funded by the Discovery Channel publishes a report on DNA from Tutankhamun and other royal mummies from the Egypt's 18th Dynasty. Their results elicit much controversy.
2012	A team led by Albert Zink reports the genome sequence of Ötzi the Iceman.
2013	A team led by Carsten Pusch at the University of Tübingen sequences DNA from five human mummies held in the university's museum.

Both of these early studies involved inserting the purified DNA fragments into bacterial cells, a process called cloning. As the bacteria divide and grow, the DNA is multiplied too, into large enough amounts to study. In the late 1980s, a technique called polymerase chain reaction (PCR) was developed, which promised an easier way to study ancient DNA. PCR enables researchers to replicate scarce DNA fragments in a test tube, a process called amplification. In 1988, Pääbo and his colleagues used it to extract DNA from the brain of a 7,000-year-old human mummy from a Florida bog called Little Salt Spring.

Researchers around the world applied the new technique to mummies as well as skeletons and fossils. They published exciting results from older and older specimens, including prehistoric plants and insects preserved in amber. In 1994, a microbiologist from Brigham Young University in Utah reported DNA from an 80 million-year-old dinosaur.

But these results were not all they seemed. Researchers did not realize at first how susceptible PCR is to contamination, particularly when used to amplify ancient DNA. DNA degrades over time, breaking into shorter and shorter fragments, so researchers who study ancient mummies or skeletons are often working with extremely tiny amounts of poor-quality DNA. The PCR reaction preferentially latches on to fresh DNA, so even a molecule or two of modern contamination—from a speck of dust in the air, or a drop of sweat—can swamp the ancient DNA in a sample and ruin a result.

When scientists checked their results, they realized that much of the so-called ancient DNA did not come from their specimens at all. The dinosaur DNA almost certainly belonged to a modern human, as did Pääbo's cloned DNA. In one study of Egyptian monkey mummies, the DNA that the researchers had amplified turned out to belong to pigeons that had nested in a storehouse where the mummies were once kept.

Researchers introduced rigorous controls to minimize the risk of contamination, such as repeating every result in two separate labs. Some leaders of the field, including Pääbo, now at the Max Planck Institute for Evolutionary Biology in Leipzig, Austria, and Eske Willerslev, head of the Centre for GeoGenetics at the Natural History Museum in Copenhagen, Denmark, stopped working on human mummies. They argued that it would never be possible to know for sure that any human DNA amplified came from the specimens and not from modern humans. Instead, they focused on the remains of prehistoric, preferably extinct, species such as mammoths, where it was easier to be sure that any results gained were authentic.

These experts saw results on Egyptian mummies as particularly controversial. DNA degrades faster in warm temperatures, so an extra problem with mummies from the hot Egyptian desert was that many researchers did not believe there was even any DNA left in them to study.

However, other groups, such as those led by Albert Zink at the EURAC Institute for Mummies and the Iceman in Bolzano, Italy, and Andreas Nerlich from the Academic Teaching Hospital Munchen-Bogenhausen in Munich, Germany, continued to work on human mummies, including those from Egypt. These researchers targeted DNA from pathogens that infected the ancient individuals. They tested hundreds of mummies, up to 5,000 years old, and reported DNA from a range of bacteria, including *Mycobacterium tuberculosis*, *Corynebacterium diphtheriae* and *Escherichia coli*, as well as the parasites responsible for malaria and leishmaniasis.

The field effectively split into two, with some groups publishing DNA results on human mummies, and others dismissing the data as flawed and down to contamination.

In 2010, a team put together by Egypt's antiquities chief Zahi Hawass published a controversial report of DNA from King Tutankhamun and other royal mummies from the 18th Dynasty of ancient Egypt. The DNA results were used to construct a family tree (see "Tutankhamun") and revealed the presence of the malaria parasite in several of the mummies, including Tutankhamun.

The team was led by Zink as well as Carsten Pusch, a geneticist at the University of Tübingen, Germany. They used a technique called DNA fingerprinting, which homes in on specific regions of the genome that vary between individuals, to give unique DNA profiles. Ancient DNA researchers including Pääbo and Willerslev were skeptical about the results. DNA fingerprinting measures the size of amplified fragments but does not provide sequences, so when using this technique it is particularly hard to know whether any DNA detected is ancient or modern.

Zink and his colleagues insisted that the results were real, suggesting that the embalming process must have helped to preserve the DNA despite the hot temperatures to which these mummies had been exposed. Recent reports by other teams of DNA from the mummies of 2,000-year-old crocodile hatchlings and cats have helped to convince the skeptics that DNA does survive, in at least some Egyptian mummies.

Hawass's team subsequently published further DNA results suggesting that an anonymous mummy dubbed Unknown Man E shared a common male lineage with the mummy of Rameses III. The authors concluded that this mummy might therefore be Rameses's son Pentawere.

In the last few years, new DNA analysis techniques have been developed, collectively known as "next-generation" sequencing. They allow researchers to sequence entire genomes rather than amplifying one fragment at a time; allow the study of DNA from older samples than before; and make it easier to spot contamination.

This is partly because these techniques don't generally rely on PCR amplification. Instead, they sequence all of the DNA in a sample as short fragments, then use a computer to stitch together these short reads into one long sequence. Because all DNA present is sampled equally, the results are less likely to be swamped by any modern sequences. It is also possible to check whether a sample contains DNA from more than one individual (a telltale sign of contamination), or whether the sequence lacks patterns of degradation that would be expected from ancient DNA.

Such techniques were used to read the genome sequence of the woolly mammoth in 2008. Big labs such as Willerslev's and Pääbo's are also using them to look again at ancient human mummies, particularly those preserved in cold conditions, reading entire genomes for samples previously beyond the limits of technology.

In 2010, Willerslev and his colleagues published the genome of a member of an extinct Eskimo group known as the Saqqaq, from 4,000-year-old tufts of hair found frozen in the permafrost at Qeqertasussuk, Greenland. The results showed that the closest living relatives of the Saqqaq are the Chukchis, who now live at the easternmost tip of Siberia, and that the owner of hair was a man with brown eyes, thick hair, and dry earwax, who was at risk of baldness in later life.

A few months later, teams led by Pääbo published two genome sequences. The first was Neandertal, using DNA from three different individuals who lived in Croatia about 38,000 years ago. The results proved that modern humans did interbreed with their Neandertal cousins, as traces of Neandertal DNA can still be seen in our genome today. The second was from a previously unknown human species that lived around the same time, using DNA from the tiny finger bone of a girl, found in a cave in the Altai Mountains of Siberia.

In 2012, a team led by Zink reported the genome sequence of Ötzi the Iceman, a 5,300-year-old mummy found frozen in the Central Eastern Alps. The DNA showed that he probably had brown eyes, type O blood, that he was lactose intolerant, and that his closest modern-day relatives now live in Sardinia and Corsica.

Willerslev is now trying to extra DNA from various mummies from south America (some preserved in warmer environments) to gain information about waves of human migration into the region, as well as from the Native American chief Sitting Bull—using a hair sample donated by his family in Dakota.

The techniques may work on Egyptian mummies too. In 2013, a team led by Pusch at Tübingen used them to sequence DNA from five human mummies held in the university's museum. Preliminary results suggest that one of the individuals may belong to an ancestral group that originated in Western Asia. They also retrieved genetic material from plants including linseed, almond, and lotus, and from the pathogens that cause toxoplasmosis and malaria.

This success suggests that in the future, it may possible to sequence entire genomes from ancient Egyptians. As next-generation technology becomes cheaper, scientists will in theory be able to sequence genomes of large numbers of mummies—moving beyond the study of individual relationships and character-istics to look at broader patterns of history and migration.

Jo Marchant

See also: Animal mummies; Cladh Hallan mummies; Crypt mummies of Sommersdorf Castle; Juanita, the Inca Ice Maiden; Ötzi the Iceman; Tutankhamun ("King Tut")

Further Reading

Aufderheide, Arthur, C. 2010. *The Scientific Study of Mummies.* Cambridge: Cambridge University Press.

Marchant, Jo. 2011. "Curse of the Pharaoh's DNA." *Nature,* April 27. http://www.nature.com/news/2011/110427/full/472404a.html.

Marchant, Jo. 2013. *The Shadow King: The Bizarre Afterlife of King Tut's Mummy.* Boston: Da Capo Press.

German Mummy Project

In 2004, during preparations for remodeling of some galleries, more than 20 human mummies were found in a basement storage area of the Reiss-Engelhorn Museums of Mannheim, Germany. Although museum documentation recorded the acquisition of the mummies from painter Gabriel von Max in the early

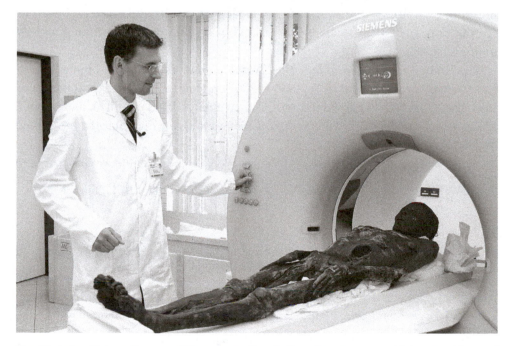

Dr. Christian Fink performs a CT scan on a female Egyptian mummy at University Hospital Mannheim, as part of the German Mummy Project. (AP Images/Manfred Rinderspacher)

1900s, all of the mummies were thought to have been lost during the heavy bombing sustained by Mannheim during World War II. A multidisciplinary collaborative research project that included biological anthropologists, radiologists, microbiologists, chemists and other scientists was formed to document and study the mummies. This collaborative research group was called the "German Mummy Project," based at the Reiss-Engelhorn Museums, with participating scientists from several countries and institutions. Mummies from museums and institutions beyond the Reiss-Engelhorn Museums mummies were included as the project expanded. The German Mummy Project ran on an informal basis until 2010, when Dr. Heather Gill-Frerking was appointed as the Scientific Research Curator to head the research.

The mandate of the German Mummy Project was three-fold: research, conservation and dissemination. The mummies were studied using gold-standard methods in the field of mummy studies, with a particular emphasis on medical imaging and restrictions on destructive testing. The mummies were also cleaned, repaired, and stabilized by an expert conservator, to ensure the long-term preservation of each individual. Although a mummy may have been preserved for centuries or millennia, deterioration will occur if the mummy is not properly conserved. The third part of the mandate of the German Mummy Project was the dissemination of the results of the research, both academically and publicly. The public aspect of dissemination came in the form of television documentaries and museum exhibitions that showcased the research results and discussed each of the mummy specimens in the wider context of discussions about mummies and mummification.

The first exhibition, *Mumien: Der Traum vom ewigen Leben*, opened at the Reiss-Engelhorn Museums in September 2007 and later toured to several museums in Germany and Italy. The exhibition was then enlarged and modified, and became *Mummies of the World: The Exhibition*, which toured several venues in the United States between 2010 and 2014.

Heather Gill-Frerking

See also: Medical imaging of mummies; Mummies of the World: The Exhibition

Further Reading

"German Mummy Project." *Mummies of the World: The Exhibition*. Accessed December 7, 2013. http://www.mummiesoftheworld.com/exhibition-preview/the-german-mummy-project.

Lobell, Jarrett A. 2010. "A Career in the Bogs." *Archaeology Magazine*, May 27. Accessed December 7, 2013. http://archive.archaeology.org/online/interviews/heather_gill_robinson.

Gliddon, George Robins

George Robins Gliddon was a British-born American diplomat and businessman, who is generally regarded as the first U.S. Egyptologist. He wrote and spoke extensively on the subject, including on mummification.

George Robins Gliddon was born in Devon, UK, on November 27, 1809, the son of John Gliddon, a merchant who became the first U.S. Vice-Consul (and then Consul) at Alexandria while his son was yet young. Growing up in Egypt, George went on to became U.S. Vice-Consul in Cairo, and through his business and Consular interests met many of the Egyptologists of the time. He was sent to the United States by the Ottoman Governor Muhammad Ali in 1838 to procure hardware for various industrial processing plants.

The Consulate closed in 1840, and Gliddon moved to the UK, where in 1841 he published a book on cotton, and another, the *Appeal to the Antiquaries of Europe on the Destruction of the Monuments of Egypt*, campaigning against the destruction of ancient monuments incidental to Muhammad Ali's industrialization program. Moving permanently to the United States in 1842, he began an extensive program of lecturing on ancient Egypt, beginning in Boston during 1842–1844. He subsequently undertook lecture tours as far west as Missouri, including the unwrapping of a crocodile mummy in Baltimore in 1845. Another was unwrapped in Boston in 1850 while Gliddon was touring an exhibition of a panoramic painting of the Nile, incorporating lectures and a display of antiquities. This unwrapping led to a degree of controversy when the mummy, confidently stated at the outset to be a "priestess," turned out, when exposed, to be a man. Two more bodies were unwrapped in 1851 in Philadelphia and a final mummy in New Orleans in 1852. Many of these mummies and their coffins were presented to local institutions, animal mummies also going from Gliddon to the Academy of Natural Sciences in Philadelphia.

At this same time, Gliddon was collaborating with the physician Josiah C. Nott (1804–1873) on *Types of Mankind* (1854), which built on the craniometric and polygenist theories of human origins of Samuel George Morton (1799–1851) that split humanity into separate species of varying intellectual capacities; Morton had dedicated his *Crania Ægyptiaca* (1844) to Gliddon. On his own, Gliddon produced a number of books on Egyptological subjects, including *Ancient Egypt: a series of chapters on early Egyptian history, archaeology and other subjects connected with hieroglyphical literature* (1843, with at least 15 later editions), and *Otia Aegyptiaca: Discourses on Egyptian Archaeology and Hieroglyphical Discoveries* (1849), which contained an extensive section on mummification.

Gliddon also made several visits to Europe and became acquainted with a wide range of European Egyptologists. In 1857 he became of Deputy Agent of the

Honduras Inter-Oceanic Railway in Honduras, but fell ill and died on November 16, 1857, in Panama while en route back to the United States on leave. Buried in Panama, his remains were later exhumed and reburied in Philadelphia.

Aidan Dodson

See also: Mummy unwrappings

Further Reading

Vivian, C. 2012. *Americans in Egypt, 1770–1915: Explorers, Consuls, Travelers, Soldiers, Missionaries, Writers and Scientists.* Jefferson NC: McFarland & Co.

Wolfe, S.J. 2009. *Mummies in Nineteenth Century America: Ancient Egyptians as Artifacts.* Jefferson, NC: McFarland & Co.

Grauballe Man

Grauballe Man is the name given to the body of a man who died in the early Iron Age in Denmark. His body was beautifully preserved because it was deposited in a peat bog, which was located just a few miles from where Tollund Man was discovered two years earlier. Though nearly two hundred "bog bodies" have been discovered in Denmark alone, few of the remains are as complete or as beautifully preserved as Grauballe Man (although Tollund Man is a notable exception). Grauballe Man's violent death and his almost perfectly preserved skin, hair, and nails have fascinated researchers and the public alike since he was unearthed. Irish poet Seamus Heaney penned "The Grauballe Man," a poem about the dramatic death and appearance Grauballe Man.

Grauballe Man was discovered in late April of 1952 in a bog near Silkeborg, Denmark, by some locals from the nearby village of Grauballe as they were cutting peat for fuel. Scientists were quickly informed, and the body was removed with a large chunk of the surrounding peat for further analysis. Because the peat cutters were not operating on an industrial scale, and because they notified experts so quickly, Grauballe Man suffered much less damage than many other bog bodies.

Grauballe Man was around the age of 30 when he died between about 400 and 200 BCE. He was probably about 5 ½ feet tall, and was strong and mostly healthy, though he did suffer from periodontal disease and a calcium deficiency, as well as the early stages of age-related degeneration (often referred to as rheumatoid arthritis) in his spine. The preservation of his hands indicated that he probably did little, if any, manual labor during his life. He had thick hair which may have been brown during life, but has been dyed red by the chemicals in the bog. No trace of clothing was found, not even an imprint of long decayed linen or plant fibers, suggesting that he was indeed naked or that his clothing had been laid nearby and decayed over the centuries. The position of his body indicates that the bog held water when he was placed there, and that he sank to the bottom of the bog quite slowly,

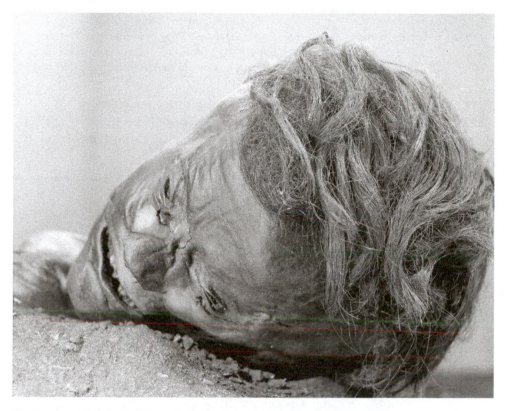

The head of Grauballe Man, who was violently killed c. 400–200 BCE by a cut to the throat from ear to ear. Possibly the victim of a sacrifice, he was perfectly preserved in a peat bog in Jutland, Denmark. (Werner Forman/Getty Images)

suggesting that Grauballe Man was dumped in the bog during the colder months. This is further strengthened by the fact that his last meal contained no fruits or greens, which could indicate that his meal was prepared during the winter or early spring, when none of these would have been available.

Like some other bog bodies found in Denmark and throughout Europe, Grauballe Man suffered a violent death. His throat was viciously cut with a single deep slice from ear to ear, which severed his esophagus, trachea, and several vital arteries, before he was thrown into the bog face-down. Although scholars at first believed that Grauballe Man's cranium and leg had been broken during his execution, more recent analysis has determined that these breaks actually occurred postmortem (i.e., after death), as the weight of the peat over the centuries slowly crushed the body. Given the violence, time of death (many festivals took place during the winter and early spring months), and the deposition of his body in a bog (a location closely tied to Norse mythology), Grauballe Man was probably the victim of human sacrifice.

1952	Grauballe Man is discovered on April 26 in a peat bog near Silkeborg, Denmark. Scientists are alerted and the body is soon removed, encased in a chunk of its surrounding peat, and transported to a museum in Aarhus for autopsy (including X-rays) and preservation.
1955	Grauballe Man is placed on display in the Moesgaard Museum in Aarhus.
2001	New research is conducted on Grauballe Man using CT scanning, 3D modeling, endoscopy, and spectroscopy, yielding new information not only about Grauballe Man but about life in Early Iron Age Denmark.

Extensive scientific examinations were carried out after the discovery of Grauballe Man. An autopsy was conducted to study the state of his organs and general health. The autopsy determined that, like Tollund Man, Grauballe Man's last meal consisted of a gruel or soup made of grains, seeds, and herbs, though with the addition of a small amount of meat. X-rays revealed the early stages of age degeneration in Grauballe Man's lower spine, as well as the decreased calcium of his bones. The papillary lines (i.e., small grooves and ridges) on Grauballe Man's hands and feet were so well-preserved that viewers at first doubted the body was actually ancient, but researchers used carbon-14 (C-14) dating to determine that he had indeed lived and died during the Early Iron Age.

In 2001, additional research was conducted on Grauballe Man using less invasive, state-of-the-art technology such as CT scanning, 3D modeling, endoscopy, and spectroscopy. Extensive and meticulous examinations of every aspect of Grabaulle Man provided volumes of information not only about Grauballe Man himself, but about what life was like during the Early Iron Age in Denmark.

The low temperature and high acidity of a peat bog combine to halt the decay process of human remains, so as soon as the body is exposed to heat and oxygen the decay process starts up again. To study and conserve bog bodies, a great deal of care and research is necessary. To preserve Grauballe Man, the tanning process begun in the bog was completed by human researchers. Various types of oil, distilled water, exposure to air, and the addition of preservatives such as glycerin and lanolin into Grauballe Man's skin also stabilized the body. More modern studies analyzed the effectiveness of these methods and improved them when possible.

Grauballe Man is currently on display at the Moesgaard Museum in Aarhus, Denmark. Since a plaster cast was made of the body as it was found before conservation, it is possible to display Grauballe Man in the same position in which he was found.

Roselyn Campbell

See also: Bog bodies; Medical imaging of mummies; Natural mummification; Tollund Man

Further Reading

Asingh, Pauline, and Niels Lynnerup, eds. 2007. *Grauballe Man: An Iron Age Bog Body Revisited*. Jutland Archaeological Society and Moesgaard Museum.

Glob, P.V. 1969. *The Bog People: Iron-Age Man Preserved*. Translated by Rupert Bruce-Mitford. Ithaca, New York: Cornell University Press.

Lauring, Palle. 1957. *Land of the Tollund Man: The Prehistory and Archaeology of Denmark*. Translated by Reginald Spink. London: Lutterworth Press.

Lobell, Jarrett A., and Samir S. Patel. 2010. "Bog Bodies Rediscovered." *Archaeology* 3 (May/June. Accessed October 23, 2013). http://archive.archaeology.org/1005/bogbodies/.

Sanders, Karin. 2009. *Bodies in the Bog and the Archaeological Imagination*. Chicago: University of Chicago Press.

van der Sanden, Wijnand. 1996. *Through Nature to Eternity: The Bog Bodies of Northwest Europe*. Translated by Susan J. Mellor. Amsterdam: Batavian Lion International.

Greenhill, Thomas

Thomas Greenhill was an English surgeon and the author of an important book on embalming, which includes one of the earliest scholarly treatments of Egyptian mummification.

He was the son of William Greenhill (d. 1681) and his wife Elizabeth Jones, being their seventh son and thirty-ninth child, all born living; however, although born after his father's death, Thomas's date of birth is uncertain, as are many facets of his life. He lived in King Street, Bloomsbury, London, where he produced his book Νεκροκηδεια, *or, The art of embalming; wherein is shown the right of burial, and funeral ceremonies, especially that of preserving bodies after the Egyptian method*, published in 1705 by subscription, and dedicated to Thomas Herbert, Eighth Earl of Pembroke (c 1656–1733). The 217 subscribers included 34 surgeons, 18 physicians and 12 apothecaries, reflecting the aim of the book, which was to professionalize embalming by making surgeons its principal practitioners, as well as to encourage more of the nobility to have their bodies embalmed. The book is arranged in three parts, or "letters," respectively on the rites of burial and funeral customs; on Egyptian embalming techniques and their cultural and geographical context; and an "Account of the Pyramids, Subterranean Vaults and Lamps of the Egyptians."

Greenhill appears to have he died in 1740.

Aidan Dodson

See also: Embalming

Further Reading

Davidson, L. A. F. 2004. "Greenhill, Thomas (fl. 1698–1732)." In Oxford *Dictionary of National Biography* 23: 601–2. Oxford: Oxford University Press.

H

Haggard, H. Rider

H. Rider Haggard was an English writer of the late nineteenth century who wrote many popular novels of exotic adventure—most famously, *King Solomon's Mines* (1885) and the subsequent Allan Quatermain series. He was an amateur egyptologist, and several of his works display a fascination with ancient Egyptian exoticism. Of these, many of his works explicitly involve mummies, and his treatment of the theme proved seminally influential on the genre.

Henry Rider Haggard was born on June 22, 1856, at Wood Farm in West Bradenham, Norfolk, to barrister William Haggard and amateur poet Ella Doventon Haggard. His fascination with Egypt started early: the boy is believed to have become familiar with William Tyssen-Amherst's (1835–1909) extensive collection of Egyptian artifacts and mummies at nearby Didlington Hall.

After failing the army entrance examination, Haggard took an unpaid position as a secretary to Sir Henry Bulwer, Lieutenant-Governor of the British colony of Natal in southeastern Africa. Haggard went to Natal in 1875. In 1876 he joined the staff of Sir Theophilus Shepstone, and was with Shepstone when he annexed the Boer republic of Transvaal for Britain. In 1878 Haggard became Registrar of the High Court in the Transvaal.

Haggard moved back to England permanently in 1881. He attempted to practice law, but also began writing fiction. Two unsuccessful novels were published in 1884 (*Dawn*—in which a female character is obsessed with her private collection of mummies and artifacts—and *The Witch's Head*). Then, inspired by Robert Louis Stevenson's *Treasure Island* and using his knowledge of Africa, Haggard wrote *King Solomon's Mines*. An adventurous tale of treasure hunters searching for a legendary diamond mine in a lost land, the book became a bestseller. As the first "lost world" novel—a subgenre in which many others have since written—it created, in protagonist Allan Quatermain, the archetypal adventurer.

No mummies are in *King Solomon's Mines*, but it does depict the discovery of a cathedral-like cave called the Hall of the Dead, where a dynasty of 27 rulers—seated at a table—are naturally preserved as stalactites.

First serialized in *The Graphic* from October 1886 to January 1887, *She: A History of Adventure* was Haggard's next (and equally successful) novel. Although not about mummies, *She* has several parallels to Victorian mummy fiction, and it influenced mummy stories that came after. The novel involves

[A] tall figure stood before us. I say a figure, for not only the body, but also the face was wrapped up in soft white, gauzy material in such a way as at first sight to remind me most forcibly of a corpse in its grave-clothes. And yet I do not know why it should have given me that idea, seeing that the wrappings were so thin that one could distinctly see the gleam of the pink flesh beneath them. I suppose it was owing to the way in which they were arranged, either accidentally, or more probably by design. Anyhow, I felt more frightened than ever at this ghost-like apparition, and my hair began to rise upon my head as the feeling crept over me that I was in the presence of something that was not canny. I could, however, clearly distinguish that the swathed mummy-like form before me was that of a tall and lovely woman, instinct with beauty in every part, and also with a certain snake-like grace which I had never seen anything to equal before. When she moved a hand or foot her entire frame seemed to undulate, and the neck did not bend, it curved.

"Why art thou so frightened, stranger?" asked the sweet voice again—a voice which seemed to draw the heart out of me, like the strains of softest music. "Is there that about me that should affright a man? Then surely are men changed from what they used to be!" And with a little coquettish movement she turned herself, and held up one arm, so as to show all her loveliness and the rich hair of raven blackness that streamed in soft ripples down her snowy robes, almost to her sandalled feet.

—From *She: A History of Adventure* by H. Rider Haggard

near-immortality, love stretching across centuries, and a fascination with well-preserved corpses. Reincarnation is the core of the story. Both widely imitated and widely parodied, *She* was the first "karmic romance"—a genre in which characters are serially incarnated, ever seeking redemption. The villain Ayesha was a new ideation of the *femme fatale*, powerful but not wholly evil; domineering, yet submissive in her undying love.

The books made Haggard wealthy and famous. He traveled extensively, including making four trips to Egypt.

With his 11th book, *Cleopatra: An Account of the Fall and Vengeance of Harmachis* (1889), Haggard returned to the themes of reincarnation and Egypt. The novel begins with the robbery of a tomb, followed by the discovery of an unusual mummy that was evidently entombed alive. The embalmed also appear in several other novels. In *The Yellow God: An Idol of Africa* (1908), Asika, a queen who has been continuously reincarnated for centuries and had many husbands, takes an English adventurer to a hall filled with "hundreds of golden men with gleaming eyes . . . now they were corpses wrapped in sheets of thin gold and wearing golden masks with eyes of crystal. . ." (Haggard 2012, 178). In yet another novel of reincarnation and romance, *The Wanderer's Necklace* (1914), a Viking-era Dane dreams of a past life in ancient Egypt. His beloved, evading Roman soldiers, flees to a tomb where she hides in the coffin that once held the mummy of her ancestress. *Queen Sheba's Ring* (1910) features a character, Professor Ptolemy Higgs, who owns a collection of antiquities, including a couple of mummies. The narrator encounters Higgs after the professor has spent the afternoon unwrapping a mummy. *Morning Star* (1910), set in ancient Egypt, incorporates a ritual in which a mummy is brought to a feast and a toast concerning the brevity of life is made.

Egypt was the setting of other works, but Haggard's only story with a true mummy theme was the novella "Smith and the Pharaohs," published as a serial in *The Strand* between December 1912 and February 1913. On a visit to the British Museum, the "Smith" of the title becomes infatuated with a sculptured head of an Egyptian queen and is inspired to take up Egyptology. He eventually locates the tomb of Queen Ma-Mé, the woman whose face he admired. Smith finds a mummified hand bearing two rings and takes his discoveries to the Cairo Museum. He is allowed to keep the mummified hand and one of the rings. He later finds himself locked in the museum overnight and—either through dream or magic—witnesses ancient royals, including his Queen Ma-Mé, coming to life and conversing. Although similar to earlier works by others, Haggard—personally conflicted by the exploitation of antiquities and violation of tombs, yet himself a collector and amateur Egyptologist—justifies Smith's modern transgressions by revealing him as a reincarnation of an ancient sculptor of royal blood.

Shaped by his colonial experience (and that of two brothers who fought in Egypt and the Sudan), Haggard viewed imperialism as a necessity. Despite cultural patronizing, Haggard traveled widely and realized the dangers of European intrusion; innately racist, he still admired Africans and Zulu culture. He was a Christian who also believed in reincarnation.

Haggard was knighted in 1912 for his research and work in agricultural reform. He died on May 14, 1925. His 68 novels and handful of shorter fiction appealed to the masses in his day and continue to influence popular fiction and film.

Paula Guran

See also: The mummy in Western fiction: Beginnings to 1922

Further Reading

Burgdett, Carol. 2004. "Romance, Reincarnation, and Rider Haggard." In *The Victorian Supernatural,* edited by Nicola Bown, Carolyn Burdett, and Pamela Thurschwell. Cambridge: Cambridge University Press.

Frost, Brian J. 2007. *The Essential Guide to Mummy Literature*. Lanham, MD: Scarecrow Press.

Haggard, H. Rider. 2000. *Diary of an African Journey: The Return of Rider Haggard.* Edited by Stephen Cohen. New York: New York University Press.

Haggard, H. Rider. 2006. *King Solomon's Mines.* Accessed December 31, 2013. http://www.gutenberg.org/ebooks/2166.

Haggard, H. Rider. 2006. *Smith and the Pharaohs and Other Tales.* Accessed December 31, 2013. http://www.gutenberg.org/files/6073.

Haggard, H. Rider. 2008. *She: A History of Adventure*. Edited by Daniel Karlin. Oxford: Oxford University Press.

Luckhurst, Roger. 2012. *The Mummy's Curse: The True History of a Dark Fantasy*. Oxford: Oxford University Press.

Stableford, Brian. 2005. "Haggard, H[enry] Rider." In *Supernatural Literature of the World: An Encyclopedia, Vol. 2, G-O*, edited by S.T. Joshi and Stefan Dziemianowicz. Westport, CT: Greenwood Press.

Hammer Films mummy series

In the late 1950s Hammer Films in England began updating the classic "monster" films of Universal Studios' Hollywood heyday. Just as Universal had made horror icons of Bela Lugosi and Boris Karloff, Hammer was to do the same for Peter Cushing and Christopher Lee. The Hammer style, however, was quite distinct, featuring bright color and intense action, trending to increased gore and nudity as the 1960s and 1970s progressed. Following the success of their initial Frankenstein and Dracula entries in 1957 and 1958, Hammer turned to the mummy, just as Universal had done in 1932.

The Mummy (1959), starring Cushing and Lee, has been discussed in detail elsewhere in this volume as a separate entry, but as the initial entry in the Hammer mummy series it deserves mention here. Unlike other Hammer and Universal films, the characters and screenplay were not based on a classic work of horror literature. Universal's 1932 *The Mummy* had been an original story, though it certainly owed elements of plot, which were uncredited, to earlier works, including Rider Haggard's *She* (1887). The later series from Universal featured the mummy Kharis, very different from Karloff's Imhotep, and there displayed elements seemingly derivative of Arthur Conan Doyle's mummy story "Lot No. 249" (1892). Despite its title, Hammer's first mummy film is not a remake of the Karloff film, but an intriguing mix of elements, scenes and characters from all of the previous Universal films, with additional original touches, such as the late Victorian setting.

Britain's Hammer Films, a.k.a. Hammer Studios, was founded in the 1930s and had already produced many movies by the time the 1950s rolled around, but, beginning with their 1957 movie *Curse of Frankenstein*, it was their reimaginings of the classic Universal Studios horror films of the 1930s and 1940s that made them legendary. Today the "Hammer Horror" brand is an iconic part of cinema history. Along with nine Dracula movies, seven Frankenstein movies, a werewolf movie, and many more, they produced four mummy movies between 1959 and 1974. The first one, 1959's *The Mummy*, was not simply a remake of Universal's classic 1932 film of the same title but a combination of elements from many Universal films, along with newly added touches. The last, 1971's *Blood from the Mummy's Tomb*, was an adaptation of Bram Stoker's classic mummy novel *The Jewel of Seven Stars*.

Maggie Kimberly fends off an attack from the mummy, played by Eddie Powell, in a scene from *The Mummy's Shroud*, directed by John Gilling for Hammer Films. (Express Newspapers/Getty Images)

Hammer did not follow the pattern set by Universal with its follow-up mummy films. Rather than produce a cycle of repetitive Kharis films, as they did with Frankenstein and Dracula well into the 1970s, Hammer made fewer mummy films, but each was unique, at least within certain conventions of plot and characterization that had become the studio's trademarks.

The Curse of the Mummy's Tomb, 1964, was written and directed by Michael Carreras, the executive producer at Hammer who had introduced science fiction and horror into their program in the mid-1950s. This deceptively simple story follows several surprising strands in its brisk 78-minute span. In 1900 Egypt the royal tomb and mummy of fictional prince Ra-Antef, son of the historical Rameses VIII, has just been found. The film starts abruptly with the brutal murder of one of the lead archaeologists. Before this gruesome event had had time to sink in, the financial backer, Alexander King, a Barnum-like showman played by brash American character actor Fred Clark, announces his plans to get rich traveling with the finds on a world tour. Protests are immediate, both from the Egyptian authorities, represented by Hashmi Bey, played by George Pastell, the modern "priest" familiar for reviving Kharis in 1959, and by the staid British archaeologist Sir Giles Dalrymple. The younger archaeologist, John Bray, played by Ronald Howard, the son of noted actor Leslie Howard, is engaged to the murdered archaeologist's daughter, Annette Dubois, and they somewhat reservedly go along with King's scheme.

During the voyage back to England the archaeologists are assaulted in a search of their staterooms. The young woman is assisted by Adam Beauchamp (pronounced Beachum), who offers to house them in England in return for associating with their work. He is told of the legend of Ra-Antef and his dissolute brother Be, who had him killed. Next we are shown a medallion, an apparent miniature of the actual Narmer palette with hieroglyphs added, that had not been found in the tomb but given to Annette by her father just before his murder. While researching this piece in Dalrymple's library, Bray is attacked by an unseen assailant and it is stolen.

At King's first show for the press, we see details of the discovery, a combination of replicas from King Tut's tomb, including objects from the earlier 1959 film, and wall scenes from the tomb of Queen Nefertari. The coffin, which earlier had been opened privately and had held the mummy, is now mysteriously empty. As he makes his way home through the fog, King is suddenly confronted by the mummy, choked, and unceremoniously tossed down several steps into the Thames. Meanwhile Bray has gone to visit Hashmi, whom he suspects of the medallion's and mummy's thefts, but this turns out to be a false lead. At the same time, the mummy has crashed through the French windows of Dalrymple's study, in a scene reminiscent of the attack on Peter Cushing five years earlier; in this instance, despite unloading his pistol into the mummy, the older archaeologist receives a crushed skull.

Next the mummy arrives at Beauchamp's home and begins strangling him, but fails to kill him when Annette, now in love with Beauchamp, distracts him. Inexplicably, the mummy leaves, after which Bray, Hashmi, and the police arrive. The heroes and villains are getting confusing at this point, which was likely the point, but it does not work well in maintaining interest. Back at Dalrymple's home a trap is set for the mummy to attack Bray, but Ra breaks a police rope net like so much string and stomps the head of Hashmi (simply to increase the body count?), but then leaves without bothering Bray.

Beauchamp next reveals to Annette, in his basement "museum" filled with Egyptian artifacts in pristine condition, that he is actually Be, the man who murdered his brother Ra-Antef, the mummy. Their father cursed Be to eternal life unless Ra-Antef, himself dead, could personally end Be's eternal existence. The medallion had been stolen by him as it contained the sacred Words of Life with which he could resurrect his brother, not just to destroy those who desecrated the tomb, but more importantly to end his increasingly miserable life. In a sewer under his home, Beauchamp is stopped from killing Annette but does achieve the death he desires at his brother's hand. Ra-Antef then pulls the solid stone ceiling down on himself, recalling the finale of the last Universal Kharis film 20 years earlier, *The Mummy's Curse* (1944).

This film differs from standard living mummy fare in one major respect. The seemingly straightforward title refers not solely to the obvious curse on those who open a mummy's tomb, a point made glibly by King throughout the first half of the movie, but to the curse of endless life placed on Be by his father. At the film's climax it is this curse that is seen to be paramount—not the curse of death, but of life. This theme had been explored in literature before, perhaps most notably in Conan Doyle's 1890 story "The Ring of Thoth," which some have seen as partial inspiration for the 1932 Karloff film. Doyle's tale, however, is more akin to the current 1964 film under discussion, centering on a man doomed to eternal life until the newly excavated mummy of his beloved is placed in a museum from which her ring containing a substance to end his life can be recovered. Tangentially, another imitation of Doyle's plot—in fact a blatant one—appeared in a 1932 story by pulp writer Arlton Eadie, "The Nameless Mummy," in which the genders were reversed and the lovers were Cleopatra and Marc Antony.

Filmed just two years later, *The Mummy's Shroud*, 1967, directed by John Gilling, begins with a lengthy omniscient narration of another ancient Egyptian rivalry between two royal brothers, the murder of the king, and the escape of his son Kah-to-bey, with the aid of the loyal slave Prem, from his pursuing uncle. On the arduous journey into the desert, the boy dies and is given a medallion which appears to be the same prop used in the previous movie. He is covered in a shroud (looking more like a small throw rug) and buried in this remote locale by Prem. Along with the opening credits, this sequence covers the first 10 minutes of the 90 minute running time.

A 1920 expedition has found a mummy originally considered Ka-to-bey but now believed to be Prem; this mummy is modeled exactly after an unnamed mummy to be seen then, as now, in the British Museum. We learn that a new expedition in search of the boy mummy has gone missing. The arrogant business-man Stanley Preston, played by John Phillips, who has underwritten and taken credit for everything, has arrived in Egypt, as his son Paul is among the missing archaeological team. Just as the tomb of the young prince is found, Preston arrives with a rescue party, though by this time head archaeologist Sir Basil Walden, played by Andre Morell, has been threatened by an Arab claiming to guard the tomb and subsequently bitten by a poisonous snake. Played by Maggie Kimberley in apparently her only starring role, the attractive female linguist Claire, whose name mirrors her apparent clairvoyance, is hesitant to translate the sacred words of Life and Death on the shroud.

Back in civilization, the two mummies are reunited. Meanwhile, Preston's megalomania leads to Walden's incarceration in an asylum and his eventual escape, to be hunted as a lunatic. He is found by a fortune teller, who happens to be the mother of the tomb guardian who reads the shroud, thus bringing Prem's mummy back to life. Walden is killed by the mummy as the old lady cacklingly predicted, and Preston, on hearing of this and the shroud's disappearance, decides it is time to leave Egypt. As further murders occur, novel ways are tried to stop the mummy, from hydrochloric acid, to attempted impaling with a camera tripod, to attack with a fire axe. The murder of Preston's assistant, played by regular Hammer character actor Michael Ripper, is tinged with a certain pathos, but the death of Preston, for which the viewer is rooting, comes as an anticlimax. As Prem goes on a final rampage after the last two desecrators of the tomb, Claire reads the Words of Death in the "ancient tongue" (which sounds more Arabic than Egyptian), leading Prem to destroy himself by crushing his own head to dust with his bare hands.

Both of the mid-1960s Hammer mummy films have elements of interest, though neither is as satisfying as the initial Hammer offering in 1959. A big part of this stems from the repeated use of by then standard plot devices, such as the illogicality of placing the means of the mummy's resurrection within immediate access to the mummy itself. A second weakness is that these mummies seem only to attack one victim at a time, then return to somnolence until called on again. Even the Hammer publicity department gave up on the possibility of anyone treating this as serious horror, and adopted the campy slogan "Beware the Beat of the Cloth-Wrapped Feet." With a little creativity, more original approaches to the mummy-as-monster genre could be forthcoming. Still, at least one writer has seen the repetitiveness of the mummy on film as part of its strength, the sequels providing "a resonant structure for his eternal return" (Kawin 2012, 132).

Hammer's fourth and final entry in the mummy series, *Blood from the Mummy's Tomb*, which was filmed in 1971, with a fall UK release but general distribution the following year, has been discussed with the entry on Bram Stoker's *The Jewel of Seven Stars*, the novel on which it is based. Though this is the only Hammer mummy film credited as an adaptation of a literary work, the mummified Tera, a beautiful but unwrapped duplicate of Margaret, recalls Ananka/Isobel from Hammer's 1959 mummy as much as anything in the Stoker novel. Margaret and her father are named Fuchs rather than Trelawney (for reasons that are unclear), but her boyfriend is Tod Browning, an apparent homage to the director of the 1931 film *Dracula*. Originally set to star, Peter Cushing had to abandon the project after the first day's filming when his wife became ill. With a week's shooting left, director Seth Holt died of a heart attack, and the film was completed by Michael Carreras. The end result is a film that many consider to be a confusing and disjointed effort. Some have called it cursed. Stoker's source novel, however, suffers from similar deficiencies, as evidenced by its disparate endings, and is clearly a challenge to translate successfully to film.

Carter Lupton

See also: Doyle, Arthur Conan; Haggard, H. Rider; *The Jewel of Seven Stars*; Lee, Christopher; *The Mummy* (1932); *The Mummy* (1959); Mummy movies; Universal Studios mummy series

Further Reading

Glut, Donald F. 1978. *Classic Movie Monsters*. Metuchen, NJ: The Scarecrow Press.

Halliwell, Leslie. 1986. *The Dead That Walk*. London: Grafton Books.

Hearn, Marcus, and Alan Barnes. 2007. *The Hammer Story: The Authorised History of Hammer Films*. Foreword by Christopher Lee. London: Titan Books.

Hunter, Jack. 2000. *House of Horror: The Complete Hammer Films Story*. 3rd ed. London: Creation Books.

Kawin, Bruce F. 2012. *Horror and the Horror Film*. London and New York: Anthem Press.

Landis, John. 2011. *Monsters in the Movies: 100 Years of Cinematic Nightmares*. New York: DK Publishing.

Lupton, Carter. 2003. "Mummymania for the Masses: Is Egyptology Cursed by the Mummy's Curse?" In *Consuming Ancient Egypt*, edited by Sally MacDonald and Michael Rice, 23–46. London: UCL Press.

Hierakonpolis

The ancient city of Hierakonpolis was an important political and religious center of Upper Egypt at the end of the predynastic and early dynastic time (4000–2800 BCE), and was important to the evolving practice of Egyptian mummification. The ancient name of the settlement was nḫn ("Nekhen"). Horus of Nekhen, a hawk deity was worshipped here, from which the Greek name Hierakonpolis originates: Ἱεράκων πόλις (hierakōn polis) "City of the hawks" (today: Al-Kom Al-Ahmar). The city is situated on the western side of the Nile, about 17 kilometers northwest of Edfu and about opposite to the city Elkab.

Naqada and Hierakonpolis were the cultural spot and settlement centers of the predynastic Naqada II period (ca. 3500–3200 BCE). Excavations in Abydos and Hierakonpolis clearly demonstrated the indigenous Upper Egyptian roots of the early civilization in Egypt. Contact with foreign countries existed, but there was no invasion. During the Naqada II period the city of Hierakonpolis became a burial ground of local elite, while the rulers had their tombs in Abydos. The nobility of Hierakonpolis called themselves the "Followers of Horus," in keeping with the city's role as home to a localized Horus cult. The importance for death and mummification rituals can be seen in the *Book of the Dead*, where in one spell the deceased declares himself to be one of these "Followers of Horus," in the double meaning of being a loyal subject to the king and the living incarnation of Horus. In his local appearance, the god Horus was worshipped from the dawn of Egyptian culture (First Dynasty) as the national god of Egypt and was closely related to the divine kingship. The Pharaohs regarded themselves as incarnation of Horus. In this early form Horus was considered to be the brother, not the son, of Isis and Osiris (regarding whom, see their respective articles in this volume).

Detail from the decorated mace head of King Scorpion, found at Hierakonpolis. (Werner Forman/Getty Images)

Hierakonpolis became one of the most important cities of Upper Egypt in the early dynasties. Later it declined to a local capital of the Third Upper Egypt Nome (District), but it remained important as a cult center. The city was of special importance during the Old, Middle and New Kingdoms. Today most of the buildings are destroyed, except for 22 New Kingdom tombs.

Hierakonpolis probably influenced the evolution of mummification. The deceased in the Predynastic Period were laid to rest in embryo-like position in oval pits and covered with sand, and the arid climate, combined with the hot and salty sand, often caused natural mummification. One female burial at Hierakonpolis (HK43, burial 85, from about 3500 BCE) shows early attempts to support natural mummification by artificial means: the limbs were fixed with bandages so that the body would not lose them, and one internal organ was removed, wrapped, and replaced to the thorax.

Hierakonpolis tomb 100, in the Wadi Abdul Suffian near Hierakonpolis, is considered to be the oldest Egyptian tomb in existence that features painted decoration on its walls, dating to Naqada II. It was discovered 1899 by F. W. Green. Thus, archaeological exploration at Hierakonpolis literally digs into the dawn, the earliest beginnings, of Egyptian culture.

Some important archaeological findings have come from the city, including the decorated mace-head of King Scorpion (Dynasty 0a, ca. 3250 BCE) and the famous palette of King Narmer (First Dynasty), found in the Horus temple by James E. Quibell in 1898. Quibell also found a life-sized copper statue of King Pepi I Meryre (ca. 2332–2283 BCE) and a golden falcon head of Horus from the Sixth Dynasty. These all underline the great importance of Hierakonpolis for the divine kingship.

Recent findings (in the year 2000) by Barbara Adams in tomb 23 at Hierakonpolis include pieces of a once life-sized statue of a man or a god and a statuette of an ibex. The most exotic finding of the predynastic cemetery is the distinctive teeth and bones of elephants (in tombs 13 and 23). Even some skin from the elephants has survived for about 5,500 years. Obviously, the city's rulers must have been rich and powerful enough to keep such exotic animals.

Hierakonpolis remains one of the most important archaeological sites for providing insight into the earliest foundations of ancient Egyptian society and culture.

Michael E. Habicht

See also: *Book of the Dead*; Egyptian mummification methods; Isis; Osiris; Seth

Further Reading

Adams, Barbara. 1976. "Ancient Hierakonpolis." *Bibliotheca Orientalis* 33: 24–25.

Adams, Barbara. 1987. *The Fort Cemetery at Hierakonpolis*. Studies in Egyptology. London: KPI.

Archaeology's Interactive Dig: Hierakonpolis. Accessed December 7, 2013. http://interactive.archaeology.org/hierakonpolis.

Rose, Mark. 2005. "Special Report: New Finds from the Elite Cemetery." *Archaeology*, April 22. Accessed December 7, 2013. http://archive.archaeology.org/online/features/hierakonpolis.

Shaw, Ian. 2003. *The Oxford History of Ancient Egypt*. New York: Oxford University Press.

Howard, Robert E.

Almost all of the writings by Texas author Robert E. Howard (1906–1936) appeared in pulp magazines, particularly *Weird Tales*, with which he is often strongly identified. From July 1925 until his suicide in June 1936, Howard appeared in *Weird Tales* no fewer than 81 times, with letters, poems, short stories, and serials; many additional pieces appeared posthumously.

Robert Ervin Howard was born in Peaster, Texas, on January, 1906, the only child of Hester Jane Ervin and Dr. Isaac Mordecai Howard. A highly intelligent child, he read widely and voraciously: his accounts describe breaking into schoolhouses to steal the books, and he read as many of the pulp magazines as he could, analyzing the stories in *Adventure*, the leading pulp magazine of the time. Howard's stories and outgoing personality made him popular with his readers, and he formed literary friendships with a number of the writers appearing in *Weird Tales*, including H. P. Lovecraft, Clark Ashton Smith, August Derleth, and E. Hoffmann Price. By the age of 30, Howard had achieved some literary success. His fiction made him the highest earning resident of Cross Plains, Texas, the small town in which he lived with his parents, and he was strong and vigorous: he boxed, wrestled, and—like Conan the Barbarian, his most famous creation—he seemed to enjoy his life to the fullest. He was a moody man, however, and perhaps mentally ill; Price said that Howard believed enemies were after him, though none were noted. Howard was also morbidly devoted to his mother and had threatened suicide

Xaltotun screamed inhumanly and rushed around the altar, dagger lifted; but from somewhere—out of the sky, perhaps, or the great jewel that blazed in the hand of Hadrathus—shot a jetting beam of blinding blue light. Full against the breast of Xaltotun it flashed, and the hills reechoed the concussion. The wizard of Acheron went down as though struck by a thunderbolt, and before he touched the ground he was fearfully altered. Beside the altar-stone lay no fresh-slain corpse, but a shriveled mummy, a brown, dry, unrecognizable carcass sprawling among moldering swathings.

Somberly old Zeiata looked down.

"He was not a living man," she said. "The Heart lent him a false aspect of life, that deceived even himself. I never saw him as other than a mummy."

—From *The Hour of the Dragon*, a.k.a. *Conan the Conqueror*, by Robert E. Howard

when she died. Concerned friends had taken away his gun, but on June 11, 1936, when Howard learned that his mother had entered terminal coma, he obtained another gun and shot himself. His mother died the next day.

As a professional writer, Howard tailored his fiction to specific magazines and their likely audience, and for *Weird Tales* many of his stories contained elements of the fantastic, and not a few made use of reanimated corpses and mummies, the two sometimes merging, as in "The Horror from the Mound" (*Weird Tales*, May 1932), which begins as a standard western, but by the time of its conclusion, the story's protagonist, Steve Brill, is involved in a life or death struggle with a Spanish *Conquistador,* a desiccated mummified vampire, newly emerged from the mound in which it has been imprisoned.

In general, Howard's mummies have simple wants: to conquer the world, kill all who would stand in the way, and enslave the survivors. This is the story of Howard's "Skull-Face" (*Weird Tales*, October–December 1929). Narrated by Steve Costigan (a name often used by Howard), it begins with Costigan as a drug addict, rescued from his addiction and recruited by a mysterious and dimly glimpsed skull-faced man. Soon enough, Costigan discovers that he saw correctly, for this man, Kathulos of Egypt, has "a skull to which no vestige of flesh seemed to remain but on which taut brownish-yellow skin grew fast, etching out every detail of that terrible death's head" (Howard 1946, 136), and as the story progresses, Kathulos is revealed to be a mummy from Atlantis. His plan is "the overthrow of the white races! His ultimate aim is a black empire, with himself as emperor of the world!" (Howard 1946, 155). Kathulos's arsenal includes a variety of psychic resources, and he can escape capture by apparently instantly resuming the form of an inanimate mummy and hiding in a mummy case, though his pursuers ultimately recognize this ruse. As one of them states, "mummies seem to weave a weird dance through the warp of the tale"

(Howard 1946, 167), a violent mangling of a metaphor that Kathulos himself might approve had he not perished in an explosion that leveled much of London.

The above formulation—conquer, kill, enslave—is also the ultimate plan of Thugra Khotan in "Black Colossus" (*Weird Tales*, June 1933), who lay long in his tomb, "awaiting the day of awakening and release" (Howard 2003, 183). Thugra Khotan has set his sights on beautiful princess Yasmela, but she has enlisted a young mercenary, Conan, against whose sword Thugra Khotan cannot stand. Evidently recognizing that the idea of reanimated villainy was too good to throw away, Howard revisited it in his only novel to feature Conan, *The Hour of the Dragon* (*Weird Tales*, December 1935–April 1936). Set in Howard's Hyborian world, the novel begins with the mummy Xaltotun of Python being reanimated by plotters who would use him to further their cause but who rapidly lose control over him. Xaltotun begins his drive toward global supremacy by overthrowing the king of neighboring Aquilonia, "the most renowned warrior among the western nations . . . an outlander, an adventurer who seized the crown by force during a time of civil strife" (Howard 2004a, 89): Conan. The majority of the novel consists of Conan escaping captivity and pursuing the magical Heart of Ahriman, the jewel that was used to reanimate Xaltotun but which has since been stolen. To his credit, Howard chose to avoid a physical conflict between Conan and Xaltotun; instead, while Conan is still on the battlefield, Xaltotun is confronted by Hadratha, a benign priest of Mitra, and Zelata, a powerful witch woman who commands wolves, and it is she who delivers the final lines over Xaltotun: "he was not a living man . . . the Heart [of Ahriman] lent him a false aspect of life, that deceived even himself. I never saw him as other than a mummy" (Howard 2004a, 250).

Conan and a mummy also figure in "The Jewels of Gwahlur" (*Weird Tales*, March 1935; original title, "The Servants of Bit Yakin"), an earlier adventure in Conan's life. He has entered the secluded kingdom of Keshan in search of the treasure known as the Teeth of Gwahlur and hoping to offer his services in a battle against the neighboring kingdom of Punt. Others are also seeking the treasure, however, and are preparing an alliance with Punt to attack and loot Keshan. Gorgula, the high priest of the Keshan, will make his decision only after consulting their mummified oracle, Yelaya, whose beauty has transcended death: she lay "silent, motionless, in breast-plates of jeweled gold, gilded sandals, and silken skirt. The lissome limbs were not rigid, a peach-bloom touched the cheeks, the lips were red . . . " (Howard 2005, 15). A moment later, the beautiful oracle opens her eyes and speaks to Conan of being a goddess. The fantastic mood is rapidly broken when Conan recognizes the mummy as a Corinthian slave girl, Muriela. Howard was perhaps inspired by Sax Rohmer's *She Who Sleeps* (Garden City, NY: Doubleday, Doran, 1928), which utilized a similar fraudulent mummy.

Solomon Kane, a sixteenth century English Puritan, and one of Howard's other notable characters, never encounters mummies during his travels, though in

"Wings in the Night" (*Weird Tales,* July 1932), the head of Goru, a friendly African murdered by harpies, sits over a hut door. Kane labors, "and between his stints he talked to the shriveled, mummified head of Goru, whose eyes strangely enough, did not change in the blaze of the sun or the haunt of the moon, but retained their life-like expression" (Howard 2004b, 316). Indeed, Goru may talk with Kane, and he may celebrate Kane's vengeance on the harpies.

A mysterious weapon that instantly mummifies humans appears briefly in "Red Nails" (*Weird Tales*, July–October 1936). It shoots "a beam of crimson fire" that hits a woman, instantly "shriveling and withering [her] like a mummy even as she fell" (Howard 2005, 278). This, however, has little to do with the plot, which concerns two cultures steeped in evil and the effects this has on them. In the post-humously published "The Noseless Horror " (*The Magazine of Horror,* February 1931), the unpleasant Sir Thomas Cameron, boasts to his guests about discovering a "most unusual mummy," one that is simply a completely dried body. Sir Thomas is killed soon after, and the mummy is revealed to have its origins in different circumstances than Sir Thomas realized. In part inspired by the writings of Poe, "The Noseless Horror" is a story that would not have been printed were it not by Howard.

Robert E. Howard was an uneven writer, and now that he is internationally popular, too much of his inferior and rejected work has been reprinted and sold on the strength of his name, but the best of his stories remain compulsively readable.

Richard Bleiler

See also: Haggard, H. Rider; Lovecraft, H. P.; The mummy in Western fiction: From 1922 to the twenty-first century; Smith, Clark Ashton

Further Reading

Howard, Robert E. 1946. *Skull-Face and Others*. Sauk City, WI: Arkham House.

Howard, Robert E. 2003. *The Coming of Conan the Cimmerian*, ed. Patrice Louinet. New York: Ballantine Books/Del Rey.

Howard, Robert E. 2004a. *The Bloody Crown of Conan*, ed. Rusty Burke. New York: Ballantine Books/Del Rey.

Howard, Robert E. 2004b. *The Savage Tales of Solomon Kane*. New York: Ballantine Books/Del Rey.

Howard, Robert E. 2005. *The Conquering Sword of Conan*, ed. Patrice Louinet. New York: Ballantine Books/Del Rey.

Howard, Robert E. 2008. *The Horror Stories of Robert E. Howard*, ed. Rusty Burke. New York: Ballantine Books/Del Rey.

Ice mummies

A particular form of mummification is represented by the preservation of dead bodies in a cold environment. Mummies that were detected in permafrost regions, glaciers, the Arctic regions, and in high altitude mountains are often referred to as "ice mummies" or "glacier mummies." The main factor in the preservation of human remains in these areas is the constantly cold temperatures that remain below 0°C for most of the year. Additionally, the very dry air that is a characteristic feature of arctic regions, most permafrost soil, and high mountains may enhance the mummification process and lead to the preservation of mummies over hundreds and thousands of years. Corpses that are found in glacial environments often still contain a considerable amount of humidity in their body tissues. In some cases this has contributed to a remarkable conservation of the skin, facial features, and other soft tissues, such as in the Tyrolean Iceman known as Ötzi and the members

The mummified body of a six-year-old boy is one of eight ice mummies found at Qilakitsoq and currently displayed in the Greenland National Museum. (Holger Leue/Getty Images)

of the Franklin expedition. The most important ice mummy findings are summarized in the following:

Arctic Mummies

In the Arctic region, despite the favorable conditions for mummification, only a few mummies have been found. The oldest find is of an approximately 50-year-old woman that was detected by Inuit hunters in Kialegak at St. Lawrence Island, in the Bering Sea of Alaska. According to her injuries, and by moss that she had inhaled, it can be assumed that she was buried alive and suffocated in her house after a landslide or earthquake. Infrared photography revealed tattoos at her lower arms. A similar scenario probably led to the death of five Inuits who were found in 1982 at Utqiagvik (Barrow), located at the northern tip of Alaska. The winter dwelling of the family has been destroyed by piles of ice that were pushed from the sea onto the shore and crushed on the wooden house. The Inuits, consisting of three women ranging from 20 to 45 years of age, a 13-year-old boy, and an 8-year-old girl, were obviously taken by surprise and killed while sleeping. One of the women was found at the entrance of the hut, where she probably tried to escape the deadly trap. During the 500 years after death, two of the women were mummified, but the other three individuals were preserved as skeletons. A paleopathological study of the mummies revealed evidence for anthracosis and possible trichinosis, and in particular multiple rib fractures with pleural effusion in both women.

Canadian Ice Man

On August 14, 1999, three sheep hunters found the mummified remains of a young man in Tatshenshini-Alsek Park in British Columbia, Canada. The young man was determined to have been about 18 or 19 years old at the time of death, and to have died approximately 300 to 550 years ago. As the mummy was found on the historic territory of the First Nations, the person was named Kwäday Dän Ts'ìnchi, which means Long Ago Person Found. Because of the importance of this unique find, which include some features comparable to the Tyrolean Iceman, he is also referred to as the Canadian Ice Man. A genetic study of tissue samples of the mummy and a comparison with 241 volunteers from the Champagne and Aishihik First Nations revealed 17 living people who are related to the Ice Man maternally.

Franklin Expedition

In 1845 an expedition to the Arctic with the goal to explore the Northwest Passage started from London. The journey was led by the Arctic explorer and Royal Navy officer Sir John Franklin, who commanded two perfectly equipped ships and a well-prepared crew. Nevertheless, between 1845 and 1848 all 129 participants died during the disastrous attempt to transverse the last untraveled section of the passage. On August 23, 1850, the graves of three seamen who had participated in the Franklin expedition were found on the Beechey Islands in the Canadian Arctic. The excavation of the tombs in 1984 and 1985 revealed the almost intact and very well preserved mummified remains of these crew members. Inside their coffins, the bodies were enclosed in a solid block of ice that, together with the permafrost environment, had helped to conserve the mummies for more than 150 years. The headboards of the graves yielded information about the exact dates of their demises: the sailors all died between January and April 1846. The scientific study of the mummies revealed a possible explanation for their cause of death. On the one hand, Franklin's crew suffered from the effects of a severe lead poisoning; the toxic metal was introduced into the food by the soldering used for sealing tin cans, which were carried on the ship as the main provisions. A further investigation showed that the three men suffered from tuberculosis and most probably died of pneumonia.

Greenland Mummies

The archeological site Qilakitsoq is located on Nuussuaq Peninsula in northwestern Greenland and is the site where eight mummified bodies were discovered in 1972. Located in two tombs, they and consisted of six woman and two children. The preservation of the corpses was thought to be a result of the low temperatures and dry air in this region, which had finally resulted in a freeze-drying process. The mummies were found fully clothed, and they belonged to the Thule culture, the direct ancestors of the Inuit of the eastern Arctic. Radio-carbon dating revealed that the people had lived around the year 1475 CE in Greenland. Scientific investigations showed that the women died between the ages of 18 and 50, and that the children were 6 months and 4 years old at time of death. Further studies demonstrated that the eight mummies were all closely related. A nasopharyngeal carcinoma was detected in one of the older women. Another interesting finding was that the four-year-old boy shows probable symptoms of Down syndrome together with evidence for a hip disorder called the Legg-Calvé-Perthes disease. Finally, five of the six women show facial tattoos, mostly curved lines on the forehead and cheeks. Some of the mummies are exhibited in the Greenland National Museum in Nuuk. On the island of Uunartoq, the mummies of three little children were found in stone graves dating to the seventeenth century.

The Tyrolean Iceman

On the September 19, 1991, the naturally mummified body of the Iceman, also referred to as "Ötzi," was discovered by two hikers in the Ötztal Alps at an altitude of 3,210 meters. This glacier mummy lived around 3300 BCE and died at an age of approximately 46 years in the high alpine area. He is now kept together with his well-preserved clothing and equipment at the Archaeological Museum in Bolzano.

Besides the well-preserved body, the presence of his clothing and equipment allowed unique insights into the living circumstances of the people in the early Copper Age in the alpine region. His equipment consists of several tools that allowed him to spend longer time away from his settlement. He was able to prepare fire and repair clothes and other items. He carried a bow (unfinished) and arrows for hunting, and he had a remarkable axe made out of an elbow-shaped wooden handle and a finely handcrafted copper blade. His clothing was made out of different furs and leather, including a cap, leggings, a loincloth, shoes and a coat. It can be assumed that his clothing was very functional and allowed him to walk up in the mountains even during cold periods.

Since his discovery in 1991, the mummy has been intensively studied using a wide variety of methodologies, included radiology and CT scan of his body, histology, isotope analysis, paleobotany, and molecular biology. In 2007 the EURAC-Institute for Mummies and the Iceman was founded in Bolzano, Italy, and all available scientific data on the Iceman was collected and critically reviewed. More recently, the Iceman was studied with different technologies, including nanotechnology of soft tissue and bone samples, spectroscopy of blood remnants at his clothing, a reevaluation of radiological data, a detailed genetic analysis of his nuclear DNA.

The different studies have shown that, based on stable isotope analysis, the Iceman grew up and lived the last years before his death in different valleys in the southern part of the Alps. The paleobotanical study and pollen analyses of samples taken from his intestines have given insights into his nutrition, his last itinerary, and the season of his death, which must have been late spring. The analyses of CT scans demonstrated the presence of healed rib fractures, degenerative arthritis, some degree of vascular calcification, and the presence of an arrowhead in his left shoulder. In 2007, a new multislice CT clearly demonstrated that the arrowhead had lacerated the left subclavian artery, leading to a fast, deadly hemorrhagic shock in the Iceman. It was further shown that the Iceman suffered from a severe brain injury that could have been caused shortly after or before the deadly arrowshot. In a recent reevaluation of radiological findings, further details on the life and death of the Iceman were revealed, including the presence of gallbladder stones and a completely full stomach. This has been interpreted as indicating that the Iceman had a big meal after he climbed up the mountains, and that he probably he felt quite safe and did not expect an attack.

In contrast to the theory that the Iceman was significantly moved or even buried at the finding site, the CT scans clearly show that the unnatural position of the left arm is not due to glacier or any other movements. This can be demonstrated by the configuration of skin folds and muscles, the intact shoulder joints, and the rotated scapula. The haematoma (collected blood) in the soft tissue of the left shoulder can be continuously followed through the arrow wound channel into the superficial tissue layers without interruption or tearing. Therefore, any displacements of these parts after death can be effectively ruled out. The fact that the cervical spine and the connection to the skull show no damage whatsoever proves that the head was not moved in a frozen state. In conclusion, within a short time after his death the Iceman was in the same position in which he would be found more than 5,000 years later.

A few years after the Iceman was found, the first studies of his mitochondrial DNA were initiated with an analysis of the so-called hypervariable (HVS1) region. In later years the entire mitochondrial genome was successfully analyzed. In a more recent study, a whole genome analysis of a bone sample from the Iceman was successfully applied. The next-generation sequencing approach revealed about 40 percent reads that mapped unambiguously to the human reference genome. Thereby, an overall coverage of the human genome of 96 percent was retrieved. A comparison with the previously published mitochondrial DNA showed a full concordance and thereby confirmed the authenticity of the ancient Iceman DNA.

Further analysis of the sequencing data revealed that the Iceman most probably had brown eyes, in contrast to the previous assumption that his eyes were blue. It also showed that the Iceman was lactose intolerant. This is of particular interest, as it represents one of the most significant genetic traits connected with the beginnings of agriculture in Europe. The advent of farming in Northern Italy is thought to have occurred between 7,000 and 6,900 years ago. Lactase persistence is associated with a polymorphism (the presence of more than one phenotype) in a certain genetic region, the MCM6 gene. In previous ancient DNA analyses, it was assumed that the derived allele was rare in the Neolithic and that it gained in frequency over the next millennia and was widespread in Central Europe by the Middle Ages. Furthermore, the Iceman genome was also analyzed for genetic risk factors, specifically for DNA sequence variations, so-called SNPs (single nucleotide polymorphisms) that are linked with different diseases. The results showed a strong genetic predisposition for an increased risk for coronary heart disease. This is of particular interest as CT scans of the Iceman had already revealed major calcification in carotid arteries, distal aorta, and right iliac artery as strong signs for a generalized atherosclerotic disease (that is, hardening of the arteries). Since his lifestyle as inferred by radiological and stable isotope data did not entail major environmental cardiovascular risk factors, the genetic predisposition could have led to the arterial calcifications. Finally, it was shown that the Iceman was infected with the pathogen for Lyme borreliosis, and the complete genome sequence provided indications for a recent common ancestry between the Iceman and present-day inhabitants of the area near the Tyrrhenian Sea.

Albert Zink

See also: Natural mummification; Ötzi the Iceman; Siberian Ice Maiden/Ukok princess

Further Reading

Aufderheide, Arthur. 2003. *The Scientific Study of Mummies*. Cambridge University Press: New York.

Dickson, James H. 2012. *Ancient Ice Mummies*. The History Press: Stroud.

Lynnerup, Niels. 2007. "Mummies." *Am J Phys Anthropol*. Suppl 45: 162–90. Review.

Wieczorek, Alfried, and Wilfried Rosendahl. 2010. *Mummies of the World*. Prestel: New York.

Imhotep

Imhotep was an historical individual who was closely associated with the construction of the Step Pyramid of the Third Dynasty King Djoser Netjerikhet (ca. 2667–2648 BCE) at Saqqara. A fragmentary base from a statue of Djoser from Saqqara lists Imhotep's titles and roles: "Seal Bearer of the King of Lower Egypt . . . Administrator of the Great Palace . . . High Priest of Heliopolis. Imhotep, builder . . . carpenter . . . sculptor . . . maker of stone vases." Little else is known of Imhotep from contemporary records, but he was clearly someone of great importance. Over a millennium after his death, Imhotep was evidently regarded as something of a culture hero. Although his patron, King Djoser, is credited as the "opener of stone" in one text, it seems that Imhotep was recognized as the creative spark behind the Step Pyramid complex. New Kingdom (ca. 1550–1070 BCE) scribes are recorded as reverentially "pouring water for Imhotep" before they started their paperwork and he is identified as the author of wisdom texts.

A limestone statue of Imhotep stands in front of an image of the Step Pyramid. (AP Images/Tim Roske)

By the first millennium BCE, Imhotep had been elevated to the full status of a deity. He is often referred to as the son of the god Ptah, appropriately the patron deity of craftsmen, and a human mother called Kheredu-ankh. Writing in

The name "Imhotep" refers to both a real historical Egyptian personage and a famous fictional character in the mummy horror genre. The historical individual was apparently a craftsman who lived during the Third Dynasty ca. 2650 BCE. He was later elevated to the status of a deity and revered for his supposed skills in the arts, writing, and medicine. The fictional character is most famous for appearing as the title character in Universal Studios' 1932 and 1999 versions of *The Mummy*, played by the actors Boris Karloff and Arnold Vosloo, respectively.

the third century BCE, the historian Manetho records the fact that the Egyptians equated Imhotep with Asclepius, the Greek god of healing, not only because of his medical skills, but also for his "invention of building in hewn stone and also for the excellence of his writings." Imhotep was frequently the subject of pious appeals, and his temple at Saqqara—the "Asclepieion," perhaps on the site of his tomb—attracted pilgrims from around the Mediterranean. His worship appears to have been linked with the cult of sacred animals at Saqqara, and his image appears on the outer bandages of several votive animal mummies. The site of neither Imhotep's tomb nor his temple has yet been positively identified.

Imhotep has also enjoyed a fantastical afterlife in fiction. In a Ptolemaic pseudo-historical inscription he is instrumental in ending a seven year famine, and in a Roman Period demotic papyrus he engages in a magical duel with an Assyrian sorceress. The earliest modern appearance of a character by that name occurs in the 1932 film *The Mummy*, where the "High Priest" Imhotep is played by Boris Karloff. After being sentenced to be buried alive for trying to revive his lover, Princess Ankhesenamun, Imhotep is accidentally disturbed when a group of modern archaeologists discover his tomb. With the help of its 1940s sequels about a separate mummy character named Kharis, the film established the horror trope of the slowly shuffling mummy, swathed in bandages (with the now iconic visual image modeled not after Imhotep but after the real mummy of King Rameses III). The name "Imhotep" also became synonymous with vengeful intent, although the audience for the 1932 film is encouraged to feel some sense of sympathy toward the film's antagonist. In the 1999 remake of *The Mummy* and its 2001 sequel, *The Mummy Returns*, the character of Imhotep, now played by Arnold Vosloo, becomes a more monstrous villain with far-reaching supernatural powers.

The fictional Imhotep's connection with secret or forbidden knowledge may echo ancient traditions; his role as a founder of Marvel Comics' law-enforcement agency S.H.I.E.L.D. is probably closer to the nature of the historical Imhotep as understood by the ancient Egyptians. For the historical figure, whose name means literally "one who has come in peace," the mummy movies have provided a quite unexpected subversion of his beneficent powers.

Campbell Price

See also: *The Mummy* (1932); *The Mummy* (1999) and *The Mummy Returns*; The mummy in popular culture

Further Reading

Day, Jasmine. 2006. *The Mummy's Curse. Mummymania in the English-speaking World*. Oxford: Routledge.

Ray, John. 2002. *Reflections of Osiris: Lives from Ancient Egypt*. Oxford: Clarendon Press.

Inca mummies

The Inca were the ruling elite of the largest Prehispanic empire in the New World. At its peak, the Inca Empire covered approximately 2,000,000 square kilometers and included an estimated 6 to 12 million people from numerous ethnic groups across much of modern-day Peru, Chile, Ecuador, Bolivia, and Argentina, and parts of Brazil and Columbia. The Inca were a relatively small ethnic group that, through military conquest, political and economic strategizing, and a shared state religion, rapidly established and controlled a very large empire from their capital city in Cusco, Peru.

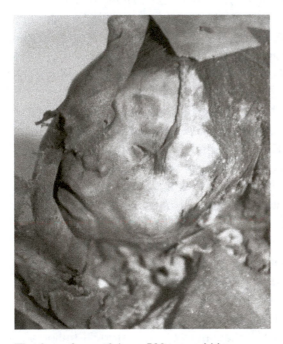

The face of one of three 500-year-old Inca mummies, the apparent victims of a ritual sacrifice, found frozen and in near-perfect condition on an Andean volcano peak in northern Argentina in 1999. (AP Images/Osvaldo Stigliano)

The Inca expansion began in the early 1400s and they continued incorporating other ethnic groups and societies into their empire until the arrival of the Spanish around 1528 CE. The last sovereign (or independent) Inca ruler, Atahualpa, was executed by Francisco Pizarro in 1533. Following the Spanish conquest of the Inca Empire, a small independent state was eventually established by the remaining Inca in Vilcabamba to the northeast of Cusco. In 1572, the last Inca ruler, Túpac Amaru, was captured and executed.

From a number of Spanish chronicles, it is known that the Inca elite did mummify rulers and their families. No Inca royal mummies have ever been found, however, because they were either purposefully destroyed by the Spanish as part of their efforts to eradicate local religious beliefs, or otherwise lost or hidden. Writing in 1609, Spanish-Inca chronicler Garcilaso de la Vega described a number of Inca royal mummies, including well-known Inca Viracocha and his descendants, which he was invited to see in a private Spanish home in Cusco in 1560:

> In the room I found five bodies of Inca rulers, three males and two females. . . . The bodies were perfectly preserved without the loss of a hair of the head or brow or an eyelash. They were dressed as they had been in life, with *llautus* [tasselled fringe worn about the head, i.e., the Inca equivalent of a European crown] on their heads but no other ornaments or royal insignia. They were buried in a sitting position . . . Padre Acosta, speaking of one of these bodies which he too saw, says in his Book VI, chapter xxi: 'The body was so complete and so well preserved with a certain bitumen that it appeared to be alive. Its eyes were made of cloth of gold, and so well fitted that one did not notice the loss of the real ones.' My own opinion is that the main operation in embalming was to take the bodies above the snow line and keep them there until the flesh dried, after which they would cover them with the bitumen Padre Acosta mentions. . . I am led to this supposition by observing that the pemmican the Indians make in all the cold countries is produced simply by placing meat in the open air until it has lost all its moisture. No salt or other preservative is used, and once dried it is kept as long as desired. . . . I remember having touched one of the fingers of [Inca] Huayna Capac, which seemed like that of a wooden statue, it was so hard and stiff. The bodies weighed so little that any Indian could carry them in his arms or his back from house to house, wherever gentlemen asked to see them. They were carried wrapped in white sheets, and the Indians knelt in the streets and squares and bowed with tears and groans as they passed. (De la Vega 2006, 40–41)

Although not part of the Inca ruling elite, mummies dating to the period of the Inca Empire have been found, most notably at Puruchuco-Huaquerones and Chachapoyas in Peru. Puruchuco-Huaquerones is located in middle region of the Rimac valley on the south coast of Peru near Lima. The region, inhabited discontinuously since 1800 BCE, was peacefully annexed and controlled by the Inca from approximately 1470 CE. The archaeological site is part of the town of Túpac Amaru, named for the last Inca ruler. The small community was founded in the late 1980s by people fleeing from guerrilla activity in the Peruvian highlands.

Archaeological excavations, with the goal of rescuing artifacts and burials from urban sprawl, began in the late 1990s. Since then, a total of 1,286 burials have been recovered, representing between 2,200 and 2,400 individuals. The burials range from complete mummification to fragmentary and poorly preserved bone. Nearly three-quarters of the cemetery remains unexcavated, and it is estimated that as many as 20,000 to 30,000 individuals may be buried at Puruchuco-Huaquerones.

The most common form of mummy bundle entailed wrapping the body in textiles and padding the bundle with cotton, and then wrapping it in textile again and filling it with cotton seeds. Several *false cabezas* have also been found. These large mummy bundles (1.0–1.6m high) are surmounted by a false head made of textile and filled with cotton, and sometimes include a wig and facial features. These large bundles typically contain multiple individuals, rather than one person. Some of the items recovered include gourds filled with maize and beans, weaving kits, weaving tools made of wood, ceramic vases, vegetable fiber mats, and bags containing vegetable offerings. Recent studies of bones, teeth, and stable isotope data suggest that, in terms of health and diet, quality of life under Inca rule for the people buried at Puruchuco-Huaquerones was reasonably good. Their diet seems to have been nutritionally adequate and, although individuals did experience periods of stress and illness, the Puruchuco-Huaquerones population was generally healthy before and after the Inca conquered the region

The Chachapoyas, also known as the "warriors of the clouds," inhabited the Amazonian Andes from around 800 CE. The Chachapoya polity included several ethnic groups and encompassed a large area of the northern Peruvian Andes, bordered by the Huallaga river to the east and the Marañón river in the west. Garcilaso de la Vega reported that the Chachapoya territory was "more than fifty leagues [250 kilometers] long and twenty [100 kilometers] broad, apart from the part that projects to Muyupampa [Moyobamba], a length of thirty leagues [150 kilometers] more." As part of their burial practice, they constructed funerary houses in the cliffs above the *Laguna de los Condores* (Lake of the Condors) on the eastern flanks of the northern Andes. Over 200 mummy bundles have been recovered and, although heavily looted, burial offerings date the site to Chachapoya (ca. 800–1470), Chachapoya-Inka (ca. 1470–1532) and early Colonial (ca. 1532–1570) times. The Chachapoya polity was conquered by the Inca Empire by 1470, after intense resistance.

Local Chachapoya burial practices involved burying the dead in remote places, e.g., in cliff houses, and decorating the defleshed bones with red paint, wrapping them in textiles, and placing the bundles in tombs. Archaeological excavations have revealed that, after the Inca conquered the local populace, they began to purposefully mummify their dead. This may reflect a change in local practices, or the presence of colonists from other parts of the Inca Empire. It is also possible that the Inca themselves began to use the cliff houses for their own burials. The Chachapoya mummies were prepared by drying and tightly binding the bodies into bundles. The anus was enlarged, the contents of the intestinal cavity were removed, and the enlarged opening was packed with cloth. The chest and rib cage were left unmodified. Most of the hair was lost in the mummification process, and the skin was treated to preserve it, probably with local plants (*poleo*, a kind of mint, and *muña*, a plant unique to the Andes), the leaves of which have been found with the mummies. Soft tissue structures of the face were packed with cotton to preserve shape, and the body was ultimately dressed and wrapped in textiles. Offerings of food and new burial wrappings covering the mummies indicate that people continued to visit the tombs, a widespread ancient Andean practice. The *Laguna de los Condores* mummies are the only Chachapoya mummies that have been found.

Radiocarbon dating confirms that the cliff houses were made by pre-Inca Chachapoyas, and that they continued to be used until after the arrival of the Spanish. The radiocarbon dates also confirm the chronology of burial styles, with mummified burials dating to the more recent Inca period. Based on archaeological evidence, it is likely that, when the Inca occupied the area, they relocated the earlier Chachapoya burials, and reused the more elaborate parts of the site for their own people, possibly including Cusco administrators, local lords and their kin, or workers brought to the region by the Inca (*mitmaqs*).

Emily Webb

See also: Juanita, the Inca Ice Maiden; Mummies of Latin America

Further Reading

Aufderheide, Arthur C. 2003. *The Scientific Study of Mummies*. Cambridge: Cambridge University Press.

Cobo, Father Bernabe. 1979. *Historia Del Nuevo Mundo*, 1653. Austin: University of Texas Press.

Cock, Guillermo A. 2002. "The Race to Save Inca Mummies." *National Geographic Magazine* 201, no. 5: 78–91.

De la Vega, Garcilaso, H. V. Livermore, and Karen Spalding. 2006. *Royal Commentaries of the Inca and General History of Peru (Abridged)*, 1609. Indianapolis: Hackett Publishing.

"Leymebamba Museum, Chachapoya, Peru." Accessed October 25, 2013. http://museoleymebamba.org/

Moseley, Michael Edward. 1997. *The Incas and their Ancestors: The Archaeology of Peru*. London: Thames & Hudson.

"Mummy Bundles of Puruchuco." 2002. *National Geographic*. Accessed October 25, 2013. http://channel.nationalgeographic.com/channel/content/inca/.

Incorruptibles

The term *Incorruptibles* refers to mummies of religious figures who died "in odor of sanctity," that is, who distinguished themselves in life for their virtues and actions. Specifically, the worship of these bodies is widespread within the Catholic

Among Roman Catholics and Eastern Orthodox Christians, the word "incorruptibles" refers to the naturally preserved bodies of deceased individuals whose lives were marked by extraordinary virtue. The verification of a body's incorruptibility is a highly formalized process, and individuals whose bodies are verified in this way are deemed to be saints. The worship of such bodies evolved out of the ancient practice of venerating holy relics and is widespread in both the Catholic and Orthodox churches.

and Orthodox Churches. The origins of this form of devotion represent an evolution of the cult of relics that appeared as a consequence of the early Christians' persecutions.

During the first centuries of the Common Era, bodies of martyrs were located in catacombs, and parts of them were transferred and venerated as sacred objects. In this respect, a great impulse was provided by the Edict of Milan in 313, through which the Roman emperors Constantine I and Licinius I granted religious liberty within their territorial holdings.

However, the golden age of relics—which may even include entire bodies—is the Middle Ages, during which time they became a sign of richness, often making the cities that possessed them into pilgrimage destinations. Thus they could be sold and even falsified, a trend that was partly halted only after the Council of Trent (1545–1563), which established that worship of a relic was dependent upon the existence of documents proving its authenticity.

Within this cult, there arose a custom of considering bodily preservation as a sign of holiness. Both entire bodies and parts of them, or even clothes or objects once belonged to the Saint, offer a dimension of corporeality (physical reality), in that their physical remains contrast with decay and indicate their victory over death. The Saint's presence is therefore represented by his body and is emphasized by the believers, who behave as if he were alive.

Preservation of such bodies could often be achieved spontaneously, due to favorable burial conditions which enhanced dehydration, providing cases of partial mummification such as Sant'Ubaldo da Gubbio (d. 1160), the Blessed Antonio Franco (d. 1626), Santa Rita da Cascia (d. 1457), and the Blessed Savina Petrilli (d. 1923), and even examples of complete mummification, including Santa Lucia (d. 304), Santa Rosa da Viterbo (d. 1251), Santa Zita da Lucca (d. 1278), the Blessed Margherita di Savoia (d. 1464), Santa Caterina da Bologna (d. 1463), and Santa Caterina da Genova (d. 1510).

However, especially in the Middle Ages, the cadavers of religious figures could also be preserved anthropogenically (by human action), to encourage a veneration initiated in life and often realized even before the official Church recognition. These include Santa Margherita da Cortona (d. 1297), Santa Chiara da Montefalco (d. 1308), the Blessed Margherita Vergine di Città di Castello (d. 1320), Santa

Caterina da Siena (d. 1380), and the Blessed Cristina da Spoleto (d. 1458). Treatments could consist of a simple external aspersion with balms and aromatics, as described in the Bible, or a more invasive procedure including evisceration, defleshing, and filling of the body cavities.

In the case of Santa Margherita da Cortona, for instance, an inspection carried out in 1988 revealed some deep incisions on the chest and abdomen, as well as on the great muscles of arms and legs, all of which were suture-closed, while Santa Chiara da Montefalco was dissected by a nun, who—with no anatomical knowledge—performed a real postmortem from the back of the corpse by a razor blade and removed the heart and viscera. Interestingly, some gross anatomic lesions were interpreted from a religious viewpoint: the opened heart showed the cross, the scourge, and the spear, and even three nails, whereas, when dry, it showed the column, the crown of thorns, and the hyssop with the sponge; the gallbladder, for its part, which was dissected a few days later, showed three stones, which were interpreted as a sign of the Trinity.

In the light of the same medieval mysticism, a sign of the Trinity was also evidenced during the dissection of the Blessed Margherita's heart, while that of Santa Veronica Giuliani (d. 1727) proved to be pierced from side to side, symbolizing the Passion of Christ.

Following the Second Vatican Council (1962–1965), relics and holy bodies are considered to be of both religious and historic value, and scientific studies may be allowed to grant these precious findings a major dignity and a proper conservation. The aim of these investigations is not only to correctly identify the bodies, but also to evaluate their preservation status, to restore the damaged ones, and to reconstruct their lives and lifestyles, as well as to diagnose some lesions and assess the possible cause of death. Currently, one of the most renowned experts in the investigation of mummified saints is Ezio Fulcheri (1952–), a pathologist at the University of Genoa who has initiated a registry for these remains.

One of the most thorough scientific studies of a Saint is that carried out on the mummy of Santa Zita da Lucca, which involved histological, radiologic, endoscopic, chemical, and molecular analyses, and allowed the diagnosis of anthracosis through the detection of coal particles in the lung, probably due to her habit of living in a kitchen, where she was constantly subjected to the smoke produced by the fireplace.

The historic and radiologic study of another Saint, the Blessed Margherita di Savoia, seems to indicate that the late woman was affected by heart and respiratory failure, further evidenced by a source mentioning edema of the lower extremities and the lack of physical strength. X-rays have demonstrated lesions consistent with rheumatic fever, a condition that notoriously bears a cardiac involvement, and this element contradicts the tradition mentioning gout as the cause of her death: this may be due to the fact that such disease was once believed to involve internal organs and even the heart.

Additionally, Santa Rosa da Viterbo whose body belongs to a young adult female, was radiologically and endoscopically investigated, and displayed the lack of the sternum, a rare condition associated to congenital disorders such as Cantrell's Syndrome, representing the only documented case of survival to such an age. Even the heart, removed in 1921, showed a ventricular diverticulum which is common in patients affected by this condition, and also a related thrombus interpreted as the most probable cause of death.

Finally, Santa Caterina Fieschi offers an example of a historic-medical approach of investigation, exclusively based on documentary sources. If on the one side these chronicles are often celebrative—e.g., by framing the pain as a fire that burns inside, representing the fervent love of God—on the other side they provide precious information on the Saint's health status, suggesting that she was probably affected by a chronic gastritis. This might have been worsened by some dietary habits aimed at mortifying her body, which later resulted in a cancer involving the abdominal organs, the liver, and the brain, as well as a gastro-enteric obstruction that led to her departure.

Dario Piombino-Mascali

See also: Mummies of Europe; Religion and mummies

Further Reading

Aufderheide, Arthur C. 2003. *The Scientific Study of Mummies*. Cambridge: Cambridge University Press.

Capasso, Luigi, Salvatore Caramiello, and Ruggero D'Anastastio. 1999. "The Anomaly of Santa Rosa." *The Lancet* 353, 9151: 504.

D'Anastasio, Ruggero, Gianpaolo Di Silvestro, Paolo Versacci, Luigi Capasso, and Bruno Marino. 2010. "The Heart of Santa Rosa." *The Lancet* 375, 9732: 2168.

Fulcheri, Ezio. 1996. "Mummies of Saints: A Particular Category of Italian Mummies." In *Human Mummies: A Global Survey of Their Status and the Techniques of Conservation*, edited by Konrad Spindler, Harald Wilfing, Elisabeth Rastbichler-Zisserning, Dieter zur Nedden, and Hans Nothdurfter, 219–230. Wien and New York: Springer.

Isis

In addition to being Egypt's most important female deity, Isis may rank as the most important of all the Egyptian gods. Her cult spread throughout the ancient world. Her name Isis or Aset is often translated as "throne." Another interpretation of Aset is "creation" or "She who has regal power" (Osing 1974).

Isis is normally represented as a woman, wearing a tight dress, with her name hieroglyph on the head. Later, from the New Kingdom onward, she was also pictured with cow horns and sun disc, similar to Hathor, the goddess of love and dance. As attributes she often holds a menat-necklace, sistrum (an ancient musical instrument), and the Ankh. The sistrum is a rattle used in rituals. In the course of history, Isis overlaid the goddess Hathor using their shared iconography. In art she is often accompanied by her sister Nephthys. Another typical image shows Isis kneeling, her hands resting on the *shen*-hieroglyph in the form of a ribbon. *Shen* stands for "protection," and the tradition of wearing an awareness ribbon is still alive today.

Isis was the daughter of Geb, god of the Earth, and Nut, goddess of the Sky. She was married to her brother Osiris. She fulfilled many roles as goddess of love, goddess of magic, and mother of the god Horus. She was believed to have more magic and be more intelligent than all the other gods. She controlled the mystery of life and was therefore of vital importance for mummification and the afterlife. She connected the world of the

A gilded wood statuette of Isis breastfeeding infant Horus. From the Treasure of Tutankhamun. (DEA/W. BUSS/Getty Images)

living, represented by Horus, with the realm of the dead, represented by Osiris.

Isis is attested from the First Dynasty (but her importance remains unclear) and had her first vital mythological role is in the Pyramid Texts (late Fifth Dynasty), where she appears as "Goddess of the North" and mourning widow at the feet of Osiris, whom she revives as a mummy to conceive her son Horus. This is the reason why Isis is often pictured at the feet of coffins (e.g., the coffins of Tutankhamun).

In the city of Khemnis she gave birth to her son Horus and healed him from a scorpion sting by using her magic. As goddess of magic, she played a pivotal role in all rituals for protecting and healing, as seen on the stelae of Horus, which contain protection spells normally invoking Isis. She raised Horus and protected him against his uncle Seth until he was grown to adulthood and able to revenge his murdered father Osiris. Isis is the archetype of a mother goddess: as mother of Horus, the god of kingship in Egypt, she was the reason why the Pharaohs declared themselves to be a "son of Isis." She plays a vital part of the myth of Osiris in Abydos in searching and reviving Osiris.

Isis was worshipped throughout Egypt, but her mythical origin is obscure since no city claimed to be her birthplace. As goddess of life, she also lacks a burial place opposite to her consort Osiris. She was not connected with a special center of worship, but was incorporated into many temples of other gods. Her famous temple in Philae (Pa ju-rek, "The Island of Time") was erected very late in Egyptian history under King Nectanebo I (379–360 BCE, 13th Dynasty) and construction continued until the Roman time. The temple of Philae, which was used until the sixth century CE, was transferred between 1977 and 1980 CE to the nearby Island Agilikia on higher ground to rescue it from the higher water level of the Aswan High Dam. Isis also had temples in foreign lands, such as the Temple of Isis in Byblos, where she was equated with the local goddess Astarte.

Isis became the supreme goddess of the ancient world during the late period and Greco-Roman time, and her cult spread over the whole Roman Empire. She incorporated many other goddesses and became an almost universal archetype of the mother goddess. Her temples in the Roman Empire were known as Isireion. The Roman writer Apuleius (ca. 125–180 CE) gave a unique insight in the cult of Isis during the Roman period in his novel *The Golden Ass*. The Horus-child sitting on the lap of Isis became the model for the Madonna with the infant Jesus.

Far from having died out in the modern world, the worship of Isis still continues today—for example, in the Fellowship of Isis and the Church of the Eternal Source.

Michael E. Habicht

See also: Anubis; Hierakonpolis; Osiris; Religion and mummies; Seth

Further Reading

Donaldson, M. D. 2003. *The Cult of Isis in the Roman Empire: Isis Invicta*. Lewiston, NY: Edwin Mellen Press.

Tiradritti, Francesco. 1998. *Isis, the Egyptian Goddess Who Conquered Rome*. Accessed December 7, 2013. –http://www.academia.edu/719626/Isis_the_Egyptian_Goddess_who _Conquered_Rome_Egyptian_Museum_of_Cairo_November_29–December_31_1998.

Wilkinson, Richard H. 2003. *The Complete Gods and Goddesses of Ancient Egypt*. London: Thames & Hudson.

Witt, R. E. 1997. *Isis in the Ancient World*, 1971. Baltimore: Johns Hopkins University Press.

J

The Jewel of Seven Stars

The Jewel of Seven Stars is an occult novel written by Bram Stoker, published in 1903 by Heinemann in London. The story details an attempt to resurrect an ancient Egyptian queen who is mysteriously linked with a modern woman. Originally from Ireland, Stoker, universally recognized today as the author of the vampire classic *Dracula* (1897), was equally well known in his lifetime as the manager of prominent Victorian stage actor Henry Irving's Lyceum Theater Co. in London. Stoker was also trained as a barrister, but he still found time to write stories and novels, a few with supernatural or occult themes, though none achieved the fame of *Dracula*. Still, his Egyptian novel has achieved a permanent though more modest fame, at least partially because of book covers that are increasingly lurid and titillating, as well as no fewer than four filmed adaptations, each more gruesome than the last.

The Jewel of Seven Stars was Stoker's first occult novel after *Dracula*. There had been earlier novels with supernatural Egyptian themes, notably Australian writer Guy Boothby's 1898 *Pharos the Egyptian*, which appeared just a year after Stoker's vampire tale. Like *Dracula*, Pharos was an ancient undead creature (in this case a mummy rather than a vampire) that represented a global threat to humanity. Boothby's novel may have helped prompt Stoker, though he was already familiar with Egyptological matters through his friendship with Oscar Wilde, whose father had traveled to Egypt and recovered mummies of his own. Another fellow writer, Hall Caine, to whom *Dracula* was dedicated, supplied further background. Additionally, then-recent interpretations of the historical female pharaoh Hatshepsut (then called Hatasu) may have provided a model on which to base some of the elements of Stoker's fictitious Tera; Amelia Edwards, one of the founders of the Egypt Exploration Fund (now Society) in London, had devoted an entire chapter to Hatshepsut in her popular 1892 book *Pharaohs, Fellahs and Explorers*, and Howard Carter had discovered her tomb in 1902. In recent years Dr. Joanne Fletcher has suggested that a mummy now in a museum in Hull, UK, but once in Whitby, may have been Stoker's inspiration in the early 1890s, but others have added further possible mummies to this evolving story.

Stoker's novel starts out as a mystery, beginning with seemingly inexplicable events much in the way of the Sherlock Holmes tales of the time. The narrator, Malcolm Ross, has been urgently awakened in the middle of the night to come to

---

Movie Adaptations of Bram Stoker's *The Jewel of Seven Stars*

1970   "The Curse of the Mummy"—Final installment of the British television anthology series "Mystery and Imagination"

1971   *Blood from the Mummy's Tomb*—Last entry in the Hammer Films mummy series

1980   *The Awakening*—Big-budget production starring the legendary Charlton Heston

1998   *Bram Stoker's The Mummy*—Low-budget shocker released to cash in on Universal Studios's imminent reboot of its classic mummy series with 1999's *The Mummy*

---

the home of a recent female acquaintance. Margaret Trelawney has discovered her father slumped in an apparent coma on the floor. His outstretched wrist, wearing a small key, is bloody from numerous parallel cuts, and the trail of blood suggests he has been dragged from his bed toward a safe. No obvious wound explains his unconsciousness, but Margaret finds a note in Trelawney's desk suggesting that he had anticipated something strange and ordering her not to remove him from the room, nor to move any item (specifically, Egyptian curios, including coffins and even a cat mummy) from its original position. Vigil is kept by multiple persons for several days, including police and doctors, but despite the precautions the comatose Trelawney is similarly attacked each night.

At this point, a new character named Corbeck is introduced. Upon hearing that Trelawney, his employer, is in a coma, Corbeck introduces himself to Ross and gives him a seventeenth-century volume by an early Dutch explorer in Egypt named Nicholas van Huyn. It recounts the discovery, in a remote "Valley of the Sorcerer," of a tomb containing a female mummy with one unwrapped hand, remarkable for its perfect preservation as well as its seven fingers. Under the hand is a large ruby shaped as a scarab beetle and containing within it a pattern of seven stars aligned as the constellation of the Plough, or Big Dipper. Van Huyn explains in his narrative that he took the jewel and later found that his Arab guides had ripped away the hand.

Corbeck tells Ross that he and Trelawney met many years ago while studying van Huyn's narrative. They managed to locate the scarab-shaped jewel in Holland, after which they mounted an expedition that eventually led to their successful rediscovery of the mysterious tomb, whose hieroglyphs, which had been undecipherable in the 1640s, were now understood to name Queen Tera, a woman who was educated in archaic magic to protect her against the priests who opposed her rule. According to the hieroglyphs, among other powers Tera's magical practice had enabled her to conquer Sleep. Her plan was to simulate death while still young and vital, and to select a time in the far future and a place to the cool north of Egypt for her physical resurrection (though her "astral" self, somewhat equated with the Egyptian ka, never actually dies).

Corbeck explains that he and Trelawney removed all items from the tomb, but then, during their subsequent journey back to the Nile, the mummy was stolen. They returned to the tomb and found their Arab guides dead, strangled by the seven-fingered hand that had been lost in van Huyn's time, but that was now reunited with the mummy.

Upon arriving back home in England, Trelawney found that during his absence his wife, whom he may not even have known was pregnant when he left, had died in childbirth at the exact moment when he found the mummy. His daughter Margaret was born shortly after her mother's death—hinting at a connection between the mummy's recovery and Margaret's life.

After relating this story, Corbeck sees the adult Margaret for the first time and realizes that she strongly resembles the ancient depictions of Tera. Trelawney suddenly awakes from his coma and tells Margaret and Ross of his Great Experiment to assist Tera in her presumed goal of resurrection. Margaret views this as a quest for a pure love in a better, cleaner world, but Trelawney says he is driven by visions of the immense knowledge mankind can reap from this woman whose consciousness has survived since antiquity. (Here and elsewhere in the book, Stoker compares and contrasts the ideas of ancient esoteric knowledge with modern science, indicating his familiarity with current occult and metaphysical movements in his day, such as theosophy and the Golden Dawn.)

Everyone transfers to Trelawney's cliffside home in Cornwall, built over a cavern facing the sea, to proceed with Trelawney's Experiment. Despite his presumed understanding of the astronomical alignments and his beliefs about Tera's purpose, there are soundings of doubt and fear, particularly from Ross. Tera's mummy is unwrapped, revealing a perfectly preserved and very beautiful woman, nude but draped in a garment that Margaret interprets as a bridal gown. The Experiment begins with the lighting of seven lamps. A green vapor rises from a special coffer and is drawn into the mummy's coffin. However, a storm begins outside, as if the elements themselves (or the Egyptian gods?) oppose the resurrection. Suddenly, a black smoke fills the chamber, the lights fail, and Ross calls out, but he receives no response. Stumbling in the dark, he finds what he believes is Margaret, but as he takes her upstairs her weight lessens, and he arrives with only the empty bridal gown of Tera. Rushing back downstairs, he finds everyone, including Margaret, dead with looks of terror on their faces.

Despite this atypically (for Stoker) downbeat and inconclusive ending, in which all of the principal characters except the narrator are left dead, Ross is left without hope, and the reader is left with uncertainty about the fate or intentions of Tera, *The Jewel of Seven Stars* received several positive reviews on its first publication. Nevertheless, in 1912, the year Stoker died, a new edition was published with significant changes. Chapter 16, a speculative section containing no action, was removed, but more significantly, the ending was changed drastically.

In the altered ending, after the black smoke clears out of the room where the Experiment is being conducted, no trace is found of Tera, but only bits of ash. Ross and Margaret get married, she wearing an Egyptian costume and thinking fondly of Tera. No one today is certain if Stoker, his wife, or an editor did the rewrite, but the "happy ending" was obviously intended to improve sales, and it became the standard form of the novel for many years, though the original last chapter, "The Great Experiment," has occasionally appeared as a separate story titled "The Bridal of Death." Since the 1990s the novel has been frequently printed with both endings.

It has also been the subject of several film adaptations. Of these, "The Curse of the Mummy" (1970), starring Isobel Black and Patrick Mower, and directed by Guy Verney, is the earliest and least well known. It was the final installment in a British television anthology series *Mystery and Imagination*. Modestly budgeted for television, this is the only film set in the correct early twentieth-century era and is closest to the feel of the novel. Characters are reduced such that Ross, a barrister in the novel, now doubles as the doctor. In ancient Egypt, Tera has a young priest (the same actor who plays Ross) killed, then herself preserved perfectly, though not wrapped, but this is all in a dream of Margaret's. Waking, she discovers her father unconscious with the bloodied arm. In simplified form, much follows the book, and Corbeck arrives, recognizing Tera in Margaret. When Trelawney awakes, he understands that Tera is speaking through Margaret, but does not grasp the dark implications. The attempt to resurrect Tera occurs in the recreated tomb in the home and results in the deaths of Trelawney and Corbeck. Ross (a reincarnation of the priest from Margaret's dream?) and Margaret are married (as in Stoker's happy ending) but she has dressed as Tera, suggesting which personality has actually survived.

Blood from the Mummy's Tomb (1971), starring Valerie Leon and Andrew Keir, and directed by Seth Holt, was the last entry in the Hammer Films mummy series. This film strays further from Stoker than *The Curse of the Mummy* did, and—in typical Hammer fashion—concentrates on gore and sex. A modern day Margaret has a boyfriend very different from the book's Malcolm Ross. Trelawney is renamed Fuchs, and Corbeck is a mysterious figure who is really the one pushing the resurrection of Tera. Three other members of the expedition that found Tera's tomb are being supernaturally killed as the "familiars" they each hold are acquired and assembled in Fuchs's basement, where Tera's body is lying. (Again the "mummy" is perfectly preserved as a beautiful woman.) Tera magically attacks Fuchs, causing his trance midway through the film. Corbeck convinces Margaret (becoming more like Tera) to stop anyone thwarting the resurrection; thus the doctor and boyfriend die. At the climax, reading a Scroll of Life—a concept pulled from Hammer's 1959 *The Mummy*—Fuchs convinces Margaret to stop Corbeck, who they stab, but during the fight with Tera, who is coming awake, Fuchs is also killed and the roof collapses on Margaret and Tera. One bandaged woman is rushed to a hospital, but is it Margaret or Tera?

The Awakening (1980)—which is discussed in more detail in a separate entry—stars Charlton Heston and Stephanie Zimbalist, and was directed by Mike Newell. A big budget production filmed evocatively in Egypt and London, the script is tailored to the star persona of Heston, who combines the characters of Trelawney and Corbeck under the latter's name. Much is made of the birth of Margaret in a lengthy prologue set 18 years before the main action, leading finally to estrangement from his wife and daughter, a new wife and life in London, fights with Egyptian officials, and numerous "coincidental" yet bloody deaths. The queen to be resurrected is here named Kara, which actually can be represented by two simple hieroglyphs. Margaret becomes increasingly "possessed" by Kara, incest between father and daughter is introduced, and all culminates in the British Museum, when Corbeck/(Trelawney) finally realizes that Kara has come to life not in the decayed mummy that crumbles in his hands, but in Margaret, unleashing an "evil bitch" on the world.

Bram Stoker's The Mummy (1998) stars Amy Locane and Louis Gossett, Jr., and was directed by Jeffrey Obrow. This modestly budgeted shocker, which is also known as *Legend of the Mummy*, had minimal theatrical release before going to video to garner some of the interest being generated by Universal's upcoming 1999 remake of *The Mummy*. Set in modern San Francisco, but true to Stoker within broad limits, this film is filled with unexplained shambling mummies, gratuitous nudity, and confused plot details. In the end, Tera has assimilated with Margaret, who has married the unsuspecting hero. This film was adapted as a graphic novel in 2010 but marketed as simply *Mummy* and attributed to Stoker as author.

In 1999 a video-only film, originally called *Ancient Evil: Scream of the Mummy*, involving college students and an Aztec mummy, was being sold under the title *Bram Stoker's The Mummy 2*, despite no affiliation with Stoker or the earlier film. An earlier budget horror film, Fred Olen Ray's 1986 *The Tomb* with Sybil Danning, is supposedly, though without credit, based on Stoker's novel, as it involves the attempted resurrection of an evil Egyptian queen, a theme that has become more common in recent low-budget films. A low-budget quickie film put out on DVD in July 2014, *The Mummy Resurrected*, before release featured a title that mirrored the look of the Brendan Fraser series, apparently to lead unwary buyers into thinking it was a sequel of some sort, but the title layout was changed on the final video package. More egregious, however, is that the film is heavily based on Stoker's novel with no acknowledgment whatsoever. A mature archaeologist, Abel Trelane (pronounced "Trelawney" as in the book but spelled in the credits as shown here) apparently is taken over by the spirit of a mummy in the opening sequence. He then meets his daughter Margaret, leader of a group of young female grad students in Egypt; he has brought a copy of an old Dutch book (van Huyn's) to lead them to a lost tomb. Trelane has not seen Margaret since childhood and is really plotting to get to the tomb of Tera to allow her evil spirit to enter his daughter. Despite the fact that one of the girls even has the surname Corbeck, absolutely no mention is ever made of Bram Stoker or his novel. For that matter, the credited writer, Joanne Spring, cannot be found on IMDB at all, suggesting the actual author of the screenplay, whoever that may be, is avoiding potential charges of plagiarism. Stoker's literary executors probably are more than pleased not to have his name associated with this travesty.

It is partly through the help of these film adaptations that the reputation of *The Jewel of Seven Stars* has been elevated in recent years. Notwithstanding its many instances of hasty writing and its clumsy plot points that keep it from being a great work, and ignoring the fact that it features no actual shambling mummy, *Jewel* has come to be generally regarded as a near-classic mummy novel.

Carter Lupton

See also: *The Awakening*; Hammer Films mummy series; Mummy movies

Further Reading

Belford, Barbara. 1996. *Bram Stoker: A Biography of the Author of Dracula*. New York: Knopf.

Glover, David. 1996. *Vampires, Mummies and Liberals: Bram Stoker and the Politics of Popular Fiction*. Durham, NC: Duke University Press.

Hearn, Marcus, and Alan Barnes. 2007. *The Hammer Story: The Authorised History of Hammer Films*. Foreword by Christopher Lee. London: Titan Books.

Stoker, Bram. 1990. "The Bridal of Death." In *Midnight Tales*, edited by Peter Haining, 151–182. London: Peter Owen.

Stoker, Bram. 1996. *The Jewel of Seven Stars*. Annotated and edited by Clive Leatherdale. Westcliff-on-Sea, Essex, UK: Desert Island Books.

Stoker, Bram. 2003. "*The Bridal of Death*." Adapted by J. B. Bonivert, in *Graphic Classics: Bram Stoker*, 119–139. Mount Horeb, WI: Eureka Productions.

Stoker, Bram. 2010. *Mummy* (Graphic Chillers). Adapted by Bart A. Thompson. London: Franklin Watts.

Juanita, the Inca Ice Maiden

Juanita, also known as the Inca Ice Maiden or the Lady of Ampato, is the name given to the frozen body of a young girl found high in the Andes Mountains of Peru. Her original name is unknown. The frigid temperatures on the mountaintop preserved the girl's body to such a degree that she almost appears to be sleeping, even though she died around 1400 CE. Her body was discovered accidentally during a climbing expedition in 1995.

The Inca ice mummy known as Juanita was discovered in 1995 in the Peruvian Andes and rapidly became one of the most famous mummies discovered in the late twentieth century. This included two famous exhibitions outside her home country of Peru. In 1996 she was transported to the United States for CT scans and DNA analysis by scientists at Johns Hopkins Hospital in Baltimore, Maryland, after which she was displayed for a month at the headquarters of the National Geographic Society in Washington, D.C. Three years later, in 1999, she was transported to Japan for a 13-month, multi-city tour.

Juanita lived during the time of the Inca Empire, which controlled much of South America from northern Ecuador to southern Chile before the arrival of the Spanish explorers and missionaries. Sacrificing children to the gods was an occasional practice for the Inca, and several other well-preserved examples of child mummies have been found on high mountains in Peru and Chile. Spanish chroniclers studying the Inca recorded that children were chosen for sacrifice because of their purity, which made them better suited to be messengers to the gods and live among deities. The location of these sacrifices was usually a high mountain in the Andes. Mountains were very important in Inca religion, and over a hundred ceremonial sites have been found at elevations exceeding 15,000 feet. The extremely high altitude, as well as the cold temperatures throughout the year, naturally mummified the bodies of these children after they died. This natural mummification preserved all of Juanita's internal organs, as well as her skin, hair, and eyelashes, and the cloth that was wrapped around her body. Because Juanita was frozen rather than desiccated, even her DNA and blood were preserved for scientists to study.

Juanita was discovered in 1995 by archaeologist and climbing enthusiast Johan Reinhard, while he and his friend, Miguel Zárate, were scaling Mount Ampato in southern Peru. Though Juanita's body had been sealed beneath the frozen ground and ice for centuries, a recent eruption of hot ash from the nearby volcano Mt. Sabancaya had caused much of the ice to melt, releasing Juanita's body from its icy grave. The climbers stumbled across what appeared to be a bundle wrapped in cloth lying in the crater of Mount Ampato. Further inspection revealed that the bundle was actually the frozen body of a young girl, wrapped in woven Inca textile. Artifacts from her grave were scattered around the crater on Mount Ampato. Even Juanita's brief exposure to the elements had caused some of her skin to shrink and dry out, so immediate action was necessary if she was to be preserved. Reinhard and Zárate carefully transported the mummy down the mountain, returning later to excavate the rest of the site where Juanita was found. Reinhard and Peruvian archaeologist José Chávez also excavated nearby sites later the same year and discovered the mummies of two more children (one male and one female) that had been offered to the Inca gods on Mount Ampato.

Juanita was probably between 11 and 14 years old when she died and in very good health with no evidence of disease. Based on her well-made clothing and excellent health, she may have been a member of an elite family, or perhaps she had been selected as a potential sacrifice early in life, and had been well-cared for so that she could be the best gift to the gods. She was curled up or kneeling in her grave, with her knees drawn to her chest and her head bowed. Despite Juanita's peaceful appearance, her death was not a serene affair. A massive blow to the head with a heavy club fractured her skull, broke part of her right eye socket, and caused her brain to hemorrhage. Although there has been some speculation that this fracturing occurred when her body was dislodged from the grave and fell down the mountain slope, the large amounts of frozen blood and the appearance of the fracture indicate that Juanita was alive when the blow was struck.

Evidence from other naturally mummified children suggested that victims may have been sedated with alcohol before death. Juanita also consumed a meal of vegetables around six to eight hours before she died. Perhaps she consumed the alcohol and vegetables as part of the rituals preceding her ultimate sacrifice to the gods.

After she died, Juanita's body was wrapped in finely made, striped Incan textiles, with a portion covering her face. She was placed in a shallow grave, within the walls of one of the stone platforms often constructed by the Inca in lieu of trying to bury offerings in the frozen ground. Even in the extreme climate, her body froze slowly, and thus her organs began the process of decomposition before they froze completely. When the ice covering her grave melted hundreds of years later, Juanita was exposed to the elements, and her mummy underwent several cycles of freezing and partial thawing, which allowed the processes of decay to take hold.

Juanita was frozen and stored temporarily at the Catholic University in Arequipa, Peru. The year after she was discovered, her body was transported to the United States to be examined by scientists at Johns Hopkins Hospital in Baltimore, Maryland. Using CT scans, the researchers compiled a virtual autopsy of Juanita's body. They also used the CT scans and small tissue samples to reconstruct information about Juanita's health, diet, and the hours before her death. Her DNA indicated that she was closely related to the Ngobe Native Americans living in Panama, as well as to modern populations native to the Andes. Radiocarbon dating, also known as carbon-14 or C-14 dating, was used to determine the approximate time period of Juanita's death.

In addition to her trip to the United States in 1996, Juanita was also transported to Japan in 1999 for a lengthy, multi-city tour. Juanita is currently on display in dark, climate-controlled case at the Museo Santuarios de Altura in Arequipa, Peru. Some of the items that originally accompanied her to her grave are also displayed.

Roselyn Campbell

See also: Genetic study of mummies; Ice mummies; Inca mummies; Medical imaging of mummies; Mummies of Latin America; Natural mummification

Further Reading

Aufderheide, Arthur C. 2003. *The Scientific Study of Mummies*. Cambridge: Cambridge University Press.

Clar, Lies. 1998. "Ice Mummies of the Inca." *Nova*. Modified November 24. Accessed October 31, 2013, http://www.pbs.org/wgbh/nova/ancient/ice-mummies-inca.html.

National Geographic. 1997. "Virtual Autopsy: The Ice Maiden, Emissary to the Gods." *Andes Expedition: Searching for Inca Secrets*. Last modified in 1997. Accessed October 31, 2013, http://www.nationalgeographic.com/features/97/andes/autopsy/intro.html.

Reinhard, Johan. 1998. *Discovering the Inca Ice Maiden*. Washington, D.C.: National Geographic Society, 1998.

Reinhard, Johan. 2005. *The Ice Maiden: Inca Mummies, Mountain Gods, and Sacred Sites in the Andes*. Washington, D.C.: National Geographic Society.

K

Karloff, Boris

The English actor Boris Karloff (1887–1969) is best known for his portrayal of Dr. Frankenstein's monster in director James Whale's film *Frankenstein* (1931), a role that was turned down by Bela Lugosi. The film was well received, and Karloff's sympathetic portrayal of the monster received so much critical praise that he became a star. Karloff's performance as the mummy Imhotep in Karl Freund's 1932 film *The Mummy* was equally memorable, emphasizing the character's "fragile and brittle qualities while nonetheless hinting at great psychic power" (Fischer, 1991).

Karloff was born in London in 1887 as William Henry Pratt, the youngest of Edward and Eliza Pratt's nine children. According to Steven Jacob's authorized biography of Karloff, his parents' relationship was stormy, and by the actor's account, Edward was an abusive father and husband, so much so that after 20 years of marriage, his mother filed for a judicial separation, a legal arrangement granted by the courts in cases of cruelty to keep the couple apart although not formally divorcing them.

Karloff made his acting debut at the age of 9 in a production of *Cinderella* staged in his home parish as part of the local Christmas festivities. Even at this age, he reveled in playing a villain, taking the role of the Demon King. As a young man, he so wanted to pursue a career in acting that he deliberately failed a consular service exam so that he could "legitimately" reject a job as a public servant. Soon after, he left for Canada and joined a touring theater group, becoming a stage actor as well as a film extra, and played minor roles in silent films until he gained recognition with his role as a murderous convict in the sound film *The Criminal Code*.

Karloff would go on to achieve fame as an actor who played monsters, and who could transform his appearance in a way rivaling that of famed character actor and "man of a thousand faces" Lon Chaney. After helping to create the definitive cinematic portrayal of Frankenstein's monster in *Frankenstein*, he laid the foundation for all other cinematic and literary representations of the mummy in *The Mummy*. Karloff's Imhotep is memorable because the monster is not the mindless, foot-dragging corpse that it would become in the later mummy series of films. Rather, the powerful magic that allows Imhotep to reanimate 3,000 years later is the force of his will and his keen intelligence, a trait we see in the creature's face when the camera first reveals his burning stare to the audience. After Imhotep is freed from

Boris Karloff's mummy makeup for 1932's *The Mummy* took eight hours to apply. (Bettmann/Corbis)

his sarcophagus, he escapes into the night and lives under the assumed identity of Ardath Bey while searching for his lost love, Princess Ankhesenamun, who has been reincarnated as Helen Grovesner (with both characters played by Zita Johann, 1904–1993). Bey is able to pass convincingly as a mortal, since the living view his wizened skin as evidence of advanced age and sun exposure rather than mummification.

Make-up artist Jack Pierce took eight hours to transform Karloff into Imhotep the mummy, twice as long as it took to turn him into Frankenstein's monster. The make-up that Karloff wore to play Imhotep was particularly uncomfortable. After Pierce glued back the actor's ears and built up the bridge of his nose, Karloff was covered in colliodon, a highly flammable and vicious solution that was then dried with a hair dryer. Next, Karloff was covered with beauty clay that Pierce carved cracks into when it hardened. To complete his costume, Karloff was wrapped in 150 yards of artificially aged linen. Although it took a great deal of time to turn Karloff into the mummy, the make-up was needed for only one scene in the film, since Freund decided to give the mummy little on-screen time so that the monster would seem more terrifying through his relative absence from view.

Removing the mummy make-up from Karloff was also painful and arduous, requiring the use of solvents and acids.

Although he was an actor, Karloff was an intensely private person who did not crave the limelight. In his authorized biography of Karloff, Steven Jacobs describes how in 1957, when Karloff found himself the subject of the television show *This Is Your Life*, he felt that the experience was "an unwelcome intrusion into his private life" (Jacobs, 2011).

June Pulliam

See also: Freund, Karl; Imhotep; *The Mummy* (1932); Universal Studios mummy series

Further Reading

Fischer, Dennis. 1991. "Karl Freund (1890–1969)." In *Horror Film Directors, 1931–1990*. Jefferson, NC: McFarland & Co.

Jacobs, Steven. 2011. *Boris Karloff: More Than a Monster. The Authorized Biography*. Sheffield, England: Tomahawk Press.

Weaver, Tom, Michael Brunas, and John Brunas. 2007. *Universal Horrors: The Studio's Classic Films, 1931–46*. Jefferson, NC: McFarland & Co.

Kharis

The ancient Egyptian mummy Kharis is a character that was originally introduced in Universal Studios 1940s series of Mummy films, which followed the wildly popular 1932 film *The Mummy* but were not sequels to it. Kharis resurfaced again in 1959 soon after Hammer Studios acquired the rights to Universal Pictures' monsters and produced its own film entitled *The Mummy*.

Kharis is the monster in *The Mummy's Hand* (1940), *The Mummy's Tomb* (1942), *The Mummy's Ghost* (1944), and *The Mummy's Curse* (1944), where he is reanimated again and again to take revenge on those who disturbed him and to seek out the reincarnation of his love, Princess Ananka. Because Kharis has considerably more on-screen time in these four films compared to the mummy scenes

Although the picture of Boris Karloff made up as a mummy in 1932's *The Mummy* may be the single most famous image of a movie mummy in the genre's history, it was actually the character of Kharis, from Universal Studios' mummy films of the 1940s, that became the iconic mute, shambling, murderous mummy monster of general popular memory. The character has effectively colonized pop culture over a span of more than 60 years. It is Kharis, for example, and not the Karloff mummy, that is the basis of the typical mummy masks, mummy costumes, and mummy decorations that have been a regular part of American Halloween celebrations since the 1950s.

of his counterpart Imhotep (played by Boris Karloff) in 1932's *The Mummy*, his character is responsible for perpetuating the iconic figure of the creature as a mute, reanimated corpse wrapped in rotting bandages who walks with a shambling gait.

In *The Mummy's Hand*, a team of archaeologists in search of the tomb of Princess Ananka accidentally unearth Kharis, an immortal who has been buried alive for several millennia. In his mortal life he served as the high priest of Karnac, but his tongue was cut out and he was mummified alive as punishment for stealing the sacred tana leaves that he hoped to use for resurrecting his lost love, Princess Ananka. Kharis fully reanimates with the help of Andoheb, a modern-day priest of Karnac who is sworn to protect Egypt's dead from outsiders such as the band of archaeologists who would rob the graves and exploit the treasures. In the next film in the series, *The Mummy's Tomb*, Andoheb sends an emissary to Mapleton, Massachusetts to revive Kharis so that he can avenge the despoiling of Princess Ananka's tomb. After killing several members of the original expedition, Kharis is caught and burned, yet he lives to kill again in *The Mummy's Ghost*, and then again in *The Mummy's Curse*.

Kharis was played by Tom Tyler (1903–1954) in *The Mummy's Hand*, and then Lon Chaney, Jr. (1906–1973) took over the role for the remaining three Mummy films. The character appears again, played by Christopher Lee, in Terence Fisher's 1959 film *The Mummy*, where he is a rough approximation of his character in the Universal mummy films.

June Pulliam

See also: *Abbott and Costello Meet the Mummy*; Chaney, Lon Jr.; *The Mummy* (1959); The mummy in popular culture; Mummy movies; *The Mummy's Ghost* and *The Mummy's Curse*; *The Mummy's Hand*; *The Mummy's Tomb*; Universal Studios mummy series

Further Reading

Cowie, Susan D., and Tom Johnson. 2002. *The Mummy in Fact, Fiction, and Film.* Jefferson, NC: McFarland & Co.

Feramisco, Thomas M. 2002. *The Mummy Unwrapped: Scenes Left on Universal's Cutting Room Floor.* Jefferson, NC: McFarland & Co.

Weaver, Tom, Michael Brunas, and John Brunas. 2007. *Universal Horrors: The Studio's Classic Films, 1931–46.* Jefferson, NC: McFarland & Co.

L

Lee, Christopher

In his long career, English actor Christopher Lee has honed the character of the villain and the protagonist to a fine, deadly edge. No other actor had played such varied roles, most having to do with the darker aspects of being human, or inhuman, as the case may be. Today, Lee is perhaps best known to audiences at large for his later career portrayal as Count Dooku in the second Star Wars franchise and the evil wizard Saruman in the Lord of the Rings trilogy directed by Peter Jackson. He came to prominence, however, in starring roles in the Hammer horror films, and his name will forever be associated with the archetypal monsters Frankenstein, Dracula, and the mummy.

Lee (Christopher Frank Carandini Lee) was born May 27, 1922 to Geoffrey Trollope Lee and Estelle Marie. His father was a decorated colonel, and his mother, a contessa, was found to be the perfect model for artists and sculptors. In school, Lee studied Greek and Latin, and then went to serve in World War II. This had a profound effect on him. He would later say the celluloid horror of the films he starred in were nothing compared to what saw in during the war. His experiences were not typical, either; he served as Special Forces officer as part of the British Special Operations Executive, a group of spies and saboteurs.

After the war, Lee and his sonorous voice took to the stage, performing in a number of operas and plays. Eventually he moved into films, often appearing as a character actor in action films such as *Captain Horatio Hornblower R. N.* (1953), *Storm Over the Nile* (1955), and *Port Afrique* (1956).

Lee's first role as a monster for the Hammer Films horror franchise was the coveted part of Frankenstein's monster in *Curse of Frankenstein* (1957). This was the first attempt at a serious faithful retelling of Mary Shelley's novel since the Universal films decades earlier, and it put Lee on the map as someone worthy to walk in

Despite his status as a bona fide horror icon, Christopher Lee has maintained for years that he never really regarded his films as horror. Instead, he says he prefers to use the same term that friend and fellow legend Boris Karloff liked to use when discussing their mutual genre: fantasy.

Reference

Landis, John. 2011. *Monsters in the Movies: 100 Years of Cinematic Nightmares*. New York: DK Publishing.

Boris Karloff's shoes. But Lee had to rely on his own imagining of the monster; the original makeup used for Karloff's performance was under copyright, and so Hammer relied on their own methods, which created an uncomfortable four-hour ordeal to apply what they wanted to be a more realistic looking corpse-like visage. Lee had no dialogue in the film, but he once told an interviewer for Cinefantastique that when he found this out prior to the start of filming, his co-star Peter Cushing consoled his friend by saying "You're lucky. I've read the script!"

His next films for Hammer would be *Horror of Dracula* (1958), the film that would not only cast Lee in one of the most archetypal villain roles of all time but typecast him—for good or ill—as an actor very much at home in the role of an antihero. Despite the relatively few lines of dialogue Lee spoke in this film, his on-screen charisma in the part of Dracula would make him a star among horror movie audiences.

Like Karloff in Universal's 1932 version, Lee plays two roles in Hammer's *The Mummy* (1959). As the ancient Egyptian priest Kharis and then as the mummy—a walking automaton under the thrall of a fanatic follower of the god Karnack—Lee gave a performance in this film that remains one of his most physical. In fact, he suffered a number of minor injuries during shooting. In one scene the mummy crashes through a set of double doors, but the prop department failed to hang them to break easily, and Lee dislocated his shoulder while busting them down. In another scene he is shot at, and the bullet effects were created by attaching charges of gun powder to his chest, which left burns on his skin.

In later interviews, Lee would describe his disappointment with the reliance of modern horror films on serial killers and gore rather than the more literary inspirations that were evidenced in the Hammer franchise. He saw his own horror films as delightful escapism and—as he once told a writer for the magazine *Famous Monsters of Filmland*—possibly less nefarious than a movie like the multiple Academy Award-winning "serious" drama *On the Waterfront* (1954) with its romantic view of "hoodlums," as he called the main characters.

Soon after what would be his most famous role as Lord Summerisle in *The Wicker Man* (1973), Lee would return again to become a character actor (playing the villain, of course). It was not until George Lucas asked him to play Count Dooku in the *Star Wars* prequel trilogy that he was once again recognized as an actor of unique talent. Peter Jackson would then cast Lee as the dark wizard Saruman in his *Lord of the Rings* trilogy. Lee had wanted to play Gandalf, one of his favorite literary characters, but while he auditioned for the part, it was given to Sir Ian McKellan. Still, Lee fully embraced his role as Saruman, which emerged as one of his best performances and a part that would fully return him to the popular consciousness and considered an icon of horror.

Peter Bebergal

See also: Hammer Films mummy series; *The Mummy* (1959); Mummy movies

Further Reading

Christopher Lee: Official Website. 2011. "Biography." Accessed December 15, 2013. http://christopherleeweb.com/pages/biography.

Hearn, Marcus, and Alan Barnes. 2007. *The Hammer Story: The Authorised History of Hammer Films*. Foreword by Christopher Lee. London: Titan Books.

Landis, John. 2011. *Monsters in the Movies: 100 Years of Cinematic Nightmares*. New York: DK Publishing.

Lenin, Vladimir

Vladimir Lenin was a revolutionary and one of the creators of the Soviet Union. When he died in 1924, his body was preserved and placed on display in the Kremlin in Moscow.

He was born Vladimir Ilych Ulyanov on April 22, 1870, to an educated family in Simbirsk, Russia. As a young man he was greatly influenced by Karl Marx's *Das Kapital* and converted to Marxism. He adopted the last name "Lenin" in 1901 while working for an underground political party. Lenin spent much of his life in

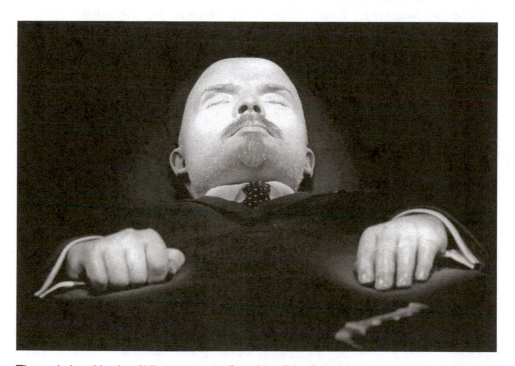

The embalmed body of Vladimir Lenin, founder of the Soviet Union, on display in his tomb on Moscow's Red Square. (AP Images/Sergei Karpukhin)

exile in Europe but returned to Russia just after the czarist regime was overthrown by the March 1917 revolution. He subsequently became leader of the new government.

In the 1920s a series of strokes incapacitated Lenin, and when he died on January 21, 1924, he was considered a national hero. His body was mummified and placed in a specially built crypt in the Kremlin so that people could view him forever, thus giving rise to the expression, "Yesterday, today, tomorrow, Lenin is always with us."

Today, Lenin's mummy appears to be well-preserved, but many have commented that the face appears waxy. This could be the result of the use of wax in the embalming procedure, but there is also an unsubstantiated rumor that the body was damaged when sewers backed up and flooded the tomb, and that it was replaced with a wax duplicate.

The Russian government has never released information about the method used to preserve Lenin's body, but the basics of the technique are known. Every 18 months the body is removed from its mausoleum and immersed in a vat of glycerol, potassium acetate, and other preservatives. After the bath, the liquid is permitted to drip off, and the body is wrapped in rubber bandages to retain the remaining preservatives. The head and hands are bathed with embalming fluid twice a week and are checked for bacteria.

Moscow's Institute for Biological Sciences, which is responsible for the preservation of Lenin's body, has sold its services for $250,000 to those who wish similar treatment. With the change in government in the former Soviet Union, it is possible that Lenin's body will be buried at some point, as funds for his preservation are no longer provided, and the scientists responsible donate their services for his upkeep.

Bob Brier

See also: Embalming

Further Reading

Atlas Obscura. 2013. "Lenin's Mausoleum." Accessed December 8, 2013. http://www.atlasobscura.com/places/lenins-mausoleum.

Lovejoy, Bess. 2013. "Vladimir Lenin." In *Rest in Pieces: The Curious Fates of Famous Corpses*, by Bess Lovejoy, 130–135. New York: Simon & Schuster.

McDonald, Mark. 2004. "Lenin Undergoes Extreme Makeover." *ArtUkraine.com*, Associated Press, March 1. Accessed December 8, 2013. http://www.artukraine.com/old/historical/lenin_makeover.htm.

Quigley, Christine. 2006. *Modern Mummies: The Preservation of the Human Body in the Twentieth Century.* Jefferson, NC: McFarland & Co.

Zbarsky, Ilya, and Samuel Hutchinson. 1999. *Lenin's Embalmers.* Translated by Barbara Bray. London: Harvill Press.

Lindow Man

Lindow Man is the remarkably well-preserved body of a man who died in Iron Age Britain between the years of 2 BCE and 119 CE. Named for the Lindow Moss bog in northwest England where the body was found, Lindow Man is one of several individuals found in the same area. The peat preserved all of the bodies extremely well, even preserving delicate eyelashes and fingernails, but Lindow Man is the most complete, and is one of the best known "bog bodies" found in Great Britain. Like some of the other bog bodies found throughout Great Britain and Europe, Lindow Man appears to have been ritually killed and then dumped into the bog.

Lindow Man's official designation is Lindow II, to differentiate him from the other bog bodies found at Lindow Moss. The remains have also been humorously dubbed "Pete Marsh." The remains were unearthed in August 1984, while workers were harvesting peat. Fragments of two or three other individuals were also discovered nearby. The remains of Lindow Man consist of the head and torso of a young man, though an upper thigh found nearby (currently labeled Lindow IV) may be from the same individual. The remainder of his body may have been unwittingly destroyed during the peat excavation process.

When he died, Lindow Man was around 25 years old, and was just under 5 ½ feet tall. He weighed somewhere between 130 and 145 pounds and had a trimmed beard and mustache and well-manicured fingernails, leading researchers to suspect that he probably did little, if any, manual labor. Like many individuals in the past, Lindow Man suffered from internal parasites, but otherwise seems to have been relatively healthy. A reconstruction of Lindow Man's facial features by an expert from the University of Manchester in 1985 revealed strong brow ridges, a straight nose, small ears, and unblemished but lined skin on his face and forehead. He had short dark brown hair, and, although his eye color is impossible to determine, he probably had blue-gray eyes, which were common among Celts of the period. Researchers were even able to reconstruct the last meal that he ate before he died: unleavened bread or a pancake containing barley and wheat. Radiocarbon dating was used to determine the approximate time period of Lindow Man's death. When he died, Lindow Man was wearing an arm band of fox skin and fur,

Lindow Man's death was an extremely violent affair. Although the exact sequence is somewhat difficult to determine, a strong blow to his back broke one of his ribs, and two blows to the top and back of his head probably originated from an axe with a narrow blade. A cord around his neck was likely used as a garrote for strangulation, breaking his neck in the process. By this time, Lindow Man was certainly dead, but his throat was cut for good measure, before he was thrown or laid face-down in the bog. The excessive violence displayed in Lindow Man's death has led many to speculate that he may have been part of a ritual killing or sacrifice.

Preserving and studying bog bodies once they are excavated is a complicated process, and the body must be handled and stored with extreme care. The environment of a peat bog, which combines very low or nonexistent levels of oxygen with high acidity, nearly halts the decay process and instead preserves the body, organs, and skin, rather like the process of tanning and preserving leather. Unearthing a bog body and exposing it to oxygen and heat immediately accelerates the process of decay. In the case of Lindow Man, the body was removed from the bog with some of the surrounding peat, to be stored at the British Museum and gradually excavated and studied. Keeping some of the peat with the body stabilized the fragile remains for transportation, and allowed the body to be excavated in controlled conditions and at a slow, careful pace. Once the peat was removed, the body was able to be analyzed and studied. CT scans, radiocarbon dating, and endoscopic examination provided extensive information about Lindow Man's life and death. After a great deal of discussion and testing, researchers determined that freeze-drying the body would provide the best way to preserve Lindow Man and prevent the remains from further decay. A specially-designed mount and display case allowed Lindow Man to be placed on display while still being kept in a carefully controlled, cool environment.

Lindow Man is currently on display in the British Museum. Although human remains from other bogs have been found in Great Britain and Europe, Lindow Man remains one of the best known examples of a bog body, and the detailed studies of his remains have illuminated many aspects of life in Iron Age England.

Roselyn Campbell

See also: Bog bodies; Medical imaging of mummies; Mummies of Europe; Natural mummification; Tollund Man

Further Reading

British Museum. 2013. "Conserving the Lindow Man." Accessed October 22. http://www.britishmuseum.org/explore/highlights/articles/c/conserving_the_lindow_man.aspx.

British Museum. 2013. "Lindow Man." Accessed October 22. http://www.british museum.org/explore/highlights/highlight_objects/pe_prb/l/lindow_man.aspx.

British Museum. 2013. "Lindow Man: What Did He Look Like?" Accessed October 22. http://www.britishmuseum.org/explore/highlights/articles/l/what_did_lindow_man_look_like.aspx.

Lobell, Jarrett A., and Samir S. Patel. 2010. "Bog Bodies Rediscovered." *Archaeology* 63, no. 3 (May/June). Accessed October 23, 2013. http://archive.archaeology.org/1005/bogbodies/.

Sanders, Karin. 2009. *Bodies in the Bog and the Archaeological Imagination*. Chicago: University of Chicago Press.

Stead, I. M., J. B. Bourke, and Don Brothwell. 1986. *Lindow Man: The Body in the Bog*. London: British Museum Publications.

Turner, R. C., and R. G. Scaife. 1995. *Bog Bodies: New Discoveries and New Perspectives*. London: British Museum Press.

van der Sanden, Wijnand. 1996. *Through Nature to Eternity: The Bog Bodies of North-west Europe*. Translated by Susan J. Mellor. Amsterdam: Batavian Lion International.

"Lost in a Pyramid; or, The Mummy's Curse"

"Lost in a Pyramid; or, The Mummy's Curse" is a short story that was first published in the January 16, 1869 issue of *New World*. The tale is one of several dozen Gothic thrillers that Louisa May Alcott (1832–1888), best known for her books for young readers, wrote either anonymously or pseudonymously, and it is one of the earliest published fictional treatments of the theme of an ancient curse visited on defilers of an Egyptian tomb.

During a visit to his cousin Evelyn, to whom he is betrothed, Paul Forsyth shows her a small gold box full of "seeds of some unknown Egyptian plant." When Evelyn asks how he came by it, Paul discloses that it is an artifact he brought back from "the Cheops" (a reference to the Great Pyramid of Giza, one of the Seven Wonders of the World). While exploring the interior of the vast pyramid, Paul and his companion, Professor Niles, become disoriented and lost. When Niles stumbles and breaks his leg, he suggests that Paul build a fire in the hope that the smoke it creates will be noted by their guide, Jumal, who left the pair earlier to engage the services of a second guide. The only available combustible material is a mummy-case, which, Paul discovers, still contains the mummy interred in it. Unwrapping the mummy, they find the gold box clasped in her hands. Paul burns the empty mummy case, and after that the mummy itself, before Jumal finds them. Niles later translates a piece of parchment that had been wrapped up with the mummy's cerements and they reveal that the body was that of "a famous sorceress who bequeathed her curse to whoever should disturb her rest." Evelyn proposes

---

Nineteenth-century American author Louisa May Alcott is more famous as the author of *Little Women*, but she also wrote several Gothic thrillers, and her 1869 short story "Lost in a Pyramid; or, The Mummy's Curse" is recognized as one of the earliest fictional treatments—or perhaps *the* earliest—of the theme of a "mummy curse," which is described in this excerpt:

> Among his spoils, Niles found a bit of parchment, which he deciphered, and this inscription said that the mummy we had so ungallantly burned was that of a famous sorceress who bequeathed her curse to whoever should disturb her rest. Of course I don't believe that curse has anything to do with it, but it's a fact that Niles never prospered from that day. He says it's because he has never recovered from the fall and fright and I dare say it is so; but I sometimes wonder if I am to share the curse, for I've a vein of superstition in me, and that poor little mummy haunts my dreams still.

that Paul plant the seeds to see what sort of plant might grow from them, but Paul—who fears that "they may be some horrible poison, or possess some evil power, for the sorceress evidently valued them, since she clutched them fast even in her tomb"—casts them into the fire.

Three months pass, and on the morning of their wedding day Paul tells Evelyn that on the night he told her of his adventure in the pyramid, he returned to the room where he destroyed the seeds and discovered that one had escaped the flames. He decided to send the seed to Niles for planting and Niles intends to take the flower grown from it to a meeting of scientists to identify it. Evelyn then tells Paul that she, too, found a seed that had gone astray and planted it herself, and she shows him the plant that has grown from it: "Almost rank in their luxuriance were the vivid green leaves on the slender purple stems, and rising from the midst, one ghostly-white flower, shaped like the head of a hooded snake, with scarlet stamens like forked tongues, and on the petals glittered spots like dew." The flower has just bloomed that morning, and Evelyn intends to wear it during the wedding ceremony. Paul cautions that Evelyn should not do so until Niles can identify the plant.

That evening, Evelyn appears to have recovered from lassitude she complained of earlier in the day, but Paul notices that her hands feel unusually cold to touch. Then a servant delivers an urgent letter to Paul, which informs him that Niles collapsed and died at the scientific conference after presenting the unusual plant, and that his corpse developed markings not unlike those of the flower. "At my desire," writes the note sender, "the mysterious plant was examined, and pronounced by the best authority as one of the most deadly poisons known to the Egyptian sorceresses. The plant slowly absorbs the vitality of whoever cultivates it, and the blossom, worn for two or three hours, produces either madness or death." By the time Paul asks if Evelyn did, in fact, wear the flower to the wedding, it is obvious that she did. She has been rendered all but comatose: "No recognition in the eyes, no word upon the lips, no motion of the hand—only the faint breath, the fluttering pulse, and wide-opened eyes, betrayed that she was alive." For the rest of her days, Forsyth attends her in her state of "death in life."

Written at the height of nineteenth-century America's interest in Egyptology and mummies, Alcott's story is possibly the first to exploit mummy lore for the purposes of horror. Mummy fiction by Alcott's predecessors—Jane Loudon Webb, Edgar Allan Poe, and Theophile Gautier—was more in the vein of fantasy or satire than horror.

Stefan R. Dziemianowicz

See also: The mummy in Western fiction: Beginnings to 1922

Further Reading

Alcott, Louisa May. 2001. "Lost in a Pyramid; or, The Mummy's Curse," 1869. In *Into the Mummy's Tomb*, edited by John Richard Stephens, 33–42. New York: Berkley Books.

Lovecraft, H. P.

H. P. Lovecraft was an American author who has come to be regarded as the leading writer of supernatural fiction in the twentieth century, and who addressed the issue of mummies in several tales written in the 1920s and 1930s.

Howard Phillips Lovecraft (born in Providence, R.I., August 20, 1890) was largely self-educated, having attended only a few years of elementary school and withdrawing from high school in 1908 without a diploma. In 1914 he began writing articles and poetry for various magazines of the United Amateur Press Association, and in 1917 he resumed the writing of weird fiction, which he had abandoned in 1908. Over the next 20 years, he wrote a relatively small body of work (about 50 original tales, several of which are of novella or short-novel length), but this work was immensely influential. Lovecraft came to focus on the theme of "cosmicism"—the notion of the insignificance of the human race in the context of the immensity (both spatial and temporal) of the universe. This is the underlying theme of the stories of the so-called Cthulhu Mythos (a term not coined by Lovecraft but by his disciple, August Derleth), in which huge and powerful "gods" or alien species have come to the earth and have had sporadic but cataclysmic encounters with human beings.

American horror writer H. P. Lovecraft may be most famous for his stories about ancient alien "gods" and slimy, tentacular, other-dimensional horrors, but he also incorporated mummies into several of his tales. One of the most notable examples is the 1935 story "Out of the Aeons," which he ghost-wrote for Hazel Heald, and which contains the following description of a particularly horrifying mummy housed in a Boston museum:

The mummy was that of a medium-sized man of unknown race, and was cast in a peculiar crouching posture. The face, half shielded by claw-like hands, had its under jaw thrust far forward, while the shriveled features bore an expression of fright so hideous that few spectators could view them unmoved. The eyes were closed, with lids clamped down tightly over eyeballs apparently bulging and prominent. Bits of hair and beard remained, and the color of the whole was a sort of dull neutral grey. In texture the thing was half leathery and half stony, forming an insoluble enigma to those experts who sought to ascertain how it was embalmed. In places bits of its substance were eaten away by time and decay. Rags of some peculiar fabric, with suggestions of unknown designs, still clung to the object.

Just what made it so infinitely horrible and repulsive one could hardly say. For one thing, there was a subtle, indefinable sense of limitless antiquity and utter alienage which affected one like a view from the brink of a monstrous abyss of unplumbed blackness—but mostly it was the expression of crazed fear on the puckered, prognathous, half-shielded face. Such a symbol of infinite, inhuman, cosmic fright could not help communicating the emotion to the beholder amidst a disquieting cloud of mystery and vain conjecture.

Lovecraft's first attempt at a mummy story is "The Nameless City" (written January 1921; first published in the *Wolverine,* November 1921). Here, a rather agitated explorer investigating the ruins of "Irem, the City of Pillars" in the Arabian desert stumbles on a city buried under the sands that contains a large number of wooden cases with glass fronts, containing the mummified remains of hideous alien creatures of a sort never seen before on earth. Although approximately human in size, their heads "violat[ed] all known biological principles." The narrator concludes that they may have been "some palaeogean species which had lived when the nameless city was alive" and that they were worshipped by the presumably human builders of the nameless city. But the narrator is appalled to discover, at the end of the story, a rushing array of the same entities, alive this time, and he is forced to conclude that they, and not any human species, had built the nameless city.

Although "The Nameless City" is not regarded as one of Lovecraft's better tales, even during his early apprentice period (1917–26), it contains a number of intriguing features that he would use to better advantage in later stories. In particular, it is one of the earliest instances in which Lovecraft depicted an alien species (although this species apparently is native to earth and did not come from outer space) whose history and achievements rival or surpass those of humanity. The story served as a kind of trial run for the much more impressive novella *At the Mountains of Madness* (written 1931; first published in *Astounding Stories,* February-March-April 1936), in which explorers to the Antarctic come upon the cryogenically preserved remains of an alien species (from outer space this time) that had come to earth millions of years ago and actually created all earth life, including the human race. But this story does not use the mummy theme even in modified form.

In early 1924, Lovecraft was commissioned by J. C. Henneberger, owner of the pulp magazine *Weird Tales,* to collaborate with the celebrated escape artist Harry Houdini (pseudonym of Ehrich Weiss, 1874–1926) on a story. The narrative was purportedly based on an actual adventure that Houdini had experienced in Egypt, when he was seized by some natives and dropped down a hole in the roof of the Temple of the Pharaohs (or Campbell's Tomb), bound and gagged; hours later, Houdini managed to escape his bonds and emerge from the pyramid. But as Lovecraft investigated this account and correlated it with what is known of the pyramids, he concluded that Houdini's story was largely or wholly fictitious, and he urged Henneberger to allow him maximum freedom in the depiction of the events. Lovecraft apparently received this freedom: although the early part of the story closely follows the series of events as Houdini had described them, the narrative gradually focuses less on Houdini's plight and more on a question that Houdini (who, in the story, is writing his account in the first person) purportedly asked himself: *"What huge and loathsome abnormality was the Sphinx originally carven to represent?"* (Lovecraft 1986, 235). Houdini discovers the answer in a surprise ending where what appears to be a strange, five-headed monster is in fact only the forepaw of an immense creature lurking under the sands of Egypt.

Because Lovecraft unexpectedly wrote the story in the first person, Edwin Baird, editor of *Weird Tales,* felt that it could not bear both Houdini's and Lovecraft's byline, so it was published under Houdini's name only as "Imprisoned with the Pharaohs" in the May-June-July 1924 issue of *Weird Tales.* When the story was reprinted in the June-July 1939 issue, Lovecraft's contribution to the story was acknowledged in an editorial note. Lovecraft's own title for the story, "Under the Pyramids," has been ascertained by consulting an advertisement that Lovecraft placed in the *Providence Journal* (March 3, 1924) noting the loss of the typescript in Union Station. (He was in the process of boarding a train to New York to marry Sonia Haft Greene.) Recent editions of Lovecraft's tales use this title.

The mummy theme is only incidental to "Under the Pyramids," but it colors the narrative effectively, creating a sense of ancient mystery and horror that serves as a backdrop to the spectacular concluding revelation. The narrator, pondering the degree to which the ancient Egyptians were obsessed with death, focuses in particular on one purported feature of what he calls "decadent priestcraft": "*composite mummies* made by the artificial union of human trunks and limbs with the heads of animals in imitation of the elder gods" (Lovecraft 1986, 234). This conception is presumably imaginary, but it sets the stage for the narrator's witnessing of living creatures who are the presumed originals of these mummies; as he states apocalyptically at one point, *"Hippopotami should not have human hands and carry torches . . . men should not have the heads of crocodiles . . ."* (Lovecraft 1986, 240).

Lovecraft's occupation as "revisionist," which ran the gamut from light copyediting to full-fledged ghostwriting, was in fact his predominant source of income, as his sales of original fiction were always sporadic and he frequently suffered painful rejections of some of his more ambitious works. Several would-be authors approached Lovecraft to write horror stories based on plot-germs they had devised, and it is in these tales that Lovecraft often wrote entire narratives based on the flimsiest of plot outlines. One such author, Hazel Heald (1896–1961), commissioned Lovecraft to write at least five stories, all of which appeared under her name in various pulp magazines.

For tracing his use of the mummy theme, the most relevant of these is "Out of the Aeons" (written 1933; first published in *Weird Tales,* April 1935). This tale concerns an ancient mummy housed in the Cabot Museum of Archaeology in Boston and an accompanying scroll in indecipherable characters. The mummy and scroll remind the narrator—the curator of the museum—of a wild tale found in the *Black Book* or *Nameless Cults* of von Junzt, which tells of the god Ghatanothoa, the mere sight of whom would cause a person's body to turn to stone and leather on the outside, while the brain inside remained perpetually alive. Von Junzt goes on to speak of an individual named T'yog who, 175,000 years ago, attempted to scale Mount Yaddith-Gho on the lost continent of Mu, where Ghatanothoa resided, and to free humanity from the god's control; he was protected from Ghatanothoa's glance by a magic formula, but at the last minute the priests of Ghatanothoa stole the parchment on which the formula was written and substituted another one for it. The antediluvian mummy in the museum, therefore, is T'yog, petrified for millennia by Ghatanothoa.

Lovecraft died in Providence, Rhode Island, on March 15, 1937. Although no book of his stories appeared in his lifetime, his work was collected in many editions after his death, and he has exercised an unparalleled influence on subsequent writers in the field of weird and supernatural fiction.

S. T. Joshi

See also: The mummy in Western fiction: From 1922 to the twenty-first century

Further Reading

Cannon, Peter. 1989. *H. P. Lovecraft*. Boston: Twayne.

Joshi, S. T. 2010. *I Am Providence: The Life and Times of H. P. Lovecraft*. 2 vols. New York: Hippocampus Press.

Joshi, S. T., and David E. Schultz. 2001. *An H. P. Lovecraft Encyclopedia*. Westport, CT: Greenwood Press.

Lovecraft, H. P. 1986. *Dagon and Other Macabre Tales*. Sauk City, WI: Arkham House.

M

Manchester Egyptian Mummy Project

The Manchester Egyptian Mummy Project was established in 1973 by Rosalie David, former Keeper of Egyptology at the Manchester Museum and now Emeritus Professor of Biomedical Egyptology at the University of Manchester. The Manchester Museum contains one of the United Kingdom's largest collections from ancient Egypt and Sudan, including 20 complete human mummies. This group formed the basis for the project, which uses a range of nondestructive scientific techniques to examine mummified tissue. Information can be extracted on ancient disease, diet, living conditions, and the process of mummification itself. The project led to the creation in 1997 of the International Ancient Egyptian Mummy Tissue Bank, which provides samples for further research. This in turn has yielded important insights into the pathology of diseases, such as schistosomiasis (also known as bilharzia), which affect modern populations and were present in ancient Egypt.

The project took up the pioneering approach of Egyptologist Margaret Murray (1863–1963), herself well-known for an association with the Manchester Museum. In 1908 Murray autopsied the Museum's "Two Brothers," the mummies of two men from an intact Middle Kingdom tomb at Deir Rifeh. One of the unwrappings was performed in front of an audience of several hundred people and was widely reported in the Manchester local press. Newspapers noted that scraps of mummy bandages were available on request as mementos for those who had attended. A meticulous report of the investigation of both brothers' remains, including contributions from medics and discussion of their tomb objects, appeared in 1910.

Building on this interdisciplinary approach, one of the first of the modern Project's many subjects was a mummy simply known by its museum accession number, "1770." The mummy was unwrapped in 1975 during a televised investigation. The project team comprised a range of specialists in areas as diverse as Egyptology, radiology, dentistry, and tropical disease. The wrappings proved to contain the poorly preserved body of a girl in her early teens, missing her lower limbs, who was perhaps the drowned victim of a crocodile attack. These had been magically "restored" by embalmers through the addition of prosthetic limbs made of mud and wooden sticks. In addition to a gilded mask, 1770 was provided with gilded finger stalls and nipple covers. The wrappings also contained an imitation phallus, raising the possibility of ancient confusion over the gender of the body.

Radiocarbon dating initially suggested that the bones of the mummy were several centuries older than the wrappings, but in light of more recent investigations the mummy has been dated to the Ptolemaic Period with possible "repairs" to wrappings carried out in the Roman Period.

Another important patient was the 25th or 26th Dynasty mummy of a lady called Asru. When her mummy was given to the Manchester Natural History Society in 1825, still within her two nested coffins, it had been fully unwrapped and lacked any of its original bandages. It was fashionable in the early-mid-nineteenth century to stage "mummy unwrappings," and it is likely that Asru had been the subject of one such macabre form of entertainment. The mummy still retained two of mummified packages of viscera, which would once have been wrapped in linen and bound up between or on her thighs. In the period when Asru died, it was a common practice to return the embalmed viscera to the chest cavity or between the legs.

Examination of the mummified packages found with Asru's body revealed that they consisted of stomach and intestines. The latter proved to be affected by a parasitic worm infestation. Worms were present in both the lining and the muscular wall of the intestine, and appear to have caused significant disease. Use of an electron microscope allowed the identification of a nematode worm, probably *Strongyloides*. This parasite is found in many tropical and subtropical countries, and enters the body through the skin when this comes into contact with contaminated soil or water. Worms pass along the veins and eventually reach the lungs, stomach, and intestines. Female worms lay eggs that are passed in feces. In conditions where hygiene is poor, the cycle begins again through contact with soil or water contaminated with feces. Symptoms of these conditions would have included coughing, wheezing, stomach ache, and diarrhea.

Further analysis revealed more of Asru's ailments. Pieces of her shriveled stomach were immersed in a 10 percent solution of buffered formalin. The dehydrated tissue was analyzed with a dissection microscope and revealed the larvae skins of *Chrysomyia albiceps*—a diphtheria-carrying fly. Asru also suffered from a parasitic bladder infection called schistosomiasis (bilharzia). This waterborne parasite can cause internal bleeding, with blood passed in the urine. Asru is likely to have been anemic due to this blood loss.

Casts of both the fingertips and toes were taken by the Greater Manchester Police using a quick-setting and flexible rubber compound, a technique later applied to modern corpses. Despite her generally poor state of health, both fingerprints and toe prints implied that Asru had led a very comfortable life. Her fingers and feet showed little sign of manual work, so it seems that her duties during life—probably in a temple—were not arduous.

A burr hole was made in the skull to allow any remaining brain tissue to be removed for histological examination. Several intact larval skins were observed within the skull and these were photographed through the endoscope and then removed with fine retrieval forceps. They appeared to be very similar to those examined from Asru's intestines, which were identified as *Chrysomyia albiceps.*

X-rays of the chest showed radiopaque tissue, which, it was thought, probably represented remains of the internal organs that the embalmers had failed to remove, but the thoracic cavities appeared to be empty. This made it suitable for examination by endoscope. There was no evidence of resin within the chest. The thin membrane (pleura) lining the inside of the chest cavity could be seen quite clearly, and appeared to be free from disease.

Radiographs of the collapsed lung tissue showed unusual striped markings, an indication of lung disease. Samples were taken using small retrieval forceps attached to the endoscope. Histological examination of this tissue revealed scarring of the pleura and the lung tissue. It also revealed that Asru not only suffered from a *Strongyloides* infestation but also had a hydatid cyst, caused by another parasitic worm, *Echinococcus*, present within the lung.

X-rays of the spine revealed a slipped-disc and a deformity of the middle finger of Asru's left hand caused by osteoarthritis. These results indicated that she had died some time in her 50s or 60s—an elderly woman for ancient Egypt. The skull of Asru, and also those of 1770 and the Two Brothers, were the subject of facial reconstructions by anatomical artist Richard Neave, allowing the public to feel a closer connection to the individuals as they may have appeared during life.

Between the 1970s and the 2000s, the Manchester Egyptian Mummy project applied its techniques—often referred to as the "Manchester Method"—to mummies in other collections. During 2012 and 2013 all of the Manchester Museum mummies were scanned using state-of-the-art CT facilities at the Manchester Children's Hospital, continuing the aims of the original project. These clarified many of the earlier X-rays and added new information about the lives, deaths and afterlives of the Manchester mummies. Many of the techniques of the project have now been extended to the Ancient Egyptian Animal Biobank, also housed in the University of Manchester.

Campbell Price

See also: Medical imaging of mummies; Mummy unwrappings

Further Reading

David, Rosalie, and Rick Archibold. 2000. *Conversations with Mummies: New Light on the Lives of the Ancient Egyptians.* London: HarperCollins.

David, Rosalie, ed. 2013. *Ancient Egyptian Mummies and Modern Science.* Cambridge: Cambridge University Press.

The Manchester Mummy (Hannah Beswick)

Hannah Beswick, "the Manchester Mummy" (1688–1758), was a wealthy Oldham resident who became recognized for her subsequent mummification following her death. Her remains were initially displayed at her surgeon's house and latterly the Museum of the Manchester Society of Natural History, before her eventual burial in 1868. Her preservation was a reflection of a personal preoccupation with mortality and a fear of being buried alive. The subsequent use of her body traces the increasingly formal and respectable atmosphere engendered within museums as ideas of curiosity and morbid voyeurism became replaced with notions of education and respectable taxonomies.

Daughter of John Beswick of Failsworth, Hannah was born in 1688 into a wealthy family. Apparently increasingly fearful of being buried alive, following an experience of her brother's near living burial, she commissioned her family physician, the Manchester surgeon Dr. Charles White (1728–1813), to ensure that a similar fate did not befall her. Popular stories indicate that Dr. White was paid a significant sum of money to embalm Hannah. However, the lack of any such explicit mention of this process within the will suggests that a briefer period of close observation was intended rather than any more permanent solution such as embalming. Nonetheless, White, a well recognized collector of curiosities (such as the skeleton of highwayman Thomas Higgins) and student of the anatomist William Hunter (1718–83) was familiar with the principles of embalming and conducted the process on Hannah.

Although the precise details of Hannah's preservation are unknown, literary scholar Zigarovich notes that Hunter's preferred process (and therefore White's probable approach) consisted of injecting the body with a mixture of vermillion,

One of the specimens which in a Natural History Museum would be classed with mammalia was the mummy of Miss Beswick. She was an 18th century lady with fear of being buried alive. With this fear in her mind she left, so it is said, her body and her money to her medical man, Mr. Charles White, with the condition that she was to be kept above ground for a century. Mr. White mummified her, and eventually the mummy was placed in the Museum. If Miss Beswick had known that her corpse would be gazed at by Manchester crowds in a Natural History Museum she would, I fancy, have preferred the risk of being buried alive to the ungenteel fate of being a specimen in a museum.

Source

Nicholson, Francis. 1915. "Inaugural Address: The Old Manchester Natural History Society and Its Museum." *Memoirs and Proceedings of the Manchester Literary and Philosophical Society* 68 (1913–14): 12. Accessed February 13, 2014. http://www.archive.org/details/memoirsproceedin58manc.

turpentine, and oil of lavender and rosemary. Following this, organs were removed and cavities packed with plaster of paris. To what extent such embalming was common in the period is still debated by scholars, but it was far from rare and had numerous historical precedents, both modern and ancient. By 1868, however, a *Manchester Guardian* report described her as embalmed with tar and swathed in bandages, leaving only her face exposed.

Following her preservation at Cheetwood, Hannah was placed within a wooden case in White's home in Sale, Ancoats Hall, where she remained until his death. One eyewitness account of her display exists; Thomas de Quincey in his *Autobiographic Sketches 1790–1803* described a visit in 1801 as a 16-year-old schoolboy to White's house, in which he claimed to have seen Hannah presented in a "common English clock case." She was later bequeathed to one Dr. Ollier, who in turn donated the remains to the recently established Museum of the Manchester Society for the Promotion of Natural History in 1828. The donation to what was ostensibly a collection focusing primarily on natural history was not as odd as it immediately appeared. Contributions to the Society provided a point of patronage and social recognition and covered a variety of objects from the obvious to the obscure and curious including other human remains such as a Peruvian mummy and one Egyptian mummy, "Asroni." (The latter, now known as Asru, is the sole survivor of the earliest human remains collected by the Society and is currently on display in the Egyptian Gallery at Manchester Museum. See "Manchester Egyptian Mummy Project.")

The wider fascination with displays of human remains continued into the nineteenth century in a variety of guises. At the more professional—and therefore respectable—end of the spectrum was the philosopher Jeremy Bentham's (1748–1832) desire to become an auto-icon and tool of anatomical education. In stark contrast were the public unwrappings that formed part of an emerging trend known as "mummymania," associated with "Egyptomania." Across Britain, Europe, and America, Egyptian remains were displayed and dissected in both private and public displays that were nominally intended to inform, but that were actually and primarily intended to entertain.

The display of Hannah Beswick in Manchester fell somewhere between these two extremes, despite the Society's focus on fauna, flora and conchology (the study of mollusc shells), Hannah Beswick highlighted the often arbitrary methods of collecting, and her designation and display as a "curiosity" emphasized this. Nonetheless, contemporary museum guides made some attempt to provide a little information about her origins, but they were unable to place her within an obvious taxonomic framework. This uneasy situation continued until the collection in its entirety was sold to the recently established Owens College (forerunner of the current University of Manchester) in 1868, as the Society was unable to continue financially or logistically.

It was at this stage, well over a century after her death, that Hannah was removed from display. Objects considered to lack an edifying or educational purpose were disposed of by the commissioner of the newly formed Manchester Museum, R. D. Darbishire. In the case of the former Manchester resident, following consultation with the Bishop of Manchester, surviving relatives and the Home Secretary, a discreet and unmarked burial took place at Harperhuy Cemetery, near Manchester. The reason given for the secrecy was the fear of grave robbers, who might seek to profit further from Hannah's notoriety. Although the worries proved unfounded, descendents viewed the incident as a scarcely creditable episode.

Following her burial, stories continued to be created around Hannah's life and death. John Timbs's 1866 *English Eccentricities,* and particularly Edith Sitwell's 1933 *The English Eccentrics*, placed her within a tradition of curiosities and increasingly the ghostly and horrific. It is this textual existence that has proved most enduring, even with all of its various inaccuracies.

Hannah Beswick's preservation, exhibition and movement through private to public viewing reflects the ability of the modern, as well as the ancient dead to have new meanings placed around them postmortem and for these in turn to evolve, become forgotten and then be rediscovered. She went from being an individual, to a source of wealth and bequests, to a curiosity, and then an inconvenience before finally being recognized as an individual again in the course of her final interment.

Robert McCombe

See also: Bentham, Jeremy; Displaying mummies; Egyptomania; Embalming; Manchester Egyptian Mummy Project; Mummy unwrappings

Further Reading

Alberti, Sam. 2009. *Nature and Culture: Objects, Disciplines and the Manchester Museum.* Manchester: Manchester University Press.

BBC. 2009. "The Strange Fame of Hannah Beswick." Last updated August 11. Accessed December 8, 2013. http://news.bbc.co.uk/local/manchester/hi/people_and _places/history/newsid_8195000/8195234.stm.

Dobson, Jessie. 1953. "Some Eighteenth Century Experiments in Embalming." *Journal of the History of Medicine and Allied Sciences* 8, no. 4: 431–441.

Grimshaw, William. 1900. "Miss Ann Beswick." *The Manchester Guardian.* May 4.

MacGregor, Arthur. 2008. *Curiosity and Enlightenment.* New Haven, CT: Yale University Press.

Rogers, Beverley. 2012. "Unwrapping the Past: Egyptian Mummies on Show." In *Popular Exhibitions, Science and Showmanship, 1840–1910*, edited by Joe Kember, John Plunkett, and Jill A. Sullivan, 199–218. London: Pickering and Chatto.

Zigarovich, Jolene. 2009. "Preserved Remains: Embalming Practices in Eighteenth-Century England." In *Eighteenth-Century Life* 33, no. 3: 65–104

Mariette, Auguste

François Auguste Ferdinand Mariette was a French scholar renowned for his Egyptological work, publications, and discoveries. Of particular relevance to the study of mummies were his discovery and clearance of the Saqqara Serapeum, the burial place of the Apis bull, as well as his unearthing of Queen Aah-hotep, his founding of the Egyptian Antiquities Service, and his establishment of the first Museum of Egyptian Antiquities in Cairo.

Mariette was born in Boulogne-sur-Mer on February 11, 1821. As a child he excelled at his studies, but was unable to complete his education as a result of his father's remarriage. At the age of 18 he traveled to England to teach French and drawing in Stratford before moving to Coventry to work in the ribbon industry. Unable to earn a living in Coventry, he returned to Boulogne in 1841 to complete his studies. He earned his Bacc. ès Lettres, with honorable mention, at Douai in only six months. He was then appointed Maître d'études at the College de Boulogne in 1841, and Professor of French in 1843. In 1842, his family received the papers of his cousin, Nestor l'Hôte, who had accompanied Jean François Champollion's expedition to Egypt. These papers inspired him to study the ancient Egyptian language. He learned Coptic and, after securing a minor post at Paris' Louvre Museum, he transcribed all of its Egyptian monuments. This work formed the basis for an inventory of Louvre's Egyptian collection. In 1850 he was sent to Egypt to acquire Ethiopic, Syriac, and Coptic manuscripts.

It was during this trip that he began his most famous work: the excavation of the Serapeum in Saqqara. Mariette discovered the monument by following the remains of sphinxes that once lined its dromos, and which are described by the Greek writer Strabo. The Serapeum consists of a series of catacombs that were dug at least as early as Egypt's 18th Dynasty (1550–1295 BCE), and were used continuously until its Ptolemaic Period (332–330 BCE). The monument was the burial place for the sacred Apis bull, the physical manifestation of an aspect of the god Ptah. The Apis bull was always a single individual animal, chosen for its sacred markings, as explained by the Greek historian Herodotus. Upon the death of this animal a period of national mourning began, and it was embalmed and buried in a granite sarcophagus in the Serapeum. These sarcophagi weighed up to 80 tons, and all but one had been robbed of its burial at the time of Mariette's work. The remaining bull mummy is now kept in Cairo's Agricultural Museum.

In 1859, an agent of Mariette discovered the intact burial of a queen named Aah-hotep (ca. 1550 BCE) in Dra Abu el Naga, in Luxor's West Bank necropolis. Inside the tomb, a gilded wooden coffin holding the queen's mummy was found. The tomb also contained many funerary items, including ceremonial weapons of Pharaoh Ahmose I, two model silver and gold barks, and a variety of historically important jewelry.

In 1858, Mariette successfully petitioned Said Pasha, the Viceroy of Egypt, to create the Service des Antiquités, which he led until 1881. This organization was dedicated to regulating the flow of antiquities from Egypt. In this position, Mariette undertook an ambitious program of excavations, employing thousands of workmen, at Sheikh Abd el Qurna, Karnak, Menshiet-Ramleh, Tell el Yahudiya, Giza, Abydos, Mit Rahina, Saqqara, Esna, Medinet Habu, Tuna, Deir el Bahri, Sais, Edfu, Mendes, and Bubastis.

In 1863, again with the support of the Egyptian government, Mariette opened the Museum of Egyptian Antiquities in Bulaq, Cairo—the first national museum in the Near East. Its current incarnation, Cairo's Egyptian Antiquities Museum, houses an important repository for ancient Egyptian mummies, as well as the nation's publicly-accessible royal mummy collection.

Mariette held many positions over the course of his career, including Commander of the Legion of Honor in 1878. He also attained many honors, including being given the title Pasha by the Egyptian government in 1879. He died in Bulaq on January 18, 1881, and his body was interred in a sarcophagus that now rests in the front garden of Cairo's Egyptian Museum.

Andrew Bednarski

See also: Brugsch, Emile; Egyptian Antiquities Museum; Napoleon and the birth of Egyptology

Further Reading

Al-Ahram Weekly Online. 2004. "A Man with a Mission." August 26-September 1. Accessed December 8, 2013. http://weekly.ahram.org.eg/2004/705/he1.htm.

Bierbrier, Morris L. 2012. *Who Was Who in Egyptology*. 4th ed. London: Egypt Exploration Society.

Marquise of Tai

This Chinese mummy, discovered in 1972 in Hunan Province, is perhaps the best preserved of all the Chinese mummies. Most Hunan tombs had been looted in the 1930s and 1940s, but two huge burial mounds near the capital, Changsha, remained untouched and were excavated by the Chinese government. After four months, a tomb containing a series of nested coffins was found, the coffins being buried in five tons of charcoal to absorb any water that might enter the tomb.

The innermost coffin contained the body of Lady Ch'eng, wife of Litsang, the Marquis of Tai, who lived 2,100 years ago. The 50-year-old woman had been buried and hermetically sealed in a solution of mercury salts that was still liquid when scientists entered the tomb. Lady Ch'eng's joints were still flexible and could be easily bent. The skin was so pliable that when touched, a depression formed and then rebounded so it could no longer be seen.

Because of the excellent preservation of the body, it was possible to perform a nearly normal autopsy to determine the cause of death. The internal organs were all in place and 16 badly worn teeth remained in her mouth. In the marquise's stomach, 138 mushmelon seeds were discovered, the remains of her last meal. Her death was probably the result of two factors occurring in sequence. First, a gallstone completely blocked the lower end of the common bile duct. Second, her arteries, especially the coronary artery, were clogged with plaque. The marquise probably died when extreme biliary distress caused a heart attack.

Bob Brier

See also: Buddhist self-mummification

Further Reading

Aufderheide, Arthur C. 2003. *The Scientific Study of Mummies*. Cambridge: Cambridge University Press.

Hall, Alice J. 1974. "A Lady from China's Past." *National Geographic* 145, no. 5: 660.

Martin, Aaron. 2008. "Conceptions of the Afterlife in Pre-Buddhist China." *Yahoo! Voices*. February 19. Accessed December 8, 2013. http://voices.yahoo.com/conceptions -afterlife-pre-buddhist-china-1009855.html?cat=34.

Medical imaging of mummies

Ancient mummies are a rich source of biomedical information. Thus, it is not surprising that diagnostic imaging has been conducted on them since as far back as the late nineteenth century. While medical imaging theoretically covers not only radiological imaging (such as X-ray and CT scan) but also microscopy-based imaging, the latter will not be addressed in this article. The application of radiological techniques on mummies has revealed a whole variety of diseases in both common and more famous mummies. It has solved many questions about possible causes of death and also provided information about types of mummification and potentially hidden artifacts. Today, diagnostic radiological techniques are a major and essential part of most scientific studies on mummies.

The "birth" of medical imaging occurred in November 1895 when the German physicist Wilhelm Röntgen became the first to detect what he termed "X-rays." Only a few months after this, in early 1896, this technique was first used by another German physicist, Walter König, who X-rayed an ancient Egyptian child mummy in the Senckenberg museum in Frankfurt. The plain X-ray of this mummy's knee region was the very first of its kind, and the image was of a surprisingly

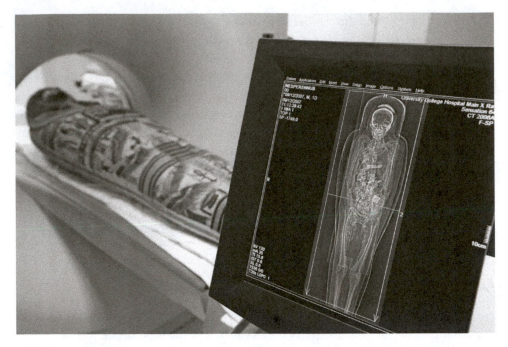

A 3,000-year-old Egyptian mummy prepares to go through a scanner at University College Hospital in central London. (AP Images/John Stillwell)

high quality. Soon after this, other researchers such as C. Thorsten Holland and A. Deoeking performed similar radiological investigations of ancient remains. So did the famous Sir Williams Flinders Petrie, who was one of the first to apply this technology to ancient Egyptian samples.

Jumping forward several decades, CT scanning—which is X–ray based—was developed in the 1970s to allow cross-sectional, high-resolution imaging, and

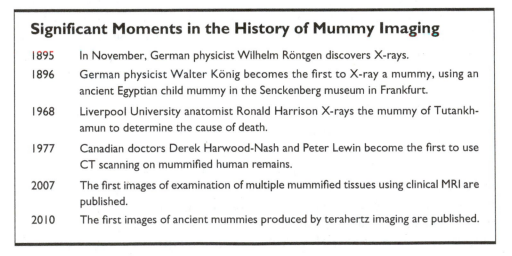

Significant Moments in the History of Mummy Imaging

1895	In November, German physicist Wilhelm Röntgen discovers X-rays.
1896	German physicist Walter König becomes the first to X-ray a mummy, using an ancient Egyptian child mummy in the Senckenberg museum in Frankfurt.
1968	Liverpool University anatomist Ronald Harrison X-rays the mummy of Tutankhamun to determine the cause of death.
1977	Canadian doctors Derek Harwood-Nash and Peter Lewin become the first to use CT scanning on mummified human remains.
2007	The first images of examination of multiple mummified tissues using clinical MRI are published.
2010	The first images of ancient mummies produced by terahertz imaging are published.

eventually it came to provide a kind of 3D data set. A few years after its very first clinical and research applications, this technology, too, was applied to mummy studies. In 1977 in Canada, D. C. F. Harwood-Nash and P. K. Lewin became the first to CT scan mummified remain. Since then, the technology evolved enormously. Endoscopic examinations—ones using endoscopes that are directly inserted into the body—have also sometimes been performed on mummies since the late 1970s (for example, by M. Manialwi and colleagues). Ultrasound imaging, by contrast, does not provide any decent results when used on mummified tissue. The very first high-resolution images of multiple mummified tissues by clinical magnetic resonance (MR) imaging were published by Frank Rühli and colleagues in 2007, and the very first terahertz images of ancient mummies were published by Lena Öhrström and colleagues in 2010.

Medical imaging is used in mummy studies for various purposes. In a manner similar to its medical applications on modern individuals, it is used in mummy studies to detect and describe pathologies (diseases) and variations in normal anatomy. Mostly pathologies in hard tissues, but also disorders in soft tissues, can be found. The list of pathologies radiologically described in ancient mummies (and in some cases verified by subsequent macroscopical, histological, or molecular analyses) is very long and basically covers all major pathologies known today. Exemplary, often traumatic or rheumatologic disease (disease affecting joints, muscles, and bones) can be found. Specific trauma is often difficult to assess in terms of its time of occurrence. Unless bone remodeling (the normal process of new bone formation) occurring at least a few days after an injury can be detected radiologically, a trauma occurring around the time of death and possibly leading to an individual's death is not distinguishable from a fracture that occurred *after* death. Also, tumors, especially bone tumors, have been found in various studies. However, it is important to bear in mind that the unique mode of preservation caused by mummification (both natural/accidental and artificial/intentional) leads to an appearance of the tissue, both to radiological imaging and the naked eye, which is quite different from a well-known clinical one. Often tissues are denser because of the loss of water and thus have a less distinct appearance, or they show unnatural cracks. It is often tricky to distinguish multiple tissues from each other, and this is one of the goals of ongoing basic research in this field. So-called pseudopathologies—structural changes that look like the result of disease but that actually resulted from normal postmortem processes—can be detected radiologically. Some are alterations that look like pathologies but are caused postmortem— for example, by environmental influences.

The interaction of imaging technologies with various types of mummies makes for some interesting variations. For example, the specific mummification and embalming techniques practiced in Ancient Egypt lead to alterations typically found in these mummies. Exemplary remnants of radio-dense embalming liquids can be found as well as alterations of the tissue due to (for example) the use of drying salts. Ice mummies, such as Ötzi the Iceman, or those from the Inca period, usually show a very good level of preservation and are therefore easier to analyze radiologically. In the case of Ötzi, the cause of death has been able to be determined (an arrow ruptured a thoracic artery and led to death by exsanguination or "bleeding out"). Without such good tissue preservation, and specifically without CT scanning, this discovery would not have been possible. Bog bodies, due to their preservation in peat, and due to the physical pressure of the soil, show a very distorted radiological appearance. Generally, such diagenetic processes (chemical and physical transformations) lead to alterations of anatomical structures and thus make radiological interpretation notoriously difficult in any mummy. Often, mummies are only partially preserved, or body parts are no longer in the original anatomical position, because of various factors, such as being disturbed and roughly handled by tomb robbers.

Besides medical assessments, anthropological issues such as sex and age can also be determined, for example, in wrapped mummies by X-ray and CT scans. Furthermore, radiological imaging can be used to find hidden artifacts or analyze clothing or other tools. Also, with the latest progress in CT technique, the resolution (and thus the later virtual reconstructions) is so good that minor dental disorders such as discrete periodontal disease or mild forms of cavities can be analyzed too.

Conventional X-ray is an easy, widely available tool to examine mummies, and it shows a high spatial resolution. That said, CT scanning has many additional technological benefits. It is a fast imaging modality; a full-body can be scanned within minutes using normal clinical routine scanners; however, some technical parameters may be slightly adjusted for such old tissues. For example, CT-guided biopsies as well as CT-based 3D stereo-lithographic reconstructions are now possible. The latter allows a facial reconstruction to be built on a skull model based on estimated soft tissue thickness and other information about a body's facial appearance. One major advantage of having CT data sets is the enormous post-processing tools available. Besides density-specific virtual reconstructions in all planes, it is also possible to measure (in so-called Hounsfield unit scales) or do other morphological calculations. The virtual unwrapping of a mummy is especially nice for exhibition to the lay public, because different structures can be removed and/or highlighted by being given different colors. Today, the resolution is so high that the type of hairstyle a mummified individual once had can be virtually determined, and inscriptions on hidden amulets can even be read. The amount of data created in such image stacks is quite large, but this can be shared among various research groups for keeping records of a sample at a particular time. If at a later stage a rescan is done, changes in preservation can theoretically be monitored.

Major advantages of diagnostic radiological imaging of mummies include the often fast initial results, the high resolution, and the noninvasive character of the procedures. The very few studies that have been done on the impact of radiological imaging on ancient tissue and DNA preservation show it to have no impact, thus making even X-ray based techniques a truly nondestructive examination method for mummies.

Furthermore, various nonstandard techniques are now used. Portable X-ray machines and mobile lorry-based CT scanners are available. Portable X-ray units are roughly the size of a suitcase and can be installed within a tomb (for example). Newer systems are even completely digitalized, thus providing immediate digital X-ray images on a connected screen. This allows a quick, high-quality conventional X-ray analysis of ancient remains in the very spot where a mummy is found, without risking the possibility of damaging or contaminating it during transportation. However, a major problem of such *in situ* (onsite) imaging is the fact that often the remains cannot be physically placed in the most appropriate way, and thus superimposition of various structures (for example, of the sarcophagus and the body) on the image may occur. This is particularly a problem when using portable conventional X-rays. But as a screening tool to record the current status of preservation, to find hidden artifacts, and to detect major pathologies, this is a very handy and cheap approach. It is used frequently at excavation sites in Egypt and in museum collections (to name just two common examples).

The use of lorry-based CT scanner was particularly highlighted as part of the examination of Pharaoh Tutankhamun in 2005 in the Valley of the Kings, Egypt. The CT scans allowed researchers to rule out several earlier claims about health and disease of the boy-king, while new theories on his presumed cause of death (femur fracture, lesion of mid-foot) could be postulated based on the high quality CT images (a total of about 1700 cross-section images of the body). Since then, almost all of the Egyptian royal mummies have been CT scanned as part of the ongoing Egyptian Mummy Project, revealing a whole range of pathologies but also providing details about the amount and type of mummification and embalming. To name another prominent example, the violent cause of death of Pharaoh Rameses III from a slit throat has been diagnosed and reconstructed specifically using CT. The quality of these trailer-based CT scans is fully comparable to the ones known from the same type of hospital-based machines.

Recently, magnetic resonance imaging (MRI) has been introduced into the research field of mummy studies as well. Since most mummies are usually very dry, the use of standard clinical MR techniques is automatically useless. However, with the introduction of new MR settings it is now possible to gain decent images of such dry tissue. Nevertheless, the use of MR is still very limited, and more comparative research on mummified tissue needs to be done to evaluate the feasibility and diagnostic impact of this challenging technology. Currently, the use of MRI is too much restricted in terms of its availability, the examination itself is time consuming and expensive, and the diagnostic impact is not good enough. Thus, CT remains the modality of choice for most current radiological studies of mummies.

Another imaging modality, terahertz imaging (as seen in similar applications in the notorious airport security body scanners) has been recently applied for the very first time on ancient mummies. It allows a rough visualization of major body structures, and in the future it could possibly be used for structural and component information.

Today the use of modern medical diagnostic imaging is an absolute must in most major mummy studies, and it reveals an enormous wealth of information about, among other things, the health and disease of these individuals, and thus on the evolution of human disease in general. With more powerful computing systems in the future, better and faster data analyses will be possible. Also, the more experience on ancient (or modern experimental) human mummified tissue we can gain, the better our ability to use medical imaging on mummies in the future will be. Despite new molecular and thus invasive technologies being available in this unique field of research, the influence of medical imaging in mummy studies will most likely become even more relevant over time.

Frank Rühli

See also: Bioanthropology Research Institute; Bog bodies; Ice mummies; Ötzi the Iceman; Swiss Mummy Project; Tutankhamun ("King Tut")

Further Reading

Chhem, Rethy K., and Brothwell, Don R. 2008. *Paleoradiology: Imaging Mummies and Fossils*. New York: Springer.

Hawass, Z., Gad, Y. Z., Ismail, S., Khairat, R., Fathalla, D., Hasan, N., Ahmed, A., et al. 2010. "Ancestry and Pathology in King Tutankhamun's Family." *JAMA* 303: 638–647.

Hawass, Z., Ismail, S., Selim, A., Saleem, S. N., Fathalla, D., Wasef, S., Gad, A. Z., et al. 2012. "Revisiting the Harem Conspiracy and Death of Ramesses III: Anthropological, Forensic, Radiological, and Genetic Study." *BMJ* (Dec 14): 345: e8268.

Hawass, Z., Shafik, M., Rühli, F. J., Selim, A., El-Sheikh, E., Abdel Fatah, S., Amer, H., et al. 2009. "Computed Tomographic Evaluation of Pharaoh Tutankhamun, ca 1300 BC." *Ann. Serv. Antiq. Egypte* 81: 159–174.

Lewin, P. K., and Harwood-Nash, D. C. 1977. "Computerized Axial Tomography in Medical Archaeology." *Paleopathology Newsletter* 17: 8–9.

Lynnerup, Niels. 2007. "Mummies." *American Journal of Physical Anthropology* suppl. 45: 162–190.

Lynnerup, Niels. 2010. "Medical Imaging of Mummies and Bog Bodies: A Mini-review." *Gerontology* 56, no. 5: 441–448.

Oehrstroem, L., Bitzer, A., Walther, M., and Rühli, F. 2010. "Terahertz Imaging of Ancient Mummies and Bone." *American Journal of Physical Anthropology* 142: 497–500.

Rühli, F. J., von Waldburg, H., Nielles-Vallespin, S., Böni, T., and Speier, P. 2007. "Clinical Magnetic Resonance Imaging of Ancient Dry Human Mummies without Rehydration." *JAMA* 298: 2618–2620.

Rühli, F. J., Hodler, J., and Böni, T. 2002. "CT-Guided Biopsy: A New Diagnostic Method for Paleopathological Research." *American Journal of Physical Anthropology* 117: 272–275.

Rühli, F., Böni, T., and Chhem, R. K. 2004. "Diagnostic Paleoradiology of Mummified Tissue: Interpretation and Pitfalls." *Canadian Association of Radiologists Journal* 55, no. 4 (October): 218–227.

Medicine and mummies

From the fifteenth century to the eighteenth, many Europeans saw mummies not merely as objects of wonder, but as medicine. When used by Shakespeare or one of his peers, "mummy" typically meant not "a mummy," but *some* mummy—an impersonal substance viewed in terms of medicine or trade. The broader context of mummy as medicine is corpse medicine, or medicinal cannibalism. Across this period thousands of Europeans, both rich and poor, swallowed or applied human blood, bone, skull, flesh, fat, and organs for medical purposes. Naturally, one significant context for this topic is cannibalism. Was this cannibalistic? Was it viewed in this way by those involved? If not, why not?

These questions themselves lead on to the rather odd historiographical status of both "mummies as medicine" and "medicinal cannibalism." For a long time, European historians seem to have been curiously reluctant to discuss these compelling topics. Relevant data was available decades ago, in books such as C.J.S. Thompson's *The Mystery and Art of the Apothecary* (1929). Yet this kind of discussion failed to spark serious debate on "mummy" as cannibalism. In 1985 Karl H. Dannenfeldt published an important article, "Egyptian Mumia." In 2003 Louise Noble discussed the question from the viewpoint of Renaissance literary studies, and in 2006 *Social History of Medicine* published an article on the cultural history of medicinal cannibalism.

It was around this time that an interesting insight began to emerge about mummy and medicinal cannibalism as topics. It became increasingly clear that

---

Although it seems almost inconceivable to most people today, from the fifteenth to the eighteenth centuries the use of crumbled, ground, and/or powdered parts of Egyptian mummies for medicinal purposes came into common use all across Europe. The practice was connected to a fundamental attitude about death and corpses that differed sharply from modern ones, and it only died out with the spread of Enlightenment-era ideas, which were employed in deliberate attempts to stamp out the practice of corpse medicine.

historians had not discussed these topics because they did not want to. The idea of Europeans as cannibals made them uncomfortable. Surprisingly, this was evident even in 2005, in an early scholarly response to a draft of the article mentioned above that was published the next year in *Social History of Medicine*. One reader suggested that the article should "drop the term cannibalism" from the title. A few decades back, this kind of unease manifested itself in much cruder ways. Quite basically, it caused historians to falsify history. Erwin H. Ackerknecht claimed in 1968 that mummy had been wholly discredited as a drug as early as the 1580s, but in fact, some Europeans were probably still using it in the 1780s.

In the sixteenth century, the naturally dry flesh of Egyptian mummies was crumbled, and then either swallowed in fluid, or pressed into a medicinal plaster that was then applied to the patient's body. It was used against cancer, ulcers, hemorrhage, epilepsy, and bruising. This last usage was perhaps the most common. The French King, Francis I (d.1547) "always carried it in his purse, fearing no accident, if he had but a little of that by him" (Jonstonus 1657, 98). In the 1570s Queen Elizabeth's surgeon, John Banister, was using and recommending it, and in the 1580s the French surgeon Ambroise Paré admitted that mummy was "the very first and last medicine of almost all our practitioners" against bruising (Paré 1585, 143). Paré himself opposed the use of mummy, but found that this marginal stance caused him problems. When, in 1580, Paré treated a Monsieur Christophe des Ursins for a fall from his horse, he used his own particular ingredients against des Ursins' injuries. On recovering consciousness, des Ursins indignantly demanded to know why mummy had *not* been applied to the bruising (Haggard 1975, 324).

Mummy medicines remained popular for over a century after Ursins voiced his complaints—so much so that certain gentlemen were using mummy as physic for their hawks. But in later decades there was a good chance that patients were swallowing a very different kind of mummy. From the early seventeenth century there were three different possibilities.

One was plain fraud. Because of the sheer demand and consequent profit motive, some unscrupulous merchants were baking up the flesh of dead lepers, beggars, or camels to resemble the genuine article. Secondly, there were "sand mummies" or "white mummies." These were new corpses, the spontaneously mummified bodies of those travelers who were either lost or suddenly overwhelmed by sandstorms in the North African deserts.

Thirdly, we have the mummy promoted by the Swiss medical reformer, Paracelsus (d.1543?). For most people in the seventeenth century, the key question was not: "should you eat people?" but rather: "what sort of person should you eat?" Paracelsus' disciples would prepare their mummy according to a version of the following recipe: "choose the carcass of a red man, whole, clear without blemish, of the age of twenty four years, that hath been hanged, broke upon a wheel, or thrust-through." This flesh should be cut into small pieces, and sprinkled with powder of myrrh and aloes, before being macerated in spirit of wine. It should then be "hung up to dry in the air," after which "it will be like flesh hardened in smoke" and "without stink" (Croll 1670, 155).

This sounds very different from the mummy of a privileged ancient Egyptian. The resultant flesh is as anonymous as that of any animal, and cured in a similar way. But this curing is itself a kind of mummification. And, whether or not we recognize this substance as "mummy," it was clearly what many doctors and patients held the word to mean in the seventeenth century. This Paracelsian mummy raises two interesting points. One is both medical and religious. Paracelsians wanted the fresh corpse of a young, healthy, red-haired man (no more than three days old, according to Paracelsus himself). Why? They evidently believed that from such a body you could consume the soul itself. To them, a three-day-old corpse was dead, but not *very* dead: its essential vitality still remained. The second point is a social one. In this era, the poor might be able to get hold of human bones or skull. And we know that they drank fresh blood (usually against epilepsy) at beheadings across Europe well into the nineteenth century. But they could not afford the Egyptian mummy that aristocrats used on their hawks, or even as fish bait. Often, they could not afford food or adequate clothing. And so, if they stole, and were caught and hung, they had a good chance of being made into medicine. In this fiercely unequal society, one of the most intimate relations between the very rich and very poor was this: the very poor were *inside* the bodies of the very rich, having been processed, sold, and swallowed as medicine.

Two big questions remain. Medicinal cannibalism arose and reached its peak just as European Christians were denouncing the tribal cannibals of the New World. First, then: how did the European medical practice escape the label of "cannibalism"? In the case of Egyptian mummy, the radically transformed qualities of such corpses probably helped soften the taboo. In the mid-sixteenth century a rabbi, David ben Zimra, was asked by fellow Jews if it was right to consume mummy. He responded that, "it is allowed, because its form has changed, and it has reverted to dust" (Patai 1964, 8–9). This could not, of course, be so easily said of Paracelsian mummy. But here, doctors and patients would often have felt that human bodies, criminal or otherwise, were elevated by the presence and power of the soul. Whatever the individual had done with their life, the body remained the pinnacle of God's creation.

It was also important that these various "mummies" were being used as medicine, not as food. In one sense, medicine could be regarded as a kind of necessary evil. Hence the memorable phrase of one seventeenth century preacher, Thomas Fuller, who emphasized that mummy was "good physic but bad food" (Fuller 1647, 100–101). Moreover, as the scientific revolution got underway, mummy medicines grew increasingly highly processed. This scientific and technological aspect of mummy must also have helped lift it over the allegedly brutish cannibalism of New World tribes. Put simply, it was a case of scientific culture over primitive nature.

Our second question is this: having thrived so long in the face of such seemingly potent taboo, when and why did the medicinal use of mummy come to an end? Significant opposition arose around the mid-eighteenth century. Yet there were notable signs of unease a hundred years before. In 1658 the author Sir Thomas Browne, lamenting the transience of even Egyptian artifacts, could write: "the Egyptian mummies, which Cambyses or Time hath spared, avarice now consumeth. Mummy is become merchandise, Mizraim cures wounds, and Pharaoh is sold for balsams" (Browne 1658, 78–79). Almost a hundred years later, the physician John Hill stated more emphatically: "the mummy and the skull alone of all these horrid medicines retain their places in the shops" (Hill 1751, 876). Although there was clearly some use of mummy even in the 1790s, the attitude of Hill and others signaled the beginning of the end for this once popular and profitable drug.

Why was its death knell sounded at this particular time? There are four key reasons, all of them bound up with the self-consciously rational, scientific, and forward-looking Enlightenment. First: many affluent patients were now much more easily disgusted. In Shakespeare's time, by contrast, the word "disgust" did not even exist in English. Secondly: this period saw the attempt to create a "medical profession." Although we now take this for granted, it did not exist in the seventeenth century. In their efforts to improve their public image, doctors became more concerned about what they prescribed. Hence the physician Robert James, in 1747, on moss of the human skull: for James, there is now "no necessity why a physician should disgrace his profession by prescribing it" (James 1747, 470–1). Thirdly and fourthly, we have Enlightenment attitudes to their arguably more religious ancestors. Mummy and corpse medicine were increasingly tabooed as backward and superstitious. More specifically, long-running attempts to isolate the human soul in anatomical and physiological terms had now largely ceased. With the soul increasingly dematerialized, the older logic of Paracelsian mummy (that you could indeed swallow the soul) naturally crumbled away. By this time, it was not just that mummy was disgusting, disgraceful, and backward. It was also that the human body was no longer *worth* eating. All four reasons are nicely captured by Hill, again: "their folly is hardly less than their beastliness, who expect good from the dung of animals, from rotten human skulls, from the moss that has grown upon them, or from the ill-preserved remains of human carcasses, which they call mummy. Reason banishes these detestable medicines, which decent delicacy should never have admitted. They were always shocking to the imagination; and they are now known to be void of efficacy" (Hill 1758, 51).

Since 2011, the marginal and misrepresented status of mummy and corpse medicine has changed significantly. Ironically, after decades of neglect, corpse medicine was in this year honored with two book-length studies: Louise Noble's *Medicinal Cannibalism in Early Modern English Literature and Culture*, and *Mummies, Cannibals and Vampires*. In following months medicinal cannibalism featured repeatedly in national and international press, radio, and television. Naturally, the hottest topic here for most people was cannibalism. Many seemed to view the subject as an intriguing dark secret of European history; some as one more piece of hypocrisy on the part of those ruling élites who had so often tabooed (or invented) the tribal cannibalism of South America, Australasia, and Africa. More conservative readers flatly refused to believe that the social élite ever did swallow mummy as medicine. As Noble has also emphasized, one of the most important modern comparisons with mummy and older corpse medicines is the black market in human organs. This is almost always highly exploitative, and often dangerous for donors. At times it seems to have prompted outright murder. For the poor in the time of Shakespeare or Charles II, Egyptian mummy was largely just some mythical drug that they could never afford. But Paracelsian mummy was, potentially, their own dead body. Then as now, there was a lot the rich could do to the poor. And then as now, one of those things was to make them into medicine.

Richard Sugg

See also: Collecting mummies; Egyptomania; Mummy unwrappings; Napoleon and the birth of Egyptology

Further Reading

Ackerknecht, Erwin H. 1968. *A Short History of Medicine*. New York: Ronald Press.

Browne, Sir Thomas. 1658. *Hydriotaphia*.

Croll, Oswald. 1670. *Bazilica Chymica*. trans. anon.

Dannenfeldt, Karl H. 1985. "Egyptian Mumia: The Sixteenth Century Experience and Debate." *Sixteenth Century Journal* 16.2: 163–80.

Fuller, Thomas. 1647. *Good Thoughts in Worse Times*.

Haggard, Howard Wilcox. 1975. *Devils, Drugs, and Doctors: The Story of the Science of Healing from Medicine-man to Doctor*. Wakefield: EP Publishing.

Hill, John. 1751. *Materia Medica*.

James, Robert. 1747. *Pharmacopœia Universalis*.

Jonstonus, Joannes. 1657. *An History of the Wonderful Things of Nature*. trans. anon.

Noble, Louise. 2003. " 'And Make Two Pasties of Your Shameful Heads': Medicinal Cannibalism and Healing the Body Politic in Titus Andronicus." *English Literary History* 70.3: 677–708.

Noble, Louise. 2011. *Medicinal Cannibalism in Early Modern English Literature and Culture*. Basingstoke: Palgrave.

Paré, Ambroise. 1952. *The Apology and Treatise of Ambroise Paré*, 1585. Edited by Geoffrey Keynes. London: Falcon.

Patai, Raphael. 1964. "Indulco and Mumia." *The Journal of American Folklore* 77.303: 3–11.

Sugg, Richard. 2006. " 'Good Physic but Bad Food': Early-Modern Attitudes to Medicinal Cannibalism and its Suppliers." *Social History of Medicine* 19:2: 225–240.

Sugg, Richard. 2011. *Mummies, Cannibals and Vampires: The History of Corpse Medicine from the Renaissance to the Victorians*. Oxford: Routledge.

Thompson, C. J. S. 1929. *The Mystery and Art of the Apothecary*. London: John Lane.

Mummies of Europe

Human remains were mummified throughout Europe, from as early as 1500 BCE until the middle of the twentieth century. The majority of European mummies were naturally mummified in bogs and church crypts. This natural preservation, however, was noted by contemporaries and artificial mummification attempted to assist or replace natural mummification processes, particularly in the case of saints and royalty.

Perhaps the best-known European mummies are the bog bodies of northern *Europe*, England, and Ireland. These natural mummies were preserved by the tanning action of sphagnum bog moss, in addition to the anaerobia, absorbance, and acidic nature of the dense peat that forms the bogs. Bodies found in these conditions have been attributed to accidental and execution drownings, murder victim disposal, executed criminal disposal, and ritual sacrifice. Bog bodies from the U.K. range in dates from 900 BCE to 1800 CE, and bog bodies from Holland and Germany typically date to around the first century CE. Exceptions include the 10,000-year-old skeletonized body of Koelbjerg Woman and World War II victims of the Russian wetlands. In general, Danish bog bodies date between 400 BCE and 400 CE, with intentional bog burials in the pre-Roman Iron Age (500 BCE–0 CE).

Different regions of Europe are famous for different types of mummies:

Northern Europe, England, and Ireland: Many bog bodies, and also many natural non-bog mummies, the latter especially numerous in Denmark, Sweden, Finland, and Greenland.

Central Europe: Primarily natural mummies produced by burial in catacombs and churches where the environment is conducive to natural preservation. Also, famously, the ice mummies found at the Tyrolean and Swiss glaciers.

Western Europe: Mummies of kings, queens, saints, and nobles, some of them naturally preserved and others aided by one or more types of intentional treatment. Western Europe is also home to the famous Guanche mummies of the Canary Islands, representing a mummification tradition extending back to 400 CE.

Southern Europe: Mummies of saints, elites, and nobles, many of them in catacombs, variously produced by natural means, artificial means, or a combination.

Eastern Europe: A long history of elite mummification (of rulers, nobles, and others) extending as far back as Siberian mummification practices of the first century BCE and as far forward as the mummification of Russian leader Vladimir Lenin in 1924.

Natural non-bog mummies are also found throughout northern Europe, particularly in Denmark, Sweden, and Finland. The Bronze Age Mound People of tenth to thirteenth century CE Denmark buried their dead in tree trunk coffins on stone platforms covered in a mound of earth, resulting in natural mummification. Numerous natural mummies have also been produced by the cold, arid environment of the Greenland, including the Thule Qilakitsoq mummies (1475 CE), the pre-Christian Pisissarfik mummies (seventeenth century CE), and the mummy of explorer Charles Francis Hall (1871 CE) buried at or below the permafrost level. Finnish and Swedish natural mummies include the eighteenth and nineteenth century CE mummies beneath Finnish churches in Ostrobothnia and the frozen remains of the Eagle North Pole balloonists lost in 1897. The peoples of Lapland also produced temporary intentional mummies when their seasonal migration cycle took them from their traditional burial sites. These bodies, simply suspended in the dry wind, were dried for transportation and future burial. Natural mummification in the United Kingdom is limited to the bodies of late medieval crusaders (ca. 1190) in St. Michael's church, Dublin and the possible mummification of bodies from Bronze Age Cladh Hallan (1100 BCE–200 BCE). Evidence suggests that the position of these bodies, now skeletonized, was altered at a time significantly after death, but they remained articulated at that time.

Central European mummies are primarily natural mummies resulting from interment in dry, well-ventilated catacombs or churches. Germany's Kreuzberg monastery produced 25 such natural mummies around 1400 CE, and the mummification of Christian von Kahlbutz (1702) was aided by burial in an oak coffin and double-walled urn. Likewise, the low temperature and constant air current of the Dominican church of Vác, Hungary, its dead laid to rest on pine shavings in pine coffins, produced approximately 250 natural mummies. The late sixteenth to eighteenth century CE catacombs of Vienna produced similar natural mummies. Austria additionally produced natural salt mummies, when early seventeenth-century mining exposed burials to raw salt ore. Central Europe's most dramatic mummies, however, are those disgorged by the Tyrolean and Swiss glaciers. Lost mountaineers are found preserved in the Alpine ice sheets, and substantial scientific study has been given to the 5,300-year-old Tyrolean Iceman, Ötzi. Switzerland has also produced natural and artificial catacomb mummies, including the natural mummies from the churches of the Dominican Friars and of St. Leonard; the sixteenth century Basel Franciscan friars laid to rest on beds of wood chips and cloth; the 1596 Baron of Sennwald hung to dry in a windy area; and the Viennese Hapsburg Queen Ana who, after her death in 1821, was eviscerated, lye-embalmed, and placed in a beech coffin.

The kings, queens, saints, and nobles of western Europe were also interred under conditions that would lead to their mummification. In fifteenth-century France, Count Nassau and his daughter were naturally mummified, while Admiral John

Paul Jones (1792) ensured his preservation by being wrapped in tinfoil and placed in a lead coffin filled with straw, hay, and alcohol. In Portugal, the saints Juliao and Tarouca and Queen Isabel of Aragon were also naturally mummified; the natural preservation seen as an indication of their purity and favor with God. Likewise, the eleventh- to thirteenth-century Spanish kings of Leon were naturally mummified, as were the noblewoman Inez Ruiz de Otalora (1607), and the saints Igorputz, Fausto, Felicia, Teresa, and Leonor. In the late thirteenth century, the kings of Leon conquered the Canary Islands, home to a millennium long (400 CE–1400 CE) tradition of artificial mummification. The Guanches people mummified their dead by evisceration and stuffing of the body cavity with sand, pine needles, and other natural materials. The body was then wrapped in goat hides, in numbers related to the individual's status, and tied to a funerary board.

Italy is home to a wide range of mummies of saints and nobles. The catacombs of Venzone (1338–1850 CE), Popoli (1734–1845), Urbania (1380–1836), Comiso, Sicily (1742–1838), Ferentillo (1500–1871), Navelli (thirteenth century), and Arezzo (late sixteenth century) all contain naturally mummified human remains as a result of hot, dry weather and cool, dry burial environments. In the catacombs of Palermo, Sicily, bodies from 1599 to the late nineteenth century were naturally mummified by drying in a hot, sealed cell for nine months, and in times of epidemic the dead would be dipped in lime or arsenic, aiding in the mummification process. The mummies of the Neapolitan kings, queens, and nobles represent a mix of natural and artificial processes. While some individuals were simply placed in coffins in a dry part of a church, others were seated over a clay drip jar for several months, washed in vinegar, and placed in a wooden box for several months prior to transfer to a permanent coffin, a treatment common for European nobility. Many of the fifteenth- and sixteenth-century individuals, however, were eviscerated (disemboweled) and excerebrated (the brains were removed); their bodies and crania packed with resin-soaked cotton or wool, lime, aromatics, or mercury-containing substances. Mummies of saints, initially the product of natural processes, were later helped toward divine preservation by zealous church officials using evisceration, balsams, and aromatics. One exceptional artificial Italian mummy dating to the second century CE (the Grottarossa mummy) was mummified in a manner reminiscent of Egyptian techniques, in spite of the Roman tradition of cremation.

Other mummies from southern Europe originated in ancient Greece and Renaissance Czechoslovakia. Natural and artificial mummies have been identified in Mycenae and Thessaloniki, including a natural mummy (1500 BCE) partially preserved by contact with a copper mask and pectoral, and an artificial mummy (300 BCE) treated with resins, wrapped in a linen shroud and bandages, and placed in a lead coffin and marble sarcophagus. In the Czech Republic, the seventeenth century aristocratic Bokuvka family and other elites were naturally mummified by the excellent ventilation of the Klatovy crypts. The social and political elite were also artificially mummified throughout the sixteenth and seventeenth centuries. Kings Premysl Otakar II, Venceslav I, Charles IV, and John of Luxemburg were eviscerated via abdominal incision, stuffed with herbs, and, in some cases, immersed in metal tanks filled with resin, potassium chloride, and potassium sulfate.

Russia and Ukraine also have a history of elite mummification, including the natural mummies of the Romanov family (1918) and composer Nicolar Rubinstein (1881) and the embalmed, paraffin-injected, and climate-controlled mummy of Vladimir Ilych Lenin (1924). Not solely a recent feature of Russian mortuary treatment, natural and artificial mummification was practiced in the Siberian steppes from the first century BCE to the fifth century CE, involving evisceration, excerebration, incision of the skin along the back to drain fluids, excarnation of the extremities (that is, removal of flesh), and restoration of the limb shape by stuffing with sedge grass. A depression was excavated to four or five meters and lined with logs, into which the body was placed in a hollow log and covered with earth, a log roof, and a mound of rock and gravel. The first rains following burial trickled down through the burial and froze permanently, and it has been suggested that processing of the body was done only during the frozen fall and winter as the burial method alone sufficed when the ground was penetrable.

Andrew Wade

See also: Bog bodies; Capuchin Catacombs of Palermo; Church of the Dead; Cladh Hallan mummies; Crypt mummies of Sommersdorf Castle; Grauballe Man; Incorruptibles; Lenin, Vladimir; Lindow Man; Mummies of Ferentillo; Mummies of Lithuania; Mummies of Venzone; Natural mummification; Ötzi the Iceman; Tollund Man; von Kahlbutz, Christian Friedrich; Windeby Girl

Further Reading

Aufderheide, Arthur C. 2003. *The Scientific Study of Mummies*. Cambridge: Cambridge University Press.

Mummies of Ferentillo

Ferentillo is a town lying in the province of Terni in the Umbrian region of central Italy, 252 meters above sea level. The borough of Precetto, located on the left side of the Nera river, holds the sixteenth-century church of Saint Stefano, built on a preexisting medieval structure. This earlier building, situated at a lower level, was used as a cemetery until the nineteenth century. It measures about 24 meters in length, 9 meters in width, and 25 meters in height. On the right-hand side of the room, four windows are visible, and the left side consists of bare rock. There, 24 human mummies, including men, women, and children, as well as 10 preserved

Mummified bodies discovered in the crypt of the Church of St. Stephen, Ferentillo, Umbria, Italy. (DEA/S. VANNINI/De Agostini/Getty Images)

heads, a coffin, and over 270 skulls, are contained and exposed. However, the original number of subjects must have been larger: some sources indicate that three of these specimens are stored in the Anatomy Museum of the Perugia University, while other samples were dissected during early investigations.

Access to the crypt is provided by a stone portal, and the room is anticipated by a small antechamber, which was probably the original apsis. On the south wall, some original frescoes are still visible. To reinforce the foundations of the upper church, pilasters were built in the middle of the chamber, which now subdivide it into two environments. Scattered in what was once the nave of the previous church, the mummified bodies are mainly in an upright position, although some of them are disposed horizontally. The majority of them are located within metal or wood-made, glass-sided display cases. At the very end, a metal shelf holds the many skulls, while at its back lie scattered human bones.

Reportedly, burials in the ground of this site were not always associated with the use of a wooden coffin, depending on the deceased's social status. Instead, dead priests were coffined and entombed in the wall. Exhumation and subsequent inspection of such remains revealed that the principle behind their spontaneous mummification was desiccation (drying out): the bodies, of a yellowish color, appeared well preserved and light; their skin was dried and said to resemble parchment, while internal organs and muscles were almost completely constrained and shrunk. Hair and nails were at times still present. According to an 1885 document, many of the bodies bore rosaries, amulets, or medals in their hands, while some showed labels at the neck, on top of which maxims on mortality and resurrection were recorded.

The Ferentillo mummies have been studied since the mid-nineteenth century by scientists aimed at shedding light on the mechanisms of mummification. These include the physicians Carlo Maggiorani (1800–1885) and Aliprando Moriggia (1830–1906), supported by the chemist Vincenzo Latini (1805–1862). The latter performed chemical analysis of the soil, reporting it as principally composed of calcium salts from limestone and clay.

According to those scholars, the hygroscopic (water-attracting) nature of the soil would have favored dehydration of the buried cadavers, while the cool and dry environment, ventilated through perpetually opened windows, would have enhanced the process. However, probably influenced by the views on the Venzone mummies (regarding which, see the separate article in this volume), they also felt that—in addition to the physical factors noted—fungal growth may have played a role in the bodies' desiccation. It may be speculated that bodies buried in a lime-rich soil were also preserved by enzyme inactivation following alteration of the degree of acidity.

A late twentieth-century biomedical study of the skin of five adult males from this collection revealed that their preservation did not prevent the occurrence of initial decomposition phenomena, as suggested by the lack of epidermis.

Historical documents from both the past two centuries, together with physical evidence, indicate that dead animals were employed to experimentally replicate the mummification process. Two birds are, in fact, still displayed in the chamber.

To sum up, very little paleopathological research was carried out on the Ferentillo mummies, but if appropriately studied, this precious treasure is bound to provide significant information on the lives, lifestyle, and deaths of this crypt's historical residents.

Dario Piombino-Mascali

See also: Mummies of Europe; Mummies of Venzone

Further Reading

Aufderheide, Arthur C. 2003. *The Scientific Study of Mummies*. Cambridge: Cambridge University Press.

Brighetti, Antonio. "Le mummie di Ferentillo." *Atti e Memorie dell'Accademia di Storia dell'Arte Sanitaria* 31, 4 (1965): 107–116.

Fulcheri, Ezio, Patrizia Baracchini, Carlo Crestani, Andrea Drusini, and Maurizio Rippa-Bonati. 1991. "Studio preliminare delle mummie naturali di Ferentillo: esame immunologico ed immunoistochimico della cute." *Rivista Italiana di Medicina Legale* 13: 171–183.

Mummies of Guanajuato

Guanajuato, an idyllic colonial town nestled in the mountains of central Mexico, is home to a unique collection of mummified humans. Guanajuato is noted for its mining industry, which during the colonial period produced about two-thirds of the world's silver. Guanajuato's name means "the mountainous place for frogs." It comes from a Purépecha word *Cuanaxhuato* with the same meaning. The nomadic Purépecha Indians of the area thought the area's mountains resembled frogs. Guanajuato was named as a UNESCO World Heritage Site in 1988 for its classic style and is filled with culture and international events. Guanajuato rests in a narrow valley, and its surface streets are very narrow, and many of the roads in and through town are actually underground tunnels.

Guanajuato is home to 111 natural mummies that are displayed at the Museo de las Momias de Guanajuato. The origin of the mummies is a fascinating story. Each of the mummified individuals was once interred in the Santa Paula Municipal Pantheon cemetery, which is adjacent to the museum. The cemetery was built in 1861. In 1865, due to overcrowding at the cemetery, a new law required families or relatives of the deceased to pay a tax for the perpetual care of the burial site. If the family moved away, if they were poor, or if there were no remaining descendants to pay the tax, the skeletal remains were exhumed and held for five years, after which time they were either cremated or buried in a mass grave, thus conserving space.

Some of the mummies that are displayed in the Mummy Museum in Guanajuato, Mexico. The mummies are more than one hundred years old and were naturally preserved by the mineral rich soil of this former silver and gold mining region. (AP Images/Daniel Jayo)

The famous mummies of Guanajuato, Mexico, currently located in the Museo de las Momias (English: Museum of the Mummies), have captured the popular imagination for many years and have become a part of pop culture literature and entertainment. For example, in the early 1970s the movie *El Santo Contra Las Momias de Guanajuato* was produced, pitting a well known Mexican wrestler, El Santo, against the supposedly "living" mummies. Legendary American science fiction writer Ray Bradbury visited Guanajuato and viewed the mummies in the 1940s, and was thus inspired to write a story titled "The Next in Line" (published in 1946), about an American married couple visiting Mexico and finding their lives impacted by the mummies. The story was later republished in the 1978 book *The Mummies of Guanajuato*, where the text was accompanied by evocative photographs of the mummies themselves. Both the El Santo movie and the Bradbury book contributed to a surge of renewed public interest in the Guanajuato mummies.

Once the exhumations began in 1865, some of the bodies were found to have mummified. These mummified remains were placed in a building adjacent to the cemetery, which remains as the location of the museum today. After a number of mummies were discovered and propped up against the walls of what appeared to be catacombs, night watchmen would make extra money charging a fee and giving tours of the mummies to people of the town. Eventually, the municipality realized that there was public interest in these mummified remains and formally established the museum in 1894. The grave tax was abolished in 1958.

During their history, the mummies of Guanajuato have been displayed and cared for in various manners. Early on, when a visit to see the mummies was more informal, they were displayed propped up against the walls of a tunnel-like series of rooms. Here visitors could touch the mummies, and some were even said to have broken off a bit of mummy as a souvenir. Sometime after the museum was established the mummies were placed in glass-enclosed wooden bunks, sometimes two or three high, and were displayed in the labyrinth of rooms within the building. Several of the mummies with a local lore or story, such as being buried alive, were displayed standing, and the special mummies of the small children, or Angelitos, were given a special display case as well.

Interest in the mummies swelled in the early 1970s when a movie, *El Santo Contra Las Momias de Guanajuato*, was produced, pitting a well-known Mexican wrestler, El Santo, against the "living" mummies. In 1978 Ray Bradbury published a book titled *The Mummies of Guanajuato* that reprinted his 1947 short story "The Next in Line," about a visit to see the Guanajuato mummies, accompanied by photographs of them. Bradbury also included a scene with mummies in a Mexican crypt (without naming them as the mummies at Guanajuato) in his 1972 novel *The Halloween Tree*. These and other popular treatments of the mummies fueled a renewed interest in this unique museum.

In 1970, major improvements were made to the displays. As interest continued to grow and funds became available, upgrades were conducted in 2006. The mummies are now seen in climate-controlled enclosures with more scientific information displayed about the lives and times of these individuals.

In 2001, National Geographic Channel's documentary series *The Mummy Road Show* featured the paleoimaging examination of 18 of the 111 mummies. In 2007, the then mayor of Guanajuato, Dr. Eduardo Romero Hicks, a physician, initiated a scientific research project involving the mummy experts from *The Mummy Road Show* as well as a forensic anthropologist. Through this initiative, called the Guanajuato Mummy Research Project, the mummies have been studied in-depth. Building on the early research in 2001, these studies took place in Guanajuato as well as in Detroit, where 36 of the mummies were allowed to become a part of a traveling display in North America. It is through the efforts of the Guanajuato Mummy Research Project that the current display at the Museo de las Momias is highly educational, informative, and no longer a voyeuristic experience.

Local lore suggested that these mummified bodies were the result of a high mineral content in the water in and around Guanajuato. Other stories suggest that the mummification was the result of being buried alive during the fears associated with a cholera epidemic of 1833. However, if either of these explanations were truly the cause of the mummification, there would be a lot more mummies in Guanajuato; only 1 in 100 of the disinterred bodies were found to be mummies.

There are several contributing factors associated with the process of mummification in Guanajuato. The altitude of Guanajuato is at 2,000 meters (6,600 feet above sea level). This creates a dry and warm climate, cooler in the winter months. Although average rainfall can reach 600 mm (23 inches) per year, most of the rainfall is seen during late spring through early fall. Guanajuato is also known for its long periods of dry spells. Given that the crypts are of a cement matrix including lime, there is great potential for removing humidity from the surrounding air. For a natural mummy to be produced in this context, rapid desiccation must take place. Current thought is that the bodies may have been buried in the dry season. Their clothes helped wick moisture away from the bodies, and this humidity was then absorbed by the cement of the surrounding crypt. The above-ground crypts at the cemetery are 7 feet high in most places, and the mummified bodies were generally from individuals occupying the centermost crypts.

This placement would decrease the potential for water leaching into the burial space either from above or from below. Another factor that may contribute is the hydration status at the time of death. These natural forces likely combined to rapidly dehydrate the body, leading to mummification of the remains. This is similar to the natural mummification process seen in crypt burials in Europe as well as in other locations.

When exhumations began, the first mummified individual to be discovered was the remains of Dr. Remigio Leroy, a French Doctor. Dr. Leroy was disinterred on June 9, 1865, and was found to be remarkably well preserved. Dr. Leroy had been entombed for five years and had no family in the local area to claim him or pay the grave tax. Exhumations continued until 1958, with any mummified bodies being taken into the museum collection. There are a wide variety of mummified remains among the collection at the Museo de las Momias, including men, women, children, and a fetus. Many of the mummies come with a "story" designed to pique the visitors' interests. For example, there is the woman who was buried alive, the women who had a cesarean section, a man who supposedly was killed by a strike to the face, and a woman who was said to have been hanged by her husband. Much of the research has shown that these are merely stories based on the postmortem appearance of the mummified bodies.

Of particular interest is a group of child and infant mummies. Their appearance is a true window into times past, as they are seen in the clothes that they were buried with. This is not the case with many of the adult bodies. The girls were dressed in a very formal manner suggesting that they were representing angels, or angelitos. The boys were often dressed as the Saint that represented the month of their birth or the month of their death. This was a common practice among the Catholic traditions of the time, indicating the child's purity and ensuring his path to heaven. Two of the infant mummies showed signs of having been autopsied, displaying sutured incision sites on the chest and abdomen. Radiographic and endoscopic study revealed that the body cavities had been filled with a packing material allowing the general shape of the infant to be maintained.

Among the collection is a mummified fetus, thought to be of about 24 weeks gestation. It is one of the smallest and youngest known mummies in the world. There are two mummies in the museum that may be related to the displayed fetal mummy. One is an adult woman approximately 40 to 50 years of age who shows signs of having had a cesarean section. Given her age estimation and given the challenges of childbearing and childbirth in this age group in this time period, if this were a cesarean procedure the fetal mummy may have been her child. Another female mummy of about 23 years of age apparently died in childbirth or during a miscarriage, presenting with a mummified placenta extruding from her vaginal region. Without DNA analysis, it is impossible to ascertain if either of these two women was associated with the mummified fetus.

The collection as a whole is extremely important as it creates a snapshot of the lives and times of nineteenth and twentieth century central Mexico. Represented among the collection are various strata of local society during the exhumation period. These were miners, soldiers, farmers, doctors, women, men, and children of Guanajuato's past. In addition to the physician, Dr. Leroy, an elegantly dressed elderly woman is mummified, complete with jewelry suggesting an upper social status. We also see persons who clearly had a hardworking life there in the mountainous region of Guanajuato. Judging from features such as healed fractures (see below), they may have been miners. Very few other places offer such a concentrated but randomly selected collection of the mummified dead from which we may continue gather valuable information.

Nearly all of the 111 mummies have been scientifically examined using paleoimaging, physical, and forensic anthropology. The findings represent what one might expect given the rocky terrain in the Guanajuato region. The primary industry was mining, a somewhat dangerous profession. Generally, the research indicated that there were many healed fractures among the collection. This can be explained by the rugged environment and the usual mode of transportation during these time periods, such as walking, mule or horseback, and wagons. Also, there was ample evidence of infectious diseases, including pulmonary adhesions and calcified lymph nodes. These findings are not surprising, tuberculosis was a common affliction, and often the cause of death, during the latter part of the nineteenth century and into the twentieth century.

Also among the conditions noted was anthracosis (black lung) from a life of inhaling smoke or coal dust. Various types of arthritis, including rheumatoid and osteoarthritis, were evident in the middle aged to older mummies. Evidence of dental disease including carries, abscesses, periodontal conditions, and pre-mortem attrition was examined. Regarding the dental conditions, one of the leading causes of death in the late nineteenth and early twentieth centuries was septicemia ("blood poisoning") brought on by dental abscesses. Where preservation of internal organs and structures was good, atherosclerosis was also present.

A few specific cases are especially noteworthy. According to local lore, one of the mummies, an elderly woman (identified as MM27) who was finely dressed for her burial was said to be a *bruja,* or witch. In life, she had a hunched over appearance, gray hair, and poor dental condition—factors that probably combined to give her a stereotypical witch-like appearance. Others said that she was a "good" witch. Scientific examination using radiography, endoscopy, computed tomography (CT), and hair analysis revealed some interesting facts about this individual. MM27's spine showed considerable arthritis, as did her hips. The spine was so affected that she had a hunched forward appearance due to compressed and collapsing vertebrae. MM27 had evidence of several dental abscesses and imaging analysis revealed calcifications in various vessels including the aortic arch and the descending aorta. Hair analysis revealed high levels of iron, lead, sulfur, tin, and mercury. The information gathered indicates that this was an elderly woman who, because of her widespread arthritis, had great difficulty in moving about. Her hair analysis suggests that she was a long-time resident of this mining area. Her burial clothes suggest that she was of middle or higher status and that she likely was an active member of the society of her time. One certain thing is that she lived a long life and was well cared for over many years prior to her death, as she would have needed assistance with activities of daily living. The "witch" moniker was likely applied when she was exhumed and put on display in the museum.

There are many wonderful stories about individual mummies at the Museo de las Momias de Guanajuato. The scientific analysis conducted sheds light on many of these individuals' lives and the times in which they lived. The Guanajuato municipality is an excellent area to explore, and the mummies are woven into their culture. The mummies can be seen at the museum, and the visit will not disappoint. These mummies are ambassadors from past times. Visitors to the museum will sense a relationship to their stories and will leave with a greater understanding of cultural differences and similarities.

Nearly all of these mummies have been examined, and in the near future, the remaining mummies of this important collection will be analyzed in an attempt to complete their life stories as much as possible.

Ronald G. Beckett and Gerald Conlogue

See also: Mummies of Latin America; Natural mummification

Further Reading

Aguilar, Louis. 2009. *Long Live the Dead: The Accidental Mummies of Guanajuato.* USA: Accidental Mummies Touring Company, LLC.

Aufderheide, Arthur C. 2003. *The Scientific Study of Mummies.* Cambridge: Cambridge University Press.

Beckett, Ronald G., and Gerald Conlogue. 2009. *Paleoimaging: Field Applications for Cultural Remains and Artifacts.* USA: CRC Press, Taylor and Francis.

Brier, Bob. 2004. *The Encyclopedia of Mummies.* 2nd ed. UK: Sutton Publishing.

The Mummy Road Show. 2001. "Much as Mummies." National Geographic Channel. Directed by Larry Engel and written by Damian F. Slattery. Hosted by Ron Beckett and Jerry Conlogue.

Mummies of Latin America

Latin America has a long and diverse history of mummification, and, while its natural mummification is predated by approximately 400 years by the North American Spirit Cave mummy, it lays claim to the oldest artificial (human-made) mummies in the world. Natural mummification in Central America occurred in Mexico, and natural and artificial mummification in South America occurred in two distinct regions: the west Amazon region (Ecuador, Venezuela, Bolivia, and Colombia) and the Andean region (largely made up of Chile and Peru).

Despite the pervasive prominence of Egyptian mummies in popular Western consciousness (a fact that owes not a little to the centrality of Egyptian mummies in the mummy movie and mummy fiction genres), Latin America is home to an extremely ancient and diverse tradition of mummification. In fact, the oldest artificial (human-made) mummies in the world come from Latin America, from the Chinchorro people of northern Chile and southern Peru. Other peoples in the same region likewise had their own mummification traditions, as did various peoples in Ecuador, Venezuela, Bolivia, and Colombia, in a collective tradition spanning six thousand years, from about 5000 BCE to 1000 CE. Many natural mummies of great historical and scientific importance have also come from Central America and South America.

The west Amazon has produced very few natural mummies as a result of the rain forest environment that is detrimental to preservation of human remains. The exception to this is a series of natural mummies found wrapped in textiles in caves in Colombia dating from 200 CE to 1520 CE and the natural mummies from the 1900 cemetery at San Bernardo . This region, however, is a source of artificial mummies and mummified, in some cases shrunken, trophy heads. Shrunken heads were produced by the Jivaro of Ecuador by removing the skin from the skull of a decapitated enemy and boiling, drying, and stretching the skin with repeated addition of hot stones and dry sand. These trophies were believed to transfer the power of the slain enemy to the victor. Although illegal, according to federal authorities, the practice of headhunting and headshrinking among the Jivaro persists to this day.

The Mundurucu of the west Amazon engaged in a similar practice, recorded since 1535, of mummifying heads with the skull intact by removing the brain, stuffing the head with cotton, and drying the head. The Cunas and Caimenes groups of Colombia produced mummified heads for commoner remains but fire-dried their chiefs, whom they wrapped in decorated cotton. The Muiscas also fire-dried their leaders, with or without eviscerating the body, before wrapping them in textiles. The Laches fire-dried corpses and filled the eviscerated body cavity with ritual items, while the Popayan flayed corpses and filled the suspended skins with ashes. The mummification of human remains among these groups was most directly related to the demonstration of social status, and mummies (mummified heads in particular) were symbols of power, often carried onto the battlefield and consulted in religious ceremonies.

Peruvian mummification occurred as early as 4000 BCE to 2000 BCE in the highlands, where the semi-flexed corpses of Preceramic peoples, wrapped in camelid mantles and red-dyed cloaks, were naturally mummified in the dry caves of Tres Vantana. The Chavin tradition peoples of the Initial/Early Horizon period (1800–200 BCE) produced mummy bundles by eviscerating the body, stuffing it with plant and animal fibers, and wrapping the tightly flexed body in "tightly spaced, horizontal, encircling, flat, braided bands" (Aufderheide 2003, 104). The Paracas peoples also produced burial bundles, although these were probably unintentionally mummified and likely limited to a priestly class of older males with a particular cranial modification style. Wrapped in clothes, cotton shrouds, and up to 15 wool blankets, the absorbent bundles were buried in *cavernas* at the bottom of deep funnel-shaped pits.

This bundle burial tradition was continued by the Nasca in the Early Intermediate and Middle Horizon periods (200 BCE–1000 CE). Heads were also mummified intentionally by the Nasca, and speculation on the motivation for this ranges from military trophies to sacrifice to ancestor worship. The heads were excerebrated (i.e., the brains were removed) via the foramen magnum, and the cheeks and mouth stuffed with cotton.

At the same time, the Moche, Tiwanaku, and Huari groups also engaged in artificial mummification. The Moche produced mummies of their rulers, eviscerating the body before burial, while the Tiwanaku and Huari produced both artificial (eviscerated) and natural mummies of the flexed bundles buried in the Bolivian highlands (Aufderheide 2003). The Chiribaya and Chancay peoples and the Moche descendants at El Brujo produced only natural, flexed bundle mummies in the Late Intermediate period (1000–1470 CE). Mummies of the Peruvian highlands were tightly flexed, with the limbs bound and the hands flat over the face, and wrapped in cords that often covered the entire mummy with apertures only for the face and toes. Mummies of the coastal areas included bundles with false heads and masks made of mud and clay, while the northern Peruvian coastal mummies were clothed and lay extended.

The mummification of the Inca royalty of the Late Horizon (1470–1534 CE) is not clearly understood, in large part due their destruction during the Spanish conquest, but it is believed that they were naturally dried on a high mountain or, possibly, smoked. The indigenous chronicler Guaman Poma, however, describes them as eviscerated and treated with balsamic substances. The Inca empire, extending into Chile, Argentina, Bolivia, and Ecuador, produced a variety of natural and artificial mummies. Commoners were typically wrapped in textiles and surrounded by a basket, resulting in natural mummification. Vreeland (1998) notes that coastal and lowland Inca mummies of this era were produced by eviscerating the corpse, covering the body in a cotton shroud, and wrapping it in cloth and cord ropes, the upper portion of which was painted to resemble a face. A distinct category of natural mummies from this period are the frozen and freeze-dried mummies of children and young adults, intoxicated and offered as mountaintop sacrifice to deities living in the skies.

The Chachapoyan people, conquered by the Inca shortly before European contact, also intentionally mummified their dead. The Chachapoya tanned the skin with organic materials, stuffed the mouth and nostrils with raw cotton, and tied the fingers and limbs to produce a tight bundle that was wrapped in wool textiles with an embroidered face. Children, infants, and neonates were also mummified in this manner, but only in adults was the abdominal cavity eviscerated *per ano* (through the anus) and the orifice plugged with cotton cloth.

Chile is home to the oldest artificial mummification in the world. The Acha Man of the Chinchorro culture is, at 7020 BCE, a close second to the Spirit Cave mummy and was naturally mummified following burial in reed mats buried in sand. By 5050 BCE, however, the Chinchorro people engaged in complex mummification rituals until 2000 BCE and artificial mummification until 1720 BCE. From approximately 5050 to 2500, corpses were defleshed and eviscerated to produce mummies of the Black type. The joints of the skeleton were reinforced with sticks and grass ropes and the overall contour of the body was roughly modeled with mud, after which the skin was replaced and painted black with manganese. Wigs and mud masks were added and the facial skin coated with manganese paste and molded with facial features. This style was replaced by the Red type of mummy from 2500 BCE to 2000 BCE In this type of mummy, the body was eviscerated through abdominal and shoulder incisions, decapitated, and excerebrated. Support sticks were inserted under the skin; soil and camelid fiber was used to fill the body cavity, and the head was reattached, complete with a human hair wig secured by a mud helmet painted red. The incisions were sutured and the body painted with red ochre, leaving the face black. During these periods everyone, regardless of age or rank, was mummified, and even neonates and embryos were treated in this manner. A subtype of Red mummy, the Bandage type, has also been described in remains from between 2620 and 2000. Similar to the Red type, this type of mummy had the skin replaced in strips resembling bandages. Around 1720 BCE (although one case exists dating to ca. 2600 BCE), the complex Black and Red mummies were replaced by a simple Mud-coated type. Some were eviscerated, while others were not, and the body was encased in a sand/cement mixture. This practice lasted for several hundred years, ending around 1500 BCE.

Special attention was paid to infant mummies, with many showing signs of repainting, implying that they were stored and displayed for a considerable time. This finding, and the high levels of arsenic in local water sources, has led to the proposition that mummification originated as a means by which to deal with the grief of the high number of abortions and preterm births associated with arseniasis (chronic arsenic poisoning). This hypothesis has not been supported in subsequent study, however, and alternative hypotheses include display as a marker of familial territory, a means to secure territory, acts of religious ideology, and symbols in ancestor worship.

Much later natural mummies exist for the Alto Ramirez (1000 BCE–350 CE), San Miguel and Gentilar (1300–1450 CE), and San Pedro de Atacama groups. The Tiwanaku/Cabuza (400–1000 CE), Chiribaya (1100–1300 Ce), and Inca (1450–1550 CE) cultures, discussed previously, were also present in Chile.

Additionally, human remains were artificially mummified, wrapped, suspended, and dried over a fire for one month in Andean Venezuela until the sixteenth century and, in Argentina, the remains of Eva Peron were embalmed following her death in 1952 CE and remain in good condition.

The deserts and caves of Mexico have also produced numerous natural mummies, including the bark-wrapped infant mummy deposited in a desert cave of the Chihuahua region between 690 and 910 CE; two mat-wrapped mummies in a west Sierra Madre cave; and the four mummies from the La Ventana cave in Chihuahua dating to around 1350 CE. Coffin burials in Tlayapacan, Morelos, and Santa Elena, Yucatan, also benefited from hot, dry, well-drained conditions, and the soil and drainage in the cemetery of Guanajuato has produced hundreds of natural mummies since its opening in 1861 CE.

Andrew Wade

See also: Chinchorro mummies; Inca mummies; Mummies of Guanajuato; Nasca mummies; Natural mummification

Further Reading

Arriaza, Bernardo T. 1995. "Chinchorro Bioarchaeology: Chronology and Mummy Seriation." *American Antiquity* 6: 35–55.

Arriaza, Bernardo T. 1996. "Preparation of the Dead in Coastal Andean Preceramic Populations." In *Human Mummies: A Global Survey of Their Status and the Techniques of Conservation*, edited by Konrad Spindler, Harald Wilfing, Elizabeth Rastbichler-Zissernig, Dieter zur Nedden, and Hans Nothdurfter, 131–140. New York: Springer.

Arriaza, Bernardo T., Cárdenas-Arroyo, Felipe, Kleiss, Ekkehard, and Verano, James W. 1998. "South American Mummies: Culture and Disease." In *Mummies, Disease, and Ancient Cultures*, 2nd ed., edited by Aidan Cockburn, Eve Cockburn, and Theodore A. Reyman, 190–236. Cambridge, UK: Cambridge University Press.

Aufderheide, Arthur C. 2003. *The Scientific Study of Mummies*. Cambridge, UK: Cambridge University Press.

Boston, Christine E. 2007. "Possible Arsenic Poisoning in Ancient Chilean Populations." MA Thesis, University of Western Ontario.

Ceruti, Constanza. 2004. "Human Bodies as Objects of Dedication at Inca Mountain Shrines (North-western Argentina)." *World Archaeology* 36: 103–122.

Guillen, Sonia. 2001/ "Keeping Ancestors Alive: The Mummies from Laguna de los Condores, Amazonas, Peru." In *Mummies in a New Millenium [sic]: Proceedings of the 4th World Congress on Mummy Studies*, edited by Niels Lynnerup, Claus Andreasen, and Joel Berglund, 162–164. Copenhagen: Danish Polar Center.

Hapke, Russel A. 1996. "An Evolution of Creativity and Ritual: The Immortalizing Craftsmanship of the Chinchorro Morticians." MA Thesis, University of Nevada, Las Vegas.

Vreeland, James M., Jr. 1998. "Mummies of Peru." In *Mummies, Disease, and Ancient Cultures*, 2nd ed., edited by Aidan Cockburn, Eve Cockburn, and Theodore A. Reyman, 154–189. Cambridge, UK: Cambridge University Press.

Mummies of Lithuania

The Dominican Church of the Holy Spirit in Vilnius, Lithuania, overlies a number of subterranean chambers that hold mummified and skeletonized human remains of both—clergy and laypeople, as well as wooden coffins and precious textiles most likely dating from the eighteenth and nineteenth centuries CE.

The crypt and its stories are part of the local folklore, and a number of ghostly tales and other anecdotes began circulating already in the mid-nineteenth century. In the fourth decade of the twentieth century, students of the local university attempted to sort the cellars. However, they did not complete the work properly, nor were scholars able to identify any written record of their activities, with the exception of two inscriptions on wooden boxes containing collected skeletal elements as well as some numbers written on the coffins and on the different rooms of the crypt.

A proper report on these mummies was only produced in 1963 by forensic scientist Juozas Markulis (1913–1987). A lecturer on the local university's medical faculty, Markulis briefly analyzed over 500 subjects, with the aim of understanding whether the remains were only historical or included some twentieth century victims, and, in this case, whether they showed evidence of torture, injuries, and/or other relevant features. He also established that most of these corpses were spontaneously mummified, except for a few exceptions that bore evidence of evisceration and the use of aromatics. Thus, while remaining unaware of his contribution to the field, Markulis initiated mummy studies in Lithuania by providing details of interest on this assemblage.

Significantly, these mummies were repeatedly moved and disturbed throughout their history as the usage of the site since the early nineteenth century was varied. The same crypt served as an alleged Napoleonic burial site in 1812. It was used as an ongoing depository for human remains. It was also a bomb shelter during the Nazi period. Because most of the remains in the crypt were accumulated in just a single cellar, and because of a change in air flow due to the installation of a glass to cover the access, most of the remains underwent significant decomposition, so that only a few mummies could be successfully retrieved during the first decade of the twenty-first century.

At the request of Church officials, and with the support of the local medical faculty, an investigation enabling the documentation, study, and curation of this historic material commenced in 2011 with the study of 23 human mummies consisting of 15 adults, 8 sub-adults, and a number of isolated body parts. Following the external inspection, each body was carefully recorded, and tissue and bone samples were obtained from those subjects that displayed loss of substance, either determined by natural decay or other postdepositional changes.

Preliminary observation of pathological features included obesity and arthritis as well as dental calculus (tartar), caries (cavities), wear, and enamel hypoplasia. Furthermore, because of their remarkable preservation status seven such bodies were CT-scanned in a branch of the local hospital to avoid any possible invasive study. Analyses revealed that those mummies were comparatively well-preserved, including some internal organs and fatty structures. Additionally, pathological conditions included extensive atherosclerosis (clotting of the arteries), tuberculosis, and pleural adhesions (fibrous growths in the lung lining) secondary to pneumonia.

The most interesting case was a female child mummy who revealed skeletal anomalies such as rickets and hydrocephalus ("water on the brain"). An association between the latter is not indicated in the literature, but it was speculated that a disabled child with hydrocephalus was not able, or possibly not permitted, to leave her house, resulting in reduced or absent exposure to sunlight and subsequent vitamin D deficiency.

The research project on the remains at the Holy Spirit church also allowed the collection of more than 100 items, including textiles and leather artifacts, which have been inspected at the Lithuanian National Museum. Most of the finds are pieces of male, female, and child clothing, headdress and footwear, and remains of sacramentalia (religious implements) and coffin equipment such as cushions and upholstery. In all likelihood, many of these textiles were made of silk, and some appeared to be embroidered or made of metal thread. The majority of these findings were rather well preserved, and even some of the colors, such as red, blue, or green, have survived until today. After that preliminary survey, it was suggested that some of these clothes were made specifically for the funerals and burial of the bodies in the crypt, since only the front halves of the clothing were discovered, with pins employed to fasten them to the coffins.

The discovery and collection of these items probably constitutes the greatest find of its kind in Lithuania's history.

Dario Piombino-Mascali and Rimantas Jankauskas

See also: Mummies of Europe; Natural mummification

Further Reading

Jankauskas, Rimantas, and Dario Piombino-Mascali. 2012. "The Lithuanian Mummy Project: Bioanthropological and Paleopathological Investigation of the Human Remains Found in the Holy Spirit Dominican Church, Vilnius." *Paleopathology Newsletter* 159: 12.

Panzer, Stephanie, Algirdas Tamošiūnas, Ramūnas Valančius, Rimantas Jankauskas, and Dario Piombino-Mascali. 2013. "Radiological Evidence of Rickets in a Lithuanian Child Mummy." *Fortschr Röntgenstr* 185: 670–672.

Mummies of the World: The Exhibition

"Mummies of the World: The Exhibition" was produced by American Exhibitions, Inc. of Boca Raton, Florida, in cooperation with the Reiss-Engelhorn Museums of Mannheim, Germany. This large touring exhibition was created to present a wide overview of mummies and mummification from around the world and from different time periods and many cultures. The aim was also, in part, to dispel the common perception that mummies are all bandage-wrapped and come from ancient Egypt. In total, the exhibition featured more than 40 human and animal mummies, presented in 6 main galleries. The collection included animals naturally preserved in various environments, ancient Egyptians, several mummies from different regions of South America, five mummies from crypts in Germany and Hungary, a bog body, and specimens prepared for medical education in the seventeenth century.

The exhibition opened July 1, 2010 at the California Science Center in Los Angeles and closed at the Maryland Science Center (Baltimore, MD) in January 2014. Other venues included the Milwaukee Public Museum (Milwaukee, WI), Franklin Institute (Philadelphia, PA), Discovery Center (Charlotte, NC), Witte Museum (San Antonio, TX), Museum of Science and Industry (Tampa, FL),

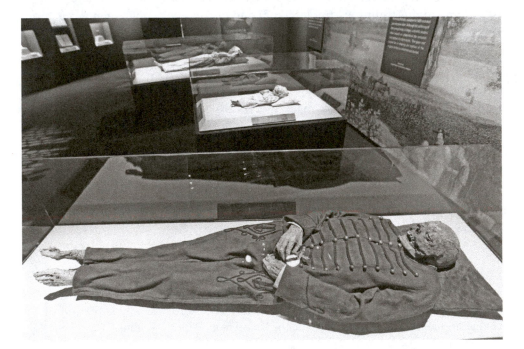

The mummified remains of Michael Orlovits, who died in 1806, and his family (according to church records in Vac, Hungary), are displayed during a press preview of the "Mummies of the World" exhibit at the Franklin Institute, June 15, 2011, in Philadelphia. (AP Photo/ Matt Rourke)

the Leonardo (Salt Lake City, UT), and the Oregon Museum of Science and Industry (Portland, OR). More than one million visitors attended the exhibition over its three and one-half year run.

The development of the exhibition was part of the three-fold mandate of research, conservation, and dissemination undertaken by the German Mummy Project. The results of multidisciplinary scientific analyses of the mummies were incorporated into the exhibition through animations derived from medical imaging, wall and label text, and interactive activities. A catalog was also created based on the research of the German Mummy Project, providing not only research and background information about every mummy in the exhibition but a detailed overview of various mummification processes and the archaeological and cultural context for mummification in some regions.

It was deemed very important to ensure that the mummies were presented in a respectful and ethical manner. The specimens in "Mummies of the World" were borrowed from more than 20 European museums and other institutions and had been held in the collections of those institutions for more than a century. The exhibition was thoroughly reviewed and approved by an ethics panel that consisted of medical ethicists, clergy of various denominations, and members of the museum and science center community. It met or exceeded the guidelines of professional associations such as the International Council of Museums (ICOM).

The main purpose of the exhibition was to showcase the wide variety of mummification that exists around the world. In particular, the mummies represented, and contextual information explained, that mummies occurred on every continent of the globe and existed from prehistoric, historic, and modern times. Furthermore, the exhibition demonstrated that both humans and animals are found in mummified forms, and that preservation of the body varies greatly, depending on various circumstances.

The storyline led the visitors through several galleries that explored the stories of the individual mummies through the science of mummification and the various techniques used for the study and interpretations of mummies. The perception of visitors was challenged throughout the exhibition, as they came face-to-face with people from the past. Visitors were encouraged to think about each mummy as a person, and through the scientific research were taught more about who the person was and how they may have lived.

Throughout the tour, the exhibition attracted visitors of all ages and from all backgrounds. The educational aspects of the exhibition were strongly emphasized, and additional material was prepared for families with children, field trip attendees, and home school students. This material was intended for parents and teachers to help prepare children for a visit to the exhibition and to help them understand that they should not be afraid of the mummies.

The exhibition also included hands-on interactive stations, such as "What does a mummy feel like?," which allowed visitors to touch panels that replicated the textures of mummified skin, embalmed skin, linen bandages, bog body bones, and mummified animal fur. Several computer-based kiosks gave visitors a chance to explore the mummies from the inside out through the CT scans and 3D animations. Visitors had the chance to look at the scans of the mummies and guess whether the person might have had tuberculosis, an injury, a tumor, or other medical conditions. While these interactive activities gave the visitors a chance to explore the mummies in more detail, the activities were designed to be unobtrusive and to maintain the respectful atmosphere of the exhibition.

Because of both its size and scope, "Mummies of the World" was a unique exhibition. The exhibition received excellent reviews in the media, and the vast majority of visitor feedback was positive. The most important aspect of the exhibition was its focus on the importance of mummies as people and on the use of modern science to the stories of those people of the past.

Anna-Maria Begerock and Heather Gill-Frerking

See also: Displaying mummies; German Mummy Project

Further Reading

Weiczorek, Alfried, and Rosendahl, Wilfried, eds. 2010. *Mummies of the World*. New York: Prestel.

Mummies of Venzone

Nestled at the junction of the Canale valley and the Tagliamento river, the historical town of Venzone lies in the Friuli region of northeastern Italy, 230 meters above sea level. This picturesque community holds a renowned collection of 15 spontaneously mummified bodies in an advanced state of desiccation, most of which date from the 1700s to the 1800s.

There, the main church, dedicated to Saint Andrew, was expanded from a preexisting structure and consecrated in 1338. Local clergy and high-status citizens were entombed inside wooden coffins in burial vaults made of bricks, constructed beneath the church pavement. Many such bodies became mummified shortly after their burial in the early nineteenth century. However, the first mummy was accidentally discovered during building works in 1647 under a stone tomb located in the exterior wall of the church, and was suggested to be of medieval date. Reportedly, it was damaged by soldiers who were eager to obtain mummy souvenirs after Napoleon's occupation of the area in 1797. Because of his spine deformity, this subject was soon nicknamed "the hunchback." However, a recent radiological study indicates that this appearance was due to a postmortem artifact.

By 1829, 18 mummies were displayed, but additional specimens were retrieved in the following years. Once exhumed, the bodies of Venzone were transferred in the crypt of the round-shaped Chapel of Saint Michael, which is located opposite the church, and were arranged in an upright stance. As a consequence of the crypt's dampness, during the mid-nineteenth century the mummies were transferred to the ground floor of the chapel, where they remained until the late twentieth century. Over time, however, their initial number was clearly reduced: one corpse was autopsied in 1828, while others were reburied, lost, or even transferred to other Italian and foreign institutions. As of 1930, a source indicates that only 22 mummies were in fact present.

In 1976 a powerful earthquake caused considerable damage to the area, destroying both the church and the chapel. Following a rescue of the remains, only 15 of them were in reasonable condition, while the remnants of the others were stored in a shed, which was later set on fire. Those 15 mummies were then treated with a formalin and phenol solution to avoid fungal and bacterial growth, and were stored in a space whose walls and pavement were also disinfected. Subsequently, they were placed in a metal hut, and later in a storage room of the rectory. Only after the reconstruction works, completed in 1998, could the remains be relocated to the chapel. At present, however, only 5 specimens are exposed to the public.

In the last decade of the past century, the mummies, belonging to both male and female adult subjects, were studied through X-rays and CT scans, and tissue samples were also submitted to biomedical investigation. In addition, the bodies were even rehydrated with glycerin and restored with a mixture of paraffin and beeswax to cover holes and defects.

As regards their mummification process, these remains were subjected to scholarly investigation beginning in the early nineteenth century. In 1831 Francesco Maria Marcolini (1779–1838), a medical doctor at the Udine Municipal Hospital, released a review of the mummies containing important details, including chemical analyses of the soil and a summary of theories by other coeval scientists. These included a moisture-absorbing soil rich in lime, with its acidic nature as well as the lack of humidity and the low temperature of the tombs as possible causes. However, Marcolini was convinced that the main explanation of the mummies' occurrence was a physicochemical one. Expanding on a suggestion put forth by physician Agostino Pagani (1769–1847), he proposed the concept that gas forming in the soil could have easily penetrated the burials and halted the cadavers' decomposition process.

Thirty years later, surgeon Pierviviano Zecchini (1802–1882) advanced an alternative biological hypothesis, suggesting fungal growth as the cause for natural mummification due to water extraction from the cadavers. To support this theory, Zecchini recalled the fact that in 1829, chemist Bartolomeo Biasoletto (1793–1859) had observed the Venzone mummies covered by a flocculent (resembling wool), soft, and roundish white fungus identified as *Hypha bombicina Pers.* The same explanation, supported by experimental data, was also put forward by physician Antongiuseppe Pari (1808–1881).

The attribution of a role of this fungus in the mummification mechanism of Venzone has remained duly accepted until recently. In 1983 the American paleopathologist Arthur C. Aufderheide (1922–2013) visited the site and was allowed to culture two specimens for fungi as well as collect soil, wood, and brick samples for biological and chemical analyses. As none of the microorganisms identified fitted the original description of *Hypha bombicina*, which was anyway insufficient to differentiate it from many other organisms in modern taxonomy, the basic conclusions of his investigations were that it is difficult to assign a major role to a fungus in the process, and that the most likely explanation for the Venzone preservation process was the well-drained limestone soil and the water protection of the tombs by the overlying church, conditions sufficient to bring about corporeal desiccation.

With their long, colorful, and unfortunate story, the Venzone mummies still intrigue scientists and laypeople, who visit this peculiar site in great numbers. These bodies remain an important biocultural and ethnographic resource, and deserve our best attention to be protected and studied in the future.

Dario Piombino-Mascali

See also: Aufderheide, Arthur Carl; Church of the Dead; Mummies of Europe; Mummies of Ferentillo; Natural mummification

Further Reading

Aufderheide, Arthur C. 2003. *The Scientific Study of Mummies*. Cambridge: Cambridge University Press.

Aufderheide, Arthur C., and Mary L. Aufderheide. 1991. "Taphonomy of Spontaneous ('Natural') Mummification with Applications to the Mummies of Venzone, Italy." In *Human Paleopathology: Current Syntheses and Future Options*, edited by Donald J. Ortner and Arthur C. Aufderheide, 79–86. Washington D.C.: Smithsonian Institution.

Baggieri, Gaspare. 2002. "The Mummies of Venzone." In *Bollettino dell'Associazione Amici di Venzone* 31.

Baggieri, Gaspare. 2012. "Protective and Consolidating Interventions on the Mummy Collection of Venzone." *Journal of Biological Research* 85, no. 1: 327–330.

Baggieri, Gaspare, and Marina di Giacomo. 2003. *The Mummies of Venzone: Morphology, Radiology and CAT Scan*. Bollettino dell'Associazione Amici di Venzone 32. Rome: MelAmi.

The Mummy! A Tale of the Twenty-Second Century

The Mummy! A Tale of the Twenty-Second Century is a satirical science fiction novel written by Jane C. Webb (1807–1858). It was published anonymously in three volumes in 1827, and it features one of the earliest fictional treatments of the mummy theme. Its author, who allowed her name to appear on subsequent printings following favorable reviews of the novel, claimed that she published the tale when her father's business failed, and she was compelled to look for a

Unable to shake off the horror that oppressed him, for he felt as though he had entered into a compact with a fiend, the priest stood immoveable, gazing at the supernatural appearance of Cheops, as he stalked across the terrace. His gaunt figure (rendered more awful by the grave-clothes that bound it) was magnified in the moonbeams, which seemed to increase, rather than to mitigate the unearthly ugliness of the apparition they shone upon. The priest was fixed in a fearful trance: in imagination, he still felt the cold and iron grasp of the Mummy, whose eyes seemed as though they were still looking into his very soul, and whose solemn accents were even now scaring his faculties. At length, however, Father Morris recovered something of his self-possession, and fled from the spot (he scarcely knew in what direction) under the fear, at every turning, of again encountering the dreaded Mummy!

—From *The Mummy! A Tale of the Twenty-Second Century* by Jane Webb Loudun

means to support herself. Webb met and married John Claudius Loudon in 1830 and, devoting herself to his field of horticulture, spent the rest of her life writing gardening manuals that became important works of reference in their field.

The Mummy! opens with an introduction in which the author claims "the Chronicle of a future age" was presented to her in a dream by a flower-crowned, winged male spirit, who urged her to "weave it into a story." The story proper begins in 2127, in a prosperous England that has reverted to a monarchy after rule by aristocracy, and later democracy, plunged the country into anarchy. By royal decree imposed by the first new queen, all queens are forbidden to marry, and their successors are chosen by popular election from among female descendants of the royal family who are between the ages of 20 and 25. The current queen, Claudia, has reigned for three years, when England is invaded by King Roderick of Ireland. Edmund Montagu, nephew of the Duke of Cornwall, hastens to repel the invaders, who are eager to return home on receiving news of an insurrection in Ireland. For this service the queen appoints Edmund general of her army to undertake a campaign against Germany, which has declared war on England.

When Edmund returns victorious from Germany his younger brother, Edric, decides to attempt some feat that will bring him distinction as well. Edric, who is interested in the natural sciences, has experimented with galvanism and is convinced that he can resuscitate a dead body. Under the instruction of his tutor, Dr. Entwerfen, Edric announces that he will travel to Egypt to reanimate the body of the mummy Cheops, and thereby answer the question whether the spirit dies with the body or remains attached to it. But Sir Ambrose has been planning to marry Edric off to Rosabella, the headstrong niece of the Duke of Cornwall whom the duke has raised in his household since some unforgiveable indiscretion that her father, the duke's brother Edgar, committed. Likewise, Sir Ambrose believes that Edmund will marry the duke's daughter, Elvira. (To complicate matters, Rosabella disdains Edric and is in love with Edmund, and Elvira is indifferent to Edmund and enamored of Henry Seymour, an Irishman traveling in England to whom she was recently introduced.) When Edric refuses to marry Rosabella, Sir Ambrose disinherits him.

The adamant Edric continues with his plans to travel to Egypt by balloon. With the help of a guide, they enter the tomb of Cheops and locate his sarcophagus. Edric uses his galvanic battery on the mummy, and when he sees that he has successfully revived it, he faints in horror. When Dr. Entwerfen revives him, they escape from the pyramid, whereupon they are arrested by local authorities as sorcerers. At their trial, the man whom they hired to watch their balloon claims, to the disbelief of the court, that he saw the mummy of Cheops steal away in the balloon. Edric and the doctor are thrown into a dungeon.

In the meantime, the mummy of Cheops—who accidentally stumbled into the basket of the balloon, setting it free—wings his way to England just as festivities for the celebration of Edmund's victory are under way. Unfamiliar with how to work a hot-air balloon, the mummy crashes into the balloons of several observers, which crash to the ground, severely injuring Queen Claudia. On the ground, Cheops escapes in the chaos, but not without terrorizing the people who see him.

With Claudia's death, Elvira is next in succession for the throne. But the haughty Rosabella decides to challenge her. She assembles a team of confidantes that includes her attendant Marianne, her confessor Father Morris, Lord Gustavus de Montfort, Lord Maysworth, Dr. Hardman, Dr. Coleman, and the Lords Noodle and Doodle. While she is in conference with Father Morris, Cheops reveals himself to them, offering to assist Father Morris in their subterfuge against Elvira.

Upon learning of her treachery, the Duke of Cornwall reprimands Rosabella, who moves into the house of Lord Gustavus. While the two political groups set about trying to use their influence to secure votes Clara, the youngest cousin of Edmund and Edric, overhears a plot between Father Morris and Dr. Coleman, who is Elvira's physician, to poison Elvira. Indeed, it is revealed later that Dr. Coleman helped to hasten the death of Queen Claudia, as part of a conspiracy by Rosabella's confederates to usurp control of the government following Rosabella's appointment of them to cabinet positions. However, Cheops advises that Rosabella will never ascend to the throne if Elvira dies, so the poisoning is stopped.

The day of the election arrives, and Elvira's chances of winning seem unlikely until Edmund champions her cause with a passionate address to the crowds that sways them in her favor. Although Elvira wins the election and appoints Edmund her prime minister, Cheops advises Father Morris that it is only a matter of time before the fickle populace will take exception to her reign and overturn her government in favor of Rosabella.

Meanwhile, Edric and Dr. Entwerfen manage to escape from their seemingly inescapable prison. After a perilous flight from Egypt—including their shipwreck on the shores of Spain and near execution by angry Spaniards—they are rescued by King Roderick, who has recently invaded Spain. Roderick informs the two men of the outcome of the election in England. When Roderick's campaign reaches Seville, Edric makes the acquaintance of M. de Mallet, an exile from Switzerland, and his daughter, Pauline, who falls in love with Edric. Dispirited by the behavior of the Spaniards in war, Roderick plans to conquer the rest of the country, appoint a new king, and return to Ireland.

Back in England, much as Cheops surmised, Elvira finds her governing criticized, and Rosabella's confederates, all of who have been placed in subordinate positions, are further sowing seeds of discord within her government. Edmund, who is increasingly frustrated at Elvira's indifference toward him, decides that he must have the law abolished that will not let the queen marry so that he can make Elvira his wife. By enacting beneficial laws, he wins the love of the people, who begin lamenting that he is not their king. But when Edmund tells Elvira that the people are willing to overturn the law, Elvira crushes him with her claim that she has given her heart to another. Although Elvira is referring to Henry Seymour, Edmund mistakenly believes that her beloved is the German Prince Ferdinand, whom Edmund befriended during his conquest of Germany. Edmund fights Ferdinand, leading to the imprisonment of both men. Hoping to advance Rosabella's cause, Father Morris spreads the rumor about the city that Elvira is in love with Ferdinand, horrifying the populace with the thought that her marriage would subject them to the rule of a foreign king.

Hoping to overturn the possible death sentence that will be imposed on both Ferdinand and Edmund, Elvira consults with Cheops, who advises her to address her subjects sternly, telling them she will not be dictated to about marrying, and demanding the freedom she needs to rule them. Her subjects are so impressed by her passion and eloquence that they accede to Elvira's request, and allow her to pardon Edmund and Ferdinand. Elvira imparts this news to her ministers, who had already all but condemned Ferdinand to death, and the trial is stopped.

While Ferdinand's trial is going on, Edmund is secretly visited in prison by Father Morris and Rosabella, who perpetuate the slander that Elvira is in love with Ferdinand. Incensed, Edmund declares that he will take Rosabella for his wife, and she and Father Morris facilitate his escape from prison. With Edmund's departure, Elvira lapses into listlessness and her government languishes, much to the outrage of her subjects. A crowd led by Edmund storms the queen's castle, and following Elvira's imprisonment, Edmund and Rosabella are proclaimed king and queen of England.

But all is not well in the court. The country is in tumult, exacerbated by Rosabella's lavishing of honors on Ferdinand to curry favor with foreign powers. Rosabella knows that Edmund does not love her, and Edmund is disgusted by his behavior. Edmund has also become estranged from his father, Sir Ambrose.

Shortly afterward, Cheops visits Clara, expressing concern over for Elvira's welfare. He urges her to travel to Ireland and secure the help of King Roderick.

Cheops helps Clara feign her death by drowning and, by a subterfuge, draws her together with Elvira and Prince Ferdinand to escape to Ireland. While they are attempting to flee the country, Roderick receives word in Spain that Elvira has been deposed. He and Edric hasten back to Ireland, mobilizing an army through the tunnel under the sea that separates the two nations. When Elvira and her retinue reach Roderick's army at the tunnel's mouth, she recognizes the king as the man who called himself Henry Seymour.

Back in London, the court is in chaos. The disillusioned Edmund has withdrawn and the haughty Rosabella is becoming increasingly unpopular. Sir Ambrose is reconciled with Edmund, but the emotional strain of the reconciliation kills him, and this tragedy drives the Duke of Cornwall mad. When Rosabella rejects any further council from Father Morris, the friar reveals that he is Edgar, Rosabella's father, having years before embraced the monastic life as penance for his murder of Rosabella's mother. Upon Roderick's arrival at the queen's castle, Marianne reveals that Rosabella is not Edgar's daughter, but the daughter she had by Edgar's servant; Marianne sold Edgar's daughter to a traveling foreigner—in fact, to M. de Mallet, who had revealed to Roderick just before his departure from Spain that Pauline was not his true child. The strain is too much for Edgar to bear and, drawing a dagger, he stabs both Marianne and himself to death. Upon seeing Elvira again, the Duke of Cornwall regains his wits. Roderick and Elvira are crowned queen and king of England, Clara marries Prince Ferdinand, and Edmund embraces the monastic life to expiate his sins.

When Edric wonders aloud what has become of Cheops, he hears a secret summons by the mummy's voice to go to the pyramids. Returning to Egypt, and entering the tomb of Cheops, he confronts the mummy still wanting to know the secrets of the tomb. But Cheops dissuades him, reminding him how much misery has been brought into the world since Edric first began his investigations. Realizing the wisdom of Cheops words, Edric asks him instead to interpret the sculptures decorating his tomb. Cheops says they depict him, as a warrior, slaying his father so that he might take his sister Arsinoë as his bride. To atone for this horrible sin, Cheops has since been periodically allowed to return to earth to assist the good and punish the malevolent. As he explains, "Under pretence of aiding them, I gave them counsels which only plunged them yet deeper in destruction, whilst the evil that my advice appeared to bring upon the good, was only like a passing cloud before the sun; it gave luster to the success that followed." Immediately after this, the mummy returns to death.

Although written several years after the end of the gothic era, *The Mummy!* was clearly influenced by the narrative design of the gothic novel. Cheops is initially made out to seem a traditional gothic villain, who is evil by nature and brings discord and misery into the lives of the virtuous. The influence of Mary Shelley's *Frankenstein* (1818), the novel considered by many to herald the end of the gothic novel's heyday, seems evident both in Edric's experiments in resuscitation with galvanism and his initial trepidation at prying into secrets that man was not meant to know. Like Frankenstein's monster, the mummy Cheops instills fear in any mortal who looks on him. But also like Frankenstein's monster, Cheops is revealed to not be malevolent by nature. The advice that Cheops gives to human confidantes is usually just a spur to how they already feel, or are predisposed to think. The satire of the novel works on several levels, but it is particularly acute in its skewering of government bureaucracy, political opportunism, and the fickleness of the public with regard to their leaders.

Despite the popularity that Loudon's novel enjoyed, it remains an anomaly that did not influence other writers to take up its theme or work variations on it.

Stefan R. Dziemianowicz

See also: The mummy in Western fiction: Beginnings to 1922

Further Reading

Webb, Jane. 1828. *The Mummy! A Tale of the Twenty-Second Century*, 2nd ed. London: Henry Colburn. https://archive.org/details/mummyataletwent02jangoog

The Mummy (1932)

Universal Studios' *The Mummy* is the most famous of all the mummy films. The role of the mummy was specifically created for Boris Karloff, who was fresh from a successful appearance as the monster in *Frankenstein*, which was a great financial success. *Dracula* was likewise successful, so producer Carl Laemmle, Jr. was looking for another horror hit, preferably an Egyptian one to capitalize on the then-recent discovery of Tutankhamun's tomb. However, unlike *Dracula* and *Frankenstein*, there was no classic mummy novel on which to base a script. In the early stages of development a treatment was written for *Cagliostro*, the story of a magician who lives for 3,000 years. The treatment was turned over to scriptwriter John Balderston, who had worked on both *Dracula* and *Frankenstein,* so that he could develop into a full-blown screenplay. In the 1920s Balderston had been a journalist sent to Egypt to cover the excavation of Tutankhamun's tomb. He recognized the widespread fascination this event had generated among the public, and soon he turned *Cagliostro* into *Im-Ho-Tep*, an Egypt-themed horror film that became *The Mummy* just before its release.

As filmed, *The Mummy* is actually a veiled adaptation of *Dracula*, which had been filmed two years earlier. Director Karl Freund had been the cinematographer for *Dracula*, and he brought this experience with him to the set of *The Mummy*. Large segments of both films are scene-by-scene parallels. There are even musical parallels, with Tchaikovsky's *Swan Lake* used as haunting background music in both films.

Universal Studios' *The Mummy*, released in 1932, was not only the first major mummy movie but the one that still remains the gold standard against which all others are judged. Here are some assorted fascinating facts about this legendary piece of cinema and mummy entertainment history:

- The finished film was an unstated reworking of Universal's *Dracula*, which was released the previous year. Karl Freund, who had worked as the cinematographer on *Dracula*, was hired to direct *The Mummy*.
- The screenwriter for *The Mummy*, John Balderston, had not only worked previously for Universal on *Dracula* and *Frankenstein* but was one of the journalists who covered the excavation of Tutankhamun's tomb in Egypt nearly a decade earlier.
- Boris Karloff's iconic mummy makeup was based on the appearance of the real-life Pharaoh Rameses III. It took eight hours to apply, and in the end it only appeared onscreen for less than one minute in the final film.
- The fictional "Scroll of Thoth" that appears in the film was actually a copy of the Egyptian *Book of the Dead* housed in the British Museum.

Balderston took full advantage of his experience covering the excavation of Tutankhamun's tomb. The name of Tutankhamun's wife's, Ankhesenamun, was used for the Egyptian princess in the movie. According to the Balderston's script, Princess Ankhesenamun died and was buried by her father, the pharaoh. Her lover, the high priest Imhotep, risked his life to steal the *Scroll of Thoth* (*Book of the Dead*) that could bring her back to life, but he was caught and buried alive in an unmarked grave. This grave is found in the present day by a museum expedition, and Imhotep is inadvertently reanimated when the *Scroll of Thoth* is read in his presence.

Significantly, many of the props in the film were patterned after real objects found in Tutankhamun's tomb. When the Scroll of Thoth appears on the screen, it is a shot of an actual copy of the Egyptian *Book of the Dead* that was housed in the British Museum. The face of the mummy itself was patterned after that of Seti II, on exhibit at the time in the Egyptian Museum in Cairo.

Because the script was continually evolving even as the production proceeded, there are some inconsistencies in the finished film. For example, it is never made clear that Helen Grosvenor, the heroine, is the reincarnation of Ankhesenamun and recognized as such by Imhotep, now resurrected in the guise of the mysterious Egyptian Ardath Bey. The reason for this ambiguity is that several scenes were cut from the final version that would have helped continuity.

The film was a huge hit with the public, and perhaps one reason for its success is that it gives the mummy an actual personality; he is not just a lunging terror. He has feelings, and in the guise of Ardath Bey he speaks well. He even has a girlfriend. When Ardath Bey magically calls Helen to the Cairo Museum, she willingly goes, happy to be reunited with her lost lover. She only balks when he explains that she must die so that she can be resurrected and join him for eternity.

The January 1933 issue of *Mystery* magazine contains the original story of *The Mummy* and makes evident last-minute changes in the script. In the magazine version, Helen is shown to have had many lives, first as the Egyptian princess Ankhesenamun, then a first-century Christian martyr, next an eighth-century barbarian queen, then a medieval lady, and finally a French aristocrat. As the film progressed, it became clear that more focus should be given to the mummy, so these scenes were cut. They may still exist somewhere in the vault of Universal Studios, but one vestige of them appears in the dramatis personae at the beginning of the movie. The credits list "The Saxon Warrior" as played by Henry Victor. The scene was cut, but not the credit.

The Mummy pioneered new techniques in movie production. The shooting schedule was only 23 days, and much of the filming as done in Red Rock Canyon, a hundred miles north of Los Angeles, because it closely resembled the Valley of the Kings in both color and topography. Little film was shot in Egypt because of the expense involved in transporting highly paid actors. Rather, a small crew was sent to Egypt to shoot background scenes, which were projected on a "process screen." The actors performed in front of this screen as the process camera synchronized with the shoot camera, so that the final composite gave the viewer the illusion that the actors were in Egypt.

Eight hours of makeup preparation were required to transform Karloff into the mummy. At 11:00 a.m. on the day the famous resurrection scene was shot, all of his facial skin was covered with cotton strips. When this had dried, it was covered with beauty mud into which wrinkles were carved to produce the ancient look. Finally, Karloff's body was wrapped with acid-dyed linen. When he stepped on the stage at 7:00 p.m. for shooting, the entire crew gasped. By 2:00 a.m. the resurrection scene was in the can, ready for posterity. Ironically, although the mummy is what virtually everybody remembers from the film, he appears in only in one scene and is on the screen for less than a minute.

Several of the actors and production people have left accounts of their experiences in the making of this film, but no one tells a funnier story than Arthur Tovey, one of the extras. Wearing black body makeup, he played one of the Nubian slaves who buried Imhotep. After the burial, pharaoh's guards hurled spears at the Nubians, killing them to assure secrecy for the resting place. To keep production costs down and the number of extras at a minimum, the two halves of the scene were shot on successive days, with the same extras playing both the Nubians and pharaoh's guards. Arthur Tovey played both and thus killed himself.

Ardath Bey's Nubian servant was played by Noble Johnson, a dog trainer. When the producers saw this imposing six-foot-four figure, they immediately enlisted him for the film, and he went on to have a successful acting career.

The reincarnated heroine was played by Zita Johann, who apparently was deeply affected by the film. She went on to write several books about reincarnation and died believing she had led many lives.

Bob Brier

See also: *Book of the Dead*; Freund, Karl; Imhotep; Karloff, Boris; Tutankhamun ("King Tut"); Universal Studios mummy series

Further Reading

Feramisco, Thomas M. 2002. *The Mummy Unwrapped: Scenes Left on Universal's Cutting Room Floor.* Jefferson, NC: McFarland & Co.

Freeman, Richard. 2009. *"The Mummy* in Context." *European Journal of American Studies* 1, document 4. Accessed December 16, 2013. http://ejas.revues.org/7566.

Glut, Donald F. 1978. *Classic Movie Monsters.* Metuchen, NJ: Scarecrow Press.

Landis, John. 2011. *Monsters in the Movies: 100 Years of Cinematic Nightmares.* New York: DK Publishing.

Mank, Gregory. 1984. "The Mummy Revisited." *Films in Review,* August/September: 414–421.

Peirse, Alison. 2013. *After Dracula: The 1930s Horror Film.* London: I. B. Tauris & Co.

Riley, Philip J., ed. 1989. *The Mummy.* Universal Filmscripts Series Classic Horror Films, Volume 7. Abescon, NJ: MagicImage Filmbooks.

Weaver, Tom, Michael Brunas, and John Brunas. 2007. *Universal Horrors: The Studio's Classic Films, 1931–46.* Jefferson, NC: McFarland & Co.

The Mummy (1959)

With the success of *Curse of Frankenstein* (1957) and *Horror of Dracula* (1958), along with an always game Christopher Lee and Peter Cushing, Britain's Hammer Films returned again to the Universal Studios monster pool in 1959 and resurrected the third of the monster triple-threat with *The Mummy.* Director Terence Fisher and screenwriter Jimmy Sangster had considerable confidence with the genre, having directed and written the previous two Hammer horror films. Rather than producing a straight remake of Universal's 1932 classic *The Mummy,* the filmmakers gathered inspiration from Universal's later films, *The Mummy's Hand, The Mummy's Tomb,* and *The Mummy's Ghost.* The resulting film is sometimes regarded as one of the least among Fisher's and Sangster's several horror collaborations, but it nevertheless offers its own (often gory and perverse) charms, and its reputation has grown over time.

Peter Cushing plays the lead role as John Banning, the son of an archeologist on a 20-year quest to find the hidden tomb of the princess Ananka, servant to the god Karnak. The film opens in Egypt in the year 1895, as the expedition has found the tomb and is preparing to open it. Just as they are about to enter, an Egyptian by the name of Mehmet Bey in a tell-tale red fez approaches and warns them to stay out of the holy resting place, since whoever "robs the graves of Egypt" will die.

They ignore him, and inside the tomb, Banning's father Stephen, played by the great character actor Felix Aylmer, finds the "Scroll of Life," a magic incantation that awakens the mummy. Stephen is instantly driven insane by the horror of it all.

Three years later, with the elder Banning confined to a mental institution, Mehmet Bey, who is revealed as the priest of Karnak, has come to London with the mummy in tow to exact vengeance on the party of archeologists for their crimes. The first appearance of the living mummy is the finest scene in the film. Christopher Lee, swathed in ancient grave wrappings, slowly rises from a swamp at Mehmet's command. Covered in slime and bandages, Lee has only his eyes to convey both menace and subservience. We soon learn that the creature was once Kharis, a priest of Karnack in ancient Egypt who fell in love with the princess Ananka (played by Yvonne Furneaux). In his attempt to raise her from the dead after she fell ill from a virus, he was punished by having his tongue removed, being wrapped in bandages, and being buried alive in her tomb to serve as her eternal guardian.

The rest of the film follows the traditional monster-movie narrative, but with Hammer's signature almost-nudity and graphic (for its era) violence. Cushing's performance is merely workmanlike, but it still exudes the charm that made him the perfect foil for Lee's sinister affect throughout their legendary string of lead appearances together in Hammer's horror films. Amid the claustrophobic Egyptian set pieces that betray Hammer's limited budget, Lee's performance as Kharis/the mummy gives everything around him an aura of authenticity and gravitas. As the mummy he works hard not to look like a Boris Karloff imitator, although that actor's classic performance in the 1932 Universal film haunts this colorful spectacle. A 1959 *New York Times* micro-review recommends the original over Hammer's, calling the latter film "woodenly directed," a comment that likely also refers to Lee's flat-footed stride.

The Hammer crew was often reticent in admitting to being influenced in any way by the original Universal films. Jimmy Sangster did once note that his script shared many similarities with Universal's later mummy films starring Lon Chaney Jr. in the title role, but he claimed never to have seen them. None of this is to say, however, that Hammer's *The Mummy* is not unique in any way. Fisher wanted the film to be more than a mere shocker, and he put noticeable care into the sets and cinematography, striving for an air of realism in Egyptological matters. One conspicuous lapse in historical accuracy, however, is seen in the fact that the references to the god Karnack do not reference an actual deity at all, but to a place. Nevertheless, the details in the tomb and in the flashback scenes to ancient Egypt convey a sense that the crew was drawing on some measure of authenticity. Even more perplexing, however, is that the figure of Kharis is never actually mummified: he is wrapped like a mummy, but instead of being subjected to the Egyptian mummification procedure he is buried alive, albeit without a tongue.

Hammer would go on to produce three more mummy-themed films up until 1971, ending with *Blood from the Mummy's Tomb*. Theirs would be the last full mummy movie franchise until the resurrection of the Universal series with the big-budget films directed by Stephen Sommers, starting in 1999 with *The Mummy*, starring Brendan Fraser and Arnold Vosloo. Today the 1959 Hammer film, despite the low status sometimes afforded to it, remains a fan favorite and is considered part of the essential Hammer horror film canon.

Peter Bebergal

See also: Hammer Films mummy series; Kharis; Lee, Christopher; Universal Studios mummy series

Further Reading

Hearn, Marcus, and Alan Barnes. 2007. *The Hammer Story: The Authorised History of Hammer Films*. Foreword by Christopher Lee. London: Titan Books.

Hunter, Jack. 2000. *House of Horror: The Complete Hammer Films Story*. 3rd ed. London: Creation Books.

iLandis, John. 2011. *Monsters in the Movies: 100 Years of Cinematic Nightmares*. New York: DK Publishing.

Steinberg, Jay. n.d. "The Mummy (1959). *Turner Classic Movies*." Accessed December 16, 2013. http://www.tcm.com/this-month/article.html?id=499693|35362.

The Mummy (1999) and The Mummy Returns

The Mummy is Stephen Sommers's comic homage to Universal Pictures' 1932 and Hammer Studios' 1959 films of the same name, incorporating elements of both stories as well as referencing *Raiders of the Lost Ark* (1981). In Sommers's film, American adventurer Rick O'Connell (played by Brendan Fraser) stumbles on the lost city of Hamunaptra, the secret burial place of the Imhotep (Arnold Vosloo), once a high priest of Osiris. The film explains in an elaborate opening sequence that Imhotep was a powerful sorcerer in ancient Egypt who was in love with the pharaoh's mistress, Anck su Namen (Patricia Velasquez). When the pharaoh discovered their relationship, the two killed him. Before the pharaoh's guards could seize her, Anck su Namen took her own life after getting Imhotep to promise that he would use his powerful magic to reanimate her. Imhotep, however, was unable to resurrect Anck su Namen before he was taken into custody by the guards, who cut out his tongue and mummified him alive as punishment for his sacrilege.

Imhotep returns to life 3,200 years later when the seals that have been holding him in place are broken by Rick and others hunting Egyptian treasures who are scornful of the old magic that guards the mummy. Free of his confinement, Imhotep reincorporates by stealing the flesh from the living; he magically removes the eyes of one of the treasure hunters, transferring them to his own empty sockets, and then repairs his withered flesh with tissue of other victims, eventually reconstituting his own young and vital body. Imhotep then kidnaps Evie Carnahan

From left: Arnold Vosloo as the mummy Imhotep, Rachel Weisz as Evie Carnahan, and Brendan Fraser as Rick O'Connell in *The Mummy* (1999). (Universal Pictures/Photofest)

(Rachel Weisz), a librarian who is part of the exploration team and Rick's love interest, to use her as a sacrifice to revive Anck su Namen. Rick defeats Imhotep in an epic battle and rescues Carnahan, and the two escape into the desert with Egyptian treasure.

There were two sequels to *The Mummy*: 2001's *The Mummy Returns* and 2008's *The Mummy: Tomb of the Dragon Emperor.* The first of these, also directed by Sommers, is widely viewed as merely recycling the plot of the first film in the franchise. In it, Rick and Evie are now married and have an eight-year-old son, Alex (Freddie Boath). An Egyptian cult resurrects Imhotep to use his power to defeat the ancient Scorpion King (Dwayne Johnson) and thus gain control of the "Army of Anubis," and this requires the retrieval of an ancient Egyptian artifact in Alex's possession. Much conflict, adventure, and mayhem ensues. In still another sequel, *The Mummy: Tomb of the Dragon Emperor* (directed by Rob Cohen), Alex (Luke Ford) is now an adult explorer who unearths a Chinese mummy in the Far East who, when reanimated, can shape-shift. Martial arts star Jet Li plays the Jade Emperor who is brought back to life by Alex's excavations.

All three films were widely released and grossed between $100 to $200 million dollars. They feature CGI special effects that graphically represent the mummy's ability to shape-shift. Brendan Fraser in his role as Rick O'Connell in The Mummy

---

When Universal Studios rebooted its long-dormant mummy series in 1999, the overall conception of the mummy mythos was radically altered. Among the changes was the introduction of a mingled tone of swashbuckling adventure and light-hearted comedy to accompany the supernatural horror of the reanimated mummy-sorcerer Imhotep.

franchise is similar to swashbuckling archaeologist Indiana Jones from the *Raiders of the Lost Ark* franchise in both his costuming and his approach to interacting with ancient cultural artifacts, which brings about monumental confrontations with supernatural forces. *The Mummy* and *The Mummy Returns* garnered tepid critical reception; while some allowed that the films were entertaining, the films were criticized as being too full of special effects while devoid of substance. *The Mummy: Tomb of the Dragon Emperor* was panned by critics as a soulless imitation of the first two.

Although further entries in this series were initially announced, in 2012 Universal Studios announced that they were scrapping these preexisting plans and would instead proceed to "reboot" the series entirely. By the close of 2013 the reboot plan was still in development, with a shifting roster of directors and actors being named from time to time in the show business press.

June Pulliam

See also: Hammer Studios mummy series; Imhotep; *The Mummy* (1932); *The Mummy* (1959); Universal Studios mummy series

Further Reading

Cowie, Susan D., and Tom Johnson. 2002. *The Mummy in Fact, Fiction, and Film*. Jefferson, NC: McFarland & Company.

Newman, Kim. 2011. *Nightmare Movies: Horror on Screen Since the 1960s*. London: Bloomsbury Publishing.

Mummy documentaries

When someone says "mummy," ears and eyes turn in that direction. Given the age-old interest in mummies among a broad popular audience, it is no surprise that today documentary television regularly brings mummy documentaries into our living rooms (and e-devices). Mummies have engaged our collective attention ever since they were first "discovered" by the modern world. The Victorian era gave birth to mummy "unrolling" or "unwrappings," in which mummies, usually Egyptians, were brought into a viewing venue to be exposed and explored with quasi-scientific intent. For those who could not travel to an exotic place, these unrollings represent the first "documentaries" using the mummy as a subject. While these early presentations certainly did expose many to the idea of mummification, they often took on a theatrical mood and amounted to little more than an avenue for voyeuristic curiosity. Often the prize or climax of these unrollings was the discovery of some amulet or jewels from within the wrappings. The human remains were of less interest.

Given the rising public interest in mummies and the phenomenon known as Egyptomania, it is no surprise that mummies found their way into the sideshow

Mummy Documentaries: A Selected Chronology

1996	*Mummies and the Wonders of Ancient Egypt*
2000	*Desert Mummies of Peru,* with Sonia Guillen; *Unwrapped: The Mysterious World of Mummies,* hosted by Bob Brier
2001	*Oldest Mummies in the World,* 2001, with Bernardo Arriaza
2001–2003	*The Mummy Road Show,* hosted by Ron Beckett and Jerry Conlogue
2002	*Pyramids, Mummies and Tombs*
2004	*Mummy Detectives,* with Bob Brier
2005–2007	*Digging for the Truth,* with Josh Bernstein
2008	*Into the Unknown,* with Josh Bernstein
2010	*Chasing Mummies,* with Zahi Hawass; *Lost Mummies of Papua New Guinea*

tents of traveling carnival troupes. Some of these were authentic Egyptian or South American mummies acquired during the vast archaeological explorations of the Victorian era. Others were simply unclaimed bodies that were mummified, usually with arsenic, and traveled extensively attached to some fantastical story line. If the sideshow man could not acquire a "real" mummy, fakes were available for purchase, coming complete with a sideshow banner and story line. Some of these sideshows were actually educational while others simply were designed to bring in revenue as they preyed on the curiosity and lack of knowledge among the attendees. The practice of displaying traveling carnival mummies did serve to inform the public, even if it was misinformation, and can be considered an early form of documentary presentation.

Documentaries are influenced by the prevalent world view and social mores of their surrounding times. With the advent of filmmaking and the public's interest in the topic, fictional presentations involving mummies found their way to theaters in 1932 with Universal Studios' classic horror movie *The Mummy*. Countless Hollywood films followed.

It was not until the early 1900s that scientists, in particular Margaret Murray and her associates, began to understand the value held within the tissues and bones of these mummified time travelers. In the early 1900s, many scientific processes were developed and applied to mummies. Tissue analysis, paleopathology reports, the discovery of the chemical composition of natron, rehydration of mummified tissue, dissections, and radiography all contributed to the enhancement of the evidence-based study of mummies. It was with thanks to these early scientific investigations that mummy science was born.

Significantly, the public began to embrace these new efforts, and the casual sideshow type of voyeurism gave way to presentations based on facts and evidence. Documentary films were all the rage in the early 1900s. These early "adventure" films were primarily focused on animals, with some delving into the anthropological realm. In the 1920s Robert Flaherty, a former explorer who turned to filmmaking, directed a documentary film called *Nanook of the North*, bringing anthropology to the movie going public, which enjoyed seeing animals unusual to their own experiences as well as seeing faraway places and peoples. The public desire for the unusual was fed by Robert LeRoy Ripley, who was known for his cartoon series and his documentation of his travel exploits. Ripley created *Ripley's Believe it or Not!*, which began as a newspaper full-page "report" and evolved into televised specials as well as a series that presented oddities, which included mummies, from around the world. Ripley presented "Atta-Boy," the likely mummified remains of a fetus from the Atacama Desert in Peru, in a 1930s book chronicling his world travel and adventures.

In the early 1950s with the development of television, and with broadcast technology improvements, more and more televised documentaries found their way into people's homes. Mummies remained a popular subject, and this interest was certainly fueled by Hollywood's depiction of mummies chasing movie stars around pyramids. Soon, documentaries dedicated to the exploration of mummies came into style.

While it is impossible to provide a complete listing of all the documentaries involving mummies, a partial list of recent efforts, along with their year of release and the names of noted mummy experts involved, would include the following: *Desert Mummies of Peru*, 2000, with Sonia Guillen; *Oldest Mummies in the World*, 2001, with Bernardo Arriaza; *Unwrapped: The Mysterious World of Mummies*, 2000, hosted by Bob Brier in three one-hour episodes; *Mummies and the Wonders of Ancient Egypt*, 1996, four episodes; *Pyramids, Mummies and Tombs*, 2002, three episodes; *Mystery of the Mummies*, three episodes; *Chasing Mummies*, 2010, ten episodes, with Zahi Hawass; *Ice Mummies*; *Digging for the Truth*, 2005–2007, with Josh Bernstein (a series with various episodes related to mummies and archaeology); *Mummy Detectives*, 2004, three episodes, with Bob Brier; *The Mummy Road Show*, 2001–2003, 40 episodes, hosted by Ron Beckett and Jerry Conlogue; *Into the Unknown* with Josh Bernstein, 2008 series with several episodes on mummies; *Lost Mummies of Papua New Guinea*, 2010, National Geographic Explorer. Again, this is only a partial and very incomplete list.

While there are many examples of excellent documentaries on the subject of mummies, the changing business of documentary television has brought about many challenges for scientists hoping to present their findings in a televised format. Science by its very nature is unpredictable. Thus, a producer may spend hours, days, weeks, and months filming a given subject and/or group of scientists with few results in terms of a marketable product. Because of the time required to film authentic documentaries on mummies, sponsors and producers now want an assurance that they will get marketable results for their dollars and time spent on a project. The realities of television financing and competition for viewership were the driving forces behind this change. The biggest change was seen in the late 1990s, flowing into the present-day "docutainment" industry. Docutainment is defined as a presentation that includes some documentary characteristics yet it is intended to both inform and entertain.

In an attempt to assure a deliverable product, many documentaries have become less about actual documentation and more about following a scripted production. In other words, many documentaries rarely "document" an event and the subjects involved, but rather direct the "action" toward some predetermined and marketable outcome. While these scripted documentaries are certainly informative and educational, the findings do not necessarily stand up to scientific scrutiny. Many such documentaries lean toward the sensationalistic, focusing on topics such as cannibalism, or the "first ever discovered," or the "oldest of its kind." Thus, documentary viewers need to watch these offerings with increased scrutiny and arm themselves with background knowledge based in the scientific literature as well as the processes associated with the scientific method. In this way the viewer will be better able to question what is being claimed as well as extract the valuable information that the documentary may contain.

Another force that has influenced mummy documentary presentations has been the "Indiana Jones" effect. Similar to what has been called the "CSI" effect, referring to the impact of the popular CSI television series franchise on actual forensic cases, the Indiana Jones effect appears to have brought about a sometimes exaggerated or fabricated sense of adventure seen in mummy documentaries. We have all seen the stereotypical appearance of some hosts in mummy documentaries who emulate Hollywood by donning the fedora hat, khaki shirt, and over-the-shoulder leather carrying pouch made famous in the Indiana Jones movie series. To be sure, mummy research in the field is very exciting and can be filled with extraordinary adventure. However, these features do not necessarily coincide with a production team's filming schedule. Thus, the "adventures" that are presented in many mummy documentaries may actually be reenactments. They may even be pure fabrications designed to fulfill a documentary's predetermined "wow" factor.

Perhaps one of the most interesting, scientific, and educational documentaries on the topic of mummies was National Geographic's *Mr. Mummy* in 1994. Doctors Bob Brier and Ronn Wade used a donated body to replicate the Egyptian mummification method using the same techniques and replicated instruments. The documentary was compelling in that there was no predetermined direction it was to take. The filmmakers documented the procedures and the scientists' reactions in real time. Nothing was set up or staged. Today the mummy, known as MUMAB, is still providing scientists with unique data related to Brier and Wade's experiment and the mummification practices of ancient Egypt.

Another excellent documentary series was *The Mysterious World of Mummies*, hosted by Bob Brier and presented in three one-hour presentations. There are several features of this "miniseries" that make it noteworthy. The material for the documentary was derived from Brier's well-researched and referenced book *The Encyclopedia of Mummies*, published in 1998 through Checkmark Books. The documentary series provided rich visual images to many of the mummies or groups of mummies described in the book. Also, the viewer was taken to many exotic locations and famous museums throughout the world where these mummies are found. Finally, the series had an excellent host in Brier, in that his storytelling style is compelling, informative, and modest, and he was willing to explore his own thinking while on camera. Brier had a way of making complex constructs accessible to the public at large without oversimplification.

As docutainment has become the norm, networks and producers do try to find a balance between entertainment value and documenting events. This is often accomplished through using a charismatic host to bring these real-life mummy stories to the public. An excellent example of success in this endeavor is seen in the work of Josh Bernstein in both his *Digging for the Truth* and *Into the Unknown* series. In these series we find a host who is engaging while bringing many topics related to archaeology and mummy science to the viewers. Having worked with Mr. Bernstein, this author can attest to the authenticity of his efforts in bringing visual and factual information to the general viewership. Bernstein is a sincere scholar on a quest for inquiry-based research and has the ability to break complex anthropological systems down making new knowledge accessible.

There are several documentaries that have also been excellent with regards to following a story as it develops, but others have not been so straightforward. This author has been involved with several documentary projects in which the director attempted to steer the scientists into making unfounded claims on camera for the sensationalistic impact those claims would have. Additionally, scientific projects have been buried within a pre-written story unfounded by facts, while others are in actuality reenactments of past adventures and do not document real-time events.

With regards to following the story as it develops, the National Geographic television documentary series *The Mummy Road Show* was interesting in that, during its production, the stories unfolded during the documentation. The episodes were then "reverse scripted" to weave together the scenes documented in the field. In this way, the reality of the individual expedition was captured. The reverse-scripted story was then designed to explain the how and why of what the viewers were seeing happened and what was learned. Of the 40 episodes that aired during its three season run, some were profound while others were somewhat flat in terms of their scientific value. This reverse scripting approach was a credit to the philosophy of National Geographic television during the series' time period as well as the production company's ethical sense of documenting what was happening rather than creating a story where there may not have been one.

It is interesting that the use of the mummy as a means of informing and educating the public has now come full circle from its earliest beginnings. When mummies were first finding their way into popular culture, the "presentations" began with unrollings and sideshows. These displays were quasi-educational and designed to entertain. Thus they had many of the characteristics of docutainment presentations. Eventually, the presentation of mummies became more scientific and less voyeuristic in nature beginning with the early twentieth century scientific scrutiny of mummified remains, with reports finding their way into scientific journals. As technology advanced, mummies were presented to the public in a much broader way through televised presentations that became the early documentaries focused on true documentation. Competition for viewership and increases in costs of production brought about the era of the scripted or predetermined documentary, assuring the networks and producers that a deliverable and sensational product was the end result. Here, the circle from docutainment, to and through true documentary intent, has now returned to docutainment. This is not to say that current documentaries involving mummified remains have become the new sideshow. Quite the contrary, there is considerable science being presented in mummy documentaries today. What it does mean is that the viewer needs to be well informed and careful not to take the entertainment facets of a presentation as fact. Even the scientific claims should be challenged with rational inquiry. A good rule of thumb may be that if a claim is made that this is the "first time we've seen this" or "this is the rarest mummy in the world," it probably is not.

Ronald G. Beckett

See also: Displaying mummies; Egyptomania; Experimental mummification; The mummy on television; Mummy unwrappings

Further Reading

Aufderheide, Arthur C. 2003. *The Scientific Study of Mummies*. Cambridge: Cambridge University Press.

Beckett, Ronald G., and Gerald Conlogue. 2005. *Mummy Dearest: How Two Guys in a Potato Chip Truck Changed the Way the Living See the Dead*. Guilford, CT: The Lyons Press.

Brier, Bob, 1998. *The Encyclopedia of Mummies*. USA: Checkmark Books.

Kilborn, RW, and John Izod. 1997. *Confronting Reality: An Introduction to Television Documentaries*. UK: Manchester University Press.

Marfo, Amma. 2007. "The Evolution and Impact of Documentary Films." *Senior Honors Project*. Paper 42. Accessed December 6, 2013. http://digitalcommons.uri.edu/srhonorsprog/42.

The Mummy Road Show. 2001–2003. National Geographic Channel.

Schweitzer, N.J., and Michael J. Saks. 2007. "The CSI Effect: Popular Fiction about Forensic Science Affects the Public's Expectations about Real Forensic Science." *Juirmetrics* 47: 357–364.

Shokrian, Rebecca. 2002. "Secrets of *The Mummy Road Show* Unraveled." *National Geographic*, March 27. Accessed October 28, 2013. http://news.nationalgeographic.com/news/2002/03/0326_0327_mummyroadshow.html.

The mummy in popular culture

Fascination with Egypt is not recent. With such a long-lived civilization, the Egyptians of the Kushite and Saite periods (ca. 700–525 BCE) looked back to Old Kingdom (ca. 2700–2200 BCE) history, art, and architecture for inspiration, restoring texts, and copying sculptural styles. The Giza pyramids were already 2,500 years old in Cleopatra's day, two millennia ago, and the Roman emperors who succeeded her as rulers of Egypt imported obelisks to Italy to adorn their Eternal City. Throughout the medieval period and Renaissance, Egypt was viewed as the original source of ancient mystical wisdom. European travelers to Egypt gradually increased from the sixteenth to the eighteenth centuries, and Egyptian themed decorative arts, furniture, and architecture slowly caught on. Napoleon's military campaign in 1798, through its resulting scholarly publications, inspired the first real wave of Egyptomania; Vivant Denon's *Voyage dans la Basse et la Haute Egypte* (1802, translated as *Travels in Upper and Lower Egypt* in 1803) provided a popular prelude to the massive volumes produced by the entire French team of "savants," *Description de l'Egypte* (1809–1829). The Rosetta Stone, found by Napoleon's men, along with a few other pieces, finally led to the decipherment of hieroglyphs by the 1820s, and Egyptology became a serious discipline.

Popular fiction on mummies appeared in Jane Webb Loudon's *The Mummy* in 1827, just five years after Champollion's initial decipherment. Books, stories, plays, and silent movies increasingly popularized Egypt—and mummies—over the next 100 years. The 1922 discovery of Tutankhamun's tomb spurred a new wave of "Tutmania," contributing to the Art Deco movement and Egyptian-inspired hairstyles, dress design, etc. The much vaunted "Curse of King Tut" also caught the public's imagination, finally fostering Boris Karloff's classic film *The Mummy* (1932), wherein the (inaccurately) reincarnated princess is Ankhesenamun, namesake of Tut's historical queen. The succeeding series of Universal mummy films of the early 1940s, all featuring the shambling mummy Kharis as the title villain, were unknown to a post–World War II generation until a package of old Universal monster movies was made available to television as "Shock Theater" in 1957, a catalyst for a variety of local TV station horror hosts on Saturdays after midnight. A year later the magazine *Famous Monsters of Filmland* debuted with features providing photos, humor, and historical background on these movies. But the young and mostly male generation, who had fed their appetite for the macabre on "questionable" horror comics from the late 1940s to the mid 1950s,

Mummy Merchandise

Among the various areas where the iconic mummy of horror and popular entertainment has invaded and colonized pop culture, none is more extensive than realm of merchandising. Since the middle part of the twentieth century, the mummy has appeared in and as all the following:

Toy models
Pez heads
Bobble heads
Action figures
Legos
Candy
Trading cards
Stickers
Magic tricks
Card games
Board games
Video games
Interactive books
Gaming miniatures
Puzzles
Costumes and masks
Clothing
Jewelry
Figurines
Museum products
Halloween decorations
Christmas ornaments

And this is just a highly selective partial list!

wanted tangible manifestations of "their" monsters, including mummies. In 1959 Topps, the originator of baseball bubble gum cards, issued trading cards depicting scenes from horror and sci-fi films with campy captions (Funny Monsters/You'll Die Laughing). By the early 1960s the merchandising of Universal's quarter century old films began in earnest.

The first phase of pop mummymania was ushered in by a Dell comic one shot from 1962 simply titled "The Mummy," with a Kharis look-alike approved by Universal Studios, but oddly the story was independent of the movies, featuring a talking mummy named Ahmed. The first two issues of *Monster World,* from 1964, each had a short comics adaptation of Karloff's *The Mummy* (1932) and the first Kharis film, *The Mummy's Hand* (1940). In 1961 Aurora, a successful plastic model kit company, launched their 1/8-scale Universal monster figure kits with Frankenstein (actually Karloff's version of the creature). The line flourished, with The Mummy appearing in 1963, based on Lon Chaney's Kharis rather than Karloff's Imhotep. A series of comical monster vehicle kits followed, among them the Mummy's Chariot in 1965. The metal injection moulds for such polystyrene kits can produce thousands of copies, and Bill Lemon's original mummy figure has been reissued numerous times by other companies, most recently in 1999. The early 1960s saw a flood of small plastic toys, games, puzzles, paint-by-number sets, pencil sharpeners, iron-on patches, pinback buttons, wallets, drinking glasses, plastic spoons and swizzle sticks (Mon-Stirs), and even bubble bath containers (Soakies) of the various Universal monsters, almost always including The Mummy, from companies such as Hasbro, Milton-Bradley, Jaymar, Marx, Colgate, and MPC. Halloween mummy costumes from Ben Cooper became common, as did rubber mummy masks, but the gold standard were the thick latex masks produced by Don Post, who produced two different versions of Chaney's Kharis in the mid 1960s, but at $35 they were far beyond the reach of most youngsters; reissued in 1999/2000, these masks were finally affordable (at $100 each) for nostalgic baby boomers.

The 1970s was not a big decade for mummy literature, either adult or juvenile, but the new wave of mummy films from Hammer Films, which had spanned the 1960s, was followed by other films in the 1970s, a decade when mummies became more popular on television, too. In addition to the standard color comics, still featuring occasional mummy stories, humorous or serious (such as Ra-Ka-Tep, created by Don Glut for his *Occult Files of Dr. Spektor*, and Marvel's *N'Kantu, The Living Mummy* and Dr. Skarab), a new style of larger format black and white horror comics—scarier, gorier and sexier (and not for younger kids)—featured mummy tales in titles like *Eerie, Creepy,* and *Psycho*. Universal mummies were no longer the standard, and a variety of small, soft-rubber "danglers" and cloth-wrapped mummy figures emerged from toy companies such as AHI, Remco, Vic's, Mego, and Lincoln. Orville the Mummy, from the TV show *Sabrina and the Groovy Goolies,* had a figural toy, as did G.I. Joe, the boy's equivalent to Barbie, in the adventure set Secret of the Mummy's Tomb. *Dungeons and Dragons* introduced early mummy role-playing miniature figures.

By the 1980s mummies had become a standard monster of modern horror, a process that had started in the 1960s when they were still part of Universal's "team." Where once Halloween had been epitomized by witches, ghosts, and goblins, it was now just as regularly typified by man-made monsters, vampires, werewolves, and mummies. Horror fiction about living mummies was on the rise with books like David Case's *The Third* Grave (1981) and Charles L. Grant's *Long Night of the Grave* (1986), culminating with *The Mummy or Ramses the Damned* from vampire fiction diva Anne Rice in 1989, which has unfortunately not been followed thus far by its promised sequel. Early video and electronic games appeared with *Oh Mummy* in 1982 from Sinclair/Gem Software and Bandai's hand held *Invaders of the Mummy's Tomb* the same year; trends with role-playing and interactive games continued.

In the late 1980s a new model maker's hobby emerged, the garage kit. Unlike the mass produced kits put out by large companies, this cottage industry was spawned by individuals who sculpted their own originals and then cast them, usually in resin in their garages or basements. Often less than 50 copies of any particular figure were made before the moulds lost their detail. Originally marketed by word-of-mouth, this has now become a significant facet of the hobby industry. Horror and science fiction are favorite topics and have allowed significant freedom in imagining various creatures. The earliest garage kit mummy may be a 1/6 Karloff Imhotep by Jeff Yagher from about 1988. Yagher, an actor as well as artist, has continued to sculpt movie mummies in various poses, his most recent in 2011. All the famous Universal and Hammer Kharis mummies, plus Arnold Vosloo's more recent Imhotep, as well as secondary characters, have been created by numerous talented artists, who have added their own, sometimes humorous interpretations of classic mummies besides developing original creations.

A new wave of mummymania emerged in the 1990s from a variety of sources. Partly it may have been due to an increased interest in Egyptology, as CT scans of mummies were being more regularly reported in the press and major discoveries like The Valley of the Golden Mummies were announced by Zahi Hawass, who also "opened" coffins in tombs on live television, shortly after his pre-fame cameo in the television drama *Legend of the Lost Tomb* (1997). The *Goosebumps* phenomenon of young adult horror novels by author R. L. Stine spawned not only imitation fun horror series by other writers but a TV show that led to massive merchandising by 1995. The mummy from Stine's best known stories, Prince Khor-Ru, was featured on cheap kids' jewelry, pencil cases, keychains, bookbags, sleeping bags, tents, pillow cases, and toy figures. In 1997 the animated show *Mummies Alive!* resulted in a series of action figures that curiously did not include the female mummy Nefertina, presumably as these were aimed at boys. In Australia, the figures were marketed as *Pharaohs Alive!* (though they were not pharaohs), and a rip-off set of cheaper figures came out as *Pharaoh Warriors*, while Lego produced a series of Egyptian toy sets with mummies for younger children in 1998. For Halloween 1997 the U.S. Post Office issued a series of 32-cent stamps highlighting famous Universal monsters, including Karloff as The Mummy; merchandise generated from this image ranged from postcards and posters to pens, pencils, erasers, kitchen magnets (metal and rubber), and lapel pins, and Kenner/Hasbro put out a related set of fairly detailed cloth-wrapped 12-inch action figures. Additionally, a variety of first day and other postmarked envelope cachets appeared with the stamp and original mummy designs. Guyana and Sierra Leone have also issued Karloff mummy stamps, and Turkmenistan produced one for the 1999 movie remake.

The announcement that Universal was remaking *The Mummy* led to a flurry of interest by other filmmakers. Suddenly surfacing on TV, video, or in theaters between 1997 and 1998 were *Under Wraps, Legend of the Lost Tomb, Bram Stoker's The Mummy, Mummies Alive!, Tale of the Mummy*, and several stand-alone television episodes, all culminating in the Brendan Fraser blockbuster in 1999, which generated numerous action figures, elaborate diorama playsets, and a major trading card series. That film in turn generated a direct sequel in 2001 which itself spun off an animated television program, and a prequel, *The Scorpion King* (2002), which as of 2012 had two follow-up films with a third filmed and scheduled for release in 2014, though the connection to mummies and Egypt was lost long ago, offering instead a fantasy mythological approach to Akkadian/Babylonian history.

Meanwhile, mummy collectibles of various types continue to appear with great frequency. Museum gift shops are a great source of items that are both fun and educational, usually based on real mummies in their collections. A series of colorful metal pencil tins from the British Museum, the first six produced in 1989, was later redesigned with new art and offered again in various sets several times; the Museum also made a jump rope with handles based on the coffin of Henutmehit. The Museum of Fine Arts in Boston developed attractive mummy coffin bookends in the 1980s and fun Russian doll style nesting coffins in 1991. The Cleveland Museum of Art offered a candle (Bakenmut) in 1995 and soon after a mouse pad and a beach towel, both from the coffin of Nesykhonsu.

Jewelry, notably earrings and small pendants, sometimes with mummies inside coffins that open, are found as cheap items on eBay and fairly pricey items in museum gift shop catalogs. Enamel pins, brightly designed, have become a new form of affordable collectible; Hard Rock Café has offered, from around the world, dozens of mummy-themed pins since 2000; the Egyptian themed HRC in Myrtle Beach alone has issued at least 20. The Disney parks produce Halloween pins, and many of their animated film characters or theme park creations have appeared as trick-or-treat mummies, some more than once, over the past decade or so. Porcelain figurines from Enesco, Hallmark, and other companies have put out all types of "cute" mummies since the 1990s; a fun whimsical piece from the Mary's Moo Moos series, "The Moommy" (1997), features a cow coffin which, when opened, emits a shrill scream. The tiny high-end Limoges boxes from France released several hand-painted coffins in the late 1990s, and the inevitable cheaper imitations have followed. Recently the Lolita collection of martini glasses offered a Mummy-tini.

Hand-blown and painted glass ornaments are a specialty of European companies Christopher Radko and Polonaise, and several attractive mummy coffins, plus even a Karloff Imhotep head, now decorate Christmas trees. As Halloween continues to grow as a major holiday decorating activity, mummy ornaments, window stickers, and lawn creations have proliferated. This mirrors the growth of mummies as typical themes of young adult and children's books. Just a handful of mummy-themed books were aimed at kids before the 1970s. By the 1980s there were over 20, which had increased to over three times that number in the 1990s and continues to grow.

Fortunately, as our knowledge of real mummies has grown, so has the information found in such stories that are passed on to the young, helping to dispel the ignorance and fear once associated with mummies. Hopefully the fascination will remain, tinged with a bit of fun.

Carter Lupton

See also: Hammer Films mummy series; Kharis; *The Mummy* (1999) and *The Mummy Returns*; The mummy in Western fiction: Beginnings to 1922; The mummy in Western fiction: From 1922 to the twenty-first century; Mummy movies; The mummy on television; Napoleon and the birth of Egyptology; Rosetta Stone; Universal Studios mummy series

Further Reading

Brier, Bob. 2013. *Egyptomania: Our Three Thousand Year Obsession with the Land of the Pharaohs*. New York: Palgrave Macmillan.

Cain, Dana. 1998. *Collecting Monsters of Film and TV*. Iola, WI: Krause Publications.

Day, Jasmine. 2006. *The Mummy's Curse: Mummymania in the English-Speaking World*. London and New York: Routledge.

Huckvale, David. 2012. *Ancient Egypt in the Popular Imagination*. Jefferson, NC: McFarland.

Luckhurst, Roger. 2012. *The Mummy's Curse: The True History of a Dark Fantasy*. Oxford: Oxford University Press.

Lupton, Carter. 2003. "Mummymania for the Masses: Is Egyptology Cursed by the Mummy's Curse?" In *Consuming Ancient Egypt*, edited by Sally MacDonald and Michael Rice, 23–46. London: UCL Press.

Marshall, John. 1999. *Collecting Monster Toys*. Atglen, PA: Schiffer Publications.

The mummy in Western fiction: Beginnings to 1922

The origin of mummies as an enduring theme in Western fiction is bound up with the major wave of Egyptomania that swept through Europe in the nineteenth century. Europe became enamored of all things Egyptian following Napoleon Bonaparte's Egyptian campaign (1798–1801) and the 1822 decipherment of the "Rosetta Stone." Egyptomania was further fueled by press coverage of the latest discoveries of Egyptologists such as those of Giovanni Belzoni (1778–1823), who—among other achievements—became the first Westerner to explore pyramid of Khufu (Cheops) at Giza. After returning to England he published a two-volume narrative and, during 1820 and 1821, exhibited a model of the tomb of Seti I in

---

A Selected Chronology of Mummy Fiction up to 1922

1827	*The Mummy! A Tale of the Twenty-Second Century* by Jane Loudon Webb
1840	"The Mummy's Foot" by Theophile Gautier
1845	"Some Words with a Mummy" by Edgar Allan Poe
1863	*The Romance of a Mummy* by Theophile Gautier
1869	"Lost in a Pyramid; or, The Mummy's Curse" by Louisa May Alcott
1886–1887	*She: A History of Adventure* by H. Rider Haggard
1890	"The Ring of Thoth" by Arthur Conan Doyle
1892	"Lot No. 249" by Arthur Conan Doyle
1903	*The Jewel of Seven Stars* by Bram Stoker
1908	"The Nemesis of Fire" by Algernon Blackwood
1914–1915	*Brood of the Witch Queen* by Sax Rohmer

London. Fiction featuring exotic Egypt soon followed, and mummies were part of the genre.

The Mummy! A Tale of the Twenty-Second Century by Jane Webb (1807–1858), later Jane Loudon, is the first novel in English featuring a mummy. Published in three volumes in 1827, it is set in an England of 2126 CE. The satirical plot involves the revived mummy of Cheops who offers wise advice. Webb's inspiration can be traced to several sources, including Belzoni, and she was certainly influenced by (and perhaps intent on countering the political and philosophical slant of) *Frankenstein*, which had been published less than a decade earlier.

Mary Wollstonecraft Godwin (1797–1852) (later Shelley) may have been the first to consider a reanimated mummy as an image of horror in English fiction. In her *Frankenstein* (1818), Victor Frankenstein, disgusted by the creature he has created, exclaims, "Oh! No mortal could support the horror of that countenance. A mummy again endued with animation could not be so hideous as that wretch" (Shelley 2008, 57).

In the 1840s, steamships made travel to Egypt easier, and mummies were brought back as souvenirs. Public and private "mummy unwrapping parties" became fashionable. American author Edgar Allan Poe (1809–1849) is credited with the first English-language short story about a mummy, "Some Words with a Mummy" (*American Whig Review,* April 1845). Poe pokes fun at mummy "unwrappings" and the "scientific" practice of galvanism—using electricity to attempt reanimation (which both Shelly and Loudon employ in their novels).

Theophile Gautier's (1811–1872) story, "The Mummy's Foot" ("*Le Pied de momie,*" *Musée des familles*, September 1840; 1st English translation, Lafcadio Hearn, 1863), explored a romantic theme as well as the magical properties of mummies in a light-hearted manner. Gautier's novel *The Romance of the Mummy* (*Roman de la Momie,* 1856; 1st English translation, Anne T. Wilbur, 1863) introduced the idea of falling in love with a still-beautiful mummy, but with no suggestion of bringing her back to life. A scroll found with the mummy, once translated, provides the main story: a "historical" tale of tragic love interwoven with the Biblical story of the Hebrews' release from Egyptian slavery.

"The Mummy's Soul," published anonymously in 1862 in *The Knickerbocker, Volume 59*, is a convoluted horrific tale of blood, mummy dust, revivification, a giant fly, and a vase stolen from a tomb. Although not explicitly mentioned, a curse is implied. In "After Three Thousand Years" by Jane Austin (*Putnam's Monthly Magazine of American Literature, Science, and Art, Vol. 12, Issue 7,* 1868), a young man steals a necklace from a mummy and presents it to a lovely but arrogant young lady. The jewelry is cursed, and ultimately the girl dons it and dies.

Both these stories predate Louisa May Alcott's "Lost in a Pyramid; or, The Mummy's Curse" (*The New World,* January 16, 1869). When rediscovered in 1998, this story was thought to be the first fiction containing the theme of a mummy's curse. In Alcott's story, the eternal rest of a powerful sorceress is disturbed, and the curse is conveyed through a seed found in the mummy's wrappings. Once planted, it blooms into a white flower that produces madness and death.

"My New Year's Eve among the Mummies," published in January 1880 in *Belgravia* Magazine, is the first known mummy-related short story in a British periodical. Author "J. Arbuthnot Wilson" was a pseudonym for Grant Allen (1848–1899). Allen obviously and amusingly satirizes Gautier's "The Mummy's Foot."

Amateur Egyptologist Sir Henry Rider Haggard (1856–1925), writing as H. Rider Haggard, wrote of ancient Egypt in several novels and short stories. Although a mummy is only peripherally involved in the best known of these works, the novel *She: A History of Adventure* (*The Graphic*, October 1886–January 1887), it does introduce some of the lore later attached to the mummy mythos, including the desire for immortal love and the highly un-Egyptian concept of reincarnation.

Arthur Conan Doyle (1859–1930) wrote two influential mummy stories. "The Ring of Thoth," published in January 1890 in *The Cornhill Magazine*, tells of Sosra, who, in ancient times, makes a chemical discovery that transforms him into a near-immortal. After having lived thousands of years, he goes to the Louvre seeking a ring wrapped with the embalmed body of his beloved whose remains are in the museum. The ring contains a poison strong enough to undo the elixir that has kept him alive. He is later discovered, dead, still tightly embracing a female mummy.

In Doyle's "Lot No. 249" (*Harper's,* October 1892), a mummy is reanimated on three brief occasions by an Oxford Egyptologist using an ancient occult spell.

The man directs the mummy to bring harm to three acquaintances. The grisly, half-unwrapped creature is frightening, but not evil; he is a tool of vengeance.

Guy Boothby (1867–1905) also wrote of a near-immortal Egyptian and his lost love in "Professor of History" (*The Graphic*, December 10, 1894). The charismatic Professor Constanides possesses hypnotic power over a modern young lady; she "remembers" herself in ancient Egypt as Nofrit, the beloved of Sinfihit. To gain eternal rest, Constanides/Sinfihit needs Cecilia/Nofrit's forgiveness, which she grants. The "professor" is found dead the next day.

Boothby was not done with the theme of eternal life after writing this story. A few years later, he began what became a series of books about the sinister Dr. Nikola and his search for immortality with *Pharos the Egyptian* (*The Windsor Magazine*, June–December 1898). A mummy and the threat of a plague are involved.

Mummy novels of the late nineteenth century were often rather odd supernatural love stories. For example, in *Iras: A Mystery,* an 1896 novel by "Theo. Douglas" (Mrs. H. D. Everett), a beautiful, ancient Egyptian virgin prefers being entranced and entombed alive rather than marry the priest Savak. Although she can be awakened in the future by a true love, Savak also tosses in a curse. Centuries later, the girl is found by Egyptologist Ralph Lavenham, who is, of course, her true love. They marry, but the evil of Savak is still at work, and Iras (as Lavenham has named her), soon turns into a wrapped mummy thousands of years old. The rest of the story consists of Lavenham trying to convince people she really existed, as, despite extensive travel, no one can testify to actually having seen the girl. Another novel from the same period, *The Romance of the Golden Star* (1897) by George Griffiths, is unusual in that the mummies are a royal Incan brother and sister, married in life over three centuries earlier, who are revived and find happiness with modern mates.

Flaxman Low, the first of many later "occult" or "psychic" detectives who became popular stock characters in horror and crime fiction, was created by "E. and H. Heron," the pseudonym of Hesketh V. Prichard (1876–1922) and his mother, Kate O'Brien Ryall Prichard (1851–1935). In "The Story of Baelbrow" (*Pearson's,* April 1898), Low discovers a mummy that is not only intermittently reanimated but is also a self-created vampire—the first combination of two literary icons.

John Silence, another occult detective, investigates strange incendiarism at a country home in Algernon Blackwood's (1869–1951) "The Nemesis of Fire" (*John Silence*, 1908). Eventually, a mummy brought to England from Egypt is found to be causing the trouble. (Blackwood's other works referencing ancient Egypt do not include mummies.)

In Bram Stoker's (1847–1912) 1903 novel *The Jewel of Seven Stars,* a modern-day heroine is psychically connected with a revivified ancient Egyptian royal.

After the discovery of a queen's tomb, her soul inhabits the body of Margaret, the daughter of an Egyptologist. The queen, Tera, awaits a full resurrection that requires that her hand—torn off in a seventeenth century tomb robbery—and a ruby containing seven seven-pointed stars be restored to her.

H. Rider Haggard's only short story with a supernatural mummy theme, "Smith and the Pharaohs," was serialized in *The Strand*, December 1912–February 1913. Rather than a mummy, a young man is first attracted to a sculptured head of an ancient queen, whose mummy he later discovers in Egypt. A dream/hallucination of the past, reincarnation, and a royal ring are elements.

The prolific English writer Arthur Sarsfield Ward (1883–1959), who became famous as Sax Rohmer, was an avid Egyptophile but only occasionally employed embalmed Egyptians in his plots, and sometimes even these turn out not to be mummies. In his novel *Brood of the Witch Queen,* however, an ancient mummy— the son of a "witch-queen"—is transformed into a living infant who grows up to be a wizard with magical knowledge of the ancients (*The Premier Magazine*, May 1914–January, 1915).

The mummy as a stock character and theme, and the mummy story as its own subgenre, were obviously well-established by the time 1922 rolled around. Then Howard Carter discovered the tomb of the ancient Egyptian pharaoh Tutankhamun in November of that year, and a whole new era in mummy fiction shortly ensued.

Paula Guran

See also: Belzoni, Giovanni; Blackwood, Algernon; Doyle, Arthur Conan; Egyptomania; Gautier, Theophile; Haggard, H. Rider; *The Jewel of Seven Stars;* "Lost in a Pyramid, or The Mummy's Curse"; Mummy unwrappings; Napoleon and the birth of Egyptology; Poe, Edgar Allan

Further Reading

Cowie, Susan D. and Tom Johnson. 2007. *The Mummy in Fact, Fiction and Film.* Jefferson, NC: McFarland & Co.

Day, Jasmine. 2006. *Mummymania in the English-Speaking World*. New York: Routledge.

Frost, Brian J. *The Essential Guide to Mummy Literature.* Lanham, MD: Scarecrow Press.

Guran, Paula. 2006. "The Mummy." In *Icons of Horror and the Supernatural: An Encyclopedia of Our Worst Nightmares*, vol. 1, edited by S.T. Joshi, 375–407. Westport, CT: Greenwood Press.

Johnson, John J., and Jared Shunin, eds. 2013. *Unearthed.* London: Jurassic London.

Luckhurst, Roger. 2012. *The Mummy's Curse: The True History of a Dark Fantasy.* Oxford: Oxford University Press.

Shelley, Mary Wollstonecraft (Godwin). 2008. *Frankenstein or the Modern Prometheus: The 1818 Text*. Oxford: Oxford University Press.

Shunin, Jared, ed. 2013. *The Book of the Dead*. London: Jurassic London.

The mummy in Western fiction: From 1922 to the twenty-first century

On the heels of the nineteenth century's explosion of Egyptomania in Europe and America, Howard Carter's 1922 discovery and decade-long exploration of Tutankhamun's tomb inspired further fascination with ancient Egypt and exerted a powerful influence on the still-developing subgenre of mummy literature. The unfounded idea of a curse attached to mummies—helped along by claims made by novelist Marie Corelli (1855–1924)—was also reinforced with the discovery and began to show up more frequently in fiction. Universal Studios' 1932 film *The Mummy*, directed by Karl Freund and starring Boris Karloff, and with a plot derived from established fictional tropes, was a project largely spurred by the cultural wave of excitement over Tutankhamun, and it in turn inspired further popularity of Egyptian/mummy motifs in written fiction.

Many Egyptian-themed novels were churned out during the 1920s and 1930s; some involved mummies, but few added to the genre or are remembered now. Fantastic versions of ancient Egypt also flourished in stories for the popular U.S. pulp magazines between 1920 and 1940. Mummies—not always Egyptian—occasionally showed up.

H. P. Lovecraft (1890–1937) ghost-wrote a novella titled "Imprisoned with the Pharaohs" (*Weird Tales* May–July 1924) under the name of the famous stage magician, Harry Houdini. In it, a fictionalized Houdini encounters horrendous half-human/half-animal mummy hybrids in a hallucination or dream that he experiences inside an Egyptian tomb. Lovecraft co-wrote, with Hazel Heald, the story "Out of the Aeons" (*Weird Tales,* April 1935), about a non-Egyptian mummy found on an island. The murderous mummy's eyes retain a horrific retinal image from the past. Lovecraft employed mummies in two other stories as well.

Clark Ashton Smith (1893–1961) wrote several stories featuring mummies. In his "The Vaults of Yoh-Vombis" (*Weird Tales*, May 1932), scientists discover an ancient Martian mummy. The same magazine published "Empire of the Necromancers" in September 1932, in which two evil magicians raise the dead in a desert land on the fictional continent of Zothique; a pair of reanimated mummies destroy the necromancers.

Robert E. Howard's (1906–1936) most famous creation, Conan the Barbarian faced off against a revived 3,000-year-old magician in *The Hour of the Dragon* (*Weird Tales*, December 1935–April 1936). Another revived mummy, "the Master," is an evil mastermind in an earlier non-Conan novel, *Skullface* (*Weird Tales*, October–December 1925).

Three stories by Robert Bloch (1917–1998), published closely together in 1936 and 1937, directly incorporate mummies. The most memorable, "Beetles," a short

A Selected Chronology of Mummy Fiction after 1922

1924	"Under the Pyramids," a.k.a. "Imprisoned with the Pharaohs," by H. P. Lovecraft
1932	"The Vaults of Yoh-Vombis" and "Empire of the Necromancers" by Clark Ashton Smith
1933	"Monkeys" by E. F. Benson; "The Mansion of Unholy Magic" by Seabury Quinn
1935	"Out of the Aeons" by H. P. Lovecraft (ghost-written for Hazel Heald)
1935–1936	*The Hour of the Dragon* by Robert E. Howard
1938	"Beetles" by Robert Bloch
1946	"The Man in Crescent Terrace" by Seabury Quinn
1947	"The Next in Line" by Ray Bradbury
1975	*Crocodile on the Sandbank* by Elizabeth Peters
1986	*The Long Night of the Grave* by Charles L. Grant
1988	*Cities of the Dead* by Michael Paine
1989	*The Mummy, or Ramses the Damned* by Anne Rice
1994	"Bubba Ho-Tep" by Joe Lansdale
1998	*Sleeper in the Sands* by Tom Holland
2000	*The Excavation* by James Rollins
2002	*A Scattering of Jades* by Alexander C. Irvine
2013	*The Book of the Dead*, edited by Jarin Shurin (the first all-original anthology of mummy fiction)

story concerning an archaeologist who suffers a terrible insectoid fate after stealing a mummy, was published in the December 1938 issue of *Weird Tales* and credited to Tarleton Fiske, a pseudonym of Bloch's.

The English writer E. F. Benson (1867–1940), who spent three years as an archaeologist in Egypt and Greece, wrote about the desecration of a mummy in his story "Monkeys" (*Weird Tales,* December 1933).

Victor Rousseau's (1879–1960) "The Curse of Amen-Ra" (*Strange Tales of Mystery of Mystery and Terror*, October 1932) contains most of the by-then clichéd tropes, including a mad Egyptologist in love with beautiful princess-mummy brought back to life, an ancient story retold within the modern era, a reincarnation, and a curse. But the action takes place on an island in the lower Chesapeake Bay. An insane asylum and deathless hawks figure in the story as well.

Mummies appeared in six of Seabury Quinn's (1889–1969) many stories featuring occult detective Jules de Gradin, published in the 1930s. In the most memorable, "The Mansion of Unholy Magic" (*Weird Tales*, October 1933), a modern-day necromancer brings a trio of mummies back to life in a rural area. Probably the best of Quinn's stories featuring mummies came later: in "The Man in Crescent Terrace" (*Weird Tales,* March 1946), De Gradin incinerates a murderous mummy in London by flicking his cigarette lighter.

Most mummy stories from the 1940s are not notable, but mention should be made of a few more. The priestly mummy in "Bones" by Donald Wollheim (1940–1990) (*Stirring Science Stories*, February 1941) is not really dead, but in suspended animation. But the ancient Egyptian experiment proves a gruesome failure when he is revived. Dennis Wheatley's (1897–1977) "Life for a Life," first published in 1943 in the collection *Gunmen, Gallants and Ghosts,* portrays a man who dreams nightly of a beautiful golden-haired mummy who drains him of life. In Ray Bradbury's (1920–2012) harrowing "The Next in Line" (*Dark Carnival*, 1947), a tourist couple visit a catacomb full of mummies in Mexico, and the wife becomes fearfully obsessed with the idea she will she will soon join the desiccated corpses.

Stories featuring mummies became less common in the 1950s and tended more toward humor than horror. Mummies were not in vogue in the 1960s, and none of the literature published is worth noting here. What little short fiction appeared in the 1970s is equally forgettable. The same is true of novels—with one exception.

Elizabeth Peters (1927–2013) helped revive interest in the theme when her turn-of-the-century Egyptologist heroine Amelia Peabody first appeared in *Crocodile on the Sandbank* (1975). Amelia solves the mystery of a supposedly animated mummy. Amelia, her husband, and their precocious son continued to uncover ancient tombs and murder mysteries—occasionally featuring mummies as part of the mix—in the popular series that followed. Its 19th (and final) entry, *A River in the Sky*, was published in 2010. Highly entertaining, the books are also historically and archaeologically accurate, as Peters was a pseudonym for Barbara Mertz, who held a PhD in Egyptology.

The genre revived a bit in the 1980s with the appearance of several worthwhile novels. These included Charles Grant's (1942–2006) 1986 novel, the fast-paced *The Long Night of the Grave*, which features a vengeful mummy murderer known as "Blackshadow." Another novel, *Cities of the Dead* (1988) by Michael Paine (1948–), is a well-researched, atmospheric book supposedly excerpted from dairies written by Howard Carter in 1903–1904. The novel pivots on the discovery of a child's mummy and deals with the mysteries of life, and life after death, rather than the walking dead.

By far the bestselling of all mummy books is Anne Rice's 1989 *The Mummy, or Ramses the Damned*. Originally conceived by Rice as a screenplay, it features revived mummies, immortal love and lust, and a preposterous plot written with a rather heavy hand, but this potboiler is still a page-turner.

In addition to novels, several instances of short mummy fiction from the 1980s and 1990s are worth noting. Two short stories from 1981, Joe R. Lansdale's (1951–) "The Mummy Buyer," which appeared in *Mike Shayne's Mystery Magazine*, May 1981, and "Colonel Stonesteel's Genuine Home-Made Truly Egyptian Mummy" (*Omni*, May 1981) by Ray Bradbury, both dealt with fake mummies. Also interesting are "The Night Comes On," written in an M. R. Jamesian style by Steve Duffy (1963–) (*The Night Comes On*, 1998), and the humorous mystery "The Mummy Case" by Carole Nelson Douglas (1944–) in which a mummified cat plays a lively role (*Cat Crimes Through Time*, 1999).

Although mummies are not the main theme, they do turn up in some suspense/mystery novel plots. The supernatural mystery *Blood Lines* (1993) by Tanya Huff (1957–) featured a mummy stalking the streets of modern Toronto. Lynda S. Robinson (1951–) set a series of mysteries in 18th Dynasty Egypt. In the first of the series, *Murder in the Place of Anubis* (1994), Robinson's "detective," Lord Meren, investigates a murder committed in a mummification workshop. *Slayer of Gods*, sixth in the series, was published in 2003.

Outside of the mystery genre, one of the few mummy novels of the 1990s worth noting is Tom Holland's *The Sleeper in the Sands* (1998), which revisits the cursed tomb theme and again uses Howard Carter as the central character.

Interest in the mummy genre was revived with Universal's 1999 "reimagining" of their 1932 film with *The Mummy* and its 2001 sequel, *The Mummy Returns*. The third and final film of the franchise, *The Mummy: Tomb of the Dragon Emperor* (2008), featured ancient Chinese mummies. Max Allan Collins wrote novelizations of all three.

Joe R. Lansdale's novella, "Bubba Ho-Tep" (*The King Is Dead/Writer of the Purple Rage*, 1994) was turned into a 2002 low-budget independent film directed by Don Coscarelli.

Of the score or so mummy novels of the twenty-first century, two stand-outs involve non-Egyptian mummies: a Peruvian in *The Excavation* (2000) by James Rollins (1961–) and a Mesoamerican mummy found in Mammoth Cave in Alexander C. Irvine's (1969–) *A Scattering of Jades* (2002). From the literary mainstream, an unusual novel *The Egyptologist* (2004) by Arthur Phillips (1969–) involves a murder-suicide related to mummies. Michael Paine took up the Universal Studios mummy character in a licensed 2006 novel *The Mummy: Dark Resurrection,* which continued the saga begun in 1932. In *The Keepsake* (USA)/*Keeping the Dead* (UK) (2008) by Tess Gerritsen (1953–), a medical examiner discovers that a mummy is not, in fact, a priceless artifact but a recent murder victim, gruesomely preserved. And, in proof that pulpish thrillers about mummies and curses are still alive, Lincoln Child's (1957–) *The Third Gate* was published in 2012.

Mummies have appeared in zombie fiction as well as the urban fantasy and steampunk-fantasy subgenres that often cross over with mystery. A few examples include David Wellington's (1971–) walking dead mummy Ptolemaus Canopus in *Monster Planet* from 2007; the revived mummy of John Wilkes Booth in *Dead Reign* (2008), third of the Marla Mason books by Tim Pratt (1976–); and the second of the Parasol Protectorate series, *Changeless* (2010), by Gail Carriger (1976–), in which a mummy's curse has a role. Moreover, mummies return in the fifth book, *Timeless* (2012).

Beginning in the 1970s and continuing into the early 2000s, a spate of mummy-themed horror fiction anthologies has been published under the guidance of various editors and editorial philosophies, with results of varying quality. *The Mummy Walks Among Us*, edited by Vic Ghidalia (1971), a compilation of pulp reprints, was probably the first all-mummy-themed anthology. *Mummy! A Chrestomathy of Cryptology*, edited by Bill Pronzini (1980), offered seven classic reprints and five originals, with the new stories all based in non-Egyptian cultures. The tales in *The Mummy: Stories of the Living Corpse*, edited by Peter Haining (1988), were all reprints. *Mummy Stories*, edited by Martin H. Greenberg (1990), included five original stories and nine reprints. *Into the Mummy's Tomb*, edited by John Richard Stephen (2001), was another rehash of reprints. *Pharaoh Fantastic*, edited by Martin H. Greenberg and Brittiany A. Koren (2002), contained thirteen original stories, only two of which were mummy related. The theme of *The Mammoth Book of Egyptian Whodunnits* (2002), edited by Mike Ashley, is apparent; five of its eighteen original Egyptological mysteries include mummies, as does the single reprint, "The Locked Tomb Mystery" by Elizabeth Peters, which first appeared in the 1989 anthology *Sisters in Crime*. In 2004, *Return from the Dead: Classic Mummy Stories*, edited by David Stuart Davies, again reprinted older stories, as did Chad Arment in *Out of the Sand* (2008). In 2013 the first all-original mummy anthology, *The Book of the Dead*, edited by Jared Shunin for the publisher Jurassic London, presented twenty new tales of the mummy and was coedited by John J. Johnston, Vice-Chair of Britain's Egypt Exploration Society. *Unearthed*, a companion volume edited by Shunin and featuring an introduction by Johnston, compiled eleven classic stories.

Mummies have continued to appear in short fiction published in other twenty-first century venues. Among the most notable so far: Lois Tilton and Noreen Doyle's "The Chapter of Coming Forth by Night" (*Realms of Fantasy*, February 2000); "The Mummies of the Motorway" by Elizabeth Ann Scarborough (*Historical Hauntings*, 2001); "The Emerald Scarab" by Keith Taylor (*Weird Tales*, Spring 2001); the hilarious "The Queen in Yellow" by Kage Baker (*Black Projects, White Knights*, 2002); John Langan's "On Skua Island" (*The Magazine of Fantasy & Science Fiction*, August 2001) "Private Grave No. 9" by Karen Joy Fowler (*McSweeney's Mammoth Treasury of Thrilling Tales*, 2003); Terry

Dowling's *The Shaddowes Box* (anthologized in *Ghosts and Gaslamps*, 2011); and the novella *The Mummy's Heart* by Norman Partridge (*Halloween: Magic, Mystery and the Macabre*, 2013).

Scores of mummy-related fiction titles were published for children and young adults in the 1990s and the first two decades of the 2000s. Some were intended to frighten, others were humorous, and quite a few were about stolen mummies. R. L. Stine (1943–) took on the theme several times in his Goosebumps (62 books, published from 1992 to 1997) and subsequent series books. Although they cannot really be called mummy-themed, Rick Riordan's (1964–) Kane Chronicles trilogy (*The Red Pyramid*, 2010; *The Throne of Fire*, 2011; *The Serpent's Shadow*, 2012), has attracted young readers to ancient Egyptian mythology.

It appears highly likely that the West's fascination with fiction involving mummies, which has come a long way and seen various interesting developments in the two centuries since the genre's birth, has a good deal of life still left in it.

Paula Guran

See also: *The Book of the Dead* (anthology); *Bubba Ho-Tep*; Corelli, Marie; Howard, Robert E.; Lovecraft, H. P.; *The Mummy* (1932); *The Mummy* (1999) and *The Mummy Returns*; Quinn, Seabury; Rice, Anne; Smith, Clark Ashton; Tutankhamun ("King Tut")

Further Reading

Cowie, Susan D. and Tom Johnson. 2007. *The Mummy in Fact, Fiction and Film*. Jefferson, NC: McFarland & Co.

Day, Jasmine. 2006. *Mummymania in the English-Speaking World*. New York: Routledge.

Frost, Brian J. *The Essential Guide to Mummy Literature*. Lanham, MD: Scarecrow Press.

Guran, Paula. 2006. "The Mummy." In *Icons of Horror and the Supernatural: An Encyclopedia of Our Worst Nightmares*, vol. 1, edited by S.T. Joshi, 375–407. Westport, CT: Greenwood Press.

Johnson, John J., and Jared Shunin, eds. 2013. *Unearthed*. London: Jurassic London.

Luckhurst, Roger. 2012. *The Mummy's Curse: The True History of a Dark Fantasy*. Oxford: Oxford University Press.

Shelley, Mary Wollstonecraft (Godwin). 2008. *Frankenstein or the Modern Prometheus: The 1818 Text*. Oxford: Oxford University Press.

Shunin, Jared, ed. 2013. *The Book of the Dead*. London: Jurassic London.

Mummy movies

A large number of mummy films deal with the same basic theme: an ancient Egyptian brought back to life to kill tomb despoilers. But the range of mummy movies extends beyond horror to mystery, comedy, adventure, historical drama,

The mummy movie series from Universal Studios and Hammer Films have long been the most prominent entries in the genre, but they are merely the tip of the proverbial iceberg, since there have been literally scores of other (and usually lesser) mummy movies produced since the very beginnings of cinema, as influenced by the already-existing traditions of mummy fiction and mummy stage plays when the movies were born in the late nineteenth century. The very first depiction of a mummy in a movie came in the 1899 short *Cleopatra's Tomb*, directed by legendary special effects pioneer George Méliès. The film is now apparently, and sadly, lost.

satire, and more. Mummy films range from family fare to juvenile schlock, including soft- and hard-core pornography, to the ridiculous, with amateurish efforts like *The Mummy Theme Park* (2000), *The Kung Fu Mummy* (2004), and *The University of Illinois vs. a Mummy* (2008), to the sublime, such as Shadi Abdel Salam's evocative Egyptian masterpiece, *The Night of Counting the Years* (1969), about the historical tomb robbing and recovery of dozens of royal mummies in the 1880s. The 1944 quirky British musical *A Night of Magic* features a fantasy romp about a young woman stepping out of a mummy coffin for a night on the town in London. The Ricky Gervais comedy *Ghost Town* (2008) has a minor subplot with Egyptologist Tea Leoni proudly describing her mummy's penis preserved in a canopic jar. In short, not all movie mummies are monsters. Nor are they all Egyptian, notable exceptions being the Mexican Aztec films of the late 1950s, *The Eternal: Kiss of the Mummy* (1999) about a Druid witch mummy, and Brendan Fraser's third mummy film, *Tomb of the Dragon Emperor* (2008), set in China.

The quintessential mummy film is the Boris Karloff classic from 1932, which ironically is not a tale of murderous horror so much as a macabre love story. This film, along with Universal's 1940s Kharis cycle, the succeeding Hammer films of the late 1950s through early 1970s, and the Brendan Fraser Indiana Jones-like adventure epics of the turn of the twenty-first century are certainly the best known of all mummy movies, and all are treated separately in this volume. The topic here is the lesser known but often intriguing variations on these scenarios.

Before motion pictures were developed in the 1890s, dramas were enacted live on stage. The earliest known mummy play, a one-act farce by W. Bayle Bernard titled *The Mummy or the Elixir of Life*, was first performed in 1833, a mere half dozen years after the publication of Jane Webb Loudon's 1827 *The Mummy: A Tale of the Twenty-second Century*, one of the earliest examples of a living mummy in modern literature. There were several other plays produced beginning in the early twentieth century, but most theatrical scenarios adopted the farce approach, apparently in the belief that living mummies cannot be taken seriously on the live stage. Early titles include *The Maid and the Mummy*, a 1904 musical; *The Mummy and the Mumps* (1925) with no actual mummy; and *The Mummy Bride* (1928). More recent theatrical offerings have included Ken Hill's *The Mummy's Tomb* (1981),

Charles Ludlam's 1984 *The Mystery of Irma Vep* (anagram for vampire), Michael Tester's *The Mummy Musical* (1996), and two completely different plays written in 1994 with identical titles, *Sherlock Holmes and the Curse of the Mummy's Tomb*, one by Fred Fondren, the other by Julian Harries. *The Curse of Tittikhamon*, a concept originally developed by Michael Armstrong for film in the 1970s, was eventually produced as a play in 1998.

From the beginning of the twentieth century, the fledgling film industry addressed the topic of living mummies. Although mummies as vengeful monsters had been developed in literature as early as Louisa May Alcott's "Lost in a Pyramid" (1869) and Arthur Conan Doyle's "Lot No. 249" (1892), the silent film mummy was often utilized, as in the early plays, as a device for humor. The very earliest depiction was a very brief use of special effects by pioneer Georges Méliès in his apparently lost *Cleopatra's Tomb* (1899). Similar early film trickery of disappearing mummies occurred in 1901's *The Haunted Curiosity Shop*. In the decade and a half beginning in 1908, when film copyrights were all but useless, no fewer than three dozen short films with mummies appeared, often with identical titles but released by different companies in France, Germany, England, and the United States. More often than not the mummies were not actual living ancients. One of these silent, which is still widely available, the 1918 German film *The Eyes of the Mummy*, is a melodrama with no obvious supernatural content. In 1923, shortly after the discovery of King Tut's tomb, a British comedy short called *Tut-Tut and His Terrible Tomb* appeared. One of the last silent mummy films was the horror/comedy short *Mummy Love* from 1926.

Throughout the 1930s and 1940s, and even beyond, mummy coffins were commonly found in mystery plots as hiding places for corpses or villains or as smuggling devices for diamonds and the like. Examples can be found in thrillers featuring Fu Manchu, Chandu the Magician, Charlie Chan, Mr. Moto, the Saint, and Sherlock Holmes. But the mummy movie as we know it today emerged with Karloff's 1932 *The Mummy;* the following year he starred in *The Ghoul*, a British film with a strong Egyptian supernatural element, but it did not have the impact of the Universal classic.

Mummy's Boys from 1936 featured the often less than funny team of Bert Wheeler and Robert Woolsey in a tomb, but there is minimal humor, at least by today's standards, and no real living mummy. Shortly thereafter appeared the classic Three Stooges short, *We Want Our Mummy* (1939), in which the trio search for the tomb of Rootin-Tootin, who turns out to be a midget mummy; though the king is not alive, Curly must masquerade as a mummy. A decade later, after the Universal Kharis series had run its course, the Stooges made another short, 1948's *Mummies' Dummies,* merely set in ancient Egypt. That same year Abbott and Costello began their series of Universal monster spoofs, which ended in 1955 with *A & C Meet the Mummy*, not the best of the series but with three mummies running around at one point: two impostors plus the "real" mummy, Klaris. Though Universal had combined many of its monsters in group films by the mid-1940s, the mummy never got this treatment. It was only much later that the mummy became part of a supernatural gang, notably in Michael Rennie's final (dismal) film, *Assignment–Terror* (1970), the fun *The Monster Squad* (1987), and *The Creeps* (1997), in which all the monsters are little people.

In 1957 a low budget British film, *Pharaoh's Curse*, was the first serious mummy horror film in well over a decade, though it made minimal impact, but just two years later Hammer Studios debuted the first color mummy with their reboot of Kharis. But even as horror in the 1960s was dominated by Hammer, cheap knock-offs were produced as well. Lon Chaney, Jr., who had played both the Wolf Man and Kharis in numerous Universal movies of the 1940s, appeared in the Mexican film *La Casa del Terror* in 1959 (reedited for American consumption in 1964 as *Face of the Screaming Werewolf*), in which he plays a mummy which is reanimated as a werewolf. A similar concept was used in *The Mummy and the Curse of the Jackal*, with an appearance by John Carradine (the priest reviving Lon Chaney's Kharis in 1942's *The Mummy's Tomb*). Here a werejackal fights a mummy on the Las Vegas strip; filmed in 1969, the film was not released to video until 1985, one year before Carradine appeared in one of his last films, Fred Olen Ray's *The Tomb*, about an evil Egyptian queen revived today, sometimes cited as unofficially inspired by Bram Stoker's *The Jewel of Seven Stars*. Several low-budget films have had similar themes in recent years, the bloodthirsty queens often exhibiting vampiric tendencies, including *Ancient Desires* (2000), *Evil Unleashed* (2003), and *Legion of the Dead* (2004).

Female mummies were not the only ones requiring blood to live. Paul Naschy, the king of Spanish horror, starred in *The Mummy's Revenge* (1973) shortly after Hammer had bowed out of the mummy business. This tale involves the resurrection, in Victorian England, of a sadistic and murderous pharaoh with the aid of a modern "priest." The Universal/Hammer formula is flipped such that the mummy actually speaks and is the dominant half of the partnership, demanding that women be supplied to provide the blood he needs for full renewal. He wants one particular woman's body to house his dead love's spirit, but after he kisses her, she shrivels into nothing, a graphic rendering of the aging of Amina/Ananka in *The Mummy's Ghost* (1944). Also in 1973 Spain produced *El Secreto de la Momia Egipcia* (more luridly, though accurately, retitled in English as *Love Brides of the Blood Mummy*); with a nineteenth century setting again, a mummy found not in bandages but dressed as an Egyptian aristocrat forces the capture of young women for his blood-thirsty needs.

By the 1980s mummy films started to develop plots or themes lifted from popular or cult cinema. *Dawn of the Mummy* (1981), filmed in Egypt on a low budget, involved several attractive fashion models; their photographer's hot lights inside a tomb revive the mummy, who has an army of flesh eating zombie mummies, obviously inspired by the then-recent *Dawn of the Dead*, the first sequel to director George Romero's zombie cult classic *Night of the Living Dead*. The following year came *Time Walker*, concerning an alien that had died in ancient Egypt and was mummified but is now revived by X-rays and wants to go home; not coincidentally, this release came just a few months after the blockbuster *E.T., the Extraterrestrial*.

In addition to several versions of Stoker's *The Jewel of Seven Stars* (treated elsewhere in this volume), other literary works have been adapted for film. The 1990 anthology horror film *Tales from the Darkside* includes a modernized version of Conan Doyle's 1892 story "Lot No. 249," which is fairly faithful to the spirit of the original, though considerably more gruesome, featuring an early but still creepy Steve Buscemi. A far less convincing pastiche is *The Mummy Lives* from Israel in 1993, which purports to be inspired by Edgar Allan Poe's 1845 satirical story "Some Words with a Mummy." It is debatable whether this dubious claim or the casting of Tony Curtis as the revived mummy counts as the more ludicrous aspect of this film.

By the late 1990s the announced big-budget remake of *The Mummy* had prompted a new wave of mummy cinema in anticipation of beating Universal to the punch. Besides the 1998 Stoker remake there was an ersatz Laurel and Hardy comedy, *For Love or Mummy* (1999). The biggest competition, however, came from Russell Mulcahy's *Tale of the Mummy* (1998, aka *Talos the Mummy*), which featured Christopher Lee, Hammer's Kharis from 40 years earlier, as the archaeologist in a prologue. A famous poster from that earlier film, showing a flashlight shining a beam through the mummy's shotgun wound, was never really seen of course in 1959, but is realized here with convincing digital effects. Unlike the Brendan Fraser film, an adventure horror comedy set fully in Egypt, the Mulcahy film was a deadly serious, dark horror film set primarily in London. For much of the film the mummy is only seen as loose bandages that can fly, kill brutally, and assume the basic shape of a mummified human. Much like the Universal remake, the mummy takes various body parts from each victim to fully rematerialize itself. The film, further complicated by concerns with planetary alignments heralding a coming Armageddon, does not end on a positive note.

Besides Brendan Fraser's *Return of the Mummy*, 2001 brought the French film *Belphegor, Phantom of the Louvre,* a reimagining of previous adaptations of a 1920s mystery novel, but in this version the "phantom" was inhabited by the spirit of an Egyptian mummy. *Night at the Museum* (2006) with Ben Stiller is not primarily a mummy film, as it involves everything from diorama statues to dinosaur skeletons coming to life, but ultimately this is all seen to be the result of a mummy's magical tablet. Hank Azaria's pharaoh in the 2009 sequel, *Battle of the Smithsonian*, does a fantastic voice imitation of a lisping, effeminate Boris Karloff. Another film that deals with both revived mummies and dinosaurs (actually pterodactyls), *The Extraordinary Adventures of Adele Blanc-Sec* (2010), concerns the imaginative escapades of the heroine of a series of French graphic novels set in the early twentieth century.

Modern CGI effects have put fantastic films within the reach of almost any would-be production company, and mummy movies continue to be churned out quickly and badly, few with lasting or even ephemeral interest. Among recent offerings are *Isis Rising: The Curse of the Lady Mummy* (2013 on Amazon Instant Video, without even a DVD release), the direct-to-DVD *Prisoners of the Sun* (2013), concerning hordes of aliens imprisoned in a buried pyramid, and *The Mummy Resurrected* (2014). The just-filmed (at the time of this writing) *Day of the Mummy* and *Frankenstein vs the Mummy*, both now in post-production, are listed as featuring the same actor, Brandon de Spain, as the mummy, though the two films do not seem to be related, based on their IMDB summaries. Possibly the most conceptually original mummy movie to date, and also the most outlandish, is *Bubba Ho-Tep* (2002), based on a story by Joe R. Lansdale and treated elsewhere in this volume. This offbeat film, ludicrously hilarious yet tinged with pathos, pairs B-movie legend Bruce Campbell as Elvis Presley (or is he a deluded Elvis impersonator?) with the widely respected actor Ossie Davis, playing an elderly man who believes himself to be JFK. The story involves an Egyptian mummy that, lost while on a tour of museums around the country, is now alive and, dressed as a cowboy, searching for souls at an old folks' home in rural Texas. The two unlikely heroes must face off with the mummy to save themselves and their fellow residents of Shady Rest.

Carter Lupton

See also: *Abbott and Costello Meet the Mummy*; *The Awakening*; *Bubba Ho-Tep*; Hammer Films mummy series; Imhotep; *The Jewel of Seven Stars*; Kharis; *The Mummy* (1932); *The Mummy* (1959); *The Mummy* (1999); The mummy in popular culture; The mummy in Western fiction: Beginnings to 1922; The mummy in Western fiction: From 1922 to the twenty-first century; The mummy on television; *The Mummy's Ghost* and *The Mummy's Curse*; *The Mummy's Hand*; *The Mummy's Tomb*; Universal Studios mummy series

Further Reading

Cowie, Susan D., and Tom Johnson. 2002. *The Mummy in Fact, Fiction and Film*. Jefferson, NC: McFarland & Co.

Glut, Donald F. 1978. *Classic Movie Monsters*. Metuchen, NJ: Scarecrow Press.

Kinnard, Roy. 1995. *Horror in Silent Films*. Jefferson, NC: McFarland & Co.

Landis, John. 2011. *Monsters in the Movies: 100 Years of Cinematic Nightmares*. New York: DK Publishing.

Smith, Stuart Tyson. "Unwrapping the Mummy: Hollywood Fantasies, Egyptian Realities." In *Box Office Archaeology: Refining Hollywood's Portrayals of the Past*, edited by Julie M. Schablitsky, 16–33. Walnut Creek, CA: Left Coast Press. Accessed December 16, 2013. http://www.academia.edu/2780165/Unwrapping_The_Mummy_Hollywood_Fantasies_Egyptian_Realities.

The mummy on television

The earliest televised mummy tale actually predates the radio broadcast of Arthur Conan Doyle's "The Ring of Thoth" in 1947 on the CBS program *Escape*. Already in the late 1930s a live drama entitled *The Mysterious Mummy Case* had been presented on NBC. Commercial television appeared after World War II, and a dramatization of Theophile Gautier's 1840 story "The Mummy's Foot" was featured on *Your Show Time* in 1949. Through the 1950s mummies were featured in similar drama, comedy, or occult/sci-fi anthologies such as *Lights Out* ("The Scarab," 1950), *Tales of Tomorrow* ("The Tomb of King Taurus," 1952), *Philco-Goodyear Television Playhouse* ("One Mummy Too Many," 1955), *Armstrong Circle Theater* ("The Mummy Complex," 1958), and *One Step Beyond* ("The Mask," 1960). Regular series with recurring characters also occasionally depicted mummies, but usually in less dramatic or supernatural ways, as in the sitcom *The Mickey Rooney Show* ("Mickey and the Mummy," 1955), and the children's program *Captain Midnight* ("Curse of the Pharaohs," 1954), a Cold War tale in which the "curse" is a ruse to keep people away from a tomb being used to store guns for an uprising at a time of political unrest in Egypt. Ronald Howard, who would star a decade later in Hammer's *Curse of the Mummy's Tomb*, played *Sherlock Holmes* for a year, and among the mysteries he solved was "The Case of the Laughing Mummy" (1954).

In 1962, the popular series *Route 66*, featured classic 1940s horror stars Peter Lorre, Boris Karloff, and Lon Chaney Jr. in "Lizard's Leg and Owlet's Wing," a fun tribute to the Universal monsters, including the Mummy, an ersatz Kharis. In its final season, *The Twilight Zone* presented "Queen of the Nile" (1964) about a movie star (Ann Blyth) who has not aged since antiquity; her Egyptian scarab sucks the life essence from men and transfers it to her. Though this was not a mummy story *per se*, the concept of eternal youth was clearly inspired by the likes of Rider Haggard's *She,* whose climax, wherein the ancient queen ages over 2,000 years suddenly, was echoed in *Twilight Zone's* first season in an episode featuring Kevin McCarthy. The BBC series *Tales of Conan Doyle* presented that author's "Lot 249" in 1967, but most television appearances during the 1960s were on the campy shows of the time like *The Munsters* ("Mummy Munster," 1965), *Get Smart* ("The Mummy," 1967), *Voyage to the Bottom of the Sea* ("The Mummy," 1967), *The Monkees* ("The Monstrous Monkee Mash," 1968), and *Dark Shadows* (1969). The highest camp of the time was to be found in *Batman*, and among the many recurring "guest villains" was Victor Buono as King Tut, a Yale professor who had been hit on the head during a student riot (another feature of the 1960s) and believed he was the reborn pharaoh. Featured in all three seasons from 1966–1968, Tut, in his first adventure, was joined by a lovely female associate,

Mummies on television have been particularly numerous in animated cartoons. This is just a sampling:

1964	"The Curse of Anubis," episode of *Adventures of Jonny Quest*
1965	"Mummies Boys," episode of *The New 3 Stooges*
1965	"Mummy Dummy," episode of *Laurel & Hardy*
1965	"Marauding Mummy," episode of *The Abbott & Costello Show*
1966–1967	"The Malevolent Mummy," episode of *New Adventures of Superman*
1967	"Ruma Tut," episode of *The Fantastic Four*
1968	"Pink Sphinx," episode of *Pink Panther* (televised 1970)
1969	"Scooby Doo & a Mummy Too," episode of *Scooby Doo, Where Are You?*
1972	"The Mummy's Tomb," episode of *Amazing Chan & the Chan Clan*
1973	"Mummy Knows Best," episode of *Goober and the Ghost Chasers*; "Alien Mummy," episode of *Super Friends*; "Mummy's Curse," episode of *Inch High, Private Eye*
1978	"I Want My Mummy," episode of *The Galloping Ghost*
1979	"The Space Mummy," episode of *Battle of the Planets*
1980	"Mummy's Worse," episode of *Captain Caveman*
1984	"The Curse of the Pharaoh," episode of *Inspector Gadget*
1987	"Sphinx for the Memories," episode of *Duck Tales*
1989	"Mummy Dearest," episode of *Garfield & Friends*
1990	"Mind Your Mummy Mommy, Mario," episode of *The Super Mario Bros. Super Show!*
1994	"Avatar," episode of *Batman: The Animated Series*
1999	"Curse of the Mummy's Tomb," episode of *Mona the Vampire*; "The Curse of the Mummy," episode of *Archie's Weird Mysteries*
2000	"The I Want My Mummy Syndrome," episode of *Men in Black: The Series*
2001	"Courage Meets the Mummy," episode of *Courage, The Cowardly Dog*
2001–2002	*The Mummy: The Animated Series* (sequel to the new Universal mummy films)
2003	*The Mummy: Secrets of the Medjai* (sequel to above series); *Beach Party Mummy, The Adventures of Jimmy Neutron: Boy Genius*
2003–2006	*Tutenstein*
2004	*Yu-Gi-Oh: Pharaoh's Memory*
2009	"Mystery of the Mumbling Mummy," episode of *Busytown Mysteries*

Nefertiti, played by Israeli actress Ziva Rodann, who had starred in the low-budget British film *Pharaoh's Curse* in 1957.

The next decade debuted auspiciously with the UK series *Mystery and Imagination*, whose final episode, broadcast on Feb 23, 1970, was "Curse of the Mummy," the first filmed adaptation of Bram Stoker's *The Jewel of Seven Stars*. Mummies and tombs appeared, but with minimal impact, in *Love, American Style* ("Love and the Monsters," 1971), *Ultraman* ("Cry of the Mummy," 1972, Japanese), *Ace of Wands* ("The Power of Atep," 1972, UK), *The Ghost Busters* ("A Worthless Gauze," 1975), the original version of *The Tomorrow People* ("The Curse of the Mummy's Tomb," 1975), *The Hardy Boys* ("The Mystery of King Tut's Tomb," 1977), and *Fantasy Island* ("The Tomb," 1978). One still-popular show from this decade is 1975's four-part "Pyramids of Mars" from the cult UK sci-fi series *Dr. Who*, best remembered for its robot mummies.

The 1970s also witnessed the growth of made-for-television movies. In 1973 one of the most interesting of these was *The Cat Creature*, scripted by Robert Bloch (*Psycho*), in which an Egyptian female spirit inflicts wounds that are seemingly caused by a cat. This has been likened to the 1942 film *The Cat People* (itself re-made in 1982), but the Egyptian theme suggests rather some influence from Sax Rohmer's 1920 novel *The Green Eyes of Bast*. The 1978 telefilm *Cruise into Terror* featured a group of TV stars and Hollywood has-beens in a sorry attempt at a horror version of the then popular *Love Boat* experience. The decade ended with another television movie, *The Curse of King Tut's Tomb* (1980), inspired partially by recent theatrical releases such as *The Awakening* and *Sphinx*, and also by the late 1970s blockbuster exhibit of Tut's treasures that had just toured the United States. Although much of this film stays true to the basic story of the discovery, many details are exaggerated, especially those involving the supposed curse. Howard Carter drives around the Valley of the Kings on a motorcycle and an attempt is made to fly some of the treasures out in a tiny plane! Characters are created whole cloth, including Eva Marie Saint's reporter/love interest and Raymond Burr's unscrupulous antiquities collector. The film concludes by saying it is for entertainment and speculation only, not historical accuracy.

Increasing numbers of mystery or sci-fi shows in the 1980s featured a curse, a mummy or a pseudo mummy as a standard plot device. These included *Quincy, M. E.* ("Dear Mummy," 1981), *Hart to Hart* ("Murder Wrap," 1981), *Buck Rogers* ("The Crystals," 1981), *Tales of the Gold Monkey* ("Trunk from the Past," 1982), *Shadow Chasers* ("The Spirit of St. Louis," 1985), *Seeing Things* ("The Eyes of Ra," 1986), *The Last Precinct* ("I Want My Mummy," 1986), and others. One of the most fun tales, "Mummy, Daddy" (1985), an early episode of Steven Spielberg's *Amazing Stories,* featured an actor who is making a mummy film and, while racing cross country to get to the hospital where his wife has gone into labor, is chased by locals who end up confronting a real mummy that lives in the nearby swamp. Soon other gruesome horror anthologies were appearing; in 1987 *Tales from the Darkside* featured two mummy episodes, "The Grave Robber" and "Beetles."

Similar trends continued into the 1990s. Mummies appeared in *Tales from the Crypt* ("Lower Berth," 1990; "Creep Course" 1993), *Father Dowling Mysteries*

("The Mummy's Curse Mystery," 1991), *Eerie, Indiana* ("America's Scariest Home Video," 1991), *Quantum Leap* ("The Curse of Ptah-hotep," 1992), *Swamp Thing* ("The Curse," 1992), *Ray Bradbury Theater* ("Colonel Stonesteel and the 'Desperate Empties,'" 1992), and more. It seemed every show featured, at some point, an Egyptian occult episode, from *Highlander* ("Pharaoh's Daughter," 1994) and *Hercules* ("Mummy Dearest," 1996) to *Sliders* ("Slide Like an Egyptian," 1997), *Night Man* ("Dust," 1999) and *Conan Doyle's The Lost World* ("Birthright," 1999). The PBS series *Poirot* featured Agatha Christie's Belgian detective in "The Adventure of the Egyptian Tomb" (1993) with essentially a fictionalized simulation of the Tut excavations, but here the "curse" was simply a device to deflect suspicion from the very human murderer. The pilot TV film for George Lucas's *Young Indiana Jones Chronicles,* subtitled *Curse of the Jackal* (1992), was partially set among Egyptian tombs and mummies, just as the original Harrison Ford film had been over a decade earlier.

By the late 1990s much TV was being aimed at younger audiences. Shows based on popular children's horror books often featured mummy stories, including *Are You Afraid of the Dark?* ("The Tale of the Guardian's Curse," 1994), *Bone Chillers* ("Mummy Dearest," 1996) and most prominently *Goosebumps* ("Return of the Mummy," 1995; "Don't Wake Mummy," 1997). Television movies similarly featured early teen protagonists, as in *The Legend of the Lost Tomb* (1997), a fictionalized search for a hidden tomb of Rameses the Great, and the Disney telefilm *Under Wraps*, in which kids try to reunite a forlorn mummy with his true love. An updated version of the British show *The Tomorrow People* starred Christopher Lee in "The Ramesses Connection" (1995).

In 1999 the series *Relic Hunter* premiered, starring Hawaiian beauty Tia Carrere as a globe-trotting professor seeking archaeological and historical artifacts for return to museums or repatriation. Several episodes involved Egyptian, often supernatural, themes, including "Afterlife and Death" (2000), "Nine Lives" (2000), "The Reel Thing" (2001), and "Out of the Past" (2001). Other shows with occult adventure elements were *So Weird* ("Meow," 2001), *Buffy the Vampire Slayer* ("Bargaining," 2001) and *Charmed* ("Y tu Mummy Tambien," 2003). R. L. Stine exhibited life after *Goosebumps* with the shows *The Nightmare Room* ("Tangled Web," 2001) and *The Haunting Hour* ("Night of the Mummy," 2012). MTV produced a mummy parody in 2001 as a spoof of the Brendan Fraser sequel *The Mummy Returns.* That same year *Murder Rooms*, a fictionalized account of the real Conan Doyle and Dr. Joseph Bell, his partial model for Sherlock Holmes, presented an episode entitled "The Kingdom of Bones," in which an Egyptian mummy proves to be a recent corpse. In 2002 the Canadian live action comedy series *I Love Mummy*, featuring Prince Nuff, debuted, ending after one season.

Most television series with mummies as the primary focus were animated, but mummies had appeared in single episodes of cartoon shows for years and in theatrical cartoons long before that, many of which later appeared on TV. Among their numerous early cartoons, silent and without color, Mutt & Jeff appeared in "Mummy O'Mine" (1926), which involved a mummy in a tomb; a similar pair called Tom & Jerry (not the cat and mouse duo from MGM) featured in "The Magic Mummy" (1933), about a stolen girl mummy who sings. The Fleischer Studio's animated *Superman* shorts, the earliest filmed incarnations of the recently created superhero, included "The Mummy Strikes" in 1943. Many theatrical cartoons were carried over to early television, including Popeye the Sailor ("A Wolf in Sheik's Clothing," 1948) and the talking magpies Heckle and Jeckle ("King Tut's Tomb," 1950). Other older characters, like Koko the Clown from *Out of the Inkwell* (created 1919), were reinvented for television with new cartoons ("Mummy's the Word," 1962). As television changed in the 1960s, new adventure-themed shows like *Jonny Quest* ("The Curse of Anubis," 1964) vied with animated versions of live action comedians such as *The New 3 Stooges* ("Mummies Boys," 1965), *Laurel and Hardy* ("Mummy Dummy," 1966), and *The Abbott and Costello Cartoon Show* ("Marauding Mummy," 1968). Boris Karloff, late in his career, added his voice to the Rankin/Bass animated TV film *Mad Monster Party* (1967), which featured a group of Universal-style monsters, including a mummy; this movie spawned an inferior sequel in 1972, *Mad, Mad, Mad Monsters*, and is more or less the spiritual inspiration for the 2012 theatrical animated film *Hotel Transylvania,* featuring an overweight Murray the Mummy.

One of the most enduring animated characters on television is the Great Dane Scooby-Doo, with a variety of incarnations of his show as well as live-action theatrical films. Almost always encountering monsters who turn out to be masked impostors, Scooby has faced his share of mummies, from the original series *Scooby-Doo, Where Are You?* ("Scooby-Doo and a Mummy Too," 1969) to *What's New, Scooby-Doo?* ("Mummy Scares Best," 2003) and the full-length animated film *Where's My Mummy?* (2005).

Several animated shows have centered on mummies. The 1997 *Mummies Alive!* featured four high-tech mummies, Ja-Kal, Rath, Armon, and Nefertina, who must protect the young boy Presley, a reincarnated pharaoh, from the evil Scarab. The show ran 42 episodes and spawned several action figures. A French comedy series produced in 2000, *Mummy Nanny*, concerned an inept teenage girl magician 5,000 years ago who mistakenly gets mummified and is then revived to become a modern babysitter. Lead actor Brendan Fraser's *The Mummy Returns* introduced his character's son, Alex, in 2001, and led that fall to the boy's TV adventures in *The Mummy: The Animated Series,* which evolved into *The Mummy: Secrets of the Medjai* in 2003. The most creative such show was *Tutenstein*, which ran from late 2003 through early 2007, with a full-length cartoon telefilm as a sort of epilogue in 2008. Reawakened in modern times, the arrogant boy pharaoh, originally created as a secondary comic book character by Jay Stephens, is always losing limbs that he reattaches; beyond the humor, Tut is constantly facing gods and demons, challenges that provide lessons on Egyptian history, religion, and mythology. *Casper's Scare School* (film 2006, series 2009/2012), aimed at younger kids, includes among the students Ra the mummy, far less obnoxious than Tut, who has perhaps been exceeded in weirdness only by Tim Burton's Mummy Boy from *The Nightmare Before Christmas* (1993) and the hamster mummy from *Frankenweenie* (2012).

Recent telefilms have focused on historical realities, but taken completely into the realm of sci-fi/fantasy. A miniseries from 2006, *The Curse of King Tut's Tomb*, unlike the 1980 TV movie of the same title, introduces all nonhistorical characters, including an Indiana Jones wannabe, in a search that involves flying demons suppressed in the underworld (parallel dimension) by King Tut in antiquity, but now released on the world again. Filmed in India and directed by Russel Mulcahy (*Talos the Mummy*, 1998), it stars one-time Tarzan Casper Van Dien, Jonathan Hyde from 1999's *The Mummy*, and Leonor Varela (*Cleopatra*, 1999); in the end all is "magically" restored to normal and Howard Carter goes on to find Tut's tomb. A series of three TV movies shot in Turkey feature a modern archaeologist/adventurer named Jack Hunter who finds a completely inaccurate mummy in *The Quest for Akhenaten's Tomb* (2008). *Sands of Oblivion* (2007) explores the intriguing premise of the excavation of Cecil B. DeMille's Egyptian set from the 1923 *Ten Commandments* in the dunes of California. This was a real project that actually began in the 1980s; objects from the dig were publicly displayed for the first time in the summer of 2013, but they showed no evidence of the mummy-like Anubis demon that stalks this film.

In addition to fictional stories, mummies have had an extensive life on television in the form of documentary programs; see the article "Mummy documentaries."

Carter Lupton

See also: *Doctor Who: Pyramids of Mars;* Mummy documentaries; The mummy in popular culture; The mummy in Western fiction: Beginnings to 1922; The mummy in Western fiction: From 1922 to the twenty-first century; Mummy movies

Further Reading

Jones, Stephen. 2000. *The Essential Monster Movie Guide: A Century of Creature Features on Film, TV, and Video*. New York: Billboard Books.

Morton, Alan. 1997. *The Complete Directory to Science Fiction, Fantasy and Horror Television Series*. Peoria, IL: Other Worlds Books.

Stanley John. 1994. *Creature Features Movie Guide Strikes Again*. 4th ed. Pacifica, CA: Creatures at Large Press.

Mummy portraits

Mummy portraits, sometimes referred to as "Fayum mummy portraits," are the painted face coverings that were incorporated into wrappings of the head, shoulders, and chest of mummies dating from Egypt's Roman Period, with mummies incorporating such portraits being discovered at a number of cemeteries throughout Egypt, from Marina el-Alamein, bordering the Mediterranean, to Diosopolis Magna (Thebes), in the south, but most prevalently in the Fayum area of Egypt.

The mummy portraits are, effectively, an updating of earlier Egyptian mummy masks, intended to fulfill the dual purpose of protecting the head of the deceased while portraying an idealized representation of the individual. Frequently executed in painted and gilt cartonnage, the handful of royal examples that have survived, such as those of Tutankhamun (reigned 1334–1325 BCE) and Psusennes I (reigned 1039–991 BCE), are finely crafted in gold and inlaid with glass paste and semiprecious stones.

The mummy portraits tended to be painted on thin wooden panels, usually cypress, sycamore, or lime, some 43.2 cm tall by 22.9 cm wide with an arched or pointed top. Following a coating of gypsum, the wood was painted in either tempera, in which the natural pigments were mixed with an adhesive such as albumen, or encaustic, in which the pigments were combined with clarified molten beeswax and applied to the panel with a "hot metal spatula" (Doxiadis 2007, 146). This latter, more frequently employed technique resulted in a thickly ridged surface in which the artist's moulding of the molten medium is clearly evident, often lending a surprisingly modern and impressionistic element to the faces.

In the years 1887–1889 and 1910–1191, William Matthew Flinders Petrie (1840–1903), the Edwards Professor of Egyptology

One of the Fayum mummy portraits depicts a boy with a floral garland in his hair, c. 200–230 CE. Found in the collection of the Brooklyn Museum, New York. (Heritage Images/Getty Images)

at University College London, excavated large numbers of mummies bearing these painted panels from the cemetery of Hawara. The majority of surviving portrait panels have been removed from their mummies for a variety of reasons, including conservation, preservation, and saleability. Fortunately, Petrie's notebooks preserve some of the archaeological contexts for the portraits that he excavated, though for many others only the panel remains.

As a result of their largely unfamiliar and apparently veristic portrayal of individuals from ancient Egypt, the so-called portraits have attracted considerable scholarly and artistic attention since the first few arrived in Europe from Saqqara in 1615. The faces of the individuals represented appear to gaze directly at the viewer, in an apparently naturalistic, though somewhat melancholy manner. They are rendered either turned slightly to the side (in earlier examples) or frontally (in the later portraits), dressed in the height of Roman fashions and having large, fluid eyes. The detailed attention of the artists to the jewelry and hairstyles of the women depicted has allowed the pieces to be dated with some certainty, based on the fashions prevalent in Rome, known from identified busts and statuary of prominent citizens and members of the Imperial family. Similarly, the tunics and facial hair of the men provide indications as to their dating. Those portraits known to hail from the cemetery of Antinoopolis, such as the fascinatingly enigmatic "Tondo of the Two Brothers," can be safely dated to a time after the founding of that city by Emperor Hadrian in 130 CE, following the death of his favorite, the eponymous Antinous, at that spot in October of that year.

Accordingly, the panel portraits may be confidently dated from the early first century to the fourth century CE, by which time mummification, as a precursor to burial, had largely ceased due to the rise of Christianity.

The faces of the men, women, and children portrayed exhibit considerable variety, and it seems evident that familial relationships may, in certain cases, be discerned, not only through facial similarities but also through reference to the archaeological context of the burials and their groupings. However, whether these portraits were painted from life remains a moot point: while certain of the better examples, such as the portrait of a woman in the Petrie Museum of Archaeology, appears, through her darkly ringed eyes and generally gaunt appearance, to reflect a terminal illness, others, though similarly realized with great effectiveness, have been suggested to represent an idealized type of youthful masculinity.

The aforementioned circular double portrait known as the "Tondo of the Two Brothers," which is presently housed in the Cairo Museum, may represent a portrait from life of the two men (whose precise relationship remains unknown, and who are depicted side by side), which had been kept in the home as an artwork before being divided and augmented for funerary purposes. Research by way of CT scan on one of the most celebrated and intact mummies still bearing a portrait panel—the youthful Artemidorus, excavated as part of what appears to be a small family group by Petrie at Hawara and now on display in the British Museum—reveals a number of basic similarities between the portrait and the deceased, although the skull of the deceased youth appears to have been somewhat more robust than that portrayed on the panel.

It seems most probable that there is no single answer to the portraiture question. The surviving paintings may, depending on individual circumstances, represent a mixture of portraits from life, idealized representations, and ready-made representations, purchased from morticians.

John J. Johnston

See also: Egyptian mummies; Egyptian mummification methods

Further Reading

Adams, B. and Walker, S. 2007. "Catalogue of the Panel Portraits in the Petrie Museum." In *Living Images: Egyptian Funerary Portraits in the Petrie Museum*, edited by J. Picton, et al., 161–270. London: Left Coast Press.

Bierbrier, M. 1997. "The Discovery of the Mummy Portraits." In *Ancient Faces: Mummy Portraits from Roman Egypt*, edited by S. Walker and M. Bierbrier, 23–24. London: British Museum Press.

Doxiadis, E. 1995. *The Mysterious Fayum Portraits: Faces from Ancient Egypt.* London: Thames and Hudson.

Doxiadis, E. 2007. "The Fayum Portraits: They Are not Art, They Are 'Truth.'" In *Living Images: Egyptian Funerary Portraits in the Petrie Museum*, edited by J. Picton, et al., 143–148. London: Left Coast Press.

Filer, J. 1998. "Revealing the Face of Artemidorus." *Minerva* 9, no. 4: 21–24.

Montserrat, D. 1993. "The Representation of Young Males in 'Fayum Portraits.'" *The Journal of Egyptian Archaeology* 79: 215–225.

Roberts, P. C. 2007. "An Archaeological Context for British Discoveries of Mummy Portraits in the Fayum." In *Living Images: Egyptian Funerary Portraits in the Petrie Museum*, edited by J. Picton, et al., 13–72. London: Left Coast Press.

Shore, A. F. 1972. *Portrait Painting from Roman Egypt.* London: The British Museum.

Walker, S. 1997. "Mummy Portraits and Roman Portraiture." In *Ancient Faces: Mummy Portraits from Ancient Rome*, edited by S. Walker and M. Bierbrier, 14–16. London: British Museum Press.

Ziegler, C. 1988. "Funerary Mask of King Psusennes." In *Gold of the Pharaohs*, edited by H. Coutts, 88–89. Edinburgh: City of Edinburgh Museums and Art Galleries.

Mummy unwrappings

Between the eighteenth century and the early twentieth century, the greatest advances in mummy studies came from mummy unwrappings: the removal of the cloth wrappings so that the bodies could be examined or dissected. Before the emergence of modern medical science as we know it, mummy unrollings were

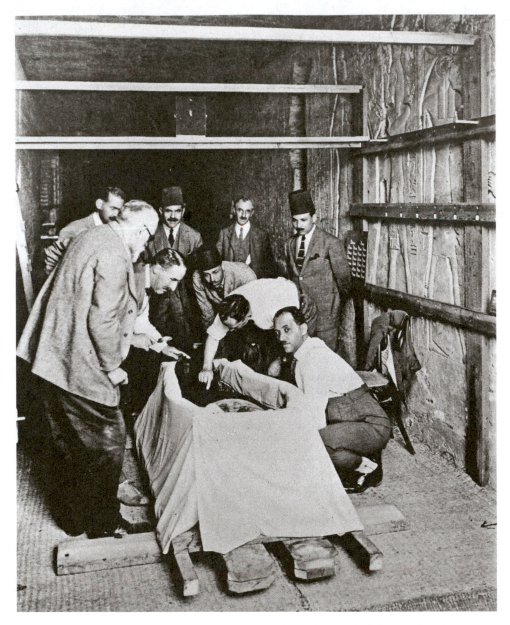

Unwrapping of the mummy of Tutankhamun in 1925. (Time Life Pictures/Getty Images)

often held in public spaces such as theaters or private homes, with invited or pay-ing audiences. The history of mummy unwrappings reveals a great deal about early mummy studies, before the arrival of modern techniques such as X-rays and CT scans.

For centuries mummies were valued in Europe as a medicine, and were ground up into a powder and swallowed, while in the Renaissance, mummies in some

European collections were regarded as works of art or curiosities. Only later did scholars begin to wonder what they might learn about the people of ancient Egypt by unwrapping their mummified bodies.

One of the earliest recorded mummy unwrappings took place in a pharmacy in Breslau (modern-day Wrocław, Poland) in 1658 and was witnessed by the German poet Andreas Gryphius. In the early eighteenth century a mummy was unwrapped at Cambridge University and recorded by the religious scholar Conyers Middleton. The first recorded mummy unwrapping in the United States took place in New York in 1824.

Some of the earliest scientific studies of mummies were carried out in France in the mid-eighteenth century by the pioneering chemist Guillaume-François Rouelle, who analyzed the materials used to embalm the mummies. In 1763 the scientist John Hadley unwrapped a mummy at his home in London in the presence of the famous doctors William and John Hunter. In this period, expert witnesses played a vital role in giving value to the knowledge gained from experiments of all kinds.

Many of the earliest mummy unwrappings were carried out by medical men. In 1794 the German doctor John Frederick Blumenbach unwrapped all the mummies in the British Museum, as well as several from private collections. He discovered that many of the smaller mummies in British collections were modern fakes.

The Italian physician Augustus Bozzi Granville carried out the first proper medical autopsy of a mummy in London in 1825. Granville recorded the wrappings in great detail and provided measurements and illustrations of the bones and other body parts. He found the remains of a tumor and concluded that ovarian cancer was the cause of death. The remains of this mummy were reexamined more recently, and it was discovered that tuberculosis most likely caused her death.

The most famous mummy unwrapper was undoubtedly Thomas "Mummy" Pettigrew, a British surgeon and scholar who unwrapped more than 50 mummies in his career, many of them in elaborate public performances. In 1834 he published *A History of Egyptian Mummies*, the first book on mummy studies. Pettigrew's mummy unwrappings became famous and were attended by leading scholars and physicians as well as aristocrats, bishops, and the general public. Pettigrew was the first mummy scholar to employ the assistance of scientific specialists: his friend, the chemist Michael Faraday, analyzed chemical samples taken from Egyptian mummies, and Pettigrew included Faraday's report in his book. In 1854 Pettigrew used his expertise from decades of mummy unwrapping to mummify the Duke of Hamilton, an enthusiastic amateur Egyptologist who wished to be buried in a sarcophagus.

Samuel Birch of the British Museum witnessed one of Pettigrew's early unwrappings as a young man. Birch later wrote to Pettigrew asking for advice on the practicalities of unwrappings, and soon he began to work independently.

An example survives of a specially printed invitation to a mummy unwrapping conducted by Birch at the home of Lord Londesborough. In the late 1860s Birch unwrapped around 20 mummies brought from Egypt to Britain by the Prince of Wales. E. A. Wallis Budge, Birch's protégé at the British Museum, also conducted mummy unwrappings.

By far the greatest number of mummy unwrappings took place in Egypt itself. The French scholar Gaston Maspero served as director of the Egyptian Department of Antiquities in the 1880s, during which time he unwrapped a considerable number of mummies, including many from the cache of royal mummies found in Deir el-Bahri in 1881. These mummies were later reexamined along with later discoveries by the Australian anatomist Grafton Elliot Smith, then Professor of Anatomy at the Cairo School of Medicine. Smith unwrapped hundreds of mummies and, together with Warren Dawson, wrote *Egyptian Mummies* (1924), the best overview of the subject since Pettigrew's book 90 years earlier.

The first recorded X-ray of a mummy was carried out in 1896, just a year after the discovery of X-rays. This began a move in mummy studies away from invasive, destructive unwrappings toward more delicate methods, such as tissue sampling and CT scans. Nonetheless unwrappings continued: in 1908 archaeologist Margaret Murray became the first woman to publicly unwrap mummies, opening two specimens at the Manchester Museum.

The history of mummy unwrapping has barely been studied, but it sheds light on the cultures of science, medicine, and archaeology around the world, particularly in Europe and the United States, from the Renaissance into the modern era.

Gabriel Moshenska

See also: Alexander, Tenth Duke of Hamilton; Dawson, Warren Royal; Manchester Egyptian Mummy Project; Medical imaging of mummies; Medicine and mummies; Pettigrew, Thomas Joseph; Smith, Grafton Elliot

Further Reading

Aufderheide, Arthur C. 2003. *The Scientific Study of Mummies*. Cambridge: Cambridge University Press.

Gange, David. 2013. *Dialogues with the Dead: Egyptology in British Culture and Religion 1822–1922*. Oxford: Oxford University Press.

Moshenska, Gabriel. 2013. "Unrolling Egyptian Mummies in Nineteenth-Century Britain." *The British Journal for the History of Science* online pre-publication. doi:10.1017/S0007087413000423

Pettigrew, Thomas Joseph. 1834. *A History of Egyptian Mummies*. London: Longman, Rees, Orme, Brown, Green, and Longman.

Sheppard, Kathleen L. 2012. "Between Spectacle and Science: Margaret Murray and the Tomb of the Two Brothers." *Science in Context* 25(4):525–49.

Smith, Graften Elliot and Warren R. Dawson. 1924. *Egyptian Mummies*. London: Allen & Unwin.

Wolfe, S.J. and Robert Singerman. 2009. *Mummies in Nineteenth Century America*. London: McFarland & Co.

Mummy's curse

The mummy's curse does not exist; the belief that it does has nevertheless dominated popular conceptions of mummies since the late nineteenth century. The lumbering, reanimated mummy that advances to exact merciless revenge on transgressors is largely the invention of Gothic fiction in the nineteenth century and the tabloid press and horror cinema in the twentieth century. The most famous curses are associated with Ancient Egypt, but they accrue to the mummified dead across the world, from Peru to Ötzi, the ice mummy discovered in a glacier in the Alps in 1991 and reported in breathless newspaper reports to be steadily killing off those associated with his discovery.

Most professional archaeologists brush aside the curse as a modern superstition imposed on ancient cultures. However, from the origins of anthropology as a scholarly discipline, there has been an evident fascination in collecting evidence or beliefs in the magical power of curses, often held by early evolutionary anthropologists as a marker of "primitive" societies. Key studies in this paradigm on sympathetic magic and the "evil eye" were published in the 1890s. In the Talmud, it is said that the curse of a scholar never fails. In the ancient cultures of Europe—in Iceland or Ireland—the curse was more associated with the wronged or oppressed, and offered a supernatural form of justice and redress to those without power. Curses associated with aristocratic families—such as the financial collapse of the Tichborne family under an interminable law-suit in the nineteenth century—continue to circulate because they are a form of class *ressentiment* (resentment, hostility).

In Egypt, only two or three actual tombs have been found containing inscriptions with anything approaching curses. Ancient Egyptians wanted to be remembered, and visitors to their funerary temples were welcomed. Many ancient cultures have formalized execration texts that contain so-called threat formulae, in which the names of enemies are invoked and ritualistically destroyed. Amulets or other devices to protect against curses are familiar from ancient Assyrian culture onward. Katherine Nordh's research on ancient Egypt suggests that threats are generally balanced with blessings: the sender praises the visitor to a tomb if she or he honors the name of the dead; the threat is attendant consequence if you do not. But even such blessing and cursing pairings were not universal in Egyptian culture and were restricted to the scribal caste.

The most famous mummy curse, which secured the global range of the myth, was the Curse of Tutankhamun. In 1922, Howard Carter discovered the largely undisturbed tomb of the 18th Dynasty boy pharaoh in the Valley of the Kings.

His patron, the Fifth Earl of Carnarvon, arranged for a global audience to witness the formal opening of the tomb in February 1923. Six weeks later, the already frail Earl died in Cairo of blood poisoning and pneumonia. Aristocratic luck was rebalanced by the curse. Rumors that he had been cursed for the transgression of an undisturbed tomb had circulated in the weeks before his death. These rumors were amplified as dread fact by journalists hungry for sensation and fed by famous writers such as Marie Corelli and Arthur Conan Doyle. It was said that a curse text written above the tomb entrance had been destroyed by Carter and Carnarvon. It was said that on Carnarvon's death, the lights in Cairo plunged into darkness. Following news reports of the "curse," it was said that the British Museum had been inundated by mummy parts and other ancient artifacts brought back by travelers and who now feared for their lives. The sixth Earl later happily amplified these accounts, claiming that his father had been warned by palm-readers of a fatal destiny in Egypt and that he had also attended Spiritualist *séances*. In the immediate years following Carnarvon's death, the press developed the logic of curse contagion by claiming a series of deaths of Egyptologists and others related to the Tutankhamun discovery as evidence of a continuing curse. Some 20 deaths were ascribed to the vengeful mummy. All this was in place long before the eventual opening of Tutankhamun's sarcophagus in 1925. Although Carter unwrapped and severely damaged the mummified body in the course of his exhaustive investigations, even managing to lose the king's penis, Carter lived on seemingly untroubled until his death in London in 1939.

The Carnarvon story found such a ready audience because a number of "real life" curse stories had already been circulating in English culture for several decades. The British Museum Egyptian Rooms were often the feverish site of speculation about allegedly cursed artifacts. The "Unlucky Mummy," for instance, was a painted mummy board for an unnamed priestess of Amen Ra, donated to the Museum in 1889 (it is in the catalogue as item 22542). It had been purchased in Luxor in the 1860s by a young gentleman traveler, Thomas Douglas Murray. Murray was severely wounded in a shooting accident near the pyramids in Cairo on the same trip, an event that gave birth to a story that the board was host either to the priestess's indignant spirit or to a dangerous malignant "elemental" that had once protected her. The story was evidently circulated in upper- and middle-class circles, and it helped that Douglas Murray was both a prominent society host who knew artists, journalists, politicians, and imperialists, and a Spiritualist who firmly believed in the spirit's survival of bodily death. In the heady atmosphere of late nineteenth century interest in "psychical research" and a magical revival that claimed to recover lost "Hermetic" secrets of Ancient Egyptian wisdom, the mummy's curse was a perfect narrative. Douglas Murray's story reenchanted the world at the end of a century supposedly marked by secularization and disenchantment.

Another well-known curse story at the end of the nineteenth century was associated with the soldier and adventurer, Walter Herbert Ingram, youngest son of the founder of the *Illustrated London News*. In 1885, Ingram had volunteered to fight in the British relief force sent south through Egypt to rescue General Gordon, besieged by an Islamic uprising against British rule in Khartoum. Ingram was at the very forefront of the attempt to reach Gordon, which notoriously failed by only two days. On his return down the Nile, Ingram acquired a sarcophagus and mummy, which he sent to England. The inscription on the outer coffin was said to contain a bloodcurdling curse (it does not). In 1889, Ingram was killed by an elephant on a hunting trip near Berbera, his body torn asunder and his remains lost in a flash-flood after burial, apparently fulfilling the terms of the curse. The coffin and mummy were gifted to Ingram's friend Sir Henry Meux, since his wife had an extensive private Egyptian collection at Theobalds Park. Inevitably, the curse transferred to the unhappy Meux couple; when the collection was sold on Susie Meux's death in 1911, it was purchased by William Randolph Hearst, another somewhat unlucky collector, who went bankrupt.

The tale of the hapless Ingram, crushed by an enraged elephant, was gleefully narrated by the young Rudyard Kipling in his first letter to Rider Haggard as something he had heard in the smoking room of the Reform Club. It is an indication that such rumors were thoroughly interwoven in colonial adventure fictions and Gothic romances of the time. Rider Haggard was obsessed with mummies, and was even sent one in the 1880s by his brother, who was an important figure in the Egyptian Army (Nesmin now resides in the National Museum of Liverpool). Haggard became a publishing phenomenon when *King Solomon's Mines* was a huge bestseller in 1885; the story ends with the discovery of the mummified leaders of a lost African kingdom. Subsequently, many of his stories, whether set in Africa, Mexico, Iceland or Peru, feature uncanny mummies and lost civilizations. The most famous of these, *She* (1886), centered on the living mummy queen Ayesha, She-Who-Must-Be-Obeyed.

Haggard collected Egyptian artifacts and was deeply respectful of Ancient Egyptian culture (even latterly believing himself to be a reincarnation of an Egyptian). His colonial romances were published during a Gothic revival, which included a substantial subset of Egyptian stories that featured vengeful reanimated mummies. The first mummy revenge tales began in the 1860s, but the genre reached its apotheosis in the 1890s in the years after the English occupation of Egypt: Conan Doyle's "Lot No. 249" (1892), Richard Marsh's *The Beetle* (1897), Guy Boothby's *Pharos the Egyptian* (1899), and Stoker's *The Jewel of Seven Stars* (1903). Sax Rohmer and other pulp writers continued the tradition into the twentieth century. Hundreds of mummy curse stories were to follow the death of Carnarvon in the new world of pulp magazines in America in the 1920s: it became the ideal subject for this mode of sensation fiction.

A new vector for the curse would emerge with the invention of the cinematograph in 1895. The first short trick film that animated a mummy (a magic trick borrowed from the music halls) first appeared in 1902, and there were many silent adaptations of *The Beetle, She,* and other Egyptian Gothics. In 1931, Universal Studios began their famous cycle of horror films, starting with *Dracula* and *Frankenstein.* These were followed by 1932's *The Mummy,* which was directed by Karl Freund and scripted by John Balderston. In 1925 Baldserston had been one of the only Western journalists left in the Valley of Kings to report on the opening of Tutankhamun's sarcophagus. The opening sequence of the film clearly echoes the rumors of King Tut's curse and further entrenched the notion that disturbing the august dead will produce murderous consequences. The logic of contagion now passed to cinema: there were several rather repetitive sequels, starting with *The Mummy's Hand, The Mummy's Tomb, The Mummy's Ghost*, and *The Mummy's Curse.* Hammer House of Horror remade *The Mummy* in 1959, and again produced three further mummy films, less sequels than reinventions of the same vengeful plot, this time shot in "terrifying Technicolor," as the posters announced. Another cycle began with Stephen Sommers's *The Mummy* (1999). The Egyptological "inaccuracies" of these melodramas continue to pain some professional archaeologists.

The success of stories of the curse of the mummy can be ascribed to the newly global mass media of the late-nineteenth century: sensation journalism, pulp magazines, and cinema. It reinvents an old tradition of aristocratic "lucks" and "curses" associated with feudal wealth. It is also, inevitably, a displaced popular account of colonial anxiety. British forces occupied Egypt for the first time in 1882, following the Urabi Rebellion. The Army was complicit in aiding the increase in collections of Egyptian artifacts in Britain, in direct competition with French, German, Dutch, and Italian smuggling operations. The Tutankhamun opening took place amidst the political chaos of a transition from British indirect rule to a native nationalist government, which turned Tutankhamun into a symbol of new, postcolonial ambition. In the last years of rule, the British were paranoid about secret societies and Islamic subversives and the English administration was subject to attack and assassination in the weeks leading up to the opening. The curse narrative suggests that artifacts that are dislodged from their rightful home become lively and uncanny: loot is the material that comes back to haunt. The museological "artifact" cannot escape the occluded history of its problematic acquisition. In early nineteenth-century public displays of mummy unwrappings, none of this dread or sense of transgression seemed to exist. It is only later, when the complexities of colonial occupation grow, that mummies start stirring under their wrappings.

Roger Luckhurst

See also: Carnarvon, Fifth Earl of (George Herbert); Carter, Howard; Corelli, Marie; Doyle, Arthur Conan; Freund, Karl; Haggard, H. Rider; Hammer Films mummy series; *The Jewel of Seven Stars*; *The Mummy* (1932); *The Mummy* (1959), *The Mummy* (1999) and *The Mummy Returns*; The mummy in Western fiction: Beginnings to 1922; The mummy in Western fiction: From 1922 to the twenty-first century; Mummy movies; Mummy unwrappings; Ötzi the Ice Man; Rohmer, Sax; Tutankhamun ("King Tut")

Further Reading

Day, Jasmine. 2006. *The Mummy's Curse: Mummymania in the English Speaking World*. London: Routledge.

Luckhurst, Roger. 2012. *The Mummy's Curse: The True History of a Dark Fantasy*. Oxford: Oxford University Press.

Nordh, Katarina. 1996. *Aspects of Ancient Egyptian Curses and Blessings: Conceptual Background and Transmission*. Uppsala: Uppsala University Press.

Smith, Stuart Tyson. "Unwrapping the Mummy: Hollywood Fantasies, Egyptian Realities." In *Box Office Archaeology: Refining Hollywood's Portrayals of the Past*, edited by Julie M. Schablitsky, 16–33. Walnut Creek, CA: Left Coast Press. Accessed December 16, 2013. http://www.academia.edu/2780165/Unwrapping_The_Mummy_Hollywood_Fantasies_Egyptian_Realities.

Tyldesley, Joyce. 2012. *Tutankhamun's Curse: The Developing History of an Egyptian King*. London: Profile Books.

The Mummy's Ghost and *The Mummy's Curse*

The Mummy's Ghost and *The Mummy's Curse*, both released in 1944, are the last two films in the Universal Films mummy franchise and the third and fourth sequels, respectively, to *The Mummy* (1932). *The Mummy's Ghost* was directed by Reginald Le Borg from a screenplay by Griffin Jay, Henry Sucher, and Brenda Weisberg. Its running time is 61 minutes. *The Mummy's Curse* was directed by Leslie Goodwins from a screenplay by Bernard Schubert. Its running time is 62 minutes.

The Mummy's Ghost opens in Mapleton, Massachusetts, the same setting for *The Mummy's Tomb* (1942). Professor Matthew Norman (Frank Reicher), the local Egyptologist, lectures a college class about the recent rampages of the mummy Kharis, who in the previous film had been brought to Mapleton to kill the surviving members of the exploration team that opened the tomb of the Princess Ananka. Ananka was the love of Kharis's life, and his mummy was cursed to protect her tomb for all eternity. Tom Hervey (Robert Lowery), a student in Professor Norman's class, later discusses the lecture with his girlfriend, Amina Mansouri (Ramsay Ames), who is of Egyptian descent and is visibly disturbed by what Tom tells her. That night, Professor Norman translates the hieroglyphics on a

In 1923 the English novelist Marie Corelli attached herself to the media frenzy surrounding the Tutankhamun discovery by issuing a warning in the British and American press about a supposed ancient Egyptian curse that would punish people who violate tombs. The impact on popular ideas about a "mummy curse" was still very much evident two decades later, in 1942, when the trailers for Universal Studios' second mummy movie, *The Mummy's Tomb*, hit theater screens and contained this ominous bit of narration: "Spawned from the depths of doom comes the most fearful monster of the ages to strike with paralyzing terror the spoilers of ancient tombs!"

casket of tana leaves left from the mummy's last appearance, and when he brews the same elixir from them that high priests of Arkam had used to revive Kharis in the two previous sequels, it summons the mummy, who strangles the professor in his study. At the same time Amina awakens from her sleep and, in a trance-like state, walks to the grounds of the professor's house, where authorities find her collapsed and unconscious.

While these events are unfolding in Mapleton, Professor Andoheb (George Zucco), a high priest of Arkam in Cairo, inducts Yousef Bey (John Carradine) into the priesthood and tasks him with traveling to America to reclaim both Kharis and the remains of the Princess Ananka, now on display at the Scripps Museum. Yousef Bey establishes himself in an abandoned mill on the outskirts of Mapleton and summons Kharis (Lon Chaney, Jr.) to him by brewing the sacred tana leaves. Yousef Bey and Kharis both sneak into the Scripps Museum one evening to perform a right of veneration for Ananka's mummy. When Kharis reaches out to touch her, her body disappears, leaving only her unwrapped bandages in the casket—proof, says Yousef Bey, that her soul has escaped to reincarnate itself in another body. An enraged Kharis rampages about the museum, and the noise of his activities summons a guard, whom he strangles to death.

Amina's distress over events involving the mummy start to take a physical toll on her, and shocks of white begin appearing in her dark hair. For the sake of her health, Tom decides to take her away from Mapleton, even though the authorities have forbidden it. The night before they are to leave Kharis makes his way to Amina's house and abducts her. Tom tracks Amina to the abandoned mill and grapples with Kharis, who knocks him unconscious. Meanwhile, Yousef Bey decides to take Amina for his bride, and when Kharis discovers the priest's duplicity he kills him. A mob of locals who have been scouring the countryside looking for Kharis make their way to the mill, but Kharis escapes just ahead of them with a visibly aging Amina in his arms. In the final scene of the movie, Kharis walks with Amina into the nearby swamps, and as the water closes over their heads, Tom and the townspeople look on helplessly.

Events in *The Mummy's Curse* are set 25 years after those in *The Mummy's Ghost*, but, inexplicably, the setting is shifted from Mapleton to the Louisiana bayous. A government project to drain a local bayou for health reasons is being held up by the superstitious fears of the workmen, who have heard stories of a supernaturally animated mummy walking into the bayou 25 years earlier, and who believe that he returns to kill on the nights of the full moon. These fears are exacerbated when a worker is found stabbed to death next to a hole in the ground in the shape of a human body. Dr. James Halsey (Dennis Moore), who has been dispatched by the Scripps Museum to recover the mummies of Kharis and the Princess Ananka from the drained swamp, confirms that a scrap of cloth found nearby is a bandage from a mummy.

Meanwhile, a subterfuge unfolds involving Dr. Halsey's Egyptian assistant, Dr. Ilzor Zandaab (Peter Coe). Zandaab is actually a high priest of Arkam who hopes to return Kharis and Ananka to Egypt. He has hired one of the workmen, Ragheb, to bring Kharis's mummy and sarcophagus to an abandoned monastery on a hill above the bayou, and Ragheb has murdered the workers who assisted him, including the man found at the work site. Zandaab revives Kharis with the tana leaf elixir, and Kharis strangles to death the caretaker of the monastery who stumbles on them during the mummy's revival.

While this is happening, a young woman emerges from the muck of a newly cleared portion of the swamp. She seems to be in a trance and incapable of speech. She is, in fact, the Princess Ananka (Virginia Christine), whose modern incarnation Kharis carried into the swamp 25 years earlier. She is rescued by Cajun Joe (Kurt Katch), the foreman on the bayou project, and is brought to the café owned by Tante Berthe (Ann Codee). Cajun Joe, Tante Berthe, and Dr. Cooper (Holmes Herbert) all are strangled to death by Kharis during his ventures to recover Ananka.

Ananka (the woman is never actually given a name in the film) is a mysterious character who shows a familiarity with ancient Egypt that she can't explain and who regularly falls in and out of trance-like states. As she explains to Dr. Halsey, she sometimes feels as though she exists in two different worlds. After several attempts, Kharis succeeds in abducting her to the monastery, where Zandaab gives her a dose of the brewed tana leaves. Meanwhile, the lustful Ragheb has lured Betty (Kay Harding), a secretary from the bayou project, to the monastery. When Zandaab finds out, he accuses Ragheb of betraying the gods of Egypt, and Ragheb kills him. This incites Kharis, who claws his way into the room that Ragheb cowers in, bringing down the roof and walls on them. Halsey and his team turn their attention to Ananka and discover that the tana leaf elixir has restored her to her ancient mummified state.

The Mummy's Ghost and *The Mummy's Curse* are notable for restoring to the story line of Universal's mummy movie franchise the romantic interest of Kharis in the Princess Ananka and Ananka's reincarnation as a modern woman, two principal plot points in 1932's *The Mummy* that were all but dispensed with in the first two sequels. As extensions of the mythology of the mummy as initially revised in *The Mummy's Hand* (1942), these two films helped reinforce the supernaturally animated mummy's place in the pantheon of iconic monsters of horror.

Stefan R. Dziemianowicz

See also: Chaney, Lon, Jr.; Kharis; *The Mummy* (1932); *The Mummy's Hand*; *The Mummy's Tomb*; Universal Studios mummy series

Further Reading

Cowie, Susan D., and Tom Johnson. 2002. *The Mummy in Fact, Fiction and Film*. Jefferson, NC: McFarland & Co.

Feramisco, Thomas M. 2003. *The Mummy Unwrapped: Scenes Left on Universal's Cutting Room Floor*. Jefferson, NC: McFarland & Co.

Glut, Donald F. 1978. *Classic Movie Monsters*. Metuchen, NJ: Scarecrow Press.

Weaver, Tom, Michael Brunas, and John Brunas. 2007. *Universal Horrors: The Studio's Classic Films, 1931–1946*. Jefferson, NC: McFarland & Co.

The Mummy's Hand

The Mummy's Hand is a film released in 1940 by Universal Pictures as the first sequel to studio's immensely popular *The Mummy*, released in 1932. It was directed by Christy Cabanne from a screenplay by Griffin Jay and Maxwell Shane and has a running time of 67 minutes.

In the first movie, the mummy of Imhotep—a prince in the royal house of ancient Egypt who attempted to bring back to life his beloved Princess Ankhesenamen and who was buried alive in her tomb for his sacrilege—is accidentally revived by modern archaeologists. In the guise of a modern Egyptian (who calls himself Ardath Bey), Imhotep seeks to unite with a contemporary young woman whom he believes to be the reincarnation of Ankhesenamen (whose remains are on exhibit in the Cairo Museum). *The Mummy's Hand* revises this back-story slightly: the prince, now named Kharis (Tom Tyler), is buried alive in his own tomb, in a cave on a hill overlooking the Valley of the Seven Jackals. Over the centuries Kharis has been kept alive by successive generations of high priests through the infusion of an elixir made with sacred tana leaves for the purpose of killing anyone who would desecrate the princess Ananka's tomb. Professor Andoheb (George Zucco) of the Cairo Museum has just been inducted as the new high priest when archaeologist Steve Banning (Dick Foran) and his sidekick Babe Jenson (Wallace Ford) find a piece of ancient pottery in a Cairo bazaar inscribed with what appears to be a map showing the tomb of Ananka. Andoheb attempts to discourage

In *The Mummy's Hand*, the character of Andoheb, who is the modern-day high priest of the ancient Egyptian cult of Karnak and the keeper of the living mummy of Kharis, becomes convinced that a young woman named Marta is the reincarnation of the ancient Egyptian princess Ankhesenamen. He offers to make her immortal with him: "You are very beautiful—so beautiful I'm going to make you immortal. Like Kharis, you will live forever. What I can do for you I can do for myself. Neither time nor death can touch us. You and I together for eternity here in the Temple of Karnak. You shall be my high priestess."

Banning from seeking out the tomb by telling him the pottery is a fake, but Banning believes otherwise, and he secures the financial support of the Great Solvani (Cecil Kelloway), an American magician traveling abroad, and his reluctant daughter Marta (Peggy Moran), to mount an expedition.

With a team of native diggers, Banning and his crew uncover the tomb of Kharis, whose mummy they find in a remarkable state of preservation. Andoheb also has access to this tomb, and he revives Kharis with a strong dose of the tana elixir and dispatches him to kill members of the expedition, including Solvani. After struggling with Solvani, Kharis carries Marta to Ananka's tomb. There, Andoheb professes his love for Marta and offers to make them both immortal with an infusion of the brewed tana leaves. Steve, meanwhile, discovers a secret passage that leads from Kharis's tomb to Ananka's. Babe shoots Andoheb and, after a brief struggle with the mummy, who is trying to reach the tana elixir that Andoheb was brewing, Steve knocks the fluid to the floor and throws the brazier at the mummy, who is quickly engulfed in flames.

Although arguably not as good a film as *The Mummy*, *The Mummy's Hand* is an important for the liberties it takes with the plot of the first movie. In *The Mummy*, after the opening sequence in which Imhotep is accidentally revived, the bandaged mummy does not appear again. In *The Mummy's Hand*, the mummy of Kharis is depicted as a bandaged, shambling monster who enforces the curse placed on those who violate the tombs of the ancient Egyptian dead. More so than *The Mummy*, *The Mummy's Hand* established the mummy as an iconic monster of horror, elevating it to the same level in the Universal Pictures pantheon as Dracula and Frankenstein's monster. The next three sequels released by Universal, and virtually every mummy film made since, have followed the mythology of the mummy created in this movie.

Stefan R. Dziemianowicz

See also: Imhotep; Kharis; *The Mummy* (1932); Universal Studios mummy series

Further Reading

Cowie, Susan D., and Tom Johnson. 2002. *The Mummy in Fact, Fiction and Film.* Jefferson, NC: McFarland & Co.

Feramisco, Thomas M. 2003. *The Mummy Unwrapped: Scenes Left on Universal's Cutting Room Floor*. Jefferson, NC: McFarland & Co.

Glut, Donald F. 1978. *Classic Movie Monsters*. Metuchen, NJ: Scarecrow Press.

Weaver, Tom, Michael Brunas, and John Brunas. 2007. *Universal Horrors: The Studio's Classic Films, 1931–1946*. Jefferson, NC: McFarland & Co.

The Mummy's Tomb

The Mummy's Tomb is a film directed by Harold Young from a screenplay by Griffin Jay and Henry Sucher. Released by Universal Pictures in 1942, it is a sequel to *The Mummy's Hand*, and it has a running time of 60 minutes.

The events of *The Mummy's Tomb* are set—for some unexplained reason—30 years after those of *The Mummy's Hand* and, in the form of a reminiscence by an elderly Steve Banning (Dick Foran) for the benefit of his family, the movie recapitulates scenes from the earlier film for its first 12 minutes. *The Mummy's Hand* ended with Professor Andoheb (George Zucco), a high priest of Arkam, shot by Banning's friend Babe Hanson (Wallace Ford), and the supernaturally animated mummy of Kharis who is under Andoheb's control, engulfed in flames. *The Mummy's Tomb,* however, reveals that Professor Andoheb (George Zucco) did not die from his gunshot wound, and that the mummy of Kharis was disfigured but not destroyed by the flames. Andoheb inducts Mehemet Bey (Turhan Bey) as the new high-priest and enjoins him to kill all living members of Banning's family and the expedition.

Mehemet Bey travels with Kharis to Banning's hometown of Mapleton, Massachusetts, and takes the job of caretaker at the local cemetery. Empowered by an elixir made from sacred tana leaves brewed on the night of the full moon, Kharis (Lon Chaney, Jr.) quickly strangles to death in rapid succession Banning, Banning's sister Jane (Mary Gordon), and Babe Hanson, who has traveled from New York City to Mapleton to attend Banning's funeral.

Upon seeing Isobel Evans (Elyse Knox), the fiancée of Banning's son John (John Hubbard), Mehemet Bey desires her for his wife and instructs Kharis to bring her to him at the cemetery. His plans to make her and himself immortal with an infusion of the tana elixir are interrupted by the arrival of a torch-bearing mob of locals, who have traced the recent spate or murders in Mapleton to Mehemet Bey. In the ensuing confrontation, Mehemet Bey is shot and killed. Kharis, who has been instructed by the priest to take Isobel elsewhere, brings her back to the Banning house. The mob follows in quick pursuit, and after John helps Isobel to escape, they torch the house and the mummy with it.

The Mummy's Tomb follows the pattern established in *The Mummy's Hand,* whose plot deviates significantly from Universal's original *The Mummy* from

1932. It deploys many of the same plot points as its predecessor, including the revival of the mummy with brewed tana leaves, the high priest who controls the mummy undone by a weakness of the flesh, and the apparent destruction of the mummy in the closing moments. The film's most significant contribution to the mummy horror canon is its shift of events from Egypt to America, bearing out the horror of a curse that strikes down those who desecrate the tombs of the ancient Egyptian dead no matter how far away they live. This was the first of three films to feature Lon Chaney, Jr. as the mummy.

Stefan R. Dziemianowicz

See also: Chaney, Lon, Jr.; Kharis; *The Mummy's Hand*; Universal Studios mummy series

Further Reading

Cowie, Susan D., and Tom Johnson. 2002. *The Mummy in Fact, Fiction and Film.* Jefferson, NC: McFarland & Co.

Feramisco, Thomas M. 2003. *The Mummy Unwrapped: Scenes Left on Universal's Cutting Room Floor.* Jefferson, NC: McFarland & Co.

Glut, Donald F. 1978. *Classic Movie Monsters.* Metuchen, NJ: Scarecrow Press.

Weaver, Tom, Michael Brunas, and John Brunas. 2007. *Universal Horrors: The Studio's Classic Films, 1931–1946.* Jefferson, NC: McFarland & Co.

N

Napoleon and the birth of Egyptology

From a Western perspective, historical interest in ancient Egyptian civilization can be traced back to Classical antiquity. People living in the landmass now known as Europe have demonstrated such interest in a multitude of forms over the past 2,000 years. The modern exploration of the country came quickly on the heels of the Enlightenment and the French Revolution, with Napoleon Bonaparte's 1798 invasion opening Egypt to scientific historical enquiry.

Ancient and Medieval peoples sought contact with ancient Egyptian civilization in a number of ways. Textual evidence for such contact can be found in the writings of Greek, and later Roman, authors who incorporated ideas from Egypt, and who wrote on Egyptian civilization. These texts discuss a wide variety of subjects, including Egyptian history, geography, culture, and mummification. They provided a starting point for Europeans interested in ancient Egypt right up until the modern era, and were particularly important sources of information for Italian scholars during the late Medieval and Renaissance periods. Ancient Egypt was also guaranteed a place in the minds of early Europeans through the role played by Judeo-Christian scripture. Familiarity with the Bible ensured a well-known starting point for Medieval Christians interested in the Near East. Information on Egypt during this period could also be found in the accounts of people who traveled through the Near East. While such texts provided a literary link to Egypt, the Crusades provided a physical one. These religious-military endeavors facilitated the transfer of people from Europe to the Near East, including Egypt, and objects and information from Egypt to Europe. One type of object from Egypt, known as *mumiya*, was, in fact, traded in Europe from the eleventh to the seventeenth centuries. This material, which comprised ground mummy parts, was widely used in Europe as an ingredient in medicines and artists' paints.

Studies of the remains of ancient Egyptian culture, including mummies, by Medieval Arabic scholars played an important, and largely unstudied, role in Renaissance and Enlightenment conceptions of Egypt. Along with the transfer of such knowledge from Egypt to Europe, the sixteenth and early seventeenth centuries saw the introduction of voyages conducted expressly for the collection and study of antiquities. European interest in Egypt also became explicit through the adoption of Egyptian motifs in art and architecture. A clear interest in the hieroglyphs found on Egyptian objects and monuments also developed during this

General Bonaparte in Egypt, 1867, by Jean-Leon Gerome. (DEA / G. DAGLI ORTI/Getty Images)

period, as evidenced by the work of Athanasius Kircher. Kircher's work prompted interest in the Coptic language and proved an important step in the development of Egyptian philology. During the seventeenth century, pyramids, the grandiose repositories for royal mummies, were the focus of study by John Greaves. His Pyramidographia (1646), which sought to quantify pyramids, may be viewed as the beginning of scientific archaeology in Egypt. In addition, a European interest in correctly locating other ancient Egyptian monuments mentioned in Classical texts developed during this period, as seen in the work of Claude Sicard. During the early 1700s, European travel to Egypt increased partly as a result of a diffusion of publications on the country, such as Frederik Ludvig Norden's *Travels in Egypt and Nubia* (1741) and Richard Pococke's *A Description of the east and some other countries* (1743). Throughout the eighteenth century, studies of ancient Egypt continued to improve, so that by the end of the century, popular and academic knowledge of Egypt, including its antiquities, natural environment, culture, and peoples, were available to Europeans long before Napoleon set foot on Alexandrian soil.

A watershed moment in the history of Egyptology occurred at the end of the eighteenth-century, when Napoleon Bonaparte shocked the world by invading Egypt, a part of the French-friendly Ottoman Empire. The roots of this invasion, however, can be found in the mid-seventeenth century. The Franco-British Treaty of 1763 significantly limited France's access to natural resources abroad. In an effort to conform to the treaty, while at the same time acquiring resources, France launched national, territorial missions of scientific exploration to previously unexploited lands. These endeavors combined the pressures of expanding empires, new technologies, and the need for resources with Enlightenment philosophical constructs. The idea of using Egypt as a source of natural resources and a base from which to harass British interests in India not only developed, it received ideological weight from Enlightenment views of the Orient, Near, and Middle East. It was these ideas and pressures that convinced Napoleon to invade Egypt in 1798.

In keeping with earlier French missions of colonization and his own Italian campaign, Napoleon attached to his army a corps of scholars. Brought primarily to create a modern infrastructure necessary for rapid colonization, and with access to the country unprecedented since antiquity, these savants came to record all aspects of the strange land: its antiquities, people, flora and fauna, arts and sciences, geography, and, of course, mummies. As the campaign and the scholars' exploration continued, the notion of pooling all these studies into one comprehensive publication was born. In 1802, with the return of the surviving French scholars to France, the government adopted the project and began the lengthy process of publishing the campaign's findings. The result is the mighty *Description de l'Egypte*, whose official, yet inaccurate, publication dates are 1809–1828. The work represented the sum of French knowledge on ancient and modern Egypt at the end of the eighteenth century. Among its many plates, and in addition to many depictions of funerary materials associated with mummies, plates 48–51 in volume II of the antiquities section accurately represent portions of human mummies viewed by Napoleon's scholars. Similarly, plates 51–55 represent animal mummies viewed by the French. The volumes of text devoted to explaining the antiquities plates also discuss Egyptian mummies at length. The Napoleonic invasion focused European attention on Egypt in an unprecedented manner: through literature, such as newspapers and periodicals; through collections of antiquities brought to Europe by the French and British armies; and through publications stemming from the invasion, such as Dominique Vivant Denon's *Voyage dans la Basse et la Haute Égypte* (1802), and the *Description de l'Egypte* itself.

The attention and resources focused on Egypt by Napoleon's military venture, as well as the resulting dissemination of information on ancient Egypt, laid the groundwork for France and Britain to launch concerted missions of exploration in the early 1800s. Henry Salt, British Consul-General to Egypt, and Bernardino Michel Maria Drovetti, French Consul-General to Egypt, largely divided Egypt into geographic spheres of influence for archaeological investigation and the accumulation of antiquities. Individuals from other countries, such as Johann Ludwig Burckhardt and Giovanni Battista Belzoni, also made significant explorations of Egypt during this period. The tradition of large-scale, ambitious publications on ancient Egypt, as established by the *Description*, also continued. This tradition included John Gardner Wilkinson's seminal *Manners and Customs of the*

Ancient Egyptians (1837), which was the result of 12 years of research in Egypt. Wilkinson's work spoke extensively about ancient Egyptian burial and mummification practices, and capitalized on Classical texts, his own observations, and depictions of scenes from monuments.

The 1800s saw many important archaeological investigations, which included mummies, which were important to the development of Egyptology. Thomas Pettigrew was a British surgeon and antiquary who took up the study of ancient Egypt, specializing in the subject of mummification. He assisted Belzoni in unwrapping a mummy in 1821 and, thereafter, took it on himself to unwrap numerous mummies until the early 1850s. Some of Pettigrew's unwrappings were open to the public, and prompted similar spectacles by others in the UK at this time. The result of such shows, unfortunately, generally was the destruction of the mummies themselves. Pettigrew published his *History of Egyptian Mummies* in 1834, which formed the first comprehensive English language treatment of Egyptian funerary archaeology. He also famously mummified Alexander Hamilton, Tenth Duke of Hamilton, in an Egyptian fashion in 1852. Within Egypt itself, François Auguste Ferdinand Mariette discovered the Serapeum, the burial place for the mummified Apis bull, founded the Egyptian Antiquities Service, which regulated the flow of antiquities from Egypt, and established the first national museum in the Near East, the latest incarnation of which is Cairo's Egyptian Antiquities Museum, home to the most important collection of royal mummies. A more infamous archaeological discovery was made in the 1870s, when a cache of royal mummies, the first find of royalty, was discovered close to the Valley of the Kings. Some of the better known Pharaohs found within it included Ahmose I, Thutmosis III, Rameses II, Rameses III, and Pinedjem I and II. The cache was originally found by a local family named Abd el Rasul, who illegally sold portions of it on the antiquities market. Once items from it raised suspicions, an investigation was launched by the Antiquities Service, the cache discovered, and its contents cleared. The story was immortalized by the 1969 Egyptian film *The Night of Counting the Years*.

Throughout the nineteenth and twentieth centuries, the professionalization of Egyptology developed in tandem with that of other sciences. Historical studies directly benefited from the resulting refinement in theories and techniques in many disciplines that accompanied this professionalization. One example is the formalization of archaeology and anthropology, two disciplines now central to Egyptology and the study of mummies. New mental tools such as these led Europeans to develop new ideas on the antiquity of the planet and mankind's presence on it. In turn, an increasingly better understanding of geological strata was complemented by new discoveries of ancient texts and languages that challenged older conceptions of mankind's history and place in the world. This refinement of methodological and conceptual tools has benefited the study of Egyptian mummies. In addition to studying mummies' aesthetic qualities, several institutions, including the British Museum and the Manchester Museum, have employed contemporary scientific tools and techniques to analyze mummified remains. X-ray radiography, CTscans, MRI, and ultrasound imaging have become increasingly common tools used by museums in the study of Egyptian mummies. In addition, investigations into single mummies now regularly incorporate interdisciplinary teams of researchers, including Egyptologists, medical doctors, physical anthropologists, chemists, imaging specialists, textile and other materials specialists, and entomologists. Mummies are also now incorporated into larger scale population studies. Such studies use sizable groups of mummies/bodies, when available, to examine and establish patterns of disease and diet across class at any one time. In addition, they analyze diseases within specific families.

The study of Egyptology, and ancient Egyptian mummies, continues, albeit in an ever-changing atmosphere of funding and academic politics. Traditional scholarly efforts to excavate and grapple with the physical remains of the culture continue apace. Yet new elements in the study of ancient Egypt, and the history of its exploration, are developing. The exclusion of Egyptians from the study of their own history, and their own mummies, for example, has been changing for quite some time. The future of exploration now resides firmly within the country of contemporary Egypt. Beyond the realm of the academic, global public interest in ancient Egypt remains strong, as suggested by the number of tourists who visit the country every year, by the number of television documentaries produced, and by the countless books published and purchased on the subject, often by Egyptologists. Academic and public interest in ancient Egypt also converge in the form of online resources. Such tools provide invaluable information to researchers in the form of republications, excavation websites, and online encyclopedia. The medium through which this information is presented also removes it from the realm of the academic library and makes it available to a broad spectrum of Internet users. Such technology increases the ways in which people interact with ancient Egypt and promises to facilitate engagement with both the ancient and modern cultures of Egypt. Strong, public interest in ancient Egypt, coupled with vibrant, scholarly work, and new technologies facilitating access to information, promise to sustain the discipline of Egyptology for generations to come. The role played by Egyptian mummies in all of this remains central.

Andrew Bednarski

See also: Alexander, Tenth Duke of Hamilton; Belzoni, Giovanni; Collecting mummies; Egyptian Antiquities Museum; Egyptian mummies; Egyptomania; Manchester Egyptian Mummy Project; Mariette, Auguste; Medical imaging of mummies; Medicine and mummies; Mummy unwrappings; Pettigrew, Thomas Joseph; Rosetta Stone

Further Reading

Aufderheide, Arthur C. 2003. *The Scientific Study of Mummies*. Cambridge: Cambridge University, 2003.

Bednarksi, Andrew. 2012. "Egyptology." In Bagnall et al., eds. *The Encyclopedia of Ancient History*. John Wiley and Sons.

Bierbrier, Morris L., ed. 2012. *Who Was Who in Egyptology*. 4th ed. London: Egypt Exploration Society.

Cockburn, Aidan, Eve Cockburn, and Theodore A. Reyman, eds. 1998. *Mummies, Disease, and Ancient Cultures*. 2nd ed. Cambridge, UK: Cambridge University Press.

David, Rosalie, ed. 2008. *Egyptian Mummies and Modern Science*. Cambridge: Cambridge University.

el-Daly, Okasha. 2008. *Egyptology: The Missing Millennia: Ancient Egypt in Medieval Arabic Writings*. London: Left Coast Press.

Ikram, Salima, ed. 2005. *Divine Creatures: Animal Mummies in Ancient Egypt*. Cairo: American University in Cairo Press.

Ikram, Salima, and Aidan Dodson. 1998. *The Mummy in Ancient Egypt: Equipping the Dead for Eternity*. London: Thames and Hudson.

Smith, Grafton E. 1912. *The Royal Mummies* (CCG). Cairo: IFAO.

Nasca mummies

The prehistoric Nasca polity inhabited the Rio Grande de Nasca Drainage on the arid south coast of Peru from approximately 1 to 750 CE. The Nasca people are best known for creating geoglyphs, often called "Nasca Lines." These immense figures, which include both animal and geometric designs, cover approximately 550 square kilometers of the desert pampa, and were designated a UNESCO World Heritage Site in 1994. The largest Nasca site is Cahuachi, a 25-hectare ceremonial center composed of numerous mounds, enclosures, and extensive cemeteries, which served as a focal point for pilgrimages, feasting, and other rituals until about 450 CE. Nasca people continued to be buried at Cahuachi for centuries after ritual activities ceased at the site. Polychrome (multicolored) ceramics, decorated with mythological figures, animals, geometric designs, and images of people and trophy heads, were also produced at Cahuachi (ca. 1–450 CE) and throughout the Nasca Drainage (ca. 450–750).

The Nasca peoples typically buried their dead in cemeteries, at Cahuachi and elsewhere in the Nasca Drainage. Most bodies are in a flexed and seated position, wrapped in one or more textiles, and accompanied by grave goods (e.g., ceramics or other keepsakes) placed in the tomb. During Early Nasca (1–450 CE), some individuals were placed in large ceramic vessels, placed in a pit, and covered with a roof of logs. During Middle (550–650) and Late Nasca (650–750), some individuals were also buried as part of multiple interments (i.e., more than one body in a tomb or pit). Other unusual burial practices include empty tombs, animal burials, bodiless graves, and a few examples of headless bodies. Because of the arid coastal Peruvian climate, soft tissue preservation for these burials is possible, even though the Nasca peoples did not purposefully mummify most individuals. An important exception was the purposeful mummification of disembodied heads, or trophy heads.

Trophy heads are skulls that have been removed from the body at or after death and intentionally modified, usually for display. Although not unique to Nasca society, the largest collection of trophy heads in the Andes does come from the Nasca polity. Nasca trophy heads, interred in caches, burials, or ritual structures, have been found in cemeteries and settlements throughout the region, as well as at Cahuachi. The over 150 documented skulls have been studied extensively. Nasca trophy heads are perforated

Nasca mummy sitting in a tomb in a pre-Inca cemetary, Nazca, Peru. (Eye Ubiquitous/Getty Images)

through the forehead, which allowed the head to be suspended by a woven cord made of cotton, vegetable fiber, or human hair. Internal tissues and muscles were removed, usually by enlarging the foramen magnum (the base of the skull), but the skin and hair were typically retained. The eye sockets and cheeks were often stuffed with cloth, and cactus spines were pierced through the skin around the mouth to cover the dentition. Nasca trophy heads are predominately young to middle-aged males, but there are several Early and Late Nasca examples of adolescent and female trophy heads.

The role of trophy-taking in Nasca society is a much-debated question, primarily focused on determining if the individuals chosen to be transformed into trophy heads were venerated ancestors or victims of conflict. The trophy heads may have played an entirely ritual role in Nasca society, perhaps taken from important ancestors and thus selected from the local Nasca population. Alternatively, trophy heads may have been taken from vanquished warriors, either foreign or from other Nasca groups, or through raiding. Based on iconographic depictions on ceramics, the role of trophy heads within Nasca society was almost certainly related in part to agricultural fertility, and trophy heads are often associated with mythical beings or shamans, and shown with plants sprouting from them or transforming into plants. They are also often found in association with coca and maize in burial contexts. Trophy head imagery became increasingly associated with themes of violence in Middle and Late Nasca, in connection with an increase in actual trophy-taking. Early scholars believed that trophies were taken from individuals, not from Nasca society who were killed or captured in battle. Other scholars have suggested that trophy heads might have been obtained through ritual battles among different groups within the Nasca polity, perhaps motivated by concerns about agricultural fertility or access to water resources, or as political symbols. Nasca warriors are represented on ceramics, and are shown with clubs, spears, and slings, as well as trophy heads.

In addition to depictions on ceramics and osteological analysis (i.e., analysis of bones), ancient DNA, hormone production, and strontium-isotope ratios and stable isotope data have also been used to investigate trophy-taking practices. Taken together, this research demonstrates that local people from the Rio Grande de Nasca Drainage were likely selected for transformation into trophy heads, and that their residential histories and diet did not differ significantly from the general populace. It is likely that the meaning of Nasca trophy heads changed through time, but chronological assignment (i.e., a knowledge of which period the various heads came from) is typically not sufficiently refined to investigate this hypothesis. Because each potential role has distinctly different implications for Nasca society, continued investigation of the origin and meaning of the trophy heads is well-warranted.

Emily Webb

See also: Mummies of Latin America

Further Reading

Conlee, Christina A. 2007. "Decapitation and Rebirth." *Current Anthropology* 48, no. 3: 438–445.

Forgey, Kathleen, and Sloan R. Williams. 2005. "Were Nasca Trophy Heads War Trophies or Revered Ancestors? Insights from the Kroeber Collection." In *Interacting with the Dead: Perspectives on Mortuary Archaeology for the New Millennium*, edited by Gordon F. M. Rakita, Jane Buikstra, Lane A. Beck, and Sloan R. Williams, 251–276. Gainesville, FL: University Press of Florida.

Proulx, Donald A. 2001. "Ritual Uses of Trophy Heads in Ancient Nasca Society." In *Ritual Sacrifice in Ancient Peru*, edited by Elizabeth P. Benson and Anita G. Cook, 119–136. Austin: University of Texas Press.

Silverman, Helaine, and Donald Proulx. 2008. *The Nasca*. The Peoples of America. Malden, MA: Blackwell Publishers.

Webb, Emily C., Christine D. White, and Fred J. Longstaffe. 2011. "Exploring Geographic Origins at Cahuachi Using Stable Isotopic Analysis of Archaeological Human

Tissues and Modern Environmental Waters." *International Journal of Osteoarchaeology* 23, no. 6: 698–715.

Natural mummification

When many people think of mummies, one of the first things that may come to mind is the Egyptian mummies. Along with these thoughts comes an image of the elaborate process used by the ancient Egyptians to intentionally preserve their dead. However, not all mummies are made intentionally. Some fall into the category of "natural mummies."

Dr. Arthur Aufderheide offers a taxonomy of mummies in his book, *The Scientific Study of Mummies*. There are four distinct classifications suggested by this taxonomy. The first is where the Egyptian mummies, and indeed many others, fit in. It is called Anthropogenic, or "artificial" mummification. Mummies who fit into this class are intentionally mummified with a concerted effort to maintain the human shape and form.

The next category (the subject of this article) is Spontaneous, or "natural" mummification. Mummies in this category are produced as a result of nature, and more specifically, by the impact of the environment where the body was laid to rest. There are many environments and conditions that will halt or greatly impede the normal process of decomposition resulting in mummified remains.

In most cases of natural mummification, there has been no attempt to preserve the body either externally or internally. With that said, natural mummies can be subdivided into two categories: Spontaneous and Spontaneous Enhanced. In the spontaneous group, chance played the biggest role. In spontaneous enhanced, however, a culture realized that their deceased were in fact being mummified by their burial practices in relation to where they were buried. The culture then

---

A taxonomy of mummies and mummification, from *The Scientific Study of Mummies* by Arthur Aufderheide:

Anthropogenic or "artificial" mummification: The intentional act of preserving the body with a concerted effort to maintain the human shape and form.

Spontaneous or "natural" mummification: When mummification occurs spontaneously through nature, via the impact of the environment where the body was laid to rest.

Spontaneous enhanced: Produced when a culture realizes that conditions in certain places are producing natural mummies, and so they decide to bury their dead in those places or others with similar conditions, but without actual treatment of the body itself.

Intermediate mummification: The temporary preservation of the body, allowing for ceremonial rituals to be planned and conducted.

intentionally buried their dead in that or a similar environment in an attempt to mummify them, thus reducing chance and enhancing the spontaneous forces. Though there was intentional placement in the right environment, there were no additional treatments as in the anthropogenic group. Spontaneous enhanced is its own category in Aufderheide's taxonomy.

The final group in the taxonomy is Intermediate mummification, which is the temporary preservation of the body, allowing for ceremonial rituals to be planned and conducted. The intermediate type of mummification was often practiced to allow relatives at a distance to travel to the ceremonial site and participate in burial traditions.

While the vast majority of natural mummies are desiccated (dry) bodies, that is not the case with all mummies who fit into this category. There are a variety of environments that can create a natural mummy. Basically, the conditions fall into two main categories: environments that enhance the desiccation process (the normal process of decomposition requires a watery medium), and environments whose specific chemistry halts the bacterial mechanisms associated with normal decay (decomposition requires a hospitable environment for microbial activity).

Cool, dry environments coupled with ventilation, like the conditions seen in caves, may halt decomposition and produce mummies. Other conditions may also produce natural mummies. Bodies in warm, dry locations with ventilation (caves or niches with extensive sun exposure), cold or warm and dry without ventilation (crypts), environments that would wick the fluids from the body, wet environments with an acidic pH (bogs), and wet (or earthy) environments with an alkaline pH (saponification) can all result in the mummification of human and animal remains. Temperature, too, can create a hostile environment for bacterial action, as in the high altitude Inca mummies from the Andes and Ötzi from the Alps.

Perhaps one of the best examples of natural mummification is seen in the mummies of Guanajuato, Mexico. Rapid desiccation helped to produce a wide variety of mummies that are on display at the Museo de las Momias de Guanajuato. Throughout Europe, natural mummies are produced in crypts below churches. Crypt mummies are not uncommon. A good example of crypt mummification is seen in the Church of the Dead in Urbania, Italy. An important aspect of crypt mummification is the crypt construction material. Often the crypts are made of rock or cement that is high in limestone concentration. The limestone acts as a natural humidity absorber, which, in turn, helps pull moisture away from the body, thereby aiding the desiccation process.

There were even natural mummies in Egypt long before the Egyptians adopted artificial mummification. The natural mummies of Egypt were rapidly desiccated by the soil they were buried in. Certain soil conditions, usually alkaline and hydrophilic, will act like a sponge drawing fluid out of and away from the body. The result is a natural mummy. Natural mummies have been found in the southwestern United States. Mummies of indigenous populations have been discovered in well-ventilated shallow caves or niches. The dry air helps wick fluid from the body, and ventilation helps conduct the moisture away from the body.

Many of the mummies of the Atacama Desert in Southern Peru and Chile have been produced through natural processes. Many of the mummies of the Chiribaya, Tiwanaku, and early Chinchorro cultures who were buried in the sand or in individual subterranean tombs were produced through natural desiccation. The Atacama Desert is one of the driest places on earth, so anything that is placed in the sand, or remains on the surface of the sand, has a high probability of being mummified. A contributing factor is the wicking action of the clothes or blankets wrapped around the deceased.

A burial environment rich in alkaline constituents like ashes can produce an interesting mummification process called saponification. Think for a moment about how soap is made. Soap is made from lye, an alkaline substance, and animal fat. Lye can be produced by mixing water with ashes. If the human body is exposed for a period of time to an alkaline yet moist environment, the body fats come in contact with the lye produced and convert to a soapy/waxy substance called adipocere (meaning fat and wax) in much the same manner that soap is produced. The process is now well understood, and it is a complex sequence of events triggered by the right environmental conditions. Although there are many saponified or partially saponified mummies throughout the world, perhaps two of the most well know are the Soap Man at the Smithsonian Institution in Washington D.C., and the Soap Lady at the Mutter Museum in Philadelphia.

Another special environment, peat bogs, can produce natural mummies. If the burial matrix is acidic, decomposition cannot proceed, as the environment is usually anaerobic, acidic, and under pressure. Temperature at the time of burial also plays a significant role in the process. These conditions create an environment in which microbial activity associated with decomposition cannot function. The state of mummification varies. Generally speaking, the skin is "tanned" and soft tissues are preserved, but the acidic environment leeches calcium from the skeletal structures. The decalcified bones, in particular the skull, have caused misinterpretations on scientific study. For example, the collapsed skull of the Grauballe Man was thought to have resulted from a blow to the head. Later research described the skull as simply collapsed from decalcification, giving it the "caved in" appearance. Mummies produced by these special conditions are referred to as "bog bodies." They are found in many places and are prevalent in Denmark, the Netherlands, Sweden, Germany, Scotland, and Ireland. Bog bodies have also been discovered in Norway, Poland, and in Florida, USA. While there are many known bog bodies, some of the more well known are the Grauballe Man, Lindow Man, Tollund Man, the Weerdinge Men, the Yde Girl, and the Windeby Girl.

A final special environment that can produce spontaneous mummification is the extreme cold found at very high altitudes or where a body can be locked in a glacial flow, such as with Ötzi. It is important to note that there are two different forms of mummies produced by extreme cold conditions: frozen and freeze-dried. Freeze drying occurs when the subject is first frozen in a high altitude environment where the atmospheric pressure is very low. The low pressure allows the frozen water in the subject to sublimate, or pass directly from the solid state of matter to a gaseous state. The liquid leaves the body without liquefying, thus reducing the possibility of microbial action, even if the body is returned to a reasonable temperature. The freeze-dried body is essentially desiccated. In contrast, a frozen body still has its water content, and when returned to temperatures above the freezing point has a great potential of continuing along the process of decay. Clearly, in either category, mummies found in these environments must be very carefully conserved or the body could be lost to decomposition. The most well-known mummies from this category are the Inca child mummies of the Andes discovered in 1999, "Juanita" the Ice Maiden discovered in 1995, and Ötzi the Iceman, found in the Alps between Austria and Italy in 1991.

In sum, natural mummies are very important to science as they were not intentionally produced, meaning they were not altered a great deal prior to burial. In contrast, artificial mummies, like the pharaohs of Egypt, have had many intrusions and procedures imposed on their bodies during the mummification process. With natural mummies, scientists can derive more accurate data since there have been few if any alterations. Also, many of the natural mummies are common people, not the elite. While we can learn a lot about ruling classes from carefully prepared artificial mummies, it is the information held in these natural mummies of everyday people that give as a chance to learn what life was like for the majority of the people of a culture during their time on earth.

Ronald G. Beckett

See also: Aufderheide, Arthur Carl; Bog bodies; Chinchorro mummies; Church of the Dead; Crypt mummies of Sommersdorf Castle; Egyptian mummies; Grauballe Man; Ice mummies; Inca mummies; Juanita, the Inca Ice Maiden; Lindow Man; Mummies of Europe; Mummies of Ferentillo; Mummies of Guanjuato; Mummies of Lithuania; Mummies of Venzone; Ötzi the Iceman; Tollund Man; Windeby Girl

Further Reading

Aufderheide, Arthur C. 2003. *The Scientific Study of Mummies*. Cambridge: Cambridge University Press.

Aufderheide, Arthur C., and Mary Aufderheide. 1991. "Taphonomy of Spontaneous ('Natural') Mummification with Applications to the Mummies of Venzone, Italy." In *Human Paleopathology: Current Syntheses and Future* Options, edited by Donald Ortner and Arthur Aufderheide, 79–86. Washington DC: Smithsonian Institution.

Beckett, Ronald G., and Gerald Conlogue. 2009. *Paleoimaging: Field Applications for Cultural Remains and Artifacts.* USA: CRC Press, Taylor and Francis.

Cockburn, Aidan, Eve Cockburn, and Theodore A. Reyman, eds. 1998. *Mummies, Disease, and Ancient Cultures.* 2nd ed. Cambridge, UK: Cambridge University Press.

The Mummy Road Show. 2001. "Muchas Mummies." Directed by Larry Engel and written by Damian F. Slattery. Hosted by Ron Beckett and Jerry Conlogue.

The Mummy Road Show. 2001. "Soap Lady." Directed by Larry Engel. Hosted by Ron Beckett and Jerry Conlogue.

Nesyamun or Natsef-amun, the Leeds Mummy

The mummy of the priest Nesyamun, Nesamun, or Natsef-amun in the collections of Leeds Museums and Galleries is arguably one of the most intensively studied ancient Egyptian mummies. The mummy was the subject of one of the earliest scientific studies of a mummy undertaken by Leeds Philosophical and Literary Society in 1825. Nesyamun was reinvestigated by a multidisciplinary team led by Dr. (now Prof.) Rosalie David as part of the Manchester Mummy Project.

Nesyamun (as the hieroglyphic inscriptions on his fine wooden coffins should now be read) was a member of the priesthood in the temple-complex of the god Amun at Karnak during the reign of Rameses XI (1099–1069 BCE). Nesyamun was a senior priest, holding important positions in the Temple of Montu. The titles in the hieroglyphic inscriptions on Nesyamun's coffin indicate he was god's-father of Montu, scribe of the temple of Montu, scribe who lays out offerings for all the gods of Upper and Lower Egypt, and scribe who keeps tally of the cattle of Amun. Nesyamun's official duties included keeping accounts and completing inventories, reports, and administrative documents. He took part in offering rituals before the statue of god, and his life was governed by special rules, such as the requirement to be ritually pure.

Nesyamun lived during politically unsettled times when the high priest of Amun, Amenhotep, came into conflict with Panehsy, the viceroy of Nubia, and there was civil war. After Panehsy's defeat, the leader of the king's army, General Piankh, took Panehsy's titles and also became high priest of Amun. Piankh's successor, Herihor, was high priest of Amun when Nesyamun was a priest at Karnak. The presence of some leather straps (no longer existing) inscribed with the cartouche of Rameses XI with Nesyamun's mummy need not suggest a secret loyalty to the Egyptian king. Having previously dressed the statue of the god in the temple of Montu, including the red leather straps with Nesyamun's mummy and coffins was presumably intended as an honor. The association with the god, no doubt, was more important than the name of the current ruler.

In 1823 wealthy Leeds banker John Blayds bought the mummy of Nesyamun from William Bullock, the showman and dealer in antiquities, who had obtained it from the Italian Giuseppe Passalacqua. Passalacqua (1797–1865), "a most successful spoliator of the tombs of the ancient Egyptians," sent two fine mummies to Trieste in 1823. One of them, comprising Nesyamun's mummy and coffins, was sold in London and acquired by Bullock and later Blayds. The mummies came from the excavation of the tombs of priests and priestesses in the causeway area of Hatshepsut's temple at Deir el-Bahri. An autopsy of Nesyamun's mummy was carried out for the council of the Leeds Philosophical and Literary Society, and John Blayds. The 60-page account of the examination of the mummy was published in 1828 as *Account of an Egyptian Mummy* by William Osburn.

In 1990 Dr. Rosalie David and the Manchester Egyptian Mummy Project studied Nesyamun again. This new work benefited from scientific advances made since the time of the first autopsy, and included radiology, CT scans, endoscopy, serology, histology (the study of the microscopic structure of tissues), dental examination, fingerprinting, and facial reconstruction.

The multidisciplinary study conducted by the Manchester Mummy team established that Nesyamun suffered from the disease filariasis, which is caused by the larvae of parasitic worms carried by mosquitoes. The worms migrate to the lymph glands and cause oedema or fluid retention, leading to the unsightly swelling known as elephantiasis. Nesyamun also had plaques of atheroma in his groin. This degenerative disease of the blood vessels, caused by a rich diet, can lead to strokes, heart attacks, and gangrene. Nerves supplying the eye muscles of Nesyamun were affected by peripheral neuritis, a condition sometimes associated with diabetes or treatments involving the use of heavy metals. X-rays of Nesyamun revealed degenerative arthritis of the neck and possibly the hip. Nesyamun's protruding tongue was not the result of a tumor or strangulation but may have been caused by an allergic reaction to a bee sting. The fingerprinting of Nesyamun's hands, removed during the 1824 investigation, showed that he died in middle age and that he had not been engaged in heavy labor. Nesyamun's teeth were badly worn, and this may have been the result of overenthusiastic dental hygiene or drinking acidic fruit beverages.

The technique of facial reconstruction, pioneered by Gerasimov and developed by John Prag and Richard Neave at the University of Manchester, was also used to create a likeness of Nesyamun. His facial features are thought to reflect strong Nubian influence on the population of Upper Egypt.

Bryan Sitch

See also: Egyptian mummies; Manchester Egyptian Mummy Project

Further Reading

David, Rosalie, ed. 1978. *Mysteries of the Mummies: The Story of the Manchester University Investigation*. New York: Macmillan.

David, Rosalie, and Edmund Tapp, eds. 1992. *The Mummy's Tale: The Scientific and Medical Investigation of Natsef-Amun, Priest in the Temple at Karnak.* London: Michael O'Mara Books.

David, Rosalie. 2005. "Natsef-Amun, Keeper of the Bulls: A Comparative Study of the Palaeopathology and Archaeology of an Egyptian Mummy." *Proceedings of the V World Mummy Congress,* edited by Emma R. Massa, 175–178. Turin: Compagnia di San Paolo.

David, Rosalie (ed.). Egyptian Mummies and Modern Science. Cambridge: Cambridge University Press, 2008.

Osburn, William. 1828. *An Account of an Egyptian Mummy presented to the Museum of the Leeds Philosophical and Literary Society by the late John Blayds drawn up at the request of the Council.* Leeds: Leeds Philosophical and Literary Society.

Wassel, Belinda. 2008. *The Coffin of Nesyamun, the "Leeds Mummy."* Leeds: Leeds Philosophical and Literary Society.

Van Dijk, Jacobus. 2000. "The Amarna Period and the Later New Kingdom." In *The Oxford History of Ancient Egypt,* edited by Ian Shaw, 272–313. Oxford: Oxford University Press.

O

Opening of the Mouth

"The Opening of the Mouth" is the name given to an ancient Egyptian ritual associated, in part, with burial practices. Attested throughout Egyptian history, the Opening of the Mouth was performed on a variety of human images, ranging from statues, to coffins, to even mummies themselves. Its ritual contents are preserved in many funerary texts, and the Opening of the Mouth scene is displayed prominently in many tombs, particularly from the New Kingdom. As part of a set of funerary rituals, the Opening of the Mouth ensured that the deceased would be able to see, speak, breathe, eat, and drink in the afterlife.

The earliest known examples of the Opening of the Mouth ritual date to the Old Kingdom, where special implements used during the ritual were found in the tombs of high officials in Memphis. These sets of ritualized tools were made of stone and included an adze (a type of woodworking tool), an arm-shaped censer, a spooned blade known as a *peseshkaf*, a serpent-headed blade, and several different types of amulets. These tools would have been used by priests during the ritual. By holding the implements up to the mouth, nose, and eyes of the mummy and reciting the religious spells associated with the ritual, the priests were ensuring the deceased would fully function and be able to receive offerings in the afterlife. Because the ancient Egyptians believe the dead continued to use their mummies in the afterlife as containers for their spirits and as vehicles for obtaining the nourishment of offerings, it was essential that the mummies of the deceased continued to function just as they had in life.

This ritualized practice continued, and throughout all of pharaonic history into the Roman Period the Opening of the Mouth ritual was performed not only on the deceased but on statuary as well. Because the ancient Egyptians believed that the deceased were connected to their personal statues found in their tombs and funerary temples, the Opening of the Mouth was performed on these statues, known as *serdabs*. These *serdab* statues, once properly treated with the Opening of the Mouth ritual, could receive offerings on behalf of the deceased, further ensuring that the deceased's needs were fully met in the afterlife.

During the later part of the Old Kingdom, written and pictorial sources for the Opening of the Mouth begin to be included in the decoration of the tomb. Beginning with simple images and only short passages of text, the practice of depicting the Opening of the Mouth continued to grow until it reached its peak in the

New Kingdom. The three of the seven most complete examples of the Opening of the Mouth ritual are part of the decoration of New Kingdom Theban tombs. These versions show that the ritual was divided into 75 episodes, or spells, each dealing with specific aspects of the body and using specific tools during their performance. As the tomb decorations grew in their elaborateness, the inclusion of the ritual tools began to decline. By the end of the New Kingdom, these tools were no longer being included in the funerary assemblages of the deceased.

Further developments of the Opening of the Mouth ritual took place during the New Kingdom. The ritual was traditionally performed with a priest, wearing a mask of Anubis, supporting the mummy or coffin, and another priest, wearing a leopard-skin garment, reciting the spells while using the prescribed tools. For the burials of the pharaohs of the New Kingdom, however, the man wearing the leopard-skin garment is no longer a priest, but rather the successor to the throne. By performing the ritual of the deceased pharaoh, the successor is affirming his legitimacy to take over the kingship of Egypt.

After the New Kingdom, the Opening of the Mouth ritual continued to be performed. During Egypt's Third Intermediate Period, funerary papyri buried with the deceased (and often wrapped in the mummy's bandages) contained images of the Opening of the Mouth being performed. The Greco-Roman Period saw an interesting expanse in the use of the ritual. No longer limited to objects of human form, the Opening of the Mouth ritual was now performed on temples so that the gods would continually be the recipients of the offerings brought there.

The Opening of the Mouth ritual continues to be a fascinating topic of study, as it reveals much about the religion of the ancient Egyptians. It shows their desire to reanimate the body to provide the deceased with offerings in the afterlife. It reveals the connection between the mummy of the deceased and the statuary of the deceased specifically designed to receive offerings. Finally, in the New Kingdom, the ritual took on an additional function of portraying the succession of legitimized rule from one pharaoh to the other.

Marissa A. Stevens

See also: Anubis; *Book of the Dead*; Coffin Texts; Egyptian mummification methods; Religion and mummies

Further Reading

Allen, James P. 2005. *The Ancient Egyptian Pyramid Texts*. Writings from the Ancient World no. 23. Atlanta: Society of Biblical Literature.

Assmann, Jan. 2001. *The Search for God in Ancient Egypt*. Ithaca: Cornell University Press.

Assmann, Jan. 2003. *The Mind of Egypt: History and Meaning in the Time of the Pharaohs*. Cambridge, MA: Harvard University Press.

Hornung, Erik. 1999. *The Ancient Egyptian Books of the Afterlife*. Ithaca, NY: Cornell University Press.

Ikram, Salima, and Aidan Dodson. 1998. *The Mummy in Ancient Egypt: Equipping the Dead for Eternity.* Thames & Hudson.

McDermott, Bridget. 2006. *Death in Ancient Egypt.* Stroud: Sutton.

Schafer, Byron E., John Baynes, Leonard H. Lesko, and David P. Silverman. 1991. *Religion in Ancient Egypt: Gods, Myths, and Personal Practice.* Ithaca: Cornell University Press.

Zandee, Jan. 1977. *Death as an Enemy According to Ancient Egyptian Conceptions.* The Literature of Death and Dying. New York: Arno Press.

Osiris

Osiris was one of the most important deities in ancient Egypt. He was both god of the dead and a fertility god. Together with Isis he was worshipped by virtual everyone in Ancient Egypt.

His name, *Us-jr*, is often translated as "throne of the Eye" (Greek: Ὄσιρις) but can be read too as *jri.t* (to do, to make) and the throne as *Ase*, "creation," and therefore as "(He) who makes the creation" (Osing 1974) or "The place of creation" (Kuhlmann 1975) or the "mighty one" (from "useru") (Wilkinson 2003).

Visually, Osiris is normally represented as a mummy with white, green, or black face and hands (green and black are both signs of fertility). He wears, like most of the male gods, a divine beard (goat-beard) and holds the regal scepters, crook, and flail like all pharaohs. He wears the Atef-crown, similar to the white crown of Upper Egypt but with ostrich feathers at either side. He often stands on the sign or symbol for the goddess Maat, who represents truth, cosmic balance, and the world order.

Several wall pictures in tombs show Osiris accompanied by a futuristic looking fetish called Imiut, a skin of a panther-like

The coffinette for the viscera of Tutankhamun, which contained the mummified liver of the king, depicts him as Osiris, holding a crook and flail. (AP Images/Ric Francis)

animal without a head, fixed on a pole. This fetish was part of funerary rites and dates back to the beginning of the Egyptian culture. Imiut is also connected with the god Anubis. Imiut was a magical protection against the evil forces of the god Seth. Two marvelous examples of this were found in the sarcophagus chamber of Tutankhamun, protecting the boy king's mummy.

Osiris probably started as a fertility god with chthonic (subterranean) connections to the underworld. He was associated with the annual flooding of the Nile River on which life in Egypt depended. Later he became the supreme God of the dead and replaced Anubis in this function. Osiris was the son of Geb, god of the Earth, and Nut, goddess of the Sky. He was married to his sister, the goddess Isis. He already appears in texts of the Fourth Dynasty and in the Pyramid Texts (Pyr. 1655a-b) of the late Fifth Dynasty and is frequently mentioned. The ancient Greek biographer and historian Plutarch described Osiris as one of the mythical divine rulers of Egypt.

Osiris was the god of the dead for the general population, while the pharaoh considered himself as the brother of Osiris and traveled after death to the stars, to the afterworld of the sun god Ra. However, with the decline of the Old Kingdom Osiris became even more important, and eventually came to be viewed as the supreme ruler of the afterlife, standing even above the pharaoh. He was the judge over the dead and the one who decided between resurrection of a person's soul in the afterworld or, in the case of wicked criminals, giving the soul to the monster Amensit or Ammut, The Devourer—a composite being composed of various different animals—which swallowed the heart of the condemned souls and utterly annihilated them. Osiris himself normally plays a passive role in myths, since he is dead. He is revenged or revived either by the King, by Horus, or, in the mystery religion centered at the holy city of Abydos, by his sister Isis.

Osiris was part of the divine triad of Abydos, together with his son Horus and his sister-wife Isis. Here the annual festival of the Myth of Osiris was celebrated. This myth is one of the most important in ancient Egyptian religion, known today mostly only by short remarks in ancient texts. A hymn to Osiris on a stela (stone monument) of Amenmose, a prince of the 18th Dynasty, is the longest text on the myth from pharaonic times. The myth was general knowledge in Ancient Egypt. Later Plutarch tells us the whole story in a Hellenistic version: Osiris was the ruler of Egypt, and his brother Seth was jealous. Nephthys, sister of Isis and wife of Set, disguised herself as Isis and received a son from Osiris: Anubis, later the god of mummification. Osiris was killed by Seth, who dismembered the body and scattered it across the world. Isis started a search and was able to find the body parts. Using magic, she was able to transform him into a revived mummy, after which she conceived a child from Osiris: Horus, the falcon-headed god. Osiris was now hidden in the underworld, but Seth was able to find him, and once again Osiris was dismembered, and once again Isis searched for the body parts.

At this point the surviving myth became unclear: either Isis buried the different parts in many locations all over Egypt or simply gave the appearance of doing so by erecting false tombs to foil any attempt to find Osiris' real burial place. Later Horus defeated Seth and revenged his father, and Seth was banned into the desert. Politically, this myth may reflect a predynastic political struggle.

In the royal funerary books of the New Kingdom (*Amduat, Book of the Gates*), Osiris unites with the sun god Ra during the deepest night to form a new, syncretistic god named Deba-Djemendy, "The united one." Out of this mystical union the sun god can gain new power for his cyclical rebirth. Osiris represents the body of Deba-Djemendy and Ra the soul. Ra stands for a cyclical, evolving eternity (Heh) while Osiris represents a static, unchanging eternity (Djed). The Djed-pillar is also the symbol of Osiris.

Osiris is also in important deity for the kingship. The deceased king became identified as Osiris, while from the Middle Kingdom onward the immortality of becoming like Osiris expanded to non-royal individuals. Osiris also has several other connections: he is the Ba-soul of the ram of Mendes and the Ba of the Apis bull of Memphis.

The custom of planting a "corn-Osiris" became a tradition from the New Kingdom onward. A plant box in the form of the mummified Osiris was filled with earth and corn seed. The growing corn symbolized the resurrection of the God.

Many Egyptian cities claimed to have a burial place and a body part of Osiris. It was said that the head of Osiris was buried in Abydos. This body relic was stored in a special container resembling a wig box on a pole. Its appearance is known in detail from a relief in the small temple of Rameses I in Abydos. The holy city of Osiris has the most mysterious temple of all Egypt: The Osireion, behind the beautifully decorated temple of the pharaoh Sety I, who carried the ancient name Akh-men-Maat-Ra-en-Us-ir ("Useful is Men-Maat-Ra [Sety I] for Osiris"). The new temple of Sety I is uncharacteristically bent into an L-shape to avoid collision with the (already existing?) Osireion behind it. This construction was probably much older and is special in its concept: the temple is made as an underground building covered by an artificial hill and surrounded by trees. It is unclear whether its central parts were built under the reign of Sety I or were in fact much older, may be even prehistoric, since they are of megalithic structure. It may have been built during the Old Kingdom. The function of the Osireion is debated: it may have been the false tomb (cenotaph) of Sety I, or the place of initiation in the mysteries of Osiris, or the fictional tomb of Osiris.

The cult of Osiris overlaid an already existing funerary necropolis god of Abydos called Khenti-Amentiu, "First of the Westerners," who appeared as a jackal similar to Anubis. The name Khenti-Amentiu became an additional name for Osiris.

Another important cult center was Busiris, where the spine of Osiris was said to be buried. In Memphis Osiris overlaid a falcon-headed local deity called Sokar and formed syncretistic appearances with him (Sokar-Osiris and Ptah-Sokar-Osiris). The city of Athribis claimed to have the heart of Osiris, while Biga, Edfu, Sebennytos, and Herakleopolis each claimed to have one of his limbs.

Osiris with his consort Isis survived the end of the pharaonic era and spread all across Greco-Roman civilization. However, a dead and mummified god was unfamiliar to foreigners, and a newly designed god named Serapis, with a Greek appearance, replaced Osiris. But the Egyptians rejected Serapis and stayed with the old iconography, while Greeks and Romans preferred the more familiar concept of Serapis. In a later version of the myth, Osiris died by drowning and became a god. From this originates the ancient belief that anyone who drowns in the Nile will become a god, too (e.g., Antinous, the friend of Emperor Hadrian, later divinized). By religious concept, Osiris belongs to that crucially significant category of gods—including Attis, Dionysus, and Jesus—who had to die and then be resurrected.

Michael E. Habicht

See also: Anubis; *Book of the Dead*; Coffin Texts; Isis; Religion and mummies; Seth

Further Reading

Eady, Dorothy (Omm Sety) and Hanny El Zeini. 1983. *Abydos: Holy City of Ancient Egypt*. Los Angeles: L. L. Co.

Griffiths, John Gwyn. 1980. *The Origins of Osiris and His Cult*. Studies in the History of Religions, no. 40. Leiden, The Netherlands: E. J. Brill.

Kuhlmann, K. P. 1975. "Zur Etymologie des Götternamens Osiris." *SÄK* 2, 1975, 135–138.

Mojsov, Bojana. 2005. *Osiris: Death and Afterlife of a God*. Malden, MA: Blackwell.

O'Connor, David. 2009. *Egypt's First Pharaohs and the Cult of Osiris*. London: Thames & Hudson.

Osing, Jiirgen. "Isis und Osiris." *MDAIK* 30, 1974, 91–114.

Ray, John. 2002. *Reflections of Osiris: Lives from Ancient Egypt*. Oxford: Clarendon Press.

Wilkinson, Richard H. 2003. *The Complete Gods and Goddesses of Ancient Egypt*. New York: Thames & Hudson.

Ötzi the Iceman

Ötzi the Iceman is a natural human Copper Age (Chalcolithic, ca. 3300 BCE) mummy, which was found in 1991 in the South Tyrolean Alps. It is the oldest known European natural mummy and is well preserved, including a high number of items of daily life equipment such as bags and tools, thus allowing a unique snapshot view into this time period. His official name is Iceman or Man from the Ice, yet he is most often also called in popular press nicknamed as Ötzi or in sometimes Frozen Fritz. Other names include the Similaun Man, the Man from

---

The Curse of Ötzi?

Egyptian mummies are not the only mummies that have been associated with the idea of a curse in the popular imagination. The ice mummy known as Ötzi or the Tyrolean Iceman is famous not only for its enormous value to science (which owes both to the body's amazingly excellent state of preservation and the number of well-preserved tools and other implements that were found with it) but also for the supposed curse that was, for a time, thought to accompany it. A number of people who were involved in its recovery and early examination died between 1992 (the year after Ötzi's discovery) and the early 2000s, sometimes in relatively unusual circumstances. For example, a forensic pathologist who had handled Ötzi's body died in a car crash in 1992 as he was traveling to give a talk about the mummy. An experienced mountaineer who had helped with the recovery of Ötzi's body died in an avalanche in 1994. The man who first discovered Ötzi died in a blizzard in 2004, the same year that a filmmaker who was producing a documentary about Ötzi died of a brain tumor as a young age. For a time rumors swirled in the popular press about a curse. It has been pointed out, however, that given the large number of people who have somehow been connected with Ötzi since 1991, on purely statistical grounds there is nothing unusual about the number of deaths among them.

---

the Hauslabjoch, *Homo tyrolensis*, or the Hauslabjoch mummy. He is currently displayed in Bolzano, Italy, in the South Tyrolean Museum of Archaeology.

On September 19, 1991, two German hikers spotted the well-preserved, mostly naked body of a human adult close to the border between Austria and Italy, near the Similaun Mountain and about 300 meters below the Hauslabjoch (a high mountain pass) in a rocky gully filled partially with water and snow. The discovery location lies at an altitude of about 3200 meters above sea level in an area most likely already known for mountain crossings during prehistoric times. Only the upper part of the body was protruding out of the melt water, and the surrounding tools and equipment were scattered over an area of about 30 square meters. At least some of the equipment seemed to be positioned in a tidy, well-organized manner, while other artifacts and pieces of clothing appeared to have been moved at least at least slightly over the millennia. Whether the body had been moved after death or whether it was discovered in the exact position and location of death remains uncertain, but some indications point toward the latter. The discovery was accidental, since the hikers were walking off the path, and since the snow depth was very low at that season.

After the hikers had informed local police, release attempts of the body were undertaken (which led to some destruction of the body and the nearby belongings) and the corpse was flown within days to the University of Innsbruck in Austria for forensic investigations. The real impact of this find—which involved the age and preservation status of the mummy and the type and amount of the belongings accompanying it—was quickly recognized, and the first scientific reports soon appeared (by Horst Seidler in *Science*, Torstein Sjovold in *Evolutionary Anthropology*, and Frank Höpfel, Werner Platzer, and Konrad Spindler in a paper presented in an international symposium at Innsbruck—all published in 1992). A more focused archaeological field campaign was also undertaken to harvest all of the artifacts, including even the smallest ones, many of which had initially been overlooked. Later re-analyses showed that the body was actually found about 90 meters on the Italian side of the border, and so it was eventually handed over to Italian authorities and transported in 1998 to his current storage location in Bolzano, Italy.

Although the body was found half-naked, parts of the original clothing were preserved either on the mummy itself or very close nearby (moved because of wind, for example). It was not treated by humans in any way for purposes of preservation around the time of death; its accidental preservation was due solely to the climatic conditions (a kind of freeze-drying) as found in other ice mummies. Most likely the corpse was rapidly covered by snow and remained that way most of the time until its discovery more than five millennia later. But the precise mechanism of mummification is still scientifically debated.

The mummy and his belongings have now been at the center of scientific research for more than two decades, and dozens of papers and books have been published. Radiocarbon dating has revealed an age more than 5,000 years, dating to around 3300 BCE, yet the precise social status, exact cultural affiliation, and original settlement of the Iceman are still mostly unknown.

The major interest among scientists has been the Iceman's medical history, including his cause of death and his genetics. There has also been much archaeological investigation of his belongings. Findings have revealed that the Iceman is an approximately 45-year-old male, about 5 feet, 3 inches tall, who most likely died violently in early summer because of a lesion of a thoracic artery by an arrow shot. Based on radiological findings, it appears that death must have been occurred on the discovery site and quite quickly due to internal bleeding and subsequent exsanguination. The head of the arrow is still visible radiologically inside the mummy. Although the shaft is no longer present, the shaft channel inside of the body contains partial blood remnants, indicating that the arrow shaft was removed around the time of death and the corpse slightly repositioned afterward. Many theories about the Iceman's death have been postulated, especially before the discovery of the arrowhead, which was not first described until 2001.

Other findings include various medical conditions and particular injuries such as, for example, hand trauma, brain trauma, rib trauma, and dental trauma. The Iceman has been medically investigated since 1991 at the University of Innsbruck and at the EURAC in Bozen several times—for example, by endoscopy and CT scan—which has revealed additional medical disorders such as arteriosclerosis (hardening of the arteries) and the presence of gallbladder stones. The mummy's intestines have specifically been highlighted in many reports in terms of their dietary (including pollen and DNA) content as well as the presence of gastrointestinal parasites. In particular, the analyzes of pollen and the content of the apparently fully-filled stomach have revealed information about the Iceman's diet (bread and game meat), including his last meal (among others, alpine ibex meat), as well as his most likely last itinerary. The dozens of skin tattoos of the Iceman have been investigated and interpreted in multiple ways—for example, as therapeutic pain-relieving attempts in areas of underlying bone degeneration. Radiogenic (strontium and lead) and stable (oxygen and carbon) isotope composition revealed that the Iceman grew up and lived before his death in various valleys in the southern part of the Tyrolean Alps close to the discovery site.

In the last few years a major focus was also on the genome (mitochondrial and nuclear DNA) of Ötzi, which revealed not only the most likely common ancestry with present-day inhabitants of the Tyrrhenian sea but also, among other things, indications about his brown eye color, lactose intolerance, and genetic predisposition for an increased risk for cardiovascular disease.

At the time of his death, the Iceman was well equipped to spend time in such an alpine environment, both in terms of climatic protection and for hunting and gathering. He not only had full multiple-layer clothing (including underwear, leggings, sophisticated shoes, and a coat) but also carried weapons (such as a longbow, arrows—which were surprisingly broken, and thus not functional—a copper axe, and a flint-bladed knife) and tools, including a frame, a probable rucksack, a retouching tool, and two birch bark baskets, one of them probably used as a fire container. In particular, the Iceman's high-quality axe has been mentioned frequently as possibly indicating an elevated social status. However, multiple controversial theories on his social status have been proposed based on the quality and quantity of his belongings.

The Iceman is covered in the public press, including film, radio, and television, on a regular basis; and, as with many other mummies, a "curse" of the Iceman has been proposed in the lay press (something for which no scientific evidence exists). Also, the idea, advanced by some, that the assemblage of the site where the Iceman was found represents a ceremonial burial place is dismissed by most scientists.

Ötzi the Iceman is now stored in a specifically dedicated temperature- and humidity-controlled cold chamber (-6° C) at the first floor of the South Tyrolean Museum of Archeology in downtown Bolzano, Italy. The complete body, along with the extensive collection of his clothing and equipment, can be viewed by the public through a small glass window in the side of the cold chamber. Furthermore, a high-resolution photoscan of the whole mummy is publicly available on the Internet. Currently, the corpse is taken regularly out of its chamber to an adjoining chamber either for scientific investigations or to maintain the thin film of iced water that coats it. The Iceman is regarded as very well kept (e.g., his current weight of currently about 13 kg is closely monitored) and does not show any major signs of decay; invasive scientific investigations are now highly restricted, and any scientific studies are coordinated locally.

The historic age, the good quality of preservation (including at the molecular level), and the vast amount of equally well-preserved daily life equipment all make the Iceman a major object of scientific research and popular interest, and will likely continue to do so in the future.

Frank Rühli

See also: Ice mummies; Medical imaging of mummies; Mummies of Europe; Natural mummification

Further Reading

Fleckinger, Angelika. 2012. *Ötzi, the Iceman: The Full Facts at a Glance*. 6th ed. Wien/ Bozen: Folio Verlag.

Iceman Photoscan. n.d. Published by EURAC Research, Institute for Mummies and the Iceman. Accessed January 4, 2014. http://www.icemanphotoscan.eu.

Ötzi at the South Tyrol Museum of Archaeology. 2013. Accessed January 4, 2014. http://www.iceman.it.

Spindler, Konrad. 2000. *Der Mann im Eis*. München: Goldmann.

Selected major scientific references can be found online at http://www.iceman.it/en/ milestones.

P

Pettigrew, Thomas Joseph

Thomas Joseph Pettigrew was a British surgeon and antiquarian who studied the history and science of embalming, particularly of Egyptian mummies. He was renowned for performing public mummy unwrappings and earned the nickname "Mummy" Pettigrew. His book *A History of Egyptian Mummies* (1834) is one of the earliest and most important books on mummies, and includes studies of human and animal mummification around the world. A collector of mummies and other antiquities and curiosities, Pettigrew spent his retirement studying archaeology until his death in 1865.

The son of a retired naval surgeon, Pettigrew was born in London in 1791 and showed an early interest in dissection and the study of anatomy. He was apprenticed to a friend of his father and became a successful surgeon as well as a respected scholar of archaeology, literature, and the history of medicine. Pettigrew married in 1812 and had 12 children, one of whom, William Vesalius Pettigrew, assisted his father in many of his mummy autopsies.

As a young man Pettigrew became fascinated by the discoveries of Ancient Egyptian remains by French and British scholars. In 1820 he met the explorer Giovanni Battista Belzoni, who was exhibiting his collection of Egyptian antiquities in London. Belzoni invited Pettigrew and some other prominent medical men to witness the unwrapping of three mummies, and shortly afterward Pettigrew purchased and unrolled a mummy of his own.

In 1833 Pettigrew was employed as a surgeon at the Charing Cross Hospital, and he used the hospital's lecture room to host his first public unrolling of two Egyptian mummies. He invited a number of famous scientists, surgeons, antiquarians, aristocrats, authors, and other distinguished men to witness the occasion. He began his performance with a lecture on the history of embalming, and he quoted classical sources relating to Egyptian mummification. Then he sawed and chiselled the mummies open, and found that one of them was partly coated in a thin layer of gold.

It was a year after this first public unrolling that Pettigrew published *A History of Egyptian Mummies*, a fascinating book that ranges across Egyptian religious beliefs, the mechanics of mummification, and the artifacts found with mummies. It also includes a section on mummification in other cultures, including the Canary Islands, Burma (now Myanmar), and Peru. In his studies of mummification,

Pettigrew was assisted by scientific friends including the pioneering chemist Michael Faraday, who analyzed the chemicals found inside mummies. Many of Pettigrew's early mummy unrollings were held in prestigious venues such as the Royal College of Surgeons and the Royal Institution, or at meetings of the British Archaeological Association. As his unrollings grew in number and popularity, some of his many enemies began to criticize Pettigrew's performances as vulgar and distasteful.

One of Pettigrew's admirers was the Duke of Hamilton, an enthusiastic amateur Egyptologist, who requested that after his death Pettigrew should mummify him. In August 1852 the Duke died at age 84, and Pettigrew duly embalmed him in the traditional Egyptian manner. The embalmed body was transported to the Hamilton Mausoleum in Scotland, where it was placed inside a sarcophagus, with Pettigrew providing Ancient Egyptian funerary rituals to accompany the ceremony. In 1921 the mausoleum began to subside and the sarcophagus was buried in a nearby cemetery.

Pettigrew's interest in mummies was by no means restricted to Egyptian examples. He acquired a range of specimens including the head of Yagan, an Aboriginal rebel leader; a body preserved in guano found on the island of Icaboe; a desiccated mummy from Tenerife; and a natural British mummy dating from the early Seventeenth Century. In January 1852 an embalmed body was found sealed behind a wall in St. Stephen's Chapel in Westminster, and Pettigrew was asked to inspect the body. The bandages were cut away and the well-preserved body of an elderly man was revealed. The mummified body was deemed to be that of William Lydewood, Bishop of St. David's, who died in 1446.

Pettigrew's reputation as a prominent and important scholar of mummies is based in part on his book and in part on his reputation as a skilled and prolific unroller. He was by most accounts a corrupt and Machiavellian character who made enemies easily, and his feuds and vendettas became legendary. Pettigrew's reputation was rescued in part by the work of his adoring biographer, Warren Dawson, himself a scholar of mummification, who drew a veil over Pettigrew's more unsavory character traits.

In his later years Pettigrew withdrew from Egyptology and the study of mummies. He served for many years as Vice-President of the British Archaeological Association, and wrote several books on antiquarian themes. Thomas Pettigrew died at his home in London in 1865 at the age of 74 and was buried in Brompton Cemetery. The auction of his possessions after his death included numerous Egyptian antiquities, including several mummified animals and an oil painting of a mummy unrolling.

Gabriel Moshenska

See also: Alexander, Tenth Duke of Hamilton; Animal mummies; Belzoni, Giovanni; Dawson, Warren Royal; Egyptian mummification methods; Embalming; Mummy unwrappings

Further Reading

Dawson, Warren Royal. 1931. *Memoir of Thomas Joseph Pettigrew F.R.C.S., F.R.S., F.S.A. (1791–1865)*. New York: Medical Life Press.

Dawson, Warren Royal. 1934. "Pettigrew's Demonstrations upon Mummies: A Chapter in the History of Egyptology." *Journal of Egyptian Archaeology* 20: 170–82.

Mayes, Stanley. 1959. *The Great Belzoni*. London: Putnam.

Moshenska, Gabriel. 2013. "Unrolling Egyptian Mummies in Nineteenth-Century Britain." *The British Journal for the History of Science* online prepublication. doi:10.1017/S0007087413000423.

Pettigrew, Thomas Joseph. 1834. *A History of Egyptian Mummies, and an Account of the Worship and Embalming of the Sacred Animals by the Egyptians, with Remarks on the Funeral Ceremonies of Different Nations, and Observations on the Mummies of the Canary Islands, of the Ancient Peruvians, Burman Priests & c.* London: Longman, Rees, Orme, Brown, Green, and Longman.

Poe, Edgar Allan

Edgar Allan Poe (1809–1849) was an American writer of poetry, fiction, and nonfiction who is credited with having published the first work of detective fiction, "The Murders in the Rue Morgue" (1841), and with having transformed the tale of Gothic horror, popular in the late-eighteenth and early-nineteenth centuries, by making its macabre events inseparable from the often aberrant psychology of his characters. Several of Poe's stories are considered proto-science fiction for their explorations of fringe sciences such as phrenology and mesmerism. As a fiction writer, Poe worked almost exclusively in short story form, whose dramatic unities he perfected. In his lifetime, Poe saw the publication of his novel *The Narrative of Arthur Gordon Pym* (1838); two major collections of short fiction, *Tales of the Grotesque*

In his 1845 story "Some Words with a Mummy," Edgar Allan Poe used an Egyptian mummy as a vehicle for exploring the themes of death and the afterlife. (Library of Congress Prints and Photographs Division[LC-USZ62-10610])

In Edgar Allan Poe's satirical short story "Some Words with a Mummy," an electrical current passed through an ancient Egyptian mummy causes it to wake up and speak indignantly to its astonished observers:

I must say, gentlemen, that I am as much surprised as I am mortified at your behavior. Of Doctor Ponnonner nothing better was to be expected. He is a poor little fat fool who knows no better. I pity and forgive him. But you, Mr. Gliddon—and you, Silk— who have traveled and resided in Egypt until one might imagine you to the manner born—you, I say who have been so much among us that you speak Egyptian fully as well, I think, as you write your mother tongue—you, whom I have always been led to regard as the firm friend of the mummies—I really did anticipate more gentlemanly conduct from you. What am I to think of your standing quietly by and seeing me thus unhandsomely used? What am I to suppose by your permitting Tom, Dick, and Harry to strip me of my coffins, and my clothes, in this wretchedly cold climate? In what light (to come to the point) am I to regard your aiding and abetting that miserable little villain, Doctor Ponnonner, in pulling me by the nose?

and Arabesque (1840) and Tales by Edgar A. Poe (1845); and the poetry collections Tamerlane and Other Poems (1827), Al Aaraaf, Tamerlane and Minor Poems (1829), Poems, by Edgar A. Poe (1831), and The Raven and Other Poems (1845). Though Poe's macabre stories represent only a small fraction of his writing, they are among his best-known works and include "The Fall of the House of Usher," "The Tell-Tale Heart," "The Black Cat," "The Pit and the Pendulum," "The Cask of Amontillado," and "Ligiea."

Death and the afterlife are common themes in Poe's stories, and in one such story, "Some Words with a Mummy" (first published in the April 1845 issue of American Review), he uses an Egyptian mummy as a vehicle for exploring these themes. Although written as a satire, the story features considerable information on ancient Egyptian funerary practices that were not common knowledge for the layman at the time (although, as Kenneth Silverman points out in his biography Edgar A. Poe: Mournful and Never-ending Remembrance, some of the story's clinical descriptions of the mummification process are paraphrased from the Encyclopedia Americana).

The narrator has just settled into bed after a sumptuous dinner when a messenger delivers a note to him from his friend Doctor Ponnonner, summoning him urgently to the doctor's residence. Ponnonner has just received permission from the Directors of the City Museum to unwrap a mummy, "one of a pair brought some years previously, by Captain Arthur Sabretash, a cousin of Ponnonner's from a tomb near Eleithias, in the Libyan Mountains, a considerable distance above Thebes, on the Nile." The mummy is expected to be very good specimen, since its coffin was never tampered with. The tomb from which the mummy coffins were retrieved was richly illustrated with paintings and bas-reliefs, and its artifacts suggest that the person buried in it was considerably wealthy.

The unwrapping begins with the narrator, Ponnonner, Mr. Gliddon, Mr. Barnes, Mr. Silk, and Mr. Buckingham in attendance. The outer layer of the coffin, which roughly measures 7 feet long, 3 feet wide, and 2 ½ feet deep, is a type of papier maché made from papyrus and decorated with paintings of funeral scenes. Interspersed among these images are glyphs thought to spell out the name of the interred, and that translate as *Allamistakeo*. Beneath an underlying layer of resin, they find a second case of the same material into which a casket of cedar has been tightly fit. Removing the body from the casket, the men find in place of the bandages and linens that would usually wrap it a papyrus sheath painted with images of the duties of the soul and its presentation to the divinities, and decorated with hieroglyphics spelling out the name of the interred and those of members of his family. They strip this away to find a well-preserved corpse with gilded finger and toe nails, wearing a necklace and belt of multicolored beads. It is determined that the body has been preserved with camphor, rather than the usual asphaltum.

The absence of any of the usual incisions through which the internal organs would have been removed mandates a dissection of the body. Owing to the late hour the men decide to put this off until the next evening, but then one of those present suggests applying electricity to the body from a voltaic pile. To the men's surprise, a current applied to the temporal muscle causes the eyelids to close, and a current to the big toe brings about a spastic kick that accidentally catapults Ponnonner out the window. The application of current to the tip of the mummy's nose completely revives it.

Speaking in primitive Egyptian that is interpreted for the group by Gliddon and Buckingham, the mummy, Count Allamistakeo, clarifies some contemporary misinformation about the past. First, that 5,050 years ago, the average lifespan was 800 years. Allamistakeo himself was 700 years old when he fell into a state of catalepsy and was embalmed alive. Embalming, at that time, was a method "to arrest *all* the animal functions subjected to the process" (Poe 1984, 457). So any person so embalmed was effectively put into a state of suspended animation. Having perfected this embalming process, the ancients decided it would be best for individuals to live their long lives in installments. A historian would be embalmed at the age of 500, and leave instructions for his descendants to revive him another 500 to 600 years hence, so that he might corrected all of the misinformation and inaccuracies that contemporary scholars impose on knowledge of the past, converting it into pure fable.

When the men then question the Count about the marked inferiority of the ancient Egyptians in their knowledge of the sciences and architecture compared to modern times, the Count offers examples from his culture that refute this assertion. Similarly, when the men tout the virtues of Democracy as a political institution, the Count tells, in a parable whose events are clearly modeled on the founding and expansion of America, how 13 Egyptian provinces, "determined all at once to be free," eventually consolidated with another 15 to 20 provinces and produced a nation given over to mob rule. By the story's end the narrator returns home, totally dispirited about life in the nineteenth century and determined to return to Ponnonner's on the morrow to "get embalmed for a couple of hundred years."

"Some Words with a Mummy" is, like "King Pest" (1835) and "Never Bet the Devil Your Head" (1841), a story in which Poe deploys elements normally considered macabre to comic effect. The story can be read as the lighter "flipside" to his more dramatic tales "The Premature Burial" (1844) and "The Facts in the Case of M. Valdemar" (1845), which explore the horrors, respectively, of burial alive and life after death.

Stefan R. Dziemianowicz

See also: Egyptomania; The mummy in Western fiction: Beginnings to 1922; Mummy unwrappings

Further Reading

Poe, Edgar Allan. 1984. *Complete Stories and Poems of Edgar Allan Poe*. New York: Doubleday.

Silverman, Kenneth. 1991. *Edgar A. Poe: Mournful and Never-ending Remembrance*. New York: Harper Perennial.

Q

Quinn, Seabury

Seabury Quinn (1889–1969) was an American pulp fiction writer distinguished as the most frequent contributor to *Weird Tales*, the landmark weird fiction pulp published from 1923 to 1954. Most famous for his tales about the occult detective Jules de Grandin, he wrote several stories that made prominent use of mummies.

Seabury Grandin Quinn was born in Washington, D.C. in 1889. He lived most of his life in there and in New York City, where he practiced law, lectured on medical jurisprudence, and edited several trade magazines, among them *Casket and Sunnyside*, a journal that served the mortuary business. Though he published over 500 works of fiction during his lifetime, his fiction writing was a sideline to his work as a lawyer and journalist.

Quinn's first known work of fiction, "Demons of the Night," appeared in the March 19, 1918 issue of *Detective Story Magazine*. Quinn wrote for both detective and weird fiction magazines (and, occasionally, adventure magazines), and he later rewrote some of his detective stories as weird tales. His debut in *Weird Tales* came in the October 1923 issue with his story "The Phantom Farmhouse" and an essay titled "Bluebeard," the latter an entry in his seven-part "Weird Crimes" series that was published up through the November 1924 issue. He followed this with a six-part essay series titled "Servants of Satan," published in the March through August 1925 issues. Quinn later worked some of the legends and lore explored in these essays into tales of the supernatural.

His contribution to the October 1925 issue of *Weird Tales*, a story titled "The Terror on the Links," introduced occult detective Jules de Grandin and his sidekick Dr. John Trowbridge, residents of Harrisonville, New Jersey, who went on to appear in 93 stories published in *Weird Tales* up through 1954. The adventures of de Grandin and Trowbridge were modeled on those of Sir Arthur Conan Doyle's Sherlock Holmes and Dr. Watson, and they featured encounters with many iconic monsters of horror—vampires, werewolves, mummies, and so on,—as well as more esoteric horrors drawn from folklore and legends from around the world.

Mummies feature in at least five of de Grandin's adventures, beginning with "The Grinning Mummy" (November, 1926). In this story, an archaeologist is bludgeoned to death while unwrapping the mummy of Anka-ma-amen. The assailant appears to have been the mummy itself, whom investigators find to be clutching a bloodstained scepter of Isis in its hand, and whose grinning lips are stained with blood. Though this appears at first to be the fulfillment of a curse put on those who would defile the mummy's tomb, de Grandin works through a series of deductions to find the real culprits: a brother and sister team of Copts who are part of a movement to revive the worship of the gods of ancient Egypt. The story is among the earliest works of fiction to evoke the death of George Herbert, Fifth Earl of Carnarvon, patron of Howard Carter's expedition to uncover the tomb of Tutankhamun, whose death in 1923 first instigated rumors of a mummy's curse.

Superstitions surrounding the Carter expedition also figure in the plot of "The Dust of Egypt" (April, 1930). In this tale, an Egyptologist is found dead in apparent fulfillment of a curse placed by the Priest Sepa on anyone who would remove his mummy from its tomb. Ultimately, de Grandin deduces that alarm over the reported deaths of members of the Carter expedition hastened the man's death by natural causes, and that the power of suggestion has similarly influenced the man's decedents, who also appear to suffering under their belief in the curse.

The mummy in "The Bleeding Mummy" (November, 1932) is deemed "unlucky": it was interred without embalming in bloodstained cerements, and three men who have come into close contact with it died after a screaming fit. De Grandin dispels the possibility of supernatural machinations when he proves that the bite of a venomous spider brought back in the mummy case is responsible for the deaths. With the help of a psychic, he establishes that the mummy is that of a priestess of Isis, who was crushed to death for refusing to lead the life of celibacy that was imposed on her.

The last two Jules de Grandin tales to feature mummies are overtly supernatural. In "The Dead-Alive Mummy" (October, 1935), a contemporary woman is mistaken as the *ka*, or discarnate soul, of a priestess of Isis mummified 3,000 years before. In fact, though she bears a striking resemblance to the image of the woman painted on the mummy case, she is just psychically sensitive to the dying thought, imbued in the mummy, that the priestess will, in time, return from the dead. De Grandin reverses the mummy's apparent absorption of the vitality of the woman through a ritual that sends its will for reanimation back into the past. "The Man in Crescent Terrace" (March, 1946) features a rampaging mummy reanimated for vengeful purposes by an evil cultist of the Esoteric Society of the Resurrection. De Grandin disposes of the monster conveniently by igniting it with his cigarette lighter.

Mummies and ancient Egyptian funerary customs are mentioned in several other Jules de Grandin stories, among them "Pledged to the Dead" (October, 1937), "The Ring of Bastet" (September, 1951), and "The Jewel of the Seven Stones" (April, 1928), which, despite its obvious evocation of Bram Stoker's Egyptian mummy novel, *The Jewel of Seven Stars* (1903), concerns a Grecian woman buried in ancient Alexandria who is resurrected in the present by a modern man's love for her. The excavation of a mummy's tomb is the backdrop for Quinn's non-Jules de Grandin novel *Alien Flesh* (1977), in which the soul of archaeologist Lynne Foster is forced to transmigrate into the body of an Egyptian woman for whose accidental death he is blamed.

Though Quinn's treatments of the mummy theme are not particularly original or imaginative, it is perhaps not a coincidence that they parallel the approach to the theme in the increasingly popular medium of film. In Quinn's three mummy tales written prior to the release of Universal's *The Mummy* in December of 1932, he rationalized the suggested supernaturalism of a mummy's curse. Written in 1946, "The Man in Crescent Terrace" seems particularly indebted to *The Mummy's Hand* (1940), *The Mummy's Tomb* (1942), *The Mummy's Ghost* (1944), and *The Mummy's Curse* (1944), all of which feature a mummy reanimated as an instrument of revenge.

Stefan R. Dziemianowicz

See also: Carnarvon, Fifth Earl of (George Herbert); Carter, Howard; *The Mummy* (1932); The mummy in Western fiction: From 1922 to the twenty-first century; Mummy's curse; Universal Studios mummy series

Further Reading

Quinn, Seabury. *The Compleat Adventures of Jules de Grandin.* Commentary by Robert Weinberg, Seabury Quinn, Jr., and Jim Rockhill. Eugenia, Ontario: Battered Silicon Dispatch Box, 2001.

"Seabury (Grandin) Quinn." 2003. *Contemporary Authors Online*, Gale. Accessed February 11, 2014. http://gdc.gale.com/gale-literature-collections/contemporary-authors.

Stableford, Brian, and David Pringle. 1998. "Quinn, Seabury." In *St. James Guide to Horror, Ghost & Gothic Writers*, 466–467. London: St. James Press.

R

Religion and mummies

A mummy is defined as a "well-preserved dead body" (Cockburn et al. 1998, 1) achieved by either natural or anthropogenic (artificial) methods, and can refer to both human and animal subjects. There are numerous beliefs surrounding mummification, many of which involve ideas and rituals concerning what happens to a living creature at the point of death and beyond. A small number of modern civilizations preserve their dead through mummification; however, the most well-known mummies were produced by ancient civilizations located across Africa, Asia, Europe, and the Americas. From the ice mummies of the Andes, sacrificial victims preserved by the natural climatic conditions in their final resting places, to the fire mummies of the Philippines and the salt mummies of Iran and China, preserved bodies have much to tell us about the culture to which they once belonged.

It can be difficult to understand the beliefs of people far removed from modern ideologies through time, geography, or cultural differences, although aspects of their beliefs still resonate in our thoughts about death and what happens to a person when they die. The notion of overcoming death is considered necessary to allow an individual to function in some way after death, and it is these beliefs and their religious basis that are discussed here, concentrating initially on the ancient Egyptians.

The ancient Egyptians are regarded as the most iconic ancient civilization to have preserved their dead through mummification and for which there is much archaeological and artistic evidence. The Egyptians lived in harmony with their environment, observing the cyclical nature of life with the annual flooding of the Nile and of night following day, with the ultimate promise of an everlasting afterlife, known as the Field of Reeds. The Egyptians believed that death was not an end, but a new beginning. Earthly life was simply a phase when many Egyptians prepared themselves for death and what came beyond. The Afterlife was considered to be a paradise, a mirror image of Egypt without the negative aspects of drought, floods, and disease, yet with the positive aspects magnified.

Much of our knowledge and understanding of ancient Egyptian religious thought comes from our interpretation of the surviving archaeological and literary evidence. It focuses on the concept of rebirth, a cycle of life encompassing all living beings, human and animal, with creation triumphant over death.

Documentary sources such as the Pyramid Texts (Old Kingdom, 2686–2160 BCE), Coffin Texts (Middle Kingdom, 2055–1650 BCE), and the *Book of the Dead* (New Kingdom, 1550–1069 BCE) form part of a large corpus of ritual texts intended to enable the deceased to achieve resurrection.

The first individual to achieve a resurrected state was considered to be the god Osiris. His myth describes how he was murdered by his jealous brother Seth and his corpse dismembered into 14 pieces and scattered around Egypt. Isis, his wife, gathered the pieces of his body, reassembled them, and wrapped the body in linen, creating the first mummiform figure. Due to his deceased state, Osiris became the god of the Afterlife as he could no longer function on earth. His name often appears as a prefix to that of the deceased to signify the transfigured state they hoped to achieve.

The Egyptians believed that by creating a mummy, the corpse (*khat*) was able to achieve the ultimate transfigured state known as *akh* and thus become like Osiris. As in the Osiris myth, the Egyptians believed it was necessary for all the physical and psychic elements of the individual to be preserved. The physical body (*sah*) itself acted as a "house" for these elements. It was essential that the *sah* was preserved in a true likeness of the person in life, which was exemplified through the use of subcutaneous packing of the skin (common during the 21st Dynasty, 1069–945 BCE) and the body cavities, false eyes to give the deceased the ability to see, and cosmetic attempts such as styling of the hair. In cases where body parts had been lost, prosthetic limbs were added to ensure that the *sah* was complete and would therefore be resurrected in its entirety.

Another physical element that required preservation was the heart (*ib*). It was positioned in the anatomical center of the body and was considered the seat of a person's emotions. Evisceration, the removal of the internal organs after death to delay the onset of putrefaction, was practiced throughout Egyptian history; however, the *ib* was commonly left *in situ* (in its original position) to ensure that the deceased could be judged in the Hall of Justice when it was weighed against the feather of *maat* or truth (*Book of the Dead*, Chapter 125). If the person had lived a good, honest life, the *ib* and *maat* would be in perfect equilibrium, signifying that the deceased was "true of voice" (*maa-kheru*) and worthy of an Afterlife. If the *ib* was not balanced with *maat*, it would be consumed by Ammut, The Devourer, a composite creature composed of a variety of animals, and thus prevent the deceased from entering the Afterlife. The Egyptians believed that the *ib* could betray the deceased at this crucial time, so they included spells from the *Book of the Dead* (Spell 30B) on a specially positioned heart scarab, which was placed on or within the mummy bundle.

Alongside the physical components, there were four psychic elements. The *ka* was thought of as the twin of the deceased and came into existence at the same time as the person it represented. At the time of death, the *ka* and the *sah* were temporarily separated, during which time the *ka* resided in an image, usually a statue, of the deceased. To achieve resurrection, the *ka* and the *sah* needed to be reunited once more through a ceremony known as the Opening of the Mouth (Chapter 23, *Book of the Dead*). This was performed on the mummy itself from the Old Kingdom onward to magically enable the individual to function in the Afterlife.

The *ba* is best described as the personality or spirit of a living being, although the Egyptians believed that inanimate objects also had a *ba*. The *ba*, depicted in the form of a bird, was able to exist after death and shared the same characteristics as the person in life. It could move about freely outside of the tomb, was capable of speech, and required sustenance. The *ba* had to return to the *sah* every night, to be reunited with its owner and thus allow the cycle to be repeated the following day. For this to happen, both the *ka* and the *ba* required that the *sah* be preserved in a true likeness of the deceased individual to aid recognition between these physical and psychic elements.

The ancient Egyptians believed that it was important to protect the name (*ren*) of a person, the most enduring symbol of individuality, so that they received eternal life. In a similar way to remembering the dead in the prayers of the living, the Egyptians believed that uttering the *ren* of the deceased, and recording it on the coffin and in tomb scenes, ensured that the individual was remembered. A person's shadow (*shut*) followed them everywhere in life, and the Egyptians believed this was a further element of the individual. Just as the *ba* could move independently outside of the person, so too could the *shut*.

Mummification was also carried out in various cultures because of a belief in the power of kinship and the notion of ancestor worship. Many believed that their deceased ancestors lived on in the world around them, enabling the living to find peace and the deceased to maintain a position within the society to which they once belonged. One such culture were the Chinchorro, who practiced artificial mummification between 7000 BCE and 1500 BCE in the deserts of northern coastal Chile. It is believed that the Chinchorro developed artificial mummification because they believed that preservation of the soul also required preservation of the physical body. They chose to introduce artificial preservation techniques (including decapitation, excerebration [removal of the brain], evisceration, amputation, skinning, defleshing, smoking, and charring among others) to positively influence the natural preservation process they witnessed, and to impose ideologies, which served to strengthen social relationships and belief systems.

The Chinchorro undoubtedly had many reasons for mummifying their dead. Mummification may have depended on an individual's position in society or as reinforcement of ethnicity. They also believed that the dead continued to play meaningful roles in the lives of the living and held a firm belief in the existence of an afterlife. Ritual acts carried out by the living following a person's passing served as a means of purification. Particular actions, such as washing the corpse and the repetition of incantations by the living, would ensure the deceased of an afterlife.

Personal and social perspectives on death are complex and multifaceted, made up in part of religious, social, genealogical, supernatural, and ritual ideologies. Most choose not to view death as a final event, instead choosing to believe that the deceased continues to exist in some form, even though their earthly lives have ended.

Preservation of the physical body through mummification occurs in some tribal communities such as the Anga tribe in Papua New Guinea, where ancestor worship is an integral part of their culture. The Anga preserve the dead by smoking the bodies, the acidity of which effectively inhibits the growth of bacteria that cause decomposition. These deceased ancestors remain pivotal members of the community in their transfigured state, although their role is overtly visible with the mummified bodies often displayed in dwellings and used in ceremonies. Such motivations and practicalities of mummification are understood through ethnographic studies, which are important in interpreting the beliefs and actions of tribal communities.

Mummification in all its guises, however it manifests itself across the boundaries of space and time, is an intentional display of the religious aspects of death. In its artificial form, it represents an intentional act to preserve the body to promote and assist the provision of a suitable afterlife for the deceased for which religion is undoubtedly a driving force. A mummy could ensure continuity of "life" between this world and the next, acting as a lifelike vessel for the psychic elements, and to provide unity for the transfigured dead. Intentionally mummified bodies are both individuals with their stories to tell and iconic and invaluable sources of information regarding the religious foundations of a civilization.

Lidija M. McKnight

See also: Anubis; *Book of the Dead*; Chinchorro mummies; Egyptian mummification methods; Isis; Opening of the Mouth; Osiris; Seth; Smoked bodies of Papua New Guinea; Summum

Further Reading

Arriaza, Bernardo. 1995. *Beyond Death: The Chinchorro Mummies of Ancient Chile.* Washington: Smithsonian Institute.

Barber, Elizabeth. 1999. *The Mummies of Ürümchi.* London: Macmillan.

Beckett, Ronald G., Ulla Lohmann, and Josh Bernstein. 2011. "A Field Report on the Mummification Practices of the Anga of Koke Village, Central Highlands, Papua New Guinea." In *Yearbook of Mummy Studies 1,* edited by Dario Piombino-Mascali, 11–17. Munich: Verlag Dr. Friedrich Pfeil.

Cockburn, Aidan, Eve Cockburn, and Theodore Reyman. 1998. *Mummies, Disease and Ancient Cultures.* 2nd ed. Cambridge: Cambridge University Press.

Taylor, John. 2001. *Death and the Afterlife in Ancient Egypt*. London: British Museum Press.

Rice, Anne

Anne Rice (born 1941) is a bestselling American novelist who is most famous as the author of the Vampire Chronicles. She has also written erotica, historical fiction, novelizations of the life of Christ, and many novels and novel series about witches, werewolves, and other supernatural creatures. Along with these, she is the author of the most popular (in terms of sales) mummy novel ever published, 1989's *The Mummy or Ramses the Damned*. Although this has, to date, been her only explicit foray into classic mummy territory, some of her other work in a supernatural and horror vein has involved and invoked themes of eternal life and immortality related to ancient Egypt.

Anne Rice was born Howard Allen Frances O'Brien on October 4, 1941, in New Orleans, Louisiana. She and her three sisters were raised there in relative poverty by her Irish Catholic family. She disliked her given name and began calling herself "Anne" in early childhood; her name was legally changed when she was six years old. She attended parochial school in New Orleans and then graduated from the public high school in Richardson, Texas, after moving there with her family as a teenager. While in Texas she met the poet Stan Rice, and they married and moved to California, where Anne earned degrees at San Francisco State College and lived somewhat in the shadow of her husband's growing literary reputation until the publication of her first novel, *Interview with the Vampire*, in 1976. Inspired partly by the death of Stan's and her daughter Michelle from leukemia at the age of 5, the novel became a bestseller, attained cult status, helped to inspire the now deeply established vampire-goth subculture in North America, and launched Rice on the road to enduring mass market literary fame.

Although she is best known as the author of the Vampire Chronicles, Anne Rice's 1989 novel *The Mummy or Ramses the Damned* is the best-selling mummy novel in history. (Bryce Lankard/Getty Images)

It was in the sequel to *Interview with the Vampire*, 1985's *The Vampire Lestat*, that Rice's interest in and use of the trope of immortality as related to ancient Egyptian esoterica and exotica (mostly of her own fictional creation) first emerged. The novel is structured as an elaborate, multileveled frame narrative, with the innermost frame telling the story of the ancient Egyptian monarchs Enkil and Akasha, who, in prehistoric Egypt, were physically invaded, inhabited, and radically transformed by unspecified supernatural spirits, and who thereby became—in Rice's fantastic/imagined history—the source and origin of vampires. The narrative also relates that the historical Enkil and Akasha were eventually mythologized in the figures of the iconic Egyptian deities Osiris and Isis. Moreover, both fell into a state of suspended animation—not as mummies but in a kind of statue-like immobility—and remained that way until, in the novel's outermost and primary frame narrative, Akasha awakens in the modern day (the 1980s), destroys the still-sleeping Enkil, and poses a supernatural threat to the entire world. This storyline continues and culminates in the third book in Rice's Vampire Chronicles, 1988's *The Queen of the Damned*.

Rice continued to develop aspects of this mythology, which might be described as "mummy-tangential," in various ways in the remainder of the Vampire Chronicles. She also mentioned mummies and mummy-related matters directly in other novels, as in the fourth entry in the Vampire Chronicles, 1992's *The Tale of the Body Thief*, where a character reads Robert Bloch's Egypt-inspired horror story "Eyes of the Mummy" (1938), and in the non-Vampire Chronicles novel *Servant of the Bones* (1996), which makes direct mention of the real-life Manchester Egyptian Mummy Project (profiled in a separate article in this volume) and its famous activities in conducting DNA analysis and medical imaging of various Egyptian mummies.

However, *The Mummy or Ramses the Damned* is Rice's most overt and extended treatment of the mummy theme, and the fact that, as mentioned, it has sold more copies than any other mummy novel in history—a result abetted by Rice's preexisting status as one of the world's most popular authors—renders it an important entry in the genre despite the widespread negative opinion of its literary merits among many critics and even general readers.

The novel's plot concerns the awakening of the ancient mummy of the pharaoh Ramses II in Edwardian England. An archaeological dig in Egypt in 1914 uncovers a tomb with an inscription that claims the occupant is Ramses II. This is confusing to the dig team, because the tomb itself dates to the first century BCE—more than a thousand years after Ramses II's death. When the archaeologist who opens the tomb, a man named Lawrence Stratford, suddenly and mysteriously dies, his companions fear they have invoked a curse by violating the tomb.

The mummy is exhumed and shipped to England, where it ends up in the British Museum, and from there the novel becomes a kind of horror soap opera. Its cast of characters includes, among others, Lawrence's daughter Julie, who is heir to his fortune; her greedy and alcoholic cousin Henry, who wants the fortune for himself; Julie's fiancé Alex; and Alex's father, the ill and elderly Elliott, Earl of Rutherford. It turns out that Henry murdered Lawrence with a poison he found in the newly discovered tomb. He tries to do the same to Julie, at which point the mummy of Ramses comes to life and saves her. The remainder of the novel details the various complications and outcomes of these inciting incidents.

Rice builds an intricate back story for Ramses, the consequences of which become central to the modern-day plot: while Ramses was reigning over Egypt as pharaoh, he learned the secret of making an elixir of immortality, and after that he used his long life to serve as an advisor to Egypt's rulers over a span of centuries. The last of these was Cleopatra, with whom he fell in love, but who fell in love herself with Mark Antony and refused Ramses' offer to become immortal with him, choosing instead to commit suicide when Antony died. In grief, Ramses had himself sealed into a tomb, which was where Lawrence Stratford found him two millennia later. The consequences of these events come to life—literally—when Ramses, accompanied by Julie and posing as an Egyptologist named Reginald Ramsey, first tours modern-day London (marveling all the while at this unfamiliar, high-technological society) and then travels to Egypt to see his homeland again. While visiting the Cairo museum, he sees a mummy that he recognizes as Cleopatra. He uses the elixir to bring her to life, but it is only partially effective, and she awakes as a monster bent on destruction. Meanwhile, throughout all of this Henry is frantically trying to convince everyone that Ramsey is really the reanimated Ramses, while Elliott begins to suspect the same as well but wants to confirm it not for purposes of revenge or monetary gain but to learn about the elixir of immortality. It all ends with Cleopatra seeking to murder Julie but then relenting and allowing herself to be killed (apparently) in a fiery car-and-train crash, while Ramses gives the elixir to Julie so that they can be together. He also gives it to Elliott. The novel closes with a revelation that Cleopatra has actually survived and is plotting revenge on Ramses.

As stated, the general opinion of *The Mummy or Ramses the Damned* is that it does not represent Rice's best work. Some readers are quite fond of it, but many others, and most of the critics and reviewers, have regarded it as an overly potboilerish piece of work that fails to engage and grip the reader with the same sense of sophisticated lushness that characterizes Rice's much of her other work. This tonal difference may have something to do with the novel's unusual origin: Rice originally planned to write it not as a novel but as a screenplay, but she changed her approach when producers in Hollywood wanted to make drastic alterations to her intended script. The resulting book is, as popular culture scholar and Rice expert Gary Hoppenstand has observed, "a modern-day pastiche of the traditional British thriller" (Hoppenstand 1997, 286) that wears its influences, both literary and cinematic, on its sleeve, ranging from the motif of the "cursed tomb," to the ancient, immortal love story, to the decision of Ramses to pose as a modern-day Egyptologist (an echo of Boris Karloff's Ardath Bey in Universal Studios' 1932 *The Mummy*). And indeed, as Hoppenstand points out, Rice herself apparently wants these influences to be noticed, since on the novel's dedication page she names, among others, "Sir Arthur Conan Doyle for his great mummy stories 'Lot No. 249' and 'The Ring of Thoth'" and "H. Rider Haggard who created the immortal *She*" (Rice 1989). In any event, the novel retains a kind of movie-like quality, as seen, for example, in the fact of its cinema-style transitions and cliffhangers.

Although *The Mummy or Ramses the Damned* ends with an explicit assertion that the story of Ramses will be continued in further books, as of early 2014 there was no indication, either at Rice's official Web site (www.annerice.com) or in the general press, that any sequel was in the works.

Matt Cardin

See also: Doyle, Arthur Conan; Haggard, H. Rider; Isis; Osiris; *The Mummy* (1932); The mummy in Western fiction: From 1922 to the twenty-first century

Further Reading

Hoppenstand, Gary. 1997. "Anne Rice's Pastiche of the British 'Thriller': Comparing The Mummy to Sir Arthur Conan Doyle's Lot No. 249." In *The Anne Rice Reader*, edited by Katherine Ramsland, 286–304. New York: Random House.

Rice, Anne. 1989. *The Mummy or Ramses the Damned*. New York: Ballantine.

Rohmer, Sax

English writer Sax Rohmer, born Arthur Henry Ward, is best known for his writings under the name of Sax Rohmer, particularly the stories featuring the Chinese master villain Fu Manchu. From the first, however, Rohmer was interested in Egypt and Egyptology, and he utilized mummies as characters and plot devices in his stories.

Arthur Henry Ward was born in Birmingham to Margaret Mary (*nee* Furey) and William Ward on February 15, 1883. In about 1886 his family moved to London, where his father worked as an office clerk, and young Arthur's formal schooling effectively concluded in 1901, upon the death of his mother. He unsuccessfully held a variety of menial jobs, working as a bank clerk, in a gas company, and as a reporter, changing his middle name to Sarsfield. He also began to write fiction, publishing his first story in 1903. He began using the name Sax Rohmer in 1905 and permanently adopted it in 1912, achieving nearly immediate success for his stories featuring the Chinese master-villain Fu Manchu.

"We discovered"—Dr. Cairn spoke very deliberately—"a certain papyrus. The translation of this is contained"—he rested the point of his finger upon the writing-table—"in the unpublished book of Sir Michael Ferrara, which lies here. That book, Rob, will never be published now! Furthermore, we discovered the mummy of a child. . . . Unaided, we performed this process upon the embalmed body of the child. Then, in accordance with the directions of that dead magician—that accursed, malignant being, who thus had sought to secure for himself a new tenure of evil life—we laid the mummy, treated in a certain fashion, in the King's Chamber of the Méydûm Pyramid."

. . . By means which are beyond my comprehension, and which alone serve to confirm his supernatural origin, he has acquired—knowledge. According to the Ancient Egyptian beliefs the Khu (or magical powers) of a fully-equipped Adept, at the death of the body, could enter into anything prepared for its reception. According to these ancient beliefs, then, the Khu of the high priest Hortotef entered into the body of this infant who was his son, and whose mother was the Witch-Queen; and to-day in this modern London, a wizard of Ancient Egypt, armed with the lost lore of that magical land, walks amongst us!

—From *Brood of the Witch Queen* by Sax Rohmer

His first publication, "The Mysterious Mummy" (*Pearson's Xmas Xtra*, 1903), begins with a series of events in the Great Portland Square Museum: a mysterious man with a hollow cough is seen to enter the Egyptian room, though not to leave. There are mysterious noises that baffle the patrolling watchmen, and the next day the fabulous Rienzi Vase is missing and a drugged policeman is found bound and gagged behind a mummy case. A seemingly impossible crime having thus been presented, an exotic background having been established, Ward thereupon explains how it was committed; in a clever twist, the narrator of the explanation is also revealed to be the master thief. For all that, "The Mysterious Mummy" is not part of a series and stands alone, it also demonstrates the directions in which Ward's narrative would often take: capable historical and/or ethnographic research, a sensational subject, seemingly inexplicable events, and then a rational (albeit improbable) conclusion, with the fantastic elements receding into the background.

Rohmer's next notable work to feature mummies is *Brood of the Witch Queen* (1918). It is not evident at first that there are mummies in the novel. Rather, it appears to be the story of a young Egyptologist, Anthony Ferrera, a thoroughly unpleasant young man who commands a variety of supernatural powers in his quest for wealth: he can project strangling hands, send beetles, control dreams, and even send fire elementals to do his bidding, and of course, his bidding involves murdering those people with money. Acting in opposition to Ferrera are Robert and Dr. Cairn. Only at the conclusion, after Ferrera's fire elemental has turned on and destroyed its master, does Dr. Cairn reveal the secret: he and Ferrera's father found a mummy, the son of a witch queen and the high priest of an Egyptian cult, and they reanimated it, setting loose the being that became Anthony Ferrera.

Tales of Secret Egypt (1918) is a collection of linked narratives, at least some of them loosely based on episodes that are said to have occurred when Rohmer and his wife Rose Elizabeth Knox, whom he married in 1909, took a much delayed honeymoon in Egypt in 1913. The first five of the *Tales of Secret Egypt* feature Neville Kernaby, the Egyptian representative of a Birmingham business. In the first of the stories, Kernaby encounters Abû Tabâh, one of the hidden masters of the Cairo who wields enormous power. (Abû Tabâh is variously referred to as the Imam and the Magician, and he is also an agent of the Egyptian Government.) For all that Egypt and its antiquities are involved in each story, the majority are romances, albeit with a touch of the weird, and mummies play active roles in only two of them. In "The Death-Ring of Sneferu," Kernaby visits the Pyramid of Méydûm in an attempt at locating a treasure. When it is not to be found, Abû Tabâh's sister is revealed to be a medium of some power, her vision revealing "a long line of dead men . . . they are of all the races of the East, and some are swathed in mummy wrappings; the wrappings are sealed with the death ring of Pharaoh" (Rohmer 1918b, 54). In "The Whispering Mummy," the painter Felix Bréton is infatuated with the beautiful dancer Yâsmîna, whom he believes is the reincarnation of a priestess of Isis. She vanishes, and a mummy tells Bréton that she died for love of him: indeed, Kernaby verifies Bréton's account and hears the same message. Alas, the truth is quite prosaic: Bréton ran afoul of the Black Darwîshes by loving Yâsmîna, and they kidnapped her and rigged a speaking tube in the mummy.

An ancient Egyptian figure of a cat—but alas, no mummies—is utilized in *The Green Eyes of Bâst* (1920), which is a mystery with a strong supernatural component that hinges on the premise of people being prenatally marked by animals. One of these psychic hybrids—she is a blend of feline and human characteristics—is from Egypt and is taking vengeance on the Coverlys, the family that rejected her.

Human mummies appeared again in *The Dream-Detective* (1926), which details some of the cases of one Moris [sic] Klaw, an antique dealer with expert knowledge of a variety of odd and esoteric subjects, including ancient Egypt. In the seventh episode, "Case of the Headless Mummies," somebody has decapitated a mummy belonging to the private collector Pettigrew, and another mummy has been mysteriously decapitated in Sotheby's auction room. While Klaw and the narrator investigate, a third mummy in Klaw's shop is decapitated. The police, embodied by Inspector Grimsby, are clueless, but Klaw has the mummies in the Egyptian Room in the Menzies Museum watched, and the malefactor is captured. The motivation for the decapitations is a search for a rare book of Egyptian ceremonial magic said to be hidden in the skull of a mummy. This information, presented without preamble or rationale, fails to convey any conviction. It should perhaps be mentioned that the second episode in *The Dream-Detective*, "Case of the Potsherd of Anubis," also utilizes an Egyptian background. The episode lacks mummies but introduces the idea that the hieroglyphs on potsherds inscribed with the figure of Anubis are a "sort of secret writing, possibly peculiar to some brother-hood" (Rohmer 1926, 20). The potsherds are held by rival collectors, and Klaw plays an unexpected role in resolving the situation. For all that they are enjoyable, the stories in *The Dream-Detective* are not particularly convincing.

She Who Sleeps (1928) reads like the rough draft of a script for an unconvincing motion picture melodrama. The story begins in New Jersey, when wealthy young Barry Cumberland—son of noted Egyptologist John Cumberland—is out driving. Instead of watching the road, he watches a beautiful young woman in a nearby house and crashes his Rolls Royce. Young Cumberland awakens in the hospital, and after nobody can identify the woman, he is soon en route to Egypt. The reason: the antiquities dealer Danbazzar has shown his father a papyrus that describes how Seti I left behind a witness to his glory, the Princess Zalithea. She has been awak-ened by successive generations of priests and is known as *She Who Sleeps but Will Awaken*, and although 2,000 years have passed since her last waking, Danbazzar having located her tomb, is prepared to awaken her. After some domestic difficul-ties—the Egyptian official Mr. Ahmed Tawwab must receive a number of bribes—Zalithea's tomb is excavated, and Barry is astonished to discover that she is identical to the woman he saw in New Jersey. He is entrusted to teach her English and, naturally, he falls in love with the beautiful, capricious, and occasionally petu-lant young woman. Upon the expedition's return to New York, Zalithea vanishes, leaving Barry heartbroken. Nevertheless, Rohmer's resolution not only allows love to triumph, it also removes the supernatural element on which the story was predi-cated, for what has hitherto seemed to be a story involving suspended animation is shown to be an elaborate plot involving forgeries, hidden entrances, and falsified identities, all done in order that a revenge can be worked on John Cumberland.

The Bat Flies Low (1935) is quasi-science fiction vaguely reminiscent of Talbot Mundy's more theosophical adventures. The story itself begins in America, with young Lincoln Hayes, president of the Western Electric Company, determined to rediscover the mysterious energy source that the Ancient Egyptians used to store sunlight, a "solar lamp." Hayes has his rivals, chief among whom is Simon Lobb, a fellow businessman, and there is also the mysterious Egyptian, Mohammed Ames Bey, a man of enormous mental power. As it is gradually revealed, Bey is in fact the leader of a secret society that knows and retains the Wisdom of the Ancients and recognizes that the modern world is not yet ready for their reintro-duction. This point is driven home when Lobb acquires a stolen solar lamp and attempts to experiment with it, causing an incredible explosion in which he perishes. Hayes has fallen in love with Hatasu, Ahmed Bey's lovely assistant, and will marry her after he is initiated into the secret society. The story itself is enjoyable and fast moving, and while it does not feature mummies, it is said to be based on fact, in which Rohmer claimed "an actual relic had existed, and an American company had employed a research team on the project" (Van Ash and Rohmer 1972, 234).

Egyptian Nights (1944, also known as *Bimbâshi Barûk of Egypt*) consists of 10 linked stories utilizing Mohammed Ibrahîm Brian Barûk, "son of a sheikh of pure lineage by his English wife" (Rohmer 1944, 23). He is physically fearless, impeccably mannered, and fluent in several languages, enabling him to enter and pass without observation through various cultures on various lands. Although several of the *Egyptian Nights* take place in the Middle East, and a portion of "Adventure in the Libyan Desert" involves a "cave of considerable size . . . artificially and roughly squared at some remote time" that is identified as "an ancient rock tomb" (Rohmer 1944, 277) the stories in *Egyptian Nights* do not involve mummies. Rather, they are mixtures of crime and romance; often, Barûk discovers motivations arising from mistakes in identity, and often, too, Barûk finds himself in opposition to the Nazis and their agents.

As the above description of *Egyptian Nights* indicates, Rohmer's fiction often strove for topicality. Thus, while mummies and Egyptology were in vogue, they figured heavily in Rohmer's fiction. As these became better understood and thus less intriguing, exciting, and romantic, mummies and the mysteries of Ancient Egypt gradually vanished from Rohmer's fiction, to be replaced by stories mirroring contemporary world events, tales in which Egypt figured as a political entity, albeit one with a romantic and exotic history. This shift is to be regretted.

The Rohmers had moved to the United States in 1947 and lived in White Plains, New York, but shortly before his death they returned to London, and Rohmer died on June 1, 1959, in London's University College Hospital, survived by his wife. In 1972 she and Cay Van Ash, her husband's former assistant, coauthored *Master of Villainy*, a biography of Sax Rohmer that has since become the standard source of biographical information about him. He was a conscientious craftsman, and even if his fantastic plots rarely withstand a second of scrutiny, the stories he told often remain lively and enjoyable.

Richard Bleiler

See also: The mummy in Western fiction: Beginnings to 1922

Further Reading
Rohmer, Sax. 1918a; 1924. *Brood of the Witch Queen*. London: C. Arthur Pearson; NY: Doubleday, Page.

Rohmer, Sax. 1918b; 1919. *Tales of Secret Egypt*. London: Methuen; New York: Robert McBride.

Rohmer, Sax. 1920. *The Green Eyes of Bâst*. London: Cassell; NY: Robert McBride.

Rohmer, Sax. 1926. *The Dream Detective*. London: Jarrolds Publishers.

Rohmer, Sax. 1928. *She Who Sleeps*. NY: Doubleday, Doran.

Rohmer, Sax. 1935. *The Bat Flies Low*. NY: Crime Club; London: Cassell.

Rohmer, Sax. 1944. *Egyptian Nights*. NY: Robert McBride; as *Bimbâshi Barûk of Egypt*. London: Robert Hale.

Van Ash, Cay, and Elizabeth Sax Rohmer. 1972. *Master of Villainy: A Biography of Sax Rohmer*. Bowling Green, OH: Bowling Green State University Popular Press.

Ward, Arthur S. 1903. "The Mysterious Mummy." *Pearson's Xmas Extra*.

Rosetta Stone

In August 1799 Pierre-François Bouchard, a French soldier in Napoleon's army, was digging a trench in the Egyptian town of el-Rashîd, known to Europeans as Rosetta, when his pick struck a large and roughly rectangular basalt stone, perhaps used to construct a wall built there about 300 years earlier. The stone had inscriptions in three languages and attracted immediate attention. It was cleaned and taken to the Institut National in Cairo, where it impressed Napoleon, who had

The Rosetta Stone, pictured here in the last stages of its conservation in the Egyptian Sculpture Gallery at The British Museum, is a granite slab dating from 196 BCE and bearing an inscription that was the key to the deciphering of Egyptian hieroglyphics. It was found by French troops in 1799 near the town of Rashid (Rosetta) in Lower Egypt. (Daniel Kalker/dpa/Corbis)

copies of the inscriptions made and distributed among scholars of languages. After the British defeated Napoleon in 1801, the antiquities collected by the French were surrendered, and the Rosetta Stone, as it was then known, was sent to England in 1802. It was put on display in the British Museum, where it remains, and where it is one of the most popular attractions, along with the museum's world-renowned collection of Egyptian mummies and artifacts.

Napoleon's efforts ensured that translations of the texts on the Rosetta Stone had already started when the stone arrived in England. The bottommost of the languages was immediately recognized as Greek, and the writing of the middle text was Demotic Egyptian. The topmost language, however, was hieroglyphics whose meaning had been lost. In 1814 the English scientist Thomas Young (1773–1829) recognized that the Egyptian writing contained both alphabetic and non-alphabetic symbols, and in 1822 the French scholar and philologist Jean François Champollion (1790–1832) announced that he had translated the inscriptions on the topmost section of the stone: he had recognized that the Demotic text included words and names that could be found in the third section, which consisted of Egyptian hieroglyphics. The Rosetta Stone was thus dated to 196 BCE, during the reign of King Ptolemy V. Its text consisted of decrees legitimizing the cult of the new ruler; it described the roles of the priests in his service, and described also the actions Ptolemy undertook to protect Egypt from rebels, punish the rebels, collect taxes, and continue the worship of the gods.

Champollion's accomplishment effectively established Egyptology as a legitimate and viable field of study. Of course Egypt was known and visited prior to this, but the hieroglyphs had not been translated, although, as Budge states, "much was written and said about them by the faddists and cranks, who were usually wholly uneducated men, and whose one idea was to prove the Egyptian inscriptions were extracts from the Bible" (Budge 1929, 198). One thus has such writers as Robert Clayton, who stated in 1753 that, "as to Sir Isaac Newton's observation of the introduction of the worship of brutes from hieroglyphics, I cannot but agree with him that the hieroglyphical method of sculpture seems to have been practiced in the lower *Egypt* before the days of Moses; and that from thence came the worship of their Gods in the various shapes of birds and beasts, and fishes, forbidden in the second commandment" (Clayton 1753, 100–101).

Or, if the hieroglyphics were not seen in biblical terms, they were patronizingly dismissed as essentially trivial, as in *The Antiquities of Egypt*, a 1753 travel guide, which stated "Every one knows that Pyramids, Obelisks, Pillars, Statues, in a word, all the publick Monuments of the *Egyptians*, were usually adorned with Hieroglyphicks; that is, symbolical Writings, either express'd in Characters unknown to the Vulgar, (and called, perhaps for this Reason, sacred Letters) or represented under the Figures of Animals, under which an hidden and parabolical Meaning was couch'd" (*Concise History* 1753, XXX).

Following Champollion's accomplishment, Egyptian history could no longer be dismissed, and it became recognized, if romanticized. Egypt was no longer merely a curiosity, a source of antiquities and mummies to be shipped elsewhere for display purposes. Rather, Egypt was a significant culture in its own right, and if to the European eyes contemporary Egypt was predominantly sand and ruins and picturesque natives, the recognition of Egypt's monumental history and the historical significance of its tombs assumed a greater importance in European narratives. In the prologue to Theophile Gautier's *The Romance of a Mummy* (*Le Roman de la momie*, 1857), one of the character dreams of opening "a tomb which neither the Shepherd Kings nor the Medes of Cambyses nor the Greeks nor the Romans nor the Arabs have explored, and which will give up its riches intact . . . and on which you will print a most learned dissertation which will give you a place by the side of Champollion, Rosellini, Wilkinson, Lepsius, and Belzoni" (Gautier 1909, 9–10).

Since the early nineteenth century, "Rosetta Stone" has been used in fiction and nonfiction as a term understood to mean a key that allows the interpretation of something else. It is presently also known as the name for a popular language-learning system, and it seems likely that Ptolemy's decree will remain the best-known term connected to the rise of Egyptiana, even if the users of the term fail to recognize its origins.

Richard Bleiler

See also: Egyptian collection, the British Museum; Napoleon and the birth of Egyptology

Further Reading

The British Museum. n.d. "The Rosetta Stone." Accessed December 16, 2013. http://www.britishmuseum.org/explore/highlights/highlight_objects/aes/t/the_rosetta_stone.aspx.

Budge, E. A. Wallis. 1929. *The Rosetta Stone in the British Museum. The Greek, Demotic and Hieroglyphic Texts of the Decree Inscribed on the Rosetta Stone Conferring Additional Honours on Ptolemy V Epiphanes (203–181 B.C.) with English Translations and a Short History of the Decipherment of the Egyptian Hieroglyphs and as an Appendix containing Translations of the Stelae of Şân (Tanis) and Tall Al-Maskhûţah*. London: The Religious Tract Society.

Caygill, Marjorie. 1999. *The British Museum: A-Z Companion*. Chicago: Fitzroy Dearborn.

Clayton, Robert. 1753. *A Journal from Grand Cairo to Mount Sinai, and Back Again. Translated from a Manuscript, written by the Prefetto of Egypt, in Company with some Missionaries de Propaganda Side at Grand Cairo*. London: Printed for William Bowyer, and sold by J. Ward Against the Royal Exchange.

A Concise History of the Antiquities of Egypt. Containing an Account of the Antient Egyptians, the Grandeur of Their Publick Buildings, Obelisks, Pyramids. 1753. London: Printed for M. Cooper, Pater-Noster Row.

Gautier, Theophile. 1909. *The Romance of a Mummy*. In *The Complete Works of Theophile Gautier*, volume III, translated and edited by Professor F. C. DeSumichrast. London and New York: Postlethwaite, Taylor and Knowles.

Royal mummies of Egypt, Part One: Third to Eighteenth Dynasties

A significant number of the mummies of the kings of ancient Egypt—or parts thereof—have survived to the present day, archaeologically excavated either from their own tombs or from secondary tombs whence they were moved in ancient times after robbery.

Royal tombs are known from the very beginning of Egyptian history, but almost all were robbed in antiquity. Human remains were particularly vulnerable, and until the beginning of the New Kingdom (the period between the sixteenth and eleventh centuries BCE) surviving remains are fragmentary at best. However, New Kingdom royal mummies were luckier than their earlier fellows in that later generations rescued them from the wrecks of their tombs and hid them in locations that survived intact until modern times, while two mummies escaped robbers altogether. Thus, we can trace the development of embalming techniques used during this time, with the interesting observation that a significant degree of innovation was employed during the last decades of the 18th Dynasty, possibly involving a short-lived use of liquid, rather than solid, natron, and subcutaneous packing (i.e., adding material beneath the skin) in the case of one body.

Those royal Egyptian mummies with a secure or probable identification are listed below in chronological order, along with any bibliographic reference(s) plus

ca. 2700 BCE	The Old Kingdom period of ancient Egypt commences with the Third Dynasty. The Pyramid Texts are the main funerary texts. Innovations in mummification include evisceration and wrapping bodies in plaster-soaked linen. The burial of Queen Hetepheres displays the earliest known use of canopic jars for storing the internal organs.
ca. 2200 BCE	The First Intermediate Period of ancient Egypt commences with the collapse of the Old Kingdom. The Coffin Texts begin to replace the Pyramid Texts.
ca. 2100 BCE	The Middle Kingdom period of ancient Egypt commences with the establishment of the 11th Dynasty. In popular religion Osiris becomes the most important deity as belief in the immortality of becoming like Osiris after death expands from royalty to the common people. The Coffin Texts are firmly established as the main funerary texts. Innovations in mummification include the widespread use of natron to dry out the body; the use of various oils, perfumes, resins; and the introduction of the cartonnage face mask.
ca. 1700 BCE	The Second Intermediate Period of ancient Egypt commences when the 13th Dynasty collapses and Egypt come under rule by the foreign Hyksos. The Book of the Dead begins to take shape and to be used in mummification rituals.

their current location and any registration number in parentheses. For information on the origin of the tomb-numbering system, see the article "Valley of the Kings." The current locations for these mummies are abbreviated as follows:

AS = Supreme Council of Antiquities store-room at Abusir
BM = British Museum
CM = Egyptian Museum, Cairo
CQ = Qasr el-Aini Medical School, Cairo
LMus = Luxor Museum
Qur = Supreme Council of Antiquities store-room at Qurna
Saq = Imhotep Museum, Saqqara
UCL = University College London.

Note that the suggestions for Further Reading at the end of this article are of a more intensely scholarly/technical nature than what accompanies many other entries in this encyclopedia, so to account for all of the references cited in the mummy descriptions below.

Also note that this article is paired with "The royal mummies of Egypt, Part 2: Nineteenth to Twenty-fifth dynasties," which continues the list begun here.

Djoser? (first king of Third Dynasty). Probably represented by a number of pieces of a mummified body, most notably the left foot, were found in the burial chamber of Djoser's Step Pyramid at Saqqara during the 1930s. The mummification technique appears typical of the Old Kingdom, although radiocarbon determinations are much later, suggesting modern contamination. (Derry 1935; CQ)

Seneferu (first king of Fourth Dynasty). Various parts of a mummy, including pieces of the skull, were found inside Seneferu's Red Pyramid at Dahshur in 1950. From their context, they seem likely to be those of the king. (Batrawi 1951; CQ)

Menkaure? (sixth king of the Fourth Dynasty). The lower part of a desiccated human body, together with a foot and some ribs and vertebrae, were found in the Third Pyramid, built by Menkaure, at Giza in 1837, in conjunction with a coffin-lid made for a reburial of the king some 2,000 years after his death. Although their archaeological context is consistent with an ancient date, radiocarbon dating seems to date the remains to the early centuries CE. (BM EA18212)

Neferefre (fifth king of the Fifth Dynasty). Fragments of the king's mummy were found in the burial chamber of his pyramid at Abusir in 1997–1998, including part of the skull, the left shoulder, and the left hand. (Strouhal 2006; AS)

Isesi (penultimate king of the Fifth Dynasty). In 1947, most of the left-hand side of a mummy was found amid the broken remains of the sarcophagus in Isesi's pyramid at Saqqara. (Strouhal and Gaballah 1993; CQ)

Unas (last king of the Fifth Dynasty). When Unas's pyramid at Saqqara was first entered in 1880, a left arm and hand, together with pieces of a skull, well-preserved and covered with skin and hair, were found. (CM)

Teti (first king of the Sixth Dynasty). When excavated in 1880, the burial chamber of Teti's pyramid at Saqqara held a shoulder and arm that had survived, more poorly embalmed than the remains of Isesi and Unas. (CM)

Pepy I (third king of the Sixth Dynasty). When entered in 1880, the Saqqara pyramid of Pepy I contained only a single hand, together with one of the four bundles holding the king's embalmed viscera. (CM)

Nemtyemsaf (Merenre) I? (fourth king of the Sixth Dynasty). A mummy was found in Nemtyemsaf I's pyramid at Saqqara-South in 1880, but its style mummification is not consistent with Old Kingdom norms; it may be a later instrusive burial. (Ridley 1983; Mende 2008; Saq [ex-CM TR2/12/25/1])

Mentuhotep II (fourth king of the 11th Dynasty). Some pieces of the skull, half the lower jaw, and some other bones of the mummy were found in the burial chamber of Mentuhotep II's temple-tomb at Deir el-Bahari in 1909. (BM EA49457)

Senwosret II (fourth king of the 12th Dynasty). Leg bones were recovered from Senwosret II's pyramid at Lahun in 1924. (UCL)

Hor (king of the 13th Dynasty). The king's body, reduced to a skeleton and damaged by robbers, but with the brain still in place, was found in his tomb at Dahshur in 1894. (De Morgan 1895: 98; CM)

Taa (Seqenenre) (penultimate king of the 17th Dynasty). The mummy was one of a large number of bodies reburied in tomb number TT320 near Deir el-Bahari early in the 22nd Dynasty and found in 1871. In this case, the king had originally been interred at Dra Abu'l-Naga. Unwrapped on June 9, 1886, the body is poorly preserved and the head covered with horrific combat-wounds. (Smith 1912: 1–6; Bietak and Strouhal 1974; CM JE26209=CG61051)

Ahmose I (first king of the 18th Dynasty). Found in TT320, and unwrapped in the 1880s, the mummy has the unusual feature of having had the brain removed through the foramen magnum (a large opening in the base of the skull) after the removal of atlas vertebra, instead of the more usual nasal route; the mummy was transferred from Cairo to the Luxor Museum in 2004. (Smith 1912: 15–18; LMus, ex-CM JE26210=CG61056)

Amenhotep I (second king of the 18th Dynasty). Found in TT320, the mummy has never been unwrapped, and still bears a cartonnage mask and floral garlands. X-rays show that it was the earliest royal mummy of the New

Kingdom to have its arms crossed at the breast. (Smith 1912: 18; Derry 1934; Harris and Weeks 1973: 30; CM JE26211=CG61058)

Thutmose II (fourth king of the 18th Dynasty). Found in TT320, and unwrapped on July 1, 1886, this mummy has skin that is covered by scabrous patches, and its arms are crossed over the chest. (Smith 1912: 28–31; JE26212=CG61066)

Thutmose III (fifth king of the 18th Dynasty). Found in TT320, originally buried in Valley of the Kings tomb KV34, and unwrapped in 1881 and 1886, the mummy was badly damaged by robbers, with the head and limbs all separated from the torso. (Smith 1912: 32–36; CM JE26213=CG 61068)

Hatshepsut? (female coruler of Thutmose III). This mummy was found in Valley of the Kings KV60, with fragments of a coffin bearing the titles of a royal nurse. It has been proposed as that of Hatshepsut on the basis of the apparent match of a tooth found in a box bearing the female king's name to roots in-situ (still in their original place) in the jaw of the mummy as revealed by CT scanning. However, there remain doubts as to the validity of the match and consequent conclusions. (Bickerstaffe 2009: 92–96; Graefe 2011; Forbes 2012; Düker 2012; CM)

Amenhotep II (sixth king of the 18th Dynasty). This mummy was found in the king's own tomb, Valley of the Kings KV35, in 1898, where the mummy had been restored after robbery during the 20th or 21st Dynasty. The mummy shows eruptions on its skin, perhaps as a result of the embalming process. It was originally left in the tomb, but its wrappings were ripped open during a robbery in 1901, with partial unwrapping occurring in 1902; the mummy was finally removed to Cairo in 1932. (Smith 1912: 36–38; CM CG61073)

Thutmose IV (seventh king of the 18th Dynasty). This mummy was found in KV35, which was used for the reburial of a number of robbed royal mummies during the 21st Dynasty; it was originally buried in Valley of the Kings tomb KV43. When it was unwrapped on March 2, 1903, its feet were found to have been broken off by robbers. (Smith 1912: 42–46; CM JE34559=CG 61073)

Amenhotep III (eighth king of the 18th Dynasty). This mummy was found in KV35 and originally buried in Valley of the Kings tomb WV22; it had been rewrapped under Panedjem I of the 21st Dynasty and was unwrapped on September 23, 1905. The mummy was very badly damaged, with most of the flesh of the head missing and the head and limbs separated from the torso. The method of mummification is unique, with resin and pieces of linen inserted under the skin and moulded into a lifelike shape. (Smith 1912: 46–51; CM JE34560=CG 61074)

Akhenaten or **Smenkhkare** (ninth/tenth king of the 18th Dynasty). This body, reduced to a skeleton by damp conditions in the tomb, was found in tomb

KV55 in 1907. There has been debate over his age at death, the majority view being in his 20s (in which case Smenkhkare), but a few examinations have proposed the 40s (in which case Akhenaten). DNA analysis suggests that the owner was the father or paternal uncle of Tutankhamun. (Smith 1912: 51–56; Harrison 1966; Filer 2002; Hawass et al. 2010; Dodson 2014: App. 3; CM CG61075)

Tutankhamun (12th king of the 18th Dynasty). The mummy of Tutankhamun was found intact in his own tomb (KV62) in 1922, but damaged by the decomposition of the sacred oils that were poured over it; it was unwrapped in 1925. There are a number of unusual features, including the apparent removal of the front of the rib-cage by the embalmers; reports of a head-injury have been disproved by CT scans. (Leek 1972; Hawass et al. 2007; in KV62)

Horemheb? (last king of the 18th Dynasty). Various skeletal remains were found in the king's tomb KV57 in 1908, some of which may have belonged to the king. (In KV57)

Aidan Dodson

See also: Egyptian mummies; Egyptian mummification methods; Napoleon and the birth of Egyptology; Royal mummies of Egypt, Part Two: Nineteenth to Twenty-fifth Dynasties; Tutankhamun ("King Tut"); Valley of the Kings

Further Reading

Batrawi, A. 1951. "The Skeleton Remains from the Northern Pyramid of Sneferu." *Annales du Service des Antiquités d'Égypte* 51: 435–40.

Bickerstaff, D. 2009. *Refugees for Eternity: The Royal Mummies of Thebes, IV: Identifying the Royal Mummies.* Loughborough: Canopus Press.

Bietak, M., and E. Strouhal. 1974. "Die Todesumstände des Pharaohs Seqenenre." *Annalen des Naturhistorisches Museums in Wien* 78: 29–52.

Bucaille, Maurice. 1990. *Mummies of the Pharaohs: Modern Medical Investigations.* New York: St. Martin's Press.

De Morgan, J. 1895. *Fouilles à Dahchour*, I. Vienna: Holzhausen.

Derry, D. E. 1934. "An X-ray Examination of the Mummy of King Amenophis I." *Annales du Service des Antiquités d'Égypte* 34: 47–8.

Derry, D. E. 1935. "Report on the Human Remains from the Granite Sarcophagus Chamber in the Pyramid of Zoser." *ASAE* 35: 28–30.

Düker, J. 2012. "Stellungnahme zur Problematik 'Zahn der Mumie Königin Hetschepsut': Molar Oberkiefer oder Unterkiefer?" *Göttinger Miszellen* 232: 135–36.

Filer, J. 2002. "Anatomy of a Mummy." *Archaeology* 55/2: 26–29.

Forbes, D. C. 2012. "The Re-Search for Hatshepsut's Mummy: Or Royal Mummies Musical Chairs Yet Again." *Kmt* 23/1: 65–73.

Graefe, E. 2011. "Der angebliche Zahn der angeblich krebskranken Diabetikerin Königin Hatschepsut, oder die Mumie der Hatschepsut bleibt unbekannt." *Göttinger Miszellen* 231: 41–43.

Harris, J. E., and K. R. Weeks. 1973. *X-Raying the Pharaohs.* London: Macdonald.

Harrison, R. G. 1966. "An Anatomical Examination of the Pharaonic Remains Purported to be Akhenaten." *Journal of Egyptian Archaeology* 52: 95–119.

Hawass, Z., Y. Z. Gad, S. Ismail, R. Khairat, D. Fathalla, N. Hasan, A. Ahmed, H. Elleithy, M. Ball, F. Gaballah, S. Wasef, M. Fateen, H. Amer, P. Gostner, A. Selim, A. Zink, and C. M. Pusch, 2010. "Ancestry and Pathology in King Tutankhamun's Family." *Journal of the American Medical Association* 303/7: 638–47.

Hawass, Z., M. Shafik, F. J. Rühli, A. Selim, E. El-Sheikh, S. Abdel Fatah, H. Amer, F. Gaballa, A. Gamal Eldin, E. Egarter-Vigl, and P. Gostner 2007. "Computed Tomographic Evaluation of Pharaoh Tutankhamun, ca. 1300 BC." *Annales du Service des Antiquités d'Égypte* 81: 159–74.

Hawass, Z., S. Ismail, A. Selim, S. N. Saleem, D. Fathalla, S. Wasef, A. Z. Gad, R. Saad, S. Fares, H. Amer, P. Gostner, Y. Z. Gad, C. M. Pusch, and A. R. Zink. 2012. "Revisiting the harem conspiracy and death of Ramesses III: anthropological, forensic, radiological, and genetic study." *British Medical Journal* 345/7888.

Leek, F. F. 1972. *The Human Remains from the Tomb of Tutʿankhamūn*. Oxford: Griffith Institute.

Mende, C. 2008. "Zum Mumienfund in der Pyramide Merenres I." *Sokar* 17: 40–43.

Ridley, R. T. 1983. "The Discovery of the Pyramid Texts." *Zeitschrift für ägyptische Sprache und Altertumskunde* 110: 74–80.

Smith, G. E. (1912) 2000. *The Royal Mummies*. Cairo: Institut français d'archéologie orientale. Reprint, London: Duckworth.

Strouhal, E. 2006. "Identification of King Raneferef According to Human Remains Found in the Burial Chamber of the Unfinished Pyramid." In *Abusir IX. The pyramid complex of Raneferef: the archaeology*, edited by M. Verner, 513–18. Prague: Czech Institute of Egyptology, Charles University.

Strouhal, E. and M. F. Gaballah 1993. "King Djedkare Isesi and his Daughters." In *Biological Anthropology and the Study of Ancient Egypt*, edited by W.V. Davies and R. Walker, 104–118. London: British Museum Press.

Royal mummies of Egypt, Part Two: Nineteenth to Twenty-fifth Dynasties

This article continues from "Royal mummies of Egypt, Part One: Third to Eighteenth Dynasties." As described there, a significant number of the mummies of the kings of ancient Egypt—or parts thereof—have survived to the present day, archaeologically excavated either from their own tombs or from secondary tombs whence they were moved in ancient times after robbery.

The royal mummies of the latter part of the New Kingdom (spanning the sixteenth through the eleventh centuries BCE), which are the subject of this article, initially revert to techniques in vogue during the middle of the 18th Dynasty, but they also show evidence that, over time, attempts were made to give the corpse a more lifelike appearance, first by applying pigment to the shriveled features, and then by providing packing in the body cavity and mechanisms for making the

ca. 1500 BCE	The New Kingdom period of ancient Egypt commences with the 18th Dynasty. Major royal figures of the period are all buried at the Valley of the Kings. The *Book of the Dead* is the primary funerary text, and is the first such text to be written on papyrus. Innovations in mummification include stuffing the body with various materials to give it a more life-like appearance.
ca. 1100 BCE	The Third Intermediate Period of ancient Egypt commences with the death of Pharaoh Rameses XI. Innovations in mummification include attempts to create a lifelike appearance using wigs, fake eyes, stuffing, and paint, as well as separate mummification of internal organs.
332 BCE	The Greco-Roman period of ancient Egypt begins when Alexander the Great invades and is accepted as the country's new ruler. Mummification continues to be practiced and is embraced by Greek settlers, but the quality of preservation begins to decline.
392 CE	The Roman emperor Theodosius I bans mummification, thus ending Egypt's 3,000-year history of embalming.

eye-sockets less sunken. The last 20th Dynasty royal mummies show the return of internal organs to the body, but subsequent developments are hidden by the absolute decay of the soft tissues of intact bodies from the Third Intermediate Period (ca. 1070–664 BCE) and the fragmentary state of the remainder.

As in Part One of this catalog of royal Egyptian mummies, those mummies with a secure or probable identification are listed below in chronological order, along with any bibliographic reference(s), plus their current location, and any registration number, in parentheses. For information on the origin of the tomb-numbering system, see the article "Valley of the Kings."

The current locations for these mummies are abbreviated as follows:

AS = Supreme Council of Antiquities store-room at Abusir
BM = British Museum
CM = Egyptian Museum, Cairo
CQ = Qasr el-Aini Medical School, Cairo
LMus = Luxor Museum
Qur = Supreme Council of Antiquities store-room at Qurna
Saq = Imhotep Museum, Saqqara
UCL = University College London.

Again, the suggestions for Further Reading at the end of this article are of a more intensely scholarly/technical nature than what accompanies many other entries in this encyclopedia to account for all of the references cited in the mummy descriptions below.

Rameses I? (first king of the 19th Dynasty). The king's coffin was found in tomb TT320, but no mummy has been identified from among those found there. A mummy acquired in the 1860s for the Niagara Falls Museum has been proposed as his and was transferred to the Luxor Museum in 2004; however, the identification is by no means secure. (Bickerstaff 2006; LMus)

Sethy I (second king of the 19th Dynasty). Found in tomb TT320 and originally buried in KV17, this mummy was unwrapped on June 9, 1886. Although separated from the body by plunderers, the head of the mummy is very well preserved; the body itself, however, is badly battered. The arms were crossed over his chest, with the hands fully open for the first time. (Smith 1912: 57–59; CM JE26213=CG61077)

Rameses II (third king of the 18th Dynasty). This mummy was found in TT320 and originally buried in KV7; it was unwrapped on June 1, 1886. Very well preserved, the mummy is that of a very old man, with poor teeth, severe arthritis, and arteriosclerosis (hardening of the arteries). It was taken to Paris in 1976 for study and conservation. (Smith 1912: 59–65; Balout and Roubet 1985; CM JE26214=CG61078)

Merenptah (fourth king of the 19th Dynasty). Found in KV35 and originally buried in KV8, this mummy was unwrapped on July 8, 1907. The face had been painted as part of the embalming process. The king suffered severely from dental problems and had severe arthritis and arteriosclerosis. (Smith 1912: 65–70; CM JE34562=CG61079)

Sethy II (fifth king of the 19th Dynasty). This mummy was found in KV35 and originally buried in KV15. It was unwrapped on September 3, 1905. Although labeled by restorers as that of the king, the mummy's identity has been questioned through its lack of resemblance to those of Sethy II's immediate ancestors. (Smith 1912: 73–81; CM JE34561=CG61081)

Siptah (seventh king of the 19th Dynasty). Found in KV35 and originally buried in KV47, this mummy was unwrapped on August 29, 1905. The mummy is unusual in that the abdominal cavity was filled with dried lichen; like Merenptah's (see above), the face was painted. The left leg is deformed: this is most probably the result of cerebral palsy. The mummy was badly damaged by plunderers, the right cheek and front teeth being smashed and the ears and the right arm broken off. (Smith 1912: 70–73; CM JE34563=CG61080)

Rameses III (second king of the 20th Dynasty). This mummy was found in TT320 and originally buried in KV11; the head was unwrapped on June 1, 1886. It was found well wrapped by restorers in antiquity, the linen carapace over the body still being in place. A CT scan has shown that Rameses III died from a slashed throat that cut back to the spine. The king is known to have been the object of a conspiracy. (Smith 1912: 84–87; Hawass et al. 2012; CM JE26208a=CG61083)

Rameses IV (third king of the 20th Dynasty). Found in KV35 and originally buried in KV2, this mummy was unwrapped on June 25, 1905, having been clumsily rewrapped by its ancient restorers. The king's own eyes had been replaced by artificial ones made of small onions during the embalming process. (Smith 1912: 87–90; CM JE34597=CG61084)

Rameses V (fourth king of the 20th Dynasty). This mummy was found in KV35, but its original place of burial is uncertain, since Rameses V's own tomb was appropriated by his successor. It was unwrapped on June 25, 1905. The skin of the well-preserved mummy is covered with raised nodules, sometimes identified as smallpox. Its thoracic cavity was stuffed with sawdust and portions of internal organs, the first example of the replacement of the viscera within the body. The face was painted red. (Smith 1912: 90–92; CM JE34566=CG 61085)

Rameses VI (fifth king of the 20th Dynasty). Found in KV35 and originally buried in KV9, this mummy was unwrapped on June 8, 1905. The body was torn to pieces by robbers, only the legs being basically intact, the hips being found where the neck ought to have been, the torso smashed, the arms hacked from the body, and the right arm lost. The head had been broken from the body, its facial skeleton proving to be totally missing, the face consisting of no more than a flap of skin above the still-intact lower jaw. Two other mummies' hands were found among the wrappings. (Smith 1912: 92–94; CM JE34564= CG61086)

Rameses IX (eighth king of the 20th Dynasty). Found in TT320 and originally buried in KV6, this mummy was partly unwrapped in 1886. The body had suffered considerable damage, its nose being missing and much of the skin badly cracked. (Forbes 1998: 646–47; CM)

Panedjem I (king of Thebes during 21st Dynasty). This mummy was found in TT320, but its original burial place is unknown; it was unwrapped on June 27, 1886. The body was not damaged by robbers. (Forbes 1998: 650–51; CM)

Pasebkhanut (Psusennes) I (third king of the 21st Dynasty). The mummy of Pasebkhanut was found intact in his tomb NRT-III at Tanis in 1940. The wrappings and flesh were totally destroyed by the damp conditions that existed within the tomb, the surviving bones being those of a very old man, who had suffered from severe dental problems and also afflicted by severe arthritis of the back. (Derry 1940/41; CQ)

Amenemopet (fourth king of the 21st Dynasty). This mummy was found intact in tomb NRT-III at Tanis in 1940. Damp had destroyed the mummy's flesh and wrappings, many of the bones having broken. The king had been a big, strongly built, man, old at death, but with sound dentition (teeth). (Derry 1942; CQ)

Siamun (sixth king of the 21st Dynasty). This mummy was found intact in tomb NRT-III at Tanis in 1939, but it was almost entirely destroyed by damp. It was identified on the basis of shabti figures found nearby—that is, the miniature figurines that were placed in tombs as part of the ancient Egyptian burial ritual, and that were meant to serve as a substitute to perform manual labor in place of the deceased individual in the afterlife.

Pasebkhanut (Psusennes) II (seventh king of the 21st Dynasty). As with Siamun above, this mummy was found intact in tomb NRT-III at Tanis in 1939, but it was almost entirely destroyed by damp. It, too, was identified on the basis of shabti figures found nearby.

Shoshenq Imia (unplaced king during the early 22nd Dynasty). This mummy was found in NRT-III in 1939, having previously been buried elsewhere and damaged by water, which had destroyed the wrappings and flesh. The king's death had been caused by an injury to the forehead, which had led to an infection that spread under the scalp and through the bone to the brain. (Derry 1939; CQ)

Harsiese (king of Thebes during the mid-22nd Dynasty). The mummy of Harsiese was found in his tomb (number 1) at Medinet Habu temple. Only a skull and a piece of arm-bone survived when the tomb was discovered in 1928; the skull contains a hole, apparently made through a surgical procedure that the king survived, to judge from the healing shown by the wound. (Hölscher 1954: 10; CQ)

Shabataka (fourth king of the 25th Dynasty). A skull and a few bones, probably belonging to the king, were found in the burial chamber of his pyramid, Ku18 at El-Kurru in the Sudan, in 1916. (Dunham 1950: 67, 118).

Aidan Dodson

See also: Egyptian mummies; Egyptian mummification methods; Napoleon and the birth of Egyptology; Royal mummies of Egypt, Part One: Third to Eighteenth Dynasties; Valley of the Kings

Further Reading

Balout, Lionel, and C. Roubet, eds. 1985. *La Momie de Ramsès: Contribution Scientifique à l'Egyptologie*. Paris: Editions Recherche sur les Civilisations.

Bickerstaff, D. 2006. "Examining the Mystery of the Niagara Falls Mummy: Was He from the Royal Mummies Cache? And Is He Rameses I?" *KMT: A Modern Journal of Ancient Egypt* 17/4: 26–34.

Bucaille, Maurice. 1990. *Mummies of the Pharaohs: Modern Medical Investigations*. New York: St. Martin's Press.

Derry, D. E. 1939. "Note on the Remains of Shashanq." *Annales du Service des Antiquités d'Égypte* 39: 549–51.

Derry, D. E. 1940/41. "An examination of the Bones of King Psusennes I." *Annales du Service des Antiquités d'Égypte* 40: 969–70.

Derry, D. E. 1942. "Report on the Skeleton of King Amenemopet." *Annales du Service des Antiquités d'Égypte* 41: 149.

Dunham, D. 1950. *The Royal Cemeteries of Kush: El Kurru*. Cambridge, MA: Harvard University Press.

Forbes, D. C. 1998. *Tombs, Treasures, Mummies: Seven Great Discoveries of Egyptian Archaeology*. Sevastopol and Santa Fe: KMT Communications.

Harris, J. E. and K. R. Weeks. 1973. *X-Raying the Pharaohs*. London: Macdonald.

Hölscher, U. 1954. *The Excavation of Medinet Habu*, V: *The Post-Ramessid Remains*. Chicago: Chicago University Press.

Smith, G.E. (1912) 2000. *The Royal Mummies*. Cairo: Institut français d'archéologie orientale. Reprint, London: Duckworth.

Ruffer, M. A.

Sir Marc Ruffer was a naturalized-British pathologist who was Professor of Bacteriology at Cairo Medical School from the 1890s to his death. He made important advances in the histological study of mummified tissue, including the identification of various diseases in ancient populations.

Marc Armand Ruffer was born at Lyons, France, on August 29, 1859, the son of the Swiss Baron Alphonse Jacques de Ruffer, a banker, and his German wife Caroline. After schooling in France and Germany, he studied at Brasenose College, Oxford, between 1878 and 1881 and then read medicine at University College London. He also studied for a short time at the Pasteur Institute in Paris, under Louis Pasteur himself. Naturalized in 1890, Ruffer became, in 1891, the first Director of the British Institute of Preventive Medicine (now the Lister Institute). While researching diphtheria, he contracted the disease himself, the results leading him to resign his post and convalesce in Egypt. Making his home at Ramleh, Alexandria, he was later appointed Professor of Bacteriology at Cairo, and has been credited with eliminating cholera from Egypt.

Like his Anatomical colleague at Cairo Medical School, Grafton Elliot Smith, he developed an interest in ancient human remains, and he produced a series of papers from 1909 onward, with some not published until after his death. The earliest group included work on the softening and rehydration of mummy tissues for microtome sectioning (i.e., being cut into very thin slices for study), and also on the discovery of the eggs of *Schistosoma haematobium bilharzia* in the kidneys of two mummies, extending the history of schistosomiasis (a disease caused by parasitic infection) back over 3,000 years. Similarly important was the identification of arterial lesions in mummies of the New Kingdom and later. With Smith,

Ruffer produced a paper identifying Pott's disease in a 21st Dynasty mummy, thus showing that tuberculosis was present at that time. A later group of papers included studies of bone-lesions, arthritis, and spondylitis (inflammation of the vertebrae), and on ancient Egyptian teeth, showing that arthritic changes were frequent and dental disease was abundant.

A set of papers were also produced on the effects of consanguineous marriage (marriage among close relatives) in the royal families of the New Kingdom and Ptolemaic Period, although marred by identifying as royal sister-wives ladies who have subsequently been shown to have been commoners. Ruffer's last paper reviewed the literature concerning prehistoric trephining (surgical perforation) of skulls, but he died before completing his work on the topic.

Appointed head of the Red Cross in Egypt in 1914, and knighted in 1916, he was sent in December of that year to Salonika to reorganize the Sanitary Service of the Greek Provisional Government. He was returning to Egypt on board the troopship HMT *Arcadian* when she was torpedoed by the German submarine UC74 on April 15, 1917, not long after *Arcadian* sailed from Greece. The ship capsized and sank within six minutes, and Ruffer was not among the 1,058 survivors out of a total aboard of 1,335.

Aidan Dodson

See also: Smith, Grafton Elliot

Further Reading

Sandison, A.T. 1967. "Sir Marc Armand Ruffer (1859–1917): Pioneer of Palaeopathology." *Medical History* 11/2: 150–56. Accessed December 17, 2013. http://journals.cambridge.org/action/displayAbstract?fromPage=online&aid=8613690.

S

Seth

The god Seth, or Set, was an important deity in ancient Egypt. Generally depicted either as a man with a dog-like head or a creature resembling a dog, Seth was associated with the desert, chaos, storms, and the color red. Seth's association with the desert also linked him to death and mummification, since tombs were typically located toward or in the desert.

Although it is uncertain exactly which type of animal Seth was supposed to represent, he seems to have been associated with some type of canid (that is, a jackal or wild dog) with tall, flat-topped ears. The other important canid deities of ancient Egypt, Anubis and Wepwaut, were more closely associated with the process of mummification, but all the canid deities had links to death and mummification. Seth's domain was the desert, particularly in southern Egypt, and this terrain, located primarily west of the Nile River, was believed to be the domain of the dead. Seth's association with the desert (often called the "Red Land" to contrast with the cultivable "Black Land" along the banks of the Nile) also made him a threat to cultivation and fertility.

Left to right: the ancient Egyptian deities Anubis, Seth, Horus, and Hathor. (siloto/iStockphoto.com)

According to Egyptian mythology, Seth was the cause of the first instance of mummification. Seth's brother, Osiris, was the ruler of Egypt during the primeval time, and he reigned with justice and wisdom. Seth was jealous of his brother, however, and so he tricked Osiris into crawling into a beautifully decorated wooden chest. When Osiris was inside the chest, Seth nailed it shut, chopped it (and Osiris) into small pieces, and flung the pieces throughout Egypt. Osiris's wife, Isis, gathered the pieces and magically put them back together again, creating the very first Egyptian mummy. Osiris became ruler of the underworld, and was depicted as a man wrapped as a mummy.

Osiris's son, Horus, grew up in hiding while his uncle Seth ruled, and when Horus was an adult he challenged Seth for the throne of Egypt. Horus and Seth fought a seemingly endless set of contests, involving much trickery, deceit, and magic, until ultimately Horus was deemed the winner and rightful king by the rest of the Egyptian gods. Seth, however, remained an important deity, and many of the kings named Rameses claimed Seth as their patron. Several pharaohs even incorporated the name of Seth into their own names, effectively tying themselves to this volatile but powerful god.

The imagery of Horus defeating Seth became an integral part of Egyptian royal iconography. Horus's defeat of Seth was used to symbolize the triumph of order over chaos, an important theme throughout Egyptian history. Pharaohs frequently had themselves depicted spearing a hippopotamus (associated with Seth) as a way to reenact and reinforce their victory over the forces of disorder.

Along with his links to chaos and disorder, Seth was also linked at various times to disease, illness, invasion by foreign forces, rebellion and turmoil. Slightly less negative was his association with cunning and with various metals, particularly iron. He was also the god of storms, bad weather, and the tempestuous sea.

Seth was associated with many qualities that seem negative: chaos, anger, violence, evil, and storms. Yet to compare Seth to the Judeo-Christian idea of a devil or Satan is to oversimplify this important deity. The Egyptians viewed Seth as a necessary balance to order and peace, since without darkness, there can be no light, and without chaos, order has no meaning. Seth could also use his propensity for violence and anger to do good. The sun god Ra, for instance, was believed to travel each night on a boat through the underworld, and it was Seth who guarded him and protected him from the many dangers, such as the serpent Apophis, that encountered in the underworld, so that the sun might rise anew every morning. The strength of Seth was such that many pharaohs invoked his name when fighting enemies or performing great feats. Thus, despite his many unpleasant characteristics, Seth was also an enormously important part of the Egyptian pantheon, and was, according to Egyptian mythology, the unwitting reason for the creation of mummification in Egypt.

Roselyn Campbell

See also: Anubis; Isis; Osiris; Religion and mummies

Further Reading
David, Rosalie. 2002. *Religion and Magic in Ancient Egypt*. New York: Penguin Books.

Pinch, Geraldine. 2004. *Egyptian Mythology: A Guide to the Gods, Goddesses, and Traditions of Ancient Egypt*. New York: Oxford University Press.

Rundle Clark, R. T. 1959. *Myth and Symbol in Ancient Egypt*. London: Thames and Hudson.

Seton-Williams, M. V. 1988. *Egyptian Legends and Stories*. London: Rubicon Press.

Wilkinson, Richard H. 2003. *The Complete Gods and Goddesses of Ancient Egypt*. London: Thames and Hudson.

Siberian Ice Maiden/Ukok princess

In the summer of 1993 the Russian archaeologist Natalia Polosmak discovered on the Ukok Plateau in the Altai Mountains, Russia, the mummy of a princess from the Pazyryk culture (ca. 980 to 200 BCE). Her tomb was located within a group of kurgans (burial mounds) that were found in a territory close to the borders of China and Russia. The burial chamber was constructed using notched wood logs that formed a small cabin. The chamber contained the burial and the grave goods. The outer surface of the tomb was covered with a mound composed of smaller sediments and a pile of rocks.

The study of the human remains inside the tomb chamber revealed that the young woman died at an age of approximately 25 years and lived about 400 BCE. She was named according to her social status and finding area as the Siberian Ice Maiden, Princess of Ukok, the Altai Lady, or the Altai Princess. The mummy was found lying on her side and slightly bended. The body was well preserved, except for the soft tissue of the face. Her upper body was decorated with beautifully prepared tattoos, including one on her left shoulder that showed a brilliant stag turning during a leap, together with the beak of a griffin and ibex horns. The princess was buried together with a wig made out of human and horse hair and a case made of light wood. She wore clothing and a silken tunic. Her burial was accompanied by six sacrificial horses that hint at her royal origin. Polosmak suggested that the young woman had probably been a female shaman.

It represents a very interesting fact that, as found in the examination of the Ice Maiden, the people of the Pazyryk culture used a highly elaborate embalming procedure for the preparation of their dead. In a first step, the inner organs were removed by cutting open the abdomen. The abdominal cavity was later filled with a mixture of sand, wool, and herbs, and the thorax was stuffed with dried peat. The brain was also removed by folding back the scalp over the right parietal bone and trepanning the skull. The cavity was then filled with vegetable substances and

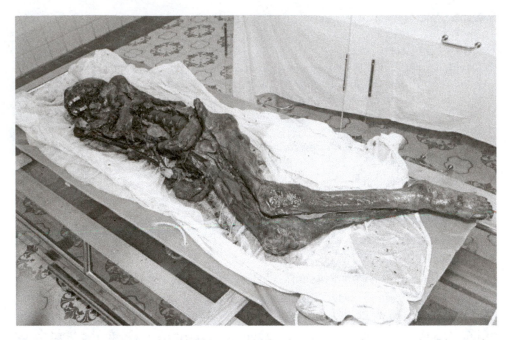

The mummified remains of the 2,500-year-old Scythian princess known as the Siberian Ice Maiden, found frozen in the permafrost of the Ukok Plateau, Pazryk region, Siberia, Russia, in 1994. (Sovfoto/Getty Images)

the skull was closed with horsehair. Traces of wax, clay, and mercury have also been detected on the skin of the mummy and were probably applied to enhance the preservation of the body and make it accessible to others who could pay their respects to the princess. (It is known from historic sources that some Scythian rulers used to "visit" their whole empire after their death. Obviously, this could only have been possible with the ruler in a mummified condition, as otherwise degradation and decomposition of the corpse would have taken place.)

The mummification process of the Siberian Ice Maiden was further supported by the specific construction of the kurgans. The subterranean log cabins were covered above ground with a layer of rubble and grass roots. This composition allowed meltwater to trickle down during the brief (two- or three-month) summer. At night, when temperatures dropped even in the summer months, the burial complex was frozen into a permanent ice lens. These circumstances further improved the preservation conditions for the human remains, and also, especially, for the organic grave goods such as clothing, carpets, leather decorations, and furs.

For conservation purposes, the Siberian Ice Princess was treated at the Moscow VILAR Research Center of Biological Structures. The scientists there—who also are in charge of the Lenin Mausoleum—managed to prevent the mummy from desiccation and darkening of the skin that happened after her removal from the burial chamber. The skin of the mummy was soaked in a preserving liquid and now allows the storage of the Altai Lady at room temperature. Currently, the mummified body is stored in the Museum of the Academy of Sciences in Novosibirsk. A facial reconstruction that was performed by Tatyana Balueva, head of the Gerasimov Ethnographic Institute of the Russian Academy of Sciences in Moscow, has led to a rather surprising result. The reconstructed face, which represents a statistical approximation of the original look of the princess based on the dimensions of the skull, did not show any Mongolian features but appeared to be much more a Caucasian type. Although this conclusion was disputed by the director of the Altai Regional Museum, a DNA analysis showed that the princess seemed not to be related to the present-day inhabitants of the Altai region. In the following years further mummies have been found in the Altai region, including the human remains of a Scythian warrior, who was buried together with his horse. Ongoing scientific studies of the mummies will provide further insights into the burial practices and the origin of this population.

Albert Zink

See also: Ice mummies; Lenin, Vladimir; Mummies of Europe

Further Reading

"Ice Mummies: Siberian Ice Maiden." 2006. Transcript for program first aired on PBS on November 24, 1998. *NOVA*. Accessed January 21, 2014. http://www.pbs.org/wgbh/nova/transcripts/2517siberian.html.

Polosmak, N. V. 2000. "Mummification and Embalming by the Pazyryk." In *The Phenomenon of the Altai Mummies*, edited by A. P. Derevyanko and V. I. Molodin, 120–124. Novosibirsk, Russia: Inst. of Archaeol and Ethnography Press.

Polosmak, Natalya, and Charles O'Rear. 1994. "A Mummy Unearthed from the Pastures of Heaven." *National Geographic*, October: 80–103.

Polosmak, N. V., and V. I. Molodin. 2000. "Pazyryk Cultural Sites on the Ukok Plateau." *Archaeology, Ethnology and Anthropology of Eurasia* 4: 66–87.

"Siberian Princess Reveals her 2,500 Hundred Year Old Tattoos." 2012. *The Siberian Times*, August 14. Accessed January 21, 2014. http://siberiantimes.com/culture/others/features/siberian-princess-reveals-her-2500-year-old-tattoos.

Smith, Clark Ashton

Much of adult writing of California poet, artist, and short story writer Clark Ashton Smith (1893–1961) appeared in *Weird Tales*, and he corresponded with *Weird Tales* mainstays H. P. Lovecraft and August Derleth, but long before the advent of *Weird Tales*, Smith had started his writing career, and his awareness of mummies revealed itself in the sonnet entitled "The Mummy" (*The Sonnet*, May–June, 1919). It describes the reawakening (or rebirth) of a mummy "from the night aeonian of the tomb/. . .reborn to mock the might of time,/While kings have built

> Confusedly, ere he opened his eyes, he became aware of an odor of bitter spices and piercing natron. Then, with the dim webs of sleep not wholly swept from his vision, he beheld, by the yellow tapers that Mouzda had lighted, a tall, mummy-like form that waited in silence beside him. The head, arms and body of the shape were wound closely with bitumen-colored cerements; but the folds were loosened from the hips downward, and the figure stood like a walker, with one brown, withered foot in advance of its fellow. . . . Then, from the thick swathings of the apparition, a voice issued indistinctly, saying: "Prepare yourself, O Nushain, for I am the first guide of that journey which was foretold to you by the stars."
> —From "The Last Hieroglyph" by Clark Ashton Smith

against Oblivion/With walls and columns of the windy sand." Nothing happens beyond this, but the poem is redolent with images of forgotten splendors of the past and concludes with a pleasant sense of impending doom. However, in a letter to George Sterling, Smith believes "The Mummy" inferior, at least to the two sonnets that the magazine's editor rejected.

Clark Ashton Smith was born on January 13, 1893, in Long Valley, California, the only child of Mary Frances Gaylord and Timeus Smith. His mother was American, from Long Valley, and Timeus was English, working a series of low-paying jobs. In 1902 Smith's parents purchased land on Indian Ridge, near Auburn, California, and built a small house that lacked electricity and indoor plumbing. The elder Smiths eventually died in this house, Mary Frances in 1935 and Timeus two years later, and although he took occasional trips, Clark Ashton Smith lived there almost until his death. In his letters, he claimed repeatedly to loathe his desolate surroundings, but he remained even when the opportunity to leave arose.

Smith's writing career began with poetry, at which he was not only talented but also appreciated, meeting and befriending the noted California poet George Sterling, and although he published prose as early as 1910, he did not seriously begin writing it until 1910, with "The Last Incantation" (*Weird Tales*, June 1930). The majority of Smith's stories occur in one of five fictional locations: Averoigne, Hyperborea, Poseidonis, Zothique, and Mars. It is Zothique, a future continent on a dying Earth, that has the realm of Tasuun and is "famous for the number and antiquity of its mummies." Naturally, these mummies figure in Smith's stories. "The Dark Eidolon" (*Weird Tales*, January 1935) is a tale of revenge and angers. The young beggar boy Narthos is trampled by Prince Zotulla and vows vengeance. He studies with Thasaidon, the god of evil, and returns as the terrifyingly potent magician Namirrha, intending to destroy the (now) Empéror Zotulla. His usage of mummies evokes splendor and horror: "then, into the hall, there filed an array of tall mummies, clad in royal cerements of purple and scarlet, and wearing gold crowns on their withered craniums . . . coming forward, the mummies said in dusty accents: 'All is made ready, and the feast awaits the arrival of Zotulla.' And the cerements of the mummies stirred and fell open at the bosom, and small rodent monsters, brown as bitumen, eyed as with accursed rubies, reared forth from the eaten hearts of the mummies like rats from their holes and chattered shrilly in human speech, replaying the words."

Tomb robbers and would-be thieves figure in "The Tale of Satampa Zeiros" (*Weird Tales*, November 1931), "The Weaver in the Vault" (*Weird Tales*, January 1934), and "Tomb Spawn" (*Weird Tales*, May 1934). Mummies *per se* do not figure in the first but partial mummification does, as Zeiros discovers that disturbing the god of the temple of Tsathoggua costs him his right hand, "leaving a strangely withered stump from which little blood issued." In "The Weaver in the Vault," King Famorgh's three henchmen, Yanur, Grotara, and Thirlain are sent to "find and bring back to Miraab whatever remained of the mummy of King Tnepreez." The three enter the ruins of the King's palace and, to their surprise, find all mummies have vanished: and only Grotara discovers the reason for the disappearances, too late to do him any good. Although they are cautioned, Milab and Marabac of "Tomb Spawn" (*Weird Tales*, May 1934) enter the tomb of Ossaru and Nioth Korghai. To get there, their journey takes them first across a land where "the hills were dark and lean, like recumbent mummies of giants," and they ride across "a powdery terrain that was like the bituminous dust of mummies." In the tomb they discover not a human body but a two-headed being, whose tentacles are in "jewel-sewn cloths of a precious purple, such as would be used for the winding of some royal mummy." Smith apparently considered this story science fiction rather than weird fiction, for he submitted it first to *Astounding Stories* and groused when they returned it.

The mummy in "The Last Hieroglyph" (*Weird Tales*, April 1935) is neither terrifying nor vicious. It is but a messenger whose statement—"Prepare yourself, O Nushain, for I am the first guide of that journey which was foretold to you by the stars"—sets Nushain the astrologer and his companions on a journey of cosmological significance. The tale is primarily of interest because Smith considered it "the concluding item of my Zothique series, if this series should ever appear between book-covers" (p. 255).

Mummies and the dead do figure in the non-Zothique stories. "The Colossus of Ylourgne" (*Weird Tales*, June 1934), a story set in Averoigne, is notable for its exuberantly grotesque and horrific central conceit. The sorcerer Nathaire vows revenge against the people of Vyones. His vengeance involves animating corpses, summoning them to him, and merging their bodies into that of the Colossus: "from the fresh bodies of the dead, which otherwise would have rotted away in charnel foulness, my pupils and familiars are making for me, beneath my instruction, the giant form whose skeleton you have beheld. My soul . . . will pass into this colossal tenement through the working of certain spells of transmigration . . ." This comes to pass, and it is up to young Gaspard du Nord, a former pupil of Nathaire who has renounced his master's teachings, to stop the rampaging monster.

Poseidonis is introduced in "The Double Shadow" (1933; *Weird Tales*, February 1939). The magician Pharpetron finds a tablet covered with indecipherable hieroglyphs. Unable to translate it, he enlists the assistance of his fellow magician Avyctes, and they succeed by sending a ghost back in time to the land of the serpent men, from whence the tablet came. With the assistance of Oigos, an animated mummy, the two magicians perform the ceremony, and though nothing initially occurs, a monstrous second shadow is soon seen creeping up on Avyctes. He is powerless to escape it, as are also Pharpetron and Oigos.

The supremely powerful magician Malygris, introduced in "The Last Incantation," returns in "The Death of Malygris" (*Weird Tales*, April 1934), when his enemy, the arch-sorcerer Maranapion, notices that Malygris has not moved or eaten in over a year and has concluded that "Malygris is dead; but by virtue of his supremacy in evil and in art magical, he sits defying the worm, still undecayed and incorrupt." Two rival sorcerers attempt to burglarize Malygris's chambers and discover that the dead Malygris remains potent, but Maranapion and his cohorts prepare spells that will cause Malygris's body to decay. The spells cast, Maranapion and his men visit Malygris, where Maranapion mockingly addresses the corrupt corpse, only to receive the following response: "Greeting, O Maranapion," replied a grave and terrible voice that issued from the maggot-eaten lips. "Indeed, I will grant thee a sign. Even as I, in death, have rotted upon my seat from the foul sorcery. . . so thou and thy fellows . . . shall decay and putrefy wholly in an hour, by the virtue of the curse that I put upon ye now." This occurs.

Smith's writing career was relatively brief, for in the late 1930s he largely abandoned writing to concentrate on his sculpture and art. In the 1950s Smith married Carolyn Jones Dorman; he left his mountain and sold the property to a real estate developer. He suffered a heart attack in 1953, followed by a number of small strokes, and died on August 14, 1961. It is tempting to be frustrated with Smith, who followed a variety of muses rather than staying with one, but these were his choices, and in the few years of his professional career, he offered a readers a unique voice and a consistent and disturbing view: the dead are often more dangerous than the living, and one interferes and interacts with them at one's peril.

Richard Bleiler

See also: The mummy in Western fiction: From 1922 to the twenty-first century

Further Reading

Bleiler, Richard. 2013. "Visionary Star Star-Treader: The Speculative Writings of Clark Ashton Smith." In *Critical Insights: Pulp Fiction of the 1920s and 1930s*, edited by Garry Hoppenstand, 66–83. Ipswich, MA: Salem Press.

de Camp, L. Sprague. 1976. "Sierran Shaman: Clark Ashton Smith." In *Literary Swordsmen and Sorcerers: The Makers of Heroic Fantasy*, 195–214. Sauk City, WI: Arkham House.

Price, E. Hoffmann. 1976. "Clark Ashton Smith: A Memoir." In *Tales of Science and Sorcery* by Clark Ashton Smith. London: Panther.

Sidney-Fryer, Donald. 1978. *Emperor of Dreams: A Clark Ashton Smith Bibliography*. West Kingston, RI: Donald M. Grant.

Sidney-Fryer, Donald. 1993. "O Amor Atque Realitas!: Clark Ashton Smith's First Adult Fiction." *The Dark Eidolon: The Journal of Smith Studies* 3:22–25. Accessed December 17, 2013. http://www.eldritchdark.com/articles/reviews/28.

Sidney-Fryer, Donald. 2011. *The Golden State Phantasticks: The California Romantics and Related Subjects*. Westchester, Los Angeles: Phosphor Lantern Press.

Smith, Clark Ashton. 1944. *Lost Worlds*. Sauk City, WI: Arkham House.

Smith, Clark Ashton. 1948. *Genius Loci, and Other Tales*. Sauk City, WI: Arkham House.

Smith, Clark Ashton. 1960. *The Abominations of Yondo*. Sauk City, WI: Arkham House.

Smith, Clark Ashton. 2003. *Selected Letters of Clark Ashton Smith*. Edited by David Schultz and Scott Connors. Sauk City, WI: Arkham House.

Smith, Grafton Elliot

G. E. Smith was an Australian-British anatomist and anthropologist of the late nineteenth and early twentieth centuries who frequently used his skills to study mummies and ancient human remains. He published the first anatomical study of the Egyptian royal mummies at the Cairo Museum. He was also involved in the infamous hoax known as the Piltdown Man, and was an active proponent for the diffusionist theories of human settlement and the spread of technology. He died of a stroke in England in 1937.

Grafton Elliot Smith was born on August 15, 1871, in New South Wales, Australia. Smith's interest in human anatomy and biology developed at an early age, and at the University of Sydney he continued his studies of anatomy and physiology. He also earned an MD by examining the anatomy and histology of the brain in nonplacental mammals, a work that earned him great acclaim. Smith traveled to England in 1896, where he continued to pursue studies of neuro-anatomy and first began to study the brains of ancient animals and humans.

In 1900, Smith was chosen to be the first anatomy professor at the Egyptian Government School of Medicine in Cairo, Egypt. While in Egypt, he became very interested in ancient Egyptian culture and mummification, and published a number of papers on the subject. Smith studied many of the mummies and human remains that were recovered during archaeological excavations in Egypt and Sudan, and was able to formulate improved ideas about mummification in ancient Egypt. These hypotheses about mummification corrected many errors of interpretation by previous scholars, and were used and improved by later researchers.

Smith is particularly known for his careful scientific examination of all the known royal Egyptian mummies housed in the Cairo Museum, and for his subsequent publication, *The Royal Mummies* (co-written with Warren Dawson). Smith was the first to apply a medical eye to many of these bodies, and he carefully unwrapped and analyzed the mummies to determine age at death, height, sex, and any medical conditions. X-ray technology was becoming available at the time, but there was some concern that the rays would damage the mummies, and thus Smith did not utilize X-rays for his study of the royal mummies. *The Royal Mummies* remains a monumental work to this day, and has only been surpassed with the invention of noninvasive imaging technology such as CT scanning.

In 1909, Smith returned to England, where he taught for many years at Manchester and at University College, London. He revolutionized anatomical studies in Great Britain, encouraging experimental studies and hands-on learning. He also continued to publish about ancient Egypt and the migration of people and ideas from Egypt into the rest of world in early human history. Smith strongly supported the diffusionist theories of the day, which held that all major human innovations had been developed in just one geographical area (in this case, Egypt or perhaps Africa), after which the technology had spread to other cultures. Although these theories of diffusion, as well as many of Smith's ideas about Egyptian culture, were eventually disproved, he was highly regarded as a scholar and a brilliant anatomist.

During this time, he also became involved with the study of the remains of the so-called Piltdown-Man. Upon examining the cranial vault (brain case) of Piltdown Man, Smith came to the conclusion that it belonged to an ape-like hominid. He had some reservations about the reconstruction of other parts of the skeleton and cranium, but his research and that of other primate specialists seemed to indicate that Piltdown Man was a representative of a very early hominid at an evolutionary stage between apes and homo sapiens. After Smith's death, however, Piltdown Man was revealed to be a well-crafted hoax, combining elements of human and ape crania and teeth. Perhaps due to Smith's formidable standing in the scientific community, his reputation remained relatively intact, and accusations of his involvement in the hoax were later dismissed.

Smith published extensively throughout his life on a variety of topics. He received many awards for his research, including a knighthood, and retired from teaching in 1936, a celebrated and well-respected scholar. After a series of small strokes, he died of another stroke on January 1, 1937, in his home at Kent in Great Britain.

Roselyn Campbell

See also: Dawson, Warren Royal; Egyptian mummies; Egyptian mummification methods; Medical imaging of mummies; Mummy unwrappings; Royal mummies of Egypt, Part One: Third to Eighteenth Dynasties; Royal mummies of Egypt, Part Two: Nineteenth to Twenty-fifth Dynasties; Ruffer, M. A.

Further Reading

Bierbrier, M. L. 2012. *Who Was Who in Egyptology*. 4th ed. London: Egypt Exploration Society.

Blunt, Michael J. 1988. "Smith, Sir Grafton Elliot (1871–1937)." *Australian Dictionary of National Biography* 11. Accessed December 18, 2013. http://adb.anu.edu.au/biography/smith-sir-grafton-elliot-8470.

David, Rosalie, and Rich Archbold. 2000. *Conversations with Mummies: New Light on the Lives of the Ancient Egyptians*. Toronto, Ontario, Canada: Black Walnut.

Dawson, Warren R. 1968. *Catalogue of Egyptian Antiquities in the British Museum, Volume I: Mummies and Human Remains*. London: Trustees of the British Museum.

Dunand, Françoise, and Roger Lichtenberg. 2006. *Mummies and Death in Egypt*. Translated by David Lorton. Ithaca: Cornell University Press.

Harris, James E., and Kent R. Weeks. 1973. *X-Raying the Pharaohs*. London: Macdonald.

Smith, Grafton Elliot. (1912) 2000. *The Royal Mummies*. Cairo: Institut français d'archéologie orientale. Reprint, London: Duckworth.

University College London Research Department of Cell and Developmental Biology. 2010. "Grafton Elliot Smith, 1871–1937." Last modified May 19. Accessed October 18, 2013, http://www.ucl.ac.uk/cdb/about/history/smith.

University College London Research Department of Cell and Developmental Biology. 2010. "Piltdown." Last modified May 19. Accessed October 18, 2013, http://www.ucl.ac.uk/cdb/about/history/piltdown.

Weiner, J.S. n.d. "Grafton Elliot Smith and Piltdown." Symposium Zoological Society London 1973. Accessed October 18, 2013. http://www.clarku.edu/~piltdown/map_prim_suspects/smith/smith_defence/smith_and_pilt.html.

Smoked bodies of Papua New Guinea

Papua New Guinea is an extremely diverse country with modern ports, advanced mining operations for copper and gold, and mummies. There are many groups within Papua New Guinea who mummified their dead, but one group stands out: the Anga. Their process is called "smoked body," which refers to their unique method of preserving their deceased.

The Anga are identified as a unique cultural group with specific linguistic and territorial boundaries. The area of the Anga cultural group includes contiguous parts of the Gulf, Central, Eastern Highlands, and Morobe provinces. The Anga were once known as the Kukukuku, a fierce warring group. Each Anga group within the cultural boundaries is known by a unique regional name. While Pidgin English is the "national language," the Anga generally speak Hamtae, and most of the Anga groups speak a different dialect from one another. The Anga are divided into linguistic tribes such as the Aseki, Kapau, Iwini, and the Baruya, and others known from ethnography. Earlier ethnographers, including Blackwood,

Mbaginta'o, Pospisil, and others, reported their findings regarding the Anga's Smoked body practices from a monolithic perspective, generalizing the mummification practices from single sites or events to the cultural group as a whole. By contrast, recent research indicates that the smoked body preparation varies to the same degree as do the dialects.

The practice of smoked body mummification is relatively current among the Anga, with the father of a village elder being one of the most recent smoked bodies produced. There is considerable pressure from Western missionaries to stop the practice. Formal cemeteries have been developed in even the most remote villages; however, some of the Anga, in particular the elders of a clan, are actively resisting these changes.

Papua New Guinea is a mountainous tropical rain forested island and is rich in biological diversity. It is difficult to imagine that mummy making could be successful in such a wet environment. The Anga had to develop a way to hold off the forces of nature that would certainly enhance decomposition. The Anga were and are masters of their environment, and they devised a very efficient and effective method of mummification.

When someone is to be mummified, the Anga begin the process by building a special smoking hut. This hut serves as the mummification chamber and helps to hold the wet environment at bay. The hut is built stilted above the ground and made from poles from the Pandanus tree. The sides are sheeted with leaves from the banana tree, with the roof being constructed from various large jungle leaves. Within the smoking hut a sling is made to hold the body to be mummified in place. Also, a fire pit is constructed. The hut is a special building used only for a single smoked body procedure.

As the hut is being constructed, body preparation begins. The first step is to open the pores of the body to allow for the seepage of body fluids. This is accomplished in two ways. First, the body is washed in warm water. Second, the body is "scrubbed" with a bristly plant called the "kukia." The abrasive nature of the kukia plant tends to remove the outermost layer of the skin. These processes encourage the release of body fluids through the dermal layers.

Prior to being placed in the smoking hut, an anal spigot is used to relieve additional body fluids that may have remained in the lower intestinal tract. The anal spigot is made from a bamboo section of the correct diameter. The bamboo is inserted into the rectum and advanced until gastric fluids are relieved.

The body is then secured to the sling within the smoking hut using strips of bush rope made from the bark of trees. Large banana leaves are spread below the sling and are filled with local clay. The clay serves as an absorbent for the fluids escaping the body. A smoky fire is started within the hut and maintained. Throughout the smoking process, additional methods are used to encourage fluid removal from the body, enhancing desiccation and staving off decomposition.

As the body remains in the sling, the kukia plant continues to be used to keep the pores open. Desiccation is further encouraged as the relatives of the deceased massaged the body, expressing body fluids. Another technique also helps remove fluids from the body: the Anga fashion bamboo knives and then puncture the gravity-dependent regions of the body, allowing trapped fluids to escape. Changing the body position from time to time assures that fluids can flow to areas of the body where they can be expressed or escape through the puncture sites.

The smoked body method is labor-intensive and can take thirty or more days to complete. The close relatives stay in the smoking hut, giving constant attention to the smoked body. The conditions within the smoking hut create a microenvironment that is required in this moist environment. Recent research indicated that the microenvironment is markedly different from the ambient conditions outside the hut. While the outside temperature hovered between 31.9 degrees C (89.42 degrees F) and 22 degrees C (71.6 degrees F), the temperature within the smoking hut reached and was maintained at around 51.7 degrees C (125.06 degrees F). Humidity also varied within the smoking hut when compared to the ambient humidity. Ambient relative humidity stayed at about 81 percent, while within the smoking hut the relative humidity was only 55 percent. These conditions not only demonstrate the characteristics of the microenvironment but also contributed to the desiccation process.

Characteristics of the smoke during the mummification process further enhance the process of preservation. The smoke was found to have a pH of 5.2, which creates a hostile environment for microorganisms. As with all smoke, formaldehyde was detected, which alters the substrate of the cadaver by encouraging the cross-bridging of collagen fibers. This alteration makes the tissues resistant to digestion by the enzymes associated with decomposition. The smoke also creates a physical barrier to insect infestation.

Once the body is mummified, a ritualistic application of red ocher clay is conducted. The clay may serve as a minor physical barrier to environmental variations and may actually continue to wick moisture from the body aiding dehydration.

The smoked bodies are then placed high in a cliff niche where they are consulted on village issues, brought down for ceremonial purposes, and serve as territory markers for a particular clan.

Scientific study of the Anga mummies indicates that while there is some variation on the smoked body procedure, the results are excellent. Physical and endoscopic examination of 33 mummies within the Anga region demonstrated that the mummification process created well-preserved individuals. The internal preservation was very high. The major variances seen were the result of how the individuals were displayed. Those residing high on a cliff, exposed to most of the elements, were the most deteriorated, while those mummies held within a protective structure remain markedly well preserved.

Ethnographic studies of the Anga and their relationship to the smoked bodies yielded a continuum of thoughts. Variation is seen among the living generations of Anga. The Anga elders still see the spiritual connection to the deceased bodies. The mummies are consulted and greatly respected. When one is introduced to a smoked body, it is as if that individual was still among the living. The elders also see the mummies as protectors, in that they continue to mark the territory for the clan. Those Anga of the middle age group understand and respect the spiritual connections seen among the elders, and they continue to see the mummies as territorial markers. Additionally, a new purpose of the mummies is being realized by this generation: mummy tourism. The middle-aged group feels that the mummies can continue to serve the village through paid visitations to see the mummies. The next generation, the young adults, see the mummies and their spiritual significance waning. The younger individuals within the village are more globally connected and see the mummies purely as a vehicle for revenue production. This group still respects the old ways but is moving forward in the twenty-first century, seeing the need for monetary gain.

It is remarkable that in this humid, wet environment, such mummies as these smoked bodies can be made. It is a testament to the will of the Anga people and their ability to adapt their environment to allow for body preservation. When asked, the Anga do not say or do not know when the smoked body practice began. As described by Yengdang, Anga village subclan leader in 2010, the common response to such questions is usually, "It is our way, it is our custom." Their dedication to their smoked bodies continues to be challenged by Western missionary efforts in the region. The missionaries suggest that the smoked body practice is unclean and against God's will. Clearly, the Anga, for the most part, disagree with the missionary teachings. It is important to note that this is a culture and a people who still today include their smoked body ancestors in village activities. There is a hope that the smoked body tradition will continue among the Anga of Papua New Guinea.

Ronald G. Beckett

See also: Embalming; Fire mummies: The Ibaloy mummies of the Philippines

Further Reading

Beckett, Ronald G. 2010. "Mastering Mummy Science." *National Geographic Magazine*, September: 140–142.

Beckett, Ronald G., and Gerald Conlogue. 2009. *Paleoimaging: Field Applications for Cultural Remains and Artifacts*. USA: CRC Press, Taylor and Francis.

Beckett, Ronald G., and Andrew Nelson, 2011. "Scientific Exploration of the Smoked Body Mummification Practice of the Anga of Koke Village, Papua New Guinea." Paper presented at the 7th World Congress on Mummy Studies, San Diego, California, June 12–16.

Beckett, Ronald G., Lohmann, Ulla, and Josh Bernstein. 2011a. "A Field Report on the Mummification Practices of the Anga of Koke Village, Central Highlands, Papua New

Guinea." In *Yearbook of Mummy Studies, Volume 1*, edited by Dario Piombino-Mascali, 11–17. Bolzano, Italy: Accademia Europea di Bolzano.

Beckett, Ronald G., Lohmann, Ulla, and Josh Bernstein. 2011b. "A Unique Field Mummy Conservation Project in Papua New Guinea." In *Yearbook of Mummy Studies, Volume 1*, edited by Dario Piombino-Mascali, 19–27. Bolzano, Italy: Accademia Europea di Bolzano.

Nelson, Andrew J., and Ronald G. Beckett. 2011. "The Meaning of Mummification among the Anga of the Aseki Region of Papua New Guinea: A Tradition in Transition." Paper presented at the 7th World Congress on Mummy Studies, San Diego, California, June 12–16.

Summum

Summum is a peculiarly American organization that comprises a winery, a religious group, and a burial society offering mummification services. It has attracted much media attention since its founding in 1975, which provides the historical information used in this essay. Summum maintains an extensive Web site that includes links to its sacred text, *SUMMUM: Sealed Except to the Open Mind*. Its 40-foot-square Summum Pyramid in Salt Lake City, Utah, serves as winery, publications office, instruction center, temple, sanctuary, and the resting place of the founder. Since 2005 there is also a mausoleum.

Claude Rex Nowell, also known as Summum Bonum Amon Ra (1944–2008), founded the religious group, reportedly because religious status was required to open a winery in the state of Utah. Summum is a tax-exempt public charity according to the rules of the Internal Revenue Service of the United States. It was active in food banks and other charitable causes during the founder's lifetime. Presently the winery permit has been withdrawn, and the organization no longer sells its "nectars" or "murh," a sexual lubricant.

Nowell was raised as a Mormon and served as a Mormon missionary. He was educated at Brigham Young University and the University of Utah and earned

Summum's non-mainstream religious beliefs, in combination with their practice of Egyptian-inspired mummification upon modern-day people and animals, have attracted a great deal of media attention in the United States, the UK, and elsewhere, including national and local coverage from the likes of CNN, NBC News, ABC News, National Geographic, *The Huffington Post*, *The Daily Mail*, and *The Los Angeles Times*. The Discovery Channel has described them as offering "the world's only commercial mummification business."

Reference

Olsen, Grant. 2012. "Religious Group Performs Mummification Rituals in Utah Pyramid." KSL.com, October 30. Accessed March 10, 2014. http://www.ksl.com/?sid=22660276.

credentials as a mortician in California. In 1980 he experienced a spiritual encounter that led him to change his name and offer instruction in the Summum Philosophy. The philosophy is an eclectic blend of popular Egyptology and New Age spiritualism pursued through meditation, wine, ecstatic sexuality, and eventual mummification. The Web site invokes figures ranging from Jesus and Gautama Buddha to Antoine de Saint-Exupéry and Morpheus from *The Matrix*. A particularly interesting source is Isha Schwaller de Lubicz (1885–1963), a prolific writer on ancient Egypt and wife of René Adolphe Schwaller de Lubicz, who surveyed Luxor. This couple was prominent in alchemy, occultism, theosophy, and right-wing politics in early twentieth-century France. Nowell's seven principles reflect his interest in the Kybalion and other early twentieth century American occult and theosophical writing.

Nowell offered mummification as a prepaid service to his adherents. He experimented with animal mummification, and examples can be viewed on the Summum Web site. By January 1993, according to a widely circulated news item, 139 clients had signed up, but none had died. In the 1990s, the mummification process was to be carried out by Dr. John Albert Chew, who then taught mortuary sciences at Miami-Dade Community College and at Lynn University, Boca Raton, Florida. Chew left his position after his experimental mummifications became national and international news. After a second incident concerning inappropriate use of cadavers in 2002, Lynn University terminated its Funeral Services Education Program. Chew and Ra traded barbs in the media with Bob Brier over the virtues of authentic Egyptian materials versus modern chemistry in the online magazine *Salon*.

Currently the Summum Web site asks prospective clients to make a "pre-need" payment for mummification services. Prepayment for funeral services is common in the United States. Clients must also make arrangements with local funeral homes and must arrange local burial. In the interval Summum pledges to provide a 90-day "transference" process that lists bathing and cleaning; evisceration; immersion of the body and organs in a baptismal font filled with "certain resins"; anointing with oil; wrapping in cotton gauze, silk, and polymer; sealing in the Pyramid; and, if desired, sealing in resin within a specially constructed "mummiform." Conventional coffins and vaults are also offered. In 2008 Nowell himself became the first human subject. Only the founder and a number of pets are illustrated as products of this process. Costs for pets are $4,000 to $28,000 for mummification and $3000 to more than $100,000 for the mummiform. Costs for human clients are $67,000 in continental United States plus the mummiform and the local arrangements and casket.

Importantly, Summum is hardly unique in introducing elements of Egyptian mummification into American funeral customs. There are many other pyramids in the United States, ranging from the huge Pyramid Arena in Memphis,

Tennessee, to the Brunswig tomb in Metairie Cemetery, New Orleans. The Mormon prophet Joseph Smith owned mummies and papyri that some scholars find worked into the *Book of Mormon*. In the nineteenth century an enterprising firm offered to store corpses in Mammoth Cave, Kentucky, to preserve them as permanently as the ancient Egyptians, and Fisk mummiform iron caskets with glass face plates were sold widely. Essayist Russell Baker recalled a moonshiner's sealed glass-topped coffin as "the fanciest mason jar ever sold in Loudon County," Tennessee (Baker 1984, 65), and even the word *hermetic* for canning jars reflects nineteenth-century mummimania. Summum is thus exercising symbols in long circulation in the United States.

Della Collins Cook

See also: Experimental mummification; Religion and mummies

Further Reading

Baker, Russell. 1984. *Growing Up*. New York: Penguin.

Colin, Chris. 2001. "Show Me the Mummy!" Salon, May 4. Accessed December 6, 2013. http://www.salon.com/2001/05/04/mummy_2.

George, Angelo I. 1994. *Mummies, Catacombs and Mammoth Cave*. Louisville: George Publishing Company.

Kimball, Stanley B. 1983. "New Light on Old Egyptiana: Mormon Mummies, 1848–71," Dialogue: A Journal of Mormon Thought 16, no. 4: 72–90.

"Not Your Parents' Funeral." 2005. *CBS News*, September 30. Accessed December 8, 2013. http://www.cbsnews.com/videos/not-your-parents-funeral.

Owsley, Douglas W., Karin S. Bruwelheide, Larry W. Cartmell, Sr., Laurie E. Burgess, Shelly J. Foote, Skye M. Chang and Nick Fielder. 2006. "The Man in the Iron Coffin: An Interdisciplinary Effort to Name the Past." *Historical Archaeology* 43, no. 3: 89–108.

Quigley, Christine. 2006. *Modern Mummies: The Preservation of the Human Body in the Twentieth Century*. Jefferson, NC: McFarland & Co.

Ravitz, Jessica. 2010. "Summum: Homegrown Spiritual Group, in News and in a Pyramid." *CNN Belief Blog*, June 11. Accessed December 8, 2013. http://religion.blogs.cnn.com/2010/06/11/summum-a-belief-system-in-the-news-%E2%80%93-and-unlike-any-other.

Summum. 2013. "Eternal Memorialization through Mummification." Accessesed December 8. http://www.summum.org/mummification/EternalMemorialization-hi.pdf.

Summum. 2013. *Summum: Mummification of Transference*. Accessed December 8, 2013. http://www.summum.org.

Swiss Mummy Project

The Swiss Mummy Project (SMP) is a scientific research project at the University of Zurich, Switzerland, with a main goal of gaining medical and historical information from ancient human mummies, primarily by the use of state-of-the-art radiological and molecular techniques.

SMP was initiated in the mid-1990s based on an MD thesis research project (see Rühli 1998). Its prime goal was to medically investigate ancient Egyptian mummies stored in Swiss collections. The team has been led since then by medical professionals, but based on its research aims, experts from other field such as anthropology, Egyptology, and radiology have been involved as well. In the first few years, about a dozen mummies from Swiss collections were investigated, an important one being, for example, the mummy "Schepenese" (Shep-en-Isis, ca. 650 BCE), which is held and displayed in the Stiftsbibliothek St. Gallen (the Abbey Library of Saint Gall, located in St. Gallen, Switzerland, which is the oldest library collection in the country). Some selected findings such as postmortem alterations due to embalming have been published, as well as a general catalog of most of the examined coffins and mummies. With time more and more international collaborations have been undertaken. People of the SMP have been involved, e.g., in diagnostic imaging and excavation projects of mummies from collections in Greece, Germany, Iran, Italy. Most famously, the SMP has performed diagnostic imaging on the mummy of King Tutankhamun in Egypt. They have also examined Ötzi the Iceman.

Currently, the project consists of about a dozen people from various professional backgrounds who are embedded in the Centre for Evolutionary Medicine at the medical faculty of the University of Zurich. The main focus of research, which is conducted on a worldwide scale through various collaborations, is to study evolutionary aspects of disease. Mostly, medically established state-of-the-art diagnostic imaging techniques (such as dual energy CT, CT-based 3D reconstructions, and histological analyses) are applied. Specific studies focus on the content of ancient Egyptian canopic jars as well as on dental disorders in ancient mummies in general. Moreover, experimental studies on the impact of mummification on fresh human tissue or the impact of radiation on desiccated human cells are explored. Ethical dimensions of work on ancient mummies are also an important part of the SMP, with the project's own Code of Ethics being applied. Finally, more and more molecular studies on ancient mummified tissue are undertaken in a dedicated ancient DNA laboratory.

So far, researchers of the SMP have been able to detect cases of extensive arteriosclerosis (hardening of the arteries), suggested bone tumors and degenerative skeletal disease, particularly in ancient Egyptian mummies. Also, anatomical variants and stress factors such as Harris lines (certain lines on bones due to injury or illness) can be regularly found. Furthermore, a major emphasis is laid on the study of new diagnostic examination technologies such as MRI or terahertz imaging. The results are presented in scientific journals and in popular media.

The SMP is a prominent example of the crucial importance of transdisciplinarity—combining medicine, science, archeology, anthropology, and Egyptology—in state-of-the-art research on ancient mummies.

Frank Rühli

See also: Experimental mummification; Genetic study of mummies; Medical imaging of mummies; Ötzi the Iceman; Tutankhamun ("King Tut")

Further Reading

Hawass Z., M. Shhafik, F. Rühli, et al. 2007. "Computed Tomographic Evaluation of Pharaoh Tutankhamun, ca. 1300 BC." *Ann Serv Antiq Egypt* 81: 159–174.

Kaufmann, I., and F. J. Rühli. 2010. "Without 'Informed Consent'? Ethics and Ancient Mummy Research." *Journal of Medical Ethics* 36, no. 10 (October): 608–613.

Leybold-Johnson, Isobel. 2009. "Swiss Research Unlocks Mummy Secrets." *Turkish Weekly*, August 18. Accessed December 19, 2013. http://www.turkishweekly.net/news/87119/-swiss-research-unlocks-mummy-secrets.html.

Lorenzi, Rossella. 2009. "Leg Mummified with Ancient Egyptian Recipe." *NBC News/Discovery News*. October 16. Accessed December 19, 2013. http://www.nbcnews.com/id/33329512.

Rincon, Paul. 2007. "Iceman 'Bled to Death on Glacier.'" *BBC News*, last updated June 6. Accessed December 19, 2013. http://news.bbc.co.uk/2/hi/science/nature/6727665.stm.

Rühli, F. J. 1998. *Paleopathological Examinations of an Ancient Egyptian Mummy from the Museum of Natural Sciences, Winterthur.* MD Thesis. University of Zurich. Dietikon, Switzerland: Juris Druck und Verlag.

The Swiss Mummy Project. 2013. Accessed December 19, 2013. http://swissmummyproject.ch.

T

Theban Necropolis

The Theban Necropolis is an area on the west bank of the Nile that contains hundreds of Egyptian tombs. Mostly used during the New Kingdom, the Theban Necropolis extended into the western desert and comprised several distinct areas, which provided space for the burials of a wide range of individuals, including pharaohs, queens, nobles, officials, priests, and workmen. It is the most extensive rock-cut necropolis in Egypt despite being contained in the relatively small area of three square kilometers.

Geographic features of the Theban Necropolis provided natural boundaries for the ancient Egyptians to delineate and allocate land for specific purposes. Because of its dry desert location and sturdy rock formations, the Theban Necropolis was the perfect setting to carve tombs deep into the hillside and bury the deceased.

One of the most impressive structures in the Theban Necropolis is the Ramesseum. Built over a period of 18 years, this is the mortuary temple of the 13th century BCE pharaoh Rameses II ("Rameses the Great"). (Terry Lawrence/Getty Images)

While certainly not common in arid regions, flash floods occasionally consumed the valley. These floods caused the destruction of several tombs, but the large amount of silt and debris deposited in the valley after the water receded also preserved and protected the entrances to several tombs. The Egyptians were aware of the potential for flooding in the valley of the Theban Necropolis, and they viewed the potential for this natural event as a sign of the necropolis's sacred importance.

The main feature of the necropolis is a high plateau with vertical cliffs that rises above the landscape. Around this plateau, 10 distinct geographical features, identified by their modern Arabic names, aid in defining parts of the necropolis.

At their base, the vertical cliffs form a semi-circle called *Deir el-Bahari*. This site prominently features the royal mortuary temples of pharaohs Montuhotep II, Hatshepsut, and Thutmose III. In addition, Deir el-Bahari also contains tombs of officials from the Middle Kingdom to the Ptolemaic Period.

Cutting through the main plateau are two wadis. The first, called *Wadi el-Muluk*, is better known by its popular name, the Valley of the Kings. This famous valley was used as the burial location of the pharaohs of the New Kingdom. Sixty-three tombs have been discovered in the valley. Almost all of the tombs were robbed in antiquity. As a result, the bodies of the royal dead were moved to a secret location elsewhere in the Theban Necropolis. Only one tomb, that of Tutankhamen, remained relatively intact, and his mummy still lies in his tomb in the Valley.

The second, smaller wadi, *Biban el-Harim*, is better known as the Valley of the Queens. Founded during the reign of Rameses I, it contains more than 70 tombs of the New Kingdom pharaohs' wives and children. It was considered the counterpart to the Valley of the Kings and was a break from the tradition of creating one tomb for a husband and wife. Even pharaohs would often set aside space in their mortuary complexes for wives during the Old and Middle Kingdoms, so the completely separate location of the Valley of the Queens is quite unique.

Near the entrance of Deir el-Bahari sits a row of low hills called *Dra' Abu el-Naga'*. Here, several New Kingdom officials built their tombs. It is also believed that the pharaohs of the 17th Dynasty used this area as their royal necropolis, although no tombs belonging to any of those kings have been positively identified. Due to pottery fragments with inscriptions, one tomb in this location is thought to be the 18th Dynasty burial of Amenhotep I, but the evidence is not conclusive.

The next few areas of the Theban Necropolis all contain a vast amount of private tombs. Collectively, these tombs are often referred to as the Tombs of the Nobles, of which there are over 400. The first of these areas lay behind the Dra' Abu el-Naga' hills and is known as the terrace of *El-Tarif*. This area is the oldest section of the Theban Necropolis, containing several mastaba tombs dating to the Old Kingdom. It was in use primarily during the First Intermediate Period, Middle

Kingdom, and Second Intermediate Period as a burial ground for local nobles and officials.

To the south of Dra' Abu el-Naga' are the areas of *El-Assasif, El-Khokha, Qurnet Murai'*, and *Sheikh Abd el-Qurna*. El-Assasif contains the tombs of nobles from the 18th, 25th, and 26th Dynasties. Five private Old Kingdom tombs and fifty noble tombs from the First Intermediate Period, New Kingdom, and Late Period have been found at El-Khokha. Qurnet Murai' housed more tombs of New Kingdom officials. Sheikh Abd el-Qurna is popularly known as the Valley of the Nobles, and it is the largest concentration of private tombs in the Theban Necropolis.

Further south of El-Khokha and Sheikh Abd el-Qurna is *Deir el-Medina*. This area housed a village where the workers who built and decorated the tombs of the Theban Necropolis lived. Not only are their houses preserved (of which the village has approximately 70), but their own tombs near the village also remain. Their burials, although modest compared to their elite and royal counterparts, exhibit some of the best craftsmanship and artistry in the Theban Necropolis and provide a wealth of information concerning the lives of the workmen and their families.

While the Theban Necropolis was used during the Old Kingdom for burying local elites, the first notable use of the area as a vast necropolis was during the 11th Dynasty during the end of the First Intermediate Period and 12th Dynasty, which marked the beginning of the Middle Kingdom. Then, larger numbers of local rulers and officials were buried in the Theban necropolis, across the river from the growing religious center of Thebes. This expanding burial practice culminated in the building of the elaborate tomb of pharaoh Montuhotep II at Deir el-Bahri.

Most of these Middle Kingdom tombs were robbed in antiquity, and little remains except for the tomb architecture itself. However, one intact 12th Dynasty burial of a man named Wah reveals much about the practice of mummification during the Middle Kingdom. He was wrapped in over 800 square meters of cloth and buried with a gold gilded mummy mask and many valuable grave goods. Some of his internal organs were removed, but the lungs and stomach remained. No canopic equipment to hold the removed organs were found in the burial.

The peak of the Theban Necropolis's use was the New Kingdom. As Thebes grew in importance as a religious capital of Egypt, the cemeteries across the river from the city and temples likewise grew. The pharaohs of this time period built their tombs in the Valley of the Kings, with other members of the royal family building nearby tombs in the Valley of the Queens. The officials, priests, and nobles of the pharaohs' courts followed suit, building their own private tombs in the Valley of the Nobles and the surrounding areas. In all, the Theban Necropolis contains around 550 tombs. Of these, there are at least 415 tombs of nobles that have been identified, but there is great potential for more tombs to be discovered.

Aside from the finds made in the Valley of the Kings, one of the most important finds in the Theban Necropolis was a cache of over 40 royal New Kingdom mummies in Deir-el Bahari. During the 21st Dynasty, these mummies, which included the bodies of Ahmose I, Amenhotep I, Thutmose I, Thutmose II, Thutmose III, Rameses I, Seti, I, Rameses II, and Rameses IX, were removed from their individual tombs in the Valley of the Kings after they had been looted and placed into a single tomb at Deir el-Bahari to prevent further desecration of the bodies. Also in the Deir el-Bahari cache, which was found by archaeologists in 1881, were the 21st Dynasty bodies of high priests and pharaohs Pinedjem I, Pinedjem II, and Siamun. All of these royal mummies are now on display in the Egyptian Museum in Cairo.

In addition, 153 mummies of the 21st Dynasty high priests of Amun and their families, known as the Bab el-Gasus cache, were found in another single tomb not far from the royal cache. Due to political difficulties and economic hardship, it was common during the Third Intermediate Period for entire families to use only one tomb, and this practice continued well into the Late Period. The mummies and their associated coffins from the Bab el-Gasus cache were divided into 17 lots and distributed to museum collections throughout the world.

Although a vast majority of the tombs (both royal and private) of the Theban Necropolis were looted in antiquity, many artifacts, coffins, and mummies still remain, and are now housed and displayed in museums worldwide. Providing a wealth of information about ancient Egypt's mortuary culture, the Theban Necropolis is a popular destination for both scholars and tourists alike.

Marissa A. Stevens

See also: Egyptian mummies; Valley of the Kings

Further Reading

Aubry, Marie-Pierre, et al. 2011. "Geological Setting of the Theban Necropolis: Implications for the Preservation of the West Bank Monuments." In *Under the Potter's Tree: Studies on Ancient Egypt Presented to Janine Bourriau on the Occasion of her 70th Birthday*. Leuven: Peeters: 81–124.

Dodson, Aidan, and Salima Ikram. 2008. *The Tomb in Ancient Egypt: Royal and Private Sepulchres from the Early Dynastic Period to the Romans*. Thames & Hudson.

Ikram, Salima, and Mathaf al-Misrī. 1997. *Royal Mummies in the Egyptian Museum*. Cairo: American University in Cairo Press.

Oakes, Lorna, Lucia Gahlin, Lorna Oakes, and Lucia Gahlin. 2002. *Ancient Egypt: An Illustrated Reference to the Myths, Religions, Pyramids and Temples of the Land of the Pharaohs*. New York: Hermes House.

Smith, G. Elliot. 2000. *The Royal Mummies (Catalogue General Des Antiquites Egyptiennes Du Musee Du Caire, Nos 61051–61100: Service Des Antiquites De L'egypte) (Duckworth Egyptology)*. Duckworth Publishers.

Snape, S. R. 2011. *Ancient Egyptian Tombs: The Culture of Life and Death*. Blackwell Ancient Religions. Malden, MA: Wiley-Blackwell.

Thomas, Elizabeth. 1966. *The Royal Necropolis of Thebes*. Trenton, NJ: Elizabeth Thomas.

Wilkinson, John Gardner. 1835. *Topography of Thebes, and General View of Egypt*. London: Murray.

Tollund Man

Tollund Man is the name given to the body of a man who died during the Early Iron Age in Denmark. When he died, Tollund Man's body was thrown into a peat moss bog, and the peat preserved his body extremely well. His hands and arms were partly skeletonized, probably as a consequence of the peat excavations that led to his discovery, but the rest of Tollund Man's body is nearly perfectly preserved, down to the miniscule grooves on his feet and the delicate skin of his lips and eyelids. Tollund Man was one of the earlier "bog bodies" discovered in Europe, and he is considered to be one of the best preserved examples of these bodies. He was the subject of a famous composition by Irish poet Seamus Heaney titled "The Tollund Man."

Tollund Man was discovered in early May of 1950, during routine harvesting of peat from a bog near Silkeborg, Denmark. It soon became apparent that the body had been placed in an already-excavated section of peat moss, indicating that inhabitants of the area were harvesting peat (probably for fuel) in the area as early as the Iron Age. The bog where Tollund Man was discovered remains waterlogged throughout the year. Combined with the acidity of peat moss and the low oxygen content of the bog, conditions are excellent for preserving human remains. While the large concentrations of this acid can cause bones to lose their calcium and become soft, the acid also preserves the surrounding skin in a process that resembles the tanning of leather.

When he died, Tollund Man was between 30 and 40 years old, and a little over 5 feet tall (though he may have shrunk somewhat from the effects of decay). Tollund Man's short hair appears red, but this is due to the chemicals in the bog rather than the original pigmentation. He had recently shaved his face, though very short

The Nobel Prize-winning Irish poet Seamus Heaney (1929–2013) wrote a famous poem about Tollund Man in the early 1970s as part of a series of poems he penned about bog bodies in Northern Europe. An audio recording of Heaney reading this poem aloud is available at various places on the Internet, including the Internet Poetry Archive: http://www.ibiblio.org/ipa/poems/heaney/the_tollund_man.php.

stubble indicates that he shaved at least 24 hours before he died. The skin of his forehead is heavily lined, and small portions of his eyebrows were preserved. Tollund Man's only clothing consisted of a pointed sheepskin leather hat, tied under his chin with leather straps, and a belt crafted out of thin strips of leather. Although Tollund Man may have originally worn other clothing of linen or flax, such cloth would most likely have left an imprint of fibers or weave on Tollund Man's skin as the cloth deteriorated; since no such pattern was found, Tollund Man likely was naked when he died, though his clothes may have been placed nearby.

Sometime between 400 and 300 BCE, Tollund Man died and was deposited into the bog. He was placed in a flexed, or fetal, position, lying on his right side. Because his right side was facing downward, it was better preserved than the left side of his body, which had suffered more decay and damage immediately after death and during the harvesting of the surrounding peat. Like Lindow Man, found in England over three decades later, Tollund Man was found with a thin cord around his neck, made of braided leather. In the case of Lindow Man, the rope was used as a garrote, but the rope around Tollund Man's neck was thicker and tied into a noose, suggesting that he was probably hanged rather than strangled. Both bogs and sacrificial hanging were important elements of Norse mythology.

The National Museum of Denmark sponsored extensive scientific examinations of Tollund Man in 1950. The remarkable preservation of the body meant that scientists could even determine the contents of Tollund Man's last meal, which he had eaten between 12 and 24 hours before death: a porridge or gruel made of barley, two kinds of flax, and knotgrass. This last meal is very similar to meals found in the other stomachs of other Iron Age bog bodies, such as Grauballe Man, which suggests that this type of gruel was a common meal at the time. Researchers also determined that Tollund Man suffered from intestinal worms, a very common ailment during the Iron Age. Several years later, when carbon-14 dating was developed for ancient remains, scientists were able to determine the approximate time frame of Tollund Man's death. After the examination, Tollund Man's head was removed from his body for preservation, since the body was viewed as less interesting and more macabre for visitors.

In 2002, the body was taken to a local hospital and scanned using a CT scanner. This technology, which creates images taken as "slices" very close together and then compiles those images into a model, is immensely valuable for studying ancient human remains without cutting or damaging the body in any way. Scientists also used an encoscope, X-rays, and both ultraviolet and infrared light to examine Tollund Man as thoroughly as possible without causing more damage to his remains. Based on these CT scans, scientists were able to further refine and correct some of the findings from the earlier study. For instance, it was conclusively shown that Tollund Man was not strangled (an early theory about his death), but was certainly hanged.

The atmosphere of the peat bog stalls decay in part because of the low temperature and lack of oxygen, so whenever bog bodies are removed and exposed to oxygen, preservation becomes an immediate and complex concern. Since conservation efforts after the body was found focused heavily on Tollund Man's head, the rest of his body decayed badly. In 1987 Silkeborg Museum used old photos to restore Tollund Man's body as much as possible, and it was reunited with his head for display. Tollund Man is currently on display at the Silkeborg Museum in Silkeborg, Denmark.

Roselyn Campbell

See also: Bog bodies; *The Book of the Dead* (anthology); Lindow Man; Medical imaging of mummies; Mummies of Europe; Natural mummification

Further Reading

Glob, P. V. 2004. *The Bog People: Iron-Age Man Preserved*, 1969. Translated by Rupert Bruce-Mitford. New York: The New York Review of Books.

Lauring, Palle. 1957. *Land of the Tollund Man: The Prehistory and Archaeology of Denmark*. Translated by Reginald Spink. London: Lutterworth Press.

Lobell, Jarrett A., and Samir S. Patel. 2010. "Bog Bodies Rediscovered." *Archaeology* 63, no. 3 (May/June). Accessed October 23, 2013. URL: http://archive.archaeology.org/1005/bogbodies/.

Sanders, Karin. 2009. *Bodies in the Bog and the Archaeological Imagination*. Chicago: University of Chicago Press.

Silkeborg Public Library, Silkeborg Museum, and Amtscentret for Undervisning. Last modified 2004. "The Tollund Man—A Face from Prehistoric Denmark." Accessed October 24, 2013, http://www.tollundman.dk.

Thorvildsen, Knud. 1962. *The Tollund Man*. Translated by Fred Mallett. Silkeborg Museum.

van der Sanden, Wijnand. 1996. *Through Nature to Eternity: The Bog Bodies of Northwest Europe*. Translated by Susan J. Mellor. Amsterdam: Batavian Lion International.

Tutankhamun ("King Tut")

King Tutankhamun (there have been many alternate spellings, including Tutankhamen and Tut-Ankh-Amon) is one of the most famous mummies in the world. The discovery of this 18th Dynasty king in 1922 was a worldwide sensation—the first (and only) pharaoh to be found intact in his tomb in Egypt's Valley of the Kings. Nearly a century later, Tutankhamun is still a household name, his fame driven by media portrayals and blockbuster museum exhibitions of the tomb's treasures, as well as a series of scientific studies on the mummy itself.

Tutankhamun was one of the last kings to rule in Egypt's rich and powerful 18th Dynasty, when the art of mummification was at its height. His predecessor

An interior view of Tutankhamun's tomb, decorated with wall paintings.
(Jim Zuckerman/Corbis)

Akhenaten rejected the multiple gods of Egypt's traditional religion, including the machinery of priests that went with it, to worship just one god, the Sun disc. He left the country's capital, Thebes, to build a new city in the desert but he died after 17 years of rule. Tutankhamun, who ruled shortly afterward (ca. 1321–1312 BCE), reversed those changes, reinstating the priests and returning to Thebes.

Tutankhamun's reign was short, and he died as a young man, aged around 18 years. He was buried—some experts say hastily—in a small tomb that was not originally meant for him, with all of his possessions, from thrones and chariots to jewelry and toys, squashed into four cramped chambers. Shortly after the funeral the tomb was broken into twice, but the thieves did not manage to enter the gold-encased shrines that protected the mummy's sarcophagus and coffins. The priests did a cursory job of cleaning up and resealed the doors.

The entrance was subsequently hidden by flood debris and forgotten about. The tomb lay untouched for more than 3,000 years, until the archaeologist Howard Carter discovered it in November 1922. Carter and his patron, the Earl of Carnarvon, had searched the Valley of the Kings for six exhausting seasons with little

The discovery and excavation of the tomb of "King Tut," as he was dubbed in the popular press, remains one of the most spectacular moments in the history of mummy studies and its interaction with popular public perceptions of what the field is about. It was both the culmination of more than century's worth of simmering Egyptomania and a seminal event in its own right that recharged the popular imagination and launched a new age of mummy entertainment and scientific investigation.

to show for their efforts. Their peers believed there was nothing left to find in the Valley, but Carter was convinced that Tutankhamun's intact tomb must be nearby.

Carter's workmen dug into the flood layer that covered the valley floor and were finally rewarded by the discovery of some steps cut into the bedrock. The steps led down to a sealed door, followed by a sloping passage that was filled with stone chippings, and a second sealed door. Carter poked his candle through a hole in the door and was amazed by the gleaming treasures within, famously remarking to Carnarvon about "wonderful things" that lay inside.

After carefully emptying the antechamber, Carter and Carnarvon tackled the sealed wall that lay beyond. It was guarded by two life-size statues of Tutankhamun and led to the pharaoh's burial chamber. They held an official opening ceremony of the chamber on February 16, 1923.

The chamber was filled by four gold-covered wooden shrines, which fitted closely inside each other. Inside those was a large pink granite sarcophagus, then three anthropoid coffins, the innermost one made from solid gold.

Carnarvon never got to see the coffins. Shortly after the burial chamber was opened, he suffered an infected mosquito bite and died from blood poisoning on April 5. The idea of a mummy's curse had already been explored in literature by authors such as Louisa May Alcott and Arthur Conan Doyle, but the high-profile death of Carnarvon, at the height of popular interest in Tutankhamun's tomb, ensured that the story became an enduring legend. It has inspired countless films, books and documentaries, and is still regularly blamed for untoward events, from the chaos of the Egyptian revolution to the mystery of a rotating statue in Manchester, UK.

The prospect of unwrapping Tutankhamun's mummy caused great excitement. As the only royal mummy found intact, it promised to reveal for the first time exactly how the ancient Egyptians buried their kings, and hopes were high that it would be in perfect condition. Little was known about Tutankhamun or the intriguing period in which he lived, and disappointingly, no written records were found within his tomb. Any information about the king's life and death would have to come from the mummy itself.

To unwrap the king, Carter enlisted the help of Douglas Derry, a Scottish anatomist based in Cairo who specialized in the study of ancient remains. The autopsy took place in the narrow entrance corridor of the tomb of Seti II, which Carter and his team used as an on-site laboratory. It was carried out over eight days starting on November 11, 1925.

The mummy wore an impressive gold burial mask and was wrapped in a linen sheet, secured by bandages around the knees, ankles, shoulders and hips. But it was not in good condition. There were signs of dampness inside the coffins, and the fabric was charred and fragile. Another problem was that unguents poured over the mummy during the funeral had set hard, gluing the body inside its gold coffin. Derry poured wax over the mummy to strengthen its coverings, then used a knife to cut from the mummy's chin down to its toes, before peeling back the outer layers.

Inside he found 143 items of jewelry, including gold sandals, a ceremonial gold apron, and a gold dagger with an iron blade, along with two other iron objects found on the mummy—the earliest examples of iron from Egypt that had ever been discovered. There were bangles, bracelets, finger rings and amulets. Over the chest alone were 35 objects at 13 different layers within the wrappings, including four gold collars featuring vultures, snakes and hawks; three scarabs; and an elaborate beaded bib.

The body itself was fragile and shrunken: for example, the flesh on its legs was just half a centimeter thick. The skin was cracked and grey. Derry estimated that Tutankhamun was slightly built, around five feet, six inches tall, and that he died aged just eighteen. The face was in good condition, with long eyelashes, pierced ears, and slightly protruding upper teeth. On the mummy's left cheek was a large round scab. Much to Carter's disappointment, there was no obvious cause of death. But the skull was particularly wide—154 mm across. It was very similar to the skull of an anonymous royal mummy from the same period found in the nearby tomb KV55, leading Derry and Carter to speculate that these two men were closely related.

Because the mummy was glued so tightly inside its coffin, the only way to remove it was to cut it into pieces before scraping those out. The hands, feet, and limbs were separated from the body, and the torso was cut in two. The pieces were placed in a wooden tray and temporarily stored in Seti II's tomb. Carter subsequently reconstructed the mummy and put the tray into the outer coffin (the inner two were taken to the Egyptian museum in Cairo). He replaced this into Tutankhamun's sarcophagus, still in the tomb's burial chamber, on October 23, 1926.

The next time the coffin was opened (officially at least) was on December 4, 1968. An anatomist from Liverpool University, UK, named Ronald Harrison X-rayed the mummy to investigate what killed the young king. The mummy had deteriorated since Carter reinterred it. The pieces were charred black instead of grey. Its arms were extended instead of folded across the chest. The head was tilted instead of straight, the ears were mostly destroyed, and the eyes were punched in.

The beaded skullcap and chest bib, which Carter is thought to have left in place, were gone. This has led experts to conclude that the tomb must have been looted at some time between 1926 and 1968, perhaps during World War II when security in the area was lax.

Harrison's results were shown in the BBC film *Tutankhamen Post Mortem* on October 25, 1969. The X-ray images showed two layers of resin inside the skull, one at the top and one at the back, suggesting that it was poured in and allowed to cool on two separate occasions. Harrison also noted two bone fragments inside the skull, as well as an area at the base of the skull that looked unusually thin. He speculated that this could be due to a brain haemorrhage, perhaps caused by a blow to the back of the head.

This statement led to the enduring idea that Tutankhamun was murdered. Several scholars have extended the theory, including the Egyptologist Bob Brier. But it has since been shown that the bone fragments were dislodged from Tutankhamun's spine after his death, and that the unusual appearance of the base of the skull was due to the radiograph being taken at a slight angle. There is no direct evidence for murder.

As well as X-raying the mummy, Harrison took home a small tissue sample. His colleague Robert Connolly used this to determine that Tutankhamun's blood group was A2MN, the same as the KV55 mummy. Tutankhamun's head was X-rayed again in 1978 by orthodontist James Harris from the University of Michigan, who X-rayed many of the royal mummies to investigate their family relationships.

A few decades later, Egypt's antiquities chief, Zahi Hawass, teamed up with U.S. media companies to fund scientific studies of the royal mummies, the results of which were then featured in hugely popular TV documentaries. On January 5, 2005, Hawass's team CT scanned Tutankhamun's mummy in a project funded by National Geographic. The researchers concluded that the pharaoh was healthy and well-nourished, with an impacted wisdom tooth. The mummy's left femur was fractured. Some members of the team argued that this could represent post-mortem damage, while others suggested that it occurred just before death, in an accident that killed the king.

This was presented as an unequivocal conclusion in *King Tut's Final Secrets*, aired by National Geographic on May 15, 2005. The CT results also featured prominently in a touring exhibition of Tutankhamun's treasures, partly funded by National Geographic, which toured across the United States and around the world starting in June 2005. A reconstruction of Tutankhamun's face based on the scans caused controversy for looking too "un-African": it was removed and replaced with a photo.

Meanwhile there were fears that the variable temperature and humidity caused by visitors to Tutankhamun's tomb might damage the mummy. On November 5,

2007, the Egyptian authorities moved it from the burial chamber into a climate-controlled glass case in the tomb's antechamber.

On February 24, 2008, a team led by Hawass—this time funded by the Discovery Channel—took samples of Tutankhamun's mummy for DNA analysis. These were analyzed in a state-of-the-art laboratory in the basement of the Egyptian museum. The samples were compared with those from other royal mummies from the period, and used to construct a family tree.

The results were published in the *Journal of the American Medical Association* (JAMA) on February 17, 2010. They also featured in a two-part documentary, aired on the Discovery Channel, titled *King Tut Unwrapped*. The researchers concluded that Tutankhamun was the son of the man found in KV55, whom they identified as Akhenaten. Two previously unidentified mummies found in tomb KV35 were reported to be Tutankhamun's grandmother (Queen Tiye) and mother (a previously unknown sister of Akhenaten). The DNA data supported the idea that two mummified fetuses found in Tutankhamun's tomb were his stillborn daughters.

The team reported that Tutankhamun was infected with malaria, and reanalyzed the CT results, this time concluding that the king had a badly deformed left foot. But almost all of these conclusions have since been questioned by other scientists. Critics argue that the DNA results could have been contaminated with modern DNA, and that the mummy's foot was probably damaged after death.

The CT scans have since been analyzed by a physician from Seattle named Benson Harer. He focuses on the fact that Tutankhamun's mummy has no chest or heart. Other researchers suggest that the chest was removed in modern times, perhaps by the looters who stole the beaded bib. But Harer uses several lines of evidence to argue that the ribs were cut when Tutankhamun's body was fresh, and that his heart was missing when he was mummified. This conclusion is supported by Connolly, who has reanalyzed Harrison's original X-rays. Harer and Connolly both believe that Tutankhamun may have died in an accident that crushed his chest, perhaps while hunting.

Shortly after the Egyptian uprising in January 2011, Hawass lost his position as Minister for Antiquities. Collaborations between the antiquities service and U.S. media companies ceased, and for now at least, all research on the royal mummies has stopped. Tutankhamun himself still lies in his glass case, covered head to toe with a plain, linen sheet. One of best-studied mummies of all time, and the details of his life, family relationships, and death, remain mysterious.

Jo Marchant

See also: Carnarvon, Fifth Earl of (George Herbert); Carter, Howard; Corelli, Marie; Genetic study of mummies; Medical imaging of mummies; *The Mummy* (1932); Mummy's curse; Royal mummies of Egypt, Part One: Third to Eighteenth Dynasties; Swiss Mummy Project

Further Reading

Brier, Bob. 1998. *The Murder of Tutankhamen: A True Story.* New York: G. P. Putnam's Sons.

Bucaille, Maurice. 1990. *Mummies of the Pharaohs: Modern Medical Investigations.* New York: St. Martin's Press.

Carter, Howard. 1927. *The Tomb of Tut.Ankh.Amen volume 2.* London: Cassell.

Carter, Howard and A. C. Mace. 1923. *The Tomb of Tut.Ankh.Amen volume 1.* London: Cassell.

Frayling, Christopher. 1992. *The Face of Tutankhamun.* London: Faber and Faber.

The Griffith Institute. n.d. *Tutankhamun: Anatomy of an Excavation.* Accessed December 19, 2013. www.griffith.ox.ac.uk/tutankhamundiscovery.html.

Leek, Frank F. 1972. *The Human Remains from the Tomb of Tut'ankhamun.* Tut'ankhamun's Tomb Series Part V. Oxford: Griffith Institute.

Marchant, Jo. 2011. "Curse of the Pharaoh's DNA." *Nature,* April 27. Accessed December 19, 2013. http://www.nature.com/news/2011/110427/full/472404a.html.

Marchant, Jo. 2011. "What Killed Tutankhamun?" *New Scientist,* January 19. Accessed December 19, 2013. http://www.newscientist.com/article/mg20927951.500-pharaonic -forensics-what-killed-tutankhamun.html.

Marchant, Jo. 2013. *The Shadow King: The Bizarre Afterlife of King Tut's Mummy.* Boston: Da Capo Press.

Tyldesley, Joyce A. 2012. *Tutankhamen: The Search for an Egyptian King.* New York: Basic Books.

U

Uhle, Max

German Archaeologist Dr. Max Uhle (1856–1944), "Father of Peruvian Archaeology" (Rowe 1954), was the first to describe the mummies of the Chinchorro culture in Chile, now dated as the oldest mummies in the world. He developed chronological sequences for pre-Columbian cultures in Peru and can be considered the founder of Latin American Studies. Uhle was the first to apply stratigraphic methods in excavations in South America and the United States.

Friedrich Max Uhle was born March 25, 1856 in Dresden. He earned a PhD in Linguistics at the University of Leipzig and worked as a curator in anthropological museums in Dresden (1881–88) and Berlin (1888–95). Influenced by his friend Alphons Stübel, a collector of mummies and artifacts from Peru, Uhle started to focus on pre-Columbian cultures of South America. In 1892 he embarked on a journey through Latin America lasting nearly 41 years.

In 1896–97 he excavated in Pachacamac, Peru, documenting assemblages that have since been heavily looted. Here, Uhle found different cemeteries with mummy bundles (humans in seated positions and wrapped in textiles), one of them with females that were strangled. In 1903 he published his findings in a pioneering book titled *Pachacamac* describing the superimposition of subsequent cultures. This changed idea, which was then widespread, of separate regional styles into a chronology for the Central Andes, which, although updated, is still in use.

In 1898 he excavated the Peruvian site Huaca de la Luna, isolating the Moche-style, which he named "proto-Chimú." His chronology, expanded by Kroeber, is still the basis for pre-Incan chronology in Peru. In 1902, while excavating Emeryville Shellmound, California, he was the first to apply the stratigraphic method in the United States. In 1906 he became director of the archaeological department of the Museo Nacional de Historia (now, Museo Nacional) in Lima, Peru.

As the "initiator of scientific archeology in Northern Chile," in 1912 he was the first to describe the mummies of the "Aborigines of Arica," now known as the Chinchorro culture, and was also the first to classify them into types. In Santiago de Chile he became director of the department of archaeology, helping to build the collections of the Museo de Etnología y Antropología.

In 1919 Uhle moved to Ecuador where, in 1925, he was given a chair at the University of Quito. He worked on collections, extended the museum, and excavated. He stayed until 1933, when he became employed by the Ibero American

Institute (IAI) in Berlin, Germany. He bequeathed significant parts of his personal effects to the IAI, but also to Philadelphia, Santiago de Chile, Lima, and Quito.

Uhle died on the May 11, 1944 in Loben, Poland. The Peruvian mummies he excavated are today in the University of California, Berkeley. The heads of the strangled females from Pachacamac are now macerated (stripped bare of flesh by decomposition) and in the Pennsylvania Medical School. Uhle's legacy is widespread in Peru, where he gives his name to many streets, a school, archaeological monuments, a museum, and a football team.

Anna-Maria Begerock

See also: Chinchorro mummies; Mummies of Latin America

Further Reading

Fleming, Stuart. 1986. "The Mummies of Pachacamac: An Exceptional Legacy from Uhle's 1896 Excavations." *Expedition* 28, no. 3: 39–45. Accessed December 19, 2013. http://www.penn.museum/documents/publications/expedition/PDFs/28-3/Fleming.pdf. PDF.

Menzel, Dorothy. 1977. *The Archaeology of Ancient Peru and the Work of Max Uhle*. R. H. Lowie Museum of Anthropology. Berkeley: University of California Press.

Rowe, John Howland. 1954. *Max Uhle 1856–1944: A Memoir of the Father of Peruvian Archaeology*. University of California Publications in American Archaeology and Ethnology 46, no. 1. Berkeley: University of California Press.

Uhle, Max. 1903. *Pachacamac. Report of the William Pepper, M.D., LL.D., Peruvian Expedition of 1896*. Philadelphia: University of Pennsylvania Press.

Universal Studios mummy series

The iconic cinematic mummy was first created and then evolved at Universal Studios in Hollywood. Over a period of nearly a quarter century, Universal's mummies went from the sublime (1932's *The Mummy* starring Boris Karloff) to the ridiculous (*Abbott & Costello Meet the Mummy,* 1955). Although Karloff's film was nowhere near the beginning of mummy cinema, it was the first talking mummy film and set the pattern for much that was to follow, initially from Universal itself. Originally developed as a story idea called "Cagliostro," about an ancient Egyptian magician/scientist who lived through the centuries through alchemy and preservative chemical injections, the story changed several times until the protagonist became a living mummy, never embalmed, but resurrected by reading aloud the Scroll of Thoth. Imhotep, namesake of a real Egyptian sage from the pyramid age, quickly dropped his mummy wrappings to masquerade as Ardath Bey, a seemingly modern, though odd, individual who, in contrast to nearly all later mummy films, actually assists archaeologists in finding the tomb of the princess Ankhesenamen (the historical name of King Tut's wife). Bey's goal is to reanimate

Universal Studios can justly be credited with having created the "mummy movie," and also the modern-day iconic mummy of popular imagination, almost single-handedly with 1932's classic *The Mummy* and its sequels in the 1940s. These films have exerted a defining influence on the reigning image of the mummy in film, fiction, and popular culture ever since, with all other versions (e.g., the Hammer Films mummy series) either drawing directly on them or otherwise standing in their debt.

the mummy like himself, but he soon finds that the "soul" has transferred to the modern Egyptian woman Helen Grosvenor.

The story uses reincarnation as a major theme, though this is not obvious in the finished film, which cut out the part of the storyline involving multiple lives the princess had experienced between ancient Egypt and the present. This theme was introduced by John Balderston, the final scriptwriter, who had changed the original storyline developed by Nina Wilcox Putnam and also Richard Schayer. Balderston was familiar enough with Egyptology to have known that reincarnation is a Hindu idea from India and would have completely baffled Egyptians, but he was also at this time developing a screenplay based on Rider Haggard's 1887 novel of the immortal *SHE*, and reincarnation was at the forefront of his thoughts. From this beginning, the notion that Egyptians believed in reincarnation was developed over and over again, such that many people today accept it as a fact. Though no credit is given in the film, the basic concept of someone alive for thousands of years with the goal of rejoining a lost love (in either eternal life or death) is not found in Haggard alone but also in Conan Doyle's 1890 story "The Ring of Thoth." A suspiciously similar tale called "The Nameless Mummy" appeared in early 1932, a few months before Balderston began finalizing *The Mummy* screenplay.

When Universal launched its 1940s series of horror films, they differed from those of the early 1930s in featuring less mood and characterization in favor of fast-paced action, sometimes laced with humor. Because Imhotep's body was blasted to dust by the goddess Isis in 1932, a different mummy was required, but the Kharis series, starting with *The Mummy's Hand* in 1940, is a reboot, not a sequel. Much the same story as the Karloff film, but set completely in Egypt, this movie alters certain details, though using flashbacks of the earlier film to save money, while inserting changes in close-ups to show Tom Tyler (see below) handling tana leaves in place of Karloff reading from the Scroll of Thoth. To allow more freedom for mayhem, the mummy itself is presented as a separate individual from the high priest who controls him; this idea of the mummy being a tool of vengeance, subject to another's will, again was first seen in a Conan Doyle story, "Lot. No. 249," from 1892, though again no credit is given. The princess is named Ananka, perhaps merely a simplified approximation of Ankhesenamen, but where did the very un-Egyptian name Kharis come from? Few writers mention this, but one has to wonder whether the name is merely the result of someone's playing with syllables until hitting on something that sounded good. One also notes that the original Universal mummy, Boris Karloff, has the sounds "Kar-Is" embedded in his name.

The first actor to play Kharis was cowboy star Tom Tyler, who is often said to have been perfect for the shambling mummy because he was beginning to be crippled by arthritis at the time he played the part. But in fact, that condition came later in his life; watch his athletic Captain Marvel the year after he played the mummy. Nevertheless Tyler was replaced by Lon Chaney, Jr. for the three Kharis sequels, all of which are set in the United States and present a single, extended storyline, though the logic connecting them from film to film defies any attempt at rational comprehension. *The Mummy's Tomb* (1942) follows *Hand* by 30 years, though why this delay occurs is unexplained. *The Mummy's Ghost* (1944) obviously occurs just a few weeks or months later, but then *The Mummy's Curse* (also 1944) has again witnessed a lapse of 25 more years. A dated document places *Hand* in 1940, the year it was filmed, so the next two take place around 1970 and the last in 1995, but obviously nothing—fashion, cars, phones—has changed. And what do these time issues even matter when geography, too, is irrelevant; in *Ghost* the mummies enter a swamp in Massachusetts, but in *Curse* they emerge from one in Louisiana. Reincarnation is reintroduced in *Ghost* as we find that the heroine is actually Ananka, aging before our eyes at the film's end, echoing the climax of Haggard's *She*. But in the follow-up, made just months later, Ananka washes off swamp mud to appear as a beautiful young woman again. Perhaps audiences who only saw these movies once in theaters, several years apart, were not as critical as modern viewers watching the movies on video multiple times.

Universal brought the mummy back one more time, in the last of their films pairing Abbott & Costello with the studio's classic monsters. But the name of the mummy became Klaris, and despite having three wrapped mummies/impostors pursuing Lou Costello at one point in the movie, the laughs were thin. Actually, the Kharis films themselves, supposedly horror vehicles, often exhibited more humor (perhaps unintentional?) in scenes where the crippled mummy just misses grabbing the victim as she's turned away and unaware of his presence.

When Hammer made their first mummy film in 1959, they were allowed by Universal to adapt the Kharis mummy, though the film actually borrows character names and details from all the Universal films spanning 1932 to 1944, although adding original details such as the Victorian English setting and a mummy which, though not actually running as in "Lot No. 249," is fast enough to pose a believable threat to healthy adults. The archaeologist's wife has a physical resemblance to Ananka, but the concept of reincarnation is mercifully not invoked. Universal's Kharis was initially actuated by priests of Karnak, suggesting (correctly) that this was a geographic area or temple location; oddly, the later films changed Karnak to the inauthentic Arkam. The 1959 Hammer version, for its part, although generally attentive to the accuracy of several Egyptological details, turned Karnak into a god, depicted as something like a mongoose.

When director Stephen Sommers rebooted the long-dormant Universal series by remaking *The Mummy* in 1999, he chose Brendan Fraser to portray an Indiana Jones-style archaeological adventurer, which paid off with a direct sequel, several spin-offs about the scorpion king, an animated television show, and a semi-related follow-up set in China. Such adventure fantasies become increasingly distant from the concept that originally spawned them 70-years earlier. At the time of this writing, talk continues of yet another reboot of Universal's mummy franchise, most recently (Nov 27, 2013) at the Internet Movie Database, which claims a release date of April 22, 2016, for an as-yet unscripted movie.

Carter Lupton

See also: *Abbott and Costello Meet the Mummy*; Chaney, Lon, Jr.; Doyle, Arthur Conan; Freund, Karl; Haggard, H. Rider; Imhotep; Karloff, Boris; Kharis; *The Mummy* (1932); *The Mummy* (1959); *The Mummy* (1999) and *The Mummy Returns*; The mummy in popular culture; Mummy movies; *The Mummy's Ghost* and *The Mummy's Curse*; *The Mummy's Hand*; *The Mummy's Tomb*

Further Reading

Cowie, Susan D., and Tom Johnson. 2002. *The Mummy in Fact, Fiction, and Film.* Jefferson, NC: McFarland & Co.

Feramisco, Thomas M. 2002. *The Mummy Unwrapped: Scenes Left on Universal's Cutting Room Floor.* Jefferson, NC: McFarland & Co.

Landis, John. 2011. *Monsters in the Movies: 100 Years of Cinematic Nightmares.* New York: DK Publishing.

Peirse, Alison. 2013. *After Dracula: The 1930s Horror Film.* London: I. B. Tauris & Co.

Weaver, Tom, Michael Brunas, and John Brunas. 2007. *Universal Horrors: The Studio's Classic Films, 1931–1946.* Jefferson, NC: McFarland & Co.

V

Valley of the Kings

The Valley of the Kings comprises a group of interconnected wadis (normally dry desert water courses) on the west bank of the river Nile opposite Luxor. They occupy an area of over 9 square kilometers, and are grouped into the "Kings' Valley" (with 3 square kilometers occupied by tombs) and the "West Valley" (0.4 square kilometers). They were used as a burial place for kings and other high-status individuals during the Egyptian New Kingdom (ca. 1550–1070 BCE), with some tombs reused during the Third Intermediate Period (ca. 1070–712 BCE). To date, 104 tombs, or the beginnings of such, have been identified, of which 64 have been given official numbers (prefixed by "KV" or "WV").

Prior to the early 18th Dynasty, royal tombs usually placed the king's burial chamber close to the monumental public element of the burial complex (the mortuary temple, often with an adjoining pyramid). However, from then until the end

The Mortuary Temple of Queen Hatshepsut in the Valley of the Kings, widely recognized as one of the great monuments of ancient Egypt. (DEA/P. LIACI/De Agostini/Getty Images)

of the 12th Dynasty, while the mortuary temple was placed on the edge of the low desert opposite the religious capital at and around Luxor, the burial itself was made in rock-cut galleries in the Valley, which was cut off from the low desert by a curtain of cliffs. This seems likely to have been prompted by a desire for increased security, as the earliest tombs in the Valley were so placed as to allow their locations to be obliterated by the flash floods that periodically penetrate it, depositing debris in the process.

The first king to be buried in the Valley was Thutmose I: there is some debate as to the identity of his original tomb (either KV20 or KV38), since he was reburied at least twice. Likewise unclear is the burial place of Thutmose II (perhaps intended to be KV42). Otherwise, all subsequent kings of the New Kingdom are known to have constructed their tombs there, with the exception of Akhenaten, who cut his at Tell el-Amarna, Smenkhkare and Neferneferuaten, who probably did so as well, and Rameses VIII, whose tomb remains unidentified.

Prior to the reign of Akhenaten, the basic form of a king's tomb was a series of galleries descending through one (later two) right-angle turns down to the burial chamber, the initial descent being interrupted by a deep shaft, which may have combined theological meaning with providing protection from any infiltration of flood-water. Some earlier burial chambers were oval (imitating the shape of the royal cartouche), but from the reign of Amenhotep II (KV35) onward a rectangular plan became standard, with a sunken crypt holding a stone sarcophagus. The canopic chest, holding the internal organs, was placed near the foot of the sarcophagus. The burial chambers of these tombs were decorated with the Book of *Amduat* (What-is-the-Underworld), depicting the sun-god's nocturnal journey, and painted as though on a papyrus scroll. The tombs also contained depictions of the king before various deities, from the reign of Thutmose IV (KV43) onward in polychrome.

Just as the kings' tombs were associated with mortuary temples on the low desert beyond the Valley, members of the nobility, priesthood, and the royal household had tomb-chapels in the hills behind the royal mortuary temples. Most had their burial chambers in the rock below them, but a few particularly favored individuals had this element of their tombs in the Valley. These actually comprise the majority of sepulchres there, but take the form of small, undecorated chambers approached by a vertical shaft or by a stairway and corridor. Since all known examples had been robbed to some degree, only a few of their owners have been identified, but those included the Vizier Amenemopet (KV48) and Yuya and Tjuiu, parents-in-law of Amenhotep III (KV46).

Amenhotep III abandoned the hitherto-used Kings' Valley branch in favor of the virgin West Valley for his tomb (WV22). It seems likely that a tomb (WV25) was begun there for his successor Amenhotep IV, but the latter (having changed his name to Akhenaten) moved the royal cemetery to his new city at Tell el-Amarna as a consequence of his religious revolution. The Valley of the Kings was once more used under Akhenaten's son Tutankhamun, although his tomb (KV62) was actually a private one, modified for a royal burial. It is possible that he had previously begun WV23 in the West Valley, which was in the event used for the interment of his successor, Ay. The decoration of these two tombs differed significantly from pre-Akhenaten tombs in both painting style and content, reflecting a widespread recasting of the decoration of funerary monuments post-Akhenaten.

The last king of the 18th Dynasty, Horemheb, inaugurated a new series of tombs in the Kings' Valley, which had a single axis and whose decoration, now carved in painted relief, supplemented the *Amduat* with additional religious compositions, which multiplied and transformed during the 19th and 20th Dynasties. Architecturally, these tombs, through to the very last, that of Rameses XI (KV4), also exhibit a steady evolution, the main motifs being a change in the orientation of the burial chamber under Rameses II (KV7) and a progressive reduction in the angle of descent after the reign of Merenptah (KV8).

The tombs in the Valley were subject to robbery from at least the latter part of the 18th Dynasty onward, but this became endemic during the latter part of the 20th Dynasty. As a result, many mummies required restoration and were gradually concentrated in a smaller number of tombs for greater security. Eventually, all those that survived, save those secreted in the tomb of Amenhotep II, were removed from the Valley altogether and, eventually, placed together in a tomb (TT320) near Deir el-Bahari early in the 22nd Dynasty.

Subsequently, a number of tombs were reused for the burial of female members of the clergy of Amun during the 22nd Dynasty, some of which survived intact until modern times. Otherwise, only a handful of tombs have been found still containing mummies, including those Tutankhamun, Amenhotep II, and Yuya and Tjuiu.

Aidan Dodson

See also: Bahariya Oasis: Valley of the Golden Mummies; Egyptian mummies; Religion and mummies; Royal mummies of Egypt, Part One: Third to Eighteenth Dynasties; Royal mummies of Egypt, Part Two: Nineteenth to Twenty-fifth dynasties; Theban Necropolis; Tutankhamun ("King Tut")

Further Reading

Dodson, Aidan. 2015. *The Royal Tombs of Ancient Egypt*. Barnsley: Pen and Sword.
Hornung, Erik. 1990. *The Valley of the Kings: Horizon of Eternity*. New York: Timken.
Reeves, Nicholas, and Richard H. Wilkinson. 1990. *The Complete Valley of the Kings*. New York: Thames and Hudson.
Weeks, Kent, ed. 2002. *The Valley of the Kings*. Vercelli: White Star.

Vatican Mummy Project

In 2007 the Department of Antiquities of Egypt and the Near East of the Vatican Museums set up the Vatican Mummy Project, coordinated by Alessia Amenta, with the aim of cataloging, studying, and restoring the collection of human mummies held in the Gregorian Egyptian Museum. The project does not include mummy bandages that arrived in the museum as separate items.

Within the Vatican Museums the project has availed itself of the collaboration of the Diagnostic Laboratory for Conservation and Restoration, the Laboratory for the Restoration of Works on Paper (for elements in *cartonnage*), and the Laboratory for the restoration of Tapestries and Fabrics (for the restoration of the bandages). Other collaborators include research workers from the Accademia Europea in Bolzano (Institute for Mummies and the Iceman), who have undertaken histological and molecular analyses, the anthropologist Dario Piombino-Mascali for bioarchaeological studies, the radiologist Stephanie Panzer, the entomologist Massimo Masetti, and the restorer Cinzia Oliva for the preservation of the bandages.

The project provides for three distinct phases in the study of each mummy:

1. Archival research, concerning both the dynamics of the acquisition and regarding any previous restoration undertaken.
2. Restoration and technical study of the bandages with relative reconstruction of the pattern of bandaging. Particular emphasis has also been given to the aspect of the "reuse" of bandages, well-evidenced by the presence of "antique darning" and various other stitching.
3. Whenever possible, an anthropological study of the body and its restoration.

The Vatican collection of Egyptian mummies holds nine complete bodies and eighteen body parts made up of heads, hands, and feet. To this two examples of so-called pseudo-mummies of children can be added.

The first mummy to be studied and restored (inv. MV 25011.6.1) belongs to a male who lived in the region of Fayoum in the Ptolemaic Period (second century BCE). The mummy arrived in the museum within a modern sarcophagus and covered by a series of inscribed and painted gilded *cartonnage* elements, used to protect the head, the chest, the upper part of the legs, and the feet; there was a garland of flowers around the neck. All these elements were probably reused, as they carry the name of a woman. The mummy had been the subject of a poor embalming, and has been restored internally by means of a consolidation of the vertebral column, although it has not been possible to reconstruct the thoracic cavity. It was later possible to determine the pattern of the original bandaging and restore it.

The second mummy to be examined (inv. MV 25004), which belongs to a young woman, had been profaned, probably in ancient times, to take any precious amulets: the bandages were found to be cut around the face, as well as those of the feet. This has allowed an in-depth "stratigraphic" study of the pattern of bandages, which turned out to be quite complex: the body was wrapped in bandages and also in four shrouds, gathered together on the chest of the mummy so as to obtain a perfect refilling of the thorax; another shroud was placed over the face. In all there were between 20 and 30 layers of bandaging.

The third mummy (inv. MV 57853), still being studied, is one of the "pseudo-mummies," which arrived in the museum covered with unrelated *cartonnage*.

Alessia Amenta

See also: Egyptian mummies; Genetic study of mummies; Medical imaging of mummies

Further Reading

Amenta, Alessia. 2009. "The Vatican Mummy Project. The Restoration of the Mummy of Ny-Maat-Re (MV 25011.6.1)." *Studien zur altägyptischen Kultur* 38: 33–43.

Amenta, Alessia. 2009–2010. "Vatican Mummy Project. Il restauro della mummia di Ni-Maat-Ra (MV 25011.6.1)." *Bollettino dei Monumenti Musei e Gallerie Pontificie* 27: 47–64.

Amenta, Alessia. 2010. "The Restoration of the Funerary Cartonnage of Ny-Maat-Re (MV 25011.6.1)." In *Decorated Surfaces on Ancient Egyptian Objects. Technology, Deterioration and Conservation (Cambridge, 6–9 September 2007)*, edited by Julie Dawson, Christina Rozeik, and Margot M. Wright, 167. London: Archetype Publications.

Amenta, Alessia, Dario Piombino-Mascali, Stephanie Panzer. Forthcoming. "Vatican Mummy Project. L'indagine paleoradiologica della mummia di Ni-Maat-Ra (MV 25011.6.1)." *Bollettino dei Monumenti Musei e Gallerie Pontificie*.

Glatz, Carol. 2010. "Keeping Mum: Preserving the Past While Still Uncovering Its Mysteries." *Catholic News Service*, March 12. Accessed December 19, 2013. http://www.catholicnews.com/data/stories/cns/1001066.htm.

Glatz, Carol. 2013. "Vatican Mummy Health Check: It's Never Too Late for an Endoscopy." *The Catholic Register*, January 18. Accessed December 19, 2013. http://www.catholicregister.org/news/international/item/15710-vatican-mummy-health-check-its-never-too-late-for-an-endoscopy.

"The Vengeance of Nitocris"

"The Vengeance of Nitocris" is a revenge story set in ancient Egypt that was first published in the August 1928 issue of the pulp magazine *Weird Tales*. It is the first published work of fiction by Thomas Lanier "Tennessee" Williams (1911–1983), written when he was 16 years old and published when he was 17. Williams was paid $35 for the story, which runs slightly less than 7,000 words long.

In the foreword to the published edition of his play *Sweet Bird of Youth* (1959), Williams attributes the origins of the story to his reading of a paragraph in the *History* of Herodotus. The paragraph in question is chapter 100 in the second book of the *History*, which reads as follows in the George Rawlinson translation of 1862:

Next, they read me from a papyrus, the names of three hundred and thirty monarchs, who (they said) were his [referring to Mên, the first king of Egypt] successors upon the throne. In this number of generations there were eighteen Ethiopian kings, and one queen who was a native; all the rest were kings and Egyptians. The queen bore the same name as the Babylonian princess, namely, Nitocris. They said that she succeeded her brother; he had been king of Egypt, and was put to death by his subjects, who then placed her upon the throne. Bent on avenging his death, she devised a cunning scheme by which she destroyed a vast number of Egyptians. She constructed a spacious underground chamber, and, on pretence of inaugurating it, contrived the following:—Inviting to a banquet those of the Egyptians whom she knew to have had the chief share in the murder of her brother, she suddenly, as they were feasting, let the river in upon them, by means of a secret duct of large size. This, and this only, did they tell me of her, except that, when she had done as I have said, she threw herself into an apartment full of ashes, that she might escape the vengeance whereto she would otherwise have been exposed. (Herodotus 1875, 164–166)

William's tale is a fairly straightforward elaboration on the events described in this paragraph. A brief prologue relates how the pharaoh—angered that the surging Nile has swept away a bridge he had been building for five years so that he could make good on his boast to one day ride his chariot across the river—has personally blown out the fires in the temple to Osiris, god of the underworld, and allowed them to remain unlit for five days. Further, he has defiled the altars of the temple, purportedly making a burnt offering of the carrion of a hyena on one. To the citizens of Thebes, this is a gross and dangerous act of desecration. Fearing the wrath of Osiris, the town's leading citizens surge as a vigilante mob toward the palace, where they confront the pharaoh, who stands on the steps leading up to it, with Nitocris, his sister, on his arm. The mob is cowed when the pharaoh descends the steps toward them, brandishing his sword. But when he stumbles on a crumbling step, and lands in a heap at the bottom of the stairs, the mob takes this as a sign from the god and falls on him, tearing his body to pieces.

A week later, the same citizens choose Nitocris as their new ruler. Nitocris, meanwhile, schemes to avenge her brother's death. All through the winter and spring, workmen, slaves, and barges under the queen's command are seen to travel down the Nile in unusually large numbers. Nitocris finally reveals that she has built a new temple to Osiris, and she invites the leading citizens of the city to a banquet to dedicate the new temple. Upon arriving, the citizens are led to a vast banquet hall beneath the temple and below the level of the river. The banquet soon becomes a bacchanal. When the guests are insensible with drink, Nitocris leaves the banquet hall, closes the slab ceiling through which the guests entered, and opens sluice gates to the river that have been built into the temple, drowning them all. As Williams writes: "And it was in the waters of the Nile, material symbol of the god Osiris, that they had died. It was magnificent in its irony!" (Williams 1985, 10–11).

In the closing paragraphs, Williams the narrator steps outside the story as a work of fiction to fulfill what he describes as "the responsibility of a historian" (Williams 1985, 11). He reports that, when the guests did not return home from the banquet, another mob of their family and friends stormed the palace the following morning, only to discover that when she returned home the evening before, Nitocris had ordered her slaves to fill her chambers with smoking ashes to smother herself. "Only her beautiful dead body remained for the mob" (Williams 1985, 12).

Discussing the story in the context of his body of work, Williams wrote that "it set the keynote for most of the work that has followed" (Williams 2009, 94). Indeed, "The Vengeance of Nitocris" features a strong-willed woman, a character type that would recur in his plays and fiction, and its grotesquerie anticipates some of the southern Gothic flourishes of his later work. And although it does not actually feature any mummies, its plot, setting, and theme of a horrific revenge exacted by ancient Egyptian royalty resonates with the classic mummy horror subgenre that was still emerging when Williams penned the tale. For this reason, "The Vengeance of Nitocris" has been repeatedly reprinted in horror anthologies focusing on mummies and ancient Egypt.

Stefan R. Dziemianowicz

See also: The mummy in Western fiction: From 1922 to the twenty-first century

Further Reading

Herodotus. 1875. *The History of Herodotus. A New English Version*. Edited with notes by G. Rawlinson. London: John Murray. Also available at the Internet Classics Archive. Accessed December 19, 2013. http://classics.mit.edu/Herodotus/history.html.

Hitchcock, Francesca M. 1995. "Tennessee Williams's 'Vengeance of Nitocris': The Keynote to Future Works." *Mississippi Quarterly* 48, no. 4: 595–608.

Williams, Tennessee. 1985. "The Vengeance of Nitocris." In *Collected Stories* by Tennessee Williams, 1–12. New York: New Directions Books.

Williams, Tennessee. 2009. *New Selected Essays: Where I Live*. New York: New Directions Books.

von Kahlbutz, Christian Friedrich

Christian Friedrich von Kahlbutz was a sixteenth-century German knight, commonly known as Knight Kabeluz, who died at the age of 52 and was found to have been naturally mummified when his body was exhumed eight decades later.

Christian Friedrich von Kahlbutz was born on March 6, 1651, in Kampehl, Germany. He married a noblewoman and had 11 children of his own. According to a local legend, he had another 30 illegitimate children who were the result of his exercising the so-called *ius primae noctis*, the feudal right to sleep with a subordinate bride on the night of her marriage. In 1690 when one of his maids, who was the bride of a shepherd, refused his privilege, the knight killed her husband. Soon afterward he was accused by the maid of assassination, but von Kahlbutz swore innocence and prophesied that, as proof of his claim, his dead body would not decay. He died on November 3, 1702, and his body was buried in an oak coffin in the family tomb located in the church of Kampehl.

During renovation of the church in 1783, the body was found well preserved in its coffin. In contrast to his other family members, the corpse of Friedrich von Kahlbutz had undergone a natural mummification process. Although the local population believed that the preservation of the body was due to divine justice, it actually represents a typical case of the spontaneous mummification that is regularly found in churches and catacombs. The factors that probably contributed to the mummification process were the anaerobic sealing of the coffin, the arid and ventilated atmosphere inside the church, the tannin of the oak wood used for the coffin, and the absorbent properties of clothing inside the burial. Moreover, it is believed that a fatal disease may have led to a consumption of the body that also enhanced the mummification process. According to historic sources, the knight suffered from a lung disease—perhaps cancer or tuberculosis—and suffocated on his own blood. However, several examinations of the mummy, including tissue analysis, have not revealed any clear evidence for the cause of death.

Von Kahlbutz's mummy has attracted many scholars, going all the way back to the late nineteenth century. The famous German pathologist Rudolf Virchow and the surgeon Ferdinand Sauerbruch studied the mummy in the 1890s, but they were not able to explain how the dead body was actually preserved. Further studies have shown that the corpse did not undergo any kind of internal or external treatment, such as embalming or the application of salts or heavy metals. A speculation that von Kahlbutz may have been poisoned with arsenic by the maid was disproved by chemical analysis.

The mummy of Christian von Kahlbutz is currently displayed in the church of Kampehl.

Albert Zink

See also: Mummies of Europe; Natural mummification

Further Reading

Auderheide, Arthur. 2003. *The Scientific Study of Mummies*. Cambridge: Cambridge University Press.

Kleiss, E. 1992. "Natural Mummies in Tombs and Catacombs." In *Proceedings of the First World Congress on Mummy Studies*, vol. 2, 829–836. Santa Cruz, Tenerife, Canary Islands: Archaeological and Ethnographical Museum of Tenerife.

W

Windeby Girl

On May 19, 1952, a body was discovered in the Domlandsmoor near the town of Windeby in northern Germany during peat cutting. The body soon became known as the "Windeby Girl." A second body was found just 20 days later and only 5 meters away from the first body. This body was dubbed the "Windeby Man." The Windeby Girl rapidly became one of the most famous bog bodies ever excavated from northern Germany. Since soon after discovery, the Windeby Girl has been part of a collection of six bodies held by the Archäologisches Landesmuseum Schloss Gottorf, in Schleswig, northern Germany. The Windeby Man, also held at the Archäologisches Landesmuseum, was not well preserved: the body has virtually no remaining skeletal material and is essentially only a thin layer of preserved soft tissue.

The Windeby Girl was discovered in the Domlandsmoor near the town of Windeby in northern Germany during peat cutting. She died 2,000 years ago during northern Germany's Iron Age. (AP Images/Daniel Roland)

The first examinations of the Windeby Girl were undertaken shortly after discovery, and were published in detail in 1958. The body is quite well preserved, although there was only a small amount of skin remaining on the chest or abdomen and no internal organs were identified through physical and radiological analysis. The brain, however, was exceptionally well preserved, although very shrunken. All of the surviving bones of the body were severely demineralized. The body was found with a woven band across the eyes, often interpreted as a blindfold. Interestingly, there were several clay pots immediately associated with the Windeby Girl, and these may have been cremation urns, since cremation was the predominant form of the disposal of the dead in this region at that time.

Radiocarbon dating of a sample taken from the fur cape around the shoulders of the Windeby Girl provided an estimated date of about 2,000 years ago, during the Iron Age of northern Germany. At the time of discovery and for decades afterward, newspaper report, popular press publications, and other media took a sensationalistic approach to the interpretation of the potential reasons for the body to have been in the bog. It was suggested that the young girl was an adulteress who had been buried in the bog as a punishment burial, following practices mentioned by the Roman historian Tacitus. It was also claimed that the Windeby Girl may have had special powers as a "seer" and prophetess, based on the presence of the "blindfold" to cover the eyes. It is, of course, difficult to find any bioarchaeological evidence that would support these interpretations. There are no written records from this region and time to offer a cultural interpretation of the "girl" as a shaman or prophetess. It is, however, possible to say that the band that was found around the eyes is a similar style and weaving technique to hairbands of the time. It is also possible to note that bog bodies shrink and move while in the bog, so it is likely that the band is not in its original position: the band may have slipped from the top of the head to the face of the Windeby Child.

Some authors went so far as to state that the girl had been strangled with her hairband or intentionally drowned, but there was no physical evidence on the body to support either of these theories. There was no evidence of ligature on the surviving neck tissues, so the possibility of strangulation could not be confirmed. While an adulteress might have been drowned in a bog in the Iron Age, there was no surviving lung tissue from the Windeby Girl available for examination to potentially confirm this idea. Furthermore, the hair on the head of the adolescent was shorter on one side of the head than on the other. Some proponents of the adulteress theory proposed that the head was shaved at the time of deposition in the bog, to shame the guilty person. There are, however, other possible explanations. It is possible that the hair was damaged during excavation, although the hair has not yet been examined to address this possibility.

In 2003–2004, the Windeby Girl was reexamined as part of a larger project to reanalyze all of the bog bodies of the Schloss Gottorf collection. During conservation following discovery in the early 1950s, the bones were removed from the body, so most of the skeleton was available for direct analysis and some of the bones were studied with CT scanning.

The original studies reported that the Windeby Girl was an adolescent female who was about 12 to 14 years old at the time of her death, but no official cause of death was determined. The recent reassessment of the skeleton and mummy determined that the body was actually that of a young male who was probably around 16 years old at the time of his death, so it is more appropriate to refer to the "Windeby Child" than the "Windeby Girl." The results of the new analyzes had important implications for the interpretation of the Windeby Child.

The reanalysis of the body, like the original examination, was not able to determine a conclusive cause of death. It is clear that the young man was delicate and perhaps very unhealthy during his life. There is evidence on the skeleton and teeth that the youth had suffered from repeated physical insults, such as periods of malnutrition or severe illness.

In terms of interpretation of the Windeby Child, it seems clear that the idea that the body belonged to someone who was being punished as an adulteress cannot be supported on the basis of any physical evidence. The body is that of a young man. The second body found in close proximity to the Windeby Child is an adult male. At the time, cemeteries in this part of northern Germany were often segregated by sex. The possibility must be considered that this area of the Domlandsmoor may well have been a burial area for males, and that the Windeby Child was simply buried there on his death. The pottery vessels found with the Windeby Child also make it difficult to support the idea of the person being buried as a punishment.

The analysis and interpretation of bog bodies is difficult and often generates even more questions. While we may never know with certainty how the Windeby Child died, or why he was put in the bog, we can perhaps restore his reputation and consider that he may not have been the immoral criminal he has been believed to be since the early interpretations of the 1950s.

Heather Gill-Frerking

See also: Bog bodies; Lindow Man; Mummies of Europe; Natural mummification; Tollund Man

Further Reading

Asingh, Pauline, and Niels Lynnerup. 2007. *Grauballe Man: An Iron Age Bog Body Revisited*. Aarhus: Moesgaard Museum and Jutland Archaeological Society.

Buell, Janet. 1997. *Bog Bodies*. New York: Twenty-First Century Books.

Gill-Frerking, Heather. 2010. "Bog Bodies: Preserved Bodies from Peat." In *Mummies of the World*, edited by A. Wieczoreck and W. Rosendahl, 60–70. New York: Prestel.

Gill-Robinson, Heather. 2005. "The Iron Age Bog Bodies of the Archaeologisches Landesmuseum, Schloss Gottorf, Schleswig, Germany." Unpublished PhD Thesis. Department of Anthropology. University of Manitoba.

Gill-Robinson, Heather. 2007. "Hidden in Plain Sight: The Story of the Windeby Child." In *ZWEIUNDVIERZIG: Festschrift für Michael Gebühr zum 65*, Geburtstag, edited by S. Burmeister, H. Derks, and J. von Richtofen, 107–112. Rahden (Westf.): Verlag Marie Leidorf.

Green, Miranda Aldhouse. 2001. *Dying for the Gods: Human Sacrifice in Iron Age and Roman Europe*. Stroud: Tempus Publishing.

Lobell, Jarrett A. 2010. "A Career in the Bogs." *Archaeology Magazine*, May 27. Accessed December 7, 2013. http://archive.archaeology.org/online/interviews/heather _gill_robinson.

Menon S. 1997. "The People of the Bog." *Discover* 18, no. 8: 60–67.

Turner, R. C., and R. G. Scaife, eds. 1995. *Bog Bodies: New Discoveries and New Perspectives*. London: British Museum Press.

van der Sanden, Wijnand. 1996. *Through Nature to Eternity: The Bog Bodies of Northwest Europe*. Translated by Susan J. Mellor. Amsterdam: Batavian Lion International.

The World Congresses on Mummy Studies

The World Congress on Mummy Studies (WCMS) is a gathering where mummy scientists and enthusiasts alike gather to share their passion, discoveries, and research. It is the only conference dedicated solely to the scientific study of mummies from all over the world, including natural, intentional, and modern mummies. While the WCMS is a lesser known scientific conference, comparatively speaking, among mummy scholars it is the most significant conference to attend, and it provides a holistic and interdisciplinary venue for research presentation and for networking and collaboration. Many would argue that the Congresses have successfully united the field and highlighted the scientific study of mummies worldwide.

The WCMS evolved from a bioanthropological project on the Guanche mummies of Tenerife, Spain, which was initiated by Arthur Aufderheide in the late 1980s. Aufderheide, most well-known for his contributions in paleopathology, visited the Canary Islands on a quest to further explore the Guanche mummies. While there, Aufderheide united with Conrado Rodríguez-Martín and Rafael González-Antón to form a working group of mummy experts. The WCMS was created to promote the integration of paleopathology, archaeology, biological anthropology, and culture history, with a focus not solely on Egyptian mummies, but rather on mummies from all over the world.

The First WCMS took place from February 3 to 6, 1992 in Puerto de la Cruz in Tenerife, Spain. Organizers have always chosen locales based on their significance to mummy studies rather than on their amenities as a conference location. Since Tenerife, seven additional WCMS have been held: Cartagena de las Indias, Columbia (1995), Arica, Chile (1998), Nuuk, Greenland (2001), Torino, Italy (2004),

Lanzarote, Canary Islands of Spain (2007), San Diego, California, USA (2011), and Río de Janeiro, Brazil (2013). The Ninth WCMS is scheduled for Lima, Peru in 2016. Attendance has generally ranged from about 200 to 300 participants for each congress.

A hallmark of the earliest congresses was their bilingual nature, with both English and Spanish being used, which united the heavily European and Egyptian worlds of mummy studies to the South American world of mummies. Paleopathological inquiry heavily influenced the earliest WCMS, as did paleogenetics, paleoparasitology, mummy conservation, mummification methods, and funerary rituals. During the Fifth WCMS, topics of local interest were incorporated into the congress, while at the Sixth WCMS sessions also include regional focuses and sub-adult mummies. With the Seventh WCMS, paleoimaging technologies and the ethics of mummy studies were added to the program schedule. The sessional and symposia topics continue to expand each year, with more diverse themes and an increase in the presentation of mummy studies using newer technologies. There has also been a marked increase in the attendance and involvement of students at the congress as well.

In 2013, the Eighth World Congress on Mummy Studies was held in Rio de Janeiro, Brazil. Paleopathology and the life history of mummies were still central themes, but sessions and symposia dedicated solely to animal mummies, 3D imaging and CT technology, chemical analyses, and the "new digital landscape" of mummies were also included. What started as a rather small gathering of mummy scholars primarily interested in paleopathology has grown with each congress to include a wider array of mummies, topics, and scientists from all over the globe. The WCMS has underlined the value in the scientific study of mummies, the collaborative nature of such research, and the necessity of focusing on mummies from many different cultures.

Alexandra R. Klales

See also: Aufderheide, Arthur Carl

Further Reading

Lynnerup, Niels, Art Aufderheide, Conrado Rodríguez-Martín, Felipe Cárdenas-Arroyo, Bernardo Arriaza, Emma Rabino-Massa, Pablo Atoche Peña, and Alana Cordy-Collins. 2012. "The World Congresses on Mummy Studies." In *The Global History of Paleopathology: Pioneers and Prospects*, ed. Jane Buikstra and Charlotte Roberts, 694–702. Oxford: Oxford University Press.

Pringle, Heather. 2001. *The Mummy Congress: Science, Obsession, and the Everlasting Dead*. New York: Hyperion.

Bibliography

General Books on Mummies

Beckett, Ron, and Jerry Conlogue. 2005. *Mummy Dearest: How Two Guys in a Potato Chip Truck Changed the Way the Living See the Dead.* Guilford, CT: The Lyons Press.

Brier, Bob. 2004. *The Encyclopedia of Mummies.* 2nd ed. USA: Checkmark Books.

Caygill, Marjorie. 1999. *The British Museum: A-Z Companion.* Chicago: Fitzroy Dearborn.

Cowie, Susan D., and Tom Johnson. 2002. *The Mummy in Fact, Fiction and Film.* Jefferson, NC: McFarland & Co.

Day, Jasmine. 2006. *The Mummy's Curse: Mummymania in the English-Speaking World.* London and New York: Routledge.

Frost, Brian J. 2007. *The Essential Guide to Mummy Literature.* Lanham, MD: Scarecrow Press.

Lovejoy, Bess. 2013. *Rest in Pieces: The Curious Fates of Famous Corpses.* New York: Simon & Schuster.

Luckhurst, Roger. 2012. *The Mummy's Curse: The True History of a Dark Fantasy.* Oxford: Oxford University Press.

MacDonald, Sally, and Michael Rice. 2003. *Consuming Ancient Egypt.* London: UCL Press.

Noble, Louise. 2011. *Medicinal Cannibalism in Early Modern English Literature and Culture.* Basingstoke: Palgrave.

Pringle, Heather. 2001. *The Mummy Congress: Science, Obsession, and the Everlasting Dead.* New York: Hyperion.

Quigley, Christine. 2006. *Modern Mummies: The Preservation of the Human Body in the Twentieth Century.* Jefferson, NC: McFarland & Co.

Sugg, Richard. 2011. *Mummies, Cannibals and Vampires: The History of Corpse Medicine from the Renaissance to the Victorians.* Oxford: Routledge.

Wieczorek, Alfried, and Wilfried Rosendahl, eds. 2010. *Mummies of the World.* Prestel: New York.

The Scientific Study of Mummies

Aufderheide, Arthur C. 2003. *The Scientific Study of Mummies.* Cambridge: Cambridge University Press.

Aufderheide, A. C., and C. Rodríguez-Martín. 1998. *The Cambridge Encyclopedia of Human Paleopathology.* Cambridge: Cambridge University Press.

Beckett, Ronald G., and Gerald Conlogue. 2010. *Paleoimaging: Field Applications for Cultural Remains and Artifacts.* Boca Raton, FL: CRC Press, Taylor and Francis.

Buikstra, Jane, and Charlotte Roberts, eds. 2012. *The Global History of Paleopathology: Pioneers and Prospects.* Oxford: Oxford University Press.

Cockburn, Aidan, Eve Cockburn, and Theodore A. Reyman, eds. 1998. *Mummies, Disease, and Ancient Cultures.* 2nd ed. Cambridge, UK: Cambridge University Press.

Piombino-Mascali, Dario, ed. 2011. *Yearbook of Mummy Studies, Volume 1.* Bolzano, Italy: Accademia Europea di Bolzano.

Spindler, Konrad, Harald Wilfing, Elisabeth Rastbichler-Zisserning, Dieter zur Nedden, and Hans Nothdurfter, eds. 1996. *Human Mummies: A Global Survey of Their Status and the Techniques of Conservation.* Wien and New York: Springer.

Mummies of Egypt

Adams, Barbara. 1987. *The Fort Cemetery at Hierakonpolis.* Studies in Egyptology. London: KPI.

Allen, Thomas. 1974. *The Book of the Dead or Going Forth by Day.* Chicago, University Chicago Press.

Andrews, Carol. 2004. *Egyptian Mummies.* London: British Museum Press.

Bickerstaff, D. 2009. *Refugees for Eternity: The Royal Mummies of Thebes, IV: Identifying the Royal Mummies.* Loughborough: Canopus Press.

Bierbrier, Morris L. 2012. *Who Was Who in Egyptology.* 4th ed. London: Egypt Exploration Society.

Brier, Bob. 1998. *The Murder of Tutankhamen: A True Story.* New York: G. P. Putnam's Sons.

Brier, Bob. 2013. *Egyptomania: Our Three Thousand Year Obsession with the Land of the Pharaohs.* New York: Palgrave Macmillan.

Bucaille, Maurice. 1990. *Mummies of the Pharaohs: Modern Medical Investigations.* New York: St. Martin's Press.

Carnarvon, Earl of, and Howard Carter. 2004. *Five Years' Explorations at Thebes: A Record of Work Done, 1907–11*. London: Kegan Paul.

Carter, Howard, and A. C. Mace. 1963. *The Tomb of Tut-Ank-Amen, Discovered by the Late Earl of Carnarvon and Howard Carter*. 3 vols. New York: Cooper Square.

Colla, Elliott. 2007. *Conflicted Antiquities: Egyptology, Egyptomania, Egyptian Modernity*. Durham: Duke University Press.

David, Rosalie. 1978. *Mysteries of the Mummies: The Story of the Manchester University Investigation*. New York: Macmillan.

David, Rosalie, ed. 2008. *Egyptian Mummies and Modern Science*. Cambridge: Cambridge University.

David, Rosalie, and Rich Archbold. 2000. *Conversations with Mummies: New Light on the Lives of the Ancient Egyptians*. Toronto, Ontario, Canada: Black Walnut.

Dawson, Warren R. 1968. *Catalogue of Egyptian Antiquities in the British Museum*, Volume I: Mummies and Human Remains. London: Trustees of the British Museum.

Dodson, Aidan. 2015. *The Royal Tombs of Ancient Egypt*. Barnsley: Pen and Sword.

Dunand, Françoise, and Roger Lichtenberg. 2006. *Mummies and Death in Egypt*. Translated by David Lorton. Ithaca: Cornell University Press.

El Mahdy, Christine. 1989. *Mummies, Myth, and Magic in Ancient Egypt*. London: Thames & Hudson.

Forbes, D. C. 1998. *Tombs, Treasures, Mummies: Seven Great Discoveries of Egyptian Archaeology*. Sevastopol and Santa Fe: KMT Communications.

Frayling, Christopher. 1992. *The Face of Tutankhamun*. London: Faber and Faber.

Gange, David. 2013. *Dialogues with the Dead: Egyptology in British Culture and Religion 1822–1922*. Oxford: Oxford University Press.

Grajetzki, Wolfram. 2007. *Burial Customs in Ancient Egypt: Life in Death for Rich and Poor*. London: Duckworth.

Harris, J. E., and K. R. Weeks. 1973. *X-Raying the Pharaohs*. London: Macdonald.

Hawass, Zahi. 2000. *Valley of the Golden Mummies*. New York: Harry N. Abrams.

Ikram, Salima. 2003. *Death and Burial in Ancient Egypt*. London: Pearson Education Limited.

Ikram, Salima, ed. 2005. *Divine Creatures: Animal Mummies in Ancient Egypt*. Cairo: American University in Cairo Press.

Ikram, Salima, and Aidan Dodson. 1998. *The Mummy in Ancient Egypt: Equipping the Dead for Eternity*. London: Thames and Hudson.

Ikram, Salima, and Mathaf al-Misrī. 1997. *Royal Mummies in the Egyptian Museum*. Cairo: American University in Cairo Press.

Leca, Ange Pierre. 1981. *The Egyptian Way of Death: Mummies and the Cult of the Immortal*. New York: Anchor Books.

Leek, Frank F. 1972. *The Human Remains from the Tomb of Tut'ankhamun*. Tut'ankhamun's Tomb Series Part V. Oxford: Griffith Institute.

Marchant, Jo. 2013. *The Shadow King: The Bizarre Afterlife of King Tut's Mummy*. Boston: Da Capo Press.

McDermott, Bridget. 2006. *Death in Ancient Egypt*. Stroud: Sutton.

Reeves, Nicholas, and Richard H. Wilkinson. 1990. *The Complete Valley of the Kings*. New York: Thames and Hudson.

Rhind, A. H. 1862. *Thebes: Its Tombs and Their Tenants*. London: Longman, Green, Longman, and Roberts.

Smith, Grafton Elliot. (1912) 2000. *The Royal Mummies*. Cairo: Institut français d'archéologie orientale. Reprint, London: Duckworth.

Taylor, John H. 2010. *Egyptian Mummies*. London: British Museum Press.

Taylor, John H., and Nigel Strudwick. 2005. *Mummies: Death and the Afterlife in Ancient Egypt; Treasures from the British Museum*. Santa Ana: Bowers Museum of Cultural Art.

Thomas, Elizabeth. 1966. *The Royal Necropolis of Thebes*. Trenton, NJ: Elizabeth Thomas.

Tyldesley, Joyce. 2005. *Egypt: How a Lost Civilization Was Rediscovered*. Berkeley and Los Angeles, California: University of California Press.

Tyldesley, Joyce. 2012. *Tutankhamen: The Search for an Egyptian King*. New York: Basic Books.

Weeks, Kent, editor. 2011. *The Valley of the Kings: The Tombs and the Funerary Temples of Thebes West*. Vercelli: White Star.

Wolfe, S. J. 2009. *Mummies in Nineteenth Century America: Ancient Egyptians as Artifacts*. Jefferson, NC: McFarland & Co.

Ancient Egyptian Religion and Mythology

Allen, James P. 2005. *The Ancient Egyptian Pyramid Texts*. Writings from the Ancient World no. 23. Atlanta: Society of Biblical Literature.

Assmann, Jan. 2001. *The Search for God in Ancient Egypt*. Ithaca: Cornell University Press.

Assmann, Jan. 2003. *The Mind of Egypt: History and Meaning in the Time of the Pharaohs*. Cambridge, MA: Harvard University Press.

Budge, E. A. 1967. *The Egyptian Book of the Dead: The Papyrus of Ani*. New York, Dover.

Champdor, Albert. 1966. *The Book of the Dead: Based on the Ani, Hunefer, and Anhai Papyri in the British Museum*. New York, Garrett publications.

David, Rosalie. 2002. *Religion and Magic in Ancient Egypt*. New York: Penguin Books.

Donaldson, M. D. 2003. *The Cult of Isis in the Roman Empire: Isis Invicta*. Lewiston, NY: Edwin Mellen Press.

Griffiths, John Gwyn. 1980 *The Origins of Osiris and His Cult*. Studies in the History of Religions, no. 40. Leiden, The Netherlands: E. J. Brill.

Hornung, Erik. 1990. *The Valley of the Kings: Horizon of Eternity*. New York: Timken.

Hornung, Erik. 1999. *The Ancient Egyptian Books of the Afterlife*. Ithaca, N.Y: Cornell University Press.

Mojsov, Bojana. 2005. *Osiris: Death and Afterlife of a God*. Malden, MA: Blackwell.

O'Connor, David. 2009. *Egypt's First Pharaohs and the Cult of Osiris*. London: Thames & Hudson.

Pinch, Geraldine. 2004. *Egyptian Mythology: A Guide to the Gods, Goddesses, and Traditions of Ancient Egypt*. New York: Oxford University Press.

Ray, John. 2002. *Reflections of Osiris: Lives from Ancient Egypt*. Oxford: Clarendon Press.

Rundle Clark, R.T. 1959. *Myth and Symbol in Ancient Egypt*. London: Thames and Hudson.

Schafer, Byron E., John Baynes, Leonard H. Lesko, and David P. Silverman. 1991. *Religion in Ancient Egypt: Gods, Myths, and Personal Practice*. Ithaca: Cornell University Press.

Seton-Williams, M.V. 1988. *Egyptian Legends and Stories*. London: Rubicon Press.

Snape, S. R. 2011. *Ancient Egyptian Tombs: The Culture of Life and Death*. Blackwell Ancient Religions. Malden, MA: Wiley-Blackwell.

Strudwick, Nigel, and John H. Taylor, eds. 2003. *The Theban Necropolis: Past, Present and Future*. London: British Museum Press.

Taylor, John. 2001. *Death and the Afterlife in Ancient Egypt*. London: British Museum Press.

Teeter, Emily. 2011. *Religion and Ritual in Ancient Egypt*. New York: Cambridge University Press.

Tiradritti, Francesco. 1998. *Isis, the Egyptian Goddess Who Conquered Rome*. Accessed December 7, 2013. –http://www.academia.edu/719626/Isis_the _Egyptian_Goddess_who_Conquered_Rome_Egyptian_Museum_of_Cairo _November_29–December_31_1998.

Wilkinson, Richard H. 2003. *The Complete Gods and Goddesses of Ancient Egypt*. London: Thames & Hudson.

Witt, R. E. 1997. *Isis in the Ancient World*, 1971. Baltimore: Johns Hopkins University Press.

Mummies of Europe

Asingh, Pauline, and Niels Lynnerup, eds. 2007. *Grauballe Man: An Iron Age Bog Body Revisited*. Jutland Archaeological Society and Moesgaard Museum.

Buell, Janet. 1997. *Bog Bodies*. New York: Twenty-First Century Books.

Fleckinger, Angelika. 2012. *Ötzi, the Iceman: The Full Facts at a Glance*. 6th ed. Wien/Bozen: Folio Verlag.

Glob, P. V. 2004. *The Bog People: Iron-Age Man Preserved*, 1969. Translated by Rupert Bruce-Mitford. New York: The New York Review of Books.

Lauring, Palle. 1957. *Land of the Tollund Man: The Prehistory and Archaeology of Denmark*. Translated by Reginald Spink. London: Lutterworth Press.

Sanders, Karin. 2009. *Bodies in the Bog and the Archaeological Imagination*. Chicago: University of Chicago Press.

Stead, I. M., J. B. Bourke, and Don Brothwell. 1986. *Lindow Man: The Body in the Bog*. London: British Museum Publications.

Thorvildsen, Knud. 1962. *The Tollund Man*. Translated by Fred Mallett. Silkeborg Museum.

Turner, R. C., and R. G. Scaife. 1995. *Bog Bodies: New Discoveries and New Perspectives*. London: British Museum Press.

van der Sanden, Wijnand. 1996. *Through Nature to Eternity: The Bog Bodies of Northwest Europe*. Translated by Susan J. Mellor. Amsterdam: Batavian Lion International.

Mummies of Latin America

Aguilar, Louis. 2009. *Long Live the Dead: The Accidental Mummies of Guanajuato*. USA: Accidental Mummies Touring Company, LLC.

Arriaza, Bernardo. 1995. *Beyond Death: The Chinchorro Mummies of Ancient Chile*. Washington: Smithsonian Institute.

Menzel, Dorothy. 1977. *The Archaeology of Ancient Peru and the Work of Max Uhle*. R. H. Lowie Museum of Anthropology. Berkeley: University of California Press.

Moseley, Michael Edward. 1997. *The Incas and their Ancestors: The Archaeology of Peru*. Thames and Hudson.

Reinhard, Johan. 1998. *Discovering the Inca Ice Maiden*. Washington, D.C.: National Geographic Society, 1998.

Reinhard, Johan. 2005. *The Ice Maiden: Inca Mummies, Mountain Gods, and Sacred Sites in the Andes*. Washington, D.C.: National Geographic Society.

Rowe, John Howland. 1954. *Max Uhle 1856–1944: A Memoir of the Father of Peruvian Archaeology*. University of California Publications in American Archaeology and Ethnology 46, no. 1. Berkeley: University of California Press.

Silverman, Helaine, and Donald Proulx. 2008. *The Nasca*. The Peoples of America. Malden, MA: Blackwell Publishers.

Uhle, Max. 1903. *Pachacamac. Report of the William Pepper, M.D., LL.D., Peruvian Expedition of 1896*. Philadelphia: University of Pennsylvania Press.

Other Mummy Groups

Barber, Elizabeth. 1999. *The Mummies of Ürümchi*. London: Macmillan.

Dickson, James H. 2012. *Ancient Ice Mummies*. The History Press: Stroud.

Jeremiah, Kenneth. 2010. *Living Buddhas: The Self-mummified Monks of Ymagata, Japan*. USA: McFarland & Co.

Mallory, J. P., and Victor H. Mair. 2008. *The Tarim Mummies: Ancient China and the Mystery of the Earliest Peoples from the West*. London: Thames & Hudson.

Picpican, Isikias. 2003. *The Igorot Mummies: A Socio-Cultural and Historical Treatise*. Quezon City: Rex Bookstore Inc.

Literary Works

Corelli, Marie. 2012. *The Soul of Lilith*, 1892. Library of Alexandria. Kindle Edition.

Corelli, Marie. 2012. *Ziska: The Problem of a Wicked Soul*, 1897. Project Gutenberg. Kindle Edition

Doyle, Arthur Conan. 1979. *The Best Supernatural Tales of Arthur Conan Doyle*. Selected and introduced by E. F. Bleiler. New York: Dover.

Gautier, Theophile. 1899. *One of Cleopatra's Nights and Other Fantastic Romances*, translated by Lafcadio Hearn. New York: Brentano's.

Gautier, Theophile. 1909. *The Romance of a Mummy*. In *The Complete Works of Theophile Gautier*, volume III, translated and edited by Professor F. C. DeSumichrast. London and New York: Postlethwaite, Taylor and Knowles.

Howard, Robert E. 2003. *The Coming of Conan the Cimmerian*, ed. Patrice Louinet. New York: Ballantine Books / Del Rey.

Howard, Robert E. 2004. *The Bloody Crown of Conan*, ed. Rusty Burke. New York: Ballantine Books / Del Rey.

Johnston, John J., and Jared Shurin, eds. 2013. *Unearthed*. London: Jurassic London.

Lansdale, Joe. 2012. *Bubba Ho-Tep*. Portland: Gere Donovan Press. Kindle book.

Poe, Edgar Allan. 1984. *Complete Stories and Poems of Edgar Allan Poe*. New York: Doubleday.

Rice, Anne. 1989. *The Mummy or Ramses the Damned*. New York: Ballantine.

Rohmer, Sax. 2010. *The Sax Rohmer Collection: 15 Novels and Short Stories in One Volume*. Alvin, TX: Halcyon Classics. Ebook.

Shurin, Jared, editor. 2013. *The Book of the Dead*. London: Jurassic London.

Smith, Clark Ashton. 2009. *The Return of the Sorcerer: The Best of Clark Ashton Smith*, edited by Robert Weinberg. Gaithersburg, MD: Prime Books.

Smith, Clark Ashton. 2014. *The Dark Eidolon and Other Fantasies*, edited by S. T. Joshi. New York: Penguin Books.

Stephens, John Richard, ed. 2001. *Into the Mummy's Tomb*. New York: Berkley Books.

Stoker, Bram. 1996. *The Jewel of Seven Stars*, annotated and edited by Clive Leatherdale. Westcliff-on-Sea, Essex, UK: Desert Island Books.

Williams, Tennessee. 1985. *Collected Stories*. New York: New Directions Books.

Mummies in the Movies

Feramisco, Thomas M. 2002. *The Mummy Unwrapped: Scenes Left on Universal's Cutting Room Floor*. Jefferson, NC: McFarland & Co.

Glut, Donald F. 1978. *Classic Movie Monsters*. Metuchen, NJ: Scarecrow Press.

Halliwell, Leslie. 1986. *The Dead That Walk*. London: Grafton Books.

Hearn, Marcus, and Alan Barnes. 2007. *The Hammer Story: The Authorised History of Hammer Films*. Foreword by Christopher Lee. London: Titan Books.

Huckvale, David. 2012. *Ancient Egypt in the Popular Imagination: Building a Fantasy in Film, Literature, Music and Art*. Jefferson, NC: McFarland.

Hunter, Jack. 2000. *House of Horror: The Complete Hammer Films Story*. 3rd ed. London: Creation Books.

Jones, Stephen. 2000. *The Essential Monster Movie Guide: A Century of Creature Features on Film, TV, and Video*. New York: Billboard Books.

Kawin, Bruce F. 2012. *Horror and the Horror Film*. London and New York: Anthem Press.

Landis, John. 2011. *Monsters in the Movies: 100 Years of Cinematic Nightmares*. New York: DK Publishing.

Miller, Cynthia J., and A. Bowdoin Van Riper, eds. 2012. *Undead in the West: Vampires, Zombies, Mummies, and Ghosts on the Cinematic Frontier*. Lanham, MD: Scarecrow Press.

Muir, John Kenneth. 2007. *Horror Films of the 1980s*. Jefferson, NC: McFarland & Co.

Newman, Kim. 2011. *Nightmare Movies: Horror on Screen Since the 1960s*. London: Bloomsbury Publishing.

Peirse, Alison. 2013. *After Dracula: The 1930s Horror Film*. London: I. B. Tauris & Co.

Riley, Philip J., ed. 1989. *The Mummy*. Universal Filmscripts Series Classic Horror Films, Volume 7. Abescon, NJ: MagicImage Filmbooks.

Schablitsky, Julie M., ed. *Box Office Archaeology: Refining Hollywood's Portrayals of the Past*. Walnut Creek, CA: Left Coast Press.

Skal, David J. 1993. *The Monster Show: A Cultural History of Horror*. New York: Penguin.

Weaver, Tom, Michael Brunas, and John Brunas. 2007. *Universal Horrors: The Studio's Classic Films, 1931–46*. Jefferson, NC: McFarland & Co.

Biographies

Ashley, Mike. 2001. *Algernon Blackwood: An Extraordinary Life*. New York: Carroll & Graf.

Belford, Barbara. 1996. *Bram Stoker: A Biography of the Author of Dracula*. New York: Knopf.

Grant, Richard E. 1975. *Theophile Gautier*. Boston: Twayne.

Hume, Ivor Noël. 2011. *Belzoni: The Giant Archaeologists Love to Hate*. Charlottesville and London: University of Virginia Press.

Jacobs, Steven. 2011. *Boris Karloff: More Than a Monster. The Authorized Biography*. Sheffield, England: Tomahawk Press.

Lycett, Andrew. 2007. *The Man Who Created Sherlock Holmes: The Life and Times of Sir Arthur Conan Doyle*. New York: Free Press.

Mayes, Stanley. 2006. *The Great Belzoni: The Circus Strongman Who Discovered Egypt's Treasures*, 1959. London: Tauris Park Paperbacks.

Reeves, Nicholas, and John H. Taylor. 1992. *Howard Carter before Tutankhamun*. London: Trustees of the British Museum.

Van Ash, Cay, and Elizabeth Sax Rohmer. 1972. *Master of Villany: A Biography of Sax Rohmer*. Bowling Green, OH: Bowling Green State University Popular Press.

Websites

Akhmim Mummy Studies Consortium. 2013. Accessed November 7. http://amscresearch.com. Official Website of the organization devoted to "advance[ing] knowledge of ancient Egyptian mummies from Akhmim and other regions" and "us[ing] our findings to increase understanding of the processes and rituals of Egyptian mummification."

Bioanthropology Research Institute. Quinnipiac University. 2013. Accessed October 28, 2013. http://www.quinnipiac.edu/institutes-and-centers/bioanthropology-research-institute. Official Website of the institute at Quinnipiac University that "conducts research in biology, archaeology, anthropology and paleopathology through paleoimaging applications including diagnostic imaging, video endoscopy, photography and laboratory analysis" on "mummified humans and animals and ancient artifacts without destruction."

The British Museum. Accessed December 20, 2013. http://www.britishmuseum.org. Official Website.

Freedman, Renée. *Archaeology's Interactive Dig: Excavating Hierakonpolis*. 2009. Accessed December 7, 2013. http://interactive.archaeology.org/

hierakonpolis. Field notes and information on the intensive archaeological excavation project at Hierakonpolis, Egypt from 2002 to 2009.

The Griffith Institute. n.d. *Tutankhamun: Anatomy of an Excavation.* Accessed December 19, 2013. www.griffith.ox.ac.uk/tutankhamundiscovery.html. Website that strives to offer "the definitive archaeological record of Howard Carter and Lord Carnarvon's discovery of the tomb of Tutankhamun." Administered by The Griffith Institute, the center for Egyptology at the University of Oxford.

Iceman Photoscan. n.d. Published by EURAC Research, Institute for Mummies and the Iceman. Accessed January 4, 2014. http://www.icemanphotoscan.eu. A high-resolution photoscan of the whole mummy of Ötzi the Iceman.

Summum. 2013. *Summum: Mummification of Transference.* Accessed December 8, 2013. http://www.summum.org. Official Website of the modern-day American religion focused around "the rites of Modern Mummification and Transference."

The Swiss Mummy Project. 2013. Accessed December 19, 2013. http://swissmummyproject.ch. Official Website of the organization, based at the University of Zurich but comprising an international team of scientists and scholars, whose aim is "to investigate ancient human mummies of multiple cultural and geographical backgrounds with state-of-the-art scientific methods."

About the Contributors

ALESSIA AMENTA is Curator of the Ancient Egyptian and Near Eastern Antiquities Department at the Vatican Museum. She has a PhD in Egyptology from the Sapienza University of Rome, where she has also done postdoctoral work in the subject. She is Director of the Vatican Coffin Project, the Vatican Mummy Project, and the Orazio Marucchi Project.

BERNARDO ARRIAZA is currently the Director of the Instituto de Alta Investigación, Universidad de Tarapacá, in Arica, Chile. He obtained his doctorate in physical anthropology at Arizona State University in 1991. He did postdoctoral work at the Smithsonian Institution, Washington, D.C. He was also a professor at the University of Nevada (1992–2004).

PETER BEBERGAL is the author of *Season of the Witch: How the Occult Saved Rock 'n' Roll* (Tarcher/Penguin, 2014) and *Too Much to Dream: A Psychedelic American Boyhood* (Soft Skull, 2011).

RONALD G. BECKETT is Professor Emeritus of Biomedical Sciences and Cofounder/Director of the Bioanthropology Research Institute at Quinnipiac University. He is a National Geographic Explorer and is coauthor, with Gerald Conlogue, of *Mummy Dearest: How Two Guys in a Potato Chip Truck Changed the Way the Living See the Dead* (2005) and *Paleoimaging: Field Applications for Cultural Remains and Artifacts* (2010). Beckett and Conlogue cohosted *The Mummy Road Show* on the National Geographic Domestic and International Channels from 2001 to 2003.

ANDREW BEDNARSKI is an historian and Egyptologist who works for the American Research Center in Egypt. In addition to his archaeological field work, he has published broadly on ancient Egyptian civilization, and is a specialist in the history of Egyptology.

ANNA-MARIA BEGEROCK studied Latin American and Mesopotamian Archaeology at the Free University of Berlin. Currently she is head of Andean Archaeology at the Spanish Institute of Mummy Studies (IECIM) in Madrid, Spain. Her research focuses on South American mummies and mummification techniques in pre-Columbian cultures. Previously she worked for the German Mummy Project in Mannheim, Germany.

RICHARD BLEILER is the Humanities Librarian at the University of Connecticut's Homer Babbidge Library.

BOB BRIER, also known as "Mr. Mummy," is an American egyptologist specializing in paleopathology. A senior research fellow at Long Island University (LIU) Post, he has researched and published on mummies and the mummification process and has appeared in many Discovery Civilization documentaries, primarily on ancient Egypt.

ROSELYN CAMPBELL received a BA and an MA in anthropology from the University of Montana and is currently earning her PhD at the Cotsen Institute of Archaeology at UCLA. Her primary research interests include bioarchaeology, Egyptian archaeology, and the analysis of violence and trauma in ancient societies.

MATT CARDIN is an author, editor, independent scholar, and college writing instructor living in Central Texas. He has a master's degree in religious studies and writes frequently about the intersection of religion, horror, psychology, creativity, consciousness, and dystopian and apocalyptic cultural trends. He has published three books of fiction and nonfiction. In addition to editing *Mummies around the World*, he has edited *Ghosts, Spirits, and Psychics: The Paranormal from Alchemy to Zombies* (ABC-CLIO, 2015) and *Born to Fear: Interviews with Thomas Ligotti* (Subterranean Press, 2014). He is founding editor of the popular blog The Teeming Brain.

JENEFER COCKITT has studied ancient Egyptian mummies since 2001 and has completed a PhD in Biomedical Egyptology at The University of Manchester focusing on the radiocarbon dating of ancient Egyptian artifacts. She has undertaken research projects on experimental mummification and ancient Nubian human remains, and is currently studying Nubian mummification techniques.

GERALD CONLOGUE is a professor of Diagnostic Imaging and Codirector of the Bioanthropology Research Institute at Quinnipiac University in Hamden, Connecticut. For 45 years his research has focused on integrating medical imaging procedures into nonmedical applications including anthropology and forensics.

DELLA COLLINS COOK is Professor of Anthropology at Indiana University. Her childhood scientific curiosity was stimulated by visiting saints relics and mummies in Europe. As an undergraduate at Cornell, she skeletonized a poorly preserved Egyptian mummy. She is interested in paleopathology, mortuary practices, and the history of anthropology.

AIDAN DODSON is a Senior Research Fellow in Archaeology at the University of Bristol, UK, and was Simpson Professor of Egyptology at the American University in Cairo for Spring 2013. He is the author of 16 books and nearly 400 articles and reviews, many focusing on Egyptian funerary archaeology.

STEFAN R. DZIEMIANOWICZ is the editor of numerous anthologies of horror fiction and numerous articles and reviews for *The Washington Post Book World*, *Publishers Weekly*, *Lovecraft Studies*, *Studies in Weird Fiction*, and other journals. He is a senior editor at Barnes & Noble, Inc. and has contributed to many reference works. He coedited, with S. T. Joshi, *Supernatural Literature of the World: An Encyclopedia* (Greenwood Press, 2005).

JONATHAN ELIAS completed his PhD at the University of Chicago specializing in research on magical inscriptions on Egyptian coffins. Since 2001, he has focused on CT scanning Egyptian mummies. He is the Director of the Akhmim Mummy Studies Consortium, a project coordinating mummy studies and forensic facial reconstructions of ancient Egyptian people.

HEATHER GILL-FRERKING has been studying aspects of mummies and mummification since 1991. She has worked with a collection of bog bodies in northern Germany, and she undertook experimental archaeology research to understand the environmental processes that lead to the preservation of bog bodies. She has also examined and analyzed mummies from South America, Egypt, and Asia.

PAULA GURAN is an anthologist and fiction editor, primarily for Prime Books, who once reviewed, interviewed, and wrote nonfiction articles for such publications as *Encyclopedia of the Vampire*, *Icons of Horror and the Supernatural*, *Supernatural Literature of the World*, *SciFi Magazine*, *SciFipedia*, *CFQ*, *Publishers Weekly*, and her own, long-defunct, award-winning newsletter *DarkEcho*.

MICHAEL E. HABICHT studied archaeology and Egyptology at the universities of Zurich and Basel. He specializes in the New Kingdom, Egyptian funerary art, tomb decoration, and mummies, and has published several books and papers on these subjects. He is currently a researcher at the University of Zurich's Centre for Evolutionary Medicine.

SALIMA IKRAM is professor of Egyptology at the American University in Cairo. She has published extensively on human and animal mummies, reinstalled the Animal Mummy Room at the Cairo Museum, been guest-curator for the Smithsonian Institution's Mummy and Ancient Egypt reinstallation, and has analyzed mummies in the field as well as in many museums and laboratories around the world.

RIMANTAS JANKAUSKAS, MD, PhD, is a Professor at the Department of Anatomy, Histology and Anthropology, Vilnius University, Lithuania. His research interests are interdisciplinary, and include bioarchaeology of the Baltic region from the Stone Age until modern times and forensic anthropology. Recently he was in charge of investigations of mummified remains in Lithuanian museums and church crypts.

JOHN J. JOHNSTON is Vice-Chair of the Egypt Exploration Society. He lectures extensively on the reception of ancient Egypt in popular culture and has contributed to the DVD/BD releases of two restored Hammer mummy films. He coedited the first all-original anthology of mummy fiction, *Book of the Dead* (Jurassic London, 2013), and his introductory essay to the companion anthology *Unearthed*, a collection of classic mummy tales, was nominated for a British Science Fiction Association Award.

S. T. JOSHI is a widely published author and editor. He has written *The Weird Tale* (1990), *Unutterable Horror: A History of Supernatural Fiction* (2012), and other works, and has edited the works of H. P. Lovecraft, Lord Dunsany, Arthur Machen, and other writers of supernatural fiction.

ALEXANDRA R. KLALES, MS (University of Manitoba), is a doctoral candidate at the University of Manitoba specializing in biological anthropology. Her doctoral research focuses on the analysis and reconstruction of mummies from Akhmim, Egypt using CT. She is an associate of the Akhmim Mummy Studies Consortium in Carlisle, Pennsylvania and is also currently adjunct faculty at two Pennsylvania colleges.

ROGER LUCKHURST is Professor of Literature at Birkbeck College, University of London. He is the author of *The Mummy's Curse: The True History of a Dark Fantasy* (Oxford University Press, 2012).

CARTER LUPTON is head of the Anthropology/History departments of the Milwaukee Public Museum. He has participated in archaeological fieldwork at Cahokia Mounds, Illinois; Laugerie Haute, France; Tell Hadidi, Syria; and

Hierakonpolis, Egypt. He is also Associate Director of the Akhmim Mummy Studies Association and he has been involved with CT studies of Egyptian mummies since 1986.

JO MARCHANT is a science journalist and author with a PhD in genetics. Her second book, *The Shadow King: The Bizarre Afterlife of King Tut's Mummy*, was published in June 2013. She lives in London.

ROBERT McCOMBE is a postdoctoral research associate at the University of Manchester. His doctoral research focused on modern uses and representations of early medieval material culture, including human remains, in museums. His wider interests lie in the history of objects and collections, engagements with preserved bodies, and ideas of identity.

LIDIJA M. McKNIGHT is a Research Associate in the KNH Centre for Biomedical Egyptology, University of Manchester. Her current research project, the Ancient Egyptian Animal Bio Bank, related conference attendances, and publications focus on the use of clinical imaging modalities and experiential mummification to study the practice of votive animal mummification.

RYAN METCALFE works at The University of Manchester, UK, and has lectured on and researched a variety of subjects related to Biomedical Egyptology. His major research interest is in the preservation of soft tissues and the effects of mummification on biomolecular and chemical analysis.

GABRIEL MOSHENSKA is Lecturer in Public Archaeology at UCL Institute of Archaeology. He works in community archaeology, the archaeology of modern conflict, and the history of archaeology. He is currently writing a biography of the surgeon, antiquarian, and mummy unroller Thomas "Mummy" Pettigrew.

KENNETH C. NYSTROM is an Associate Professor at the State University of New York at New Paltz. His dissertation research examined the consequences of the Inca conquest of the Chachapoya, and subsequently he has published several papers on the Chachapoya, including a consideration of their mummification and funerary behavior.

MIKE PARKER PEARSON is Professor of British Later Prehistory at the Institute of Archaeology, University College London. He has excavated on archaeological sites around the world from Madagascar to Easter Island, but in recent years his main research focus has been Stonehenge. His 20-year project in the Outer Hebrides covered all periods from the Bronze Age to the Vikings and included the Bronze Age settlement of Cladh Hallan, where he found formerly mummified skeletons, the first evidence for mummification in prehistoric Britain. Mike is well known for his work on funerary archaeology and has written many books on this and other subjects.

DARIO PIOMBINO-MASCALI, PhD, collaborates with the most prestigious institutions devoted to the study of mummified remains. He serves as honorary inspector of the cultural heritage of Sicily and as curator of the Capuchin Catacombs of Palermo. He is also a visiting scientist at Vilnius University and an explorer with the National Geographic Society.

CAMPBELL PRICE is Curator of Egypt and Sudan at the Manchester Museum. He received his BA, MA, and PhD in Egyptology from the University of Liverpool, where he is an Honorary Research Fellow. His research interests focus on Egyptian sculpture and public perceptions of Egyptology in museum settings.

JUNE PULLIAM teaches courses on horror literature and Young Adult fiction at Louisiana State University. She has authored (with Anthony Fonseca) three volumes of *Hooked on Horror, Read On . . . Horror,* and *The Encyclopedia of the Zombie: The Walking Dead in Popular Culture and Myth* as well as articles on George Romero's *Land of the Dead, The Twilight Saga, The Hunger Games Trilogy,* Roald Dahl, and teen female lycanthropes in Young Adult fiction. She edits *Dead Reckonings: A Review Magazine for the Horror Field.*

FRANK RÜHLI (MD, PhD) is Professor of Anatomy and head of the Center for Evolutionary Medicine and the Swiss Mummy Project, University of Zurich, Switzerland. He has excavated or investigated mummies in Egypt, Iran, Botswana, and elsewhere; delivered invited lectures and provided expert opinion on Tutankamun, Ötzi, and more; and published dozens of scientific mummy articles, books, and book chapters.

CAROLYN SHEFCYK is a graduate student at the University of Saint Joseph pursuing a master's degree and certification in elementary education. She currently volunteers in a first grade classroom. She studied English at UCONN in her undergraduate years. In her spare time she enjoys creative writing and reading science fiction.

BRYAN SITCH is Deputy Head of Collections at the Manchester University Museum and has worked in museums in northern England for over 20 years. He has experience of a wide range of material, including ancient Egyptian collections. At Leeds he was responsible for the mummy of Nesyamun.

MARISSA A. STEVENS is a PhD student of Egyptology at UCLA. In addition to her own research on 21st Dynasty funerary papyri, she also works as both a research assistant for Dr. Kathlyn Cooney's 21st Dynasty coffins project and a teaching assistant for the Department of Near Eastern Languages and Cultures.

RICHARD SUGG is the author of five books, including *Mummies, Cannibals and Vampires: the History of Corpse Medicine from the Renaissance to the Victorians* (Routledge, 2011). He lectures in Renaissance literature at Durham University. He is currently completing *The Real Vampires*, and beginning research into the history of the poltergeist.

ANDREW WADE is an anthropological bioarchaeologist, codeveloper of the IMPACT Mummy Database, and founder of the Mummipedia Project. His research focuses on cultural change, sociopolitical interactions, and identity formation examined through large-scale studies of mummification features, and on the nondestructive imaging techniques used to gather this biocultural information.

EMILY WEBB is an archaeological scientist who received her doctoral degree from the University of Western Ontario, London, Canada. Her doctoral research focused on investigating ancient lifeways in coastal South America, as revealed through bioarchaeology and biogeochemical analyzes. Currently, she is a postdoctoral research assistant in the School of Chemistry, University of Bristol, UK.

ALBERT ZINK is director of the Institute for Mummies and the Iceman in Bolzano, Italy. He is responsible for the scientific investigation of the well-known Tyrolean Iceman popularly known as Ötzi. He has specialized in the ancient DNA detection of infectious diseases in ancient human skeletons and mummies, and he is editor of the *Anthropologischer Anzeiger* and associate editor of the *International Journal of Paleopathology.*

Index

Note: Page numbers in bold font indicate main entries.